# Time Out

# Paris

**timeout.com/paris**

**Published by Time Out Guides Ltd,** a wholly owned subsidiary of Time Out Group Ltd.
Time Out and the Time Out logo are trademarks of Time Out Group Ltd.

© **Time Out Group Ltd 2008**
Previous editions 1989, 1990, 1992, 1995, 1997, 1998, 1999, 2000, 2001, 2002, 2003, 2004, 2005, 2006, 2007.

10 9 8 7 6 5 4 3 2 1

**This edition first published in Great Britain in 2008 by Ebury Publishing**
A Random House Group Company
20 Vauxhall Bridge Road, London SW1V 2SA

**Random House Australia Pty Limited** 20 Alfred Street, Milsons Point, Sydney, New South Wales 2061, Australia
**Random House New Zealand Limited** 18 Poland Road, Glenfield, Auckland 10, New Zealand
**Random House South Africa (Pty) Limited** Isle of Houghton, Corner Boundary
Road & Carse O'Gowrie, Houghton 2198, South Africa

Random House UK Limited Reg. No. 954009

**For further distribution details, see www.timeout.com**

ISBN: 978-1-84670-050-7

A CIP catalogue record for this book is available from the British Library

Printed and bound by Firmengruppe APPL, aprinta druck, Wemding, Germany

The Random House Group Limited supports The Forest Stewardship Council (FSC), the leading international forest
certification organisation. All our titles that are printed on Greenpeace approved FSC certified paper carry the FSC
logo. Our paper procurement policy can be found at http://www.rbooks.co.uk/environment

**Time Out Guides Limited**
**Universal House**
**251 Tottenham Court Road**
**London W1T 7AB**
**Tel + 44 (0)20 7813 3000**
**Fax + 44 (0)20 7813 6001**
**Email guides@timeout.com**
**www.timeout.com**

## Contributors

**Introduction** Jonathan Derbyshire. **History** Jonathan Derbyshire, Andrew Hussey. **Paris Today** Andrew Hussey. **Architecture** Natasha Edwards. **Peripheral Vision** Rich Woodruff. **Where to Stay** Julien Sauvalle (*Small and salubrious* Natasha Edwards). **Sightseeing** Jonathan Derbyshire, Natasha Edwards, Andrew Hussey, Rich Woodruff, Alison Culliford. **Restaurants** Rosa Jackson. **Cafés & Bars** Iris Mansour (*12-bar booze* Alison Culliford). **Shops & Services** Alison Culliford (*Market forces* Rosa Jackson; *Bargain hunt* Iris Mansour). **Festivals & Events** Iris Mansour (*Up all night* Jonathan Derbyshire). **Cabaret, Circus & Comedy** Anna Brooke. **Children** Natasha Edwards. **Dance** Estelle Ricoux. **Film** Rich Woodruff. **Galleries** Natasha Edwards. **Gay & Lesbian** Robert Vallier. **Music: Classical & Opera** Stephen Mudge. **Music: Rock, Roots & Jazz** David McKenna. **Nightlife** Ben Osborne. **Sport & Fitness** Rich Woodruff. **Theatre** Anna Brooke. **Trips Out of Town** Anna Brooke. **Directory** Alexia Loundras, Rich Woodruff.

**Maps** john@jsgraphics.co.uk, except pages 415, 416.

**Photography by** Karl Blackwell, except: pages 12, 21 akg-images/Erich Lessing; page 27 AP/PA Photos; page 28 AGIP RA/Lebrecht Music & Arts; page 34 Horacio Vilalobos/epa/Corbis; page 104 Oliver Knight; pages 128, 163 Keystone France, Camera Press London; page 142 Catherine Helie/© Gallimard; page 162 Associated Press; page 267 Jean-Christophe Godet; page 275 Shaun Botterill/Getty; page 276 David Lefranc; page 295 Stéphane Dabrowki/CF; page 323 Thierry Ardouin/ Cité de la musique; page 327 Oliver Viex, Sekence.net; page 333 Phillippe Perusseau/epa/Corbis.

The following image was provided by the featured establishment: page 291.

**The Editor would like to thank** all contributors to previous editions of *Time Out Paris*, whose work forms the basis for parts of this book.

The editor travelled to Paris with Eurostar (08705 186 186; www.eurostar.com).

# Contents

# Introduction

Paris is being reborn – and nothing symbolises that rebirth quite like 104, an enormous arts and media centre that will open in summer 2008 in a building that used to be home to the city's undertakers.

104 is part of an elaborate scheme to revive the north-east of Paris; in particular, an area wedged between a grim expanse of railway goods yards and the suburb of Aubervilliers. Modelled on the successful regeneration of the 13th arrondissement on the Left Bank of the Seine, the plan is to turn this previously desolate neighbourhood into a cultural hub, with a multiplex arthouse cinema not far from 104, as well as shops and affordable social housing.

The driving force behind all this change is Socialist mayor Betrand Delanoë, who shows every sign of doing for Paris in the 21st century what Baron Haussmann did for it in the 19th. Haussmann changed the face of the city by driving his great, monumental boulevards through its heart; Delanoë is transforming Paris by turning its gaze out towards its previously neglected suburbs.

In 2006, the first tramway to be opened in Paris in nearly a century enhanced the connections between the city and its southern satellites. The plan for the north-east also includes the tram, plus a series of walkways crossing the *périphérique*, the eight-lane motorway that currently marks the limits of Paris 'proper'.

Delanoë also wants to cover the ring road and plant it with trees, a project in keeping with his attempts to turn the entire city green. Since he came to power in 2001, Paris has acquired 32 hectares of new parks and gardens, where previously it had lagged behind more extensively cultivated cities like London or Rome.

Most significant of all, though, has been Delanoë's attempt to tame the traffic in Paris. In summer 2007, he launched Vélib, a free bicycle scheme that was an immediate and unambiguous success. Thronging with cyclists using the standard-issue grey bikes, today the streets of Paris look more like Beijing than Brussels or Berlin.

For all this change, however, some things stay the same – as anyone taking to a bike will soon see. Paris is a world capital built on a human scale, with an unrivalled concentration of galleries and museums all within easy reach of each other, whether you're on two wheels or two feet. It's also a remarkably diverse city, a jumble of villages really, all of them pungently, defiantly distinctive. And now they're easier to explore than ever.

## ABOUT TIME OUT CITY GUIDES

This is the 16th edition of *Time Out Paris*, one of an expanding series of more than 50 guides produced by the people behind the successful listings magazines in London, New York, Chicago, Sydney and many more cities around the world. Our guides are all written and updated by resident experts who have striven to provide you with all the most up-to-date information you'll need to explore Paris, whether you're a local or a first-time visitor.

## THE LOWDOWN ON THE LISTINGS

We've tried to make this book as useful as possible. Addresses, telephone numbers, websites, transport information, opening times, admission prices and credit card details have all been included in the listings, as have details of other selected services and facilities. However, owners and managers can change their arrangements at any time. Before you go out of your way, we strongly advise you to call and check opening times and other particulars. While every effort has been made to ensure the accuracy of the information contained in this guide, the publishers cannot accept responsibility for any errors it may contain.

## PRICES AND PAYMENT

Prices are given in euros, and have been verified with each venue or business listed. We've noted whether shops, hotels, restaurants and other establishments accept credit cards, but have only listed the majorcards – namely American Express (AmEx), Diners Club (DC), MasterCard (MC) and Visa (V). Many businesses will also accept other cards, such as Maestro. Note that the Visa card is referred to locally as *la Carte Bleue*.

The prices we've supplied should be treated as guidelines, not gospel. Fluctuating exchange rates and inflation can cause charges, particularly in shops and restaurants, to change

rapidly. If prices vary wildly from those we've quoted, ask whether there's a good reason, then please email to let us know. We aim to give the best and most up-to-date advice, and we always want to know if you've been badly treated or overcharged.

## THE LIE OF THE LAND

To make both book and city easier to navigate, we've divided Paris into areas. They are: The Seine & Islands; The Louvre; Opéra to Les Halles; The Champs-Elysées & Western Paris; Montmartre & Pigalle; Beaubourg & the Marais; Bastille & Eastern Paris; North-East Paris; The Latin Quarter; St-Germain-des-Prés & Odéon; Montparnasse & Beyond; The 7th & Western Paris; and the 13th arrondissement. These are our own breakdowns, and not the official arrondissements you will see signposted around town. However, every address listed in the book includes an arrondissement number.

We have also included details of the nearest public transport option(s) and a reference to the series of fully indexed colour maps at the back of this guide, which start on page 396. The precise locations of hotels (●), restaurants (●) and cafés and bars (●) have all been pinpointed on these maps; the section also includes a transport map and a street index.

## TELEPHONE NUMBERS

The area code for Paris and the Ile-de-France is 01. All phone numbers listed in this guide take this code unless stated. We've identified premium-rate and mobile numbers, which will incur extra calling costs.

The country code for France is 33. To dial numbers as given in this book from abroad, use your country's exit code (00 in the UK, 011 in the US) or the + symbol (on many mobile phones), followed by the country code, followed by the number as listed, minus the initial 0. For more on phones, including information on free and premium-rate numbers, *see p379*.

## ESSENTIAL INFORMATION

For all the practical information you might need for visiting the city, including customs and immigration information, disabled access, emergency telephone numbers, the lowdown on the local transport network and a list of useful websites, turn to the Directory at the back of this guide. It starts on page 360.

## LET US KNOW WHAT YOU THINK

We hope you enjoy *Time Out Paris*, and we'd like to know what you think of it. We welcome tips for places that you consider we should include in future editions, and take notice of your criticism of our choices. You can email us at guides@timeout.com.

There is an online version of this guide, along with guides to more than 50 other international cities, at **www.timeout.com**.

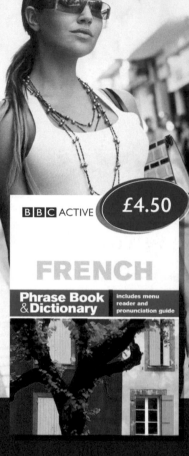

# In Context

## Features

**Eglise St-Sulpice**. *See p160.*

*Retable de Saint Denis* by Bellechose.

# History

## From Caesar to Sarkozy.

The earliest settlers seem to have arrived in Paris around 120,000 years ago. One of them lost a flint spear-tip on the hill we now call Montmartre, and the still dangerous-looking weapon is to be seen today in the Stone Age collection at the **Musée des Antiquités Nationales** (*see p182*). There was a Stone Age weapons factory under present-day Châtelet, and the redevelopment of Bercy in the 1990s managed to unearth ten Neolithic canoes, five of which are now high and dry in the **Musée Carnavalet** (*see p134*). The fluctuating level of the river probably forced people to dwell on one of the area's many hills.

By 250 BC, a Celtic tribe known as the Parisii had put the place on the map. The Parisii were river traders, wealthy enough to mint gold coins. The **Musée de la Monnaie de Paris** (*see p157*) has an extensive collection of their small change. Their most important *oppidum*,

a primitive fortified town, was located on an island in the Seine, which is generally thought to have been what is today's Ile de la Cité.

### ROMAN PARIS

A superb strategic location and the capacity to generate hard cash were guaranteed to attract the attention of the Romans. Julius Caesar arrived in southern Gaul as proconsul in 58 BC and soon used the pretext of dealing with invading barbarians to stick his Roman nose into the affairs of northern Gaul. The Gauls didn't appreciate the attention, and in 54 BC the Eburones from the Meuse valley rebelled against the Romans. Other tribes joined in: in 52 BC the Parisii rose up with the rest of Gaul.

Caesar had his hands full dealing with the great Gaul marauder Vercingetorix, so he sent his general Labienus with four legions and part of the cavalry to secure the passage of the Seine

at Lutetia, as they called Paris. The Gauls were massacred, although a contingent of Parisii escaped to be defeated later at the Battle of Alesia with Vercingetorix. The subsequent surrender of Vercingetorix left the Paris region and the rest of Gaul in Roman hands.

Roman Lutetia was a prosperous town of around 8,000 inhabitants. Apart from centrally heated villas and a temple to Jupiter on the main island (the remains of both are visible in the **Crypte Archéologique**; *see p91*), there were the sumptuous baths (now the **Musée National du Moyen Age**; *see p148*) and the 15,000-seater **Arènes de Lutèce** (*see p153*).

## CHRISTIANITY

Christianity arrived in around 250 AD in the shape of Denis of Athens, who went on to become the first bishop of Paris. Legend has it that when he was decapitated by Valerian on Mons Martis, the mount of the martyrs (today better known as Montmartre), Denis picked up his head and walked with it to what is now St-Denis, to be buried there. The event is depicted in Henri Bellechose's *Retable de Saint-Denis*, now exhibited in the **Louvre** (*see pp93-100*).

> 'With the arrival of the Huns, the people of Paris prepared to flee. They were dissuaded by a feisty woman named Geneviève, famed for her piety.'

Gaul was still a tempting prize. Waves of barbarian invaders – Alamans, Francs and others – began crossing the Rhine from 275 onwards. They sacked more than 60 cities in Gaul, including Lutetia, where the population was massacred and the buildings on the Montagne Ste-Geneviève were pillaged and burned. The bedraggled survivors used the rubble to build a rampart around the Ile de la Cité and to fortify the forum, although few citizens remained in the shadow of its walls.

It was at this time that the city was renamed Paris. Protected by the Seine and the new fortifications, its main role now was as a rear base for the Roman armies defending Gaul, and it was here in 360 that Julian was proclaimed emperor by his troops. In the same year, the first Catholic council of Paris was held, condemning the Arian branch of Christianity as heresy. The city's inhabitants, however, had concerns more pressing than theology.

Around 450, with the arrival of the Huns in the region, the people of Paris prepared once again to flee. They were dissuaded by a feisty

woman named Geneviève, famed for her piety. Seeing the walls of the city defended against him, no less a pillager than Attila the Hun turned back and was defeated soon afterwards.

## CLOVIS

In 464 Paris managed to resist another siege, this time by the Francs under Childeric. However, by 486, after a further blockade lasting ten years, Geneviève had no option but to surrender the city to Childeric's successor, Clovis, who went on to conquer most of Gaul and founded the Merovingian dynasty. He chose Paris as capital of his new kingdom, and it stayed that way until the seventh century, in spite of various conflicts among his successors.

Under the influence of his wife, Clotilde, Clovis converted to Christianity. He founded, and was buried in, the basilica of the Saints Apôtres, later rededicated to Ste Geneviève when the saviour and future patron saint of Paris was interred there in 512. All that remains of the basilica today is a single pillar in the grounds of the modern Lycée Henri IV; but there's a shrine dedicated to Ste Geneviève and some relics in the fine Gothic church of **St-Etienne-du-Mont** (*see p151*) next door. Geneviève and Clovis had set a trend. The Ile de la Cité was still the heart of the city, but, under the Merovingians, the Left Bank was the up-and-coming area for fashion-conscious Christians, with 11 churches built here in the period (against only four on the Right Bank and one on the Ile de la Cité). Not everyone was sold on the joys of city living, though. From 614 onwards, the Merovingian kings preferred the *banlieue* at Clichy, or wandered the kingdom trying to keep rebellious nobles in check. By the time one of the rebels, Pippin 'the Short', decided to do away with the last Merovingian in 751, Paris was starting to look passé.

Pippin's son, Charlemagne, built his capital at Aix-la-Chapelle, while his successors, known as the Carolingian dynasty, moved from palace to palace, consuming the local produce.

Paris, meanwhile, was doing nicely as a centre for Christian learning, and had grown to a population of 20,000 by the beginning of the ninth century. This was the high point in the political power of the great abbeys like St-Germain-des-Prés, where transcription of the Latin classics was helping to preserve much of Europe's Roman cultural heritage. Power in the Paris area was exercised by the counts of Paris.

## THE VIKINGS

In 845 the Vikings appeared before the walls. Unopposed, the Norsemen sacked the city, and King Charles II, 'the Bald', had to cough up 7,000 pounds of silver to get them to leave.

**UK–Paris. Frequent flights from 9 airports.**

**AIR FRANCE KLM**                                    **www.airfrance.co.uk**

Recognising a soft touch when they saw one, the Vikings returned to sack the city repeatedly between 856 and 869, burning churches with heathen abandon. Better late than never, Charles organised the defence of the city and fortified bridges were built the Grand Pont over the northern branch of the Seine and the Petit Pont over the southern, blocking the passage of the Viking ships further upstream.

In 885, Gozlin, Bishop of Paris, had just finished repairing the Roman walls when the Vikings showed up once again; this time they found the city defended against them. After a siege lasting a year, King Charles III, 'the Fat', arrived at the head of an army but, deciding that discretion is indeed the better part of valour, handed over 700 pounds of silver and politely invited the Norsemen to pillage some other part of his kingdom. The Count of Paris, Eudes, having performed valiantly in the siege of 885 and 886, was offered the royal crown when Charles was deposed in 888. Although the Carolingians recovered the throne after Eudes' death in 898, his great-nephew, Hugues Capet, was elected King of France in 987, adding what remained of the Carolingian dominions to his territories around Paris.

### PARIS FINDS ITS FEET

Under the Capetian dynasty, although Paris was now at the heart of the royal domains, the city did not yet dominate the kingdom. Robert 'the Pious', king from 996 to 1031, stayed more often in Paris than his father, restoring the royal palace on the Ile de la Cité, while Henri I (1031-60) issued more of his charters in Paris than in Orléans. In 1112 the abbey of **St-Denis** (*see p179*) replaced St-Benoît-sur-Loire as principal monastery, so confirming the pre-eminence of Paris over Orléans.

Paris itself still consisted of little more than the Ile de la Cité and small settlements under the protection of the abbeys on each bank. On the Left Bank, royal largesse helped to rebuild the abbeys of St-Germain-des-Prés, St-Marcel and Ste-Geneviève, although it took more than 150 years for the destruction wrought there by the Vikings to be fully repaired. The Right Bank, where mooring was easier, prospered from river commerce, and three boroughs grew up around the abbeys of St-Germain-l'Auxerrois, St-Martin-des-Champs and St-Gervais. Bishop Sully of Paris began building the cathedral of Notre-Dame in 1163.

The growing complexity of government during the 12th century, and the departure of kings on crusades, meant the administration tended to stay in the Palais de la Cité and the royal treasure in the fortress of the Temple. The wisdom of this approach was confirmed by the disaster of Fréteval in 1194, where King Philippe-Auguste was defeated by Richard the Lionheart, losing much of his treasure and his archives in the process.

The **Sorbonne** – seat of Left Bank learning since the 13th century. *See p17.*

This minor hiccup aside, the reign of Philippe-Auguste (1180-1223) was a turning point in the history of Paris. Before, the city was a confused patchwork of royal, ecclesiastical and feudal authorities, exercising various powers, rights and privileges. Keen to raise revenues, Philippe favoured the growth of the guilds, especially the butchers, drapers, furriers, haberdashers and merchants: so began the rise of the bourgeoisie.

He also ordered the building of the first permanent market buildings at Les Halles, and a new city wall, first on the Right Bank to protect the commercial heart of Paris, and later on the Left Bank. At the western end of the wall, Philippe built a castle, the Louvre, to defend the road from the ever-menacing Normandy, whose duke was also King of England.

## A GOLDEN AGE

Paris was now the principal residence of the king and the uncontested capital of France. No longer threatened by foreign invasion, the city found itself overrun by a new and altogether deadlier menace that exists to this day: lawyers. And barristers, bailiffs, prosecutors, sergeants, accountants, judges, clerks and all the bureaucratic trappings of royal government.

To accommodate the rapidly growing royal administration, the Palais de la Cité, site and symbol of power for the previous thousand years, was remodelled and enlarged. Work was begun by Louis IX (later St Louis) in the 1240s, and later continued under Philippe IV ('le Bel'). This architectural complex, of which the **Ste-Chapelle** (*see p92*) and the nearby **Conciergerie** (*see p91*) can still be seen, was inaugurated with great pomp at Pentecost 1313.

# Slaughterhouse city

The trigger for the St Bartholomew's Day massacre was a marriage. On 18 August 1572 Marguerite de Valois, a Catholic, was set to marry Henri de Bourbon, a Protestant aristocrat (and soon to become the future King Henri IV). Invitations were sent out to all the great families of France and the festivities were expected to last several weeks; great balls were to be held in the Louvre, Hôtel de Ville and Hôtel de Bourbon.

This was a marriage brokered by Catherine de Médicis, with the strategic aim of uniting the two opposed religious forces in a union which supported the Crown. Although most Protestants had declared that their only goal in Paris was freedom of worship, the royal family had long feared their potential to overthrow the sovereign. This threat, it was anticipated, would be dissolved in blessed marital union. The capital was packed with Protestant and Catholic nobility for celebrations organised by Catherine.

As the clock struck 2am on 24 August, the slaughter of Protestants began in earnest. 'Kill them all,' declared King Charles IX, 'so that none shall reproach me for it.'

The first task was to get rid of the Protestant leader Coligny properly. This was done by the duc de Guise and his men, who slit his throat and then dangled his severed head from the window of his apartment with a rope. Guise's men then marched through the streets with bloodied weapons, dragging the mutilated corpse of Coligny with them, exhorting the population to rise and commit

murder. Coligny's balls were ripped off and thrown into the Seine, followed by his headless corpse. He was fished out and hung by his feet for several days at Montfaucon.

From the Louvre to the backstreets of Ile de la Cité and the Latin Quarter, a madness swept through the city. The ordinary people of Paris were overwhelmingly Catholic and the Protestants their aristocratic overseers (over the years many of the leading Parisian families had converted to Protestantism in disgust at the venality of government and the court). It was now time to settle accounts.

Most of the important murders, at least from a political point of view, took place in the opening hours of the massacre. The dead and dying were not men at arms, but gentlemen come to a wedding, poor artisans and workers, the elderly, women, children and babies. Pezou, a butcher by profession and a captain faithful to Guise, prided himself on killing human beings like beasts and boasted of slitting the throats of more than 120 Protestants in a few hours, and throwing the bodies into the Seine with his own strength.

Within days, the Seine was so swollen with bodies that they floated back on to the banks of the river almost as soon as they were thrown in. It was impossible to bury this many dead and huge pits were dug instead of graves to soak up the human detritus. The King laughed when his captains reported that Paris could not swallow all these Protestants.

*Andrew Hussey is the author of* Paris: The Secret History *(see p384).*

Philippe invited Edward II of England and his queen, Isabelle of France. The English were impressed: they soon came back for a long stay.

The palace was quickly filled with functionaries, so the king spent as much of his time as he could outside Paris at the royal castles of **Fontainebleau** (*see p349*) and, especially, **Vincennes** (*see p180*). The needs of the plenipotentiaries left behind to run the kingdom were met by a rapidly growing city population, piled into rather less chic buildings.

Paris was also reinforcing its identity as a major religious centre: as well as the local clergy and dozens of religious orders, the city was home to the masters and students of the university of the **Sorbonne** (established in 1253; *see p153; photo p15*), who were already gaining a reputation for rowdiness. An influx of scholars from all over Europe gave the city a cultural and intellectual cachet it was never to lose.

By 1328 Paris was home to approximately 200,000 inhabitants, making it the most populous city in Europe. However, that year was also notable for being the last of the medieval golden age: the dynasty of Capetian kings spluttered to an inglorious halt when Charles IV died without an heir. The English quickly claimed the throne for the young Edward III, the son of Philippe IV's daughter. Refusing to recognise his descent through the female line, the late king's cousin, Philippe de Valois, claimed the French crown as Philippe VI. So began the Hundred Years War between France and England – a war that in fact would go on for 116 years.

**TROUBLES AND STRIFE**

To make matters worse, the Black Death (bubonic plague) ravaged Europe from the 1340s. Those not finished by the plague had to contend with food shortages, ever-increasing taxes, riots, repression, currency devaluations and marauding mercenaries. Meanwhile, in Paris, the honeymoon period for the king and the bourgeoisie was coming to an end. Rich and populous, Paris was expected to bear the brunt of the war burden; and as defeat followed defeat (notably the disaster at Crécy in August 1346), the bourgeoisie and people of the city were increasingly exasperated by the futility of the sacrifices they were making for the hideously expensive war. To fund the conflict, King Jean II tried to introduce new tax laws – without success. When the king was captured by the English at Poitiers in 1356, his problems passed to his 18-year-old son, Charles.

The Etats Généraux, consultant body to the throne, was summoned to the royal palace on the Ile de la Cité to discuss the country's woes. The teenage king was besieged with angry demands for reform from the bourgeoisie, particularly from Etienne Marcel, then provost of the local merchants. Marcel seized control of Paris and began a bitter power struggle with the crown; in 1357, fearing widespread revolt, Charles fled to Compiègne. But as he ran, he had Paris blockaded.

Marcel called on the peasants, who were also raging against taxes, but they were quickly crushed. He then called on Charles 'the Bad' of Navarre, ally to the English, but his arrival in Paris made many of Marcel's supporters nervous. On 31 July 1358, Marcel was murdered, and the revolution was over. As a safeguard, the returning Charles built a new stronghold to protect Paris: the Bastille.

By 1420, following the French defeat at Agincourt, Paris was in English hands; in 1431 Henry VI of England was crowned King of France in Notre-Dame. He didn't last. Five years later, Henry and his army were driven back to Calais by the Valois king, Charles VII. Charles owed his grasp on power to Jeanne d'Arc, who led the victorious French in the Battle of Orléans, only to be betrayed by her compatriots, who decided she was getting too big for her boots. She was captured and sold to the English, who had her burned as a witch.

By 1436 Paris was once again the capital of France. But the nation had been nearly bled dry by war and was still divided politically, with powerful regional rulers across France continuing to threaten the monarchy. Outside the French borders, the ambitions of the Austrian Habsburg dynasty represented a serious threat. In this general atmosphere of instability, disputes over trade, religion and taxation were all simmering dangerously in the political background.

**RENAISSANCE AND REFORMATION**

In the closing decades of the 15th century, the restored Valois monarchs sought to reassert their position. A wave of building projects was the public sign of this effort, producing such masterpieces as St-Etienne-du-Mont, **St-Eustache** (*see p115*) and private homes like the Hôtel de Cluny (which today houses the Musée National du Moyen Age) and the **Hôtel de Sens**, which now accommodates the **Bibliothèque de Forney** (for both, *see p136*). The Renaissance in France had its peak under François I. As well as being involved in the construction of the magnificent châteaux at Fontainebleau, Blois and Chambord, François was equally responsible for transforming the Louvre from a fortress into a royal palace. He held open house for such luminaries as Leonardo da Vinci and Benvenuto Cellini. He also established the Collège de France to

encourage humanist learning outside the control of the clergy-dominated universities.

Despite burning heretics by the dozen, François was unable to stop the spread of Protestantism, launched in Germany by Martin Luther in 1517. Resolutely Catholic, Paris was the scene of some horrific violence against the Huguenots, as supporters of the new faith were called. The picture was complicated by the political conflict between the Huguenot Prince de Condé and the Catholic Duc de Guise.

By the 1560s the situation had degenerated into open warfare. Catherine de Médicis, the scheming Italian widow of Henri II, was the real force in court politics. It was she who connived to murder prominent Protestants gathered in Paris for the marriage of the king's sister on St Bartholomew's Day (23 August 1572). Catherine's main aim was to dispose of her powerful rival, Gaspard de Coligny, but the situation got out of hand, and as many as 3,000 people were butchered. Henri III attempted to reconcile the religious factions and eradicate the powerful families directing the conflict, but the people of Paris turned against him and he was forced to flee. His assassination in 1589 brought the Valois line to an end.

### THE BOURBONS

The throne of France being up for grabs, Henri of Navarre declared himself King Henri IV,

launching the Bourbon dynasty. Paris was not impressed. The city closed its gates against the Huguenot king, and the inhabitants endured a four-year siege by supporters of the new ruler. Henri managed to break the impasse by having himself converted to Catholicism (and was later heard to quip, *'Paris vaut bien une messe'* – Paris is well worth a mass).

Henri set about rebuilding his ravaged capital. He completed the **Pont Neuf** (*see p87*), the first bridge to span the whole of the Seine. He commissioned place Dauphine and the city's first enclosed residential square – the place Royale – now **place des Vosges** (*see p135*). The square was the merry scene of jousting competitions and countless duels.

Henri also tried to reconcile his Catholic and Protestant subjects, issuing the Edict of Nantes in 1598, effectively giving each religion equal status. The Catholics hated the deal, and the Huguenots were suspicious. Henri was the subject of at least 23 attempted assassinations by fanatics of both persuasions. Finally, in 1610, a Catholic by the name of François Ravaillac fatally stabbed the king while he was stuck in traffic on rue de la Ferronnerie.

### TWO CARDINALS

Since Henri's son, Louis XIII, was only eight at the time of his father's death, the widow, Marie de Médicis, took up the reins of power. We can

**Eglise St-Sulpice.** *See p20.*

thank her for the **Palais du Luxembourg** (*see p160*) and the 24 paintings she commissioned from Rubens, now part of the Louvre collection.

Louis took up his royal duties in 1617, but Cardinal Richelieu, chief minister from 1624, was the man who ran France. Something of a schemer, he outwitted the king's mother, his wife (Anne of Austria) and a host of princes and place-seekers. Richelieu helped to strengthen the power of the monarch, and he did much to limit the independence of the aristocracy. The cardinal was also a great architectural patron. He commissioned Jacques Lemercier to build what is now the **Palais-Royal** (*see p106*), and ordered the rebuilding of the Sorbonne.

The Counter-Reformation was at its height, and lavish churches such as the baroque **Val-de-Grâce** (*see p151*) were an important reassertion of Catholic supremacy. The 17th century was 'Le Grand Siècle', a time of patronage of art and artists, even if censorship forced the brilliant mathematician and philosopher René Descartes into exile.

The first national newspaper, *La Gazette*, hit the streets in 1631; Richelieu used it as a propaganda tool. The cardinal founded the **Académie Française** (*see p156*), a sort of literary think-tank, which is still working, slowly, on the dictionary of the French language that Richelieu commissioned from them in 1634. Richelieu died in 1642; Louis XIII

followed suit a few months later. The new king, Louis XIV, was five years old. Anne of Austria became regent, with the Italian Cardinal Mazarin, a Richelieu protégé, as chief minister. Rumour has it that Anne and Mazarin may have been married. Mazarin's townhouse is now home to the **Bibliothèque Nationale de France – Richelieu** (*see p108*).

Endless wars against Austria and Spain had depleted the royal coffers and left the nation drained by exorbitant taxation. In 1648 the royal family was chased out of Paris by a popular uprising, 'la Fronde', named after the catapults used by some of the rioters. Parisians soon tired of the anarchy that followed. When Mazarin's army retook the city in 1653, the boy-king was warmly welcomed. Mazarin died in 1661 and Louis XIV, now 24 years old, decided he would rule France without the assistance of any chief minister.

### SHINE ON, SUN KING

The 'Roi Soleil', or Sun King, was an absolute monarch. 'L'état, c'est moi' (I am the State) was his vision of power. To prove his grandeur, the king embarked on wars against England, Holland and Austria. He also refurbished and extended the Louvre, commissioned **place Vendôme** (*see p106*) and **place des Victoires** (*see p109*), constructed the **Observatory** (*see p165*) and laid out the *grands boulevards* along the lines of the old city walls. The triumphal arches at **Porte St-Denis** and **Porte St-Martin** (for both, *see p112*) date from this time too. His major project was the palace at **Versailles** (*see p351*), a massive complex that drew on the age's finest architectural, artistic and landscape-design talents. Louis moved his court there in 1682.

Louis XIV owed much of his brilliant success to the work of Jean-Baptiste Colbert, nominally in charge of state finances, but eventually taking control of all the important levers of the state machine. Colbert was the force behind the Sun King's redevelopment of Paris. The Hôtel des Invalides was built to accommodate the crippled survivors of Louis' wars, the **Salpêtrière** (*see p175*) to shelter fallen women. In 1702 Paris was divided into 20 *quartiers* (not until the Revolution was it re-mapped into arrondissements). **Le Procope** (*see p156*), the city's first café, opened in 1686. Although its original proprietor, Francesco Procopio dei Coltelli, would no longer recognise it since a 1989 facelift, the place is still in business. Colbert died in 1683, and Louis' luck on the battlefield ran out. Hopelessly embroiled in the War of the Spanish Succession, the country was devastated by famine in 1692.

The Sun King died in 1715, leaving no direct heir. His five-year-old great-grandson, Louis XV, was named king, with Philippe d'Orléans as regent. The court moved back to Paris. Installed in the Palais-Royal, the regent set about enjoying his few years of power, hosting lavish dinners that degenerated into orgies. The state, meanwhile, remained chronically in debt.

## THE ENLIGHTENMENT

Some of the city's more sober residents were making Paris the intellectual capital of Europe. Enlightenment thinkers such as Diderot, Montesquieu, Voltaire and Rousseau were all active during the reign of Louis XV. Literacy rates were increasing – 50 per cent of French men could read, 25 per cent of women – and the publishing industry was booming.

The king's mistress, Madame de Pompadour, encouraged him to finance the building of the Ecole Militaire and the laying out of place Louis XV, known to us as **place de la Concorde** (*see p106*). The massive church of **St-Sulpice** (*see p160; photo p18*) was completed in 1776. Many of the great houses in the area bounded by rue de Lille, rue de Varenne and rue de Grenelle date from the first half of the 18th century. The private homes of aristocrats and wealthy bourgeois, these would become the venues for numerous salons, the informal discussion sessions often devoted to topics raised by Enlightenment questioning.

The Enlightenment spirit of rational humanism finally took the venom out of the Catholic–Protestant power struggle, and the increase in public debate helped to change views about the nature of the state and the place and authority of the monarchy. As Jacques Necker, Louis XVI's finance minister on the eve of the Revolution, put it, popular opinion was 'an invisible power that, without treasury, guard or army, gives its laws to the city, the court and even the palaces of kings'. Thanks to the Enlightenment, and an ever-growing burden of taxation on the poorest strata of society to prop up the wealthiest, that power would overturn the status quo for good.

## THE FRENCH REVOLUTION

Louis XVI had poor control of his country's swelling problems, and French intervention in the Seven Years War and the American War of Independence had left the country practically bankrupt. Subsequent attempts to introduce new taxes met with strong opposition from the bourgeoisie. After a ruined harvest and a harsh winter, bread prices soared, as did discontent. Springtime in 1789 brought riots on the rue du Faubourg-St-Antoine, where factory workers' wages had been cut. The *parlements*, or high courts, urged Louis to call a meeting of the Etats Généraux – the representative body for the First Estate (the clergy), the Second Estate (the nobility) and the Third Estate (the bourgeoisie and commoners).

On 5 May 1789, the king reluctantly faced the Etats at Versailles. The Third Estate, which had as many members as the other two combined, demanded that the three merge into a single assembly, with one vote per member. Louis refused. On 20 June the Third Estate reconvened on the playing courts at the Jeu de Paumes at Versailles and swore to establish a national constitution. The embattled Louis eventually conceded and allowed the Etats to form the Assemblée Nationale. But behind the scenes, the king was gathering troops to disband the assembly; and on 12 July he publicly, and foolishly, dismissed the commoner's ally, finance minister Jacques Necker, prompting a violent counter-coup.

> **'The crowd marched on the Bastille prison and proceeded to tear it down. Only seven prisoners were imprisoned there, but the symbolic victory was immense.'**

On 13 July Camille Desmoulins, a young unemployed lawyer, empassioned an angry crowd gathered in the Palais-Royal garden to take action. The next day, the crowd pillaged Les Invalides for arms, marched on the Bastille prison and proceeded to tear it down. Only seven prisoners were imprisoned there, but the symbolic victory was immense (and enduring, as the annual *quatorze juillet* celebrations show; *see p277*). A chastened Louis came to Paris on 17 July to acknowledge the crowds at the Hôtel de Ville.

The establishment of the constitution forged ahead, and sparked furious debate. Tax breaks for the nobility and clergy were abolished, the country was divided into local governments and Roman Catholic Church property was seized. Two Paris convents hosted two newly formed political clubs. On the Left Bank, at a 13th-century Franciscan convent (some parts of which are still standing at 15 rue de l'Ecole de Médicine), the Cordeliers club charged its members, mostly the poor *sans-culottes* (so called because they couldn't afford breeches), a few cents to hear monarchy-bashing speeches by its leading lights. These included the figures of Desmoulins and Marat. On the

Right Bank, the more radical Jacobins, who included the likes of Mirabeau, Danton and Robespierre, took up residency in a Dominican convent on rue St-Honoré, later knocked down by Napoleon.

One of Louis' original problems, the price of bread, had not budged. In October a mob of starving women marched the 12 miles (19km) to Versailles and demanded that the king come to Paris. He promised to send the women grain, an offer they rejected by decapitating some of his guards. Louis wisely transferred to the Tuileries. In the months that followed, the Jacobins roused powerful Republican feeling. Fearing greater danger at home and hoping to gain support abroad, the king and his family attempted to flee Paris on 20 June 1791. With Louis disguised as a valet, they got as far as Varennes, where a commoner recognised Louis' face from his portrait on a coin. Louis, Marie-Antoinette and family were brought back to

Paris in disgrace, crowds throwing things at their coach, and poking their heads through the window and spitting.

On 14 September Louis accepted the new constitution, and the Revolution appeared to be over. But other monarchies were plotting to reinstate the king. In 1792 Austrian and Prussian troops invaded France, gaining rapidly on Paris with easy victories against a weak French army. The Republicans, rightly, suspected Louis of conspiring with the enemy, and scrabbled together their own army to capture him, ringing out the cannons on Pont Neuf to enrol the public. On the morning of 10 August, the Tuileries palace rang with gunfire. Swiss guards enlisted to defend the king put up a staunch fight, but were hacked to death along with all the palace staff. Two bloody days later, the royal family was incarcerated in the Temple prison by the radical Commune de Paris, headed by Danton, Marat and Robespierre.

*Liberty Leading the People* by Delacroix.

Rampant suspicion about possible traitors led the Revolutionaries to the gates of the city's prisons. They invaded, and murdered 2,000 so-called traitors, including the Princess of Lamballe, whose head was stuck on a spike and paraded past the royal family at the Temple. The monarchy was abolished on 22 September; the king was executed on 21 January. A trial, Robespierre claimed, was out of the question, since it would put 'the Revolution itself in the dock'. The guillotine, a symbol of the Revolution's brutality (in fact, invented by Dr Guillotin as a humane method of execution) stood at the place de la Révolution and took thousands of heads, including that of Louis' widow, Marie-Antoinette, almost a year later. She awaited her fate in a wallpapered prison cell at the Conciergerie.

There was precious little dignity to this particular period of the Revolution. Within the Revolutionary Convention, which had replaced the Assemblée Nationale, the Jacobins had expelled the monarchist Girondins (a young Girondist, Charlotte Corday, retaliated by stabbing Marat to death at his home) and were gathering dictatorial momentum. Headed by 'l'incorruptible' Robespierre, the Jacobins in September 1793 vowed to wage terror against all rebels, Girondins and dissidents. In the Great Terror of 1794, the guillotine was transferred to place du Trône Renversé ('Overturned Throne', now place de la Nation), and sliced through 1,300 necks in just six weeks. The bodies were dumped in the Picpus garden (now the **Cimetière de Picpus**; *see p139*). The tumbrils, or two-wheeled carts, that carried the dead away were painted green to disguise their bloody load.

Almost everybody wanted the Terror to end. The French army had successfully beaten off foreign forces, and the incessant killing began to look unnecessary. Robespierre and his cohorts attempted some democratic reform, but most people wanted them gone. On 28 July 1794 he was executed, and the reign of terror collapsed. The biggest and bloodiest revolution was finally over.

## NAPOLEON

Amid the post-Revolutionary chaos, power was divided between a two-housed Assembly and a Directory of five men. The French public reacted badly to hearing of England's unsuccessful attempts to promote more popular rebellion; when a royalist rising in Paris needed to be put down, a young officer from Corsica was the man to do it: Napoleon Bonaparte.

Napoleon quickly became the Directory's right-hand man. When they needed someone to lead a campaign against Austria, he was the man. Victory saw France – and Napoleon – glorified. After a further, aborted campaign to Egypt in 1799, Napoleon returned home to put down another royalist plot, made himself the chief of the newly governing three-man Consul – and by 1804 was emperor.

After failing to squeeze out the English by setting up the Continental System to block trade across the Channel, Napoleon waged massive wars against Britain, Russia and Austria. On his way to the disaster of Moscow, Napoleon gave France the *lycée* educational system, the Napoleonic Code of civil law, the Legion of Honour, the Banque de France, the **Pont des Arts** (*see p87*), the **Arc de Triomphe** (*see p117*), the **Madeleine** church (he re-established Catholicism as the state religion; *see p109*), **La Bourse** (*see p109*) and **rue de Rivoli**. He was also responsible for the centralised bureaucracy that still manages to drive the French mad.

As Russian troops – who had chased Napoleon's once-mighty army all the way from Moscow and Leipzig – invaded France, Paris itself came under threat. Montmartre, then named Montnapoléon, had a telegraph machine at its summit, one that had given so many of the emperor's orders and transmitted news of so many victories. The hill fell to Russian troops. Napoleon gave the order to blow up the city's main powder stores, and thus Paris itself. His officer refused. Paris accommodated carousing Russian, Prussian and English soldiers while Napoleon was sent to exile in Elba.

A hundred days later, he was back, leading an army against Wellington and Blücher's troops in the midsummer mud of Waterloo, near Brussels. A further defeat saw the end of him. Paris survived further foreign occupation. The diminutive Corsican died on the South Atlantic prison island of St Helena in 1821.

## ANOTHER ROUND OF BOURBONS

Having sampled revolution and military dictatorship, the French were now ready to give monarchy a second chance. The Bourbons got back in business, briefly, in 1815 in the person of Louis XVIII, Louis XVI's elderly brother. Several efforts were made to adapt the monarchy to the new political realities, though the new king's Charter of Liberties was not a wholly sincere expression of how he meant to rule. Liberal intellectual activity flourished nevertheless, with figures such as the caricaturist Daumier regularly poking satirical fun at the bourgeoisie.

When another brother of Louis XVI, Charles X, became king in 1824, he decided that enough royal energy had been wasted trying to reconcile the nation's myriad factions. It was

time for a spot of old-fashioned absolutism. But the forces unleashed during the Revolution, and the social divisions that had opened as a result, were not to be ignored – the people were happy to respond with some old-fashioned rebellion. In the 1830 elections, the liberals won a hefty majority in the Chamber of Deputies, the legislative body. Charles's unpopular minister Prince Polignac, a returned émigré, promptly dissolved the Chamber, announced a date for new elections and curtailed the number of voters. Polishing off this collection of bad decisions was the 26 July decree abolishing the freedom of the press. The day after its issue, 5,000 print workers and journalists filled the streets and three newspapers went to press. When police tried to confiscate copies, they sparked a three-day riot, 'les Trois Glorieuses', with members of the disbanded National Guard manning the barricades. On 30 July Charles dismissed Polignac, but it was too late. He had little choice but to abdicate, and fled to England. As French revolutions go, it was a neat, brief affair.

Another leftover from the *ancien régime* was now winched on to the throne – Louis-Philippe, Duc d'Orléans, who had some Bourbon blood in his veins. A father of eight who never went out without his umbrella, he was eminently acceptable to the newly powerful bourgeoisie. But the poor, who had risked their lives in two attempts to change French society, were unimpressed by the new king's promise to embrace a moderate and liberal version of the Revolutionary heritage.

**THE NINETEENTH CENTURY**

Philosopher Walter Benjamin declared Paris 'the capital of the 19th century', and he had a point. Though it was smaller than its global rival of London, in intellectual and cultural spheres it reigned supreme. On the demographic front, its population doubled to one million between 1800 and 1850. Most of the new arrivals were rural labourers, who had come to find work on the city's ever-expanding building sites. Meanwhile, the middle classes were doing well, thanks to the relatively late arrival of the industrial revolution in France, and the solid administrative structures inherited from Napoleon. The poor were as badly off as ever, only now there were more of them. The back-breaking hours worked in the factories would not be curbed by legislation: 'Whatever the lot of the workers is, it is not the manufacturer's responsibility to improve it,' said one trade minister. In Left Bank cafés, a new bohemian tribe of students derided the materialistic government. Workers' pamphlets and newspapers, such as *La Ruche Populaire*,

gave voice to the starving, crippled poor. A wave of ill feeling was gradually building up against Louis-Philippe.

On 23 February 1848, hundreds of Parisians – men, women and students – moved along the boulevards towards a public banquet at La Madeleine. The king's minister, François Guizot, had forbidden any direct campaigning by opposition parties in the forthcoming election, so the parties held banquets instead of meetings.

One diarist of the time noted that some of the crowd had stuffed swords and daggers underneath their shirts, but the demonstration was largely peaceful – until the troops stationed on the boulevard des Capucines opened fire, igniting a riot.

> **'As barricades sprang up all over the city, Louis-Philippe abdicated and a liberal provisional government declared a republic.'**

As barricades sprang up all over the city, a trembling Louis-Philippe abdicated and a liberal provisional government declared a republic. The virtual epidemic of poverty and unemployment was stemmed by creating national *ateliers*, or workshops, but such 'radical' reforms made the right extremely nervous. A conservative government took power in May 1848, and shut down the *ateliers*. A month later, the poor were back in the streets. Some 50,000 took part in the 'June Days' protests, which were quite comprehensively crushed by General Cavaignac's troops. In total, about 1,500 Parisians died and some 5,000 were deported.

As the pamphleteer Alphonse Karr said of the revolution's aftermath, 'plus ça change, plus c'est la même chose' (the more things change, the more they stay the same). In December 1848 Louis Bonaparte – nephew of Napoleon – was elected president. By 1852 he had moved into the Tuileries palace and declared himself Emperor Napoleon III. Victor Hugo called him Little Napoleon, but the diminutive Bonaparte held on to power for 22 years – significantly longer than his 'bigger' diminutive forebear.

**THE SECOND EMPIRE**

The emperor appointed a lawyer as *préfet* to mastermind the reconstruction of Paris. In less than two decades, prefect Georges-Eugène Haussmann had created the most magnificent city in Europe. His goals included better access to railway stations, better water supplies, an

extended sewer system and a long list of new hospitals, barracks, theatres and *mairies*. It was a colossal, revolutionary project, and it transformed the capital. Haussmann created a network of wide, arrow-straight avenues that were better ventilated and more hygienic than the narrow streets they replaced – particularly in the old quarters on the islands and just off the Seine, whose rapid improvement would see the largest slum clearance ever accomplished in Europe. Now, with their unobstacled vistas, these streets were far more aesthetic. Their dimensions also had political advantages: the streets would be harder to barricade, and troops would be able to reach the scene of any future insurrection faster and in greater numbers. (Boulevard de Sébastopol, in particular, was conceived as a military fast track to the centre.)

So synonymous is Haussmann with the city's recasting, and with a certain architectural style, that he's sometimes believed to have designed the buildings himself. He was indeed a formidable administrator, but no civil engineer: architectural detail he left to others. Shrewdly, he refused to employ the official architects of the day and hired instead more modest practitioners – people like Gabriel Davioud – who were much easier to command. The tree-lined streets radiating out from place Charles-de-Gaulle are the classic expression of Haussmann's vision, while the rich mix of styles in Charles Garnier's **Opéra** (*see p110*) is often seen as typical of Second Empire self-indulgence.

Not everyone was happy. Haussmann's works destroyed thousands of buildings, including beautiful Middle Ages monuments; on the whole of Ile de la Cité only Notre-Dame survived. Entire residential areas were wiped off the map, and only the owners of the buildings themselves were compensated; tenants were merely booted out and left to fend for themselves. Writers and artists lamented the loss of the more quirky Paris they used to know, and criticised the unfriendly grandeur of the new city. But there was no going back.

Napoleon III's meddling foreign policy would be his downfall. After his initially successful Crimean War of the mid 1850s, he tried in vain to impose the Catholic Maximilian as ruler of Mexico. Maximilian's execution was the subject of Edouard Manet's famous painting. Manet would be the precursor of the burgeoning Impressionist movement, which would include Monet, Renoir, Degas and Cézanne. The emperor's next misadventure, the Franco-Prussian War of 1870, divided the figureheads of this artistic movement. They either fought or fled. Monet's stay in London marked him: he

discovered the light techniques used by Turner. Once the war was over, Manet, Monet and Renoir would move to bucolic, riverside locations, to experiment with the contrasting use of colours and light. Artists flocked to Paris to emulate them. Impressionism begat Fauvism and Matisse, Cubism and Picasso. Paris was the centre of the art world.

At home, the city's rapid industrialisation saw the rise of Socialism and Communism amid the disgruntled working classes. Napoleon III gave limited rights to trade unions. Abroad, though, the now constitutional monarch was a disaster. A sick man, dominated by his wife Eugénie, he allowed himself to be drawn into a war with Prussia. France was soon defeated. At Sedan, in September 1870, 100,000 French troops were forced to surrender to Bismarck's Prussians; Napoleon III himself was captured, never to return.

## 'Paris held out, starving, for four brave months, its citizens picking rats from the gutter for food.'

The war continued, and back in Paris, a provisional government hastily took power. Elections gave conservative monarchists the majority, though the Paris vote was firmly Republican. Former prime minister Adolphe Thiers assumed executive power. Meanwhile, Prussian forces marched on Paris and laid siege to the city. Paris held out, starving, for four brave months, its citizens picking rats from the gutter for food. Léon Gambetta, a young politician, escaped in style (by hot-air balloon) but failed to raise an army in the south. In January 1871 the provisional government signed a bitter armistice that relinquished the industrial heartlands of Alsace and Lorraine and agreed to pay a five-million-franc indemnity. German troops would stay on French soil until the bill was paid.

But with occupying army camps stationed around their city, Parisians considered the treaty a dishonour and remained defiant. Thiers ordered his soldiers to enter the city and strip it of its cannons, but the insurgents cut them short. The new government scuttled off to the haven of Versailles, while on 26 March Paris elected its own municipal body, the Commune, so called in memory of the spirit of 1792. The 92 members of the Commune hailed from the left and working classes; their agenda was liberal (schools would be secularised, debts suspended) but war-like (Germany must be defeated). Paris itself was given a little makeover: the column

projecting Napoleonic glory into place Vendôme was pulled down, and statues of the great emperor were smashed all over town.

Thiers would not stand by and watch. Artillery fire picked at the Communards' sandbag barricades on the edges of Paris, and the suburbs fell by 11 April. In the sixth week of fighting, troops broke in through the Porte de St-Cloud and covered the springtime city in blood. The ill-equipped Communards faced a massacre: some 25,000 were killed in a matter of days. In revenge, around 50 hostages were taken and shot, including the Archbishop of Paris. The infamous *pétroleuses*, women wielding petrol bombs, burned off their anger, torching the Tuileries and the Hôtel de Ville. On the ultimate day of *la semaine sanglante*, 28 May, 147 Communards were trapped and shot in **Père-Lachaise cemetery** (*see p146*), against the 'Mur des Fédérés', still an icon of the Commune struggle. The dead were buried in the streets, the prisons crammed with 40,000 Communards; thousands were deported, many to penal colonies in New Caledonia.

### THE THIRD REPUBLIC

Out of the ruins of the Second Empire rose the Third Republic, a hasty compromise given little chance of survival even by those who supported it. In fact, its makeshift constitution was to survive until 1940, thus becoming the most enduring – so far – in modern French history.

Thanks mainly to the huge economic boost provided by colonial expansion in Africa and Indo-China, the horrors of the Commune were soon forgotten in the self-indulgent materialism of the turn of the century. The **Eiffel Tower** (*see pp168-174*) was built as the centrepiece of the 1889 Exposition Universelle. For the next Exposition Universelle, in 1900, the **Grand Palais** (*see p118*) and **Petit Palais**, the **Pont Alexandre III** (*see p87*) and the Gare d'Orsay (now the **Musée d'Orsay**; *see pp168-174*) were built to affirm France's position as a world power, and the first line of the métro opened, linking porte Maillot and Vincennes. The first cinema had opened (1895), and clubs like the **Moulin Rouge** (*see p281*) were buzzing. The lurid life of Montmartre, depicted by Toulouse-Lautrec – and its cheap rents – would attract the world's artistic community.

In 1894 a Jewish army officer, Captain Alfred Dreyfus, was dismissed in disgrace from the army and deported to Devil's Island, convicted of selling secrets to the Prussians. The affair rocked the establishment to its roots. Emile Zola famously championed Dreyfus' cause in *J'Accuse!*, an open letter to President Faure. The Catholic right wing sided with the army, and lost heavily when Dreyfus was proven innocent.

### THE GREAT WAR

Against the backdrop of the major European powers attempting to outdo each other to industrialise and carve up the atlas, France and England came to a political understanding in 1904: the Entente Cordiale. With the inclusion of Russia, this became the Triple Entente, which was slowly stacking up against the Triple Alliance of Germany, Italy and Austro-Hungary. Nationalist tensions rose as European empires crumbled. On 3 August 1914 Germany declared war on France. Although the Germans never made it to Paris in World War I – German troops were stopped 20 kilometres (12 miles) short of the city thanks to the French victory in the Battle of the Marne – the artillery was audible. Paris, and French society as a whole, suffered terribly, despite ultimate victory.

The nations gathered at Versailles to make the peace and established new European states. The League of Nations was formed. Artists responded to the horrors and absurdity of the conflict with Surrealism, a movement founded in Paris by André Breton, a doctor who had treated troops in the trenches and embraced Freud's theories of the unconscious. In 1924 Surrealism had a manifesto, a year later its first exhibition. Again, artists (and photographers), including Dali and Man Ray, flocked to Paris. By now Montmartre was too dear, and Montparnasse, south of St-Germain, became the hub of artistic life. The interwar years were a whirl of activity in artistic and political circles. Paris became the avant-garde capital of the world, recorded by Hemingway, F Scott Fitzgerald and Gertrude Stein, who had made the city their home and source of inspiration.

Meanwhile, the Depression unleashed a wave of political violence, Fascists fighting Socialists and Communists for control. The 1936 election of Léon Blum's Front Populaire saw the introduction of such social benefits as paid holidays for workers. At the same time, many writers were leaving Paris for Spain to cover – and, indeed, to take part in – the Civil War. Across the German border, the contentious territories of Alsace-Lorraine – and the burden of the World War I peace agreements signed in Paris – became one of many bugbears held by the new chancellor, Hitler. As war broke out, France believed that its Maginot line would hold strong against the German threat. The Nazis simply bypassed it through Belgium.

### WORLD WAR II

Paris was in German hands within weeks of the start of hostilities. The city fell without a fight. A pro-German government was set up in Vichy, a spa resort with enough hotels to accommodate the number of administrators. It was headed by

the ageing World War I hero Marshall Pétain, popularly known as the 'Victor of Verdun', while a young army officer, Charles de Gaulle, went to London to organise the Free French opposition. For those happy to get along with the German army, the period of the Occupation presented few hardships and, indeed, some good business opportunities. Food was rationed, and tobacco and coffee went out of circulation, but the black market thrived. In other ways, life went on much as before: each month during the winter of 1939-40, 800,000 Parisians still managed to go to the cinema.

For those who resisted, there were the Gestapo torture chambers at avenue Foch or rue Lauriston. The Germans further discouraged uncooperative behaviour with executions: one victim, whose name now adorns a métro station, was Jacques Bonsergent, a student caught fly-posting and shot because he refused to reveal the names of his friends who escaped.

Paris was also a bad place in which to be Jewish. The Vichy government was so eager to please the Germans, it organised anti-Semitic measures without prompting from the occupier. As of the spring of 1941, the French authorities deported Jews to the death camps, frequently via the internment camp at Drancy. Prime Minister Pierre Laval claimed it was a necessary concession to his Third Reich masters. (Laval would later flee to Spain, be refused political asylum by Franco and be handed to the Americans. After a failed attempt at poisoning himself, he was shot in 1945.)

In July 1942, 12,000 Jewish French citizens were rounded up in the Vélodrome d'Hiver, a sports complex on quai de Grenelle, and then dispatched to Auschwitz. (In July 1994 a memorial to the victims was finally erected near the site of the long-demolished sports arena.)

## THE LIBERATION

Paris survived the war practically unscathed, ultimately thanks to the bravery of one of its captors. On 23 August 1944, as the Allied armies of liberation approached the city, Hitler ordered his commander, Dietrich von Choltitz, to detonate the explosives that had been set all over town in anticipation of a retreat. Von Choltitz refused. On 25 August, French troops, tactfully placed at the head of the US forces, entered the city, and General de Gaulle led the parade down the Champs-Elysées.

Writers and artists swept back into Paris to celebrate and seek out old haunts. Hemingway held court at the Ritz and Scribe hotels with the great journalists of the day, clinking glasses with veterans of the Spanish Civil War such as photographer Robert Capa and George Orwell. Picasso's studio was besieged by well-wishers.

However, the Liberation was by no means the end of France's troubles. De Gaulle was the hero of the hour, but relations between the interim government he commanded and the Resistance – largely Communist – were still tricky. Orders issued to *maquis* leaders in the provinces were often ignored. The Communists wanted a revolution, and de Gaulle suspected them of hatching plans to seize Paris prior to August 1944.

Meanwhile, de Gaulle knew that he had to commit every available French soldier to the march on Germany, or risk being sidelined by the other allies after the war. With no military forces to spare for domestic law and order, he had to leave homeland security to the very people – the 'patriotic militias' – who were most likely to be at least sympathetic to the Communist cause; or, even more dubiously, gendarmes who had previously worked with the occupying power.

When it came to rebuilding the country, the uncomfortable compromises multiplied – even to the point of injustice. Companies that had worked with the Germans were the best equipped, and thus the most useful; and while a handful of collaborating industrialists, including the motor-vehicle baron Louis Renault, were imprisoned, many got off scot-free. In any case, recovery was slow to come. There were shortages of everything. Food was as hard to come by as it had been during the war; indeed, many complained they had been better off under the Germans. Medical supplies were inadequate, as were basic necessities. Even in the ministries, paper was so scarce that correspondence had to be sent out on Vichy letterhead with the sender crossing out 'Etat Français' at the top and writing 'République Française' instead. It was a poor state of affairs.

## THE FOURTH REPUBLIC

On 8 May 1945, de Gaulle made a broadcast to the nation to announce Germany's surrender. Paris went wild. Cars hooted their horns, church bells rang, sirens wailed, artillery boomed and low-flying aircraft zoomed overhead. Crowds packed out the Champs-Elysées, and the city's fountains were switched back on. It was the party to end all parties.

The euphoria didn't last. There were strikes. And more strikes. Liberation had proved to be a restoration, not the revolution the Communists, now the most powerful political force in the land, had hoped for. The Communist Party was, in at least one respect, as pragmatic as everyone else: it did its utmost to turn parliamentary democracy to its advantage, to wit, getting as many of the top jobs as it could. (It even lobbied to get members into the Académie Française.)

# Patriots and traitors

Not all Parisians found the German Occupation during World War II a burden. This was especially true of writers. During the war a number of notable pro-Nazi intellectuals emerged. These writers – including Robert Brasillach, Lucien Rebatet and Pierre Drieu La Rochelle – often styled themselves as 'true voices of Paris', though their ideological line had been set in Berlin, where many of them had moved when hostilities first broke out. During the Occupation, Brasillach's journal *Je Suis Partout* came to the forefront, alongside the newspaper *Au Pilori*, as the leading organ of the Right and the remnants of the self-hating French Left. Among journalists who came over to the collaborationist side without shame or hesitation were Abel Bonnard, Fernand de Brinon and Jean Luchaire.

The strategy of Otto Abetz, the German ambassador, was to court those writers, intellectuals and politicians who had formerly been or indeed still were associated with the Left, but were now disillusioned by the wreckage of the Parisian political landscape. This explained the apparently anomalous situation in 1941 and 1942 when well-known writers of left-wing sympathies – including the likes of Raymond Queneau, Marguerite Duras, Simone de Beauvoir, Albert Camus and Jean-Paul Sartre – found themselves published and even lauded in Occupied Paris.

The former Surrealist turned Communist Louis Aragon finally came to proper national prominence with his 'patriotic poems' which, reactionary in both form and content, echoed Victor Hugo's calls for national solidarity against the oppressor. For example, in the 1943 poem 'Du poète à son parti', Aragon presented a peculiarly Parisian marriage of Communism and patriotism. It evaded the censor and had genuinely popular appeal.

Although a handful of intellectuals chose not to publish at all during the war, most writers and artists were able to function almost as if nothing untoward had happened. Sometimes this was because the censor simply failed to discern anything significantly anti-German in the work (this was said to be the reason that Sartre's 1942 play *Les Mouches*, 'The Flies', received a positive critical reception, with German critics turning a blind eye to its allegorical references to the Occupation).

Courting French writers was intended by the Germans to prevent the emergence of literary martyrs, and it also had the effect of reducing much of the literary output of the period to mere impotent rage: political and philosophical debates centred on issues of defeat, suffering and silence, but rarely engaged directly with the enemy. Proof, the collaborationist Right argued, that the French model of enlightenment and egalitarianism had been no more than a dangerous illusion that had brought the country to disaster.

*Andrew Hussey is the author of* Paris: The Secret History *(see p384).*

# Maydays

For much of the tumultuous month of May 1968, President de Gaulle was away on a state visit to Romania. Rumours that he was scared to come back began to circulate among students and striking workers. But on the night of 24 May, as he had done during previous crises, the French leader decided to address the nation. He spoke to the strikers directly and contemptuously, accusing them of 'shitting in their own beds'. He didn't concede to any of their demands, but did admit that the old stranglehold on power had to be broken, and that there was a need for a 'mutation in our society... a more extensive participation of everyone in the conduct and result of the activities which concern them.'

This rousing speech did nothing to stop the momentum of the conflict, though. On the night of 24 May barricades went up across France, and in Paris some 30,000 demonstrators marching towards the place de la Bastille found their path blocked by police. They began tearing up paving stones, grabbing café chairs and tables and anything else they found in their path, hurling them at police.

Meanwhile, de Gaulle had left the country once more. As rumours of his resignation spread, he was in fact meeting his generals stationed on the Rhine to reassure himself of their support if the revolution ever came.

The moment never arrived. Instead, at 4.30pm on 30 May, de Gaulle spoke again to the French people. This time he announced there would be elections within 40 days, stating there would be 'civic action against subversion' and warning the people about the threat of 'totalitarian communism'. With a huge sense of relief, the patriotic France that was de Gaulle's natural constituency rose as one: there was a triumphant parade of thousands up the Champs-Elysées, waving *tricolores* and chanting 'France back to work' and 'Clean out the Sorbonne'.

In the occupied Sorbonne, the 'revolutionary festival' had long since degenerated into a nightmare, with the hard core of 'political' students alarmed to find themselves rubbing shoulders with drug dealers, whores and sundry other petty criminals. A group of mercenaries called the 'Katangais', made up of army deserters and thugs, organised a 'defence committee' and tried to impose some sort of order, but their violence was too much for the students to stomach. They were expelled in the first weeks of June.

The defenceless 'commune' was eventually taken over by the police on 16 June. The historic battle for Utopia had ended.

*Andrew Hussey is the author of* Paris: The Secret History *(see p384).*

The pragmatism stopped, however, at its tendency to see Fascists and fifth columnists in every shadow; the French Communist leader, Maurice Thorez, would travel around town only in an armoured limousine with bodyguards in tow, for fear of assassination attempts. A general election was held on 21 October 1945. The Communists secured 159 seats, the Socialists got 146 and the Catholic Mouvement Républicain Populaire got 152. A fortnight later, at the Assemblée Nationale's first session, a unanimous vote was passed maintaining de Gaulle in his position as head of state – but he remained an antagonistic leader. His reluctance to take a firm grip on the disastrous economic situation alienated many intellectuals and industrialists who had once been loyal to him, and his characteristic aloofness only made the misgivings of the general populace worse. He, on the other hand, was disgusted by all the political chicanery – what he called its *pourriture*, or rot. On 20 January 1946, de Gaulle abruptly resigned.

France, meanwhile, looked to swift industrial modernisation under an ambitious plan put forward by internationalist politician Jean Monnet. Although the economy and daily life remained grim, brash new fashion designer Christian Dior put together a stunning collection of strikingly simple clothes: the New Look. Such extravagance horrified many locals, but the fashion industry boomed. Meanwhile, the divisions in Paris between its fashionable and its run-down working-class areas became more pronounced. The northern and eastern edges – areas revived only in the late 20th century by a taste for retro, industrial decor and cheap rent – were forgotten about.

Félix Gouin, the new Socialist premier, quickly nationalised the bigger banks and the coal industry. But the right wing was growing, and there was even a rise of royalist hopes. A referendum was held in May 1946 to determine the crucial tenet of the Fourth Republic's constitution: should the Assemblée Nationale have absolute or restricted power? The results were a narrow victory for those who, like de Gaulle, had insisted the Assemblée's power should be qualified. De Gaulle's prestige increased, but it was to be another 12 years, and a whole new constitution – the Fifth Republic – before he got his hands back on the levers of power. He spent much of his *'passage du désert'* writing his memoirs.

### THE ALGERIAN WAR AND MAY 1968

The post-war years were marked by the rapid disintegration of France's overseas interests – and her rapprochement with Germany to create what would become the European Community.

When revolt broke out in Algeria in 1956, almost 500,000 troops were sent in to protect national interests. A protest by Algerians in Paris on 17 October 1961 led to the deaths of hundreds of people at the hands of the city's police (*see p128* **Battle of Algiers**). The extent of the violence was officially concealed for decades, as was the use of torture against Algerians by French troops. Algeria became independent in 1962.

Meanwhile, the slow, painful discoveries of collaboration in World War II, often overlooked in the rush to put the country back on its feet, were also being faced. The younger generation began to question the motives of the older one. De Gaulle's Fifth Republic was felt by many to be grimly authoritarian. Some, certainly, believe that he designed it to be an elected monarchy, which is interesting when you consider that it's the constitution still in use to this day.

> **'The talk of politics grew across the campuses, turning against the government's stranglehold on the media and President de Gaulle's poor grasp of the economy.'**

In the spring of 1968, students unhappy with overcrowded university conditions took to the streets of Paris at the same time as striking Renault workers. These *soixante-huitards* sprang the greatest public revolt in French living memory. For that, and for the left, at least, the revolutionaries of 1968 are still revered as heroes. At the time, they were students crammed into universities that had been somewhat cheaply expanded in order to accommodate them. The talk of politics grew across the campuses, turning against the government's stranglehold on the media and President de Gaulle's poor grasp of the economy. Ministers did indeed at the time have a sinister habit of leaning on the leading newspaper editors of the day, and television was dubbed 'the government in your dining room'. Inflation was high, and the gap between the working classes and the bourgeoisie was becoming a chasm.

But still, de Gaulle echoed many when he said the events of May 1968 were simply *'incompréhensible'*. The touchpaper was lit at overcrowded Nanterre university, on the outskirts of Paris, where students had been protesting against the war in Vietnam and the tatty state of the campus.

On 2 May, exhausted by the protests, the authorities closed the university down and threatened to expel some of the students. The next day, a sit-in was held in sympathy at the Sorbonne. Police were called to intervene, but made things worse, charging into the crowd with truncheons, tear gas and a comprehensive lack of judgement. The city's streets were soon flooded with thousands of incensed student demonstrators, now officially on strike. The trade unions followed, as did the *lycées*. By mid May nine million people were on strike: factories all over the country were occupied by workers.

On 24 May, de Gaulle intervened – naturally, via the nation's television sets (*see p28* **Maydays**). His speech warned of civil war and pleaded for people's support. It didn't go down well: riots broke out, with students storming the Bourse, only to be thwarted by more police tear gas. Barricades sprang up all over the Latin Quarter, which had become something of a battleground, with the Odéon theatre and the Sorbonne's amphitheatre packed every night with activists and students.

Five days later, as the street violence reached its peak, de Gaulle fled briefly to Germany and Prime Minister Pompidou sent tanks to the edges of Paris. But the crisis didn't quite reach such extremes. Pompidou conceded pay rises of between seven and ten per cent and increased the minimum wage; the country went back to work. A general election was called for 23 June, by which time the right had gathered enough red-fearing momentum to gain a safe majority.

## MITTERRAND

Following the presidencies of Georges Pompidou and Valéry Giscard d'Estaing, the Socialist François Mitterrand took up the task in 1981. The verdict on Mitterrand is still not in: the early part of his presidency saw him introducing some radical political and economic reforms, but the necessities of pragmatism and compromise led to their reversal, and he left the Socialist Party in some disarray. At any rate, Mitterrand made a big difference to Paris – visitors to the city can thank him for his *Grands Projets* without worrying about suggestions that they might represent a most unrepublican form of self-aggrandisement. Mitterrand was responsible for IM Pei's Louvre **pyramid** (*see p93*), the **Grande Arche de la Défense** (*see p183*), the **Opéra Bastille** (*see p315*) and the more recent **Bibliothèque Nationale de France – François Mitterrand** (*see p177*).

## CHIRAC, BUSH AND IRAQ

France may still boast the world's fourth-largest economy, the nuclear deterrent and a permanent seat on the UN Security Council, but her influence on the world stage had been waning for years until President Chirac, flushed from re-election and well aware he was on to a PR winner, stood up in early 2003 to oppose the US-led invasion of Iraq. France's official disapproval of George Bush culminated in the threat to use her Security Council veto against any resolution authorising the use of force without UN say-so, a move inspired by Chirac's hunger for an international role, his fear of the consequences among France's five million Muslims of an attack on Iraq, traditional Gallic anti-Americanism, and a genuine belief that this particular war at this particular time in this particular place was wrong.

Whatever the reason, it did Chirac no harm at all. His personal approval ratings soared at home, at one stage breaking the 80 per cent barrier, and abroad he became the darling of the Islamic world, Africa, Asia and large swathes of continental Europe. He also acquired a most-hated-man status in America, rivalled only by Osama Bin Laden and Saddam Hussein, but that was a small price to pay.

> **'During the heatwave of August 2003, Chirac did not deign to open his mouth, still less cut short his holiday in Canada.'**

Chirac's domestic popularity couldn't last. His prime minister, Jean-Pierre Raffarin, and the centre-right government began attacking some of France's more prized national institutions with a programme of long-overdue reforms, starting with the state pension system.

The obvious fact that a steadily greying population coupled with fewer people in work equals serious pension shortfall did not prevent some of the largest nationwide protests France has seen since 1995, with striking métro staff, hospital workers, postmen, teachers and rubbish collectors creating havoc and bringing the capital to a virtual standstill.

Planned restrictions on the uniquely Gallic, exceptionally generous (and thus heavily indebted) system of unemployment benefit for out-of-work performing-arts professionals led to a further round of protests, as well as the cancellation of France's equivalents of Edinburgh and Glyndebourne, the Avignon and Aix summer cultural festivals.

Then came the official mismanagement and aloofness that characterised the two-week heatwave of August 2003, during which as many as 14,000 elderly people died. Government ministers put their heads in the

# Key events

## EARLY HISTORY

**250 BC** Lutetia founded on the Ile de la Cité by a Celtic tribe, the Parisii.
**52 BC** Paris conquered by the Romans.
**AD 260** St Denis executed on Mount Mercury.
**360** Julian, Governor of Lutetia, is proclaimed Roman Emperor by his troops.
**451** Attila the Hun nearly attacks Paris.
**496** Frankish king Clovis baptised at Reims.
**508** Clovis makes Paris his capital.
**543** Enormous Benedictine monastery of St-Germain-des-Prés founded.
**635** King Dagobert establishes international Fair of St-Denis.
**800** Charlemagne becomes first Holy Roman Emperor. Moves his capital from Paris to Aix-la-Chapelle (Aachen).
**845-880** Paris sacked by the Vikings.
**987** Hugues Capet, Count of Paris, becomes King of France.

## THE CITY TAKES SHAPE

**1136** Abbot Suger begins the construction of the Basilica of St-Denis.
**1163** Building of Notre-Dame begins.
**1181** Philippe-Auguste establishes a new market at Les Halles.
**1190-1202** Philippe-Auguste constructs a protective city wall.
**1215** University of Paris is recognised by Rome with the Papal Charter.
**1246-48** Louis IX (later St Louis) constructs Sainte-Chapelle.
**1253** Sorbonne founded.
**1340** Hundred Years War with England begins – lasting 116 years.
**1357** Revolt by Etienne Marcel.
**1364** Charles V moves royal court to the Louvre and builds Bastille and Vincennes fortresses.
**1420-36** Paris under English rule.
**1422** Henry V of England dies at the Château de Vincennes.
**1463** First printing press in Paris.

## THE WARS OF RELIGION AND AFTER

**1528** François I, the Renaissance King, begins rebuilding the Louvre.
**1572** 23 August: the brutal massacre of Protestants on St Bartholemew's Day.
**1589** Henri III assassinated.
**1593** Henri IV converts to Catholicism, ending Wars of Religion.
**1605** The construction of place des Vosges and Pont Neuf.

**1610** Henri IV assassinated.
**1635** Académie Française founded.
**1643** Cardinal Mazarin becomes regent.
**1648-53** Paris under continual threat by the 'Fronde' rebellion.
**1661** Louis XIV begins personal rule – and the transformation of Versailles; the fall of Fouquet.
**1667** Paris given its first street lighting.
**1671** Building of Les Invalides.
**1672** Creation of the Grands Boulevards on line of Charles V's city wall. Portes St-Denis and St-Martin built.
**1680** Comédie Française founded.
**1682** Louis XIV transfers court to Versailles.

## ROYALTY TO REPUBLICANISM

**1700** Beginning of the 15-year War of the Spanish Succession.
**1715** Death of Louis XIV; Philippe d'Orléans becomes regent.
**1753** Place Louis XV (later place de la Concorde) begun.
**1785** Fermiers Généraux Tax Wall built.
**1789** The first meeting of Etats Généraux since 1614.
**1789** 14 July: Paris mob takes the Bastille. Oct: Louis XVI forced by protesters to leave Versailles for Paris.
**1791** 21 June: Louis XVI attempts to escape Paris – unsuccessfully.
**1792** September Massacres. 22 Sept: Republic declared. Royal statues removed.
**1793** Execution of Louis XVI and Marie-Antoinette. Louvre museum opens to the public.
**1794** The Terror – 1,300 heads fall in six weeks. July: Jacobins overthrown; Directoire takes over. A young officer from Corsica, Napoleon Bonaparte, is its right-hand man.
**1799** Napoleon returns from Egypt to stage a military coup – becomes First Consul.
**1804** Napoleon crowns himself emperor in a grand ceremony at Notre-Dame.
**1806** Napoleon commissions the building of the Arc de Triomphe.
**1814** Napoleon defeated; Russian army occupies Paris; Louis XVIII grants the Charter of Liberties.
**1815** Napoleon regains power (the 'Hundred Days'), before defeat at Waterloo. Bourbon monarchy restored, with Louis XVIII.
**1830** July: Charles X overthrown; Louis-Philippe of Orléans becomes king.
**1836** Completion of Arc de Triomphe.

**1838** Daguerre creates first daguerreotype photos. Paris gradually becomes a global centre for visual arts.
**1848** Louis-Phillppe overthrown, replaced by Second Republic. Most men get the vote. Louis-Napoleon Bonaparte elected President.

## CULTURAL EVOLUTION
**1852** Louis-Napoleon declares himself Emperor Napoleon III: Second Empire. Bon Marché, first department store, opens.
**1853** Haussmann made Préfet de Paris.
**1862** Construction of Palais Garnier begins. Hugo's Les Misérables published.
**1866** Le Figaro daily newspaper founded.
**1870** Prussian victory at Sedan; siege of Paris. Napoléon III abdicates.
**1871** Commune takes over Paris; May: la semaine sanglante.
**1874** First Impressionist exhibition in Nadar's atelier on bd des Capucines.
**1875** Bizet's Carmen at Opéra Comique.
**1889** Exposition Universelle on the centenary of Revolution: Eiffel Tower built. Moulin Rouge opens. Montmartre becomes the artistic hub.
**1894-1900** Dreyfus case polarises opinion.
**1895** Dec: world's first public film screening by the Lumière brothers at the Jockey Club, now the Hôtel Scribe.
**1900** Exposition Universelle: Grand Palais, Petit Palais, Pont Alexandre III built. First métro line opened.

## THE WORLD WAR YEARS
**1914** As World War I begins, Germans beaten back from Paris at the Marne.
**1918** 11 Nov: Armistice signed in the forest of Compiègne.
**1919** Peace conference held at Versailles.
**1927** La Coupole opens in Montparnasse. Paris again the cultural and literary powerhouse as writers and artists flock here in the interwar years. Surrealism flourishes.
**1934** Fascist demonstrations.
**1936-37** France elects Popular Front under Léon Blum; first paid workers' holidays.
**1940** Germans occupy Paris. 18 May: de Gaulle's call to arms from London. Life in occupied Paris goes on.
**1941-42** Mass deportations of Paris Jews.
**1944** Aug: Paris liberated.
**1946** Fourth Republic established. Women given the vote.
**1947** Christian Dior launches the New Look. Marshall Plan gives post-war aid to France.

**1949** Simone de Beauvoir's The Second Sex is published.
**1955-56** Revolt begins in Algeria; demonstrations on the streets in Paris.
**1957** Opening of CNIT in new La Défense business district.
**1958** De Gaulle President: Fifth Republic.

## EUROPEAN UNION AND NEW WORLD ORDER
**1958** France founder member of what would become the European Economic Community – today's European Union.
**1962** Algerian War ends.
**1968** May: student riots and workers' strikes in Paris and across France.
**1969** De Gaulle resigns, Georges Pompidou becomes President.
**1973** Boulevard Périphérique inaugurated.
**1977** Centre Pompidou opens. Jacques Chirac wins first mayoral elections.
**1981** François Mitterrand elected President; abolition of the death penalty.
**1989** Bicentenary of the Revolution: Louvre Pyramid and Opéra Bastille completed.
**1995** Jacques Chirac elected President.
**1997** General election: Socialist government elected under Lionel Jospin.
**2001** Socialist Bertrand Delanoë elected Mayor of Paris, and begins to introduce a series of crowd-pleasing civic projects.
**2002** National Front leader Jean-Marie Le Pen's success in the first round of the presidential elections paves the way for Jacques Chirac's landslide re-election. Jean-Pierre Raffarin becomes Prime Minister.
**2003** Chirac threatens to veto any US-led attempt to authorise military action against Iraq. Proposals to reform state pension and unemployment benefit cause widespread strikes. More than 14,000 die during the August heatwave.
**2004** Muslim headscarves and other symbols banned from French schools. Massive gains for the Socialists in regional elections.
**2005** French voters reject the proposed new EU constitution. Raffarin replaced by former foreign minister Dominique de Villepin. The deaths of two North African teenagers in October spark massive riots in the banlieue.
**2006** Chirac lifts state of emergency in January. The unpopular CPE employment bill is withdrawn after three months of strikes and protests.
**2007** Nicolas Sarkozy elected President.

sands, and Chirac did not deign to open his mouth, still less cut short his holiday in Canada. The popularity of president and prime minister plummeted to all-time lows, from which they have barely recovered.

The national mood stayed gloomy through 2004, and the clouds darkened further in 2005, as Paris surprisingly lost its Olympic bid, French voters said No in the referendum on the European Constitution and a poll found only 32 per cent of respondents willing to express confidence in their president. Commentators and analysts warned that France could be about to enter its worst period of social unrest for over a decade. Even Jean-Pierre Raffarin's inevitable resignation after the referendum and his replacement by former foreign minister and Chirac loyalist Dominique de Villepin brought no immediate improvements.

Then, in October 2005, the accidental deaths of two North African teenagers in Clichy-sous-Bois sparked riots that spread through the *banlieue* like wildfire. Cars were torched and rioters ran amok through the streets, battling with the police – a state of affairs inflamed when Interior Minister Nicolas Sarkozy described the rioters as '*racaille*' or 'rabble'. Eventually Chirac declared an official state of emergency that was only lifted in January 2006. Then, in March, trouble flared once again, this

time provoked by an unpopular new employment bill, the CPE – which, after three months of strikes and street protests, the government was forced to withdraw.

## VICTORY FOR SARKOZY

Despite – or perhaps because of – his provocations during the riots, Sarkozy was elected president in May 2007, beating the rather lacklustre Socialist candidate Ségolène Royal. Aside from a few desultory molotov cocktails hurled in place de la Bastille on the night of the election, reaction on the Left to Sarkozy's victory was characterised more by bemusement than anger. The President took advantage of this and wrong-footed his opponents in his early days in power with a policy of '*ouverture*' or openness, inviting left-wing politicians, notably Bernard Kouchner who became Foreign Minister, to join his government.

It remains to be seen how Sarkozy will seek to leave his mark on the French capital. But the early signs suggest that he may surprise those critics who regard him as a philistine. In a speech at the opening of the **Cité de l'Architecture** (*see p117*), Sarkozy invited several of the world's top architects, including Norman Foster and Richard Rogers, to brief him on ways of renewing the built environment in Paris.

Talking tough: **Nicolas Sarkozy** was elected President in May 2007.

# Paris Today

Don't believe the reports of this city's demise.

These days, it seems that Parisians like nothing more than to declare that the city they love is dead, or at least dying. The media regularly complain that Paris is being strangled by traffic and pollution, and threatened by a new influx of outsiders from Eastern Europe and other dangerous corners of the globe. They also moan that culture is being undermined by globalisation, the process that brought Starbucks and basketball to the city, wiping out the traditional spaces of old-style urban intercourse. Paris culture has been replaced with 'Parisiana', a kitsch tourist version of the city. As property prices in the centre rise beyond the reach of most ordinary people, social commentators now write despairingly of Paris as a *'ville-musée'* ('museum city') and *'Paris desemparigoté'* – Paris without Parisians.

Partly as a reaction against such developments, it has recently become a craze among black and Arab youths from the poorer parts of the city and its run-down suburbs to come into the shopping malls of central Paris – Les Halles, La Défense – to cause trouble. Dressed like Black Americans, but with the accents and manners of West Africa and the Maghreb, these kids stage pitched battles, terrifying shoppers and workers alike. Like the rhetorical violence in rap music – at which these suburbanites excel – the aim is to shock the jaded spectator into feeling something, anything.

The social theorist Marc Augé has tried to explain all this by arguing that the city is now made up of 'non-spaces' – shopping malls, car parks, business districts and so on – which contradict everything which Paris, in its eclectic intimacy, has previously represented. The only appropriate response, he says, is alienation or violent rebellion. Meanwhile, the architectural historian Paul Virilio wittily but despairingly describes how the city is defined no longer by its outer ring road but rather by anti-terrorist devices at the airports.

# Delanoë's war on the car

Paris has always been a place in search of a transport policy. In the Middle Ages, the city was already known to provincials as a confusing and dangerous labyrinth, and visitors who had neither a trusted guide nor prior knowledge of the place were warned to stay well away. Little wonder that the likes of Jules Verne, the 19th-century father of science fiction, dreamt of a future city in which citizens would move around freely in engineless trains or their own personal helicopters.

As it happens, Verne's vision of a clean and efficient Paris, where motor traffic and pollution are reduced to a minimum, looks like being realised, partially at least, under the guiding hand of Socialist mayor Bertrand Delanoë. Delanoë came to power with two grand projects: first, to solve the accommodation crisis in Paris, which has seen large parts of the city depopulated due to high property prices; and second, to diminish the primacy of the car.

Even before he came to power Delanoë questioned why 94% of Paris road surfaces should be occupied by private motorists. Since then he has announced, and has begun to deliver, a series of measures designed to make Paris largely car-free and therefore one of the cleanest and most pleasant cities in the world. These included building the first new tramway in Paris since the 1930s and a significant increase in the number of lanes used exclusively by buses, taxis and bicycles. Delanoë also introduced restrictions on parking in the city centre, coupled with reduced parking rates in residential areas, and, most recently, the introduction of a cheap bicycle scheme (*see p164* **Easy rider**).

At the height of the heatwave in 2003, when it seemed that every breath you took was full of poison, nobody in their right mind could have argued against Delanoë's vision for cleaning the city. The free bike scheme has been a roaring success, and it is noticeable that it has been taken up by Parisians of all generations and classes. There have been teething troubles, of course: people are quite happy, for example, to freewheel down the hills of Belleville and Ménilmontant, but no one wants to cycle back, which means discreet lorry-loads of bikes being hauled up the hill each evening.

There are still dissenting voices, however. Strangely, some of the most strident and occasionally convincing arguments have come from the political left. Last year, *Les Temps Modernes*, the journal founded by Jean-Paul Sartre and still an important influence on the Paris intelligentsia, published an article by the veteran poet and philosopher Michel Deguy entitled '*La Destruction de Paris*'. Deguy hit a number of raw nerves in this piece, arguing that Paris no longer looks like a great, cosmopolitan city but rather resembles a mediocre provincial capital, with a sense neither of grandeur nor of history. Deguy then raised the stakes further with a rant that had a direct appeal to all Parisians of a leftist bent, describing Delanoë's measures as a way of controlling and policing the city. Making Paris safe and clean is also to make it banal, a crime that no true Parisian could condone. The 'new Green', Deguy argued, is a hypocritical puritan who does not understand the inner life of the city.

The arguments about Delanoë's transport measures are similar to those about smoking in public places. There is a hard core of libertarians who resist them in the name of freedom, poetry or whatever; but nearly everyone else is happy not to be choked to death. More to the point, much more so than London or New York – the cities which Paris sees as its only true rivals – this is still a city where life can be lived on a human scale.

But despite what the carpers, critics and cynics say, the city isn't dead just yet. You'll find the proof of this in walking the streets. Indeed, one of the finest places to start a walk in Paris, and thereby – day or night – restore your faith in the contemporary city, is at the head of rue de la Gaîté, next to the Gaîté métro station itself in the heart of the 14th arrondissement. There is nothing particularly auspicious about this starting point. You are surrounded by the everyday staples of early 21st-century Paris life – an *épicerie*, a sushi bar, an Arab café good for smoking *nargileh*, a *café-tabac* and, half-hidden in the doorway of a massage parlour called Le Palais du Plaisir, the side entrance to a well-known brothel. It is worth remembering that until the end of the 19th century, this was the edge of Paris, the *barrière* Montparnasse beyond which lay green fields and the bucolic paradise of *la campagne*, rarely visited though much fantasised about by Parisians of the era.

As is the case with all the borderlands of Paris – from Clichy in the west to Pigalle and Montmartre in the north – the main activities in this part of the city have always been sleaze and fun. Little has changed: you can still eat mussels at the Brussels bar or visit any number of the tiny theatres and cabarets that flourish here. Only the whores have gone.

Sex is still on the agenda, however: at the bottom of rue de la Gaîté, discreetly sheltered from boulevard Edgar Vavin, is the famous *échangiste* (or swingers') club Le Sphinx. This place has been here since the 1930s, but really became famous in the 1990s when it featured in the novels of Michel Houellebecq, who wrote with Sadean precision about the Paris underworld of *échangisme*. At one time, Houellebecq was a frequent guest here with his wife, before she had a nervous breakdown and filed for divorce. Through the blacked-out windows of the club you could, if you felt like it, gaze over the long field of graves that is the Cimetière Montparnasse. The corpse of Samuel Beckett is there somewhere.

Across the street, no less glamorous and discreet than Le Sphinx, is the lesbian club Le Monocle. Like its neighbour, this has been here since the 1930s. Georges Brassaï famously took photographs of stern-looking women dressed in military gear in each other's arms, as well as the sweeter, blonder lipstick lesbians of the day.

There is also a distinctly East European air around here, at the crossroads with rue d'Odessa. Trotsky and Lenin lived in the neighbourhood. All of the three cafés are good to linger at, although La Liberté has the best beer (cold Leffe) and offers the best view of the artists' street fair and the occasional flea market that accompanies it.

This part of Paris was also home to French immigrants, mainly from Brittany, for whom the Gare Montparnasse around the corner was their first sight of the big city. This explains the cinema called La Bretagne, as well as the plethora of cheap crêperies. The Celtic theme is continued into rue du Maine, where a tiny shop sells books in Breton, Scots and Irish Gaelic and Welsh. Indeed, this is probably the only place in Paris where you can buy a copy of the newspaper *Y Cymro* ('The Welshman') and *An Poblacht* (the official organ of Sinn Fein).

Stepping across the street towards rue Delambre is to take a journey into a different world. This is Surrealist territory, the ground stalked by the poet André Breton and his acolytes, who believed that if only we would follow our desires to their ultimate conclusion and meaning, a revolution in the consciousness of humanity would surely follow. Breton lived for a while around here and dined regularly at La Coupole, just around the corner on the main boulevard. The poet Apollinaire, who gave the world the word 'Surreal', also lived and died here.

The Surrealist legacy lives on in the window of a dusty and apparently austere antiques shop called Garance. As you peer through the grimy *vitrine*, you start to realise that each of the tiny, delicate figures for sale at astronomical prices is doing something extremely rude.

## 'Paris still offers all the delicious and exhausting extremes of urban life.'

These include figurines of fiendishly grinning, masturbating monks, nymphs worshipping an outsize phallus and copulating goblins. The Surrealists would have loved the childish and malicious spirit of it all, but who buys these things? How this shop has managed to stay open so long is one of Paris's many mysteries.

This walk takes you through just a small section of a large metropolis; however, it's also a way of drifting through space and time which lets you in on the imaginative life of the city. It also reveals the real history of Paris which is, as the poet Jean de Boschère puts it, a movement between the '*clair*' and the '*obscur*'; it is visible in the streets, he writes, as the endless play of polarities – shadow and light, past and present.

This explains the passion, glamour and fanaticism which are, and always have been, an integral part of daily life in this ancient place. The new lifestyles, new politics and new forms of violence and pleasure shaping the city are a reminder that Paris still offers all the delicious and exhausting extremes of modern urban life.

# Architecture

Ten centuries of architectural innovation.

Paris is a city of architectural statements. Long before Haussmann's boulevards, Henri IV created the first planned squares, while Louis XIV's minister Colbert boosted the royal image with triumphal arches. When Paris expanded it did so in organised leaps, absorbing rural villages lying outside the city walls in roughly concentric circles. Yet despite its apparent uniformity (largely a result of the predominance of golden stone), the city's architecture has often been marked by radical experimentation.

## ROMANESQUE TO GOTHIC

Medieval Paris congregated on the Ile de la Cité and the Latin Quarter, following the broad lines of the Roman city. Although the clusters of medieval housing built around Notre-Dame were razed by Haussmann in the 19th century (see p41), much of the medieval street plan remains. A few churches survive as examples of simple Romanesque architecture, including **St-Germain-des-Prés** (see p156), with the

rounded arches of its tower, the apse of St-Martin-des-Champs (now part of the **Musée des Arts et Métiers**), and the well-preserved interior of **St-Julien-le-Pauvre** (see p148) – a pilgrim pit stop in the late 12th century.

The Gothic trademarks of pointed arches, ogival vaulting and flying buttresses – allowing the multiplication of windows and spanning of large areas by stone – had their beginning at the **Basilique St-Denis** (see p179), begun in the 12th century and completed in the 13th by master mason Pierre de Montreuil. **Notre-Dame** (see p89) continued the style with its rich, delicate rose windows and fine, tendon-like buttresses (not to mention its characterful menagerie of gargoyles). Montreuil's **Sainte-Chapelle** (see p92), built 1246-48, represents the peak of Gothic design, reducing stonework to a minimum between the expanses of stained glass. The Flamboyant Gothic style that followed saw a host of decoration. **Eglise St-Séverin** (see p148), with its twisting spiral

column, is particularly original. Civil architecture can be seen in the impressive vaulted halls of the **Conciergerie** (*see p91*). The **Tour Jean Sans Peur** (*see p115*) is a rare fragment of an early 15th-century mansion, while the city's two finest medieval mansions are the Hôtel de Cluny (now the **Musée National du Moyen-Age**; *see p148*) and the **Hôtel de Sens** (*see p136*) in the Marais. Although still distinctly Gothic in form and decoration, they set the pattern for Paris's later *hôtels particuliers*, with the main building set back behind a courtyard.

## RENAISSANCE

Italianate town planning, with its ordered avenues, neat squares and public spaces, came late to Paris. It was instigated by François I towards the end of his reign, when he realised the beneficial effects that a well organised urban landscape could have on trade. He installed Leonardo da Vinci at Amboise, brought over Primaticcio and Rosso to work on his palace at **Fontainebleau** (*see p350*), and began transforming the **Louvre** with the Cour Carrée. The **Eglise St-Etienne du Mont** and the massive **Eglise St-Eustache** display a transitional style, adding the classical motifs of the Renaissance over an essentially Gothic structure. Aristocratic quarters were established in St-Germain and the newly developing Marais; the latter holds the **Hôtel Carnavalet** (*see p135*) and the **Hôtel de Lamoignon** (24 rue Pavée, 4th), the finest examples of Renaissance mansions to be found in Paris.

## THE ANCIEN REGIME

Henri IV, France's first Bourbon king, took control of Paris after a long siege. He found the city knee-deep in bodies and broken buildings. Public projects were promptly organised to restore order; timber was banned, to be replaced by brick and stone, while bridges over the Seine were cleared of the houses and shops that dangerously cluttered their paths. The Pont Neuf's construction was speeded up with a new levy on wine imports.

**Place Dauphine** (1st) and **place des Vosges** (*see p135*) reflected Henri's taste for Italian classicism – the latter irresistibly elegant, with its symmetrical design, red brick vaulted galleries and pitched roofs. Attributed to, among others, royal architect Louis Métezeau and his brother Clément, it set the model for geometrical town squares and influenced Inigo Jones's Covent Garden and the squares of Bloomsbury.

Nouveaux riches flocked to build mansions in the Marais and the Ile St-Louis. Those in the Marais follow a symmetrical U-shaped plan, with a secluded courtyard: look through the

archways to the *cour d'honneur* of the **Hôtel de Sully** (*see p133*) or the **Hôtel Salé** (*see p132*), where façades are richly decorated, in contrast with the face they present to the street.

The **Palais du Luxembourg** (*see p160*), built in the 1620s by Salomon de Brosse in Italianate style for Marie de Médicis, combines classic French château design with elements of the Pitti palace in Marie's native Florence. The 17th century was a high point in French power and the monarchy desired buildings that reflected its grandeur. The **Eglise du Val-de-Grâce** (*see p151*), designed by Mansart and finished by Jacques Lemercier, is one of the city's grandest examples of baroque architecture, with its painted dome and barley-sugar columns. Great architects emerged under court patronage: de Brosse, François Mansart, Libéral Bruand and landscape architect André le Nôtre, who redesigned the Tuileries gardens and planned the Champs-Elysées. But even at **Versailles** (*see p350*), baroque never reached the decorative excesses of Italy or Austria, as French architects followed Cartesian principles of harmony and balance, with the emphasis on space and volume.

Under Colbert, Louis XIV's chief minister, the creation of stage sets to magnify the Sun King's power proceeded apace. **The Louvre** (*see p96* **Who built the Louvre?**) grew as Claude Perrault created the sweeping west wing, while Hardouin-Mansart's sweeping, circular **place des Victoires** (*see p109*) and **place Vendôme** (*see p106*), an elegant octagon, were both designed to show off equestrian statues of the king.

## ROCOCO AND NEO-CLASSICISM

In the early 18th century, the Faubourg St-Germain overtook the Marais as the city's most fashionable quarter, as the nobility built smart mansions with tall windows and elegant wrought ironwork. The finest example of frivolous rococo decoration is the **Hôtel de Soubise** (60 rue des Francs-Bourgeois, 3rd), with panelling, plasterwork and paintings by celebrated decorators of the day, including Boucher, Restout and van Loo.

Under Louis XV, a number of sumptuous buildings were commissioned, among them **La Monnaie** (now the **Musée de la Monnaie de Paris**; *see p157*), the **Panthéon** (*see p153*), the **Ecole de Droit** (place du Panthéon, 5th) and many new theatres. Soufflot's Panthéon, like Jacques-Ange Gabriel's neo-classical **place de la Concorde** (*see p106*), was inspired by the majestic monuments of ancient Rome, as were the toll gates put up in 1785 by Nicolas Ledoux (still visible at Nation,

Denfert-Rochereau and Parc Monceau) for the Mur des Fermiers Généraux.

## THE 19TH CENTURY

The street fighting of the revolution left Paris in a dilapidated state, with royal statues pulled down and churches converted into 'temples of reason' or grain stores. Napoleon redressed this situation with a suitably pompous vision to make Paris the most beautiful city in the world. He confiscated land from the aristocracy and the Church for development, and went on a massive building spree. As well as five new bridges, including the **Pont d'Austerlitz** (5th/12th) and **Pont d'Iéna** (7th/16th) and 56 ornamental fountains (such as the Fontaine de Mars), he built the **Eglise de la Madeleine**, a mock Greek temple in honour of the Grande Armée, plus a rash of self-aggrandising statues and arches, most notably the **Arc de Triomphe** (*see p117*) and the shamelessly gaudy **Arc du Carrousel** (*see p102*). One of his more practical commissions was the **Canal de l'Ourcq** (*see p143*) – an addition that would help improve the city's appalling water supply.

Bonaparte's nephew Louis Napoleon, envious of London's energy and the glory of ancient Rome, decided that Paris once again needed a makeover. In 1853 he appointed Baron Haussmann as the *prefet* of Paris. A fearsome administrator rather than a professional architect, Haussmann faced problems of sanitation, sewage and traffic-clogged streets. Bestowing upon himself the honorific 'demolition artist' (others preferred the less flattering 'Alsatian Attila'), he set about bringing order to the city's chaotic street plan, cutting broad, long boulevards through the urban fabric. An estimated 27,000 houses were razed in the process, including many of the patrician Left Bank *grands hôtels*, which made way for the boulevard St-Germain. The Haussmannian apartment block has endured, its utilitarian lines set off by rows of wrought-iron balconies.

Haussmann also introduced English-style public parks, such as the **Buttes-Chaumont** (*see p146*), prisons, hospitals, train stations and sewers. Amid the upheaval, one building epitomised the grand style of the Second Empire: Charles Garnier's sumptuous **Palais Garnier** opera house (1862-75; *see p315*).

Haussmann could also be an innovator, persuading Baltard to build the new market pavilions at Les Halles in lacy iron rather than stone. Iron frames had already been used by Henri Labrouste in his lovely reading room at the **Bibliothèque Ste-Geneviève** (1844-50; 10 place du Panthéon, 5th), and they became increasingly common: stations such as Hittorf's **Gare du Nord** (1861-65; *see p142*) and

Hidden gem: **Hôtel de Sully**.

Laloux's Gare d'Orsay (now **Musée d' Orsay**; *see p172*) are simply shells around an iron frame, allowing spacious, light-filled interiors. The most daring iron construction of them all was, of course, the **Eiffel Tower** (*see 173*). When it was built in 1889, it was the tallest structure in the world.

## EARLY 20TH CENTURY

An outburst of extravagance for the 1900 Exposition Universelle marked the beginning of the 20th century. The **Train Bleu** brasserie in the Gare de Lyon (*see p206*) is an ornate example of the heavy, florid Beaux Arts style of this period. Art nouveau at its most fluid and flamboyant can be seen in Hector Guimard's instantly recognisable métro stations and his 1901 **Castel Béranger** (*see p122* **The path to modernity**).

All of this was a long way from the roughly contemporary work of Henri Sauvage. After designing several Paris apartment blocks, he went on to create a large social housing project in **rue des Amiraux** (18th), tiled artists' studios-cum-flats in **rue La Fontaine** (16th), and the more overtly art deco 1920s extension of **La Samaritaine** (19 rue de la Monnaie, 1st). Funded by philanthropists, social housing began to be put up citywide, such as the Rothschilds' estate in **rue de Prague** in the 12th arrondissement.

# Reach for the sky?

For a city that boasted the world's tallest building at the end of the 19th century, Paris has since been a remarkably timid competitor in the race for the skies. But with a shortage of housing and office space, the skyscraper is back on the agenda. In 1960, the 67m (220ft), 23-storey 33 rue Croulebarbe in the 13th arrondissement was the city's first high-rise residential block, designed by Edouard Albert. During the next decade, tower blocks went up in clusters at Les Olympiades, along the Fronts de Seine and in the 19th. The 210m (690ft), 57-storey Tour Montparnasse (1969-73; *pictured*) put paid to that. Still the tallest building in France (excluding the Eiffel Tower and various radio masts), it symbolised the end of the old Montparnasse of alleyways and artists' studios, and was loathed for its monolithic form and failure to integrate with

the urban fabric. President Giscard d'Estaing (never a fan of modern architecture) slapped a ban on building anything over 37m (121ft) in Paris – far lower than monuments such as Le Panthéon at 83m (272ft) or the dome of Les Invalides at 105m (345ft).

So could the skyscraper return to the city? Current mayor Bertrand Delanoë is known to be in favour, though the Greens (on whom he depended for election in 2001) are against. In February 2007, 12 architectural teams were invited to participate in a '*réflexion sur les hauteurs*' in Paris. Three development zones were identified: around Porte de la Chapelle, Bercy, and Massena in the ZAC Paris Rive Gauche (*see p177* **In the zone**). All three are close to the Périphérique, where the tower is seen as the answer to traffic pollution as it means cleaner air for apartments above the office floors. The report is yet to be published and may not come out before the municipal elections in March 2008. In any case, given the density of central Paris, its large number of listed buildings and the shortage of land for construction, it seems unlikely the Tour Montparnasse will have a rival any time soon.

High rise is coming to the fringes, though, notably at La Défense, where several new skyscrapers are planned. Most well publicised is the 300m (984ft) Tour Phare by Californian architectural practice Morphosis, with its assymetrical shape and glass skin that shifts with the sun. Others include the 300m (984ft) Gothic-spired Generali Tower by Valode et Pistre; the 180m (590ft) triangular Granite Tower by Christian de Portzamparc; and Philippe Chiambaretta's spiralling PB22 duo – 270m (885ft) and 160m (525ft). These are all pawns in the political rivalry between La Défense (nicknamed 'Sarkoville') in the UMP-controlled Hauts de Seine and Socialist Paris.

Clearly the historic centre doesn't equate with La Défense, a business district created in the 1950s. But perhaps the real question, given the banality of the majority of tower blocks shooting up around the world, is not one of size but of quality.

### THE MODERN MOVEMENT

After World War I, two names stand out by virtue of their innovation and influence: Auguste Perret and Le Corbusier. A third architect, Robert Mallet-Stevens, is unrivalled for his elegance. Paris is one of the best cities in the world for Modern Movement houses and

studios (many in the 16th and Montparnasse, areas that were being built up at the time, and western suburbs like Boulogne and Garches), but also in a more diluted form for town halls and schools built in the socially minded 1930s.

Perret stayed largely within a classical aesthetic, but experimented with reinforced

concrete structures. Le Corbusier tried out his ideas in private houses, such as the **Villa Savoy** in Poissy and **Villa La Roche** in the 16th (now **Fondation le Corbusier**; *see p124*). His **Pavillon Suisse** at the **Cité Universitaire** (*see p166*) and **Armée du Salut** hostel (12 rue Cantagrel) in the 13th can be seen as an intermediary point between these villas and his Villes Radieuses mass housing schemes, which became so influential and so debased in projects across Europe after 1945.

Other notable Modern Movement buildings include Adolphe Loos' house for Dadaist poet Tristan Tzara in avenue Junot, supposedly the epitome of his maxim 'ornament is crime'. Meanwhile the new love of chrome, steel and glass found its way into art deco cafés and brasseries such as **La Coupole** (*see p216*). As in the 19th century, world fairs provided an excuse for grandiose state architecture, with a return to monumental classicism in the Palais de la Porte Dorée, built for the 1931 Exposition Coloniale, and the Palais de Chaillot and Palais de Tokyo built for the 1937 Exposition Internationale.

### POST-WAR PARIS

The aerodynamic aesthetic of the post-war era yielded the 1958 **UNESCO building** (*see p174*) by Bernard Zehrfuss, Pier Luigi Nervi and Marcel Breuer, and the beginnings of **La Défense** (*see p183*) with the same architects' **CNIT** building, then the largest concrete span in the world. In the 1960s and '70s, tower blocks sprouted in the suburbs and new towns to replace the dismal *bidonvilles* (shanty towns) that had served as immigrant housing. Inside the city, redevelopment was limited, although new regulations allowed taller buildings, notably in the 13th and 19th; and the raised '*dalle*' style of architecture of Les Olympiades (13th) and Centre Beaugrenelle (15th) did away with the conventional idea of a street plan.

President Georges Pompidou embraced modernity too, disastrously in the case of the expressways along the Seine, and more benignly in the form of Piano and Rogers' high-tech **Centre Pompidou** (*see p131*), which opened in 1977 and was the first of the daring prestige projects that subsequently became a trademark of modern Paris. But Pompidou's successor, Valéry Giscard d'Estaing, found the skyscraping style of projects such as the place des Fêtes distasteful, and prevented the Paris horizon from rising any higher.

### THE 1980S AND BEYOND

President François Mitterrand's *grands projets* dominated the 1980s and '90s, as he sought to leave his stamp on the city with Jean Nouvel's

**Institut du Monde Arabe** (*see p154*), IM Pei's **Louvre Pyramid** (*see p93*) and Johan Otto Von Sprecklesen's **Grande Arche de la Défense** (*see p183*), as well as Carlos Ott's more dubious **Opéra Bastille** (*see p315*), Dominique Perrault's **Bibliothèque Nationale** (*see p177*) and Chemetov & Huidobro's **Bercy** (*see p139*) finance ministry. Stylistically, the buzzword was 'transparency', from Pei's pyramid to Nouvel's **Fondation Cartier** (*see p163*) with its clever slices of glass. Christian de Portzamparc pursued a more eclectic postmodern style with his **Cité de la Musique** (*see p314*) – a series of geometrical blocks set around a colourful internal street.

The city also invested in public housing; of note are the developments around **Parc de la Villette** (*see p144*) and **Parc André-Citroën** (*see p174*), Piano's red tile and glass ensemble in **rue de Meaux** (19th), and La Poste's apartments for postal workers designed by young architects such as Frédéric Borel.

### THE 21ST CENTURY

*The age of the grands projets is over, although* Jacques Chirac managed to squeeze one last legacy project into his reign with the completion of Nouvel's **Musée du Quai Branly** (*see p171* **Windows on the world**) in 2006. Nouvel is also behind the new Philharmonic concert hall at La Villette (*see p313* **Music hall**), but younger architects are making their mark too: Manuelle Gautrand's **Citroën** showcase on the Champs-Elysées, for instance, cleverly plays on the firm's chevrons logo in a fine example of architecture as branding.

The vast Seine Rive Gauche development in the 13th arrondissement is at last taking shape, with a mixture of office, residential and university buildings designed by an army of French and international architects.

A number of exciting projects suggest that adventurous architecture is returning to the capital. There's Frank Gehry's cloud-like **Louis Vuitton Art Foundation** in the Bois de Boulogne and the **Cité de la Mode et du Design** (opening spring 2008), where duo Jakob and MacFarlane have crowned the concrete framework of the Magasins d'Austerlitz with a green wave, creating a venue for fashion shows, design shops, roof terraces, restaurants and riverside promenades. There's even hope for the unloved Forum des Halles, following the recent announcement of the winner of the competition for its redevelopment: Patrick Berger and Jacques Anziutti's **La Canopée**, a striking, green glass, glow-in-the-dark jungle roof that will provide a flowing, organic interface between the shopping centre and transport exchange beneath and the gardens above.

MAC/VAL.

# Peripheral Vision

Paris is finally acknowledging its suburbs.

Traditionally, Parisians avoid the suburbs (*banlieue*) at all costs. The heart of the city has earned an international reputation for cultural eclecticism, gastronomic excellence and vibrant nightlife, the *banlieue* has more often been associated with poverty, crime and social disaffection. Even if a handful of outer-city agglomerations (Neuilly-sur-Seine, St-Cloud, Versailles, St-Germain-en-Laye) conform to the anglophone idea of leafy, prosperous suburbia, the prevailing connotations of the word *banlieue* are almost wholly negative.

The reasons for such a divide are historical as much as geographical, but today there is some indication that attitudes are beginning to change. The mairie has begun to pursue a more active role in working with its neighbouring communities; suburban areas have recently welcomed major new cultural venues; and Parisians themselves are starting to venture beyond the Périphérique in search of leisure, as well as more affordable accommodation.

## RIOTS AND REGENERATION

The ambivalent relationship between Paris and its *banlieue* can be traced back to the period immediately after World War II, when the baby boom and a significant influx of immigrants led the government to develop high-rise housing estates (*cités*) in the vicinity of suburban factories. When the economy plummeted in the 1970s, the populations of these estates found themselves struggling with factory closures and unemployment. While the wealthier moved to more desirable areas, the remaining residents were effectively left stranded in a suburban desert. Unsurprisingly, this predicament left them feeling angry and resentful, emotions that were violently articulated during the prolonged *banlieue* riots of November 2005.

Those living in the city centre, meanwhile, have traditionally felt unconcerned by the problems of the *banlieusards*. Unlike most modern cities, Paris has rigidly defined limits. Since 1860, the city has been composed of the

same 20 arrondissements over the same 105 square kilometres (40 square miles). While just over two million people live in Paris, the *agglomération de Paris* ('Greater Paris') is home to almost ten million. The city of Paris is an administratively independent *département* (No.75) in its own right, while the *banlieue* is divided into another seven *départements*, each subject to its own budgetary imperatives and with its own social and political agenda. In 1973, these administrative divisions were given physical expression by the completion of the city's outer ring road, the Périphérique, which forms a barrier between Paris and its surrounding suburbs.

Despite all this history, recent economic and cultural developments have started to reshape Parisians' relationship with the *banlieue*. First and foremost among these factors is the inexorable rise of property prices in the city centre. Apartment prices in Paris have increased by 79.7 per cent in the last five years. Consequently Parisians, especially those with children, have taken their search for less expensive property to the suburbs, where certain areas registered a 76 per cent increase in the volume of annual house sales between 2006 and 2007. The nearer suburbs have also become a financially attractive option for businesses, while those areas well served by public transport have welcomed a series of

new mid-range hotels. In the Hauts-de-Seine *département*, more than 20 three- and four-star hotels have opened in the last five years.

### CULTURE IN THE CITES

Another striking recent trend has been the opening of major cultural venues in the *banlieue*. Paris has always been renowned for its museums, theatres and music. The suburbs, meanwhile, have certainly fostered cultural output, but generally in minority forms expressing anger or disaffection (rap music, *beur* literature or *cinéma de banlieue*). Today, however, the *banlieue* plays host to a number of more mainstream cultural venues, of which the most prominent is undoubtedly the MAC/VAL (*see p180*) contemporary art museum in the south-east suburb of Vitry-sur-Seine.

> ## 'Even the city's notoriously snobbish art establishment has been enticed beyond the Périphérique.'

MAC/VAL was opened in November 2005, just days after the riots ended, and has since earned itself a fearsome reputation for artistic savvy. Such is its pull that even the city's notoriously snobbish art establishment has

been enticed beyond the Périphérique to see what all the fuss is about. The museum's main objective is to make art fun and accessible to people who don't normally visit galleries. To this end it has low admission prices and long opening hours (until 9pm on Thursdays), and aims to demystify contemporary art by organising regular 'meet the artist' events.

In fact, unbeknown to most Parisians, the *département* of Val-de-Marne, which encompasses Vitry-sur-Seine, has been actively supporting and buying contemporary art for over 20 years, and MAC/VAL is the fruit of this investment. The museum's permanent collection offers a stunning snapshot of artistic creation in France from 1950 to the present, including installations by Gilles Barbier, Jesús Rafael Soto and Christian Boltanski. Vitry-sur-Seine also ranks third in France in terms of contemporary art installations in public spaces. The most famous of the town's 110 open-air works is Jean Dubuffet's *Chaufferie avec cheminée* ('Boiler with chimney') on place de la Libération.

If MAC/VAL is spearheading the cultural upsurge in the *banlieue*, it is closely followed by a number of other galleries and arts venues. In the south, the Centre d'art contemporain de Brétigny has gained international renown for its commitment to the plastic arts, while the contemporary art museum in the eastern suburb of Noisy-le-Sec boasts a partnership with the Centre Pompidou. Contrary to the elitism of many Parisian galleries, these venues promote entertainment, education and accessibility via hands-on workshops and guided tours for adults and children.

Performance arts are also enjoying a suburban boom, led by the Centre National de la Danse in northern Pantin (*see p290*) and the MC 93 theatre in Bobigny (*see p341*), which has a highly eclectic programme, often putting on plays in their original language with on-stage surtitles. Meanwhile, in spring, the Banlieues Blues festival (*see pp274-278*) brings world-famous jazz, blues and soul musicians to a host of suburban venues. A prestigious new music and dance school will open in Noisy by the end of 2008, and St-Denis will welcome the Cité Européenne du Cinéma in 2010. The brainchild of movie director Luc Besson, the cinema complex will house nine production studios and promises to give the national film industry – and the surrounding area – a massive boost. Besson was also behind an initiative to bring art house films to poorer neighbourhoods: in 2007, the Cannes et Banlieues festival offered free movie premieres from the Cannes film festival to ten Parisian *banlieues*.

## THE FUTURE'S GREEN

Such cultural innovations make encouraging news for suburban communities, both economically and by helping to change the attitudes of Parisians. Perhaps the most heartening evolution of all for suburban mayors, however, is the newfound, dedicated commitment of the city authorities to help break down the long-standing physical divisions between Paris and its *banlieue*. Since coming to power in 2001, Paris mayor Bertrand Delanoë has based many of his flagship public transport policies around improving links with the suburbs.

Inaugurated in December 2006, the city's first tramway in almost a century connects with a number of Métro and RER lines that run to the nearby *banlieue*. Over the next 15 years, several Métro lines are to be extended to reach beyond the Périphérique, while the high-tech line 14 could eventually stretch as far as Gennevilliers in the north and Orly airport in the south. Delanoë has also backed the creation of a boat network that will unite Seine-side communities in the suburbs with the city centre. A test phase begins in 2008, with the creation of a six-station route between the Gare d'Austerlitz and the eastern *banlieue* of Maisons-Alfort. If the project proves a success, the service will be extended to Suresnes in the west and Vitry in the east. Plans are also afoot to develop suburban stations for the highly popular Vélib bike hire initiative (*see p164* **Easy rider**).

As proof of its good intentions, the mairie has signed co-operation agreements with a number of local boroughs. Ivry-sur-Seine in the south-east has thus worked closely with the capital's 13th arrondissement in a major urban development project that has helped transform the area around the Seine-side quays into a major university and business centre (*see p177* **In the zone**).

Perhaps the clearest sign of the mairie's willingness to unite Paris with its *banlieue* is the project to cover the Périphérique. By covering sections of the frequently congested ring road with landscaped gardens and sports fields, mayor Delanoë hopes at the same time to improve the quality of life of the 100,000 Parisians who live alongside its eight lanes of traffic. The first area to gain relief from pollution, as well as pedestrian access to its local *banlieue*, was the north-eastern Porte des Lilas at the beginning of 2007. Delanoë's ultimate vision is of a wholly subterranean Périphérique, and a city that is united with its suburbs across a porous border of green spaces. Perhaps, then, people would talk not of Paris and its *banlieue*, but of a wholly unified '*Grand Paris*'.

# Where to Stay

**Hôtel de Crillon**. *See p51.*

# Where to Stay

Sumptuous palaces, discreet mini-hotels and high-end design at budget prices.

*Vive la France!* Despite growing competition from Barcelona, New York, Beijing, London and Rome, Paris remains the most visited city in the world. Last year, some 27 million tourists came to have a peek at the Eiffel Tower, between them occupying over 76,000 rooms in more than 1,450 hotels. But rather than resting on their laurels, the city's hoteliers continue to strive for excellence, ensuring that Paris retains pole position.

The long-established luxury palaces now face a challenge from several smaller, cosier newcomers such as the exclusive **Hôtel Particulier Montmartre** and **Jays Paris** (*see p76* **Small and salubrious**), which draw their inspiration from the global success of boutique hotels. Last year saw the opening of several much-awaited hotspots, including the **Five Hôtel** in the Latin Quarter and Left Bank fashionista paradise the **Bellechasse** – the latest hotel to be 'dressed' by designer Christian Lacroix.

If your wallet won't even stretch to a drink in the lounge of one of the more ostentatious establishments, look no further than Franck Altruie's chain of boutique hotels for affordable, stylish rooms (*see p55* **Boutique bargains**). The selection below should provide options even for those who might previously have feared that pitching a tent in the Camping du bois de Boulogne (2 allée du Bord-de-l'Eau, 16th, 01.45.24.30.31) was their only choice.

## CLASSIFICATION AND FACILITIES

Hotels are graded according to an official star rating system designed to sort palace from pit stop – but we haven't followed it in this guide. Said star ratings usually reflect room size and the mere presence of a lift, and are not always indicative of other important factors such as decor, staff or atmosphere. Instead, we've divided the hotels by area, then listed them in four categories, according to the price for one night in a double room with en suite shower/bath: Deluxe over €350; Expensive €220-€350; Moderate €120-€219; Budget up to €119. We provide a list of services below the description of each hotel. For **gay hotels**, *see p308*.

## IN THE KNOW

Note that all hotels in France charge an additional room tax (*taxe de séjour*) of around €1 per person per night, sometimes included in the rate. Hotels are often booked solid during the major trade fairs (January, May, September), and it's hard to find a quality room during Fashion Weeks (January, March, July and October). At quieter times, including July and August, hotels often offer special deals at short notice; phone ahead or check websites. Same-day reservations can be made in person for a nominal commission at the Office de Tourisme de Paris (*see p379* **Tourist information**).

Several websites offer discount booking: www.parishotels.com guarantees the lowest prices online, (up to 70 per cent off); and www.ratestogo.com offers big discounts on last-minute reservations. And remember that making your reservation via your hotel's website can make it 50 per cent cheaper, even in the trendiest places.

## The Islands

### Expensive

#### Hôtel du Jeu de Paume

*54 rue St-Louis-en-l'Ile, 4th (01.43.26.14.18/fax 01.40.46.02.76/www.jeudepaumehotel.com). M° Pont Marie.* **Rates** €180-€255 single; €275-€350 double; €435-€545 suite; €18 breakfast. **Credit** AmEx, DC, MC, V. **Map** p409 K7 ❶
With a discreet courtyard entrance, 17th-century beams, private garden and a unique timbered breakfast room that was once a real tennis court built under Louis XIII, this is a charming and romantic hotel. These days it is filled with an attractive array of modern and classical art. A dramatic glass lift and catwalks lead to the rooms, which are simple and tasteful, the walls hung with Pierre Frey fabric. *Bar. Gym. Internet (€10/hr wireless). Room service.*

#### Paris Yacht

*Quai de la Tournelle, 5th (06.88.70.26.36/www. paris-yacht.com). M° Maubert Mutualité.* **Rates** (breakfast included) €300 double. **No credit cards.** **Map** p409 K7 ❷
If you're looking to add a twist to your Paris experience, the Paris Yacht might be the place for you. Bobbing peacefully on the Left Bank opposite the Ile

---

❶ Green numbers given in this chapter correspond to the location of each hotel as marked on the street maps. *See pp400-409.*

Saint Louis, this two-cabin houseboat can accommodate up to four guests (welcomed with a bottle of champagne from the owners). Reservations are for between three and six nights, but it's possible to extend your stay according to availability. The terrace on the upper deck provides the ideal setting for a romantic dinner. But it's not a good option for sufferers of seasickness.
*Internet (free wireless). TV.*

## Moderate

### Hôtel des Deux-Iles

*59 rue St-Louis-en-l'Ile, 4th (01.43.26.13.35/ fax 01.43.29.60.25/www.deuxiles-paris-hotel. com). M° Pont Marie.* **Rates** €150 single; €170 double; €11 breakfast. **Credit** AmEx, MC, V. **Map** p409 K7 ❸

This peaceful 17th-century townhouse offers 17 soundproofed, air-conditioned rooms done out in vaguely colonial style. Attractive features include a tiny courtyard off the lobby and a vaulted stone breakfast area. All the rooms were freshened up in 2007, with new decoration and refurbished bathrooms. The equally pleasant Hôtel le Lutèce, which is located at nearby no.65 (01.43.26.23.52), is run by the same management.
*Concierge. Internet (€8/hr shared terminal or €12/ 2 hrs wireless). Room Service. TV.*

## Budget

### Hospitel Hôtel Dieu

*1 pl du Parvis-Notre-Dame, 4th (01.44.32.01.00/ fax 01.44.32.01.16/www.hotel-hospitel.com). M° Cité or Hôtel de Ville.* **Rates** €99 single; €110

Luxury comes as standard at the magnificent **Hôtel de Crillon**. *See p51.*

double; €11extra bed; €8 breakfast. **Credit** MC, V.
**Map** p408 J7 ④
Hospitel has 14 recently renovated, spotless rooms
with colourful contemporary decor and a limited
view of the spires of Notre-Dame. It's used by families of the Hôtel Dieu hospital's in-patients and
staff; they usually take up about half the hotel's
capacity. A medical smell is present but not strong,
bathrooms are quite large, and you couldn't ask for
a better sightseeing base in all of Paris. Prices have
gone up during the last year, but it's still good value
for money.
*Disabled-adapted rooms. Internet (€4/hr wireless).
No smoking throughout. Room service.TV.*

## The Louvre & Palais-Royal

### Deluxe

#### Hôtel Costes
*239 rue St-Honoré, 1st (01.42.44.50.00/fax
01.42.44.50.01/www.hotelcostes.com). M° Concorde
or Tuileries.* **Rates** €400-€750 single or double;
€1,450 suite; €30 breakfast. **Credit** AmEx, DC,
MC, V. **Map** p401 G5 ⑤
If attitude is more important than service, this temple of stylish notoriety is for you. Just don't even
think of whipping out your autograph book, no matter how many A-listers you might find at the low-lit
bar. The Costes boasts one of the best pools in Paris,
a sybaritic Eastern-inspired affair with its own
underwater music system. The same management
is also responsible for the sleek Hôtel Costes K in the
16th, complete with a fabulous spa.
*Bars (2). Business centre. Concierge. Disabled-
adapted rooms. Gym. Internet (free wireless).
No-smoking rooms. Parking (€30). Pool (indoor).
Restaurant. Room service. Spa. TV.*
**Other locations** Hôtel Costes K, 81 av Kléber, 16th
(01.44.05.75.75).

#### Hôtel de Crillon
*10 pl de la Concorde, 8th (01.44.71.15.00/fax
01.44.71.15.02/www.crillon.com). M° Concorde.*
**Rates** €605 single; €695-€890 double; €1,160-
€8,200 suite; €47 American breakfast, €32
continental breakfast. **Credit** AmEx, DC, MC, V.
**Map** p401 F4 ⑥
The height of neo-classical European magnificence,
the Crillon lives up to its *palais* reputation with decor
strong on marble, mirrors and gold leaf. The
Michelin-starred Les Ambassadeurs (*see p194*) has
an acclaimed chef, Jean-François Piège, and a brand
new kitchen with a glassed-in private dining area
for groups of no more than six who wish to dine
amid the bustle of the 80-strong kitchen staff. The
Winter Garden tearoom has a gorgeous terrace,
while classes by the city's top floral designers teach
guests how to recreate the chic flower arrangements
seen throughout the hotel. *Photos p49.*
*Bar. Business centre. Concierge. Gym. Internet
(free wireless). No-smoking rooms. Parking
(free). Restaurants (2). Room service. TV.*

#### Hôtel Ritz
*15 pl Vendôme, 1st (01.43.16.30.30/fax
01.43.16.45.38/www.ritzparis.com). M° Concorde
or Opéra.* **Rates** €710-€810 single or double;
€910-€9,120 suite; €47 American breakfast, €36
continental breakfast, €46 Japanese breakfast,
€65 Ritz breakfast. **Credit** AmEx, DC, MC, V.
**Map** p401 G4 ⑦
This, the grande dame of Paris hotels, has proffered
hospitality to Coco Chanel, the Duke of Windsor,
Proust, and Dodi and Di. Today's guests have the
choice of 162 bedrooms, of which 56 are suites, from
the romantic Frédéric Chopin to the glitzy Impérial.
There are plenty of corners in which to strike poses
or quench a thirst, from Hemingway's elegant cigar
bar and the plush Victorian champagne bar to the
Ancient Greece-themed poolside hangout.
*Bars (3). Business centre. Concierge. Gym.
Internet (€26/day wireless; €24/day high speed).
No-smoking rooms. Parking (€44). Pool (indoor).
Restaurants (2). Room service. Spa. TV.*

## The best Hotels

### For flawless design
**Hôtel des Académies et des Arts** (*see p74*), **Hôtel de Sers** (*see p59*) and **Hôtel le A** (*see p59*).

### For gilded grandeur
**Four Seasons George V** (*see p57*), **Hôtel de Crillon** (*see p51*), **Le Meurice** (*see p53*) and **Hôtel Ritz** (*see p51*).

### For the glitterati
**Hôtel Amour** (*see p57*), **Hôtel Costes** (*see p51*), **Murano Urban Resort** (*see p65*) and **Le Sezz** (*see p62*).

### For a room with a view
**Hôtel de la Trémoille** (*see p61*), **Hôtel Royal Fromentin** (*see p63*), **Hôtel du Panthéon** (*see p71*) and **Terrass Hôtel** (*see p63*).

### For a peaceful hideaway
**Jays Paris** (*see p61*), **Hôtel de l'Abbaye** (*see p73*), **Hôtel Daniel** (*see p59*) and **Regents Hôtel** (*see p74*).

### For spa aficionados
**Hôtel Ritz** (*see p51*), **Hôtel Royal Monceau** (*see p59*), **InterContinental Paris Le Grand** (*see p54*) and **Le Meurice** (*see p53*).

### For the cheapest of the cheap
**Blanche Hôtel** (*p65*), **Hôtel de Lille** (*p54*), **Hôtel de Roubaix** (*p66*) and **Hôtel Eldorado** (*p65*).

# www.parisaddress.com

# short term apartment rental in Paris

**Live in Paris like a true Parisian!**
You wish to live Paris from "within",
like a true Parisian?
Saint-Germain-des-Prés,
the Latin Quarter, the Marais...

Paris Address invites you to
discover picturesque and
lively central Paris apartments.

Prices all included,
instant availability
an easy-booking
on the website.

### Hôtel Sofitel le Faubourg

*15 rue Boissy-d'Anglas, 8th (01.44.94.14.14/fax 01.44.94.14.28/www.sofitel.com). M° Concorde or Madeleine.* **Rates** €300-€395 single; €400-€530 double; €515-€995 suite; €2,000 apartment; €28 breakfast. **Credit** AmEx, DC, MC, V. **Map** p401 F4 **8**

This hotel is close to all the major couture boutiques, which is no surprise as it used to house the *Marie Claire* offices. The rooms have Louis XVI armchairs, large balconies, walk-in wardrobes and Roger & Gallet smellies in the bathrooms; for shopping widowers, there's a small gym and a hammam. It's quiet too: the street has been closed to traffic since 2001 because the American embassy is on the corner. *Bar. Business centre. Concierge. Disabled-adapted rooms. Gym. Internet (€16/day high speed; pay as you go wireless). No-smoking rooms. Parking (€29). Restaurant. Room service. TV.*

**Other locations** Sofitel Arc de Triomphe, 14 rue Beaujon, 8th (01.53.89.50.50); Sofitel Champs-Elysées, 8 rue Jean Goujon, 8th (01.40.74.64.64); Hôtel Scribe, 1 rue Scribe, 9th (01.44.71.24.24).

### Le Meurice

*228 rue de Rivoli, 1st (01.44.58.10.10/fax 01.44. 58.10.15/www.lemeurice.com). M° Tuileries.* **Rates** €520-€620 single; €620-€910 double; €840-€12,000 suite; €48 American breakfast, €36 continental breakfast. **Credit** AmEx, DC, MC, V. **Map** p401 G5 **9**

With its extravagant Louis XVI decor and intricate mosaic tiled floors spruced up in a lengthy facelift, Le Meurice looks absolutely splendid. All its 160 rooms are done up in distinct historical styles; among the 36 suites (25 full and 11 junior), the Belle Etoile on the seventh floor provides 360-degree panoramic views of Paris from its terrace. You can relax by the Winter Garden to the strains of regular live jazz performances; for more intensive intervention, head over to the lavishly appointed spa with its *vinothérapie* treatments – or get grape products into your bloodstream at the gorgeous Bar Fontainebleau. *Bar. Business centre. Concierge. Disabled-adapted rooms. Gym. Internet (€30/day wireless). No-smoking rooms. Restaurants (2). Room service. Spa. TV: DVD.*

## Moderate

### Hôtel Brighton

*218 rue de Rivoli, 1st (01.47.03.61.61/fax 01.42.60.41.78/www.esprit-de-france.com). M° Tuileries.* **Rates** €154-€190 single; €190-€246 double; €289 suite; €16 buffet breakfast, €10 continental breakfast. **Credit** AmEx, DC, MC, V. **Map** p401 G5 **10**

With several rooms overlooking the Tuileries garden, the Brighton is great value (book well ahead for a good view). All faux-marble and mosaic decor, the recently restored hotel was opened at the start of the 20th century as the Entente Cordiale got under way. *Bar. Concierge. Disabled-adapted rooms. Internet (€5/45mins wireless). No-smoking rooms. Room service. TV.*

### Hôtel Mansart

*5 rue des Capucines, 1st (01.42.61.50.28/fax 01.49.27.97.44/www.esprit-de-france.com). M° Madeleine or Opéra.* **Rates** €155-€315 single or double; €17 extra bed; €12 continental breakfast. **Credit** AmEx, DC, MC, V. **Map** p401 G4 **11**

This spacious hotel has real style, with a light, roomy lobby decorated in murals inspired by formal gardens. The 57 bedrooms feature pleasant fabrics, antiques and paintings; five rooms have an excellent view of the square. *Bar. Concierge. Internet (€5/45mins wireless). Room service. TV.*

### Hôtel des Tuileries

*10 rue St-Hyacinthe, 1st (01.42.61.04.17/fax 01.42.61.04.17/fax 01.49.27.91.56/www.hotel-des-tuileries.com). M° Tuileries.* **Rates** €140-€210 single; €150-€240 double; €230-€260 triple; €14 breakfast. **Credit** AmEx, DC, MC, V. **Map** p401 G5 **12**

The fashion pack adores this 18th-century hotel, located in prime shopping territory. There's a comfy *Ab Fab* feel, with ethnic rugs and a smattering of animal prints and bright art, combined with antique furniture, exposed beams and a listed staircase. *Concierge. Internet (€10/hr shared terminal or wireless). TV.*

### Le Relais Saint-Honoré

*308 rue St-Honoré, 1st (01.42.96.06.06/fax 01.42.96.17.50/www.relaissainthonore.com). M° Tuileries.* **Rates** €196 double; €290-€330 suite; €12 breakfast. **Credit** AmEx, DC, MC, V. **Map** p401 G5 **13**

Hôtel Concorde St-Lazare. See p54.

There are 13 rooms and two suites with elegant, traditional decor in this 17th-century hotel. The attention to detail is immaculate – although lack of customer care sometimes lets the side down. *Concierge. Internet (free shared terminal & wireless). No-smoking rooms. TV.*

## Budget

### Hôtel du Cygne
*3 rue du Cygne, 1st (01.42.60.14.16/fax 01.42. 21.37.02/www.hotelducygne.fr). M° Etienne Marcel/RER Châtelet Les Halles.* **Rates** €85-€105 single; €100-€120 double; €110-€130 twin; €140-€165 triple; €8 breakfast. **Credit** MC, V. **Map** p402 J5 ⓮
This traditional hotel in a 17th-century building offers 20 compact, cosy and simple rooms embellished with touches such as antiques and home-made furnishings. It's on a pedestrian street in the bustling Les Halles district, so light sleepers might prefer the rooms that overlook the courtyard.
*Internet. TV.*

### Hôtel de Lille
*8 rue du Pélican, 1st (01.42.33.33.42). M° Palais Royal Musée du Louvre.* **Rates** €38-€55 single; €50-€60 double; twin €75; extra bed €10; €5 breakfast. **No credit cards. Map** p402 H5 ⓯
A tiny hotel with 14 clean, spacious rooms in belle époque style. Its sibling, the Hôtel du Petit Trianon (01.43.54.94.64) in the 6th, has similar rates.

## Opéra to Les Halles

## Deluxe

### Hôtel Ambassador
*16 bd Haussmann, 9th (01.44.83.40.40/fax 01.42.46.19.84/www.hotelambassador-paris.com). M° Chaussée d'Antin or Richelieu Drouot.* **Rates** €250-€600 double; €600-€1,000 suite; €60 extra bed (free under-12s); €24 buffet breakfast, €12 continental breakfast. **Credit** AmEx, DC, MC, V. **Map** p401 H4 ⓰
If you're looking for vintage style but can't face another gilded Louis XIV interior, check into this historic, Haussmann-era hotel, which mixes traditional furniture with contemporary decor. The lowlit Lindbergh Bar is named after the pilot who dropped in for a celebratory drink and cigar after his solo transatlantic flight in 1927. The hotel is ideally situated for shopping at the *grands magasins*. *Bar. Business centre. Concierge. Disabled-adapted rooms. Gym. Internet (€7/30mins shared terminal; free wireless). No-smoking rooms. Restaurant. Room service. TV.*

### Hôtel Concorde St-Lazare
*108 rue St-Lazare, 8th (01.40.08.44.44/fax 01.42.93.01.20/www.concordestlazare-paris.com). M° St-Lazare.* **Rates** €190-€500 double; €600-€1,200 suite; €24 breakfast. **Credit** AmEx, DC, MC, V. **Map** p401 G3 ⓱

Guests here are cocooned in soundproofed luxury. The 19th-century Eiffel-inspired lobby is a historic landmark: the high ceilings, marble pillars and sculptures look much as they have for over a century. Rooms are spacious, with double entrance doors and exclusive Annick Goutal toiletries; the belle époque brasserie, Café Terminus, and sexy Golden Black Bar were designed by Sonia Rykiel. Guests have access to a nearby fitness centre. *Photo p53.*
*Bar. Business centre. Concierge. Internet (€10/day shared terminal; free wireless). No-smoking rooms. Parking (€24). Restaurant. Room service. TV.*

### Hôtel Edouard VII
*39 av de l'Opéra, 2nd (01.42.61.56.90/fax 01.42. 61.47.73/www.edouard7hotel.com). M° Opéra.* **Rates** €445-€545 single; €505-€595 double; €645-€1,800 suite; €23 breakfast. **Credit** AmEx, DC, MC, V. **Map** p401 G4 ⓲
Owned by the same family for five generations, this refined hotel includes some delightfully artful touches such as Murano glass lights, smooth wood features and modern sculptures in the entrance hall. The stylish bar and restaurant Angl'Opéra is decked out in dark mahogany and comfortable stripes. Some of the individually decorated bedrooms offer wonderful balcony views of the Garnier opera house.
*Bar. Concierge. Gym. Internet (€14/day high speed). No-smoking rooms. Restaurant. Room service. TV.*

### Hôtel Westminster
*13 rue de la Paix, 2nd (01.42.61.57.46/fax 01.42.60.30.66/www.warwickhotels.com). M° Opéra/RER Auber.* **Rates** €350-€630 single or double; €800-€3,000 suite; €28 buffet breakfast, €23 continental breakfast. **Credit** AmEx, DC, MC, V. **Map** p401 G4 ⓳
This luxury hotel near place Vendôme has more than a touch of British warmth about it, no doubt owing to the influence of its favourite 19th-century guest, the Duke of Westminster (after whom the hotel was named; the current Duke reportedly still stays here). The hotel fitness centre has a top-floor location, with a beautiful tiled steam room and views over the city, while the cosy bar features deep leather chairs, a fireplace and live jazz at weekends.
*Bar. Concierge. Gym. Internet (€20/day high speed or wireless). No-smoking rooms. Parking (€25). Restaurant. Room service. Spa. TV.*

### InterContinental Paris Le Grand
*2 rue Scribe, 9th (01.40.07.32.32/fax 01.42. 66.12.51/www.paris.intercontinental.com). M° Opéra.* **Rates** €350-€640 double; €900-€1,600 suite; €30 breakfast. **Credit** AmEx, DC, MC, V. **Map** p401 G4 ⓴
This 1862 hotel is the chain's European flagship – but, given its sheer size, perhaps 'mother ship' would be more appropriate: this landmark establishment occupies the entire block (three wings, almost 500 rooms) next to the opera house; some 80 of the honey-coloured rooms overlook the Palais Garnier.

# Boutique bargains

Gone are the days when a budget hotel room in Paris meant suspicious sheets, yellowing wallpaper and a solitary bidet in the corner. For a long time, the city lacked anything much between cheap, often grotty hotels and its opulent deluxe palaces. But that was before 2003, when Franck Altruie opened the **Général Hôtel** (*see p67*) in the heart of the then unregarded République quarter. He's since made two further additions to his mini empire, the **Quartier République, Le Marais** (*see p69*) and the **Quartier Bastille, Le Faubourg** (*see p67*). Like their elder sibling, both offer comfort and hip design at reasonable prices.

Altruie says that when the Général opened 'almost everyone from the industry said that it would never work in a neighbourhood like this.' As it turned out, the hotel became one of the first establishments in Eastern Paris to be awarded three stars in the official French rating scale. The trend shows no sign of stopping, as upmarket hotels sprout in unlikely neighbourhoods. The **Kube Rooms & Bar** (*see p63*), for example, settled where it was least expected: in the Goutte d'Or, an area which is best known for its insanitary squats and drug dealers.

These days, travellers aren't just interested in location; design is almost as important, even for those on a budget. Altruie, together with minimalist designer Jean-Philippe Nuël (who had already worked miracles for the Sofitel and Hilton chains), understood this very well when conceiving the visual identity of Le Général and the two Quartiers. Bright spaces, purity of line, a combination of wood and steel and subtle touches of colour are all characteristic.

Despite being the cheapest of the chain, the Quartier République boasts exposed brick walls in a cosy breakfast room, plus a sauna and a small fitness centre. The Quartier Bastille, meanwhile, has a leafy patio where you can almost forget you're in one of the busiest areas of the city. The rooms, like those at Le Général, have some witty details to welcome the weary traveller: the signature Granny Smith apple shining on the pillow, for instance, or the rubber duck in the bathroom. Technology has not been overlooked either, with flat-screen TV and Wi-Fi as standard.

In autumn 2008, a previously neglected corner of the 20th arrondissement will welcome the **Mama Shelter**, a massive glass and concrete building designed by architect Roland Castro in tandem with Philippe Starck. It is already being touted as the next big thing and promises to offer 172 rooms starting from as little as €69 a night (www.townshelter.com).

**Quartier Bastille, Le Faubourg.**

The space under the vast *verrière* is one of the best oases in town, while the hotel's restaurant and elegant coffeehouse, the Café de la Paix (*see p222*), poached its chef, Laurent Delarbre, from the Ritz. You can have lunch here during the week or, for a relaxing daytime break, head to the I-Spa for its seawater treatments.

*Bar. Business centre. Concierge. Gym. Internet (€12/day high speed or free wireless). No-smoking rooms. Parking (€40). Restaurants (2). Room service. Spa. TV.*

### Park Hyatt Paris-Vendôme

*5 rue de la Paix, 2nd (01.58.71.12.34/fax 01.58.71.12.35/www.paris.vendome.hyatt.com). M° Opéra.* **Rates** €700 single or double; €910-€3,500 suite; €34-€44 breakfast. **Credit** AmEx, DC, MC, V. **Map** p401 G4 ㉑

A luxurious mix of mahogany, pale limestone, matt gold and neutral fabrics under high ceilings, with rough bronze sculptures serving as light sconces and doorknobs, makes this hotel a favourite among fashion editors. Rooms have plush Bang & Olufsen TVs and spa-like bathrooms, split into a huge dressing area and artful shower/ bath zone. There's a circular gourmet restaurant, Le Grill, where guests can watch chefs at work in the open kitchen, and a courtyard for dining in summer.

*Bar. Business centre. Concierge. Disabled-adapted rooms. Gym. Internet (pay as you go high speed or €19/12hrs wireless). No-smoking rooms. Parking (free). Restaurants (2). Room service. Spa. TV.*

Northern chic: the cool **Kube Rooms & Bar** is located in the Goutte d'Or. *See p63.*

## Moderate

### Hôtel Amour

*8 rue Navarin, 9th (01.48.78.31.80/fax
01.48.74.14.09/www.hotelamour.com). M° St-
Georges.* **Rates** €100 single; €130-€200 double;
€12 continental breakfast. **Credit** AmEx, MC, V.
**Map** p402 H2 ㉒
Opened in 2006, this boutique hotel is a hit with the
in crowd. Each of the 20 rooms is unique, decorated
to the theme of love by a coterie of contemporary
artists and designers such as Marc Newson, M&M,
Stak, Pierre Le Tan and Sophie Calle. Seven of the
rooms contain artists' installations, and two others
have a private bar and a large terrace on which to
hold your own party. The late-night brasserie
has an outdoor garden, and the crowd is young,
beautiful and loves to entertain.
*Bar. Internet (free wireless). No-smoking rooms only.
Restaurant.*

### Hôtel Arvor Saint Georges

*8 rue LaFerrière, 9th (01.48.78.60.92/fax 01.48.
78.16.52/www.arvor-hotel-paris.com). M° St-Georges.*
**Rates** €95-€120 single; €105-€150 double; €150-
€180 suites; €9 breakfast. **Credit** AmEx, DC, MC, V.
**Map** p402 H2 ㉓
Don't be put off by the slightly austere façade;
the owner intended it this way to contrast with the
homely atmosphere that reigns once you're through
the door. Although you're right in the middle of the
city, the hotel has the relaxing feel of a quiet country
house. The decor is delicate and uncluttered, and
most of the 30 spacious rooms, including six suites,
overlook the rooftops (no.503 has the best view of the
Eiffel Tower). The small terrace is the ideal spot to
take a break from the Paris buzz.
*Internet (free wireless). No-smoking rooms. TV.*

### Hôtel Langlois

*63 rue St-Lazare, 9th (01.48.74.78.24/fax
01.49.95.04.43/www.hotel-langlois.com). M° Trinité.*
**Rates** €105-€120 single; €120-€140 double; €140
twin; €180 suite; €20 extra bed; €12 breakfast.
**Credit** AmEx, DC, MC, V. **Map** p401 H3 ㉔
Built as a bank in 1870, this *belle époque* building
became the Hôtel des Croisés in 1896. In 2001, after
featuring in the Jonathan Demme film *Charade*, it
changed its name to Hôtel Langlois in honour of
the founder of the Cinémathèque Française. Its 27
spacious, air-conditioned bedrooms are decorated
in art nouveau style; the larger ones have delightful
hidden bathrooms.
*Internet (free wireless). Room service. TV.*

### Résidence Hôtel des Trois Poussins

*15 rue Clauzel, 9th (01.53.32.81.81/fax
01.53.32.81.82/www.les3poussins.com). M° St-
Georges.* **Rates** €139 single; €154 double; €174-
€226 triple; €226 quad; €189-€241 studios with
kitchenette; €10 breakfast. **Credit** AmEx, DC,
MC, V. **Map** p401 H2 ㉕

Just off the beaten track in a pleasant *quartier*, and
within walking distance (uphill) of Montmartre, the
Résidence offers hotel accommodation in the traditional manner, and also has some rare self-catering
studios for people who'd rather cook than eat out.
Decor is traditional, with a preference for yellow.
Mention *Time Out Paris* on reservation to benefit
from a 15% discount.
*Concierge. Disabled-adapted room. Internet (€4/hr
wireless). Room service (night-time only). TV.*

## Budget

### Hôtel Chopin

*10 bd Montmartre or 46 passage Jouffroy, 9th
(01.47.70.58.10/fax 01.42.47.00.70/www.hotel-
chopin.com). M° Grands Boulevards.* **Rates** €55-€81
single; €88-€102 double; €120 triple; €7 breakfast.
**Credit** MC, V. **Map** p402 J4 ㉖
Handsomely set in a historic, glass-roofed arcade
(*see p107* **Safe passage**), the Chopin's original 1846
façade adds to its old-fashioned appeal. The 36
rooms are quiet and functional, with salmon walls
and green carpet.
*TV.*

### Hôtel Madeleine Opéra

*12 rue Greffulhe, 8th (01.47.42.26.26/fax
01.47.42.89.76/www.hotel-madeleine-opera.com).
M° Havre-Caumartin or Madeleine.* **Rates** €85-€91
single; €86-€92 double; €109 triple; €7 breakfast.
**Credit** MC, V. **Map** p401 G4 ㉗
This bargain hotel is located just north of the Eglise
Madeleine, in the heart of the city's theatre and
*grands magasins* districts. Its sunny lobby sits
behind a 200-year-old façade that was once a
shopfront. The 24 rooms are perhaps a touch basic,
but still nice enough, and breakfast is brought to
your room every morning.
*Internet (€5/45mins wireless). Room service
(morning). TV.*

# Champs-Elysées & western Paris

## Deluxe

### Four Seasons George V

*31 av George-V, 8th (01.49.52.70.00/fax
01.49.52.70.10/www.fourseasons.com). M° Alma
Marceau or George V.* **Rates** €700-€910 single;
€730-€940 double/twin; €1,350-€11,000 suite; €45
American breakfast, €33 continental breakfast,
€48 Japanese breakfast. **Credit** AmEx, DC, MC, V.
**Map** p400 D4 ㉘
There's no denying that the George V is serious
about luxury: chandeliers, marble and tapestries;
(over) attentive staff; glorious flower arrangements;
divine bathrooms; and ludicrously comfortable beds
in some of the largest rooms in all of Paris. The
Versailles-inspired spa includes whirlpools, saunas

and a menu of treatments for an unabashedly metrosexual clientele; non-guests can now reserve appointments. It's worth every euro.
*Bar. Business centre. Concierge. Disabled-adapted rooms. Gym. Internet (€22/24hrs high speed). No-smoking rooms. Parking (€40). Pool (indoor). Restaurants (2). Room service. Spa. TV.*

### Hôtel le A
*4 rue d'Artois, 8th (01.42.56.99.99/fax 01.42. 56.99.90/www.paris-hotel-a.com). M° Franklin D. Roosevelt or St-Philippe-du-Roule.* **Rates** €355-€431 single, double or twin; €485-€640 suite; €640 apartment; €23 buffet breakfast, €16 continental breakfast. **Credit** AmEx, DC, MC, V. **Map** p401 E4 ㉙
The black-and-white decor of this designer boutique hotel provides a fine backdrop for the models, artists and media types hanging out in the lounge bar area; the only splashes of colour come from the graffiti-like artworks by conceptual artist Fabrice Hybert. The 26 rooms all have granite bathrooms, and the starched white furniture slip covers, changed after each guest, make the smallish spaces seem larger than they are. The dimmer switches are a nice touch – as are the lift lights changing colour at each floor.
*Bar. Concierge. Disabled-adapted rooms. Internet (€5/45mins wireless). No-smoking rooms. Room service. TV.*

### Hôtel Daniel
*8 rue Frédéric-Bastiat, 8th (01.42.56.17.00/fax 01.42.56.17.01/www.hoteldanielparis.com). M° Franklin D. Roosevelt or St-Philippe-du-Roule.* **Rates** €350 single; €410-€490 double; €540-€740 suite; €24 continental breakfast, American breakfast. **Credit** AmEx, DC, MC, V. **Map** p401 E4 ㉚
A romantic hideaway close to the monoliths of the Champs-Elysés, the city's new Relais & Châteaux is decorated in chinoiserie and a palette of rich colours, with 26 rooms cosily appointed in *toile de Jouy* and an intricately hand-painted restaurant that feels like a courtyard. At about €50 a head, the gastronomic restaurant Le Lounge, run by chef Denis Fetisson, is a good deal for this neighbourhood; the bar menu is served at all hours.
*Bar. Concierge. Disabled-adapted rooms. Internet (free wireless). No-smoking rooms. Parking (€25). Restaurant. Room service. TV.*

### Hôtel Fouquet's-Barrière
*46 av George-V, 8th (01.40.69.60.00/fax 01.40. 69.60.05/www.lucienbarriere.com). M° George V.* **Rates** €690-€910 double; €1,500-€8,500 suite; €46 American breakfast, €35 continental breakfast. **Credit** AmEx, DC, MC, V. **Map** p400 D4 ㉛
This grandiose five-star is built around the famous fin-de-siècle brasserie Le Fouquet's. Five buildings form the hotel complex, housing 107 rooms (including 40 suites), upmarket restaurant Le Diane, a spa, indoor pool and a rooftop terrace for hire. Jacques Garcia, of Hôtel Costes fame, was responsible for the interior design, which retains the Empire style of the exterior while incorporating luxurious modern

touches inside – flat-screen TVs and mist-free mirrors in the marble bathrooms, for example. And, of course, it's unbeatable for location – right at the junction of avenue George-V and the Champs-Elysées.
*Bar. Business centre. Concierge. Disabled-adapted rooms. Gym. Internet (free high speed & wireless). No-smoking rooms. Parking (€45). Pool (indoor). Restaurants (2). Room service. Spa. TV.*

### Hôtel Plaza Athénée
*25 av Montaigne, 8th (01.53.67.66.67/fax 01.53.67.66.66/www.plaza-athenee-paris.com). M° Alma Marceau.* **Rates** €595 single; €720-€820 double; €995-€18,000 suite; €48 American breakfast, €36 continental breakfast. **Credit** AmEx, DC, MC, V. **Map** p400 D5 ㉜
This palace is ideally placed for power shopping at Chanel, Vuitton, Dior and other avenue Montaigne boutiques. Material girls and boys will enjoy the high-tech room amenities such as remote-controlled air-con, internet and video-game access on the TV via infrared keyboard, and mini hi-fi. The stylish bar full of rock stars and hotshots has modern decor, matched by a cool cocktail list and staff who know what service is.
*Bar. Business centre. Concierge. Disabled-adapted rooms. Gym. Internet (€15/hr high speed & wireless). No-smoking rooms. Parking (€25). Restaurants (2; 4 in summer). Room service. TV.*

### Hôtel Royal Monceau
*37 av Hoche, 8th (01.42.99.88.00/fax 01.42. 99.89.90/www.royalmonceau.com). M° Charles de Gaulle Etoile.* **Rates** €560-€750 double; €980-€3,650 suite; €32-€45 breakfast. **Credit** AmEx, DC, MC, V. **Map** p400 D3 ㉝
As if the acres of opulent marble and tapestries, a romantic, Michelin-starred garden restaurant and sumptuous health spa with mosaic-tiled pool weren't luxury enough, the historic Royal Monceau palace upped the ante with a complete renovation by Costes' darling Jacques Garcia in early 2006. The peaceful rooms have plush, tastefully muted decor.
*Bar. Business centre. Concierge. Disabled-adapted rooms. Gym. Internet (€20/day high speed). No-smoking rooms. Parking (€30). Pool (indoor). Restaurants (1). Room service. Spa. TV.*

### Hôtel de Sers
*41 av Pierre-1er-de-Serbie, 8th (01.53.23.75.75/fax 01.53.23.75.76/www.hoteldesers.com). M° Alma Marceau or George V.* **Rates** €550-€650 double; €900-€2,300 suite; additional bed €100; €35 American breakfast, €29 continental breakfast. **Credit** AmEx, DC, MC, V. **Map** p400 C5 ㉞
Behind its stately 19th-century façade, the Hôtel de Sers is an ambitious mix of minimalist contemporary furnishings (often in deep reds and mauves; nothing too austere), with a few pop art touches. Original architectural details such as the grand staircase and reception complete the picture.
*Bar. Concierge. Disabled-adapted rooms. Gym. Internet (free high speed & wireless). No-smoking rooms. Parking (€50). Restaurant. Room service. TV.*

## Hôtel de la Trémoille

*14 rue de la Trémoille, 8th (01.56.52.14.00/fax 01.40.70.01.08/www.hotel-tremoille.com). Mº Alma-Marceau.* **Rates** €460-€540 single or double; €600-€1,000 suite; €26 breakfast. **Credit** AmEx, DC, MC, V. **Map** p400 D4 ⑤

New director Olivier Lordonnois has pushed La Trémoille to another level. The recent opening of a new restaurant-bar-lounge and improved spa and fitness facilities have made this four-star deluxe a serious competitor to the other palaces nearby. The 93 flawless rooms are decorated to evoke no fewer than 31 different 'atmospheres', and the bathrooms are filled with Molton Brown products. A unique feature is the 'hatch', which enables room service to deliver your meal without disturbing you.

*Bar. Business centre. Concierge. Disabled-adapted rooms. Gym. Internet (free high speed). No-smoking rooms. Restaurant. Room service. Spa. TV.*

## Hôtel de Vigny

*9-11 rue Balzac, 8th (01.42.99.80.80/fax 01.42.99.80.40/www.hoteldevigny.com). Mº George V.* **Rates** €395 single; €440-€495 double; €575-€850 suite; €25-€32 breakfast. **Credit** AmEx, DC, MC, V. **Map** p400 D3 ⑥

One of only two Relais & Châteaux in the city, this hotel has the feel of a private, plush townhouse. Although it's just off the Champs-Elysées, the Vigny pulls in a discerning, low-key clientele. Its 37 rooms and suites are decorated in tasteful stripes or florals, with marble bathrooms. Enjoy dinner in the art deco Baretto restaurant, or a cup of tea in the library.

*Bar. Concierge. Internet (€7/hr high speed). No-smoking rooms. Parking (€23). Restaurant. Room service. TV.*

## Jays Paris

*6 rue Copernic, 16th (01.47.04.16.16/fax 01.47.04.16.17/www.jays-paris.com). Mº Kléber or Victor Hugo.* **Rates** €390 superior suite; €530 deluxe suite. **Credit** MC, V. **Map** p400 C4 ⑦

Introducing a new concept on the Paris hotel scene, Jays is a luxurious *'boutique-apart'* hotel that trades on a clever blend of antique furniture, modern design and high-tech equipment (*see p76* **Small and salubrious**). The five suites all have a kitchenette, and a cosy salon is available to welcome in-house guests and their visitors. The balcony is the only place for a cigarette since the establishment was made entirely smoke-free.

*Bar. Concierge. Internet (free high speed & wireless). No-smoking rooms. Parking (€15). Room service. TV.*

## Pershing Hall

*49 rue Pierre-Charron, 8th (01.58.36.58.00/fax 01.58.36.58.01/www.pershinghall.com). Mº George V.* **Rates** €450-€540 double; €750-€1,070 suite; €26 continental breakfast. **Credit** AmEx, DC, MC, V. **Map** p400 D4 ⑧

The refreshing mix of 19th-century grandeur and contemporary comfort makes Pershing Hall feel quite large, but this luxury establishment is really a cleverly disguised boutique hotel with just 26 rooms. Fashionable locals frequent the stylish bar and restaurant terrace, nicely set off by a dramatic vertical garden. Designed by Andrée Putman, the neat bedrooms emphasise natural materials, with stained grey oak floors and fine mosaic-tiled bathrooms with geometric styling and copious towels.

*Bar. Concierge. Gym. Internet (free high speed & pay as you go wireless). No-smoking rooms. Restaurant. Room service. Spa. TV.*

Le Sezz. See p62.

### Le Sezz

*6 av Frémiet, 16th (01.56.75.26.26/fax
01.56.75.26.16/www.hotelsezz.com). Mº Passy.*
**Rates** €280 single; €330 double; €440-€600 suite;
€25 continental breakfast. **Credit** AmEx, DC, MC, V.
**Map** p404 B6 ❸

Le Sezz opened its doors in 2005 with 27 sleek, luxurious rooms and suites – the work of acclaimed French furniture designer Christophe Pillet. The understated decor represents a refreshingly modern take on luxury, with black parquet flooring, rough-hewn stone walls and bathrooms partitioned off with sweeping glass façades. The bar and public areas are equally sleek and chic. *Photo p61.*
*Bar. Concierge. Internet (free wireless). No-smoking rooms. Parking (€20). Room service. Spa. TV.*

## Expensive

### Hôtel Pergolèse

*3 rue Pergolèse, 16th (01.53.64.04.04/fax 01.53.
64.04.40/www.hotelpergolese.com). Mº Argentine.*
**Rates** €220-€380 single or double; €18 breakfast.
**Credit** AmEx, DC, MC, V. **Map** p400 B3 ❹

The Pergolèse was one of the first designer boutique hotels in town, but still looks contemporary a decade or so after being kitted out by Rena Dumas-Hermès with Philippe Starck furniture and rugs by Hilton McConnico. Rooms feature pale wood details, Bang & Olufsen TVs and cool, white-tiled bathrooms.
*Bar. Concierge. Internet (pay as you go wireless). No-smoking rooms. Room service. TV.*

### Hôtel Square

*3 rue de Boulainvilliers, 16th (01.44.14.91.90/
fax 01.44.14.91.99/www.hotelsquare.com).
Mº Passy/RER Avenue du Pdt Kennedy.* **Rates**
€300-€380 single or double; €480-€600 suite;
€22 breakfast. **Credit** AmEx, DC, MC, V.
**Map** p404 A7 ❶

Located in the upmarket 16th, this courageously modern hotel has a dramatic yet welcoming interior, and attentive service that comes from having to look after only 22 rooms. These are decorated in amber, brick or slate colours, with exotic woods, quality fabrics and bathrooms seemingly cut from one huge chunk of Carrara marble. View the exhibitions in the atrium gallery or mingle with the media types at the hip Zebra Square restaurant and DJ lounge bar.
*Bar. Concierge. Disabled-adapted rooms. Internet (free wireless). No-smoking rooms. Parking (€20). Restaurant. Room service. TV.*

## Moderate

### Hôtel Elysées Ceramic

*34 av de Wagram, 8th (01.42.27.20.30/fax
01.46.22.95.83/www.elysees-ceramic.com). Mº Charles
de Gaulle Etoile.* **Rates** €190 single; €210 double;
€240 triple; €260 quad; €25 extra bed; €10 breakfast.
**Credit** AmEx, DC, MC, V. **Map** p400 D3 ❷

Situated between the Arc de Triomphe and place des Ternes, this comfortable hotel has a listed art nouveau ceramic façade dating from 1904; inside, the theme continues with a ceramic cornice around

Hôtel du Petit Moulin. *See p65.*

the reception. Of the 57 rooms, 29 have been renovated in sophisticated chocolate or pewter tones with art nouveau-inspired wallpaper and light fixtures; at the time of writing, the remaining rooms were scheduled to follow by the end of 2007. Outside is a terrace garden perfect for taking afternoon tea or evening cocktails.
*Bar. Concierge. Internet (€10/hr shared terminal; €8/hr wireless). Room service (breakfast only). TV.*

### Hôtel Regent's Garden

*6 rue Pierre-Demours, 17th (01.45.74.07.30/ fax 01.40.55.01.42/www.hotel-paris-garden.com). M° Charles de Gaulle Etoile or Ternes.* **Rates** €170 single; €199-€279 double; €14 breakfast. **Credit** AmEx, DC, MC, V. **Map** p400 C2 ❹❸

This elegant hotel – built for Napoleon III's physician – features appropriately Second Empire high ceilings and plush upholstery, and a lounge overlooking a lovely walled garden. There are 39 large bedrooms, some with gilt mirrors and fireplaces. An oasis of calm ten minutes from the Champs-Elysées.
*Concierge. Internet (€5/hr shared terminal; free wireless). No-smoking rooms. Parking (€14). Room service (daytime only). TV.*

## Montmartre & Pigalle

### Deluxe

### Hôtel Particulier Montmartre

*23 avenue Junot, 18th (01.53.41.81.40/ fax 01.42.58.00.87/www.hotel-particulier-montmartre.com). M° Lamarck Caulaincourt.* **Rates** €390-€590 suite. **Credit** MC, V. **Map** p401 H1 ❹❹

Those lucky (and wealthy) enough to manage to book a suite at the Hôtel Particulier Montmartre will find themselves in one of the city's hidden gems (*see p76* **Small and salubrious**). Nestled in a quiet-passage off rue Lepic, in the heart of Montmartre, this sumptuous Directoire-style house is dedicated to art, with each of the five luxurious suites personalised by an avant-garde artist. The private garden conceived by Louis Bénech (famous for the Tuileries renovation) adds the finishing touch to this charming hideaway.
*Concierge. Internet (free wireless). No-smoking rooms. Room service. TV.*

### Expensive

### Kube Rooms & Bar

*1-5 passage Ruelle, 18th (01.42.05.20.00/fax 01.42.05.21.01/www.kubehotel.com). M° La Chapelle.* **Rates** €250 single; €300-€400 double; €500-€750 suite; €25 buffet breakfast, €18 continental breakfast, €32-€42 brunch (Sun). **Credit** AmEx, DC, MC, V. **Map** p402 K1 ❹❺

The younger sister of the Murano Urban Resort (*see p65*), Kube is an edgier and more affordable design hotel. Like the Murano, it sits behind an unremarkable façade in an unlikely neighbourhood – in this case, the ethnically diverse Goutte d'Or. The Ice

Kube bar serves up vodka in glasses that, like the bar itself, are carved from ice; drinkers pay €38 to down all the vodka they like in 30 minutes. Also on the menu: 'apérifood' and 'snackubes' by culinary designer Pierre Auge. The 'art brunch' on Sundays introduces an artist each month, with DJ music and a 35-foot buffet. Access to the 41 rooms is by fingerprint identification technology. *Photos p56.*
*Bars (2). Concierge. Disabled-adapted rooms. Gym. Internet (free wireless). No-smoking rooms. Parking (€30). Restaurant. Room service. TV.*

### Terrass Hôtel

*12-14 rue Joseph-de-Maistre, 18th (01.46.06.72.85/fax 01.44.92.34.30/www.terrass-hotel.com). M° Place de Clichy.* **Rates** €270-€320 double; €320-€360 suite; €17 buffet breakfast. **Credit** AmEx, DC, MC, V. **Map** p401 H1 ❹❻

There's nothing particularly spectacular about this classic hotel, but for those willing to pay top euro for the best views in town, Terrass fits the bill. Ask for room 704 and you can lie in the bath and look at the Eiffel Tower (and people up the Eiffel Tower can – in theory – see you in the bath). Julien Rocheteau, trained by Ducasse, is at the helm of gastronomic restaurant Diapason; in fine weather, opt for a table on the seventh-floor terrace, open June to September.
*Bar. Concierge. Disabled-adapted rooms. Internet (€3/hr shared terminal; free wireless). No-smoking room(s). Restaurant. Room service. TV.*

### Moderate

### Hôtel Royal Fromentin

*11 rue Fromentin, 9th (01.48.74.85.93/fax 01.42.81.02.33/www.hotelroyalfromentin.com). M° Blanche or Pigalle.* **Rates** €129 single; €149 double or twin; €169 triple; €219 quad; €8 breakfast. **Credit** AmEx, DC, MC, V. **Map** p401 H2 ❹❼

Wood panelling, art deco windows and a vintage glass lift echo the hotel's origins as a 1930s cabaret hall; its theatrical feel attracted Blondie and Nirvana. It's just down the road from the Moulin Rouge, and many of its 47 rooms overlook Sacré-Coeur. Rooms have been renovated in French style, with bright fabrics and an old-fashioned feel.
*Bar. Concierge. Internet (free shared terminal & wireless). No-smoking rooms. TV.*

### Timhotel Montmartre

*11 rue Ravignan, 18th (01.42.55.74.79/fax 01.42.55.71.01/www.timhotel.fr). M° Abbesses or Pigalle.* **Rates** €130-€160 double; €165-€210 triple; €250 suite; €8.50 breakfast. **Credit** AmEx, DC, MC, V. **Map** p401 H1 ❹❽

The location adjacent to picturesque place Emile-Goudeau makes this one of the most popular hotels in the Timhotel chain. It has 59 nice rooms, comfortable without being plush; try to bag one on the fourth or fifth floor for stunning views over Montmartre. Special offers are often available at quieter times of year; ring for details.
*Internet (€7/hr wireless). No-smoking rooms. TV.*

## Budget

### Blanche Hôtel

*69 rue Blanche, 9th (01.48.74.16.94/fax 01.49.95.95.98). M° Blanche.* **Rates** €39-€68 single; €49-€99 double; €88-€106 triple; €94-€115 quad; €6 breakfast. **Credit** AmEx, MC, V. **Map** p401 G2 (49)

If you're prepared to forgo frills and don't mind the rather racy aspect of the neighbourhood, this is a good-value bet. The interior is far from palatial and features less-than-luxurious 1970s furniture, but the rooms are a good size and there's a bar in the lobby.

*Bar. Concierge. TV in some rooms.*

### Hôtel Eldorado

*18 rue des Dames, 17th (01.45.22.35.21/fax 01.43.87.25.97/www.eldoradohotel.fr). M° Place de Clichy.* **Rates** €33-€57 single; €55-€80 double; €65-€90 triple; €6 breakfast. **Credit** AmEx, DC, MC, V. **Map** p401 G1 (50)

This eccentric hotel is decorated with eccentric flea market finds. The Eldorado's winning features include a wine bar, one of the best garden patios in town and a loyal fashionista following.

*Bar. Internet (free wireless). Restaurant.*

### Hôtel Ermitage

*24 rue Lamarck, 18th (01.42.64.79.22/fax 01.42.64.10.33/www.ermitagesacrecoeur.fr). M° Lamarck Caulaincourt.* **Rates** (incl breakfast) €81 single; €94 double; €118 triple; €138 quad. **No credit cards. Map** p402 J1 (51)

This 12-room townhouse hotel stands on the calm, non-touristy north side of Montmartre, only five minutes from Sacré-Coeur. Rooms are large and endearingly overdecorated, with bold floral wallpaper; those higher up have fine views.

*No-smoking rooms. Parking (€15). Room service (morning only).*

### Hôtel Roma Sacré-Coeur

*101 rue Caulaincourt, 18th (01.42.62.02.02/fax 01.42.54.34.92/www.hotelroma.fr). M° Lamarck Caulaincourt.* **Rates** €70-€100 single; €100-€170 double; €7.80 breakfast. **Credit** AmEx, DC, MC, V. **Map** p402 H1 (52)

This hotel is located on the trendier, north side of Montmartre, far from the postcard shops and coach parties, but still within walking distance (uphill) of Sacré-Coeur. From the tiny lobby, a whimsical, AstroTurf-covered staircase leads to the 57 pastel rooms; the priciest enjoy views of the basilica. Air-conditioned rooms cost an extra €10 per day.

*Concierge. Internet (€5/45mins wireless). TV.*

# Beaubourg & the Marais

## Deluxe

### Murano Urban Resort

*13 bd du Temple, 3rd (01.42.71.20.00/fax 01.42.71.21.01/www.muranoresort.com). M° Filles du Calvaire or Oberkampf.* **Rates** €360 single; €440-€650 double; €750-€2,500 suite; €25-€32 breakfast; €46-€55 brunch (Sat and Sun). **Credit** AmEx, DC, MC, V. **Map** p409 L5 (53)

Behind this unremarkable façade is a super-cool and supremely luxurious hotel, popular with the fashion set for its slick lounge-style design and high-tech flourishes – including coloured light co-ordinators that enable you to change the mood of your room at the touch of a button. The handsome bar has a mind-boggling 140 varieties of vodka to sample, which can bring the op art fabrics in the lift to life and make the fingerprint access to the hotel's 43 rooms and nine suites (two of which feature private pools) a late-night godsend.

*Bar. Concierge. Gym. Internet (free wireless). No-smoking rooms. Parking (€35). Restaurant. Room service. TV.*

## Expensive

### Hôtel Bourg Tibourg

*19 rue du Bourg-Tibourg, 4th (01.42.78.47.39/ fax 01.40.29.07.00/www.hotelbourgtibourg.com). M° Hôtel de Ville.* **Rates** €160 single; €220-€250 double; €350 suite; €14 breakfast. **Credit** AmEx, DC, MC, V. **Map** p409 K6 (54)

The Bourg Tibourg has the same owners as Hôtel Costes (*see p51*) and the same interior decorator – but don't expect this jewel box of a boutique hotel to look like a miniature replica. Aside from its enviable location in the heart of the Marais and its fashion-pack fans, here it's all about Jacques Garcia's neo-Gothic-cum-Byzantine decor – both impressive and imaginative. Exotic, scented candles, mosaic-tiled bathrooms, luxurious fabrics in rich colours and the cool contrast of crisp white linens create the perfect escape from the outside world. There's no restaurant or lounge – posing is done in the neighbourhood bars.

*Concierge. Disabled-adapted rooms. Internet (free wireless). Room service. TV.*

### Hôtel du Petit Moulin

*29 rue de Poitou, 3rd (01.42.74.10.10/fax 01.42.74.10.97/www.hoteldupetitmoulin.com). M° St-Sébastien Froissart.* **Rates** €190-€360 suite; €15 continental breakfast. **Credit** AmEx, DC, MC, V. **Map** p409 L5 (55)

Within striking distance of the Musée Picasso and the hip shops situated on and around rue Charlot, this listed, turn-of-the-century façade masks what was once the oldest *boulangerie* in Paris, lovingly restored as a boutique hotel by Nadia Murano and Denis Nourry. The couple recruited no lesser figure than fashion designer Christian Lacroix for the decor, and the result is a riot of colour, trompe l'oeil effects and a savvy mix of old and new. Each of its 17 exquisitely appointed rooms is unique, and the walls in rooms 202, 204 and 205 feature swirling, extravagant drawings and scribbles taken from Lacroix's sketchbook. *Photo p62.*

*Bar. Concierge. Internet (€5/45mins wireless). Parking (free). Room service. TV.*

## Moderate

### Hôtel de la Bretonnerie

*22 rue Ste-Croix-de-la-Bretonnerie, 4th
(01.48.87.77.63/fax 01.42.77.26.78/www.
bretonnerie.com). Mº Hôtel de Ville.* **Rates** €120-
€180 single or double; €180-€205 triple; €180-
€205 suite; €9.50 breakfast. **Credit** MC, V.
**Map** p409 K6 ❺❻
With its combination of wrought ironwork, exposed
stone and wooden beams, the labyrinth of corridors
and passages in this 17th-century *hôtel particulier* is
full of historic atmosphere. Tapestries, rich colours
and the occasional four-poster bed give the 29 suites
and bedrooms individuality. The location is convenient too, with the bars, shops and museums of the
Marais just a short stroll away.
*Concierge. Disabled-adapted room. Internet (free
wireless). TV.*

### Hôtel Duo

*11 rue du Temple, 4th (01.42.72.72.22/fax
01.42.72.03.53/www.duoparis.com). Mº Hôtel de
Ville.* **Rates** €135-€155 single; €200-€300 double;
€350-€430 suite; €14 breakfast. **Credit** AmEx, DC,
MC, V. **Map** p406 K6 ❺❼
Formerly the Axial Beauborg, this stylish boutique
hotel, decorated with white marble floors, mud-
coloured walls, crushed-velvet sofas and exposed
beams, is close to the Centre Pompidou. Rooms are
not large, but exude refinement and comfort.
*Bar. Concierge. Disabled-adapted rooms. Gym.
Internet (free high speed). Sauna. TV.*

### Hôtel St-Louis Marais

*1 rue Charles-V, 4th (01.48.87.87.04/fax
01.48.87.33.26/www.saintlouismarais.com).
Mº Bastille or Sully Morland.* **Rates** €99 single;
€115-€140 double; €140 triple; €160 suite;
€10 breakfast. **Credit** AmEx, DC, MC, V.
**Map** p409 L7 ❺❽
Built as part of a 17th-century Célestin convent, this
peaceful hotel had its bathrooms redone and Wi-Fi
internet access installed in 2005. Rooms are compact
and cosy, with wooden beams, tiled floors and simple, traditional decor; book a more expensive one if
you're claustrophobic.
*Concierge. Internet (€5/hr wireless). No-smoking
rooms. Parking (€18). Room service (breakfast
only). TV.*
**Other locations** *Hôtel St-Louis Bastille, 114 bd
Richard Lenoir, 11th (01.43.38.29.29); Hôtel St-
Louis Opéra, 51 rue de la Victoire, 9th
(01.48.74.71.13).*

### Hôtel St-Merry

*78 rue de la Verrerie, 4th (01.42.78.14.15/fax
01.40.29.06.82/www.hotelmarais.com). Mº Châtelet
or Hôtel de Ville.* **Rates** €160-€230 double; €335-
€407 suite; €11 breakfast. **Credit** AmEx, MC, V.
**Map** p406 K6 ❺❾
The Gothic decor of this former presbytery attached
to the Eglise St-Merry is ideal for a Dracula set, with
wooden beams, stone walls and plenty of iron –

behind the door of room no.9 an imposing flying
buttress even straddles the carved antique bed. On
the downside, the historic building has no lift and
only the suite has a TV.
*Concierge. Internet (€2/day wireless). No-smoking
rooms. Room service. TV (suite only).*
**Other locations** *Hôtel Saintonge Marais, 16 rue
de Saintonge, 3rd (01.42.77.91.13).*

## Budget

### Grand Hôtel Jeanne d'Arc

*3 rue de Jarente, 4th (01.48.87.62.11/fax
01.48.87.37.31/www.hoteljeannedarc.com). Mº
Chemin Vert or St-Paul.* **Rates** €60-€84 single;
€84-€97 double; €97 twin; €117 triple; €146 quad;
€6 breakfast. **Credit** MC, V. **Map** p409 L6 ❻⓪
This hotel's strong point is its location on a quiet
road close to pretty place du Marché-Ste-Catherine.
Recent refurbishment has made the reception area
striking, with a huge mirror adding the illusion of
space. Rooms are colourful and, for the price, well-
sized and comfortable.
*Internet (€1/hr wireless). No-smoking rooms. TV.*

### Hôtel Paris France

*72 rue de Turbigo, 3rd (01.42.78.00.04/fax
01.42.71.99.43/www.paris-france-hotel.com). Mº
Temple.* **Rates** €76 single; €89-€129 double; €109-
€137 triple; €25 extra bed; €6 continental breakfast.
**Credit** AmEx, DC, MC, V. **Map** p402 L5 ❻①
A great central location, sweet lift, spruce staff and
clean, pleasant rooms are on offer here. The attic has
views of Montmartre and (if you lean out far enough)
the Eiffel Tower.
*Bar. Internet (free wireless). No-smoking rooms. TV.*

### Hôtel de Roubaix

*6 rue Greneta, 3rd (01.42.72.89.91/fax 01.42.
72.58.79/www.hotel-de-roubaix.com). Mº Arts
et Métiers or Réaumur Sébastopol.* **Rates** (incl
breakfast) €60-69 single; €77-€79 double; €80-€82
twin; €94 triple. **Credit** MC, V. **Map** p402 K5 ❻②
You're two blocks from the Centre Pompidou, the
Marais and the trendy shops of rue Etienne-Marcel,
with an immaculately clean bathroom, television,
telephone and even a lift. So why are the rates so
low? Could be the granny-friendly decor or the
squishy mattresses; but since the hotel's 53 rooms
are invariably fully booked, it seems that no one is
too discouraged.
*Concierge. Internet (pay as you go high speed).
No-smoking rooms. TV.*

### Hôtel du Septième Art

*20 rue St-Paul, 4th (01.44.54.85.00/fax
01.42.77.69.10/www.paris-hotel-7art.com). Mº Pont
Marie or St-Paul.* **Rates** €65 single; €85-€145
double; €100-€145 twin; €135-€165 triple; €165-
€185 quad; €8 breakfast. **Credit** AmEx, DC, MC, V.
**Map** p409 L7 ❻③
A good address for film freaks on a budget. Ideally
located in a lively part of the Marais, the quaint
façade hides a treasure trove of cine-memorabilia,

which takes up most of the reception space. Exposed brick walls and devoted staff make for a friendly, cosy atmosphere. The decor in the bedrooms isn't exactly groundbreaking, but everything is clean and well equipped.

*Bar. Gym. Internet (€5/hr shared terminal; free wireless). TV.*

## Bastille & eastern Paris

### Expensive

#### Hôtel Marceau Bastille

*13 rue Jules César, 12th (01.43.43.11.65/fax 01.43.41.67.70/www.hotelmarceaubastille.com). M° Bastille.* **Rates** €350-€450 single or double. **Credit** AmEx, DC, MC, V. **Map** p407 M7 🖾

This slick boutique hotel offers 55 rooms divided into two different styles: 'urban' or '*écolo*' (eco-friendly), some with a balcony. The bar-lounge, overlooking a pleasant bamboo-planted patio, is surrounded by a gallery which exhibits the works of contemporary artists.

*Bar. Concierge. Disabled-adapted rooms. Gym. Internet (free wireless). No-smoking rooms. Room service (6pm-midnight). TV.*

### Moderate

#### Le Pavillon Bastille

*65 rue de Lyon, 12th (01.43.43.65.65/fax 01.43. 43.96.52/www.pavillonbastille.com). M° Bastille.* **Rates** €150-€195 single, double or twin; €220-suite; €12 breakfast. **Credit** AmEx, DC, MC, V. **Map** p407 M7 🖾

The best thing about this hotel is its location between the Bastille opera house and the Gare de Lyon. The 25 rooms may be small, but you're a stone's throw from the Viaduc des Arts, where an elevated garden has replaced the railroad's tracks and arty boutiques now occupy the arches.

*Bar. Disabled-adapted room. Internet (€12/hr wireless). No-smoking rooms. TV.*

### Budget

#### Le Quartier Bastille, Le Faubourg

*9 rue de Reuilly, 12th (01.43.70.04.04/fax 01.43.70.96.53/www.lequartierhotelbf.com). M° Faidherbe Chaligny or Reuilly-Diderot.* **Rates** €103-€118 single; €118-€148 double; €12 breakfast. **Credit** AmEx, DC, MC, V. **Map** p407 P7 🖾

Within walking distance of the Opéra Bastille and the Canal St-Martin, Le Quartier Bastille is a branch of Franck Altruie's chain of budget design hotels (*see p55* **Boutique bargains**).

*Disabled-adapted rooms. Internet (free wireless). No-smoking rooms. Parking (€18). TV.*

## North-east Paris

### Moderate

#### Le Général Hôtel

*5-7 rue Rampon, 11th (01.47.00.41.57/fax 01.47.00.21.56/www.legeneralhotel.com). M° République.* **Rates** €145-€165 single; €275-€205 double; €205-€235; €245-€275 suite; €16 breakfast. **Credit** AmEx, DC, MC, V. **Map** p402 L5 🖾

There's not enough room to swing a suitcase at the cosy **Hôtel St-Louis Marais**.

# Hôtel Saint-Germain-des-Prés

★ ★ ★

Situated in one of the Paris' most coveted positions, Hotel Saint Germain des Prés provides a cool haven with a feel of a chic Paris pied a terre.

Built in the 18th century as a gracious townhouse, the hotel retains many period details and original architectural features.

Today Hotel Saint Germain is a landmark of unique character and 21st century timeless elegance. A choice of interesting people the world over.

# Rates from €170.00 to €325

## HOTEL SAINT GERMAIN-DES-PRES

36 rue Bonaparte
75006 Paris
France

**Tel  00.33.1.43.26.00.19**

**Fax  00.33.1.40.46.83.63**

**For your booking :**
www.hotel-paris-saint-germain.com
**or**
hotel-saint-germain-des-pres@wanadoo.fr

A fashionable find near the nightlife action, Le Général is notable for its remarkably moderate rates (*see p55* **Boutique bargains**). *Photos p70. Bar. Business centre. Concierge. Disabled-adapted rooms. Gym. Internet (free wireless). No-smoking rooms. Sauna. TV.*

### Mercure Terminus Est

*5 rue du 8-Mai 1945, 10th (01.55.26.05.05/fax 01.55.26.05.00/www.mercure.com). M° Gare de l'Est.* **Rates** €124-€208 single; €134-€228 double; €260-€350 suite; €31 extra bed; €14 continental breakfast. **Credit** AmEx, DC, MC, V. **Map** p402 K3 ⑱
Located opposite the Gare de l'Est, this great railway hotel combines modern interior design with elements that evoke the classic age of steam: leather luggage handles on the wardrobes, retro bathroom fittings and a library in the lobby. The 200 rooms and public areas all offer Wi-Fi internet access. *Bar. Disabled-adapted rooms. Gym. Internet (€3.50/hr wireless). No-smoking rooms. Room service (noon-midnight). TV.*

## Budget

### Hôtel Beaumarchais

*3 rue Oberkampf, 11th (01.53.36.86.86/fax 01.43.38.32.86/www.hotelbeaumarchais.com). M° Filles du Calvaire or Oberkampf.* **Rates** €75-€90 single; €75-€90 double or twin; €170-€190 triple; €150-€170 suite; €10-€12 continental breakfast. **Credit** AmEx, MC, V. **Map** p409 L5 ⑲
This contemporary hotel is in the Oberkampf area, not far from the Marais and Bastille. Its 31 rooms are brightly decorated with colourful walls, bathroom mosaics and wavy headboards; breakfast is served on the tiny garden patio or in your room. *Concierge. Internet (free high speed & wireless). Room service. TV.*

### Le Quartier République, Le Marais

*39 rue Jean-Pierre Timbaud, 11th (01.48.06.64.97/ fax 01.48.05.03.38/www.lequartierhotelrm.com). M° Parmentier or République.* **Rates** €87-€95 single; €92-€105 double, €10 buffet breakfast. **Credit** AmEx, DC, MC, V. **Map** p403 M4 ⑰
Despite its slightly misleading name (the hotel isn't exactly located in the Marais), the younger sibling of Le Général and Le Quartier Bastille offers the most wallet-friendly rates of the three (*see p55* **Boutique bargains**). *Concierge. Disabled-adapted rooms. Gym. Internet (free wireless). No-smoking rooms. Sauna. TV.*

## The Latin Quartier & the 13th

## Moderate

### Five Hôtel

*3 rue Flatters, 5th (01.43.31.74.21/fax 01.43. 31.61.96/www.thefivehotel.com). M° Les Gobelins or Port Royal.* **Rates** €160 single; €190-€280 double;

€330- suite; €15 buffet breakfast. **Credit** AmEx, MC, V. **Map** p406 J9 ⑰
The rooms in this stunning boutique hotel may be small, but they're all exquisitely designed, with Chinese lacquer paint and velvety fabrics. Fibre optics built into the walls create the illusion of sleeping under a starry sky, and you can choose among four different fragrances to subtly perfume your room (the hotel is entirely non-smoking). Guests staying in the suite have access to a private garden with a jacuzzi. *Concierge. Internet (free wireless). No-smoking rooms. TV.*

### Hôtel la Demeure

*51 bd St-Marcel, 13th (01.43.37.81.25/fax 01.45.87.05.03/www.hotel-paris-lademeure.com). M° Les Gobelins.* **Rates** €165-€197 double; €230 suite; €13 breakfast. **Credit** AmEx, DC, MC, V. **Map** p406 K9 ⑰
This comfortable, modern hotel on the edge of the Latin Quarter is run by a friendly father and son. It has 43 air-conditioned rooms with internet access, plus suites with sliding doors to separate sleeping and living space. The wrap-around balustrades of the corner rooms offer lovely views of the city, and bathrooms feature either luxurious tubs or shower heads with elaborate massage possibilities. *Internet (€8/hr; free wireless). No-smoking rooms. Parking (€17). TV.*

### Hôtel des Grandes Ecoles

*75 rue du Cardinal-Lemoine, 5th (01.43.26.79.23/ fax 01.43.25.28.15/www.hotel-grandes-ecoles.com). M° Cardinal Lemoine.* **Rates** €110-€130 single; €110-€135 double; €20 extra bed; €8 continental breakfast. **Credit** MC, V. **Map** p406 K8 ⑰
A breath of fresh air in the heart of the Latin Quarter, this country-style hotel has 51 old-fashioned rooms set around a leafy garden where breakfast is served in the summer. The largest of the three buildings houses the reception area and a stylish breakfast room with a gilt mirror and piano. *Concierge. Disabled-adapted rooms. Internet (€2/hr wireless). No-smoking rooms. Parking (€30).*

### Hôtel de la Sorbonne

*6 rue Victor-Cousin, 5th (01.43.54.58.08/fax 01.40.51.05.18/www.hotelsorbonne.com). M° Cluny La Sorbonne/RER Luxembourg.* **Rates** €70-€170 single or double; €8 breakfast. **Credit** AmEx, DC, MC, V. **Map** p408 J8 ⑰
This cosy hotel features wooden floors, beams and a fireplace in the salon. The 39 rooms are pale green or lavender, with cheerful geranium-filled window boxes. Bathrooms are tiny; those with shower are preferable to those with a gnome-sized tub. *Concierge. Internet (free wireless). No-smoking rooms. TV.*

### Select Hôtel

*1 pl de la Sorbonne, 5th (01.46.34.14.80/fax 01.46.34.51.79/www.selecthotel.fr). M° Cluny La Sorbonne.* **Rates** (incl breakfast) €179-€225 double; €249 triple. **Credit** AmEx, DC, MC, V. **Map** p408 J8 ⑮

**Le Général Hôtel.** *See p67.*

Located at the foot of the Sorbonne, this 68-room hotel contains an appealing blend of modern art deco features, traditional stone walls and wooden beams. The winter garden and airy common areas have recently been redone in a contemporary style. *Bar. Concierge. Internet (wireless). No-smoking rooms. Room service (until 10pm). TV.*

## Budget

### Familia Hôtel
*11 rue des Ecoles, 5th (01.43.54.55.27/fax 01.43.29.61.77/www.hotel-paris-familia.com). M° Cardinal Lemoine or Jussieu.* **Rates** (incl breakfast) €84-€125 single; €100-€131 double; €159 triple; €181 quad. **Credit** AmEx, DC, MC, V. **Map** p406 J8 ⑦
This old-fashioned Latin Quarter hotel has balconies hung with tumbling plants and walls draped with replica French tapestries. Owner Eric Gaucheron offers a warm welcome, and the 30 rooms have personalised touches such as sepia murals, cherry-wood furniture and stone walls. The Gaucherons also own the Minerve next door – book in advance for both. *Concierge. Internet (free wireless). Parking (€20). TV.*
**Other locations** Hôtel Minerve, 13 rue des Ecoles, 5th (01.43.26.26.04).

### Hôtel les Degrés de Notre-Dame
*10 rue des Grands-Degrés, 5th (01.55.42.88.88/ fax 01.40.46.95.34/www.lesdegreshotel.com). M° Maubert-Mutualité or St-Michel.* **Rates** (incl breakfast) €95 single; €115-€170 double; €30 extra bed. **Credit** MC, V. **Map** p406 J7 ⑦
On a tiny street across the river from Notre-Dame, this vintage hotel is a gem. Its ten rooms are full of character, with original paintings, antique furniture and exposed wooden beams (nos.47 and 501 have views of the cathedral). It has an adorable restaurant and, a few streets away, two studio apartments that the owner rents to preferred customers only. *Bar. Internet (free wireless). No-smoking rooms. Restaurant. Room service (noon-midnight). TV.*

### Hôtel Esmeralda
*4 rue St-Julien-le-Pauvre, 5th (01.43.54.19.20/ fax 01.40.51.00.68). M° Maubert Mutualité or St-Michel.* **Rates** €35 single; €65-€95 double; €110 triple; €120 quad; **Credit** AmEx, MC, V. **Map** p408 J7 ⑦
An offbeat piece of historic Paris, the Esmeralda has 19 floral rooms with antique furnishings and aged wallpaper, as well as the uneven floors and wonky staircase you'd expect in a building that's been here since 1640. Book ahead: the eight rooms overlooking Notre-Dame are popular with honeymooners.

### Hôtel de Nesle
*7 rue de Nesle, 6th (01.43.54.62.41/fax 01.43.54.31.88/www.hoteldenesleparis.com). M° Odéon.* **Rates** €55-€85 single; €75-€100 double; €15 extra bed; no breakfast. **Credit** MC, V. **Map** p408 H6 ⑦

Only nine of the 20 rooms are en suite, but all are decorated with colourful murals, and many overlook a charming garden courtyard. *Internet (€15 shared terminal). Parking (€15).*

### Hôtel du Panthéon
*19 pl du Panthéon, 5th (01.43.54.32.95/fax 01.43.26.64.65/www.hoteldupantheon.com). M° Cluny La Sorbonne or Maubert Mutualité/RER Luxembourg.* **Rates** €90-€285 single, double or triple; €12 breakfast. **Credit** AmEx, DC, MC, V. **Map** p408 J8 ⑳
The 36 rooms of this elegant hotel are beautifully decorated with classic French *toile de Jouy* fabrics, antique furniture and painted woodwork. Some enjoy impressive views of the Panthéon; others squint on to a hardly less romantic courtyard, complete with chestnut tree. *Internet (free wireless). No-smoking rooms. TV.*

### Hôtel Résidence Gobelins
*9 rue des Gobelins, 13th (01.47.07.26.90/fax 01.43.31.44.05/www.hotelgobelins.com). M° Les Gobelins.* **Rates** €63-€73 single; €83-€87 double; €98 triple; €110 quad; €8 breakfast. **Credit** AmEx, MC, V. **Map** p406 K10 ㉛
A tiny lift leads to colourful rooms, equipped with satellite TV and telephone. The breakfast room overlooks a private garden, and there's free internet at the reception. The hotel is entirely non-smoking. Friendly service. *Internet (free shared terminal). No smoking throughout. TV.*

### Hôtel Résidence Henri IV
*50 rue des Bernardins, 5th (01.44.41.31.81/fax 01.46.33.93.22/www.residencehenri4.com). M° Cardinal Lemoine.* **Rates** €85-€230 single or double; €140-€340 apartment; €6 breakfast. **Credit** AmEx, DC, MC, V. **Map** p406 K8 ㉜
This belle époque style hotel has a mere eight rooms and five apartments, so guests are assured of the staff's full attention. Peacefully situated next to leafy square Paul-Langevin, it's minutes away from Notre-Dame. The four-person apartments come with a handy mini-kitchen featuring a hob, fridge and microwave – although you may be reduced to eating on the beds in the smaller ones. *Concierge. Internet (free wireless). No-smoking rooms. TV.*

## St-Germain-des-Prés & Odéon

## Deluxe

### L'Hôtel
*13 rue des Beaux-Arts, 6th (01.44.41.99.00/fax 01.43.25.64.81/www.l-hotel.com). M° St-Germain-des-Prés or Mabillon.* **Rates** €255-€640 double; €540-€740 suite; €18 continental breakfast. **Credit** AmEx, DC, MC, V. **Map** p408 H6 ㉝
Guests at the sumptuously decorated L'Hôtel are more likely to be models and film stars than the starving writers who frequented it during Oscar

Wilde's last days. Under Jacques Garcia's careful restoration, each room has its own special theme: Mistinguett's *chambre* retains its art deco mirror bed, and Oscar's deathbed room has, appropriately, been decorated with green peacock murals. Don't miss the cellar swimming pool or *fumoir*.
*Bar. Concierge. Internet (shared terminal; free wireless). Pool (indoor). Restaurant. Room service (until 11pm). Sauna. TV.*

### Hôtel Lutetia
*45 bd Raspail, 6th (01.49.54.46.46/fax 01.49.54.46.00/www.lutetia-paris.com). M° Sèvres Babylone.* **Rates** €400-€600 double; €750-€3,000 suite; €27 breakfast. **Credit** AmEx, DC, MC, V. **Map** p405 G7 ㉞
This historic Left Bank hotel is a masterpiece of art nouveau and early art deco architecture that dates from 1910. It has a plush jazz bar and lively brasserie with views of the chic Bon Marché store across the street. Its 250 rooms, revamped in purple, gold and pearl grey, maintain a 1930s feel. Big-name guests in years gone by have included Pablo Picasso, Josephine Baker and Charles de Gaulle. It was also Abwehr HQ during the Nazi occupation.
*Bar. Business centre. Concierge. Gym. Internet (€18/day high speed; free wireless). No-smoking rooms. Restaurants (2). Room service. TV.*

### Villa d'Estrées
*17 rue Git-le-Coeur, 6th (01.55.42.71.11/fax 01.55.42.71.00/www.villadestrees.com). M° St-Michel.* **Rates** €235-€315 suite; €265-€355 suite; €485-€670 apartment; €10 breakfast. **Credit** AmEx, DC, MC, V. **Map** p408 J6 ㉟
Jewel colours, sumptuous fabrics, stripes and patterns are the hallmarks of this polished boutique hotel – there's nothing at all minimalist about Villa d'Estrées, which was designed by Jacques Garcia. Each of the ten rooms and suites is individually decorated, all with a nod to Empire style and a crisp, slightly masculine feel.
*Bar. Concierge. Internet (free wireless). No-smoking rooms. Restaurant. Room service (until 10pm). TV.*

## Expensive

### Hôtel de l'Abbaye
*10 rue Cassette, 6th (01.45.44.38.11/fax 01.45.48.07.86/www.hotelabbayeparis.com). M° Rennes or St-Sulpice.* **Rates** (incl breakfast) €232-€367 double or twin; €427-€519 suite. **Credit** AmEx, MC, V. **Map** p405 G7 ㊱
A monumental entrance opens the way through a courtyard into this tranquil hotel, originally part of a convent. Wood panelling, well-stuffed sofas and an open fireplace in the drawing room make for a relaxed atmosphere, but, best of all, there's a surprisingly large garden where breakfast is served in the warmer months. The 44 rooms are tasteful and luxurious, and the suites have rooftop terraces.
*Bar. Concierge. Internet (€12/2hrs; free shared terminal). Room service. TV.*

### Relais Saint-Germain
*9 carrefour de l'Odéon, 6th (01.43.29.12.05/fax 01.46.33.45.30/www.hotel-paris-relais-saint-germain.com). M° Odéon.* **Rates** (incl breakfast) €210 single; €275-€360 double; €380-€420 suite. **Credit** AmEx, DC, MC, V. **Map** p408 H7 ㊲
The rustic, wood-beamed ceilings remain intact at the Hotel Relais Saint-Germain, a 17th-century hotel bought and renovated by much-acclaimed chef Yves Camdeborde (originator of the *bistronomique* dining trend) and his wife Claudine. Each of the 22 rooms offers a different take on eclectic provençal charm, and the marble bathrooms are huge by Paris standards. Guests get first dibs on a highly sought-after seat in the 15-table restaurant Le Comptoir next door (*see p213*).
*Bar. Concierge. Internet (free high speed & wireless). No-smoking rooms. Restaurant. Room service (until 10pm). TV.*

### La Villa
*29 rue Jacob, 6th (01.43.26.60.00/fax 01.46.34.63.63/www.villa-saintgermain.com). M° St-Germain-des-Prés.* **Rates** €265-€325 double; €445-€485 suite; €40 extra bed; €16 breakfast. **Credit** AmEx, DC, MC, V. **Map** p408 H6 ㊳
Refreshingly modern and stylish, the charismatic La Villa features cool faux crocodile skin on the bedheads and crinkly taffeta over the taupe-coloured walls. Wonderfully, your room number is projected on to the floor outside your door; very useful for any late-night, drunken homecomings. Keep a look out for some excellent offers on last-minute bookings during the year.
*Bar. Concierge. Internet (€5/30mins high speed; €12/hr wireless). No-smoking rooms. Room service (until midnight). TV.*

## Moderate

### Le Clos Médicis
*56 rue Monsieur-le-Prince, 6th (01.43.29.10.80/fax 01.43.54.26.90/www.closmedicis.com). M° Odéon/RER Luxembourg.* **Rates** €160 single; €205-€250 double; €290 triple or duplex; €490 suite; €13 breakfast. **Credit** AmEx, DC, MC, V. **Map** p408 H8 ㊴
Designed more like a stylish, private townhouse than a hotel, Le Clos Médicis is located by the Luxembourg gardens: perfect if you fancy starting the morning with a stroll among the trees. The hotel's decor is refreshingly modern chic, with rooms done out in taffeta curtains and chenille bedcovers, and antique floor tiles in the bathrooms. The cosy lounge has a working fireplace.
*Bar. Concierge. Internet (free high speed & wireless). No-smoking rooms. TV.*

### Grand Hôtel de l'Univers
*6 rue Grégoire-de-Tours, 6th (01.43.29.37.00/fax 01.40.51.06.45/www.hotel-paris-univers.com). M° Odéon.* **Rates** €130-€185 single; €150-€280 double or twin; €10 breakfast. **Credit** AmEx, DC, MC, V. **Map** p408 H7 ㊵

Making the most of its 15th-century origins, this hotel features exposed wooden beams, high ceilings, antique furnishings and toile-covered walls. Manuel Canovas fabrics lend a posh touch, but there are also useful services such as a laptop for hire. The same helpful team runs the Hôtel St-Germain-des-Prés nearby, which has a medieval-themed room and the sweetest attic in Paris.

*Bar. Concierge. Internet (€8/hr shared terminal; free wireless). No-smoking rooms. TV.*
**Other locations** *Hôtel St-Germain-des-Prés, 36 rue Bonaparte, 6th (01.43.26.00.19).*

### Hôtel du Globe
*15 rue des Quatre-Vents, 6th (01.43.26.35.50/fax 01.46.33.62.69/www.hotel-du-globe.fr). Mº Odéon.* **Rates** €95-€140 single; €110- €150 double; €180 family room; €10 breakfast. **Credit** MC, V. **Map** p408 H7 ⑤

The Hôtel du Globe has managed to retain much of its 17th-century character – and very pleasant it is too. Gothic wrought-iron doors take you through into the florid corridors, while an unexplained suit of armour supervises guests from the tiny salon. The rooms with baths are somewhat larger than those with showers – all 14 of them underwent complete renovation in 2004. There's even a four-poster bed to be had if you ask for it upon reservation.
*Internet (free wireless). TV.*

### Hôtel des Saints-Pères
*65 rue des Sts-Pères, 6th (01.45.44.50.00/fax 01.45.44.90.83/www.espritfrance.com). Mº St-Germain-des-Prés.* **Rates** €145-€295 double; €305-€355 suite; €13.50 breakfast. **Credit** AmEx, MC, V. **Map** p405 G7 ㉜

Built in 1658 by one of Louis XIV's architects, this discreet hotel now occupies an enviable location near St-Germain-des-Prés' designer boutiques. It boasts a charming garden and a sophisticated, if small, bar. The most coveted room is no.100 (€325), with its fine 17th-century ceiling by painters from the Versailles School; it also has an open bathroom, so you can gaze at scenes from the myth of Leda and the Swan while you scrub.
*Bar. Concierge. Internet (€10/hr shared terminal & wireless). TV.*

## Budget

### Regents Hôtel
*44 rue Madame, 6th (01.45.48.02.81/fax 01.45.44.85.73). Mº St-Sulpice.* **Rates** €80 single; €80-€110 double; €110 triple; €125 quad; €7 breakfast. **Credit** AmEx, MC, V. **Map** p408 G8 ㉝

This discreet hotel located in a quiet street is a lovely surprise, its courtyard garden used for breakfast in the warmer months. The reception rooms are a sunny provençal blue and yellow, and the bedrooms are comfortable, with new bathrooms. Some have small balconies.
*Concierge. Room service (breakfast only). TV.*

## Montparnasse

## Expensive

### Hôtel des Académies et des Arts
*15 rue de la Grande Chaumière, 6th (01.43.26.66.44/fax 01.40.46.86.85/www.hotel-des-academies.com). Mº Notre-Dame des Champs, Raspail or Vavin.* **Rates** €220-€285 single or double; €15 breakfast. **Credit** AmEx, DC, MC, V. **Map** p405 G7 ㉞

Reopened in early 2007 after a full refurbishment, this small boutique hotel scores highly on style. There are cosy salons, fireplaces and an extensive collection of art books. The 20 immaculate rooms are individually designed around four themes (Paris, Actor, Man Ray or Rulhmann), and offer some wonderful views over the rooftops or down on to the spectacular Jérôme Mesnager mural in the courtyard.
*Concierge. Disabled-adapted room. Internet (free shared terminal & wireless). TV.*

## Moderate

### Hôtel Aviatic
*105 rue de Vaugirard, 6th (01.53.63.25.50/ fax 01.53.63.25.55/www.aviatic.fr). Mº Montparnasse Bienvenüe or St-Placide.* **Rates** €149-€265 double; €310-€355 suite; €199-€265; €14 breakfast. **Credit** AmEx, DC, MC, V. **Map** p405 F8 ㉟

This historic hotel has tons of character, from the Empire-style lounge and garden atrium to the bistro-style breakfast room. The polished floor in the lobby (watch your feet) and the hints of marble and brass lend an impressive touch of glamour. The pricier Supérieure rooms have such extras as bathrobes and a modem connection.
*Concierge. Internet (€15/hr wireless). Parking (€27). TV.*

### Hôtel Istria Saint-Germain
*29 rue Campagne-Première, 14th (01.43.20.91.82/ fax 01.43.22.48.45/www.istria-paris-hotel.com). Mº Raspail.* **Rates** €80-€190 single or double; €10 breakfast. **Credit** AmEx, DC, MC, V. **Map** p405 G9 ㊱

Behind this unassuming façade is the place where the artistic royalty of Montparnasse's heyday – the likes of Man Ray, Marcel Duchamp and Louis Aragon – once lived. The Istria Saint-Germain has been modernised since then, but it still has plenty of charm, with 26 bright, simply furnished rooms, a cosy cellar breakfast room and a comfortable communal area. Film fans should take note: the tiled artists' studios next door featured in Godard's *A Bout de Souffle.*
*Concierge. Disabled-adapted room. Internet (€3/15mins shared terminal; €6/hr wireless). No-smoking rooms. Parking (€24). Room service. TV.*

## Budget

### Hôtel Delambre

*35 rue Delambre, 14th (01.43.20.66.31/fax 01.45.38.91.76/www.hoteldelambre.com). M° Edgar Quinet or Vavin.* **Rates** €80-€115 single; €95-€115 double; €150-€160 suite; €12 extra bed; €9 breakfast. **Credit** AmEx, MC, V. **Map** p405 G9 ⑨
Occupying a narrow slot in a small street between Montparnasse and St-Germain, this hotel was home to surrealist André Breton in the 1920s. Today it's modern and friendly, with cast-iron details in the 13 rooms and newly installed air-conditioning. The mini suite in the attic, comprising two separate rooms, is particularly pleasing – if not really suitable for the more generously framed. *Disabled-adapted room. Internet (€9/hr wireless). No-smoking rooms. TV.*

## The 7th & western Paris

## Deluxe

### Le Bellechasse

*8 rue de Bellechasse, 7th (01.45.50.22.31/fax 01.45.51.52.36/www.lebellechasse.com). M° Assemblée Nationale or Solferino/RER Musée d'Orsay.* **Rates** €340-€490 single or double. **Credit** AmEx, MC, V. **Map** p405 F6 ⑨
A former *hôtel particulier*, the Bellechasse fell into the hands of Christian Lacroix, already responsible for the makeover of the Hôtel du Petit Moulin (*see p65*). It reopened in July 2007, duly transformed into a trendy boutique hotel. Only a few steps away from the Musée d'Orsay, it offers 34 splendid – though rather small – rooms, in seven different decorative styles. It's advisable to book early as the Bellechasse promises to be *the* hit of 2008. *Bar. Internet (free shared terminal & wireless). No-smoking rooms. TV.*

### Le Montalembert

*3 rue Montalembert, 7th (01.45.49.68.68/fax 01.45.49.69.49/www.montalembert.com). M° Rue du Bac.* **Rates** €370-€470 double; €600-€830 suite; €1,300 apartment; €24 breakfast. **Credit** AmEx, DC, MC, V. **Map** p405 G6 ⑨
Grace Leo-Andrieu's impeccable boutique hotel opened in 1990 and is a benchmark of quality and service. It has everything that *mode* maniacs (who flock here for Fashion Week) could want: bathrooms stuffed with Contemporel toiletries, a set of digital scales and 360° mirrors to check out that all-important figure. Decorated in pale lilac, cinnamon and olive tones, the entire hotel has Wi-Fi access and each room is equipped with a flat-screen TV. Clattery two-person stairwell lifts are a nice nod to old-fashioned ways in a hotel that is otherwise *tout moderne. Bar. Concierge. Internet (free shared terminal or €29/day wireless). No-smoking rooms. Restaurant. Room service. TV.*

## Expensive

### Hôtel Duc de Saint-Simon

*14 rue de St-Simon, 7th (01.44.39.20.20/fax 01.45.48.68.25/www.hotelducdesaintsimon.com). M° Rue du Bac.* **Rates** €220-€275 double; €385-€395 suite; €15 breakfast. **Credit** AmEx, DC, MC, V. **Map** p405 F6 ⑩
A lovely courtyard leads the way into this popular hotel situated on the edge of St-Germain-des-Prés. Of the 34 romantic bedrooms, four have terraces over a closed-off, leafy garden. It's perfect for lovers, though if you can do without a four-poster bed, there are more spacious rooms than the Honeymoon Suite. *Bar. Concierge. Internet. (free shared terminal & wireless). No-smoking rooms. Room service. TV.*

## Moderate

### Hôtel La Bourdonnais

*111-113 av de la Bourdonnais, 7th (01.47.05.45.42/fax 01.45.55.75.54/www.hotellabourdonnais.com). M° Ecole Militaire.* **Rates** €103-€130 single; €170-€185 double or twin; €185 triple; €195 quad; €225 suite; €12 breakfast. **Credit** AmEx, DC, MC, V. **Map** p404 D7 ⑩
The Bourdonnais feels more like a traditional French bourgeois townhouse than a hotel, with 56 bedrooms decorated in rich colours, antiques and Persian rugs. The main lobby opens on to a jungle-like winter garden and patio, where guests take breakfast. *Concierge. Internet (€10/hr shared terminal or pay as you go). Parking (€15). TV.*

### Hôtel Lenox

*9 rue de l'Université, 7th (01.42.96.10.95/fax 01.42.61.52.83/www.lenoxsaintgermain.com). M° St-Germain-des-Prés.* **Rates** €150-€170 double; €265-€280 duplex; €310 triple; €14 breakfast. **Credit** AmEx, DC, MC, V. **Map** p405 G6 ⑩
The location may be the seventh, but this venerable literary and artistic haunt is unmistakeably part of St-Germain-des-Prés. The art deco-style Lenox Club Bar, open to the public, features comfortable leather club chairs and jazz instruments on the walls. Bedrooms, reached by an astonishing glass lift, have more traditional decor and city views. *Bar. Concierge. Internet (€10/hr shared terminal & wireless). No-smoking rooms. Room service (from 5.30pm). TV.*

## Budget

### Hôtel Eiffel Rive Gauche

*6 rue du Gros-Caillou, 7th (01.45.51.24.56/fax 01.45.51.11.77/www.hotel-eiffel.com). M° Ecole Militaire.* **Rates** €75-€115 single; €75-€125 double; €95-€145 triple; €105-€175 quad; €9.50 breakfast. **Credit** MC, V. **Map** p404 D6 ⑩
The provençal decor and warm welcome make this a nice retreat. For the quintessential Paris view at a bargain price, choose to stay on one of the upper floors:

# Small and salubrious

**Jays Paris.**

Luxury accommodation used to mean palace hotels with concierges, legions of staff and splendid salons. Today, however, a new trend has emerged: a small, selective cocoon, high on design, personal service and discretion.

First of the breed was **3 Rooms** (5 rue de Moussy, 4th, 01.44.78.92.00), opened in 2004 by fashion designer Azzedine Alaia. Three sophisticated minimalist apartments, in an 18th-century building in the Marais, are furnished with Alaia's own enviable collection of modern design classics. There's also a fully equipped kitchen, comfortable bedding and all the necessary high-tech trappings; plus the discreet service of factotum Patrice. A hit with the fashion world and design buffs, this is an insider address where you live as if in your own flat – though one where you eat at and sit on the sort of pieces usually found in design galleries and museums.

Then there's **Jays Paris** (*see p61*), a miniature boutique hotel opened in 2006 in a 19th-century house near the Arc de Triomphe. With just five bright, spacious rooms decorated à la chinoise, Louis XVI or Provençal, this is the most conventional and businesslike of the new breed and attracts an almost entirely Anglophone clientele.

Cosiest of the lot is **6 Mandel** (6 av Georges-Mandel, 16th, 01.42.27.27.93, www.naturelei.com), which has just one *chambre d'hôte*, as part of the showroom and home office of landscape designer Jean-Christophe Stoerkel. There's an impression of greenery everywhere in this neo-Gothic house. The idea here is 'lots of warmth and quality', in the resolutely modern interior and in the welcome: after an initial booking on the internet, Stoerkel follows up with a phone call to find out which paper you want in the morning, what you like for breakfast and your specific preference for flowers in the room. Beyond the bedroom itself, with its purple velvet, brocade and raw silk fabrics, pale mint walls and Eiffel Tower view, you can colonise the kitchen or enjoy the changing displays of textiles, furniture and artworks.

You have to ring the bell by the (unlabelled) black gate and cross a lawn to reach the **Hôtel Particulier Montmartre** (*see p63*), a white stucco townhouse hidden down an alley near the 'witches' stone' between rue Lepic and exclusive avenue Junot. Here sometime curator and collector Morgane Rousseau has invited five artists 'to reflect on the theme of the traveller' in order to create a cosy, cosseted hotel where guests can live and breathe contemporary art. Art books scattered around the house and artists' videos to borrow add to the experience.

you can see the Eiffel Tower from nine of the 29 rooms. All feature Empire-style bedheads and modern bathrooms. Outside, there's a tiny, tiled courtyard with a bridge. A nearby sister hotel in the 15th, the Hôtel Eiffel Villa Garibaldi (01.56.58.56.58), has equally modest rates.
*Concierge. Internet (€6/30mins shared terminal or free wireless). TV.*

## Youth accommodation

### Auberge Internationale des Jeunes
*10 rue Trousseau, 11th (01.47.00.62.00/fax 01.47.00.33.16/www.aijparis.com). M° Ledru-Rollin.* **Rates** (incl breakfast, per person) *Mar-June, Sept-Oct* €15. *July, Aug* €17. *Nov-Feb* €13. **Credit** AmEx, MC, V. **Map** p407 N7 ⓴

Cleanliness is a high priority at this large (120 beds) hostel close to Bastille and within easy distance of the Marais. Rooms accommodate between two and four people, and the larger ones have their own shower and toilet. With the lowest hostel rates in central Paris, the place does tend to fill up fast in summer, but advance reservations can be made. Although the hostel is open all hours without any late-night curfew, the rooms are closed for cleaning every day between 10am and 3pm.
*Internet (€6/hr shared terminal). Microwave.*

### Auberge Jules-Ferry
*8 bd Jules-Ferry, 11th (01.43.57.55.60/fax 01.43.14.82.09/www.hihostels.com). M° République.* **Rates** (incl breakfast & linens, per person) €21. **Credit** MC, V. **Map** p402 M4 ⓹

This friendly IYHF hostel has 100 beds in rooms for two to six. There's no need – indeed, no way – to make advance bookings. No curfew, though rooms are closed between 10am and 2pm.
*Internet (€6/hr shared terminal).*

### BVJ Paris/Quartier Latin
*44 rue des Bernardins, 5th (01.43.29.34.80/fax 01.53.00.90.91/www.bvjhotel.com). M° Maubert Mutualité.* **Rates** (incl breakfast, per person) €28 dorm; €40 single; €30 double. **No credit cards**. **Map** p406 J7 ⓶

The BVJ hostel has 121 beds with homely tartan quilts in clean but bare modern dorms (for up to ten) and rooms with showers. There's also a TV lounge and a work room in which to write up your journal.
*Internet. (€4/hr shared terminal)*
**Other locations** BVJ Paris/Louvre, 20 rue Jean-Jacques-Rousseau, 1st (01.53.00.90.90).

### MIJE
*6 rue de Fourcy, 4th (01.42.74.23.45/fax 01.40.27.81.64/www.mije.com). M° St-Paul.* **Rates** (incl breakfast, per person; €2.50 obligatory membership) €28 dorm (18-30s); €45 single; €33 double; €29 triple. **No credit cards**. **Map** p409 L6 ⓷

MIJE runs three 17th-century Marais residences – one is a former convent – that provide the most attractive hostel sleeps in Paris. Its plain, clean rooms have snow-white sheets and sleep up to eight; all have a shower and basin. The Fourcy address has its own restaurant (evenings only). Curfew is 1am unless you arrange otherwise with reception. *Internet (€6/hr shared terminal).*
**Other locations** *(same phone) 11 rue du Fauconnier, 4th; 12 rue des Barres, 4th.*

## Bed & breakfast

### Alcove & Agapes
*Le Bed & Breakfast à Paris, 8bis rue Coysevox, 18th (01.44.85.06.05/fax 01.44.85.06.14/www.bed-and-breakfast-in-paris.com).*

This B&B booking service offers over 100 *chambres d'hôte* (€75-€195 for a double, including breakfast; triple, quad and quint rooms available too) with hosts who range from artists to grannies. Extras can include anything from dinner to cooking classes or tours of Paris. The multilingual website provides good descriptions and photos of each property.

### Good Morning Paris
*43 rue Lacépède, 5th (01.47.07.28.29/fax 01.47.07.44.45/www.goodmorningparis.fr).*

This company has 100 rooms in the city. Prices range from €56 to €96 for one person, €69 to €109 for doubles and around €109 for larger rooms for two or three. It also has apartments for two to four people, from €99 to €125. Two-night minimum stay.

## Apart-hotels & flat rental

A deposit is usually payable on arrival. Small ads for private short-term lets run in the fortnightly anglophone *FUSAC* (www.fusac.fr).

### Citadines Apart'hotel
*Central reservations 01.41.05.79.79/fax 01.41.05.78.87/www.citadines.com.* **Rates** €110-€615. **Credit** AmEx, DC, MC, V.

The 16 modern Citadines complexes across Paris (including around the Louvre and Opéra) tend to attract a mainly business clientele. Room sizes vary from slightly cramped studios to quite spacious two-bedroom apartments, all with a kitchenette and dining table suitable for those with children. Rates depend on neighbourhood, size of apartment and length of stay; although you can book for as little as one night, there are discounts for longer stays.

### Paris Appartements Services
*20 rue Bachaumont, 2nd (01.40.28.01.28/fax 01.40.28.92.01/www.paris-apts.com). M° Sentier.* **Open** 9am-6pm Mon-Fri. *Key pick-up* 24hrs. **Rates** (5-night minimum stay) €83-€150 studio; €135-€214 2-room apartment. Monthly prices on request. **Credit** AmEx, MC, V.

This organisation specialises in short-term rentals, offering furnished studios and one-bedroom flats in the 1st to 4th districts, with a weekly maid service and a 24-hour helpline manned by bilingual staff. A daily breakfast service and cleaning can be arranged.

# Cruises on the Seine

Lunch Cruise        Dinner Cruise        Sightseeing Cruises

Mazarine image - Crédits Photos : P. Hamon, D. Vijelovic, M. Monteaux.

## The most Parisian of trips...

During a sightseeing outing, lunch or dinner, music and songs accompany the cruise and you discover the emotion and enchantment of Paris - majestic during the day and magical at night.
Board for a unique and unforgettable meeting with Paris...

**At the foot of the Eiffel Tower**

Port de la Bourdonnais, 75007 Paris - 00 33 (1) 46 99 43 13
www.bateauxparisiens.com
Métro : Bir-Hakeim ou Trocadéro - RER C : Champ de Mars

Bateaux Parisiens

# Sightseeing

## Features

# Introduction

Just capital.

Paris is a compact capital: neatly contained inside the Périphérique and divided by the Seine into Left and Right Banks, with Ile de la Cité and Ile St-Louis to add interest. Dead central, and almost self-contained, is the world's most famous art museum, the Louvre.

We have divided **Sightseeing** into 14 chapters: **The Seine & Islands** (*pp86-92*); **The Louvre** (*pp93-100*); **Opéra to Les Halles** (*pp101-115*); **The Champs-Elysées & western Paris** (*pp116-124*); **Montmartre & Pigalle** (*pp125-129*); **Beaubourg & the Marais** (*pp130-136*); **Bastille & eastern Paris** (*pp137-140*); **North-east Paris** (*pp141-146*); **The Latin Quarter** (*pp147-154*); **St-Germain-des-Prés & Odéon** (*pp155-160*); **Montparnasse & Beyond** (*pp161-167*); **The 7th & western Paris** (*pp168-174*); **The 13th arrondissement** (*pp175-177*) and **Beyond the Périphérique** (*pp178-184*). The main sections are also sub-divided by areas that, roughly, follow district guidelines, starting from the centre and working out. To cut to the chase, follow our recipe for a potted Paris break (*see pp84-85* **Saturday night, Sunday morning**).

You can get a good feel for Paris even on a day's sightseeing trip – something you can't say of many capital cities – and while its famed beauty certainly doesn't extend to every last nook and cranny, there are few streets here that are not worth walking along.

Walking: that's the key. The Paris métro is a world champion among public transport networks and merits a ride in its own right; the local buses are clean, frequent and cheap; and there are plenty of guided tours (*see p84*) to take you around the sights. By all means, time permitting, try them all. But your best chance of hearing this city's heartbeat lies in putting one foot in front of the other, above ground, among the people who live and work here Alternatively, take to two wheels, thanks to **Vélib'**, the free bike scheme launched in July 2007 by the mairie. *See p164* **Easy rider**.

The city's 20 districts spiral out, clockwise and in ascending order, from the Louvre. These are the arrondissements, the pieces that together make a jigsaw puzzle compared by the novelist Julien Green to medical models of the human brain. Each piece has its peculiar connotations. Fifth: intellectual. Sixth: chic.

16th: affluent and stuffy. Tenth, 11th: post-industrial bar hubs. 18th, 19th, 20th: lively and multicultural. Rightly or wrongly, residents are often assessed, at least at first encounter, by their postcodes – and many will tell you that Paris is not a city but, in fact, a collection of distinct villages. *See p142* **Street poetry**.

## Museums

The Louvre (*see p93-100*) is so vast that it tends to overshadow the city's 100-plus museums. The **Centre Pompidou**, **Musée d'Orsay** and **Musée Marmottan** are almost as famous, and you shouldn't miss the world-class ethnic art on show at the **Musée du Quai Branly** and the **Institut du Monde Arabe**. The city's science museums are equally impressive, from the **Musée des Arts et Métiers** to the high-tech, child-friendly **Cité des Sciences et de l'Industrie** at La Villette. For lovers of the avant-garde, there's the innovative **Palais de Tokyo**, which houses the **Musée d'Art Moderne de la Ville de Paris**.

The reason for the rich trove is tied up with French history. After the Revolution, the huge royal collections became the property of the state; then came the 19th-century zeal for *grand tourisme* – although the ownership of foreign plunder is a matter of current debate. Both the French state and the city put large sums into the upkeep and expansion of collections, while tiny, unique private museums, like the **Musée Edith Piaf** or **Musée de l'Eventail**, struggle.

The big openings in 2007 were the **Cité de l'Architecture et du Patrimoine** at the **Palais de Trocadéro** and the **Cité Nationale de l'Histoire de l'Immigration** at the **Palais de la Porte d'Orée**. 2008 sees the unveiling of the **Cité de la Mode et du Design**, as part of an exciting development by the Seine in the 13th arrondissement (*see p177* **In the zone**).

### MUSEUM TICKETS AND PASSES

The most economical way to visit a large number of museums is the **Paris Museum Pass** (www.parismuseumpass.fr), formerly known as the Carte Musées et Monuments. The one-day version has been discontinued, but the pass is available in two-day (€30), four-day (€45) and six-day (€60) formats. It allows you

# Welcome to the neighbourhood

landmarks, the subterranean Forum des Halles shopping mall.

### Ile de la Cité
The bullseye of the capital, where its history begins – home to the law courts, Notre-Dame and a dinky flower market.

### Ile St-Louis
You'd need a pile of euros to buy property on this island of calm, but it costs nothing to explore its charming streets and small, characterful shops.

### Madeleine
Moneyed but lacking in character, this is where you'll find fab food shops and any number of hotels.

### The Marais
With ancient buildings and a street plan largely unmolested by Haussmann, this is great pedestrian territory. The Marais is the heartland of Jewish and gay Paris, full of boutiques, art galleries and bars.

### Ménilmontant
A thriving centre of alternative Paris, awash with artists' studios and trendy cafés.

### Montmartre
The highest point in the city also has one of its densest concentrations of tourists. The views and Sacré-Coeur should be seen, of course – but then strike out from the crowds and explore the unabashedly romantic side streets and stairways.

### Montparnasse
There's just enough of a good-time feel here after dark to recall the area's artistic heyday in the 1920s and '30s. Bars, restaurants and cinemas are abundant.

### Pigalle
Sex shops and neon: that's the popular image of Pigalle. True, there's a lot of both – but the area has been cleaning up its act in recent years, with the relandscaping of major thoroughfares.

### St-Germain-des-Prés
Intellectual heritage and some of the most expensive cups of coffee in the city are to be found here. The district is now best known for fashion houses and luxury brands, though a few publishers remain.

### Bastille
No so much revolutionary, these days, as creative; the area around iconic place de la Bastille is stocked with record shops, music venues (such as the opera house) and a handful of decent bars.

### Belleville
One of the city's most multicultural areas: Chinese shops rub up against halal and kosher grocers, and there's a busy street market on Tuesday and Friday mornings.

### Bercy
Entertainment is a strong point, especially cinema: Bercy is the new home for the Cinémathèque Française, housed in a building by Frank Gehry.

### Grands Boulevards
Less a distinct quarter than a curving east-west stripe across several others. At the western end it's all large-scale consumerism in the *grands magasins*; to the east are seediness, buzz and exotic food shops.

### Les Halles
Once the city's wholesale food market, now home to one of its unloveliest architectural

Sightseeing

admission into more than 60 museums and monuments in Paris, including the Louvre, Musée National Picasso and Cité des Sciences et de l'Industrie (though you will have to pay extra for special exhibitions), and also allows you to jump queues. The card is sold at participating museums and monuments, as well as tourist offices. In our listings, **PMP** indicates venues where the card is accepted.

The Galeries Nationales du Grand Palais also now operate an annual pass, the aptly named **Sésame** (www.rmn.fr), which grants handy queue-jumping rights, unlimited entry and various other discounts (€74 couples; €42 solo; €22 13-25s).

Museums often offer reduced admission for students, children and the over-60s; bring identification to prove your status. In any case, all permanent collections at municipal-run museums are free, and a reduced rate is usually applicable on Sundays. All national museums are completely free of charge on the first Sunday of the month.

## MUSEUM OPENING HOURS

Most national museums close on Tuesdays; most municipal museums close on Mondays. To avoid the crowds, visit on weekdays, or take advantage of the late-night opening that most of the big museums offer. Pre-booking is essential before 1pm at the Grand Palais, and it's also possible to pre-book the Louvre, the Luxembourg and major exhibitions. Most ticket counters will close 30 to 45 minutes before the official closing time.

Thousands turn out for the annual **Journées du Patrimoine** (see p277) in September to see behind the normally closed doors of some of the capital's oldest and most beautiful buildings.

## TEMPORARY EXHIBITION VENUES

Non-museum exhibition centres include the **Grand Palais** and **Palais du Luxembourg**, and a host of smaller institutions offering well-priced or free exhibitions. Check *L'Officiel des spectacles* for details. Cultural centres include: **Centre Culturel Calouste Gulbenkian** (Portugal; 51 av d'Iéna, 16th, 01.53.23.93.93); **Centre Culturel Irlandais** (Ireland; 5 rue des Irlandais, 5th, 01.58.52.10.30); **Centre Culturel Suisse** (Switzerland; 32-38 rue des Francs-Bourgeois, 3rd, 01.42.71.44.50); **Centre Wallonie-Bruxelles** (Belgium; 127 rue St-Martin, 4th, 01.53.01.96.96); **Institut Finlandais** (Finland; 60 rue des Ecoles, 5th, 01.40.51.89.09); **Institut Néerlandais** (Holland; 121 rue de Lille, 7th, 01.53.59.12.40); and **Maison de l'Amérique Latine** (Latin America; 217 bd St-Germain, 7th, 01.49.54.75.00).

**Sightseeing**

## The best Sights

### For 19th-century ingenuity
**Canal d'Ourcq** (*p143*), **Canal St-Martin** (*p143*), **Gare du Nord** (*p142*), **Musée des Arts et Métiers** (*p134*) and **Pavillon de l'Arsenal** (*p136*).

### For architecture and design
**Cité de l'Architecture et du Patrimoine** (*p117*), **Fondation Le Corbusier** (*p124*), **Fondation Pierre Bergé Yves Saint Laurent** (*p118*), **Galerie-Musée Baccarat** (*p118*), **Musée des Arts décoratifs** (*p105*), **Musée Galliera** (*p119*) and **Palais de Tokyo** (*p120*).

### For children's attractions
**Bois de Boulogne** (*p124*), **Cinéaqua** (*p117*), **La Cité des Sciences et de l'Industrie** (*p143*), **Eiffel Tower** (*p173*), **Grande Galerie de l'Évolution** (*p154*), **Jardin du Luxembourg** (*p160*), **Jardin des Plantes** (*p154*), **Palais de la Découverte** (*p120*), **Parc des Buttes-Chaumont** (*p146*) and **Parc Montsouris** (*p167*).

### For intriguing oddities
**Les Catacombes** (*p166*), **Les Egouts de Paris** (*p173*), **Musée de l'Erotisme** (*p127*), **Musée de l'Eventail** (*p142*), **Musée des Lettres et Manuscrits** (*p160*), and **Musée National de la Marine** (*p119*).

### For Roman remains
**Arènes de Lutèce** (*p153*), **Musée National du Moyen Age – Thermes de Cluny** (*p148*), **rue Cujas** (*p147*) and **rue St-Jacques** (*p147*).

### For views of Paris
**Arc de Triomphe** (*p117*), **Eiffel Tower** (*p173*), **Institut du Monde Arabe** (*p154*), **Observatoire de Paris** (*p165*), **Sacré-Coeur** (*p126*) and **Tour Montparnasse** (*p166*).

### For world-class art
**Centre Pompidou** (*p131*), **Musée Maillol** (*p170*), **Musée Marmottan – Claude Monet** (*p124*), **Musée National Rodin** (p172), **Musée d'Orsay** (p172) and **Musée National Picasso** (*p135*).

# Saturday night, Sunday morning

You've got a mere 48 hours to spend in the city of light. As well as the must-see list of iconic sights – the Eiffel Tower, Notre-Dame, Arc de Triomphe, the Louvre, the Musée d'Orsay, Sacré-Coeur – there are some other delights worth squeezing into a swift *séjour*. Here are a few ideas.

## Day one

Start the day with mouthfuls of crispy, buttery flakes and soft, squishy dough – in other words, a croissant from **Au Levain du Marais** (32 rue de Turenne, 3rd), an easy stroll from beautiful 17th-century place des Vosges. Sip an espresso at one of several cafés that sit facing the square.

Now for a look at a bit more of the Marais. Traditionally the Jewish quarter, it's abuzz with culture, retail and bars. Many of its imposing *hôtels particuliers* – old aristocratic mansions – now house important cultural institutions like the **Musée Carnavalet** (*see p134*), **Musée National Picasso** (*see p135*) and **Maison Européenne de la Photographie** (*see p136*). Boutique hunters, meanwhile, will find rich pickings in the streets leading off the main shopping thoroughfare of rue des Francs-Bourgeois. The area is also an enclave of contemporary art galleries and, around rue Vieille-du-Temple, a thriving bar scene, straight and gay.

There are several unsung panoramas in Paris. The **Institut du Monde Arabe** (*see p154*), a behemoth glass building designed by French superstar architect Jean Nouvel, has a fine collection of Middle Eastern art and a rooftop café with fabulous views looking down the Seine. Clambering up to the small temple that marks the summit of the **Parc des Buttes-Chaumont** (*see p146*) reveals beautifully landscaped swathes of green below, and miles of city beyond. Save **Sacré-Coeur** (*see p126*) for dusk, when the tourists have largely departed and the night lights have begun to glimmer.

Meander along the stone quays that border the Seine and leaf through old *revues* and tatty paperbacks at the riverside *bouquiniste* stalls (*see p241*), which are folded away into their green boxes at night. From the quays you can either hop on a sightseeing boat, or pause to explore the islands. The **Mémorial des Martyrs de la Déportation** (*see p92*) on the Ile de la Cité is an under-visited tribute to the people deported to concentration camps in World War II. On the Ile St-Louis, the deliciousness of the ice-cream from **Berthillon** (31 rue St-Louis-en-l'Ile, 4th, 01.43.54.31.61) is no secret; if the weather's warm, you'll have to queue.

Evenings start with aperitifs. Join the sociable crowd on the terrace seats at **Le Bar du Marché** (*see p236*) and watch the Left Bank people-traffic pass by over a kir, served by one of the eccentric, dungaree-wearing waiters. By now, you're almost certainly in the mood for a little nocturnal revelry. Cross the river to the **Rex** nightclub (*see p330*)

## Guided tours

For boat tours, *see p90*.

## Coach tours

### Les Cars Rouges

*01.53.95.39.53/www.carsrouges.com*. **Departs** *from Trocadéro. Summer* every 8-15mins 9.30am-8.50pm daily. *Winter* every 10-20mins 9.30am-7.30pm daily. **Tickets** €22; €11 4-12s. **No credit cards.**
Red buses follow a set tour of the major monuments. Hop on at any of nine stops. Recorded commentary.

### Cityrama

*4 pl des Pyramides, 1st (01.44.55.61.00/ www.pariscityrama.com)*. M° *Palais Royal Musée du Louvre*. **Departs** *Summer* 10am, 11.30am, 1.30pm, 3.30pm daily. *Winter* 10am, 11.30am, 2pm daily. **Tickets** €26; €13 4-11s. **Credit** AmEx, DC, MC, V.

Another double-decker outfit with multilingual recorded commentary.

### Paris L'OpenTour

*13 rue Auber, 9th (01.42.66.56.56/www.paris-opentour.com)*. M° *Havre-Caumartin/RER Auber*. **Departs** *Apr-Oct* every 10-15mins 9.20am-6pm daily. *Nov-Mar* every 25-30mins 9.45am-4pm daily. **Tickets** 1 day €26. 2 days €29; €13 4-11s. **Credit** AmEx, DC, MC, V.
Green, open-top buses with recorded commentary in English and French. Hop on at any of 50 stops.

### Paris Vision

*214 rue de Rivoli, 1st (01.42.60.30.01/www.parisvision.fr)*. M° *Tuileries*. **Departs** times vary. **Tickets** €19-€163; €13.30-€114.10 under-12s. **Credit** AmEx, DC, MC, V.
Large air-conditioned coaches tour the sights – make sure you get a top-deck seat. Commentary is basic, and trips last between two hours and a full day.

for an electronica blowout. Post-dancefloor hunger pangs can be satiated at welcoming Les Halles bistro **La Poule au Pot** (10 rue de Vauvilliers, 1st, 01.42.36.32.96), which thoughtfully stays open until 6am. Near the Champs-Elysées, meanwhile, you'll find **La Maison de l'Aubrac** (37 rue Marbeuf, 8th, 01.43.59.05.14), a bonhomie-filled outpost of the Auvergne, grilling *côte du boeuf* to perfection until 7am, every day of the week.

Finish your *nuit blanche* in style with a coffee at gorgeous art deco brasserie **Le Vaudeville** (29 rue Vivienne, 2nd, 01.40.20.04.62), which opens its doors from 7am.

### Day two

Cross the Pont des Arts and head south through the narrow Left Bank streets to St-Sulpice church, then stroll to the **Jardin du Luxembourg** (*see p160*), pull up two green chairs (this is the accepted protocol – you need the extra one as a footrest) and size up the park life: children sailing toy boats past the ducks on the central pond, t'ai chi groups doing bizarre stretches and old-timers playing unhurried chess. The adjacent museum, the **Musée National du Luxembourg** (*see p160*), hosts world-class art exhibitions – Botticelli, Modigliani and so on.

Amble along the tree-lined **Canal St-Martin**, crossing from side to side over its romantic green bridges, to explore little shops and waterside cafés. On Sundays, traffic is outlawed from the quai de Valmy and the bar-lined quai de Jemmapes, to be replaced by streams of in-line skaters, cyclists and baby buggies. Boutiques such as princessy outfitter **Stella Cadente** (93 quai Valmy, 10th, 01.42.09.27.00) and kitsch merchants **Antoine et Lili** (*see p253*) are both open on Sundays. For coffee and a slice of chocolate cake, drop by wood-floored, chandeliered café **Le Sporting** (3 rue des Récollets, 10th, 01.46.07.02.00); if you'd prefer a swift *demi* near the water, go for friendly **L'Atmosphère** (*see p231*) across the road.

Modern art lovers should make a point of visiting the wonderful collection at the **Musée de l'Art Moderne de la Ville de Paris** (*see p118*), which is neighbour to dynamic contemporary art space the **Palais de Tokyo** (*see p120*). From here you can walk to the Champs-Elysées and take a nighttime hike up the Arc de Triomphe to see the lights of the avenue stretching into the city.

As a parting gesture, sink into a comfy Chesterfield and relax with an expertly shaken cocktail at the classy neo-colonial **China Club** (50 rue de Charenton, 12th, 01.43.43.82.02).

### WEEKEND TRAVEL TIPS

Buy a *carnet* of ten tickets (€10.90) if you're staying in the city for less than two days; for long weekends it's worth investing in a *coupon hebdomadaire*, or weekly pass, for €15.90. You can use either on the métro, RER and buses.

---

## Two-wheeled tours

### City-bird
*08.26.10.01.00/www.city-bird.com.* **Tickets** €70-€100. **Credit** AmEx, DC, MC, V.
A friendly and knowledgeable driver weaves you through the traffic on a motorbike, supplying the history while the sights whizz by.

### Fat Tire Bike Tours
*01.56.58.10.54/www.fattirebiketoursparis.com. Meet at Pilier Sud, Tour Eiffel, Champs de Mars, 7th. M° Bir-Hakeim.* **Departs** *Bike day tour* mid Feb-May & mid Sept-mid Dec 11am daily; June-mid Sept 11am, 3pm daily. *Bike night tour* Mar & 1st 2wks Nov 7pm Tue, Thur, Sat, Sun; Apr-15 Nov 7pm daily. *Segway day tour* mid Feb-30 Nov 10.30am daily. *Segway night tour* Apr-Oct 6.30pm daily. **Tickets** *Day* €24; €22 students. *Night* €28; €26 students. *Both* €48; €44 students. *Segway* €70. **No credit cards.**

Paris, Versailles and Giverny by chunky bike or Segway scooter. Walking tours and bike hire too.

### Paris à vélo, c'est sympa!
*22 rue Baudin, 11th (01.48.87.60.01/ www.parisvelosympa.com). M° Richard Lenoir.* **Departs** times vary. **Tickets** €34; €28 13-26s; €18 under-12s. **Credit** MC, V.
Multilingual themed cycle tours include nocturnal Paris and Paris at dawn. Reservations only. Bike hire available, from €10 for a half day or €13 for a day.

---

## Walking tours
*See also above* **Cityrama** and **Fat Bike Tours.**

### Paris Walking Tours
*01.48.09.21.40/www.paris-walks.com.* **Departs** 10.30am, 2.30pm daily. **Tickets** €10. Credit MC, V.
Led by long-term resident expatriates, daily walks explore areas like the Marais and the old Left Bank.

# The Seine & Islands

A working river overlooked by some of the most expensive real estate in Paris.

Pont Neuf.

## The Seine

The Seine is more than just a transport route and tourist attraction; it also splits the city in two, a division that is as much psychological as it is physical. The Right Bank is perceived as briskly mercantile, whereas the image remains of the Left Bank as chic and intellectual. The Seine is still used to transport building materials by barge, and as the wealth of boat tours attests (*see p90* **Sightseeing from the Seine**), it's a must-see feature for any visitor.

However, it hasn't always been so. For much of the 19th and 20th centuries, the Seine was barely given a second thought by anyone who wasn't working on it or roaring along its quayside roads. Then, in the 1980s, the banks along the stretch now known as quai François-Mitterrand became a popular gay cruising area (dubbed 'Tata Beach'), and in 1990 UNESCO added 12 kilometres (7.5 miles) of Paris riverbank to its World Heritage register. Parc Tino-Rossi was created on the Left Bank, where waterside tango became a regular event. Then the floating venues – Batofar (*see p326*) and its ilk – became super-trendy; and in the last ten years, it's been one Seine-side cultural attraction after another. Stretches of riverside roads are closed on Sundays to give cyclists and rollerskaters free rein (*see p334* **Capital cruising**), port de Javel becomes an open-air dancehall in the summer, and there's the

summer riverside jamboree of Paris-Plage (*see p177* **In the zone**), Mayor Delanoë's inspired attempt to bring a bit of the south of France to the city – sand, palm trees, loungers, beach huts and all.

## The bridges

From the honey-coloured arches of the ancient Pont Neuf to the swooping lines of the Passerelle Simone-de-Beauvoir, the city's 37 bridges are among the most seductive reasons to visit the city, offering as they do some of the best vistas of the cityscape.

The date of the very first construction traversing the Seine is lost in the mists of time, but there was already a bridge on the site of today's Petit Pont in the first century BC, when the Parisii Celts ran their river trade and toll-bridge operations. The Romans put up a cross-island thoroughfare in the shape of a reinforced bridge to the south of Ile de la Cité, and another one north of it (where Pont Notre-Dame now stands), thus creating a straight route all the way from Orléans to Belgium.

The city's *ponts* have been bombed, bashed by buses, boats and barges, weather-beaten and even trampled to destruction: in 1634 the Pont St-Louis collapsed under the weight of a religious procession. During the Middle Ages, the handful of bridges linking the islands to the riverbanks were lined with shops and houses,

but the flimsy wooden constructions regularly caught fire or got washed away. Petit Pont sank 11 times before councillors decided it would be a good idea to ban building on top of bridges. Pont Neuf was inaugurated in 1607 and has been standing sturdy, gargoyles a-goggle, ever since. This was the first bridge to be built with no houses to obstruct the view of the river.

It had a raised stretch of road at the edge to protect walkers from traffic and horse dung (the new-fangled 'pavement' soon caught on); the semicircular alcoves that now make handy pit stops for lovers were once filled with teeth-pullers, peddlers and *bouquinistes* (*see p243*).

The 19th century saw a boom in bridge-building – 21 were built in all, including the city's first steel, iron and suspension bridges. Pont de la Concorde used up what was left of the Bastille after the storming of 1789; the romantic Pont des Arts was the capital's first solely pedestrian crossing (built in 1803 and rebuilt in the 1980s). The most glitteringly exuberant bridge is Pont Alexandre III, with its finely wrought lamps, garlanding and gilded embellishments. More stolidly practical is Pont de l'Alma, with its Zouave statue. This has long been a popular flood-level measure: when the statue's toes get wet, the state raises the flood alert and starts to close the quayside roads; when he's up to his ankles in Seine, it's no longer possible to navigate the river by boat. This offers some indication of how devastating the great 1910 flood must have been, when the plucky Zouave disappeared up to his neck – as did large areas of central Paris.

The 20th century also saw some spectacular additions to the line-up. Pont Charles-de-Gaulle, for example, stretches resplendent like the wing of a huge aeroplane, and iron Viaduc d'Austerlitz (1905) is striking yet elegant as it cradles métro line 5. The city's newest crossing, the Passerelle Simone-de-Beauvoir, is a walkway linking the Bibliothèque Nationale to the Parc de Bercy in the 12th arrondissement.

## Ile de la Cité

*In the 1st & 4th arrondissements.*

The Ile de la Cité is where Paris was born around 250 BC, when the Parisii, a tribe of Celtic Gauls, decided to found a settlement on this convenient bridging point of the Seine). Romans, Merovingians and Capetians followed, in what became a centre of political and religious power right into the Middle Ages: royal authority at one end, around the Capetian palace; the Church at the other, by Notre-Dame.

When Victor Hugo wrote his *Notre-Dame de Paris* in 1831, the Ile de la Cité was still a bustling quarter of narrow medieval streets and

tall houses: 'the head, heart and very marrow of Paris'. Taking the metaphor literally, Baron Haussmann performed a marrow extraction when he supervised the expulsion of 25,000 people from the island, razing tenements and some 20 churches, and leaving behind large, official buildings – the law courts, the **Conciergerie**, Hôtel-Dieu hospital, the police headquarters and the cathedral. The lines of the old streets are traced into the parvis in front of **Notre-Dame**.

Perhaps the most charming spot on the island is the western tip, where Pont Neuf spans the Seine. Despite its name, it is in fact the oldest remaining bridge in Paris, begun under the reign of Henri III and Catherine de Médicis in 1578 and taking 30 years to complete. Its arches are lined with grimacing faces, said to be modelled on some of the courtiers of Henri III. In 1991, the bridge (or rather a full-size facsimile of it) starred in Leos Carax's budget-busting film *Les Amants du Pont Neuf.*

Down the steps is a leafy triangular garden, square du Vert-Galant. You can take to the water here on the **Vedettes du Pont Neuf** (*see p90* **Sightseeing from the Seine**). In the centre of the bridge is an equestrian statue of Henri IV; the original went up in 1635, was melted down to make cannons during the Revolution, and replaced in 1818. On the bridge's eastern side, place Dauphine, home to restaurants, wine bars and the ramshackle Hôtel Henri IV, was built in 1607, on what was then a sandy bar that flooded every winter. It was commissioned by Henri IV, who named it in honour of his son, the future King Louis XIII. The brick and stone houses, similar to those in place des Vosges (though subsequently much altered to accommodate sun terraces), look out over the quays and square. The third, eastern side was demolished in the 1860s, when the new Préfecture de Police was built. Known by its address, quai des Orfèvres, it was immortalised on screen by Clouzot's film and Simenon's Maigret novels. It's a tranquil, secluded spot.

The towers of the Conciergerie dominate the island's north bank. Along with the Palais de Justice, it was originally part of the Palais de la Cité, residential and administration complex of the Capetian kings. It occupies the site of an earlier Merovingian fortress and, before that, the Roman governor's house. Etienne Marcel's uprising prompted Charles V to move the royal retinue to the Louvre in 1358, and the Conciergerie was assigned a more sinister role as a prison for those awaiting execution. The interior is worth a visit for its prison cells and the vaulted Gothic halls. On the corner of boulevard du Palais, the Tour de l'Horloge, built in 1370, was the first public clock in Paris.

*Sightseeing*

**Sainte-Chapelle,** Pierre de Montreuil's masterpiece of stained glass and slender Gothic columns, nestles amid the nearby law courts. Enveloping the chapel, the Palais de Justice was built alongside the Conciergerie. Behind elaborate wrought-iron railings, most of the present buildings around the fine neo-classical entrance courtyard date from the 1780s reconstruction by Desmaisons and Antoine. After passing through security, you can visit the Salle des Pas Perdus, busy with plaintiffs and barristers, and sit in on cases in the civil and criminal courts. The Palais is still the centre of the French legal system, though it's rumoured that the law courts will one day be moved to the 13th or 15th arrondissement.

Across boulevard du Palais, behind the Tribunal du Commerce, place Louis-Lépine is occupied by the Marché aux Fleurs, where horticultural suppliers sell flowers, cacti and exotic trees. On Sundays, they are joined by caged birds and small animals in the Marché aux Oiseaux. The Hôtel-Dieu, east of the market place, was founded in the seventh century. During the Middle Ages your chances of survival here were, at best, slim; today the odds are much improved. The hospital originally stood on the other side of the island facing the Latin Quarter, but after a series of fires in the 18th century it was rebuilt here in the 1860s.

Notre-Dame cathedral dominates the eastern half of the island. On the parvis in front of the cathedral, the bronze 'Kilomètre Zéro' marker is the point from which distances between Paris and the rest of France are measured. The **Crypte Archéologique** hidden under the parvis gives a sense of the island's multi-layered past, when it was a tangle of alleys, houses, churches and cabarets. Despite all the tourists, Notre-Dame is still a place of worship, and holds its **Assumption Day procession** (see p274), Christmas Mass (see p278) and Nativity scene on the parvis.

Walk through the garden by the cathedral to appreciate its flying buttresses. To the north-east, a medieval feel persists in the few streets untouched by Haussmann, such as rue Chanoinesse, rue de la Colombe and rue des Ursins, though the crenellated medieval remnant on the corner of rue des Ursins and rue des Chantres was redone in the 1950s for the Aga Khan. The capital's oldest love story unfolded in the 12th century at 9 quai aux Fleurs, where Héloïse lived with her uncle Canon Fulbert, who had her tutor and lover, the scholar Abélard, castrated. Héloïse was sent to a nunnery. Behind the cathedral, in a garden at the eastern end of the island, is the **Mémorial des Martyrs de la Déportation**, remembering those sent to Nazi concentration camps.

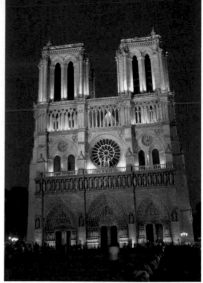

Gothic grandeur: **Cathédrale Notre-Dame.**

## Cathédrale Notre-Dame de Paris

*Pl du Parvis-Notre-Dame, 4th (01.42.34.56.10/ www.cathedraledeparis.com). M° Cité/RER St-Michel.* **Open** 8am-6.45pm daily. *Towers* Apr-Sept 10am-6.45pm daily. Oct-Mar 10am-5.30pm daily. **Admission** free. *Towers* €7.10; €5.10 18-25s; free under-18s. PMP. **Credit** MC, V. **Map** p406 J7.

A masterpiece of Gothic architecture, Notre-Dame was commissioned in 1160 by Bishop Maurice de Sully, who wanted to rival the smart new abbey that had just gone up in St-Denis. It replaced the earlier St-Etienne basilica, built in the sixth century by Childebert I on the site of a Gallo-Roman temple to Jupiter. Notre-Dame was constructed between 1163 and 1334, and the amount of time and money spent on it reflected the city's growing prestige. Pope Alexander III may have laid the foundation stone; the choir was completed in 1182, the nave in 1208; the west front and twin towers went up between 1225 and 1250. Chapels were added to the nave between 1235 and 1250, and to the apse between 1296 and 1330. The cathedral was plundered during the French Revolution, and then rededicated to the cult of Reason. The original statues of the Kings of Judah from the west front were torn down by the mob (who believed them to represent the kings of France) and rediscovered only during the construction of a car park in 1977 (they're now in the Musée National du Moyen-Age; see p148). By the 19th century, the cathedral was looking pretty shabby.

Victor Hugo, whose novel *Notre-Dame de Paris* had been a great success, led the campaign for its restoration. Gothic revivalist Viollet-le-Duc restored Notre-Dame to her former glory in the mid 19th century, although work has been going on ever since, with the replacement and cleaning of damaged and eroded finials and sculptures. Although Reims was

# Sightseeing from the Seine

Most boats depart from the quays in the 7th and 8th arrondissements, at the foot of the Eiffel Tower, and go on a circuit around the islands, first along the Left Bank and past the Latin Quarter and Notre-Dame, then along the Right Bank, past the Marais and the Louvre.

## Bateaux-Mouches

*Pont de l'Alma, 8th (01.42.25.96.10/ 01.42.25.02.28/www.bateaux-mouches.fr). M° Alma-Marceau.* **Departs** *Apr-Sept* every 15 mins 10am-11pm daily. *Oct-Mar* every 45mins 11am-9pm daily. **Admission** €9; €4 under-12s, over-65s; free under-4s. **Credit** AmEx, MC, V.

If you're after a whirlwind tour of the essential sights and don't mind crowds of tourists and schoolchildren, this, the oldest cruise operation on the Seine, is the one to go for. Still, the four languages that are crammed into the canned commentary and the high speed of the boat mean you get only the basic facts.

## Bateaux Parisiens

*Tour Eiffel, port de la Bourdonnais, 7th (01.46.99.43.13/www.bateauxparisiens. com). RER Champ de Mars.* **Departs** *Apr-Nov* every 30mins 10am-11pm daily. *Dec-Mar* every hr 10am-10pm daily. **Admission** €10; €5 under-12s; free under-3s. **Credit** AmEx, MC, V.

BP's trimarans are smarter boats than most, and jaunty Paris music flavours your cruise. Competent staff provide a live commentary in French, plus good English and Spanish. The glass-topped boats should be avoided on sunny days, however, as they rapidly turn into floating greenhouses.

## Batobus Tour Eiffel

*08.25.05.01.01/www.batobus.com.* Boats stop at Tour Eiffel (port de la Bourdonnais), Musée d'Orsay, St-Germain-des-Prés (quai Malaquais), Notre-Dame, Jardin des Plantes, Hôtel de Ville, Louvre and Champs-Elysées (Pont Alexandre III). **Departs** every 15-30mins. *Feb-mid Mar, Nov-early Jan* 10.30am-4.30pm daily. *Mid Mar-May, Sept-Oct* 10am-7pm daily. *June-Aug* 10am-9.30pm daily. Closed 3 wks Jan. **Admission** *Day pass* €11; €7 reductions; €5 under-16s. *2-day pass* €13; €8 reductions; €6 under-16s. *5-day pass* €16; €10 reductions; €7 under-16s. *Annual pass* €50; €30 under-16s.

A public transport and sightseeing hybrid, this is a pleasurable way to cruise through the city, with eight hop-on, hop-off stops between the Eiffel Tower and the Jardin des Plantes. The polite staff and the presence of some Parisians make this a classier choice. It can be combined with L'Open Tour on a two-day ticket that gives you unlimited access to the 50 bus stops and eight boat stops.

## Canauxrama

*13 quai de la Loire, 19th (01.42.39.15.00/ 01.42.39.11.24/www.canauxrama.fr).* **Departs** *All year* Port de l'Arsenal (50 bd de la Bastille, 12th, M° Bastille) 9.45am, 2.30pm daily. *Apr-Sept* Bassin de la Villette (13 quai de la Loire, 19th, M° Jaurès) 9.45am, 2.45pm daily. **Admission** *Mon-Fri* €14; €8 6-12s; €11 students and reductions; free under-6s Mon-Fri. *Sat, Sun* all tickets €14 after noon.

If the Seine palls, take a trip up the city's second waterway, the Canal St-Martin. The tree-lined canal is a pretty and characterful sight, and the 150-minute trip even goes underground for a stretch, where the tunnel walls are enlivened by a coloured light show. Reservations must be made in advance; also call for cruises between the Musée d'Orsay and La Villette.

## Vedettes de Paris

*Port de Suffren, 7th (01.47.05.71.29/ 01.47.05.74.53/www.vedettesdeparis.com). M° Bir-Hakeim.* **Departs** *Easter-Oct* every hr 10am-10pm daily. *Nov-Easter* every hr 11am-6pm daily. **Admission** €10; €4 5-12s; free under-4s.

Open boats give the most unobstructed views, and the recorded commentary can be avoided by choosing the children's cruise: the French-only tour guide on board soon tires of the bridge-naming game.

## Vedettes du Pont-Neuf

*Sq du Vert-Galant, 1st (01.46.33.98.38/ 01.43.29.86.19/www.vedettesdupontneuf. com). M° Pont Neuf.* **Departs** *Mar-Oct* every 30-45mins 10.30am-10.30pm daily. *Nov-Feb* every 45mins 10.30am-10pm Mon-Thur; 10.30am-10.30pm Fri-Sun. **Admission** €11; €6 under-12s; free under-4s.

You can sit inside just a foot or two above water level or outside on the top deck – where you may get drenched by pranksters throwing water from bridges as you pass underneath.

the coronation church of the French kings, that didn't deter others with monarchical pretensions: in 1430 Henry VI of England was crowned here; Napoleon made himself Emperor here in 1804; and in 1909 it hosted the beatification of Joan of Arc.

Despite its heavy restoration, the west front remains a high point of Gothic art for the balanced proportions of its twin towers and rose window, and the three doorways with their rows of saints and sculpted tympanums: the *Last Judgement* (centre), *Life of the Virgin* (left) and *Life of St Anne* (right). Inside, take a moment to admire the long nave with its solid foliate capitals and high altar with a marble *Pietà* by Coustou; the choir was rebuilt in the 18th century by Robert le Cotte but is surrounded by medieval painted stone reliefs depicting the Resurrection (south) and Nativity (north). Religious paintings, known as 'the Mays' because they were donated by the guilds on 1 May every year, hang in many of the side chapels, while the Treasury contains ornate bishops' copes, church plate and reliquaries designed to hold the Crown of Thorns (which long sat in Sainte-Chapelle; *see p92*). To truly appreciate the masonry, climb up the towers (only a limited number can ascend at one time). The route runs up the north tower and down the south. Between the two you get a close-up view of the gallery of chimeras – the fantastic birds and leering hybrid beasts designed by Viollet-le-Duc along the balustrade, including the pensive Stryga, who looks down from the first corner. After a detour to see the Bourdon (the massive bell), a spiral staircase leads to the top of the south tower, from where you can see pretty much every monument in Paris. *Photo p89.*

### La Conciergerie

*2 bd du Palais, 1st (01.53.40.60.97). M° Cité/ RER St-Michel Notre-Dame.* **Open** *Mar-Oct* 9.30am-6pm daily. *Nov-Feb* 9am-5pm daily. **Admission** €6.50; €4.50 18-25s, students; free under-18s (accompanied by an adult). *With Sainte-Chapelle* €10; €8 reductions. PMP. **Credit** MC, V. **Map** p408 J6.

Marie-Antoinette was imprisoned here during the Revolution, as were Danton and Robespierre before their executions. The Conciergerie looks every inch the forbidding medieval fortress, yet much of the pseudo-medieval façade was added in the 1850s. The 13th-century Bonbec tower, built during the reign of St Louis, the 14th-century twin towers, César and Argent, and the Tour de l'Horloge all survive from the Capetian palace. The visit takes you through the Salle des Gardes, the medieval kitchens with their four huge chimneys, and the Salle des Gens d'Armes, an impressive vaulted Gothic hall built between 1301 and 1315 for Philippe 'le Bel'. After the royals moved to the Louvre, the fortress became a prison under the watch of the Concierge. The wealthy had private cells with their own furniture, which they paid for; others crowded on beds of straw. A list of Revolutionary prisoners, including a hairdresser, shows that not all victims were nobles. In Marie-Antoinette's cell, the Chapelle des Girondins, are her crucifix, some portraits and a guillotine blade.

### La Crypte Archéologique

*Pl Jean-Paul II, 4th (01.55.42.50.10). M° Cité/RER St-Michel Notre-Dame.* **Open** 10am-6pm Tue-Sun. **Admission** €3.30; €2.20 over-60s; €1.60 13-26s; free under-14s. PMP. **Credit** (€15 minimum) MC, V. **Map** p406 J7.

Hidden under the forecourt in front of the cathedral is a large void that reveals bits and pieces of Roman quaysides, ramparts and hypocausts, medieval cellars, shops and pavements, the foundations of the Eglise Ste-Geneviève-des-Ardens (the church where Geneviève's remains were stored during the Norman invasions), an 18th-century foundling hospital and a 19th-century sewer, all excavated since the 1960s. It's not always easy to work out exactly which wall,

La Conciergerie.

column or staircase is which – but you do get a vivid sense of the layers of history piled one atop another during 16 centuries. There are plans to extend the crypt to uncover part of the foundations of the Merovingian cathedral, west of the present one.

## Mémorial des Martyrs de la Déportation

*Sq de l'Ile de France, 4th (01.46.33.87.56). M° Cité/ RER Châtelet or St-Michel Notre-Dame.* **Open** *Winter* 10am-noon, 2-5pm daily. *Summer* 10am-noon, 2-7pm daily. **Admission** free. **Map** p406 J7.
This sober tribute to the 200,000 Jews, Communists, homosexuals and *Résistants* deported to concentration camps from France in World War II stands on the eastern tip of the island. A blind staircase descends to river level, where simple chambers are lined with tiny lights and the walls are inscribed with verse. A barred window looks on to the Seine.

## Sainte-Chapelle

*6 bd du Palais, 1st (01.53.40.60.97). M° Cité/RER St-Michel Notre-Dame.* **Open** *Mar-Oct* 9.30am-6pm daily. *Nov-Feb* 9am-4.30pm daily. **Admission** €7.50; €4.80 18 25s, students; free under-18s (accompanied by an adult). PMP. *With Conciergerie* €10; €8 reductions. **Credit** MC, V. **Map** p408 J6.
Devout King Louis IX (St Louis, 1226-70) had a hobby of accumulating holy relics (and children: he fathered 11). In the 1240s he bought what was advertised as the Crown of Thorns, and ordered Pierre de Montreuil to design a suitable shrine. The result was the exquisite Flamboyant Gothic Sainte-Chapelle. With 15m (49ft) windows, the upper level, intended for the royal family and the canons, appears to consist almost entirely of stained glass. The windows depict hundreds of scenes from the Old and New Testaments, culminating with the Apocalypse in the rose window; on sunny days, coloured light dapples the stone. The lower chapel, with its star-painted vaulting, was for the use of palace servants.

# Ile St-Louis

*In the 4th arrondissement.*
The Ile St-Louis is one of the most exclusive residential addresses in the city. Delightfully unspoiled, it offers fine architecture, narrow streets and pretty views from the tree-lined quays, and still retains the air of a tranquil backwater, curiously removed from city life.

For hundreds of years, the island was a swampy pasture belonging to Notre-Dame, known as Ile Notre-Dame and used as a retreat for fishermen, swimmers and courting couples. In the 14th century Charles V built a fortified canal through the middle, thus creating the Ile aux Vaches ('Island of Cows'). Its real-estate potential wasn't realised until 1614, though, when speculator Christophe Marie persuaded Louis XIII to fill in the canal (present-day rue Poulletier) and plan streets,

bridges and houses. The island was renamed in honour of the king's pious predecessor, and the venture proved a huge success, thanks to architect Louis Le Vau, who from the 1630s built fashionable new residences along the quai d'Anjou, quai de Bourbon and quai de Béthune, as well as the **Eglise St-Louis-en-l'Ile**. By the 1660s the island was full up; its smart reception rooms were set at the front of courtyards to give residents riverside views.

Rue St-Louis-en-l'Ile – lined with fine historic buildings that now house quirky gift shops and gourmet food stores (many of them open on Sunday), quaint tearooms, stone-walled bars, restaurants and hotels – runs the length of the island. The grandiose Hôtel Lambert at no.2 was built by Le Vau in 1641 for Louis XIII's secretary, and has sumptuous interiors by Le Sueur, Perrier and Le Brun. At no.51 – Hôtel Chenizot – look out for the bearded faun adorning the rocaille doorway, which is flanked by stern dragons supporting the balcony. There's more sculpture on the courtyard façade, while a second courtyard hides craft workshops and an art gallery. Across the street, the Hôtel du Jeu de Paume at no.54 was once a tennis court; at no.31, famous ice-cream maker Berthillon still draws a crowd. There are great views of the flying buttresses of Notre-Dame at the western end from the terraces of the Brasserie de l'Ile St-Louis (*see p207* **Water with your meal?**) and the Flore en l'Ile café. A footbridge crosses from here to the Ile de la Cité.

Baudelaire wrote part of *Les Fleurs du Mal* while living at the Hôtel de Lauzun at no.17 quai d'Anjou; he and fellow poet Théophile Gautier also organised meetings of their dope-smokers' club here. A couple of centuries earlier, Racine, Molière and La Fontaine resided as guests of La Grande Mademoiselle, cousin of Louis XIV and mistress of the Comte de Lauzan. The *hôtel*, built in 1657, stands out for its scaly sea-serpent drainpipes and trompe-l'oeil interiors. At no.6 quai d'Orléans, meanwhile, the Adam Mickiewicz library-museum (01.43.54.35.61, open 2-6pm Thur) is dedicated to the Romantic poet, journalist and campaigner for Polish freedom, who had set off for Poland to catch the failed 1831 uprising, only to find himself unable to cross the border. He came to Paris to write poems and political pamphlets, all kept here.

## Eglise St-Louis-en-l'Ile

*19bis rue St-Louis-en-l'Ile, 4th (01.46.34.11.60). M° Pont Marie.* **Open** 9am-noon, 3-7pm Tue-Sun. **Map** p409 L7.
The island's church was built between 1664 and 1765, following plans by Louis Le Vau and later completed by Gabriel Le Duc. The baroque interior boasts Corinthian columns and a sunburst over the altar, and sometimes hosts classical music concerts.

# The Louvre

Extravagant architecture and extraordinary art.

Much like the building itself, the Louvre's collections were built up over the centuries. They encompass a rich visual history of the western world, from Ancient Egypt and Mesopotamia to the 19th century. Indeed, one of the most impressive things about the Louvre is the way it juxtaposes architecture and content. Look up from a case of Greek or Roman antiquities and you might see an 18th-century painted ceiling, or two doves by Braque. In the Egyptian department you'll find Louis XIV's bedchamber, complete with gilded bed, while Renaissance art is housed in the Grande Galerie, where the Sun King performed the 'scrofula ceremony', blessing the sick. In between exhibits, the Louvre's long windows afford stunning views of the building's façades, formal gardens and beautiful interior courtyards.

Some 35,000 works of art and artefacts are on show, divided into eight departments and housed in three wings: Denon, Sully and Richelieu. Under the light-flooded atrium of the glass pyramid, each wing has its own entrance, though you can pass from one to another. Treasures from the Egyptians, Etruscans, Greeks and Romans each have their own extensive galleries in the Denon and Sully wings, as do Middle Eastern and Islamic works of art. The first floor of Richelieu is taken up with European decorative arts from the Middle Ages up to the 19th century, including room after room of Napoleon III's lavish apartments.

The main draw, though, is the painting and sculpture. Two glass-roofed sculpture courts contain the famous Marly horses on the ground floor of Richelieu, with French sculpture below and Italian Renaissance pieces in the Denon wing. The Grand Galerie and Salle de la Joconde (home to the *Mona Lisa*), like a mini Uffizi, run the length of Denon's first floor with French Romantic painting alongside. Dutch and French painting occupies the second floor of Richelieu and Sully. Jean-Pierre Wilmotte's minimalist galleries in the Denon wing were designed as a taster for the **Musée du Quai Branly** (*see p171* **Windows on the world**), with art from Africa, the Americas and Oceania.

So where did all the art come from? The spoils of Napoleon's campaigns are one part. Much of the royal collection was presented as offerings to the ruling monarchs and acted as diplomatic sweeteners. The talent of Leonardo da Vinci was fought over as a commodity and sign of prestige during the reign of Louis XII, who petitioned for a portrait in Lombardy even as Milan was being sacked by his troops. It was François I who brought an entire Italian court to France, resulting in a rich collection of then contemporary art and antiquities that included the *Mona Lisa*. Some treasures were bequeathed to the state in lieu of death duties; others are acquired in an ongoing process by the Réunion des Musées Nationaux. The Louvre itself became a museum in 1793, its revolutionary opening to the people a true expression of the art-for-all ethic still in force every first Sunday of the month, when entrance to the museum is free.

Mitterrand's Grand Louvre project expanded the museum two-fold by throwing out the Ministry of Finance and other government offices that once inhabited the Cour Napoleon (*see p96* **Who built the Louvre?**). But the organisation and restoration of the Louvre is still very much a work in progress: check the website or lists in the Carrousel du Louvre to see which galleries are closed on certain days to avoid missing out on what you really want to see. The museum is also subtly moving with the times and trying to strike a healthy balance between highbrow culture and accessibility. Photography was banned in 2005 at the request of mainly French visitors, who complained that it interfered with their enjoyment; meanwhile, the link with Dan Brown's *Da Vinci Code* has been embraced with a dedicated audio guide. Laminated panels found throughout provide a surprisingly lively commentary, and the superb website is a technological feat unsurpassed by that of any of the world's major museums.

## ADVANCE TICKETS AND ENTRANCE

IM Pei's glass pyramid is a wonderful piece of architecture, but it's not the only entrance to the museum – there are three others to choose from. Buying a ticket in advance means you can go in directly via the passage Richelieu off rue de Rivoli, or via the Carrousel du Louvre shopping mall (there are steps down either side of the Arc de Triomphe du Carrousel, at 99 rue de Rivoli or from the métro). Advance tickets are valid for any day, and are available from the Louvre website or from branches of **Fnac** and **Virgin Megastore** (for both, *see p272*). You can buy one at the Virgin in the Carrousel du Louvre

Sightseeing

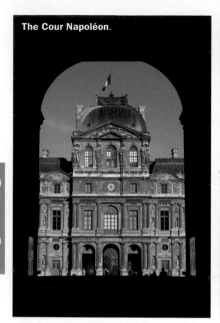

**The Cour Napoléon.**

and use it immediately. Another option is to buy a ticket at the Cour des Lions entrance (closed Fridays) in the south-west corner of the complex, convenient for the Italian collections. The Louvre is also accessible with the all-in **Paris Museum Pass** (*see p80*). Finally, don't forget that the Louvre is closed on Tuesdays.

### OTHER TIPS
● The Louvre's website, much of which is in English, is an unbeatable resource for planning your visit. Every single work on display is photographed, and you can search the website's Atlas database by room, artist or theme.
● Pick up a map at the information desk. The eight collections are colour-coded on it, and signs point the way to the most popular exhibits. Leaflets suggesting various thematic trails are also available. *Destination Louvre* (€7.50), from the Réunion des Musées Nationaux shop in the Carrousel du Louvre, is a good English-language guide.
● Laminated cards in each room provide useful background information. Audioguides (€5; ID must be left) are available at the main entrances in the Carrousel du Louvre.
● Don't attempt to see more than two collections in one day. Your ticket is valid all day and you can leave and re-enter as you wish.
● Evening visits can be made on Wednesdays and Fridays till 9.45pm. On Fridays after 6pm

entry is free for the under-26s, but if you plan to make several visits, the Carte Louvre Jeunes, at €15 for the year, is worth getting.
● Some rooms are closed on a weekly basis – check on 01.40.20.51.51 or at www.louvre.fr.
● Save your shopping for the end. The RMN bookshop and separate souvenir shops are open an hour after closing, except when the museum stays open late.

### The Louvre
*Rue de Rivoli, 1st (01.40.20.50.50/recorded information 01.40.20.51.51/disabled access 01.40.20.59.90/www.louvre.fr). M° Palais Royal Musée du Louvre.* **Open** 9am-6pm Mon, Thur, Sat, Sun; 9am-10pm Wed, Fri. **Admission** *Permanent collections* €9 (incl entry to the Musée Delacroix but not shows at the Salle Napoléon); €6 6-9.45pm Wed, Fri; free under-18s at all times, under-26s 6-9.45pm Fri, all 1st Sun of mth. PMP. *Exhibitions* €8.50. *Combined ticket* €13; €11 6-9.45pm Wed, Fri. **Credit** AmEx, MC, V. **Map** p403 G5.

### REFRESHMENTS
Take your pick from **Richelieu**, **Denon** or **Mollien** cafés; the latter is just off the Mollien staircase and has a terrace. Under the pyramid there's a sandwich bar and the smart **Grand Louvre** restaurant, serving sophisticated French cuisine. The **Restorama**, in the Carrousel du Louvre, has self-service outlets. The terrace of **Café Marly** (*see p220*) serves pricey brasserie fare and cocktails.

## The collections

### History of the Louvre

*Sully: lower ground floor. Shown as dark brown on Louvre maps.*

Here you can explore the medieval foundations of the Louvre, dating back to Philippe-Auguste's reign (*see p96* **Who built the Louvre?**). Uncovered in 1985 during excavations for the Grand Louvre project, they include the remains of the moat that once surrounded the fort and the pillars of two drawbridges; the La Taillerie tower, with heart symbols cut into the stone by masons; and the outside of the dungeons. A well and a portion of ground have been left undisturbed, showing artefacts just as they were found, and a scale model shows the fortress at the time of Charles V. An exhibition in the Saint-Louis room – a guard room from the era of Philippe-Auguste, discovered in 1882 – recounts the history of the Louvre through rare archaeological finds, as well as an unfinished staircase and carved pillars.

### Ancient Egypt

*Denon: lower ground floor; Sully: lower ground, ground & 1st floors. Green on Louvre maps.*

Announced by the pink granite Giant Sphinx (1898-1866 BC), the Egyptian department divides into two routes. The Thematic Circuit on the ground floor presents Nile culture (fishing, agriculture, hunting, daily and cultural life, religion and death). One of the big draws is the Mastaba of Akhethetep, a decorated burial chamber from Sakkara dating back to 2400 BC. Six small sphinxes, apes from Luxor and the lion-headed goddess Sekhmet recreate elements of temple complexes, while stone sarcophagi, mummies, amulets, jewellery and entrails form a vivid display on funeral rites. A display of Egyptian furniture (room 8, ground floor) dating from 1550-1069 BC contains pieces that look almost contemporary in design.

On the first floor the Pharoah Circuit is laid out chronologically, from the Seated Scribe and other stone figures of the Ancient Empire, via the painted figures of the Middle Empire, to the New Empire, with its animal-headed statues of gods and goddesses, hieroglyphic tablets and papyrus scrolls. Look for the statue of the god Amun protecting Tutankhamun, and the black diorite 'cube statues' of priests and attendants. The collection, one of the largest hoards of Egyptian antiquities in the world, has its origins in Napoleon's Egyptian campaign of 1798 and 1799, as well as the work of Egyptologist Jean-François Champollion, who deciphered hieroglyphics in 1824. The Coptic gallery, on the lower ground floor, houses textiles and manuscripts.

### Oriental antiquities

*Richelieu: lower ground & ground floors; Sully: ground floor. Yellow on Louvre maps.*

This section deals with Mesopotamia, Persia and the Levant from the fifth millennium BC to the first century AD. The huge Mesopotamian rooms contain glistening diorite sculptures from the Akkad dynasty and Gudea from the third millennium BC; in some cases, only the feet have survived intact. Make sure you don't miss the serene alabaster sculpture of Ebih-II, the superintendant of Mari (room 1b), and the earliest evidence of writing, in the form of fourth-century BC Sumerian tablets (room 1a). The Hammurabi Code, an essential document of Babylonian civilisation, is a black basalt stele recording 282 laws beneath reliefs of the king and the sun god; it's one of the most ancient collections of laws in the history of mankind (room 3). Next come two breathtaking palace reconstructions: the great court, c713 BC, from the palace of Sargon II at Khorsabad (in present-day Iraq), with its giant bearded and winged bulls and friezes of warriors and servants (room 4); and the palace of Darius I at Susa (now Iran), c510 BC, with its glazed-brick reliefs of archers, lions and griffins (room 12). The double-bull-headed column was one of 36 such gigantic supports at the palace. Entering the Iranian section, you find 5,000-year-old statues from Susa housed in the circular room 8, and a fine view of the Cour Napoleon. The Levantine section includes Cypriot animalistic vases and carved reliefs from Byblos.

### Islamic arts

*Richelieu: lower ground floor. Turquoise on Louvre maps.*

The Islamic decorative arts on show include early glassware, tenth- to 12th-century dishes decorated with birds and calligraphy, traditional Iranian blue-and-white wares, Iznik ceramics, intricate inlaid metalwork from Syria, tiles, screens, weapons and funerary steles. The highlight is three magnificent 16th-century kelims. In 2005 a Saudi prince, Prince Walid bin Talal, gave over €17 million – one of the largest donations in French cultural history – for a new Islamic wing to be built as an extension to the southern wing. It's expected to open by 2009.

### Greek, Roman & Etruscan antiquities

*Denon: lower ground & ground floors; Sully: ground & 1st floors. Blue on Louvre maps.*

The *Winged Victory of Samothrace*, a headless Greek statue dating from the second century BC, stands sentinel at the top of the grand staircase, giving an idea of its original dramatic impact on a promontory overlooking the Aegean sea. This huge department is made up

*Sightseeing*

# Who built the Louvre?

### Philippe-Auguste (1180-1223)
Philippe-Auguste built a medieval castle on the site of a seventh-century Roman kennel in 1190. In the centre was a dungeon, which also served as a treasure trove. The remains of Philippe-Auguste's Louvre were discovered under the Cour Carré in 1985.

### Louis IX (Saint-Louis) (1226-70)
The Salle Saint-Louis is thought to date from the saintly king because of the carvings on the pillars.

### Charles V (1364-80)
Records show that Charles turned the Louvre into a sumptuous palace. Little of it survived the Hundred Years War, however.

### François I (1515-47)
Having razed the medieval tower, François had Pierre Lescot build a new wing fit for a Renaissance prince.

### Henri II (1547-59)
Henri II added the Pavillon du Roi, the earliest example of a mansard-style roof. The Salle des Caryatides and Escalier Henri II date from this era.

### Charles IX (1560-74)
Charles carried on the work of Lescot. During this period, Catherine de Médicis had the Tuileries palace built. Thus began the 'Grand Dessein', the plan to unite the two palaces finally realised by Napoleon III 30 years before the Tuileries burned down.

### Henri III (1574-89); Henri IV (1589-1610)
To Charles IX's Petite Galerie, the two Henris added the perpendicular Grande Galerie, a display of power and order along the Seine.

### Louis XIII (1610-43)
Louis commissioned Jacques Lemercier to continue the Lescot wing on the western side of the Cour Carrée. Lemercier created a mirror image of Lescot's work, with the Sully Pavilion taking pride of place in the middle.

### Louis XIV (1643-1715)
Louis XIV added three sides to the Cour Carrée to complete the square. Place du Carrousel, now a traffic roundabout, is named after an equestrian event held here in 1662.

### Napoleon (1799-1815)
Despite crediting himself in his memoirs with the 'construction of the Louvre', Napoléon built only one wing, along rue de Rivoli (galleries now occupied by the **Musée des Arts Décoratifs**; see p105), and filled the museum with plunder from his military expeditions. He also erected the handsome Arc de Triomphe du Carrousel.

### Napoleon III (1852-70)
Most of the Cour Napoléon was built in the Second Empire by Louis Visconti and Hector Lefuel. With Baron Haussmann at the helm, the whole project was completed in four years (1852-56). The stone decoration is more ornate than that of the 17th-century parts – note Denon's central *pavillon* with a statue of the Emperor in the middle.

### François Mitterand (1981-95)
Mitterand will be remembered for the daring Grand Louvre project. He evicted the Ministry of Finance and opened the Richelieu wing, doubling exhibition space. His most inspired move, however, was making IM Pei's glass pyramid the main entrance. A spiral staircase descends into the Carrousel du Louvre, with shops, restaurants and an exhibition hall.

### Jacques Chirac (1995-2007)
It would have been hard for Chirac to top the achievements of his predecessor, so he commissioned the **Musée du Quai Branly** instead (see p171 **Windows on the world**). The Salle des Etats and the Cour d'Apollon were renovated on Chirac's watch.

of pieces amassed by François I and Cardinal Richelieu, plus the Borghese collection (acquired in 1808), and the Campana collection of thousands of painted Greek vases and small terracottas. Endless dark rooms on the first floor harbour small bronze, silver and terracotta objects, but the really exciting stuff is on the ground floor. The grandiose, vaulted marble rooms are a fitting location for masterpieces such as the 2.3m (7.5ft) *Athena Peacemaker* and the *Venus de Milo* (room 12), and overflow with gods and goddesses, swords and monsters.

Also on the ground floor are artefacts from the Etruscan civilisation of south-central Italy, spanning the seventh century BC until submission to the Romans in the first century AD. The highlight is the painted terracotta Sarcophagus of the Cenestien Couple (c530-510 BC), which illustrates a smiling couple reclining at a banquet. Key Roman antiquities include a vivid relief of sacrificial animals, intricately carved sarcophagi, mosaic floors and the Boscoreale Treasure: magnificent silverwork excavated at a villa near Pompeii. Pre-classical Greek art on the lower ground floor includes a large Cycladic head and Mycenean triad.

## French painting

*Denon: 1st floor; Richelieu: 2nd floor;*
*Sully: 2nd floor. Red on Louvre maps.*
There are around 6,000 of the most famous paintings in the world on show here, the most impressive being the huge 18th- to 19th-century canvases hanging in the Daru and Mollien rooms in the Denon wing, serving Classicism and Romanticism respectively. Here, art meets politics with David's enormous *Sacre de Napoléon*, Gros's propagandising *Napoléon Visitant le Champ de Bataille d'Eylau* and Delacroix's flag-flying *La Liberté Guidant le Peuple*. Géricault's beautiful but disturbing *Le Radeau de la Méduse* illustrates the grisly true story of the abandoned men who resorted to cannibalism and murder after a famous shipwreck in 1816, while his generals on flame-eyed horses fuel the myth of the dashing French officer. Biblical and historical scenes rub shoulders with aristocracy and grand depictions of great moments in mythology. Ingres' *Grande Odalisque* is also found here, along with a new Ingres acquisition, a portrait of the Duc d'Orléans.

In the Richelieu wing you can find the earliest known non-religious French portrait, an anonymous depiction of French king Jean Le Bon (c1350); the *Pietà de Villeneuve-les-Avignon*, later attributed to Enguerrand Quarton; Jean Clouet's *Portrait of François I* (marking the influence of the Italian Renaissance on portraiture); and various works from the Ecole de Fontainebleau, including the anonymous *Diana the Huntress*, an elegant nude who strangely resembles Diane de Poitiers, mistress of Henri II. Poussin's religious and mythological subjects epitomise 17th-century French classicism, and are full of erudite references for an audience of cognoscenti. His works spill over into the Sully wing, where you'll also find Charles Le Brun's wonderfully pompous *Chancellier Séguier* and his four grandiose battle scenes, in which Alexander the Great is a suitable stand-in for Louis XIV.

The 18th century begins with Watteau's *Gilles* and the *Embarkation for Cythera*. Works by Chardin include sober still lifes, but also fine figure paintings. If you're used to the sugary images of Fragonard, don't miss the *Fantaisies*, which forgo sentimentality for fluent, broadly painted fantasy portraits, intended to capture moods rather than likenesses. Also in the Sully wing are sublime neo-classical portraits by David, Ingres' *La Baigneuse* and *Le Bain Turc*, portraits and Orientalist scenes by Chassériau, and landscapes by Corot.

## French sculpture

*Richelieu: lower ground & ground floors.*
*Light brown on Louvre maps.*
French sculpture is displayed in and around the two covered courts created by the Grand Louvre scheme. A tour of the medieval regional schools takes in the *Virgins* from Alsace, 14th-century figures of Charles V and Jeanne de Bourbon that once adorned the exterior of the Louvre, and the late 15th-century tomb of Philippe Pot, an effigy of a Burgundian knight carried by eight black-clad mourners. Fine Renaissance memorials, fountains and portals include Jean Goujon's friezes from the Fontaine des Innocents. In the Cour Marly, pride of place goes to Coustou's *Chevaux de Marly*, rearing horses being restrained by their grooms, plus two earlier equestrian pieces by Coysevox. Hewn from single blocks of marble, they were sculpted for the royal château at Marly-le-Roi before being moved to the Tuileries gardens, where copies now stand. In Cour Puget are the four bronze captives by Martin Desjardins, Clodion's rococo frieze and Pierre Puget's twisting, baroque *Milo of Croton*. Amid the 18th-century heroes and allegorical subjects, look out for Pigalle's *Mercury* and *Voltaire*.

## Italian & Spanish painting

*Denon: 1st floor. Red on Louvre maps.*
Starting from the Sully end of the Denon wing, three rooms of fragile frescoes by Botticelli, Fra Angelico and Luini, and 13th- to 15th-century Florentine paintings on wood by Cimabue, Giotto, Fra Angelico and Lippi, open the Italian department, before you move into the long,

skylit Grande Galerie. To the right, the Salle des Sept Mètres has highlights of the Sienese school, including Simone Martini's *Christ Carrying the Cross* and Piero della Francesca's *Portrait of Sigismondo Malatesta*. Now that the *Mona Lisa* has moved, there is no need to bowl along the Grande Galerie at speed in your haste to see her, missing the wonders on either side. Most notably, about a quarter of the way along on the left are Leonardo's *Virgin of the Rocks*, *Virgin and Child with Saint Anne* and *Saint-Jean Baptiste*, which form part of the Northern Italian section, along with Bellini's *Calvary* and *Portrait of a Man* and Raphael's *Portrait of Dona Isabel de Requesens*. The first turning on the right after the da Vincis leads into the Salle de La Joconde, whose toffee-coloured brushed concrete walls provide a suitably golden setting for Veronese's monumental, lavish *Wedding at Cana*, his *Crucifixion* and *Sainte Famille* and other Venetian masterpieces such as Lotto's *Adulterous Woman* and red-robed *Christ Carrying the Cross*, Tintoretto's *Suzanne Bathing* and Bassano's earthy canvases. Don't miss the exquisite Titians hidden behind the *Mona Lisa* on her stand-alone wall. A trip back down the Passage de Mollien, containing 16th-century cartoons, frames Giorgio Vasari's *Annunciation*, revealing how much better it is to stand back and look at these paintings. In between the two in the Grande Galerie are Arcimboldo's famous *Four Seasons*, various Bronzinos and Caravaggios, plus 17th-century works by Albani, Carracci and Reni. A small Spanish section takes in *Christ on the Cross Adored by Two Donors* by El Greco and his contemporary Jusepe de Ribera's *Club Foot*.

## Graphic arts

*Denon: 1st floor; Sully: 2nd floor.*
*Pink on Louvre maps.*
The Louvre's huge collection of drawings includes works by Raphael, Michelangelo, Dürer, Holbein and Rembrandt. However, owing to their fragility, drawings are not shown as permanent exhibits. Four galleries (French and Northern schools on the 2nd floor; Italian and the latest acquisitions on the 1st) feature changing exhibitions. Other works can be viewed in the Salle de Consultation only upon written application to the management (01.40.20.52.51, fax 01.40.20.53.51).

## Italian, Spanish & Northern sculpture

*Denon: lower ground & ground floors.*
*Light brown on Louvre maps.*
Michelangelo's *Dying Slave* and *Captive Slave* (sculptures planned for the tomb of Pope Julius II in Rome) are the real showstoppers here, but other Renaissance treasures include a painted marble relief by Donatello, Adrien de Vriesse's bronze *Mercury and Psyche*, Giambologna's *Mercury* and the ethereal *Psyche Revived by Cupid's Kiss* by Antonio Canova. Benvenuto Cellini's *Nymph of Fontainebleau* relief is on the Mollien staircase. Napoleon III's former stables were reopened in 2004 to house princely collections of statuary acquired by Richelieu and the Borghese and Albani families during the 17th and 18th centuries. The statues, either copies of classical works or heavily restored originals, demonstrate the relationship between antique and modern sculpture. The height of the room also allows oversized works such as *Jupiter* and *Albani Alexander* to be displayed. Northern sculpture, on the lower ground floor, ranges from Erhart's Gothic *Mary Magdalene* to the neo-classical work of Thorvaldsen, while pre-Renaissance Italian pieces include Donatello's clay relief *Virgin and Child*.

## Northern schools

*Richelieu: 2nd floor; Sully: 1st floor.*
*Red on Louvre maps.*
Northern Renaissance works include Flemish altarpieces by Memling and van der Weyden, Bosch's fantastical, proto-surrealist *Ship of Fools*, Metsys' *The Moneylender and his Wife*, and the northern mannerism of Cornelius van Haarlem. The Galerie Médicis houses Rubens' Médicis cycle; Marie de Médicis, the widow of Henri IV, commissioned the 24 canvases for the Palais de Luxembourg in the 1620s. They blend historic events and classical mythology for the glorification of the queen, never afraid to put her best features on public display. Look out for Rubens' more personal portrait of his second wife, *Hélène Fourment and her Children*, plus van Dyck's *Charles I and his Groom* and David Teniers the Younger's peasant-filled townscapes.

Dutch paintings in this wing include early and late self-portraits by Rembrandt, his *Flayed Ox* and the warmly glowing nude *Bathsheba at her Bath*. There are Vermeer's *Astronomer* and *Lacemaker* amid interiors by De Hooch and Metsu, and the meticulously finished portraits and framing devices of Dou, plus works from the Haarlem school. German paintings in side galleries include portraits by Cranach, Dürer's *Self-Portrait* and Holbein's *Anne of Cleves*.

The rooms of Northern European and Scandinavian paintings include Caspar David Friedrich's *Trees with Crows*, the sober, classical portraits of Christian Købke, and pared-back views by Peder Balke. A fairly modest but high-quality British collection located on the first floor of the Sully includes landscapes by Wright of Derby, Constable and Turner, and portraits by Gainsborough, Reynolds and Lawrence.

The Denon wing.

## Decorative arts

*Richelieu: 1st floor; Sully: 1st floor.*
*Magenta on Louvre maps.*

The decorative arts collection runs from the Middle Ages to the mid-19th century, often with royal connections, and includes entire rooms decorated in the fashion of the day. Many of the finest medieval items came from the treasury of St-Denis, amassed by the powerful Abbot Suger, counsellor to Louis VI and VII, among them Suger's 'Eagle' (a porphyry vase), a serpentine plate surrounded by precious stones, and the sacred sword of the kings of France, dubbed 'Charlemagne's Sword' by the Capetian monarchs as they sought to legitimise their line.

The Renaissance galleries take in ornate carved chests, German silver tankards and the *Hunts of Maximilien*, a dozen 16th-century tapestries depicting the months, zodiac and hunting scenes. Seventeenth- and 18th-century French decorative arts are displayed in superb panelled rooms, and include characteristic brass and tortoiseshell pieces by Boulle. Displays then move on to French porcelain, silverware, watches and scientific instruments. Napoleon III's opulent apartments, used until the 1980s by the Ministry of Finance, have been preserved, with chandeliers and upholstery intact. Next to the Denon wing, the Galerie d'Apollon reopened in 2004 after four years of restoration. A precursor to the Hall of Mirrors at Versailles, it was built for Louis XIV and is a showcase of talents from this golden age: architecture by Louis Le Vau, painted ceilings by Charles Le Brun and sculpture by François Girardon, the

Marsy brothers and Thomas Regnaudin. Napoleon III then commissioned Delacroix to paint the central medallion, *Apollo Vanquishing the Python*, and now it houses the crown jewels and Louis XIV vases. Merry-Joseph Blondel's *Chute d'Icare* graces the ceiling of an anteroom of the adjacent Rotonde d'Apollon.

## African, Asian, Oceanic & American arts

*Denon: ground floor. White on Louvre maps.*

A new approach to '*arts premiers*' is seen in these eight rooms in the Pavillon des Sessions, prefiguring the Musée du Quai Branly. The spare, modern design of Jean-Michel Wilmotte allows each of the 100 key works to stand alone in something midway between an art gallery and a museum. The pure aesthetics of such objects as a svelte Zulu spoon with the breasts and buttocks of a woman, a sixth-century BC Sokoto terracotta head, a recycled iron sculpture of the god Gou that anticipates Picasso, and a pot-bellied, terracotta Chupicaro from Mexico can be appreciated in their own right. Computer terminals with mahogany benches offer visitors multimedia resources.

## Temporary exhibitions

Major new exhibitions are shown in the Salle Napoléon. The 2008 programme includes a retrospective of drawings by Gabriel de Saint-Aubin (28 Feb-26 May), a collection of artefacts inspired by the legend of Babylon (14 Mar-2 June) and an exhibition of photographs of the Louvre taken during World War II.

# Opéra to Les Halles

The historic centre of royal power in Paris is now the city's commercial powerhouse.

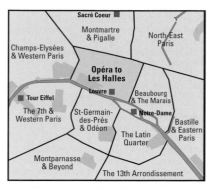

## Tuileries & Palais-Royal

*In the 1st arrondissement.*

Once the monarchs had moved from the Ile de la Cité to spacious new quarters on the Right Bank, the Louvre and, later, the palaces of the **Tuileries** and **Palais-Royal** became the centres of royal power.

**The Louvre** (*see p93-99*) still exerts considerable influence today: first as a grandiose architectural ensemble, a palace within the city; and, second, as a symbol of the capital's cultural pre-eminence. What had been simply a fortress along Philippe-Auguste's city wall in 1190 was transformed into a royal residence with all the latest Gothic comforts by Charles V; François I turned it into a sumptuous Renaissance palace. For centuries it was a work in progress: everyone wanted to make their mark – including the most monarchical of presidents, François Mitterrand, who added IM Pei's glass pyramid, doubled the exhibition space and added the Carrousel du Louvre shopping mall, auditorium and food halls (*see p96* **Who built the Louvre?**).

The palace has always attracted crowds: first courtiers and ministers; then artists; and, since 1793, when it was first turned into a museum, art lovers – though the last department of the Finance Ministry moved out as late as 1991. Around the Louvre, other subsidiary palaces grew up: Catherine de Médicis commissioned Philibert Delorme to begin work on one in the Tuileries; Richelieu built the Palais Cardinal, which later became the Palais-Royal.

On place du Louvre, opposite Claude Perrault's grandiose western façade of the Louvre, is **Eglise St-Germain-l'Auxerrois**, once the French kings' parish church and home to the only original Flamboyant Gothic porch in Paris, built in 1435. Mirroring it to the left of the belfry is the 19th-century neo-Gothic 1st arrondissement town hall, with its fanciful rose window and classical porch. Next door is the stylish **Le Fumoir** (*see p221*), with a Mona Lisa of its own: Amaretto, orange juice and champagne. You can walk to the Louvre from here, through the ornate Cour Carrée, although the main museum entrance is now the pyramid, or from métro Palais Royal Musée du Louvre.

Across rue de Rivoli from the Louvre, past the **Louvre des Antiquaires** antiques emporium (*see p269*) and nightspot **Le Cab** (*see p331*), stands the understatedly elegant **Palais-Royal**, once Cardinal Richelieu's private mansion and now the Conseil d'Etat and Ministry of Culture. After a stroll in its quiet gardens, it's hard to believe that this was once the most debauched corner of the capital and the starting point of the French Revolution.

In the 1780s the Palais was a boisterous centre of Paris life, where aristocrats and the financially challenged inhabitants of the *faubourgs* rubbed shoulders. The coffee-houses in its arcades generated radical debate: here Camille Desmoulins called the city to arms on the eve of Bastille Day (*see p277*); and after the Napoleonic Wars, Wellington and Field Marshal von Blücher lost so much money in the gambling dens that Parisians claimed they had won back their entire dues for war reparations. Only haute cuisine restaurant **Le Grand Véfour** (*see p189*), founded as Café de Chartres in the 1780s, survives from this era, albeit with decoration from a little later. The **Comédie Française** theatre ('La Maison de Molière'; *see p343*) stands on the south-west corner. The company, created by Louis XIV in 1680, moved here in 1799. Molière himself is honoured with a fountain on the corner of rue Molière and rue de Richelieu. Brass-fronted Café Nemours on place Colette – Colette herself used to buy cigars from old-fashioned A la Civette nearby (157 rue St-Honoré, 1st, 01.42.96.04.99) – is another thespian favourite; standing in front of it, the métro entrance by

artist Jean-Michel Othoniel, all glass baubles and aluminium struts, is a kitsch take on Guimard's celebrated art nouveau métro entrances.

Today, the stately arcades of the Palais-Royal house an eclectic succession of antiques dealers, philatelists, specialists in tin soldiers and musical boxes – and fashion showcases. Here you'll find the recently opened European flagship of renowned New York designer **Marc Jacobs** (*see p247*), chic vintage clothes specialist **Didier Ludot** (*see p256*) and the elegant perfumery **Salons du Palais-Royal Shiseido** (*see p265*). Passing through the arcades to rue de Montpensier, the neo-rococo Théâtre du Palais-Royal and the centuries-old café **Entr'acte** (*see p221*), you'll find narrow, stepped passages that run between here and rue de Richelieu.

On the other side of the palace towards Les Halles is galerie Véro-Dodat. Built by rich *charcutiers* during the Restoration, it has wonderfully preserved neo-classical wooden shopfronts. Right where rue St-Honoré meets rue Croix-des-Petits-Champs, look out for a controversial new steel lattice that the architect Francis Solers has placed across the façade of a Haussmann-era Ministry of Culture annexe.

At the western end of the Louvre, by rue de Rivoli, are the **Musée des Arts décoratifs**, the **Musée de la Mode et du Textile** and the **Musée de la Publicité**. All of these are administered independently of the Musée du Louvre, but were refreshed as part of the Grand Louvre scheme. Across place du Carrousel from the Louvre pyramid, the Arc du Carrousel, a mini-Arc de Triomphe, was built in polychrome marble for Napoleon from 1806 to 1809. The chariot on the top was originally drawn by the antique horses from San Marco in Venice, snapped up by Napoleon but returned in 1815. From the arch, the extraordinary axis along the **Jardin des Tuileries**, the **Champs-Elysées** (*see p116*) up to the **Arc de Triomphe** (*see p117*) and on to the **Grande Arche de la Défense** (*see p183*) is plain to see.

The Jardin des Tuileries stretched as far as the Tuileries palace, until that was destroyed in the 1871 Paris Commune. The garden was laid out in the 17th century by André Le Nôtre and remains a pleasure area, with a **funfair** (*see p285*) in summer; it also serves as an open-air gallery for modern art sculptures. Overlooking focal **place de la Concorde** is the **Musée de l'Orangerie**, reopened in May 2006 after a complete renovation; and the **Jeu de Paume**, built as a court for real tennis, now a centre for photographic exhibitions.

The stretch of rue de Rivoli running beside the Louvre towards Concorde was laid out by Napoleon's architects Percier and Fontaine from 1802 to 1811, and is notable for its arcaded façades. It runs in a straight line between place

**Palais-Royal**. *See p106.*

de la Concorde and rue St-Antoine, in the **Marais** (*see p130*); at the western end it's filled with tacky souvenir shops – though old-fashioned hotels remain, and there are also gentlemen's outfitters, bookshop **WH Smith** (*see p243*) and tearoom Angelina (*see p220*). The area was inhabited by English aristocrats, writers and artists in the 1830s and '40s after the Napoleonic Wars, sleeping at **Le Meurice** (*see p53*), buying the daily English newspaper published by bookseller **Galignani** (*see p243*), and dining in the fancy restaurants of the Palais-Royal.

Place des Pyramides, at the junction of rue de Rivoli and rue des Pyramides, contains a gleaming gilt equestrian statue of Joan of Arc. One of four statues of her in the city, it's fêted as a proud symbol of French nationalism every May Day by supporters of the Front National.

Ancient rue St-Honoré, running parallel to rue de Rivoli, is one of those streets that changes style as it goes along: smart shops line it near place Vendôme, small cafés and inexpensive bistros predominate towards Les Halles. The baroque **Eglise St-Roch** is still pitted with bullet holes made by Napoleon's troops when they crushed a royalist revolt in 1795. With its old houses, adjoining rue St-Roch still feels wonderfully authentic; a couple of shops are built into the side of the church. Further up stands Chapelle Notre-Dame de l'Assomption (1670-6), now used by the city's Polish community, its dome so disproportionately large that locals dubbed it *sot dôme* ('stupid dome'), a pun on 'Sodom'. Concept store **Colette** (*see p250*) brought some glamour to what was once a staid shopping area, drawing a swarm of similar stores in its wake. All are ideally placed for the fashionistas and film stars who touch down at **Hôtel Costes** (*see p51*).

Opposite Colette is rue du Marché-St-Honoré, which once led to the covered Marché St-Honoré, since replaced by offices, in a square lined with trendy restaurants; to the north, rue Danielle-Casanova boasts 18th-century houses.

Further west along rue St-Honoré lies the wonderful, eight-sided **place Vendôme** and a perspective stretching from rue de Rivoli up to **Opéra** (*see p109*). At the end of the Tuileries, place de la Concorde, originally laid out for the glorification of Louis XV, is a masterclass in the use of open space, and spectacular when lit up at night. The winged Marly horses (only copies as the originals are in the Louvre) frame the entrance to the Champs-Elysées.

Smart rue Royale, leading to the **Madeleine** (*see p109*), has tearoom **Ladurée** (*see p225*) and the famed restaurant Maxim's (3 rue Royale, 1st, 01.42.65.27.94), with its fabulous art nouveau interior. Rue Boissy d'Anglas proffers stylish shops and the trendy Buddha

**Sightseeing**

Place Vendôme. *See p106.*

Bar (no.8, 1st, 01.53.05.90.00); while sporting luxuries at **Hermès** (*see p246*) on rue du Fbg-St-Honoré (a westward extension of rue St-Honoré), and high-end designs at **Yves Saint Laurent** (*see p250*), Gucci (no.2, 1st, 01.44.94.14.70), Chloé (no.54, 1st, 01.44.94.33.00) and others set the plush tone.

## Eglise St-Germain-l'Auxerrois

*2 pl du Louvre, 1st (01.42.60.13.96). M° Louvre Rivoli or Pont Neuf.* **Open** 9am-7pm Mon-Sat; 9am-8.30pm Sun. **Map** p406 H6.

The architecture of this former royal church spans several eras: most striking is the elaborate Flamboyant Gothic porch. Inside, there's the 13th-century Lady Chapel and a canopied, carved bench by Le Brun made for the royal family in 1682. The church achieved notoriety on 24 August 1572, when its bell rang to signal the St Bartholomew's Day massacre (*see p16* **Slaughterhouse city**).

## Eglise St-Roch

*296 rue St-Honoré, 1st (01.42.44.13.20). M° Pyramides or Tuileries.* **Open** 9am-7pm daily. **Map** p401 G5.

Begun in the 1650s in what was then the heart of Paris, this long church was designed chiefly by Jacques Lemercier; work took so long, the church was consecrated only in 1740. Famed parishioners and patrons are remembered in funerary monuments: Le Nôtre, Mignard, Corneille and Diderot are all here, as are busts by Coysevox and Coustou, Falconet's statue *Christ on the Mount of Olives* and Anguier's superb *Nativity*. Bullet marks from a 1795 shoot-out between royalists and conventionists still pit the façade, recently scrubbed clean as part of an ongoing programme of restoration.

## Jardin des Tuileries

*Rue de Rivoli, 1st. M° Concorde or Tuileries.* **Open** 7.30am-7pm daily. **Map** p401 G5.

Between the Louvre and place de la Concorde, the gravelled alleyways of these gardens have been a chic promenade ever since they opened to the public in the 16th century; and the popular mood persists with the funfair that sets up along the rue de Rivoli side in summer. André Le Nôtre created the prototypical French garden with terraces and central vista running down the *Grand Axe* through circular and hexagonal ponds. When the Tuileries palace was burned down during the Paris Commune in 1871 (*see p24*), the park was expanded. As part of Mitterrand's Grand Louvre project, fragile sculptures such as Coysevox's winged horses were transferred to the Louvre and replaced by copies, and the Maillol sculptures were returned to the Jardins du Carrousel; a handful of modern sculptures has been added, including bronzes by Laurens, Moore, Ernst, Giacometti, and Dubuffet's *Le Bel Costumé*. Replanting has restored parts of Le Nôtre's design and replaced damaged trees, and there's a specialist gardeners' bookshop by place de la Concorde.

## Jeu de Paume

*1 pl de la Concorde, 8th (01.47.03.12.50/www. jeudepaume.org). M° Concorde.* **Open** noon-9pm Tue; noon-7pm Wed-Fri; 10am-7pm Sat, Sun (last admission 30mins before closing). **Admission** €6; €3 reductions. **Credit** MC, V. **Map** p401 F5.

The Centre National de la Photographie moved into this site in 2005. The building, which once served as a tennis court, has been divided into two white, almost hangar-like galleries. It is not an intimate space, but it works well for showcase retrospectives. A video-art and cinema suite in the basement offers new digital installation work, plus feature-length films made by artists. There is also a sleek café and a decent bookshop. The Jeu de Paume's smaller site is the former Patrimoine Photographique at the Hôtel de Sully (*see p133*).

## Musée des Arts Décoratifs

*107 rue de Rivoli, 1st (01.44.55.57.50/ www.lesartsdecoratifs.fr). M° Palais Royal Musée du Louvre or Pyramides.* **Open** 11am-6pm Tue, Wed, Fri; 10am-6pm Sat, Sun. Closed some hols. **Admission** (with Musée de la Mode & Musée de la Publicité) €8; €6.50 18-25s; free under-18s. PMP. **Credit** MC, V. **Map** p402 H5.

Taken as a whole along with the Musée de la Mode et du Textile and Musée de la Publicité (for both, *see p106*), this is one of the world's major collections of design and the decorative arts. Located in the west wing of the Louvre since its opening a century ago, the venue reopened in 2006 after a decade-long, €35-million restoration, both of the building and of 6,000 of the 150,000 items donated mainly by private collectors. The major focus here is French furniture and tableware. From extravagant carpets to delicate crystal and porcelain, there is much to admire. Clever spotlighting and black settings show the exquisite treasures – including *châtelaines* made for medieval royalty and Maison Falize enamel work – to their best advantage. Other galleries are categorised by theme: glass, wallpaper, drawings and toys. There are cases devoted to Chinese head jewellery and the Japanese art of seduction with combs. Of most immediate attraction to the layman are the reconstructed period rooms, ten in all, showing how the other (French) half lived from the late 1400s to the early 20th century. The museum is privately run – hence its high-end contemporary design shop 107Rivoli (01.42.60.64.94, open 11am-7pm Mon, 10am-7pm Tue-Sun), which is a world away from tacky caps and key rings.

## Musée de la Mode et du Textile

*107 rue de Rivoli, 1st (01.44.55.57.50/www. lesartsdecoratifs.fr). M° Palais Royal Musée du Louvre or Pyramides.* **Open** Exhibitions 11 am-6pm Tue-Fri; 10am-6pm Sat, Sun. **Admission** €8; €6.50 18-25s; free under-18s. PMP. **Credit** MC, V. **Map** p402 H5.

This municipal fashion museum holds Elsa Schiaparelli's entire archive and hosts exciting themed exhibitions. Dramatic black-walled rooms

make a fine background to the clothes, while video screens and a small cinema space shows how the clothes move, as well as interviews with the creators.

## Musée de l'Orangerie

*Jardin des Tuileries, 1st (01.44.77.80.07/ www.musee-orangerie.fr). M° Concorde.* **Open** 12.30-7pm Mon, Wed, Thur, Sat, Sun; 12.30-9pm Fri. **Admission** €6.50; €4.50 18-25s; free under-18s. PMP. **Credit** MC, V. **Map** p401 F5.

The long-delayed reopening of this Monet showcase finally took place in 2006, and the Orangerie is now firmly back on the tourist radar: beware long queues. Stylistically, the new look is utilitarian and fuss-free, with the museum's eight, tapestry-sized *Nymphéas* (water lilies) paintings housed in two plain oval rooms. They provide a simple backdrop for the astonishing, ethereal romanticism of Monet's works, painted late in his life. Depicting Monet's 'jardin d'eau' at his house in Giverny, the *tableaux* have an intense, dreamy quality – partly reflecting the artist's absorption in the private world of his garden. Downstairs, the Jean Walter and Paul Guillaume collection of Impressionism and the Ecole de Paris is a mixed bag of sweet-toothed Cézanne and Renoir portraits, along with works by Modigliani, Rousseau, Matisse, Picasso and Derain.

## Musée de la Publicité

*107 rue de Rivoli, 1st (01.44.55.57.50/www. lesartsdecoratifs.fr). M° Palais Royal Musée du Louvre or Pyramides.* **Open** 11am-6pm Tue, Wed, Fri; 11am-9pm Thur; 10am-6pm Sat, Sun. **Admission** (with Musée des Arts Décoratifs & Musée de la Mode) €8; €6.50 18-25s; free under-18s. PMP. **Credit** MC, V. **Map** p402 H5.

The upstairs element of the trio of museums in the Louvre west wing, the advertising museum has a distressed interior by Jean Nouvel. Only a fraction of the vast collection of posters, promotional objects and packaging can be seen at one time; vintage posters are accessed through the multimedia space.

## Palais-Royal

*Pl du Palais-Royal, 1st. M° Palais Royal Musée du Louvre.* **Open** Gardens 7.30am-8.30pm daily. **Admission** free. **Map** p402 H5.

Built for Cardinal Richelieu by Jacques Lemercier, the building was once known as the Palais Cardinal. Richelieu left it to Louis XIII, whose widow Anne d'Autriche preferred it to the chilly Louvre and rechristened it when she moved in with her son, the young Louis XIV. In the 1780s the Duc d'Orléans, Louis XVI's fun-loving brother, enclosed the gardens in a three-storey peristyle and filled it with cafés, shops, theatres, sideshows and accommodation to raise money for rebuilding the burned-down opera. In contrast to Versailles, the Palais-Royal was a place for people of all classes to mingle and its arcades were a trysting venue. Daniel Buren's modern installation of black-and-white striped columns graces the main courtyard, while the stately buildings around it house the Conseil d'Etat and Ministry of Culture. *Photos pp102-103.*

## Place de la Concorde

*1st/8th. M° Concorde.* **Map** p401 F5.

This is the city's largest square, its grand east-west perspectives stretching from the Louvre to the Arc de Triomphe, and north-south from the Madeleine to the Assemblée Nationale across the Seine. Royal architect Gabriel designed it in the 1750s, along with the two colonnaded mansions astride rue Royale; the west one houses the chic Hôtel de Crillon (*see p51*) and the Automobile Club de France, the other is the Naval Ministry. In 1792 the centre statue of Louis XV was replaced with the guillotine for Louis XVI, Marie-Antoinette and many more. The square was embellished in the 19th century with sturdy lamp-posts, the Luxor obelisk (from the Viceroy of Egypt), and ornate tiered fountains that represent navigation by water. The best view is by night, from the terrace by the Jeu de Paume.

## Place Vendôme

*1st. M° Opéra or Tuileries.* **Map** p401 G4.

Elegant place Vendôme got its name from a *hôtel particulier* built by the Duc de Vendôme that stood on the site. Opened in 1699, the eight-sided square was conceived by Hardouin-Mansart to show off an equestrian statue of the Sun King, torn down in 1792 and replaced in 1806 by the Colonne de la Grande Armée. Modelled on Trajan's Column in Rome and featuring a spiral comic strip illustrating Napoleon's military exploits, it was made from 1,250 Russian and Austrian cannons captured at the Battle of Austerlitz. During the 1871 Commune this symbol of 'brute force and false glory' was pulled down; the present column is a replica. Hardouin-Mansart only designed the façades, with their ground-floor arcade and giant Corinthian pilasters; the buildings behind were put up by nobles and speculators. Today the square houses sparkling jewellers and top fashion houses, as well as the Justice Ministry and the Hôtel Ritz (*see p51*), from where Diana and Dodi Al-Fayed set off on their last journey. At No.12, you can visit the Grand Salon where Chopin died in 1849; its fabulous allegorical decoration dates from 1777 and has been restored as part of the new museum above the jewellers Chaumet (01.44.77.26.26). *Photos p104.*

## The Bourse

*In the 1st & 2nd arrondissements.*

Far less frenzied than Wall Street, the city's traditional business district is squeezed between the elegant calm of the Palais-Royal and shopping hub the **Grands Boulevards** (*see p111*). Along rue du Quatre-Septembre, **La Bourse** (the stock exchange) is where financiers and stockbrokers beaver away in grandiose buildings. The Banque de France, France's national central bank, has occupied the 17th-century Hôtel de Toulouse since 1811, its long gallery still hung with Old Masters. Nearby, fashion and finance meet at stylish **place des Victoires**, designed by Hardouin-

# Safe passage

**Passage Jouffroy.**

Substantial portions of the second arrondissement, off rue St-Denis and boulevard Montmartre, are honeycombed with iron-and-glass arcades or *passages*. Large numbers of these glass-covered thoroughfares were thrown up in a frenzy of property speculation in the early part of the 19th century. Forerunners of the department store and the shopping mall, the original arcades were lined with cafés and restaurants as well as shops. They were technologically advanced too, using the latest iron construction methods, as well as being laboratories for early experiments with gas lighting.

A guide book of the period describes the typical Paris arcade as a 'world in miniature, in which customers will find everything they need.' However, it wasn't only consumers who were fascinated by these streets under glass: French literature from the middle of the 19th century on is full of hymns to the arcades. Balzac evoked the hawkers and booksellers of the Galerie de Bois, in the gardens of the Palais Royal, in his novel *Illusions perdues*, and 20 years later, in 1867, Zola set his tale of adultery, *Thérèse Raquin*, in the passage du Pont-Neuf. Zola described this arcade on the Left Bank, which connected rue Mazarine to rue de Seine, as a 'narrow, dark corridor ... with a flat, glazed roof black with grime.'

The passage du Pont Neuf hasn't survived (it was razed in 1912); nor has the passage de l'Opéra, the subject, as well as the setting, of a lengthy section of Louis Aragon's surrealist masterpiece *Le Paysan de Paris* ('Paris Peasant').

Aragon saw in the 'great glass coffin' of the passage de l'Opéra a kind of royal road to the urban unconscious. It is troubling, he wrote, that these covered galleries are called *passages*, as if it weren't permitted for anyone to stop in them for 'more than an instant.' The arcades, he concluded, were temples to a 'cult of the ephemeral'.

That was certainly how the German cultural theorist Walter Benjamin, who shared Aragon's obsession with the *passages*, understood them – as the natural habitat of that distinctively 19th-century figure, the *flâneur*. The peripatetic urban dandy could spend his life of leisure under the glass roofs of the arcades, protected from the weather and the traffic.

The surviving *passages* still afford ample opportunity for unhurried *flânerie*. You can get a sense of what Aragon's passage de l'Opéra must have been like from **passage des Panoramas**, just off boulevard Montmartre. One of the oldest arcades, it's a rather gloomy labyrinth of stamp dealers, secondhand bookshops and Indian restaurants. Its neighbour **passage Jouffroy** is altogether more prepossessing, with an especially impressive vaulted roof and several interesting specialist shops. Most notable of these is **MGW Segas** (34 passage Jouffroy, 9th, 01.47.70.89.65, www.canesegas.com), dealer in antique canes and walking sticks, and a reminder that the arcades were once the focus of the luxury goods trade in Paris.

Mansart, forming an intimate circle of buildings today dedicated to fashion. West of the square is shop-lined galerie Vivienne, the smartest of the covered passages in Paris, adjoining galerie Colbert. Also look out for temporary exhibitions at the **Bibliothèque Nationale de France – Richelieu**. You can linger at the luxury food and wine merchant **Legrand** (*see p263*), or head along passage des Petits-Pères to admire the 17th- to 18th-century Eglise Notre-Dame-des-Victoires, the remains of an Augustine convent, featuring a cycle of paintings around the choir by Carle van Loo.

Rue de la Banque leads to the Bourse, behind a commanding neo-classical colonnade. The area has a relaxed feel – it's dead at weekends – but animated pockets exist at places like Le Vaudeville (29 rue Vivienne, 2nd, 01.40.20.04.62) and Gallopin (40 rue Notre-Dame-des-Victoires, 2nd, 01.42.36.45.38), busy brasseries favoured by stockbrokers and journalists. Rue des Colonnes is a quiet street lined with graceful porticos and acanthus motifs dating from the 1790s; its design nemesis, the 1970s concrete-and-glass HQ of Agence France-Presse, the nation's biggest news agency, stands on the other side of busy rue du Quatre-Septembre. Although most newspaper offices have moved elsewhere, *Le Figaro* is still based in rue du Louvre. From the corner of rue Montmartre and rue du Croissant, take a look at the Café du Croissant, where Socialist politician Jean Jaurès was assassinated in 1914.

## Bibliothèque Nationale de France – Richelieu & Musée du Cabinet des Médailles

*58 rue de Richelieu, 2nd (01.53.79.59.79/www.bnf.fr). M° Bourse.* **Open** Galeries Mansart/Mazarine, exhibitions only 10am-7pm Tue-Sat; noon-7pm Sun. Cabinet des Médailles 1-5.45pm Mon-Fri; 1-4.45pm Sat; noon-6pm Sun. **Admission** Galeries prices vary. Cabinet des Médailles free. **Credit** AmEx, MC, V. **Map** p402 H4.

The history of the French National Library begins in the 1660s, when Louis XIV moved manuscripts that couldn't be housed in the Louvre to this lavish Louis XIII townhouse, formerly the private residence of Cardinal Mazarin. The library was first opened to the public in 1692, and by 1724 it had received so many new acquisitions that the adjoining Hôtel de Nevers had to be added. Some of the original painted decoration by Romanelli and Grimaldi can still be seen in Galeries Mansart and Mazarine, now used for temporary exhibitions (and closed otherwise). The highlights, however, are the two circular reading rooms: the Salle Ovale, which is full of researchers, note-takers and readers, and the magnificent Salle de Travail, a temple to learning, with its arrangement of nine domes supported on slender columns clearly influenced by the Ottoman architecture of the Levant. The latter is now hauntingly empty, as most of its books have since been relocated to the Bibliothèque Nationale – François Mitterrand (*see p177*).

On the first floor is the Musée du Cabinet des Médailles, a modest two-room collection of coins and medals, including Greek, Roman and medieval

Originally a trade centre for coffee and sugar: the **Bourse de Commerce**. *See p115.*

examples. There is also a miscellany of other items, including Merovingian king Dagobert's throne, Charlemagne's chess set and small artefacts from the Classical world and ancient Egypt.

## La Bourse
*Palais Brongniart, pl de la Bourse, 2nd (01.49.27. 55.55/www.bourse-de-paris.fr). M° Bourse.* **Open** Guided tours call 1 wk in advance. **Admission** €8.50; €5.50 reductions. **No credit cards.** **Map** p402 H4.

After a century at the Louvre, the Palais-Royal and rue Vivienne, in 1826 the Stock Exchange was transferred to the Bourse, a dignified testament to First Empire classicism designed at Napoleon's behest by Alexandre Brongniart. It was enlarged in 1906 to create a cruciform interior, where brokers buzzed around a central enclosure, known as the *corbeille* ('basket' or 'trading floor'). Computers have made the design obsolete, but the pace remains frenetic.

## Place des Victoires
*1st, 2nd. M° Bourse.* **Map** p402 H5.
This circular square, the first of its kind, was designed by Hardouin-Mansart in 1685 to show off a statue of Louis XIV that marked victories against Holland. The original statue was destroyed after the Revolution (although the massive slaves from its base are now in the Louvre), and replaced in 1822 with an equestrian statue by Bosio. Among the occupants of the grand buildings that encircle the 'square' are fashion boutiques Kenzo and Victoire.

## Opéra & Grands Boulevards
*In the 2nd, 8th, 9th & 10th arrondissements.*

## Opéra & Madeleine

Charles Garnier's wedding-cake **Palais Garnier** is all gilt and grandeur, as an opera house should be. Garnier was also responsible for the ritzy **Café de la Paix** (*see p222*) and the **InterContinental Paris Le Grand** (*see p54*) overlooking place de l'Opéra. Behind, in the Jockey Club (now the Hôtel Scribe), the Lumière brothers held the world's first public cinema screening in 1895. Outfitter Old England (no.12, 9th, 01.47.42.81.99), just opposite on boulevard des Capucines, with its wooden counters, Jacobean-style ceilings and old-style goods and service, could have served as their costume consultants. The **Olympia** concert hall (*see p320*), the legendary venue of the Beatles, Piaf and anyone in *chanson*, was knocked down, but rose again nearby. Over the road at no.35, pioneering portrait photographer Nadar opened a studio in the 1860s, frequented by names such as Dumas père, Offenbach and Doré. In 1874 it hosted the first Impressionists' exhibition. Pedestrianised rue Edouard-VII, laid out in 1911, leads to the octagonal square of the

same name with Landowski's equestrian statue of the monarch. Through an arch, another square contains the belle époque **Théâtre de l'Athénée-Louis Jouvet.**

The **Madeleine**, a monument to Napoleon's army, guards the end of the boulevard. At the head of rue Royale, its classical portico mirrors the **Assemblée Nationale** (*see p170*) on the other side of place de la Concorde over the river, while the interior is a riot of marble and altars. Well worth a browse are extravagant delicatessens **Fauchon, Maison de la Truffe** (for both, *see p264*) and other luxury food shops; here, too, is haute cuisine restaurant **Senderens** (*see p197*).

Landmark department stores **Printemps** (*see p241*) and the **Galeries Lafayette** (*see p240*), which opened just behind the Palais Garnier in the late 19th century, also deserve investigation. Behind the latter stands the Lycée Caumartin, designed as a convent in the 1780s by Bourse architect Brongniart, and later one of the city's most prestigious schools. West along boulevard Haussmann is a small square containing the **Chapelle Expiatoire** dedicated to Louis XVI and Marie-Antoinette.

## Chapelle Expiatoire
*29 rue Pasquier, 8th (01.42.65.35.80). M° St-Augustin.* **Open** 1-5pm Thur-Sat. **Admission** €2.50; free under-18s. PMP. **Map** p401 F3.
The chapel was commissioned by Louis XVIII in memory of his executed predecessors, his brother Louis XVI and Marie-Antoinette. Their remains, along with those of 3,000 victims of the Revolution, including Camille Desmoulins, Danton, Malesherbes and Lavoisier, were found in 1814 on the exact spot where the altar stands. The year after, the bodies of Louis XVI and Marie-Antoinette were transferred to the Basilique St-Denis (*see p179*); the pair are now represented by marble statues, kneeling at the feet of Religion. Every January ardent (if currently unfulfilled) royalists gather here for a memorial service.

## Eglise de la Madeleine
*Pl de la Madeleine, 8th (01.44.51.69.00/www.eglise-lamadeleine.com). M° Concorde or Madeleine.* **Open** 9am-7pm daily. **Map** p401 G4.
The building of a church on this site began in 1764, and in 1806 Napoleon sent instructions from Poland for Barthélémy Vignon to design a 'Temple of Glory' dedicated to his Grand Army. After the emperor's fall, construction slowed and the building, by now a church again, was finally consecrated in 1845. The exterior is ringed by huge fluted Corinthian columns, with a double row at the front, and a frieze of the Last Judgement just above the portico. Inside are giant domes, an organ and pseudo-Grecian side altars in a sea of multicoloured marble. The painting by Ziegler in the chancel depicts the history of Christianity, with Napoleon prominent in the foreground. It's a favourite venue for society weddings.

**Sightseeing**

## Eglise St-Augustin

*46 bd Malesherbes, 8th (01.45.22.23.12). Mº St-Augustin.* **Open** Sept-June 10am-6pm Mon-Fri; 10 am-7.30pm Sat, Sun. July, Aug 10am-12.45pm, 3.30-6pm Tue-Fri; 10am-noon, 4-7.30pm Sat; 10am-noon, 4.30-6pm Sun. **Map** p401 F3.

St-Augustin, designed between 1860 and 1871 by Victor Baltard, architect of the defunct Les Halles pavilions, is not what it seems. The domed, neo-Renaissance stone exterior is merely a shell: inside is an iron vault structure; even the decorative angels are cast in metal. Impressive paintings by Adolphe William Bouguereau hang in the transept

## Musée de la Franc-Maçonnerie

*16 rue Cadet, 9th (01.45.23.20.92). Mº Cadet.* **Open** 2-6pm Tue-Fri; 1-5pm Sat. Closed 2wks July, Aug, 1wk Sept. **Admission** €2; free under-12s. **No credit cards.** **Map** p402 H3.

Tucked away at the back of the French Masonic Great Lodge, this museum opened in 1973. It traces the history of French freemasonry, from stonemasons' guilds to prints of masons General Lafayette and 1848 revolutionary leaders Blanc and Barbès.

## Musée de l'Opéra

*Palais Garnier, 1 pl de l'Opéra, 9th (01.40. 01.24.93). Mº Opéra.* **Open** Oct-June 10am-5.30pm daily. July-Sept 10am-4.30pm daily. **Admission** €7; €4 10-25s, students, over-60s; free under-10s. **No credit cards. Map** p401 G4.

The Palais Garnier houses temporary exhibitions relating to current opera or ballet productions, and a permanent collection of paintings, scores and bijou opera sets housed in period cases. Entrance includes a visit to the auditorium, if rehearsals permit.

## Musées des Parfumeries-Fragonard

*9 rue Scribe, 9th (01.47.42.04.56) & 39 bd des Capucines, 2nd (01.42.60.37.14). Mº Opéra.* **Open** 9am-6pm Mon-Sat (Mar-Oct rue Scribe open 9.30am-4pm Sun). **Admission** free. **Map** p401 G4.

Two museums showcase the collection of perfume house Fragonard: five rooms at rue Scribe range from Ancient Egyptian ointment flasks to Meissen porcelain scent bottles; the second museum has bottles by Lalique and Schiaparelli.

## Palais Garnier

*1 pl de l'Opéra, 9th (08.92.89.90.90/www. operadeparis.fr). Mº Opéra.* **Open** 10am-5pm daily. Guided tours in English (01.40.01.22.63) 11.30am & 2.30pm daily July-Aug; Wed, Sat & Sun Sep-June. **Admission** €8; €4 reductions. Guided tours €12; €6-€10 reductions. **Credit** AmEx, MC, V. **Map** p401 G4.

Brimming with gilt and red velvet, the Opera House designed by Garnier is a monument to Second Empire high society. The opera company had been founded by Louis XIV in 1669, moving home after fires and assassination attempts. In 1860 a tender for a grander – and safer – new opera house was

Gilt and grandeur: the **Palais Garnier**.

launched. It was won by then unknown 35-year-old Charles Garnier, who described opera as 'a temple with art for divinity' and designed his new building with the auditorium as a sanctuary and the foyer as a nave. Delayed by money, fire, the Franco-Prussian War and the Paris Commune, it wasn't inaugurated until 1875. The comfortably upholstered auditorium seats more than 2,000 people – and the exterior is just as opulent, with sculptures of music and dance on the façade, Apollo topping the copper dome and nymphs bearing torches. Carpeaux's sculpture *La Danse* shocked Parisians with its frank sensuality; in 1869 someone threw a bottle of ink over its marble thighs. The original is now safe in the Musée d'Orsay (*see p172*), where there is also a massive maquette of the building. The Garnier hosts productions of opera and ballet (*see p291* and *p315*). The Grand Foyer, its mirrors and parquet, coloured marble, moulded stucco, sculptures and allegorical paintings by Baudry have all been magnificently restored. You can also visit the Grand Escalier; the auditorium with its false ceiling painted by Chagall in 1964, and red satin and velvet boxes; as well as the library and museum – once the emperor's private salons, where he could arrive directly by carriage on the ramp at the rear of the building.

## Quartier de l'Europe

With its streets named after European cities, the area from Gare St-Lazare towards place de Clichy was the Impressionists' quarter. In those days it epitomised modernity, with the station, which opened in 1837, serving the line from Paris to St-Germain-en-Laye (it was rebuilt in the 1880s). The long shabby commuter hub has had a revamp; a glass dome now disgorges travellers from the métro interchange. The adjoining **Hôtel Concorde St-Lazare** (*see p54*) was the city's first great station hotel, with a grandiose hallway built by Eiffel in 1889 for visitors to the Exposition Universelle as he was putting up his Tower. Monet, who lived nearby in rue d'Edimbourg, depicted the steam age in *La Gare St-Lazare* and *Pont de l'Europe*; Pissarro and Caillebotte painted views of the new boulevards, and Manet had a studio on rue de St-Petersbourg. Rue de Budapest remains a red-light district; rue de Rome, or '*rue des luthiers*', has long been home to stringed-instrument makers. East of St-Lazare stands the **Eglise de la Trinité**.

### Eglise de la Trinité

*Pl Estienne-d'Orves, 9th (01.48.74.12.77). M°
Trinité.* **Open** 11am-8pm Mon-Sat; 10.30am-8pm Sun. **Map** p401 G3.
Noted for its tiered bell tower, this neo-Renaissance church was constructed between 1861 and 1867 by Théodore Ballu. Composer Olivier Messiaen (1908-92) was organist here for over 30 years.

## The Grands Boulevards

Contrary to popular belief, the string of Grands Boulevards between Madeleine and République (des Italiens, Montmartre, Poissonnière, Bonne-Nouvelle, St-Denis, St-Martin) was not built by Baron Haussmann, but by Louis XIV in 1670, replacing the fortifications of King Philippe-Auguste's city wall. Their ramparts have left their traces in the strange changes of levels, with stairways climbing up to side streets at the eastern end. The boulevards burgeoned after the French Revolution, as residences, theatres and covered passages were put up on land repossessed from aristocrats and monasteries. To this day they offer a glimpse of the city's divergent personalities – a stroll from Opéra to République leads from luxury shops to St-Denis prostitutes – and the phrase *théâtre des boulevards* is still used for lowbrow theatre. Between boulevard des Italiens and rue de Richelieu is place Boïeldieu and the **Opéra Comique** (*see p315*), where Bizet's *Carmen* was premièred in 1875.

The 18th-century Hôtel d'Angny, now the town hall of the 9th arrondissement, was once home to the infamous *bals des victimes*, where every guest had to have a relative who had lost their head to the guillotine. The **Hôtel Drouot** auction house (*see p112*) is ringed by antiques shops, coin- and stamp-dealers and wine bar Les Caves Drouot, where auction-goers and valuers congregate.

There are several grand *hôtels particuliers* on rue de la Grange-Batelière, which leads on one side down the curious passage Verdeau, occupied by antiques dealers, and on the other back to the boulevards via passage Jouffroy. With its grand, barrel-vaulted glass-and-iron roof, this is home to the lovely **Hôtel Chopin** (*see p57*), shop windows of doll's houses, antique walking sticks, art books and film posters, and the colourful entrance of the **Grévin** waxworks (*see p286*).

Over the boulevard, passage des Panoramas is the oldest remaining covered arcade in Paris (*see p107* **Safe passage**). When it opened in 1800, panoramas – vast illuminated circular paintings – of Rome, Jerusalem, Athens, London and other cities drew large crowds. Today it contains tearoom L'Arbre à Cannelle (no.57, 2nd, 01.45.08.55.87), coin- and stamp-sellers, furniture-makers and old-fashioned printer Stern (no.47), established here since 1840. The passage leads into a tangle of other little passages and the stage door of the Théâtre des Variétés (7 bd Montmartre, 2nd, 01.42.33.11.41), a pretty neo-classical theatre, where Offenbach premièred *La Belle Hélène*.

**Sightseeing**

Rue du Faubourg-Montmartre is home to celebrated belle époque *bouillon* Chartier (no.7, 9th, 01.47.70.86.29), which serves up hundreds of meals a day to the budget-minded. The street is also part of a significant Jewish quarter, less well known than the Marais, that grew up in the 19th century (*see p134* **Kosher quarter**). There are several kosher bakers, restaurants and France's largest synagogue at 44 rue de la Victoire (01.45.26.95.36), an opulent Second Empire affair completed in 1876. Cobbled Cité Bergère, constructed in 1825 with desirable residences, now houses budget hotels, though the pretty iron-and-glass *portes-cochères* remain. On rue Richer stands the art deco Folies-Bergère (no.32, 9th, 08.92.68.16.50), only sporadically used for cabaret revues. To the south of boulevard Bonne-Nouvelle lies **Sentier** (*see below*), while to the north rue du Faubourg-Poissonnière is a mixture of rag-trade outlets and *hôtels particuliers*.

Back on the boulevard is evidence of a move north of the Marais by trendsetting hubs, including DJ Laurent Garnier's fief **Le Rex** (*see p330*) and chic **De la Ville Café** (*see p223*). East of here are Louis XIV's twin triumphal arches, the **Porte St-Martin** and **Porte St-Denis**, which were erected to commemorate his military victories.

### Le Grand Rex

*1 bd Poissonnière, 2nd (01.45.08.93.58/reservations 08.92.68.05.96/www.legrandrex.com). Mᵒ Bonne Nouvelle.* **Tour** *Les Etoiles du Rex* every 5mins 10am-7pm Wed-Sun; daily during school hols. **Admission** €8; €7 under-16s. Tour & film €12. **Credit** AmEx, MC, V. **Map** p402 J4.
Opened in 1932, this huge art deco cinema was designed by Auguste Bluysen with fantasy Hispanic interiors by US designer John Eberson. Go behind the scenes in the crazy 50-minute guided tour, which includes a presentation about the construction of the auditorium and a visit to the production room, complete with nerve-jolting Sensurround effects.

### Hôtel Drouot

*9 rue Drouot, 9th (01.48.00.20.20/www.drouot.fr). Mᵒ Richelieu Drouot.* **Open** 11am-6pm Mon-Sat. Auctions 2pm Mon-Sat. **Map** p402 H3.
A spiky aluminium-and-marble concoction is the unlikely location for France's second largest art market – though it's now rivalled by Sotheby's and Christie's. Inside, escalators take you up to a number of small salerooms, where everything from medieval manuscripts and antique furniture to oriental arts, modern paintings, posters, jewellery and fine wines might be up for sale. Details of forthcoming auctions are published in the weekly *Gazette de l'Hôtel Drouot*, sold at newsstands.
**Other locations** Drouot-Montaigne, 15 av Montaigne, 8th (01.48.00.20.80); Drouot Nord, 64 rue Doudeauville, 18th (01.48.00.20.99).

### Porte St-Denis & Porte St-Martin

*Rue St-Denis/bd St-Denis, 2nd/10th; 33 bd St-Martin, 3rd/10th. Mᵒ Strasbourg St-Denis.* **Map** p402 K4.
These twin triumphal gates were erected in 1672 and 1674 at important entry points to the city as part of Colbert's strategy to glorify Paris and celebrate Louis XIV's victories on the Rhine. Modelled on the triumphal arches of Ancient Rome, the Porte St-Denis is based on a perfect square with a single arch, bearing Latin inscriptions and decorated with military trophies and battle scenes. Porte St-Martin bears allegorical reliefs of Louis XIV's campaigns.

## Les Halles & Sentier

*In the 1st & 2nd arrondissements.*
Les Halles is the geographic centre of Paris, an ugly nexus of commerce and entertainment, with a massive RER-métro interchange as its centrepiece. The area is due for a makeover in the coming years, however.

For centuries, Les Halles was the city's wholesale food market. Covered markets were set up here in 1181 by King Philippe-Auguste; in the 1850s Baltard's spectacular cast-iron and glass pavilions were erected. In 1969 the market was relocated to the southern suburb of Rungis. Baltard's ten pavilions were knocked down (one was saved and now stands at Nogent-sur-Marne; *see p180*), leaving a giant hole. After a long political dispute, it was filled in the early 1980s by the miserably designed **Forum des Halles** underground shopping and transport hub and the unloved Jardin des Halles.

East of the Forum, in the middle of place Joachim-du-Bellay, stands the Renaissance Fontaine des Innocents. The canopied fountain has swirling stone reliefs of water nymphs and titans by Jean Goujon (the ones you see today are copies; the originals are in the Louvre). It was inaugurated for Henri II's arrival in Paris in 1549 on the traditional royal route along rue St-Denis. It was moved and reconstructed here when the nearby Cimetière des Innocents, the city's main burial ground, was demolished in 1786 after flesh-eating rats started gnawing into people's living rooms, and the bones were transferred to the catacombs.

Pedestrianised rue des Lombards is a beacon for live jazz, with **Sunset/Sunside**, **Baiser Salé** and **Au Duc des Lombards** (for all, *see pp322-323*) to choose from. In 1610, King Henri IV was assassinated by a Catholic fanatic named François Ravaillac on nearby rue de la Ferronerie. Today, the street has become an extension of the Marais gay circuit. The ancient, easternmost stretch of rue St-Honoré runs into the southern edge of Les Halles. The Fontaine du Trahoir stands at the

**Eglise St-Eustache.** *See p115.*

Sightseeing

corner with rue de l'Arbre-Sec. Opposite, the Hôtel de Truden (52 rue de l'Arbre-Sec) was built in 1717 for a rich wine merchant; in the courtyard on rue des Prouvaires, the market-traders' favourite **La Tour de Montlhéry** (*see p193*) serves up meaty fare through the night. Fashion chains line the commercial stretch of the rue de Rivoli south of Les Halles. Running towards the Seine, ancient little streets such as rue des Lavandiers-Ste-Opportune and

rue Jean-Lantier show a different side of Les Halles. Between rue de Rivoli and the Pont Neuf is department store La Samaritaine, currently closed for safety reasons. Next door, a former section of it contains the chic Kenzo flagship, spa and the Philippe Starck-designed **Kong** restaurant and bar (*see p221*), offering more great views. From here, quai de la Mégisserie, lined with horticultural suppliers and pet shops, leads towards **Châtelet** (*see p130*).

Undergound shopping at **Forum des Halles**.

Looming over the northern edge of the Jardin des Halles is the massive **Eglise St-Eustache**, with Renaissance motifs inside and chunky flying buttresses outside. At the western end of the gardens is the circular, domed **Bourse de Commerce**. In front of it, an astrological column is all that remains from a grand palace belonging to Marie de Médicis that stood here.

The empire of French designer **Agnès b** (*see p253*) stretches along most of rue du Jour, with streetwise outlets such as **Kiliwatch** (*see p255*) clustered along the buzzing rue Tiquetonne. On rue Etienne-Marcel, the restored **Tour Jean Sans Peur** is a weird Gothic relic of the fortified medieval townhouse of Jean Sans Peur, duke of Burgundy.

Busy, pedestrianised rue Montorgueil is lined with grocers, delicatessens and pavement cafés. Some historic façades remain from when this was an area in which the well-heeled and the working class mingled: Pâtisserie Stohrer (no.51, 2nd, 01.42.33.38.20), founded in 1730 and credited with the invention of the sugary *puits d'amour*; Le Rocher de Cancale (no.78, 01.42.33.50.29); and, back towards Les Halles, the golden snail sign hanging in front of L'Escargot Montorgueil (no.38, 01.42.36. 83.51), a restaurant established in 1832.

Stretching north, bordered by boulevard de Bonne-Nouvelle to the north and boulevard Sébastopol to the east, lies Sentier, the historic garment district, while cocky rue St-Denis has long relied on strumpets and strip joints. The tackiness is unremitting along its northern continuation, rue du Fbg-St-Denis.

Rue Réaumur houses striking art nouveau buildings with metal structures constructed as industrial premises in the early 1900s. Between rue des Petits-Carreaux and rue St-Denis is the site of the medieval Cour des Miracles – a refuge where paupers would 'miraculously' regain use of their eyes or limbs. An disused aristocratic estate, it was a sanctuary for the underworld until it was cleared out in 1667.

Sentier's streets and passages buzz with porters shouldering linen bundles, while sweatshops churn out passable copies of catwalk creations. Streets such as rue du Caire, rue d'Aboukir and rue du Nil reflect the Egyptian craze that followed Napoleon's Egyptian campaign in 1798 and 1799 – look out too for the sphinx heads and mock hieroglyphics at 2 place du Caire.

### Bourse de Commerce
*2 rue de Viarmes, 1st (01.55.65.55.65). M° Louvre Rivoli.* **Open** *tour groups* 9am-6pm Mon-Fri. **Admission** free. **Map** p402 J5.
Housing the Paris chamber of commerce, this trade centre for coffee and sugar was built as a grain market in 1767. The circular building was then covered

by a wooden dome, replaced by an avant-garde iron structure in 1809. It is sadly underused, though plans have been mooted to turn it into a hotel, restaurant or museum. *Photo p108.*

### Eglise St-Eustache
*Rue du Jour, 1st (01.42.36.31.05/www.st-eustache. org). M° Les Halles.* **Open** 9am-7.30pm daily. **Map** p402 J5.
This massive, barn-like church, built between 1532 and 1640, has a Gothic structure but Renaissance decoration in its façade and Corinthian capitals. Among the paintings in the side chapels are a *Descent from the Cross* by Luca Giordano; contemporary pieces by John Armleder were added in 2000. Murals by Thomas Couture adorn the 19th-century Lady chapel. There is a magnificent 8,000-pipe organ, and free recitals are held at 5.30pm on Sundays. *Photos p113.*

### Forum des Halles
*1st. M° Les Halles/RER Châtelet Les Halles.* **Map** p402 J5.
The labyrinthine mall and transport interchange extends three levels underground and includes the Ciné Cité multiplex cinema (*see p294*), the Forum des Images (*see p296*) and a swimming pool (*see p340*), as well as clothing chains, a branch of Fnac (*see p272*) and the Forum des Créateurs, a section for young designers. Despite an open central courtyard, a sense of gloom prevails. All should change by 2012, with a new landscaping of the whole area.

### Pavillon des Arts
*Les Halles, 101 rue Rambuteau, 1st (01.42.33. 82.50). M° Châtelet.* **Open** 11.30am-6.30pm Tue-Sun. **Admission** €5.50; €4 students; €2.50 14-26s; free under-14s. **No credit cards. Map** p402 K5.
This gallery in Les Halles hosts exhibitions on anything from photography to local history.

### Tour Jean Sans Peur
*20 rue Etienne-Marcel, 2nd (01.40.26.20.28/www. tourjeansanspeur.com). M° Etienne Marcel.* **Open** Termtime 1.30-6pm Wed, Sat, Sun. School hols 1.30-6pm Tue-Sun. Tour 3pm. **Admission** €5; €3 7-18s, students; free under-7s. Tour €8. **No credit cards. Map** p402 J5.
This Gothic turret (1409-11) is the remnant of the townhouse of Jean Sans Peur, duke of Burgundy. He was responsible for the assassination of his rival Louis d'Orléans, which sparked the Hundred Years' War and saw Burgundy becoming allied to the English crown. Jean had this show-off tower added to his mansion to protect him from vengeance by the aggrieved widow and her husband's followers, known as the 'Armagnacs'. In 1419 he was assassinated by a partisan of the dauphin, the future Charles VII. You can climb the tower, which has rooms leading off the stairway. Carved vaulting halfway up depicts naturalistic branches of oak, hawthorn and hops, symbols of Jean Sans Peur and Burgundian power. The huge mansion originally spanned Philippe-Auguste's city wall.

**Sightseeing**

# The Champs-Elysées & Western Paris

Extreme wealth, magnificent museums and early modernist architecture.

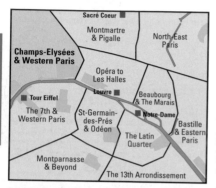

Sacré Coeur ■

Montmartre & Pigalle

North-East Paris

**Champs-Elysées & Western Paris**

Opéra to Les Halles

■ Tour Eiffel

Louvre ■

Beaubourg & The Marais

The 7th & Western Paris

St-Germain-des-Prés & Odéon

■ Notre-Dame

Bastille & Eastern Paris

The Latin Quarter

Montparnasse & Beyond

The 13th Arrondissement

## Champs-Elysées

*In the 8th & 16th arrondissements.*
The Champs-Elysées remains a symbolic gathering place: sporting victories, New Year's Eve, displays of military might on 14 July – all are celebrated here. Over the past decade, the avenue has undergone a renaissance, thanks initially to the facelift – including underground car parks and granite paving – instigated by Jacques Chirac.

Chi-chi shops and chic hotels have set up in the 'golden triangle' (avenues George-V, Montaigne and the Champs): **Louis Vuitton** (*see p247*), **Chanel** (*see p245*), **Jean-Paul Gaultier** (*see p246*), **Ladurée** tearoom (*see p225*), and the Marriott (70 av des Champs-Elysées, 8th, 01.53.93.55.00) and **Pershing Hall** (*see p61*) hotels. The **Four Seasons George V** (*see p57*) has undergone a revamp, while fashionable restaurants such as Spoon, Food & Wine (12 rue de Marignan, 8th, 01.40.76.34.44) draw an affluent and screamingly fashionable pack. Crowds line up for the glitzy **Le Lido** cabaret (*see p279*), the now commercialised **Queen** nightclub (*see p331*) and numerous cinemas, or stroll down the avenue to floodlit **place de la Concorde** (*see p106*). The famous **Drugstore Publicis** (*see p241*) is where locals head to stock up on late-night wines and groceries. Founded by an advertising agency back in the 1960s,

it was recently given a rather tacky cladding of swirly metal bars by American architect Michele Saee.

This great spine of western Paris started life as an extension to the Tuileries, laid out by Le Nôtre in the 17th century. By the Revolution, the avenue had reached its full extent, but it was during the Second Empire that it became a focus for fashionable society, military parades and royal processions. Bismarck was so impressed when he arrived with the conquering Prussian army in 1871 that he had a replica, the Ku'damm, built in Berlin, and Hitler's troops made a point of marching down it in 1940, as did their Allied counterparts four years later.

The lower, landscaped reach of the avenue hides two theatres and elegant restaurants Laurent (41 av Gabriel, 8th, 01.42.25.00.39) and Ledoyen (1 av Dutruit, 8th, 01.53.05.10.01), housed in fancy Napoleon III pavilions. At the Rond-Point des Champs-Elysées, nos.7 (now the Artcurial gallery bookshop and auction house) and 9 give visitors some idea of the magnificent mansions that once lined the avenue. From here on, it's platinum cards and stick-thin women aplenty, as avenue Montaigne rolls out a full deck of fashion houses.

Models and magnates nibble on the terrace at fashionable eaterie L'Avenue (no.41, 8th, 01.40.70.14.91). You can admire the lavish **Hôtel Plaza Athénée** (*see p59*) and Auguste Perret's innovative 1911-13 **Théâtre des Champs-Elysées** concert hall (*see p316*), with an auditorium painted by Maurice Denis and lights by Lalique. Since 1990 it has been topped by the sleek glass-fronted Maison Blanche restaurant (no.15, 8th, 01.47.23.55.99) with views across the Seine to the Eiffel Tower.

South of the avenue, the glass-domed **Grand Palais** and Petit Palais, both built for the 1900 Exposition Universelle and still used for major art exhibitions, create a magnificent vista across the elaborate Pont Alexandre III to Les Invalides, both of which underwent major renovations in 2005. The rear wing of the Grand Palais opening on to avenue Franklin-D-Roosevelt contains the **Palais de la Découverte** science museum.

To the north of the avenue lie more smart shops, antiques dealers and officialdom; on circular place Beauvau, wrought-iron gates herald the Ministry of the Interior. The

(also known as *La Marseillaise*). In 1840 Napoleon's ashes were carried under it on their way to Les Invalides; French troops finally got their victory march through it at the end of World War I. In 1921

France's Unknown Soldier was buried here, and the annual Bastille Day military procession begins here (*see p277*). Manic drivers race around the square, so cross via the pedestrian underpass before climbing the stairs for a wonderful view atop the arch.

### Cimetière de Passy
*2 rue du Commandant-Schloesing, 16th (01.53.70.40.80). M° Trocadéro.* **Open** *16 Mar-5 Nov* 8am-5.30pm Mon-Fri; 8.30am-5.30pm Sat; 9am-5.30pm Sun. *6 Nov-15 Mar* 8am-6pm Mon-Fri; 8.30am-6pm Sat; 9am-6pm Sun. **Map** p400 B5.
Since 1874 this has been one of the most desirable Paris locations in which to be laid to rest. Here you'll find composers Debussy and Fauré, painters Manet and his sister-in-law Berthe Morisot, writer Giraudoux, and various generals and politicians.

### Cinéaqua
*2 av des Nations Unies, 16th (01.40.69.23.23/ www.cineaqua.com). M° Trocadéro.* **Open** 10am-8pm daily. **Admission** €19.50; €15 students; €12.50 3-12s; free under-3s. **Credit** MC, V. **Map** p400 B5.
Opened in 2006, this aquarium and three-screen cinema is a wonderful attraction and a key element in the renaissance of the once moribund Trocadéro. Many have baulked at the admission price, though.

### Cité de l'Architecture et du Patrimoine
*Palais de Chaillot, 1 pl du Trocadéro, 16th (01.58.51.52.85/www.citechaillot.fr). M° Trocadéro.* **Open** noon-8pm Mon, Wed, Fri; noon-10pm Thur; 11am-7pm Sat, Sun. **Admission** €7; €5 18-25s; free under-18s. **Credit** MC, V. **Map** p400 B5.
Opened in 2007 in the eastern wing of the Palais de Chaillot, this new architecture and heritage museum impresses principally by its scale. The expansive ground floor is filled with life-size mock-ups of French cathedral façades and heritage buildings, while interactive screens place the models in context. Upstairs, darkened rooms house full-scale copies of medieval and Renaissance murals and stained-glass windows. The indisputable highlight of the modern architecture section is the walk-in replica of an apartment from Le Corbusier's Cité Radieuse in Marseille. Temporary exhibitions are housed in the large basement area.

### Fondation d'Enterprise Paul Ricard
*12 rue Boissy d'Anglas, 8th (01.53.30.88.00/ www.fondation-enterprise-ricard.com). M° Concorde.* **Open** 10am-7pm Mon-Fri. **Admission** free. **Map** p401 F4.
The Pastis firm promotes modern art, notably with the Prix Paul Ricard – young French artists shortlisted by an independent curator for an annual prize – to coincide with FIAC (*see p278*) each autumn.

### Fondation Mona Bismarck
*34 av de New-York, 16th (01.47.23.38.88/www. monabismarck.org). M° Alma Marceau.* **Open** 10.30am-6.30pm Tue-Sat. Closed Aug. **Admission** free. **Map** p400 C5.

**Sightseeing**

The Fondation provides a chic setting for eclectic exhibitions, from Etruscan antiquities to folk art. From February to May 2008 it hosts an exhibition of contemporary art from Sri Lanka, to coincide with the 60th anniversary of that country's independence.

## Fondation Pierre Bergé Yves Saint Laurent

*3 rue Léonce-Reynaud, 16th (01.44.31.64.00/ www.fondation-pb-ysl.net). M° Alma Marceau.* **Open** *Exhibitions* 11am-5.30pm Tue-Sun. Closed Aug. **Admission** €5; €2.50 students, 11-16s; free under-10s. **Credit** AmEx, MC, V. **Map** p400 D5.
When Yves Saint Laurent bowed out of designing in 2002, he reopened his fashion house as this foundation, exhibiting Picasso and Warhol paintings with the dresses they closely inspired. Every sketch and every *toile* has been carefully catalogued, and many of Saint Laurent's friends and clients have presented the designer with the dresses he created for them, stored in the upper floors at precisely 18 degrees centigrade and a hygrometric level of 50%.

## Galerie-Musée Baccarat

*11 pl des Etats-Unis, 16th (01.40.22.11.00/ www.baccarat.fr). M° Boissière or Iéna.* **Open** 10am-6pm Mon, Wed-Sat. **Admission** €7; €3.50 students; free under-18s. **Credit** *Shop* AmEx, DC, MC, V. **Map** p400 C4.
Designer Philippe Starck has created a neo-rococo wonderland in the former mansion of the Vicomtesse de Noailles. From the red carpet entrance with a chandelier in a fish tank to the Alchemy room, which was decorated by Gérard Garouste, there's a play of light and movement that makes Baccarat's work, past and present, sing. See items by great designers Georges Chevalier and Ettore Sottsass, services made for princes and maharajahs, and monumental show-off items made for the great exhibitions of the 1800s. The opulent Le Cristal Room restaurant (01.40.22.11.10) has a two-month waiting list.

## Galeries Nationales du Grand Palais

*3 av du Général-Eisenhower, 8th (01.44.13.17.17/ reservations 08.92.68.46.94/www.rmn.fr/galeries nationalesdugrandpalais). M° Champs-Elysées Clemenceau.* **Open** 10am-8pm Mon, Thur-Sun; 10am-10pm Wed; pre-booking compulsory before 1pm. **Admission** *Before 1pm with reservation* €11.10. *After 1pm without reservation* €10; €8 18-26s; free under-13s. **Credit** MC, V. **Map** p401 E5.
Built for the 1900 Exposition Universelle, the Grand Palais was the work of three different architects, each of whom designed a façade. During World War II it accommodated Nazi tanks. In 1994 the magnificent glass-roofed central hall was closed when bits of metal started falling off, although exhibitions continued to be held in the other wings. After major restoration, the Palais reopened in 2005. Shows in 2008 include a comprehensive exhibition of paintings by Gustave Courbet.

## Musée d'Art Moderne de la Ville de Paris

*11 av du Président-Wilson, 16th (01.53.67.40.00/ www.mam.paris.fr). M° Alma Marceau or Iéna.* **Open** 10am-6pm Tue-Sun. **Admission** *Temporary exhibitions* €4.50-€9; €2.50-€4.50 14-26s; free under-13s. **No credit cards.** **Map** p406 H7.
The monumental 1930s building that houses the city's modern art collection reopened in 2006 with a Pierre Bonnard exhibition. The museum is strong on the Cubists, Fauves, the Delaunays, Rouault and Ecole de Paris artists Soutine, Modigliani and van Dongen. Major shows in 2008 will include retrospectives of the work of German figurative artist AR Penck (February-May) and the British painter Bridget Riley (June-September).

## Musée de la Contrefaçon

*16 rue de la Faisanderie, 16th (01.56.26.14.00). M° Porte Dauphine.* **Open** 9am-12.30pm, 2-5.30pm Mon, Wed-Sun. **Admission** €6; €3 students; free under-12s. **No credit cards.** **Map** p400 A4.

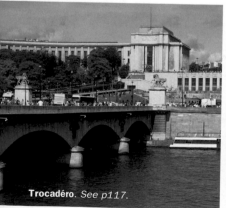

Trocadéro. *See p117.*

This museum was set up by the French anti-counterfeiting association with the aim of deterring forgers – but playing spot-the-fake with brands such as Reebok, Lacoste and Vuitton is fun for visitors too.

## Musée Dapper

*35bis rue Paul-Valéry, 16th (01.45.00.01.50/ www.dapper.com.fr). M° Victor Hugo.* **Open** 11am-7pm Mon, Wed-Sun. **Admission** €6; €3 students, 16-25s; free under-16s. **Credit** MC, V. **Map** p400 B4.
Named after the 17th-century Dutch humanist Olfert Dapper, the Fondation Dapper began as an organisation dedicated to preserving sub-Saharan art. Reopened in 2000, the venue created by Alain Moatti houses a performance space, bookshop and café. Each year it stages two African-themed exhibitions.

## Musée Galliera

*10 av Pierre-1er-de-Serbie, 16th (01.56.52.86.00). M° Iéna.* **Open** *Exhibitions* 10am-6pm Tue-Sun. **Admission** (incl audio-guide) €7.50; €3.50 14-26s; free under-14s. **Credit** MC, V. **Map** p400 D5.
This look at clothes through history takes an academic approach to its subject. Housed in a *hôtel particulier* built by Eiffel, the Galliera has a huge costume collection: 1,300 garments from the 18th century alone. It has links with the fashion industry, and its initiative with young designers shows examples of innovative work the moment it hits the shops.

## Musée de l'Homme

*Palais de Chaillot, 17 pl du Trocadéro, 16th (01.44.05.72.72/www.mnhn.fr). M° Trocadéro.* **Open** 9.45am-5.15pm Mon, Wed-Fri; 10am-6.30pm Sat, Sun. **Admission** €7; €5 reductions; free under-14s. **Credit** *Shop* MC, V. **Map** p400 B5.
The human department of the Muséum National d'Histoire Naturelle (*see p287*) considers human evolution, genetic diversity, and the reasons for and consequences of the population explosion. The prehistoric department covers from 3.7 million years ago to the Bronze Age, with artefacts including the skeleton of Lucy and the skull of the Man of Tautavel.

## Musée National des Arts Asiatiques – Guimet

*6 pl d'Iéna, 16th (01.56.52.53.00/www.museeguimet. fr). M° Iéna.* **Open** 10am-5.45pm Mon, Wed-Sun (last entry 5.15pm). **Admission** €6; €4 students, 18-25s, all Sun; free students, under-18s, all 1st Sun of mth. PMP. **Credit** *Shop* AmEx, DC, MC, V. **Map** p400 C5.
Founded by industrialist Emile Guimet in 1889 to house his collection of Chinese and Japanese religious art, and later incorporating oriental collections from the Louvre, the museum has 45,000 objects from Neolithic times onwards, in a voyage across Asian religions and civilisations. Lower galleries focus on India and South-east Asia, centred on stunning Hindu and Buddhist Khmer sculpture from Cambodia. Don't miss the Giant's Way, part of the entrance to a temple complex at Angkor Wat. Upstairs, Chinese antiquities include mysterious jade discs and a bronze, elephant-shaped Shang dynasty pot. Afghan glassware, Tibetan mandalas and Moghul jewellery also feature.

## Musée National de la Marine

*Palais de Chaillot, 17 pl du Trocadéro, 16th (01.53.06.69.53/www.musee-marine.fr). M° Trocadéro.* **Open** 10am-6pm Mon, Wed-Sun. **Admission** €9; €7 under-25s, over-60s; €5 6-18s; free under-6s, under-18s to main collection. PMP. **Credit** *Shop* MC, V. **Map** p400 B5.
French naval history is outlined in detailed models of battleships and Vernet's series of paintings of French ports (1754-65). There's also an imperial barge, built when Napoleon's delusions of grandeur were reaching their zenith in 1810.

## Palais de Chaillot

*Pl du Trocadéro, 16th. M° Trocadéro.* **Map** p400 C5.
The immense pseudo-classical Palais de Chaillot was constructed by Azéma, Boileau and Carlu for the 1937 international exhibition, with giant sculptures of *Apollo* by Henri Bouchard and *Hercules* by Albert Pommier, and inscriptions by Paul Valéry.

It stands on the foundations of an earlier complex put up for the 1878 World Fair. With two sweeping wings astride the central esplanade, it houses the Musée National de la Marine and what's left of the Musée de l'Homme (for both, *see p119*). In the east wing are the Théâtre National de Chaillot, and the Cité de l'Architecture et du Patrimoine (*see p117*).

## Palais de la Découverte

*Av Franklin-D.-Roosevelt, 8th (01.56.43.20.21/ www.palais-decouverte.fr). M° Champs-Elysées Clemenceau or Franklin D. Roosevelt.* **Open** 9.30am-6pm Tue-Sat; 10am-7pm Sun (last entry 30mins before closing). **Admission** €7; €4.50 5-18s, over-60s, students under 26; free under-5s. *Planetarium* €3.50. **Credit** AmEx, MC, V. **Map** p401 E5.

The city's original science museum houses designs dating from Leonardo da Vinci's time to the present day. Models, real apparatus and audio-visual material bring the displays to life, while permanent exhibits cover astrophysics, astronomy, biology, chemistry, physics and earth sciences. The pertinent Planète Terre section highlights the latest developments in meteorology, while one room is dedicated to the sun. There are shows at the Planetarium too, and 'live' experiments take place at weekends and during school holidays.

## Palais de Tokyo: Site de Création Contemporaine

*13 av du Président-Wilson, 16th (01.47.23.54.01/ www.palaisdetokyo. com). M° Alma Marceau or Iéna.* **Open** noon-midnight Tue-Sun. **Admission** €6; €4.50 concessions; free under-18s, art students. **Map** p400 B5.

When it opened in 2002, many thought the Palais' stripped-back interior with visible air-conditioning and lighting was a design statement. In fact, it was a practical answer to tight finances. The 1937 building has now come into its own as an open-plan space with a skylit central hall, hosting exhibitions, installations, fashion shows and performances. Extended opening hours and a funky café have succeeded in drawing a younger audience, and the roll-call of artists is impressive (Pierre Joseph, Frank Scurti, Wang Du and others). The name dates back to the 1937 Exposition Internationale, but is also a reminder of links with a new generation of artists from the Far East.

## Monceau & Batignolles

*In the 8th & 17th arrondissements.*

**Parc Monceau**, with its neo-antique follies and large lily pond, lies at the far end of avenue Hoche (the main entrance is on boulevard de Courcelles, the circular pavilion by Ledoux). Three museums capture the extravagance of the area when it was newly fashionable in the 19th century: the **Musée Jacquemart-André**, with its Old Masters, the **Musée Nissim de Camondo** (superb 18th-century decorative arts), and the **Musée Cernuschi** (Chinese art).

There are some nice exotic touches too, such as the unlikely red lacquer Galerie Ching Tsai Too (48 rue de Courcelles, 8th), built in 1926 for a dealer in oriental art near the wrought-iron gates of Parc Monceau, or the onion domes of the Russian Orthodox **Alexander Nevsky Cathedral** on rue Daru. Built in the mid 19th century, when a stay in Paris was essential to the education of every Russian aristocrat, it is still at the heart of an émigré little Russia.

Famed for its stand during the 1871 Paris Commune, the Quartier des Batignolles to the north-east towards place de Clichy is more working class, housing the rue de Lévis market, tenements lining the deep railway canyon and square des Batignolles park, with the pretty Eglise Ste-Marie-de-Batignolles looking on to a semi-circular square. It's fast becoming trendy, with a restaurant scene to match.

## Alexander Nevsky Cathedral

*12 rue Daru, 17th (01.42.27.37.34). M° Courcelles.* **Open** times vary. **Map** p400 D3.

All onion domes, icons and incense, this Russian Orthodox church was completed in 1861 in the neo-Byzantine Novgorod-style of the 1600s, by the tsar's architect Kouzmin, responsible for the Fine Arts Academy in St Petersburg. Services, on Sunday mornings and Orthodox saints' days, are in Russian.

## Cimetière des Batignolles

*8 rue St-Just, 17th (01.53.06.38.68). M° Porte de Clichy.* **Open** *16 Mar-6 Nov* 8am-5.45pm Mon-Fri; 8.30am-5.45pm Sat; 9am-5.45pm Sun & public hols. *7 Nov-15 Mar* 8am-5.15pm Mon-Fri; 8.30am-5.15pm Sat; 9am-5.15pm Sun & public hols.

Squeezed inside the Périphérique are the graves of poet Paul Verlaine, Surrealist André Breton, and Léon Bakst, costume designer of the Ballets Russes.

## Musée Cernuschi

*7 av Velasquez, 8th (01.53.96.21.50/www.cernuschi. paris.fr). M° Monceau or Villiers.* **Open** 10am-5.45pm Tue-Sun. **Admission** free. Temporary exhibitions €7; €5 concessions; €3.50 14-26s; free under-18s. **Map** p401 E2.

Since the banker Henri Cernuschi built a *hôtel particulier* by the Parc Monceau for the treasures he found in the Far East in 1871, this collection of Chinese art has grown steadily. The museum has been expanded to twice its size, and was reopened back in 2005 with a total exhibition area of 3,200sq m (34,500sq ft) and 1,000 exhibits. The fabulous displays range from legions of Han and Wei dynasty funeral statues to refined Tang celadon wares and Sung porcelain.

## Musée Jacquemart-André

*158 bd Haussmann, 8th (01.45.62.11.59/www. musee-jacquemart-andre.com). M° Miromesnil or St-Philippe-du-Roule.* **Open** 10am-6pm daily. **Admission** €9.50; €7 7-17s, students; free under-7s. **Credit** AmEx, MC, V. **Map** p401 E3.

Parc Monceau.

Long terrace steps and a stern pair of stone lions usher visitors into this grand 19th-century mansion, home to a collection of equally stately *objets d'art* and fine paintings. The collection was built up by Edouard André and his artist wife Nélie Jacquemart, using money inherited from his rich banking family. The mansion was made to order to house their art hoard, which includes Rembrandts, Tiepolo frescoes and various works by Italian masters Uccello, Mantegna and Carpaccio. The visit unfolds in style, from the richly decorated ground floor past a marble winter garden and up a double spiral staircase. The adjacent tea room, with its fabulous tottering cakes, is a favourite with the smart lunch set.

### Musée Nissim de Camondo

*63 rue de Monceau, 8th (01.53.89.06.40/www. ucad.fr).* M° *Monceau or Villiers.* **Open** 10am-5pm Wed-Sun. **Admission** €6; €4.50 18-25s; free under-18s. **PMP. Credit** AmEx, MC, V. **Map** p401 E3.
Put together by Count Moïse de Camondo, this collection is named after his son Nissim, killed in World War I. Moïse replaced the family's two houses near Parc Monceau with this palatial residence and lived here in a style in keeping with his love of the 18th century. Grand first-floor reception rooms are filled with furniture by craftsmen of the Louis XV and XVI eras, silver services, Sèvres and Meissen porcelain, Savonnerie carpets and Aubusson tapestries.

### Parc Monceau

*Bd de Courcelles, av Hoche, rue Monceau, 8th.* M° *Monceau.* **Open** *Nov-Mar* 7am-8pm daily. *Apr-Oct* 7am-10pm daily. **Map** p401 E2.
Surrounded by grand *hôtels particuliers* and elegant Haussmannian apartments, Monceau is a favourite with well-dressed children and their nannies. It was laid out in the 18th century for the Duc de Chartres

in the English style, with a lake, lawns and a variety of follies: an Egyptian pyramid, a Corinthian colonnade, Venetian bridge and sarcophagi.

## Passy & Auteuil

*In the 16th arrondissement.*
West of l'Etoile, the extensive 16th arrondissement is the epitome of bourgeois respectability, with grandiose apartments and exclusive residences lining the private roads. It is also home to some seminal examples of modernist architecture (*see p122* **Paris promenade**), plus several of the city's most important museums.

When Balzac lived at no.47 rue Raynouard in the 1840s, Passy was a country village (it was absorbed into the city in 1860) where the rich came to take cures at its mineral springs – a history alluded to by rue des Eaux. The novelist's former abode, **Maison de Balzac**, is open to the public. The **Musée du Vin** is of interest if only for its setting in the cellars of the wine-producing Abbaye de Minimes, destroyed in the Revolution. Rue de Passy, formerly the village high street, and parallel rue de l'Assomption, are the focus of local life, with fashion shops and *traiteurs*, the department store Franck et Fils (80 rue de Passy, 16th, 01.44.14.38.00) and a pricey covered market.

The former Passy station is now restaurant La Gare (19 chaussée de la Muette, 16th, 01.42.15.15.31). Ladies who shop stop by the lovely art deco La Rotonde café (12 chaussée de la Muette, 16th, 01.45.24.45.45) or stock up on cakes at Japanese *pâtisserie* Yamazaki

# Paris promenade
## The path to modernity

Fondation Le Corbusier.

In stark contrast with its current rather snooty image, the 16th arrondissement in the early 1900s was a hotbed of avant-garde architecture and experimentation. This walk explores the artists' studios, apartment blocks and luxury villas that sprung up in a district that had only recently been incorporated into Paris proper.

Start on rue La Fontaine at the **Castel Béranger** (❶ see p124), the Art Nouveau masterpiece of Hector Guimard – before dropping in for an early coffee break at the whimsically pretty **Café Antoine** at no.17 (❷), inserted into another Guimard building with clever wrap-around corners. Next admire the rampart tendrils sprouting from the wrought-iron fence of the **Hôtel Mezzara** (❸), at no.60, also designed by Guimard, for textile manufacturer Paul Mezzara. Further along at no.65, don't miss the polychrome-tiled 1926-28 artists' **Studio Building** (❹) by Modernist maverick Henri Sauvage.

Turning right into avenue Mozart, you'll find Guimard's former home at **no.122** (❺), where he lived with his American artist wife Adeline

Oppenheim. On the corner as you turn left into rue Jasmin stands the imposing Beaux-Arts style apartment building – just the sort of neo-Renaissance frippery against which Guimard was rebelling. Turn right into rue Henrich Heine, then left along rue du Dr Blanche. Here you'll find the **Fondation Le Corbusier** (❻; see p124), housed in two villas designed by the architect in 1923, which draws architectural pilgrims from the world over. The interior reveals his mastery of multiple viewpoints, fluidity of space and surprising use of colour.

Just off rue du Dr Blanche, turning right into **Rue Mallet-Stevens** (❼), stand six exclusive Cubist houses by Robert Mallet-Stevens, the glamorous architect and designer who best combined the elegance of Art Deco with the rigour of Modernism. Back at **no.5 rue du Dr Blanche** (❽) are artists' studios by Pierre Patout, decorator of luxury cruise liner *Normandie* (Art Deco was also known as *le style paquebot*).

Head right down rue de l'Assomption, then left onto avenue Mozart and right onto rue de Passy at M⁰ La Muette, with glitzy Art Deco brasserie La Rotonde on the corner. Next to Passy covered market, take rue Duban, then rue Singer towards the river onto rue Raynouard. **Nos.51-55** (❾) were designed by Auguste Perret in reinforced concrete, cunningly tinted golden yellow to match Paris stone. Best known for the Théâtre des Champs-Elysées (see p316), this building contained apartments and Perret's

(6 chaussée de la Muette, 16th, 01.40.50.19.19). A curiosity are three wooden dachas on Villa Beauséjour, built by Russian craftsmen for the 1867 Exposition Universelle and rebuilt here.

West of the former high society pleasure gardens of the Jardin du Ranelagh you'll find the **Musée Marmottan**, with its superb collection of Monet's late water-lily canvases, other Impressionists and Empire furniture.

Next to the Pont de Grenelle stands the circular **Maison de Radio-France**, the giant home of state broadcasting. You can attend concerts (see p314) or take a tour around its endless corridors; employees nickname the place 'Alphaville', after the Jean-Luc Godard film. From here, in more upmarket Auteuil, you can head up rue Fontaine, the best place to find art nouveau architecture by Hector Guimard

Sightseeing

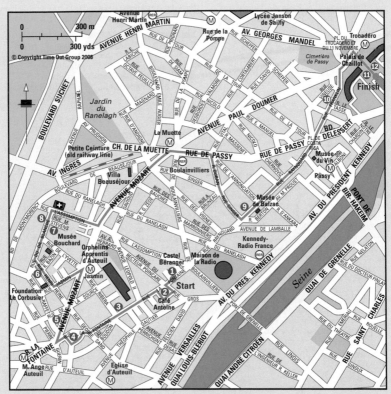

architectural offices. Turn left on rue Raynouard, past the Maison de Balzac (*see p124*), and cross place du Costa Rica into rue Benjamin-Franklin.

There's more Perret at **no.25bis** (⑩) where, behind the leaf-motif tiles, the 1904 building was one of the first to be constructed around a concrete frame. The revolutionary structure freed up the floor plan from load-bearing walls, creating the light, airy spaces associated with Modernism – as well as giving all the occupants a view of the Seine.

The walk ends at Trocadéro with the **Palais de Chaillot** (⑪; *see p119*), an example of gigantesque 1930s state classical revival. It was designed by Léon Azéma, Louis-Hippolyte Boileau and Jacques Carlu for the Exposition Universelle of 1937, with two curved wings, giant bronze sculptures by Henri Bouchard and Pommier and quotations by Paul Valéry. Pop into the **Cité de l'Architecture** (⑫; *see p117*), in the east wing, for a more thorough tour of French architectural history, from Romanesque... to the future.

(*see p122* **Paris promenade**), of métro entrance fame. He also designed the less ambitious nos.19 and 21. At no.96 pay homage to Marcel Proust. This is the house where he was born.

Nearby, the **Fondation Le Corbusier** occupies two of the architect's avant-garde houses in square du Dr-Blanche (*see p122* **Paris promenade**). A little further up rue

du Dr-Blanche sculptor Henri Bouchard himself commissioned the studio and house that is now the dusty Atelier-Musée Henri Bouchard. Much of the rest of Auteuil is private territory, with exclusive streets of residences off rue Chardon-Lagache; the studio of 19th-century sculptor Jean-Baptiste Carpeaux remains, looking rather lost, at no.39 boulevard Exelmans. The top storey was later added by Guimard.

West of the 16th, across the Périphérique, sprawls the parkland of **Bois de Boulogne**. At porte d'Auteuil are the romantic **Serres d'Auteuil** and sports venues the **Parc des Princes**, home of football club **Paris St-Germain** (for both, *see p335*), and **Roland Garros** (*see p333*), host of the French Tennis Open. Another attraction will open in 2009: the Fondation Louis-Vuitton, to be housed in a new Frank Gehry glass construction.

### Bois de Boulogne

*16th. M° Les Sablons or Porte Dauphine.*
Covering 865 hectares, the Bois was once the Forêt de Rouvray hunting grounds. It was landscaped in the 1860s, when artificial grottoes and waterfalls were created around the Lac Inférieur. The Jardin de Bagatelle (route de Sèvres à Neuilly, 16th, 01.40.67.97.00) is famous for its roses, daffodils and water lilies, and contains an orangery that rings to the sound of Chopin in summer. The Jardin d'Acclimatation (*see p288*) is a children's amusement park, complete with a miniature train, farm, rollercoaster and boat rides. The Bois also boasts two racecourses (Longchamp and Auteuil; *see p339* **A day at the races**), sports clubs and stables, and restaurants, including Le Pré Catelan (route de Suresnes, 16th, 01.44.14.41.14).

Today there are plans to reduce the traffic and replant some of the scrubby woodland. The opening of the Fondation Louis-Vuitton in 2009 should also change the character of the area. For the time being, it attracts picnickers and dog walkers, with a boating lake and nearby cycle hire, but by night it's transformed into a parade ground for transsexuals and swingers of every stripe.

### Castel Béranger

*14 rue La Fontaine, 16th. M° Jasmin.* Closed to the public.
Guimard's masterpiece of 1895-98 epitomises art nouveau in Paris (*see p122* **Paris promenade**). From outside you can see his love of brick and wrought iron, asymmetry and renunciation of harsh angles not found in nature. Green seahorses climb the façade, and the faces on the balconies are thought to be self-portraits, inspired by Japanese figures, to ward off evil spirits.

### Fondation Le Corbusier

*Villa La Roche, 8-10 square du Dr-Blanche, 16th (01.42.88.41.53/www.fondationlecorbusier.fr). M° Jasmin.* **Open** 1.30-6pm Mon; 10am-12.30pm, 1.30-6pm Tue-Thur; 10am-12.30pm, 1.30-5pm Fri; 10am-5pm Sat. Closed Aug. **Admission** €3-€4; €2 students; free under-14s. **No credit cards.**
This house, designed by Le Corbusier in 1923 for a Swiss art collector, shows the architect's ideas in practice, with its stilts, strip windows, roof terraces and balconies, built-in furniture and an unsuspected use of colour inside: sludge green, blue and pinky beige. A sculptural cylindrical staircase and split volumes create a variety of geometrical vistas;

inside, Le Corbusier's own neo-Cubist paintings and furniture sit alongside pieces by Perriand. Adjoining Villa Jeanneret houses the foundation's library.

### Le Jardin des Serres d'Auteuil

*3 av de la Porte d'Auteuil, 16th (01.40.71.75.23). M° Porte d'Auteuil.* **Open** *Winter* 10am-5pm daily. *Summer* 10am-6pm daily. **Admission** free.
These romantic glasshouses were opened in 1895 to cultivate plants for Paris parks and public spaces. Today there are seasonal displays of orchids and begonias. Look out for the steamy tropical pavilion with palms, birds and Japanese ornamental carp.

### Maison de Balzac

*47 rue Raynouard, 16th (01.55.74.41.80/www.paris.fr/musees). M° Passy.* **Open** 10am-6pm Tue-Sun. **Admission** €4; €3 reductions; €2 14-26s; free under-13s. **Credit** MC, V. **Map** p404 B6.
Honoré de Balzac rented this apartment in 1840 to escape his creditors. Converted into a museum, the collection of mementos is spread over several floors. Memorabilia includes first editions and letters, plus portraits of friends and the novelist's mistress Mme Hanska, with whom he corresponded for years before they married. Along with a 'family tree' of his characters that extends across several walls, you can see Balzac's desk and the monogrammed coffee pot that fuelled all-night work on his epic *Comédie Humaine*.

### Musée Marmottan – Claude Monet

*2 rue Louis-Boilly, 16th (01.44.96.50.33/www.marmottan.com). M° La Muette.* **Open** 10am-5.30pm Tue-Sun (last entry 5pm). **Admission** €8; €4.50 8-25s; free under-8s. **Credit** MC, V.
Originally a museum of the Empire period left to the state by collector Paul Marmottan, this old hunting pavilion has become a famed holder of Impressionist art thanks to two bequests: the first by the daughter of the doctor of Manet, Monet, Pissarro, Sisley and Renoir; the second by Monet's son Michel. Its Monet collection, the largest in the world, numbers 165 works – including the seminal *Impression Soleil Levant* – plus sketchbooks, palette and photos. A special circular room was created for the breathtaking late water lily canvases; upstairs are works by Renoir, Manet, Gauguin, Caillebotte and Berthe Morisot, 15th-century primitives, the Wildenstein collection of medieval manuscripts, a Sèvres clock and a collection of First Empire furniture.

### Musée du Vin

*Rue des Eaux, 16th (01.45.25.63.26/www.musee duvinparis.com). M° Passy.* **Open** 10am-6pm Tue-Sun. **Admission** (with guidebook and glass of wine) €9; €7 over-60s; €5.70 students; free under-14s, diners in the restaurant. **Credit** Shop, restaurant AmEx, DC, MC, V. **Map** p404 B6.
Here the Confrères Bacchiques defend French wines from imports and advertising laws. In the cellars of an old wine-producing monastery are displays on the history of viticulture, with waxwork peasants, old tools, bottles and corkscrews. Visits finish with a wine tasting and, a paid extra, a meal.

# Montmartre & Pigalle

Head north for the city's highest point – and some of its lowest culture.

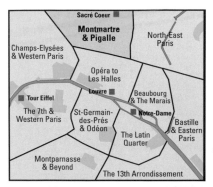

Sacré Coeur ■

**Montmartre
& Pigalle**

North East
Paris

Champs-Elysées
& Western Paris

Opéra to
Les Halles

Louvre ■

■ Tour Eiffel

Beaubourg
& The Marais

The 7th &
Western Paris

St-Germain-
des-Prés
& Odéon

■ Notre-Dame

Bastille
& Eastern
Paris

The Latin
Quarter

Montparnasse
& Beyond

The 13th Arrondissement

## Montmartre

*In the 18th arrondissement.*

Perched on a hill (or *butte*), Montmartre is the highest point in Paris, its tightly packed houses spiralling round the mound below the oversized, sugary-white dome of **Sacré-Coeur**. Despite the thronging tourists, it is surprisingly easy to fall under the spell of this, the most unabashedly romantic district of Paris. Climb quiet stairways, peer down narrow alleys and into ivy-covered houses and deserted squares, and explore streets s uch as rue des Abbesses, rue des Trois-Frères and rue des Martyrs, with their cafés, quirky boutiques and bohemian residents.

For centuries, Montmartre was a tranquil village packed with windmills. When Haussmann sliced through the city centre in the middle of the 19th century, working-class families started to move out and peasant migrants poured into an industrialising Paris from across France. The population of Montmartre swelled. The *butte* was absorbed into the city of Paris in 1860, but remained proudly independent. Its key role in the Commune in 1871, fending off government troops, is marked by a plaque on rue du Chevalier-de-la-Barre.

Artists moved into the area from the 1880s. Renoir found subject matter in the cafés and *guinguettes*. Toulouse-Lautrec enthusiastically patronised the local bars and immortalised its cabarets in his famous posters; later it was frequented by Picasso and artists of the Ecole de Paris, Utrillo and Modigliani.

You can start a wander from Abbesses métro station, one of only two in Paris (along with Porte Dauphine) to retain its original art nouveau metal-and-glass awning designed by Hector Guimard. Across place des Abbesses is art nouveau St-Jean-de-Montmartre church, a pioneering reinforced concrete structure studded with turquoise mosaics around the door. Along rue des Abbesses and adjoining rue Lepic, which winds its way up the hill, are food shops, wine merchants and cafés, including the ever-popular Le Sancerre (*see p227*), and offbeat boutiques. The famous Studio 28 cinema (*see p297*), opened in 1928 and still going strong, is where Luis Buñuel's controversial Surrealist classic *L'Age d'Or* had its riotous premiere in 1930.

In the other direction from Abbesses, at 11 rue Yvonne-Le-Tac, is the Chapelle du Martyr where, according to legend, St Denis picked up his head after his execution in the third century (hence the name Montmartre – martyr's mount). Rue Orsel, with a typical local cluster of retro design, ethnic and second-hand clothes shops, leads to place Charles-Dullin, where a cluster of cafés overlook the respected Théâtre de l'Atelier (1 pl Charles-Dullin, 18th, 01.46.06.49.24).

Up the hill, the cafés of rue des Trois-Frères are a popular spot for an evening drink. The street leads into sloping place Emile-Goudeau, whose staircases, wrought-iron streetlights and old houses are particularly evocative of days gone by. The Bâteau Lavoir, a piano factory that stood at No.13, witnessed the birth of Cubism. Divided into a warren of studios in the 1890s for impoverished artists of the day, it was here that Picasso painted *Les Demoiselles d'Avignon* in 1906 and 1907, when he, Braque and Juan Gris were all residents. The building burned down in 1970, but has since been reconstructed.

On rue Lepic, which winds up the hill from rue des Abbesses, are the village's two remaining windmills: the Moulin du Radet, which was moved here in the 17th century from its hillock in rue des Moulins near the Palais-Royal; and the Moulin de la Galette, site of the celebrated dancehall famously depicted by Renoir (now in the Musée d'Orsay; *see p172*) and today a smart restaurant. Vincent van Gogh and his beloved brother Theo resided at No.54 from 1886 to 1888.

On tourist-swamped place du Tertre at the top of the hill, portrait painters compete to sketch you or flog lurid sunset views of Paris; nearby Espace Dalí (11 rue Poulbot, 18th, 01.42.64.40.10) offers a slightly more illustrious alternative. Round here, or so legend has it, the bistro concept was born in the early 1800s, when Russian soldiers shouted '*Bistro!*' ('Quickly!') to be served. Just off the square is the oldest church in the district, St-Pierre-de-Montmartre, whose columns have grown bent with age. Founded by Louis VI in 1133, it is an example of early Gothic, in contrast to its extravagant neighbour, the basilica of Sacré-Coeur.

For all its kitsch and swarms of tourists, though, Sacré-Coeur is well worth the visit for its sheer 19th-century excess. Rather than the main steps, take the staircase down rue Maurice-Utrillo to pause on a café terrace on the small square at the top of rue Muller, or wander down through the adjoining park to the Halle St-Pierre. The old covered market is now used for shows of naïve art, but the surrounding square and streets, known as the Marché St-Pierre, are packed with fabric shops.

On the north side of place du Tertre in rue Cortot is the quiet 17th-century manor that houses the **Musée de Montmartre**, dedicated to the neighbourhood and its former famous inhabitants. Dufy, Renoir and Utrillo all used to have studios in the entrance pavilion. Nearby in rue des Saules is the Montmartre vineyard, planted by local artist Poulbot in 1933 in commemoration of the vines that once covered the area. The grape harvest here every autumn is a local highlight, celebrated with great pomp.

Further down the hill, amid rustic, shuttered houses, is the Au Lapin Agile cabaret (*see p281*). This old meeting point for local artists got its name from André Gill, who painted the inn sign of a rabbit 'lapin A. Gill'.

A series of squares leads to rue Caulaincourt, crossing the **Cimetière de Montmartre** (enter on avenue Rachel, reached by stairs from rue Caulaincourt or place de Clichy). Winding down the back of the hill, avenue Junot is lined with exclusive residences, such as the avant-garde house built by Adolf Loos for Dadaist poet Tristan Tzara at No.15, exemplifying his Modernist maxim: 'Ornament is crime.'

### Cimetière de Montmartre

*20 av Rachel, access by staircase from rue Caulaincourt, 18th (01.53.42.36.30). M° Blanche or Place de Clichy.* **Open** *6 Nov-15 Mar* 8am-5.30pm Mon-Sat; 9am-5.30pm Sun & public hols. *16 Mar-5 Nov* 8am-6pm Mon-Sat; 9am-6pm Sun & public hols. **Admission** free. **Map** p401 G1.
Truffaut, Nijinsky, Berlioz, Degas, Offenbach, German poet Heine and Surrealist painter Victor Brauner are all buried here. So too are La Goulue,

the first great cancan star and model for Toulouse-Lautrec, celebrated local beauty Mme Récamier, and the consumptive heroine Alphonsine Plessis, inspiration for Dumas' *La Dame aux Camélias* and Verdi's *La Traviata*. Flowers are still left for pop diva and gay icon Dalida, who used to live on nearby rue d'Orchampt.

### Musée d'Art Halle St-Pierre

*2 rue Ronsard, 18th (01.42.58.72.89/www.halle saintpierre.org). M° Anvers.* **Open** *Jan-July, Sept-Dec* 10am-6pm daily; *Aug* noon-6pm Mon-Fri. **Admission** €7; €5.50 students, 4-26s; free under-4s. **Credit** *Shop* MC, V. **Map** p402 J2.
The former covered market in the shadow of Sacré-Coeur specialises in *art brut*, *art outsider* and *art singulier* from its own and other collections. Shows for the beginning of 2008 include a retrospective of Paris naïve artist Yolande Fièvre, who died in 1983, and an exhibition on American intellectual Varian Fry.

### Musée de Montmartre

*12 rue Cortot, 18th (01.49.25.89.37/www.musee demontmartre.fr). M° Abbesses or Lamarck Caulaincourt.* **Open** 11am-6pm Wed-Sun.
**Admission** €7; €5.50 students, over-60s; free under-10s. **Credit** *Shop* MC, V. **Map** p402 H1.
At the back of a garden, this 17th-century manor displays the history of the hilltop, with rooms devoted to composer Gustave Charpentier and a tribute to the Lapin Agile cabaret, with original Toulouse-Lautrec posters. There are paintings by Suzanne Valadon, who had a studio above the entrance pavilion, as did Renoir, Raoul Dufy and Valadon's son Maurice Utrillo.

### Sacré-Coeur

*35 rue du Chevalier-de-la-Barre, 18th (01.53.41.89.00/www.sacre-coeur-montmartre.com). M° Abbesses or Anvers.* **Open** *Basilica* 6am-10.30pm daily. *Crypt & dome* Winter 10am-5.45pm daily. Summer 9am-6.45pm daily. **Admission** free. *Crypt & dome* €5. **Credit** MC, V. **Map** p402 J1.
Work on this enormous mock Romano-Byzantine edifice began in 1877. It was commissioned after the nation's defeat by Prussia in 1870, voted for by the Assemblée Nationale and built from public subscription. Finally completed in 1914, it was consecrated in 1919 – by which time a jumble of architects had succeeded Paul Abadie, winner of the original competition. The interior boasts lavish mosaics, and there's a fine view from the dome.

## La Goutte d'Or

The area north of Barbès Rochechouart métro station was used by Zola as a backdrop for *L'Assommoir*, his novel set among the district's laundries and absinthe cafés. Today, heroin has replaced absinthe as the means of escape.

La Goutte d'Or is primarily an African and Arab neighbourhood, and can seem like a colourful slice of the Middle East or a state

La Fourmi.

under perpetual siege due to the frequent police raids (*see p128* **Battle of Algiers**). Down rue Doudeauville you'll find lively ethnic music shops, while rue Polonceau contains African grocers and Senegalese restaurants. Mayor Delanoë has tried to attract young designers to the area by designating rue des Gardes 'rue de la mode', while square Léon is the focus for La Goutte d'Or en Fête (*see p276*) in June, which brings together local musicians. Some of them, such as Africando and the Orchestre National de Barbès, have become well known across Paris. A market sets up under the métro tracks along boulevard de la Chapelle on Monday, Wednesday and Saturday mornings , with stalls of exotic vegetables and rolls of African fabrics.

Further north, at porte de Clignancourt, is the city's largest flea market, the Marché aux Puces de Clignancourt (*see p271* **Bargain Hunt**).

## Pigalle

*In the 9th arrondissement.*
Pigalle is Paris's centre of sleaze. Despite a police crackdown, which sought to eliminate tourist rip-offs and rough-ups, passers-by may still be hassled by barkers and hawkers trying to corral them into some peep show or other.

In the 1890s Toulouse-Lautrec's posters of Jane Avril at the Divan Japonais, Chat Noir and Moulin Rouge, and of *chansonnier* Aristide Bruant, immortalised the area's cabarets and were landmarks of art and advertising. At the end of the 19th century, of the 58 buildings on rue des Martyrs, 25 were cabarets (a few, such as the drag shows Michou and Madame Arthur, remain today); others were *maisons closes*. But it's still a happening street: Le Divan Japonais is now Le Divan du Monde (*see p318*), a club and music venue; a hip crowd packs into La Fourmi (*see p226*) opposite; and up the hill there's a cluster of *atelier*-boutiques where designers have set up their sewing machines at the back of the shop. Along the boulevard, behind its bright red windmill, the Moulin Rouge (*see p281*), once the image of naughty 1890s Paris, is now a cheesy tourist draw. Its befeathered dancers still cancan and cavort across the stage, but are no substitute for La Goulue and Joseph Pujol – *le pétomane* who could pass wind melodically. In stark contrast is the Cité Véron next door, a cobbled alley with a small theatre and cottagey buildings, among them 6bis where writer and jazz musician Boris Vian lived between 1953 and 1958. The famous Elysée Montmartre music hall today has an array of concerts (*see p318*) and club nights, but the Folies Pigalle (*see p329*) nightspot retains undeniable Pigalle flavour with its after-parties and drag queens.

### Musée de l'Erotisme
*72 bd de Clichy, 18th (01.42.58.28.73/www.musee-erotisme.com). M° Blanche.* **Open** 10am-2am daily. **Admission** €8; €6 students. **Credit** MC, V. **Map** p401 H2.

# Battle of Algiers

It could be argued that Paris is the greatest centre of North African culture in the world; it just happens not to be in Africa. Certainly, it is possible to spend much of your time in Paris immersed in the languages, food, politics, literature and culture of the Maghreb – and this is not confined to the formerly ghettoised areas of the city (Barbès or Belleville). But the apparent ease with which Parisians accept North African culture these days does not disguise contemporary racism or the bitter legacy of the war for independence in Algeria.

The greatest influx of North Africans to Paris came after World War II and settled in those parts of the city already known to the pre-war generation from the Maghreb, who had long been viewed with suspicion and made the object of police surveillance. Indeed, the police had set up a special brigade in 1925 to control the North African population. This unit was dissolved in the wake of the Liberation, its staff of ex-colonials turning out to have been suspiciously close to the Gestapo.

North Africans in Paris were quick to realise that many of the promises of racial tolerance made after the Liberation were never going to be kept. There were frequent complaints, from both Left and Right, about the incompatibility of Islam and 'European civilisation', and the North Africans' alleged propensity for violent crime.

At the height of the Algerian War of Independence in the 1950s and 1960s, the instinctive reaction of the Paris police was to crack down on all Algerians, and indeed anyone of North African appearance. This policy had terrible consequences on 17 October 1961, when tens of thousands of Algerians gathered in the centre of the city to demonstrate for independence. The police response was ruthless. On the pont de Neuilly a skirmish between demonstrators and the security forces turned into a fully fledged riot, when heavily armed police charged into the crowd, killing two and wounding many more. The police then began to kill more Algerians, throwing their bodies into the Seine. And there was more to come: in February 1962, a demonstration for peace turned violent as police again charged demonstrators. This time nine people were killed and hundreds were injured in the crush at métro Charonne.

The Paris public soon became heartily sick of this endless and apparently unstoppable cycle of violence. When De Gaulle finally granted Algeria its independence in that same year, most Parisians greeted the move more with relief than with any sense that justice had been done.

To be North African, and particularly Algerian, in Paris these days is to have a dual identity: it is to be part of the cultural mainstream and yet an 'outsider'. It's one of the more striking paradoxes of French cultural life, therefore, that Zinédine Zidane – the son of Algerian immigrants – is often voted among the 'most popular Frenchmen of all time'.

Seven floors of erotic art and artefacts amassed by collectors Alain Plumey and Joseph Khalif. The first three run from first-century Peruvian phallic pottery through Etruscan fertility symbols to Yoni sculptures from Nepal; the fourth gives a history of Paris brothels; and the recently refurbished top floors host exhibitions of modern erotic art. In the basement you'll find titillations such as a vagina dinner plate.

## La Nouvelle Athènes

Just south of Pigalle and east of rue Blanche lies this mysterious and often overlooked quarter, dubbed the New Athens when it was colonised by a wave of artists, writers and composers in the early 19th century. Long-forgotten actresses and *demi-mondaines* had mansions built here; some are set in tiny rue de la Tour-des-Dames, which refers to one of the many windmills owned by Couvent des Abbesses. To glimpse more of these miniature palaces, wander through the adjoining streets and passageways, such as rue St-Lazare (the painter Paul Delaroche lived at No.58) and rue de La Rochefoucauld.

Just off rue Taitbout is square d'Orléans, a remarkable housing estate built in 1829 by the English architect Edward Cresy. These flats and studios attracted the glitterati of the day, including writer George Sand and her lover Chopin. In the house built for Dutch painter Ary Scheffer in nearby rue Chaptal, the **Musée de la Vie Romantique** displays Sand's mementos.

The **Musée Gustave Moreau** on rue de La Rochefoucauld is reason alone to visit, featuring the artist's cramped apartment and magnificent studio. Fragments of bohemia can still be gleaned in the area, although the Café La Roche, where Moreau would meet Degas for drinks and rows, has been downsized to La Joconde (57 rue Notre-Dame-de-Lorette, 9th, 01.48.74.10.38). The area is steeped in history: Degas painted most of his memorable ballet scenes in rue Frochot, while Renoir hired his first proper studio at 35 rue St-Georges. A few streets away in Cité Pigalle, a collection of studios, is van Gogh's last Paris house (No.5), from where he moved to Auvers-sur-Oise. There is a plaque here, but nothing marks the building in rue Pigalle where Toulouse-Lautrec sat and slowly drank himself to an early grave.

The area around the neo-classical Eglise Notre-Dame-de-Lorette, built in the form of a Greek temple, was built up in Louis-Philippe's reign and was famous for its courtesans or *lorettes*, elegant ladies named after their haunt of rue Notre-Dame-de-Lorette. In 1848, Gauguin was born at No.56; from 1844 to 1857, Delacroix had a studio at No.58. The latter then moved to place de Furstemberg in the 6th (now Musée Delacroix; *see p157*). Rue St-Lazare still contains some delightfully old-fashioned shops and bistros, including perfumer Détaille 1905 (*see p268*), and bistro Chez Jean (No.8, 01.48.78.62.73). The lower stretch of rue des Martyrs is packed with tempting food shops, while a little further up the hill you should look out for the prosperous residences of the Cité Malesherbes and avenue Trudaine. The circular place St-Georges was home to the true Empress of Napoleon III's Paris: the Russian-born Madame Païva. She lived in the neo-Renaissance No.28, thought to be outrageous at the time of its construction. 'La Païva' shot herself in the head after a passionate affair with the millionaire cousin of Chancellor Otto von Bismarck.

### Musée Gustave Moreau

*14 rue de La Rochefoucauld, 9th (01.48.74.38.50/ www.musee-moreau.fr). M° Trinité.* **Open** 10am-12.45pm, 2-5.15pm Mon, Wed-Sun. **Admission** €5; €3 18-25s, all Sun; free under-18s. PMP. **Credit** MC, V. **Map** p401 G3.

This wonderful museum combines the small private apartment of Symbolist painter Gustave Moreau (1825-98) with the vast two-floor gallery he built to display his work – set out as a museum by the painter himself, and opened in 1903. Downstairs shows his obsessive collector's nature with family portraits, Grand Tour souvenirs and a boudoir devoted to the object of his unrequited love, Alexandrine Durem. Upstairs is Moreau's fantasy realm, which plunders Greek mythology and biblical scenes for canvases filled with writhing maidens, trance-like visages, mystical beasts and strange plants. Printed on boards that you can carry around are the artist's lengthy, rhetorical and mad commentaries. Don't miss the trippy masterpiece *Jupiter et Sémélé* on the second floor.

### Musée de la Vie Romantique

*Hôtel Scheffer-Renan, 16 rue Chaptal, 9th (01.55.31.95.67/www.vie-romantique.paris.fr). M° Blanche or St-Georges.* **Open** 10am-6pm Tue-Sun. Tearoom May-Oct 11.30am-5.30pm Tue-Sun. **Admission** €7; €3.50 18-26s; free under-14s. **Credit** AmEx, DC, MC, V. **Map** p401 G2.

When Dutch artist Ary Scheffer lived in this small villa, the area thronged with composers, writers and artists. Aurore Dupin, Baronne Dudevant (George Sand) was a guest at Scheffer's soirées, and many other great names crossed the threshold, including Chopin, Delacroix and Liszt. The museum is devoted to Sand, although the watercolours, lockets, jewels and plastercast of her right arm that she left behind reveal little of her ideas or affairs. But the house itself is quite lovely, decorated with restraint and good taste. A couple of ancillary buildings are used for temporary exhibitions, and there's a pretty rose garden and a conservatory that serves as a café.

Sightseeing

# Beaubourg & the Marais

Modern art, medieval architecture, museums and lots of shopping.

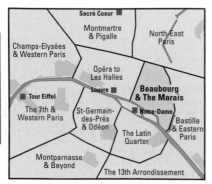

Between boulevard Sébastopol and the Bastille are Beaubourg – site, since 1977, of the Centre Pompidou – and the Marais, largely built between the 16th and 18th centuries and now jam-packed with boutiques, museums and bars.

## Beaubourg & Hôtel de Ville

*In the 4th arrondissement.*
Modern architecture in Paris really took off with the **Centre Pompidou**, designed by Richard Rogers and Renzo Piano. This benchmark of inside-out high-tech is as much of an attraction as the **Musée National de l'Art Moderne** within. The piazza outside attracts street performers and pavement artists, while the reconstructed **Atelier Brancusi**, the sculptor's studio, which he left to the state, was moved here from the 15th arrondissement. On the other side of the piazza, rue Quincampoix houses galleries, bars and cobbled passage Molière, with its old shopfronts and the Théâtre Molière (01.44.54.53.00). Beside the Centre Pompidou is place Igor-Stravinsky and the Fontaine Stravinsky – full of spraying kinetic fountains, and a colourful snake by the late artists Nikki de St-Phalle and Jean Tinguély – and the red-brick **IRCAM** music institute (*see p314*), also designed by Renzo Piano.
The church of St-Merri (78 rue St-Martin, 4th, 01.42.71.93.93), whose Flamboyant Gothic façade has an androgynous demon leering

over the doorway, sits on the south side of the square. Inside are a carved wooden organ loft, the joint contender (along with one in **Eglise St-Séverin**; *see p148*) for the oldest bell in Paris (1331), and 16th-century stained glass.
South of here stands the spiky Gothic **Tour St-Jacques**. Towards the river, on the site of the Grand Châtelet (a fortress put up in the 12th century to defend Pont au Change), place du Châtelet's Egyptian-themed fountain is framed by twin theatres designed by Davioud as part of Haussmann's urban improvements in the 1860s. They are now two of the city's main arts venues: the **Théâtre de la Ville** (*see p316 and p344*) and **Théâtre du Châtelet** (*see p291 and p323*), an opera and concert hall.
Beyond Châtelet, the **Hôtel de Ville** (city hall), has been the symbol of municipal power since 1260. The equestrian statue out front is of 14th-century merchant leader and rebel Etienne Marcel. Revolutionaries made the Hôtel de Ville their base in the 1871 Commune, but it was set on fire by the Communards themselves and wrecked during savage fighting. It was rebuilt according to the original model, on a larger scale, in fanciful neo-Renaissance style, with knights in armour along the roof and statues of French luminaries dotted all over the walls. The square outside was formerly called place de Grève, after the nearby riverside wharf where goods were unloaded for market. *Grève* has come to be the French word for 'strike', thanks to the number of demonstrations and protests that gathered here. During the 16th-century Wars of Religion, Protestant heretics were burned in the square, and the guillotine stood here during the Terror, when Danton, Marat and Robespierre made the Hôtel de Ville their own seat of government. Today the square hosts an ice rink every December (*see p278*) and screenings of major sports events. Across the road stands the Bazar de l'Hôtel de Ville department store, or **BHV** (*see p240*).

### Atelier Brancusi
*Piazza Beaubourg, 4th (01.44.78.12.33/www. centrepompidou.fr). M° Hôtel de Ville or Rambuteau.* **Open** 2-6pm Mon, Wed-Sun. **Admission** free. **Credit** AmEx, V. **Map** p406 K6.

When Constantin Brancusi died in 1957 he left his studio and its contents to the state, later rebuilt by the Centre Pompidou. His fragile works in wood and plaster, the endless columns and streamlined bird forms, show how Brancusi revolutionised sculpture.

## Centre Pompidou
## (Musée National d'Art Moderne)

*Rue St-Martin, 4th (01.44.78.12.33/www.centre pompidou.fr). M° Hôtel de Ville or Rambuteau.*
**Open** 11am-9pm (last entry 8pm) Mon, Wed-Sun (until 11pm some exhibitions); 11am-11pm Thur.
**Admission** Museum & exhibitions €10; €8 18-25s; free under-18s, 1st Sun of mth (museum only). PMP.
**Credit** AmEx, DC, MC, V. **Map** p406 K6.

The primary colours, exposed pipes and air ducts make this one of the best-known sights in Paris. The then-unknown Italo-British architectural duo of Renzo Piano and Richard Rogers won the competition with their 'inside-out' boilerhouse approach, which put air-conditioning, pipes, lifts and the escalators on the outside, leaving an adaptable space within. The multi-disciplinary concept of modern art museum (the most important in Europe), library, exhibition and performance spaces and repertory cinema was also revolutionary. When the centre opened in 1977, its success exceeded all expectations. After a two-year revamp, the centre reopened in 2000 with an enlarged museum, renewed performance spaces, vista-rich Georges restaurant and a mission to get back to the stimulating interdisciplinary mix of old. Entrance to the forum is free (as is the library, which has a separate entrance), but you now have to pay to go up the escalators.

The Centre Pompidou (or 'Beaubourg') holds the largest collection of modern art in Europe, rivalled only in its breadth and quality by MOMA in New York. Sample the contents of its vaults (50,000 works of art by 5,000 artists) on the website, as only a fraction – about 600 works – can be seen for real at any one time. There is a partial rehang each year. For the main collection, buy tickets on the ground floor and take the escalators to level four for post-1960s art. Level five spans 1905 to 1960. There are four temporary exhibition spaces on each of these two levels (included in the ticket). Main temporary exhibitions take place on the ground floor, in gallery two on level six, in the south gallery, level one and in the new Espace 315, devoted to the under-40s.

On level five, the historic section takes a chronological sweep through the history of modern art, via Primitivism, Fauvism, Cubism, Dadaism and Surrealism up to American Color-Field painting and Abstract Expressionism. Masterful ensembles let you see the span of Matisse's career on canvas and in bronze, the variety of Picasso's invention, and the development of cubic orphism by Sonia and Robert Delaunay. Others on the hits list include Braque, Duchamp, Mondrian, Malevich, Kandinsky, Dalí, Giacometti, Ernst, Miró, Calder, Magritte, Rothko and Pollock. Don't miss the reconstruction of a wall of André Breton's studio, combining the tribal art, folk art, flea-market finds and drawings by fellow artists that the Surrealist artist and theorist had amassed. The photography collection also has an impressive roll call, including Brassaï, Kertész, Man Ray, Cartier-Bresson and Doisneau.

Level four houses post-'60s art. Its thematic rooms concentrate on the career of one artist or focus on movements such as Anti-form or *arte povera*. Recent acquisitions line the central corridor, while at the far end you can find architecture and design. Video art and installations by the likes of Mathieu Mercier and Dominique Gonzalez-Foerster are in a frequently changing room devoted to *nouvelle création. See also p43, p286 and p295.*

**Sightseeing**

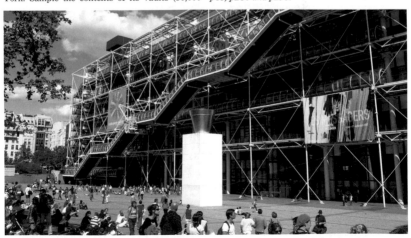

Inside out: Richard Rogers' spectacular **Centre Pompidou**.

## Hôtel de Ville

*29 rue de Rivoli, 4th (01.42.76.43.43/www.paris.fr).*
*M° Hôtel de Ville.* **Open** 10am-7pm Mon-Sat.
**Map** p406 K6.

Rebuilt by Ballu after the Commune, the palatial, multi-purpose Hôtel de Ville is both the heart of the city administration and a place to entertain visiting dignitaries. Free exhibitions are held in the Salon d'Accueil (open 10am-6pm Mon-Fri); the rest of the building, accessible only by weekly guided tours (book in advance), features parquet floors, marble statues, crystal chandeliers and painted ceilings.

## Tour St-Jacques

*Square de La-Tour-St-Jacques, 4th. M° Châtelet.*
**Map** p406 J6.

Loved by the Surrealists, this solitary Flamboyant Gothic belltower with its leering gargoyles is all that remains of the St-Jacques-La-Boucherie church, built for the powerful Butchers' Guild in 1508-22. The statue of Blaise Pascal at the base commemorates his experiments on atmospheric pressure, carried out here in the 17th century. A weather station now crowns the 52m (171ft) tower, not open to the public.

## The Marais

*In the 3rd & 4th arrondissements.*

The narrow streets of the Marais contain aristocratic *hôtels particuliers*, art galleries, boutiques and stylish cafés, with beautiful carved doorways and early street signs carved into the stone. The Marais, or 'marsh', started life as a piece of swampy ground inhabited by a few monasteries, sheep and market gardens. This was one of the last parts of central Paris to be built up. In the 16th century the elegant Hôtel Carnavalet and Hôtel Lamoignon sparked the area's phenomenal rise as an aristocratic residential district; Henri IV began building **place des Vosges** in 1605. Nobles and royal officials followed, building smart townhouses where literary ladies such as Mme de Sévigné held court. The area fell from fashion a century later; many of the narrow streets remained unchanged as mansions were transformed into workshops, crafts studios, schools, tenements, and even, on rue de Sévigné, a fire station. Several can be visited as museums, others can be seen only on walking tours or during the **Journées du Patrimoine** (*see p277*). The Marais is a favourite spot for a Sunday stroll, as many of the shops are open – though if you come during the week you have more chance of wandering into some of the elegant courtyards.

Rue des Francs-Bourgeois, crammed with impressive mansions and original boutiques, runs like a backbone right through the Marais, becoming more aristocratic as it leaves the food shops of rue Rambuteau behind. Two of the most refined early 18th-century residences are

Hôtel d'Albret (no.31), a venue for jazz concerts during the **Paris Quartier d'été** festival (*see p277*), and the palatial Hôtel de Soubise (no.60), the national archives. Begun in 1704 for the Prince and Princesse de Soubise, it has interiors by Boucher and Lemoine and currently hosts the **Musée de l'Histoire de France**, along with the neighbouring Hôtel de Rohan. There's also a surprising series of rose gardens. On one side of its colonnaded Cour d'Honneur, architect Delamair incorporated the turreted, medieval gateway of the Hôtel de Clisson, visible on rue des Archives. Facing the Archives Nationaux, the Crédit Municipal (no.55) still acts as a sort of municipal pawnshop: people bring in goods for cash; items never reclaimed are sold off at auction. On the corner of rue Pavée is the austere Renaissance Hôtel Lamoignon, with a magisterial courtyard adorned with Corinthian pilasters. Built in 1585, it now contains the Bibliothèque Historique de la Ville de Paris (no.24, 01.44.59.29.40). Further up, the **Musée Carnavalet** runs across the Hôtel Carnavalet and the Hôtel le Peletier de St-Fargeau. The Hôtel Carnavalet set the pattern for many of the *hôtels* to follow, with its U-shaped plan behind an entrance courtyard; the façade reliefs of the four seasons are possibly by Jean Goujon.

At its eastern end, rue des Francs-Bourgeois leads into the beautiful brick-and-stone place des Vosges. At one corner is the **Maison de Victor Hugo**, where the writer lived from 1833 to 1848. An archway in the south-west corner leads to the **Hôtel de Sully**, accommodating the Patrimoine Photographique. Designed in 1624, the building belonged to Henri IV's minister, the Duc de Sully. Its two beautifully proportioned courtyards contain reliefs of the four seasons and a rare, surviving orangery.

Several other important museums are also found in sumptuous *hôtels*. The Hôtel Salé on rue de Thorigny, built in 1656, was nicknamed ('salty') after its owner, Fontenay, who collected the salt tax. Beautifully restored and extended to house the **Musée National Picasso**, it has an elegant courtyard adorned with sphinxes and a baroque stairwell carved with garlands, imperial busts and gambolling cupids. Nearby, the pretty Hôtel Donon, built in 1598, contains the **Musée Cognacq-Jay** with its remarkable 18th-century panelled interiors, while the Hôtel Guénégaud contains the **Musée de la Chasse et de la Nature** hunting museum.

The Marais has also long been a focus for the Jewish community (*see p134* **Kosher quarter**). Jews were expelled from France in the Middle Ages, but when they were granted citizenship after the Revolution, the Marais became their point of arrival. Today Jewish businesses are clustered along rue des Rosiers,

rue des Ecouffes and rue Pavée (where there's a synagogue designed by Guimard). Originally made up mainly of Ashkenazi Jews, who fled the pogroms in Eastern Europe at the end of the 19th century (many were later deported during World War II), the community expanded in the 1950s and '60s with a wave of Sephardic Jewish immigration after French withdrawal from North Africa. As a result, there are now many falafel shops alongside long-established Central European Jewish bakers and delis such as **Finkelsztajn** (*see p263*).

The lower ends of rue des Archives and rue Vieille-du-Temple are the centre of café life – including **Petit Fer à Cheval** and **La Perle** (for both, *see p229*) – and the hub of the gay scene. Bars such as the **Open Café** (*see p307*) draw gay crowds for the early-evening happy hour. In their midst, at 22-26 rue des Archives, the 15th-century Cloître des Billettes is the only surviving Gothic cloister in Paris.

Workaday rue du Temple is full of surprises. Near rue de Rivoli, cinema **Le Latina** (*see p297*) specialises in Latin American films and holds tango balls in the room above. At no.41, an archway leads into the former Aigle d'Or coaching inn, now the **Café de la Gare** café-théâtre (*see p281*). Further north, at no.71, the grandiose Hôtel de St-Aignan, built in 1650, contains the **Musée d'Art et d'Histoire du Judaïsme**. The majestic courtyard with giant Corinthian pilasters, oval galleried staircase and traces of fresco in the café hint at just how splendid this must have been before it was converted into a town hall, workshops and a warren of apartments, prior to being rescued in the 1990s. The top end of rue du Temple and adjoining streets such as rue des Gravilliers are packed with costume jewellery, handbag and rag-trade wholesalers in what is the city's oldest Chinatown. The Quartier du Temple was once a fortified, semi-independent entity under the Knights Templar, until the order grew so powerful it rivalled the monarchy and was suppressed in 1313. Their Tour du Temple, a monastery under the Knights Hospitalier de St-Jean, became a prison in the Revolution, and held the royal family in 1792. The church and keep have been replaced by square du Temple and the Carreau du Temple clothes market.

The north-west corner of the Marais hinges on the **Musée des Arts et Métiers**, a science museum with early flying machines displayed in the 12th-century chapel of the former priory of St-Martin-des-Champs, and the adjoining Conservatoire des Arts et Métiers. Across rue St-Martin on square Emile-Chautemps, the Théâtre de la Gaîté Lyrique is currently undergoing renovation and will reopen in 2010 as a centre for contemporary music and the

'digital arts'. Among the ancient buildings here, no.3 rue Volta, once considered the oldest house in Paris, is now thought to date from the early 17th century, in defiance of the then laws against half-timbered structures. A much older house is at 51 rue de Montmorency, built in 1407 by notorious alchemist Nicolas Flamel.

Despite the Marais' rise to fashion, the less gentrified streets around the northern stretch of rue Vieille-du-Temple towards place de la République are awash with designers on the rise and old craft workshops (*see p249* **Marais à la mode**). Rue Charlot, housing an occasional contemporary art gallery at the passage de Retz at no.9 (01.48.04.37.99), is typical of the prevailing trend. At the top, the Marché des Enfants-Rouges (once an orphanage whose inhabitants were attired in red uniforms) is one of the city's oldest markets, founded in 1615 (*see p261* **Market forces**).

### Hôtel de Sully
*62 rue St-Antoine, 4th (01.42.74.47.75). M° St-Paul.* **Open** noon-6.30pm Tue-Fri; 10am-6.30pm Sat, Sun. **Admission** €5; €2.50 reductions. **Credit** MC, V. **Map** p409 L7.
Along with the Jeu de Paume (*see p105*), the former Patrimoine Photographique forms part of the two-site home for the Centre National de la Photographie.

### Maison de Victor Hugo
*Hôtel de Rohan-Guéménée, 6 pl des Vosges, 4th (01.42.72.10.16/www.paris.fr/musees). M° Bastille or St-Paul.* **Open** 10am-6pm Tue-Sun. **Admission** free. *Exhibitions* prices vary. **Credit** MC, V. **Map** p409 L6.
Victor Hugo lived here from 1833-48, and today the house is a museum devoted to the life and work of France's favourite son. On display are his first editions, nearly 500 drawings and, more bizarrely, the great man's home-made furniture.

### Musée d'Art et d'Histoire du Judaïsme
*Hôtel de St-Aignan, 71 rue du Temple, 3rd (01.53.01.86.60/www.mahj.org). M° Rambuteau.* **Open** 11am-6pm Mon-Fri; 10am-6pm Sun. Closed Jewish hols. **Admission** €6.80; €4.50 18-26s; free under-18s. **Credit** Shop MC, V. **Map** p409 K6.
It is fitting that a museum of Judaism should be lodged in one of the grandest mansions of the Marais, for centuries the epicentre of local Jewish life (*see p134* **Kosher quarter**). It sprung from the collection of a private association formed in 1948 to safeguard Jewish heritage after the Holocaust. Pick up a free audio-guide in English to help you navigate through displays illustrating ceremonies, rites and learning, and showing how styles were adapted across the globe through examples of Jewish decorative arts. Photographic portraits of modern French Jews, each of whom tells his or her own story on the audio soundtrack, bring a contemporary edge. There are documents and paintings relating to the emancipation of French Jewry after the

# Kosher quarter

The closure in 2006 of Jo Goldenberg's famous Paris restaurant and delicatessen in rue des Rosiers marked the end of an era in the history of the city's Jewish community. This narrow street in the Marais had been the focus of Jewish life in Paris since shortly after the Revolution, when Jews were granted full citizenship rights. From the second half of the 19th century, the surrounding area, known in Yiddish as the 'pletzl' (or 'little place'), saw waves of Ashkenazi Jewish immigrants fleeing pogroms in Poland and the Hapsburg Empire. Between the wars cultural and commercial life in the 'pletzl' flourished – a renaissance that was brutally cut short by the rounding-up and subsequent deportation of French Jews by the Nazis (with the collusion of the French police) in 1941 and 1942. Along with other Ashkenazi bakers and delis, Goldenberg's, which opened in the early 1950s, was a relic of a way of life that had for the most part disappeared – more or less overnight.

The area retained its Jewish character after the war, though by the late 1950s it was the accents and manners of the Maghreb, rather than *Mitteleuropa*, that predominated as Sephardic Jewish immigrants from Tunisia set up businesses here. Today, a handful of shops still selling 'Yiddish sandwiches' cling on as falafel joints multiply seemingly by the day.

In fact, the demise of Goldenberg's merely confirmed that the real centre of Jewish Paris now lies to the north-east, in Belleville. It was there, in a working-class neighbourhood that had already welcomed the Ashkenazi overflow from the Marais, that most of the Tunisian Jews settled in the 1950s and '60s. Walk along and you'll pass a succession of kosher butchers, delicatessens and restaurants all run by Jews of Tunisian origin.

Revolution and the Dreyfus case, from Zola's *J'Accuse!* to anti-Semitic cartoons. Paintings by the early 20th-century avant-garde include works by El Lissitsky and Chagall. The Holocaust is marked by Boris Taslitzky's stark sketches from Buchenwald and Christian Boltanski's courtyard memorial to the Jews who lived in the building in 1939, 13 of whom died in the camps.

## Musée des Arts et Métiers

*60 rue Réaumur, 3rd (01.53.01.82.00/www.arts-et-metiers.net). M° Arts et Métiers.* **Open** 10am-6pm Tue, Wed, Fri-Sun; 10am-9.30pm Thur. **Admission** €6.50; €4.50 students; free under-18s. PMP. **Credit** V. **Map** p402 K5.

After the monks of St-Martin-des-Champs lost their heads in the Revolution, Abbé Henri Grégoire kept his by thinking up a new use for the building – as a repository of technological marvels that could act as a 3D encyclopedia for investors and industrialists in the new republic. The collection has since expanded to fill three floors of a neighbouring modern building with glass cases of beautifully crafted scientific instruments, from astrolabes to steam engines, plus reconstructions of famous inventors' workshops. It's pretty dry and static, though, and not child-friendly. The exception is the restored church, the earliest example of Paris Gothic, which removes invention from the realm of science and presents it as some sort of divinely inspired alchemy. Here, in soaring ecclesiastical surrounds, you'll find an original Foucault's Pendulum, set in motion at noon and 5pm daily, Blériot's biplane, a model of Bartholdi's Statue of Liberty and Alain Prost's Formula 1 Renault.

## Musée Carnavalet

*23 rue de Sévigné, 3rd (01.44.59.58.58/www.paris.fr/musees). M° St-Paul.* **Open** 10am-6pm Tue-Sun. **Admission** free. *Exhibitions* €7; €5.50 over-60s; €3.50 14-26s; free under-13s. **Credit** *Shop* AmEx, MC, V. **Map** p409 L6.

Here, 140 chronological rooms depict the history of Paris, from pre-Roman Gaul to the 20th century. Built in 1548 and transformed by Mansart in 1660, this fine house became a museum in 1866, when Haussmann persuaded the city to preserve its beautiful interiors. Original 16th-century rooms house Renaissance collections, with portraits by Clouet

Sightseeing

and furniture and pictures relating to the Wars of Religion. The first floor covers the period up to 1789, with furniture and paintings displayed in restored, period interiors; neighbouring Hôtel Le Peletier de St-Fargeau covers the period from 1789 onwards. Displays relating to 1789 detail that year's convoluted politics and bloodshed, with prints and memorabilia, including a chunk of the Bastille prison. There are items belonging to Napoleon, a cradle given by the city to Napoleon III, and Proust's cork-lined bedroom.

## Musée de la Chasse et de la Nature

*Hôtel Guénégaud, 62 rue des Archives, 3rd (01.53.01.92.40/www.chassenature.org). M° Rambuteau.* **Open** 11am-6pm Tue-Sun. **Admission** €6; €4.50 18-25s; free under-18s. **Map** p409 K5.

Housed on three floors of a 17th-century mansion, this museum reopened in 2007 after a two-year overhaul. It's a store of everything from ornate hunting weapons to studies by Alexandre-François Desportes, including his portrait of Louis XIV's hunting dogs.

## Musée Cognacq-Jay

*Hôtel Donon, 8 rue Elzévir, 3rd (01.40.27.07.21/www.paris.fr/musees). M° St-Paul.* **Open** 10am-6pm Tue-Sun. **Admission** free. **Map** p409 L6.

This cosy museum houses a collection put together in the early 1900s by La Samaritaine founder Ernest Cognacq and his wife Marie-Louise Jay. They stuck mainly to 18th-century French works, focusing on rococo artists such as Watteau, Fragonard, Boucher, Greuze and pastellist Quentin de la Tour, though some English artists (Reynolds, Romney, Lawrence) and Dutch and Flemish names (an early Rembrandt, Ruysdael, Rubens), plus Canalettos and Guardis, have managed to slip in. Pictures are displayed in panelled rooms with furniture, porcelain, tapestries and sculpture of the same period.

## Musée de l'Histoire de France

*Hôtel de Soubise, 60 rue des Francs-Bourgeois, 3rd (01.40.27.60.96/www.archivesnationales.culture. gouv.fr/chan). M° Hôtel de Ville or Rambuteau.* **Open** 10am-12.30pm, 2-5.30pm Mon, Wed-Fri; 2-5.30pm Sat, Sun. **Admission** €3; €2.30 18-25s; free under-18s. **Credit** V. **Map** p409 K6.

Generally housed in one of the grandest Marais mansions, the Hôtel de Rohan, this museum is currently undergoing renovation. In the meantime, documents and artefacts covering everything from the founding of the Sorbonne to an ordinance about umbrellas are displayed in the neighbouring Hôtel de Soubise. Its rococo interiors, decorated for the Prince and Princesse de Soubise in the 1730s, feature paintings by Boucher and van Loo.

## Musée National Picasso

*Hôtel Salé, 5 rue de Thorigny, 3rd (01.42.71.25.21/www.musee-picasso.fr). M° Chemin Vert or St-Paul.* **Open** Oct-Mar 9.30am-5.30pm Mon, Wed-Sun. Apr-Sept 9.30am-6pm Mon, Wed-Sun. **Admission** €6.50 Mon-Sat; €4.50 Sun; free under-18s, 1st Sun

of mth. PMP. *Exhibitions* prices vary. **Credit** *Shop* AmEx, MC, V. **Map** p409 L6.

Picasso's paintings, sculptures, collages, drawings and ceramics are shown off in style in this stately Marais mansion, complete with sweeping staircase. The collection, donated to the state by Picasso's family in lieu of inheritance tax, gives a panorama of his career from precocious early sketches to later stylistic whimsies, via delightful oddities such as a papier-mâché goat. Many of the 'greatest hits' hang in other state-owned Paris museums, but to get a feeling for Picasso's artistic development this is the best resource in the city. (Photography, one of his late conquests, is the only under-represented medium.) From a haunting, blue-period self-portrait and rough studies for the *Demoiselles d'Avignon*, the collection moves to Picasso's Cubist and classical phases, the surreal *Nude in an Armchair* and assorted portraits of his abundant lovers, in particular Marie-Thérèse and Dora Maar. A small covered sculpture garden displays pieces that sat around Picasso's studio until his death, and there is a pleasant summer café.

## Place des Vosges

*4th. M° St-Paul.* **Map** p409 L6.

Paris's first planned square was commissioned in 1605 by Henri IV and inaugurated by his son Louis XIII in 1612. With harmonious red-brick-and-stone arcaded façades and steeply pitched slate roofs, it differs from the later pomp of the Bourbons. Laid out symmetrically with carriageways through the taller Pavillon de la Reine on the north side and Pavillon du Roi on the south, the other lots were sold off as concessions to royal officials and nobles (some façades are imitation brick). It was called place Royale prior to the Napoleonic Wars, when the Vosges was the first region of France to pay its war taxes. Mme de Sévigné, salon hostess and letter-writer, was born at no.1bis in 1626. At that time the garden hosted duels and trysts; now it attracts children from nearby nursery school.

## The St-Paul district

In 1559 Henri II was fatally wounded jousting on today's rue St-Antoine, marked by Pilon's marble *La Vierge de Douleur* in the **Eglise St-Paul-St-Louis**. South of rue St-Antoine is the sedate residential area of St-Paul, lined with dignified 17th- and 18th-century façades. The linked courtyards of Village St-Paul house antiques sellers (*see p269*). On rue des Jardins-St-Paul is the largest surviving section of the **fortified wall of Philippe-Auguste** (www.philippe-auguste.com), complete with towers. King Philippe-Auguste (1165-1223), the first great Paris builder since the Romans, enclosed his city within this great wall; another chunk is at 3 rue Clovis (5th), and odd remnants of towers are dotted around the Marais, rue du Louvre and St-Germain-des-Prés. The infamous poisoner Marquise de Brinvilliers, who killed

**Sightseeing**

her father and brothers to inherit the family fortune, lived at Hôtel de Brinvilliers (12 rue Charles-V) in the 1630s.

By St-Paul métro station on the corner of rue François-Miron and rue de Fourcy is the Hôtel Hénault de Cantorbe, renovated and given a minimalist modern extension as the **Maison Européenne de la Photographie**. Down rue de Fourcy towards the river, across a medieval formal garden, you can see the rear façade of the Hôtel de Sens, a rare medieval mansion built as the Paris residence of the Archbishops of Sens in the 15th century, with a lovely array of turrets. It houses the **Bibliothèque Forney** (1 rue du Figuier, 01.42.78.14.60, closed Mon & Sun), specialising in exhibitions of applied arts and graphic design.

Near Pont Sully are square Henri-Galli, with a rebuilt piece of Bastille prison, and the **Pavillon de l'Arsenal**, built by a rich timber merchant to put on art shows, and home to displays relating to Paris architecture.

Winding rue François-Miron leads you back towards the Hôtel de Ville. At 17 rue Geoffroy-l'Asnier, the Mémorial du Martyr Juif Inconnu is being extended as part of the **Mémorial de la Shoah**, a museum, memorial and study centre devoted to the Holocaust that opened in 2005. As you pass no.26, note the Cité des Arts complex of artists' studios, and the ornate lion's head and giant shell motif on the doorway of the 17th-century Hôtel de Châlon-Luxembourg. At 11 and 13 rue François-Miron, two half-timbered houses probably date from the 14th century, although they were heavily rebuilt in the 1960s. Rue du Pont-Louis-Philippe contains jewellers, designer furniture and gift shops, while stepped rue des Barres boasts tearooms overlooking the spiky chevet of the **Eglise St-Gervais-St-Protais**.

### Eglise St-Gervais-St-Protais
*Pl St-Gervais, 4th (01.48.87.32.02). Mº Hôtel de Ville.* **Open** times vary. **Map** p409 K6.
Gothic at the rear and classical at the front, this church also has an impressive Flamboyant Gothic interior, most of which dates from the 16th century. The nave gives an impression of enormous height, with tall columns that soar up to the vault. There are plenty of fine funerary monuments, especially the baroque statue of Chancellor Le Tellier.

### Eglise St-Paul-St-Louis
*99 rue St-Antoine, 4th (01.42.72.30.32). Mº St-Paul.* **Open** 8am-8pm daily. **Map** p409 L7.
This domed baroque Counter-Reformation church is modelled, like all Jesuit churches, on the Chiesa del Gesù in Rome. Completed in 1641, it features a single nave, side chapels and a three-storey hierarchical façade featuring statues of Saints Louis, Anne and Catherine – all replacements. The provider of

confessors to the kings of France, the Eglise St-Paul-St-Louis was richly endowed until Revolutionary iconoclasts pinched its treasures, including the hearts of Louis XIII and XIV. Afterwards, in 1802, it was converted back into a church, and today it houses Delacroix's *Christ in the Garden of Olives*.

### Maison Européenne de la Photographie
*5-7 rue de Fourcy, 4th (01.44.78.75.00/www.mep-fr.org). Mº St-Paul.* **Open** 11am-7.30pm Wed-Sun. **Admission** €6; €3 students, 8-26s; free under-8s, all 5-8pm Wed. **Credit** MC, V. **Map** p409 L6.
Probably the capital's best photographic centre, hosting retrospectives by Larry Clark and Martine Barrat, along with work by emerging photographers. The building, an airy mansion with a modern extension, contains a huge permanent collection. The venue organises the biennial Mois de la Photo and the Art Outsiders festival of new media web art in September.

### Le Mémorial de la Shoah
*17 rue Geoffroy-l'Asnier, 4th (01.42.77.44.72/ www.memorialdelashoah.org). Mº St-Paul or Pont Marie.* **Open** 10am-6pm Mon-Wed, Fri-Sun; 10am-10pm Thur. *Research centre* 10am-5.30pm Mon-Wed, Fri, Sun; 10am-7.30pm Thur. **Admission** free. **Map** p409 K6.
Airport-style security checks mean queues, but don't let that put you off. The Mémorial du Martyr Juif Inconnu is an impressively presented and moving memorial to the Holocaust. Enter via the Wall of Names, where limestone slabs are engraved with the first and last names of each of the 76,000 Jews deported from France from 1942 to 1944 with, as an inscription reminds the visitor, the say-so of the Vichy government. The excoriation continues in the basement-level permanent exhibition, which documents the plight of French and European Jews through photographs, written texts, films and individual stories: 'The French,' reads one label (captioning is also handily given in English), 'were not particularly interested in the fate of French Jews at this point.' Expect to spend the remainder of your day in deep contemplation.

### Pavillon de l'Arsenal
*21 bd Morland, 4th (01.42.76.33.97/www.pavillon-arsenal.com). Mº Sully Morland.* **Open** 10.30am-6.30pm Tue-Sat; 11am-7pm Sun. **Admission** free. **Credit** *Shop* MC, V. **Map** p409 L7.
The setting is a fantastic 1880s gallery with an iron frame and glass roof; the subject is the built history of Paris; the result is disappointing. The ground floor houses a permanent exhibition on the city's development, but space and funds are lacking to the extent that exhibits are limited to a few storyboards, maps and photos, and three city models set into the floor (done far more impressively at the Musée d'Orsay). Upstairs you'll find temporary displays on local building projects, a library and a *vidéothèque*.

# Bastille & Eastern Paris

Revolutionary tradition, a lively bar scene and lots of green space characterise this corner of the city.

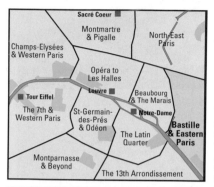

## Bastille

*Mainly in the 11th and 12th arrondissements.*
**Place de la Bastille** has been a potent symbol of popular rebellion ever since the storming of the eponymous prison that inaugurated the Revolution in 1789. Although still a gathering point for demonstrations, as well as being the setting for the Bastille Day ball every July (*see p277*), the area was transformed in the 1980s with the arrival of the **Opéra Bastille** (*see p315*) along with fashionable cafés, restaurants and bars. The site of the prison itself is now a bank, while the gap left by the prison ramparts forms the present-day square, dominated by the imposing curved façade of the Opéra. Opened in 1989 on the bicentenary of Bastille Day, the venue remains controversial, criticised for its poor acoustics and design. South of the square is the Port de l'Arsenal marina, where the Canal St-Martin meets the Seine. The canal continues underground north of the square, running beneath boulevard Richard-Lenoir, site of a lively outdoor market on Sunday mornings.

Rue du Fbg-St-Antoine has been the heart of the furniture-makers' district for centuries. Gaudy furniture showrooms still line the street, though they now compete with clothes shops and bars. Cobbled rue de Lappe typifies the shift, as the last remaining furniture workshops hold out against theme bars overrun at weekends by suburban adolescents. Pockets of bohemian resistance remain on rue de

Charonne, however, with the Pause Café (*see p231*) and its busy terrace, bistro Chez Paul (No.13, 11th, 01.47.00.34.57) and dealers in colourful 1960s furniture. Rues des Taillandiers and Keller are a focus for record stores, streetwear shops and fashion designers.

Narrow street frontages hide cobbled alleys, lined with craftsmen's workshops or quirky bistros dating from the 18th century. Note the cours de l'Ours, du Cheval Blanc, du Bel Air (and hidden garden) and de la Maison Brûlée, the passage du Chantier on rue du Fbg-St-Antoine, the rustic-looking passage de l'Etoile d'Or and the passage de l'Homme, with wooden shopfronts on rue de Charonne. This area was originally located outside the city walls on the lands of the Convent of St-Antoine (parts of which survive as the Hôpital St-Antoine). In the Middle Ages, skilled furnituremakers not belonging to the city's restrictive guilds earned the neighbourhood a reputation for free thinking that was cemented a few hundred years later during the Revolution.

Further down rue du Fbg-St-Antoine is place d'Aligre, home to a rowdy, cheap produce market, a more sedate covered food hall (*see p261* **Market forces**) and the only flea market within the city walls, where a handful of *brocanteurs* sell junk and old books. The road ends in the major intersection of place de la Nation, another grand square. It was originally called place du Trône, after a throne that was positioned here when Louis XIV and his bride Marie-Thérèse entered the city in 1660. After the Revolution, between 13 June and 28 July 1799, thousands were guillotined on the site, their bodies carted to the nearby **Picpus Cemetery** (*see p139*). The square still has two of Ledoux's toll houses and tall Doric columns from the 1787 Mur des Fermiers-Généraux. In the centre stands Jules Dalou's sculpture *Le Triomphe de la République*, erected for the centenary of the Revolution in 1889. East of place de la Nation, broad cours de Vincennes has a market on Wednesday and Saturday mornings and kerb-crawlers by night.

North of place de la Bastille, boulevard Beaumarchais divides Bastille from the Marais. East of place Voltaire, on rue de la Roquette, which heads east towards the **Ménilmontant**

# Homing instinct

Like many of the city's green spaces, the square de la Roquette near Père-Lachaise has always attracted its fair share of pigeons. Now, though, the 11th arrondissement garden has gone one step further by providing the birds with their very own home. This is no attempt to boost local communications by honing a fleet of message-carrying pigeons; rather, the new pigeon house is part of a city-wide strategy to control the pigeon population and put a stop to avian pollution.

The Mairie de Paris plans to build a so-called 'pigeonnier contraceptif' in each of the city's 20 arrondissements, picking out locations that are particularly blighted by infestations of feral birds. Thanks to the pigeon houses, city officials can more easily control the growth of the pigeon population.

In each pigeonnier, only the first batch of eggs each year is left to hatch; subsequent batches (usually six to eight per female pigeon) are neutralised and then replaced in the nest, in order to encourage the birds to stay. The pigeon houses also allow municipal authorities to monitor the birds' health and to quickly remove any carcasses.

The initiative was conceived as a response to the nuisances caused by the city's estimated 80,000 pigeons. Foremost among these inconveniences is, you've guessed it,

bird shit. Beyond their obvious unsightliness, pigeon droppings are highly acidic, which means they can cause serious damage to the stonework used in most traditional Paris buildings. The birds can also transmit diseases to humans, including salmonella and respiratory infections.

In response to the problem pigeons, the Mairie set up a trial pigeon house back in 2003 at Porte de Vanves. As well as providing a humanitarian way to restrict local pigeon numbers, the pilot pigeonnier proved highly effective in allowing officials to clean up droppings, which were always concentrated around the nest. Following the success of this trial, it was decided to make pigeon houses a city-wide feature.

For the pigeonnier at square de la Roquette, around 60 pigeons were initially captured and placed in the house. After a month's acclimatisation period, during which the birds were kept locked inside, the wooden box was reopened. With a large number of pigeons now firmly installed, a park official stops by once a week to top up food and water supplies, and to wipe down the surrounding area. Pigeon lovers should be warned that only authorised personnel are allowed to feed the pigeons; those caught thowing crumbs to the birds face a fine of up to €450.

area (*see p145*) and **Père-Lachaise** cemetery (*see p146*), a small park and playground marks the site of the prison de la Roquette, where a plaque remembers the 4,000 Resistance members imprisoned here in World War II.

## La Maison Rouge – Fondation Antoine de Galbert

*10 bd de la Bastille, 12th (01.40.01.08.81/www.la maisonrouge.org). M° Quai de la Rapée.* **Open** 11am-7pm Wed-Sun. **Admission** €6.50; €4.50 students, 13-25s; free under-13s. **Credit** MC, V. **Map** p406 M7.
Founded by collector Antoine de Galberg, and set in a former printworks, the Red House is an independently run space that alternates monographic shows of contemporary artists' work with pieces from different private art collections.

## Place de la Bastille

*4th/11th/12th. M° Bastille.* **Map** p407 M7.
Nothing remains of the prison that, on 14 July 1789, was stormed by revolutionary forces. Though there were only seven prisoners left, the event provided the rebels with arms and gave the insurrection momentum. The prison was quickly torn down, its stones used to build Pont de la Concorde. Parts of the foundations can be seen in the métro, while some of the reconstructed tower stands at sq Henri-Galli, near Pont de Sully (4th). The Colonne de Juillet, topped by a gilded *génie* of Liberty, is a monument to Parisians who fell in the revolutions of July 1830 and 1848.

# Bercy & Daumesnil

The **Viaduc des Arts** is a former railway viaduct along av Daumesnil; its glass-fronted arches enclose a row of craft boutiques and workshops. Above sprout the blooms and bamboo of the **Promenade Plantée**, which continues through the Jardin de Reuilly and east to the **Bois de Vincennes**.

Eglise du St-Esprit is a copy of Istanbul's Hagia Sofia, while the nearby **Cimetière de Picpus** contains the graves of many of the victims of the Terror, as well as American War of Independence hero General La Fayette. Just before the Périphérique, the **Palais de la Porte Dorée** was built in 1931 for the Exposition Coloniale. It features striking, if politically incorrect, reliefs on the façade and two beautiful art deco offices designed by Ruhlmann. Originally the Musée des Colonies, then the Musée des Arts d'Afrique et d'Océanie (its collections now absorbed by the Musée du Quai Branly, *see p171* **Windows on the world**), it is the new home of the **Cité Nationale de l'Histoire de l'Immigration**. There's also an aquarium in the basement.
As recently as the 1980s, wine was unloaded from barges at Bercy, but after redevelopment this stretch of the Seine is now home to the vast

Ministère de l'Economie et du Budget and, to the west, the **Palais Omnisports de Paris-Bercy** (*see p318* and *p333*). To the east is the Bercy Expo exhibition and trade centre. In between lie the modern **Parc de Bercy** and the former American Center, built in the 1990s by Frank Gehry. It has since reopened as the **Cinémathèque Française** (*see p295* **A sanctuary for cinephiles**). At the eastern edge of the park is **Bercy Village**, where warehouses have been restored and opened as shops and cafés. The result is lively, if somewhat antiseptic; typical is mainstream **Club Med World** (*see p331*). Another conversion is the Pavillons de Bercy, with the **Musée des Arts Forains**, a collection of fairground rides and carnival salons.

## Bois de Vincennes

*12th. M° Château de Vincennes or Porte Dorée.*
This is Paris's biggest park, created, like the Bois de Boulogne in the west, when the former royal hunting forest was landscaped by Alphand for Baron Haussmann. There are boating lakes, a Buddhist temple, a racetrack, restaurants, a baseball field (*see p336*) and a small farm. The park also contains the city's main zoo (*see p288*), now largely closed because of lack of maintenance, and the Cartoucherie theatre complex (*see p342*). The Parc Floral (*see p285*) is a cross between a botanical garden and an amusement park. Jazz (*see p323*) and classical concerts take place on summer weekends. Amusements include Paris-themed crazy golf, with water drawn from the Seine, plus an adventure playground. Next to the park stands the imposing Château de Vincennes, where England's Henry V died in 1422.

## Cimetière de Picpus

*35 rue de Picpus, 12th (01.43.44.18.54). M° Daumesnil, Nation or Picpus.* **Open** 15 Apr-14 Oct 2-6pm Tue-Sun. 15 Oct-14 Apr 2-4pm Tue-Sun. **Admission** €2.50. **No credit cards. Map** p407 Q8.
Redolent with revolutionary associations, both French and American, this cemetery in a working convent is the resting place for the thousands of victims of the Revolution's aftermath, guillotined at place du Trône (now place de l'Ile-de-la-Réunion) between 14 June and 27 July 1794. At the end of a walled garden is a graveyard of aristocratic French families. In one corner is the tomb of General La Fayette, who fought in the American War of Independence and was married to the aristocratic Marie Adrienne Françoise de Noailles. Clearly marked are the sites of two communal graves, and you can discern the doorway where the carts arrived. It was only thanks to a maid who had seen the carts that the site was rediscovered, including the cemetery and adjoining convent, founded by descendants of the Noailles family. In the chapel, two tablets list the names and occupations of the executed: 'domestic', 'farmer' and 'employee' figure alongside 'lawyer' and 'prince and priest'.

Parc de Bercy.

## Cité Nationale de l'Histoire de l'Immigration – Palais de la Porte Dorée

*293 av Daumesnil, 12th (01.58.51.52.00/www. histoire-immigration.fr). M° Porte Dorée.* **Open** 10am-5.30pm Tue-Fri; 10am-7pm Sat-Sun. **Admission** €3; €2 18-25s; free under-18s. *Aquarium* €4.50; €3 under-25s. **PMP. No credit cards.**
Until recently the old Musée des Arts d'Afrique et d'Océanie was the temporary home of the Cité de l'Architecture, since moved to the Palais de Chaillot *(see p117)*. It now houses a new Ellis Island-style museum devoted to the history of immigration in France. Designed for the 1931 Exposition Coloniale, this fine building has an art deco bas-relief glorying in France's colonial past. However, the museum's collection, comprising photographs, artworks and objects belonging to immigrants, offers a different version of the last two centuries of French history.

## Eglise du St-Esprit

*186 av Daumesnil, 12th (01.44.75.77.50/www.st-esprit.org). M° Daumesnil.* **Open** 9.30am-noon, 3-7pm Mon-Fri; 9.30am-noon, 3-6pm Sat; from 9am Sun. **Map** p407 P9.
Behind a red-brick exterior cladding, this unusual 1920s concrete church follows a square plan around a central dome, lit by a scalloped ring of windows. Architect Paul Tournon was directly inspired by the Hagia Sofia cathedral in Istanbul, though rather than mosaics, the inside is decorated with frescoes by Maurice Denis and others.

## Musée des Arts Forains

*53 av des Terroirs-de-France, 12th (01.43.40.16.22/ www.pavillons-de-bercy.com). M° Cour St-Emilion.* **Open** groups only, min 15 people, by appointment. **Admission** €11.50. **No credit cards. Map** p407 P10.
Housed in a collection of Eiffel-era, iron-framed wine warehouses is a fantastical collection of 19th- and early 20th-century fairground attractions. The venue is hired out for functions on most evenings,

and staff may well be setting the tables when you visit. Of the three halls, the most wonderful is the Salon de la Musique, where a musical sculpture by Jacques Rémus chimes and flashes in time with the 1934 Mortier organ and a modern-day digital grand piano playing *Murder on the Orient Express*. In the Salon de Venise you are twirled round on a gondola carousel; in the Salon des Arts Forains you can play a ball-throwing game that sets off a race of moustachioed waiters or brave the Vélocipède, a nightmarish carousel of penny farthings. The venue is open only to groups of 15 or more, but individuals can visit as part of a guided tour. Call ahead.

## Parc de Bercy

*Rue de Bercy, 12th. M° Bercy or Cour St-Emilion.* **Open** *Winter* 8am-5.30pm Mon-Fri; 9am-5.30pm Sat, Sun. *Summer* 8am-9pm Mon-Fri; 9am-9pm Sat, Sun. **Map** p407 N9/10.
Created in the 1990s, the Bercy park features a large lawn, a grid with square rose, herb and vegetable plots, an orchard, and gardens laid out to represent the four seasons.

## La Promenade Plantée

*Av Daumesnil, 12th. M° Gare de Lyon or Ledru-Rollin.* **Map** p407 M8/N8.
The railway tracks atop the Viaduc des Arts were replaced in the late 1980s by a promenade planted with roses, shrubs and rosemary. It continues at ground level through the Jardin de Reuilly and the Jardin Charles Péguy on to the Bois de Vincennes.

## Le Viaduc des Arts

*15-121 av Daumesnil, 12th (www.viaduc-des-arts.com). M° Gare de Lyon or Ledru-Rollin.* **Map** p407 M8/N8.
Glass-fronted workshops in the arches beneath the Promenade Plantée provide a showroom for furniture and fashion designers, picture-frame gilders, tapestry restorers, porcelain decorators, and chandelier, violin and flute makers. Design industry body VIA holds exhibitions of work at Nos.29-35.

# North-east Paris

Home to some of the city's grandest arrivals and departures.

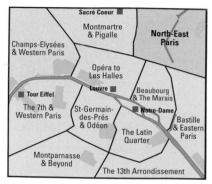

The other side of place de la République from the aristocratic Marais lies the more proletarian north-east. Here, charming *quartiers* stand cheek by jowl with grotty ones, and modern housing developments rub shoulders with relics from the old villages of Belleville, La Villette, Ménilmontant and Charonne.

## Fbg-St-Denis to Gare du Nord

*In the 10th arrondissement.*
North of Porte St-Denis and Porte St-Martin, two of the oldest thoroughfares leading out of the city, rue du Fbg-St-Denis and rue du Fbg-St-Martin, traverse an area that was transformed in the 19th century by the railways, when it became the site of the Gare du Nord and Gare de l'Est. The grubby rue du Fbg-St-Denis is almost souk-like with its food shops, narrow passages and sinister courtyards. Garishly lit passage Brady is a surprising piece of India in Paris, full of restaurants, hairdressers and costume shops, while the art deco passage du Prado is more a continuation of the Sentier rag trade. The rue du Fbg-St-Martin follows the trace of the Roman road out of the city, and is full of children's clothes wholesalers, atmospheric courtyards and the ornate Mairie for the tenth. Rue des Petites-Ecuries ('Little Stables Street') was once known for saddlers, but now has shops, cafés and jazz venue **New Morning** (*see p322*), and is home to Turkish and Afro-Caribbean communities.

Rue de Paradis is known for its porcelain and glass outlets, while rue d'Hauteville shows traces of the area's grander days (notably the **Petit Hôtel Bourrienne**, at no.58, a Consulaire-style apartment open to the public). Opposite, the Cité Paradis is an alley of early industrial buildings. At the top of the street are the twin towers and terraced gardens of the **Eglise St-Vincent-de-Paul**. Behind, on rue de Belzunce, are bistro **Chez Michel** (*see p208*) and offshoot Chez Casimir at no.6 (10th, 01.48.78.28.80). On boulevard Magenta, Marché St-Quentin, built in the 1860s, is one of the city's few remaining cast-iron, covered market halls.

Boulevard de Strasbourg was cut through in the 19th century to create a vista up to the Gare de l'Est. At no.2, a neo-Renaissance creation houses the last fan-maker in Paris and the **Musée de l'Eventail**. Towards the station, Eglise St-Laurent (69 bd de Magenta, 119 rue du Fbg-St-Martin, 10th) is one of the city's oldest churches, an eclectic composition with a 12th-century tower, Gothic nave, baroque lady chapel, 19th-century façade and 1930s stained glass. Between the Gare de l'Est and **Canal St-Martin** are the restored **Couvent des Récollets** and Square Villemin park.

### Couvent des Récollets

*148 rue du Fbg-St-Martin, 10th. Mº Gare de l'Est.*
**Map** p402 L3.
Founded as a monastery in the 17th century when still outside the city walls, this barracks, spinning factory and hospice was a military hospital from 1860 to 1968. Left empty, the convent was squatted by artists, Les Anges des Récollets, in the early 1990s. The buildings were renovated and reopened in 2004. One half, the Maison des Architectes, hosts a garden café and architectural debates. The other is the Centre International d'Accueil et d'Echanges des Récollets: 85 studios and duplexes for foreign 'creators' – artists and researchers (from painters to neurobiologists) – invited to stay here for extended periods. In rehabilitating the building, architect Frédéric Vincendon left traces of its history: the ghostly 17th-century stonework, 20th-century reinforced concrete columns and squatters' graffiti.

### Eglise St-Vincent-de-Paul

*5 rue Belzunce, 10th (01.48.78.47.47). Mº Gare du Nord.* **Open** 2-7pm Mon; 8am-noon, 2-7pm Tue-Fri; 8am-noon, 2-7.30pm Sat; 9.30am-noon, 4.30-7.30pm Sun. **Map** p402 K2.
Set at the top of terraced gardens, this church was begun in 1824 by Lepère and completed in 1844 by Hittorff. The twin towers, pedimented Greek temple portico and sculptures of the four evangelists along

# Street poetry

The English historian Richard Cobb, an inveterate Francophile, once observed that most of the literature about Paris – and there's a lot of it – is in fact set in the 'quarters and villages' that, jumbled together, make up the French capital. Even in a city as relatively compact as Paris, there's a strong sense of localism, with the individual *quartiers* retaining distinctive identities.

However, Cobb lamented the fact that *his* 'village', the tenth arrondissement, lacked an extensive literature when compared to the 'fashionable literary quarters' of Paris, or to working-class areas such as Belleville and Ménilmontant, which were patronised by 'populist' writers. It 'possesses no literature,' he wrote, and has been 'sung about by no

poet.' He was presumably thinking about Balzac, whose hymn to the mid-19th century shopping arcades depicts a 'great poem of display' stretching from 'the Madeleine to the gate of St-Denis', at the very threshold of the tenth arrondissement.

Cobb was too modest to mention either his essay 'Paris Xe', which was a memoir of his 1930s sojourn in a shabby-genteel family home at 26 boulevard Bonne-Nouvelle and an elegantly compressed history of the steep decline of a previously *haut-bourgeois* neighbourhood; or *The Streets of Paris*, in which his words accompanied Nicholas Breach's atmospheric photographs of hidden corners of the north-east of the city.

But now the tenth *does* have its own 'poet': an unexpected hit of the '*rentrée littéraire*' season in the autumn of 2007 was Thomas Clerc's book about the district, *Paris, musée du XXIe siècle*. It's a kind of urban travelogue, written as a paragraph-less stream of consciousness punctuated by brief '*poèmes de site*', verses written on the hoof that record Clerc's encounters as he tramps, in strict alphabetical order, the arrondissement's 155 streets, squares, avenues and boulevards.

Clerc's book mixes, in more or less equal measures, personal reminiscence (he recalls a former mistress of his who insisted on buying bread in Arab-owned bakeries, as a gesture of 'solidarity'), political economy and ethnography (an area whose pre-war population was predominantly eastern European and Jewish is now home to significant concentrations of immigrants from China, West Africa and the Maghreb). In doing so, Clerc does what Cobb hoped someone would one day do – he treats the tenth with the 'imaginative sympathy and careful observation' that has for many centuries been lavished on its more celebrated neighbours.

the parapet are in high classical mode. The interior has a splendid double-storey arcade of columns, murals by Flandrin and church furniture by Rude.

### Gare du Nord
*Rue de Dunkerque, 10th (08.91.36.20.20). M° Gare du Nord.* **Map** p402 K2.
The grandest of the great 19th-century train stations (and Eurostar terminal since 1994) was designed by Hittorff between 1861 and 1864. A conventional stone façade, with Ionic capitals and statues repre-

senting towns served by the station, hides a vast iron-and-glass vault. The airy refurbishment of the suburban section by rue du Fbg-St-Denis makes the Eurostar's glass-topped digs look a little drab.

### Musée de l'Eventail
*2 bd de Strasbourg, 10th (01.42.08.90.20/www.anne hoguet.fr). M° Strasbourg St-Denis.* **Open** 2-6pm Mon-Wed (Mon-Fri during school hols). *Children's activities* Wed afternoons. Closed Aug. **Admission** €6; €4 under-26s; €3 8-12s; free under-8s. **No credit cards.** **Map** p402 K4.

Anne Hoguet keeps the tradition of her ancestors alive in this arcane museum in a 19th-century apartment, a fan-maker's *atelier* since 1805. One room houses the tools of the trade; beside it is Hoguet's studio, where she works on fans for fashion and the stage. The former *salle d'exposition*, lined in blue silk, is where the collection of almost 1,000 historic fans – from 18th-century fans to modern versions – is shown in glass cases and stored in cabinets.

### Petit Hôtel Bourrienne

*58 rue d'Hauteville, 10th (01.47.70.51.14). M°*
*Bonne Nouvelle or Poissonnière.* **Open** *Guided visits*
*1-15 July, Sept* noon-6pm daily. Rest of year by appointment Sat. **Admission** €7. **No credit cards**.
**Map** p402 K3.
A rare example of the Consulaire style, this small *hôtel particulier* was built in 1789-98. It was occupied by Fortunée Hamelin, born (like her friend the Empress Josephine) in Martinique, and notorious for parading topless down the Champs-Elysées. A bedroom boudoir painted with tropical birds was her only decoration before the site was taken over by Louis Fauvelet de Bourrienne, Napoleon's private secretary. He had it decorated according to the latest fashion, making sure to keep his political options open (the dining room ceiling is painted with motifs favourable to both monarchy and empire).

## Canal St-Martin to La Villette

*In the 10th & 19th arrondissements*
Canal St-Martin, built between 1805 and 1825, begins at the Seine at Pont Morland (where there's a small marina at Port de l'Arsenal), disappears underground at Bastille, hides under boulevard Richard-Lenoir, then emerges after crossing rue du Faubourg-du-Temple, east of place de la République. Rue du Faubourg-du-Temple itself, once the country lane that led to Belleville, is scruffy and cosmopolitan, lined with cheap grocers and discount stores, hidden courtyards and stalwarts of Paris nightlife: **Le Gibus** (*see p329*), Brazilian bar-restaurant **Favela Chic** (*see p332*) and the vintage dancehall **La Java** (*see p332*), as well as the Palais des Glaces (no.37, 10th, 01.42.02.27.17), which programmes seasons of French comics.

The first stretch of the canal, lined with shady trees and crossed by iron footbridges and locks, has the most appeal. The quays are traffic-free on Sundays. Many canalside warehouses have been snapped up by artists and designers or turned into loft apartments. You can take a boat as far as La Villette.

East of here, the Hôpital St-Louis (entrance rue Bichat) was commissioned in 1607 by Henri IV to house plague victims, and was built as a series of isolated pavilions in the same brick-and-stone style as **place des Vosges**

(*see p135*), far enough from the town to prevent risk of infection. Behind the hospital, the rue de la Grange-aux-Belles housed the Montfaucon gibbet, put up in 1233, where victims were hanged and left to the elements. Today the street contains music cafés **Chez Adel** (*see p320*) and L'Apostrophe (no.23, 10th, 01.42.08.26.07). East of the hospital, the lovely cobbled rue Ste-Marthe and place Ste-Marthe have a provincial air, busy at night with multi-ethnic eateries like **Le Panier** (*see p234*).

North, on place du Colonel-Fabien, is the headquarters of the Parti Communiste Français, a modernist masterpiece built between 1968 and 1971 by Brazilian architect Oscar Niemeyer with Paul Chemetov and Jean Deroche. The canal disappears briefly again under place de Stalingrad, a locale best avoided after dark. The square was landscaped in 1989 to showcase the Rotonde de la Villette, one of Ledoux's grandiose 1780s toll houses that once marked the boundary of Paris; it now displays exhibitions and archaeological finds.

Here the canal widens into the Bassin de la Villette, and the new developments along the quai de Loire and further quai de la Marne, as well as some of the worst 1960s and '70s housing in the colossal blocks that stretch along rue de Flandres. At 104 rue d'Aubervilliers, the old Pompes Funèbres – former municipal undertaker – is being turned into a multimedia art space, scheduled to open in September 2008 (*see p300* **Arty undertaking**).

At the eastern end of the basin is an unusual 1885 hydraulic lifting bridge, Pont de Crimée. Thursday and Sunday mornings add vitality with a market at place de Joinville. East of here, the Canal de l'Ourcq (created in 1813 to provide drinking water, as well as for freight haulage) divides: Canal St-Denis runs north towards the Seine, while Canal de l'Ourcq continues east through La Villette and the suburbs. Long the city's main abattoir district, still reflected in the Grande Halle de la Villette and in some of the old meaty brasseries along boulevard de la Villette, the neighbourhood has been revitalised since the late 1980s by the postmodern **Parc de la Villette** leisure and education complex, with the **Cité des Sciences et de l'Industrie** science museum (which also incorporates the **Cité des Enfants**; *see p289* **The appliance of science**), and the **Cité de la Musique** concert hall (*see p314 and p321*).

### La Cité des Sciences et de l'Industrie

*La Villette, 30 av Corentin-Cariou, 19th*
*(01.40.05.70.00/www.cite-sciences.fr). M° Porte de*
*la Villette.* **Open** 10am-6pm Tue-Sat; 10am-7pm Sun.
**Admission** €8; €6 7-25s, over-60s; free under-7s.
PMP. **Credit** MC, V. **Map** p403 inset.

The ultra-modern science museum at La Villette pulls in five million visitors every year. Explora, the permanent show, occupies the upper two floors, whisking visitors through 30,000sq m (320,000sq ft) of space, life, matter and communication: scale models of satellites including the Ariane space shuttle, planes and robots, plus the chance to experience weightlessness, make for an exciting journey. In the Espace Images, try the delayed camera and other optical illusions, draw 3D images on a computer or lend your voice to the *Mona Lisa*. The hothouse garden investigates futuristic developments in agriculture and bio-technology. The lower floors host exhibitions; the Cité des Enfants runs workshops for children. *See pp283-289.*

## Musée de la Musique

*Cité de la Musique, 221 av Jean-Jaurès, 19th (01.44.84.44.84/www.cite-musique.fr). M° Porte de Pantin.* **Open** noon-6pm Tue-Sat; 10am-6pm Sun. **Admission** €7; €5.60 18-26s; free under-18s, over-60s. PMP. **Credit** AmEx, MC, V. **Map** p403 (inset).
Alongside the concert hall, this innovative music museum houses a gleamingly restored collection of instruments from the old Conservatoire, interactive computers and scale models of opera houses and concert halls. Visitors are supplied with an audio guide in a choice of languages, and the musical commentary is a joy, playing the appropriate instrument as you approach each exhibit. Alongside the trumpeting brass, curly woodwind instruments and precious strings are more unusual items, such as the Indonesian gamelan orchestra, whose sounds influenced the work of Debussy and Ravel. Concerts in the amphitheatre use historic instruments from the collection.

## Parc de la Villette

*Av Corentin-Cariou, 19th (01.40.03.75.75/ www.villette.com). M° Porte de la Villette. Av Jean-Jaurès, 19th. M° Porte de Pantin.* **Map** p403 inset.
La Villette's programmes range from avant-garde music to avant-garde circus. Once the city's main cattle market and abattoir, it was to be replaced by a high-tech slaughterhouse but instead was transformed into the Cité des Sciences et de l'Industrie, a futuristic, interactive science museum. Outside you'll find the shining, spherical La Géode IMAX cinema (*see p294*) and the Argonaute submarine. Dotted with red pavilions, or *folies*, the park was designed by Swiss architect Bernard Tschumi and is a postmodern feast (guided tours 08.03.30.63.06, 3pm Sun in summer). The *folies* serve as glorious giant climbing frames, as well as a first-aid post, burger bar and children's art centre. Kids shoot down a Chinese dragon slide, and an undulating suspended path follows the Canal de l'Ourcq. As well as the lawns, which are used for an open-air film festival in summer, there are ten themed gardens bearing evocative names such as the Garden of Mirrors, of Mists, of Acrobatics and of Childhood Frights (all of this can be terribly spooky if you lose your way en route to the Cabaret Sauvage nightclub venue; *see p332*). South of the canal are the Zénith (*see p318*), used for rock concerts, and the Grande Halle de la Villette – now used for trade fairs, exhibitions and September's high profile jazz festival (*see p277*). It is flanked by the Conservatoire de la Musique and the Cité de la Musique, with rehearsal rooms, concert halls and the Musée de la Musique (*see left*). This is also the site of a new concert hall for the Orchestre de Paris, due to open in 2012 (*see p313* **Music hall**).

Belleville.

## Belleville, Ménilmontant & Charonne

*In the 11th, 19th & 20th arrondissements.*

When the city boundaries were expanded in 1860, Ménilmontant, Belleville and Charonne, once villages that provided Paris with fruit, wine and weekend escapes, were all absorbed. They were built up with housing for migrants, first from rural France and later from former colonies in North Africa and South-east Asia. The main tourist attraction is **Père-Lachaise** cemetery, but the area also encompasses one of the city's most beautiful parks, the romantic **Buttes-Chaumont**. Despite attempts to dissipate workers' agitation by splitting the village between the 11th, 19th and 20th administrative districts, Belleville became the centre of opposition to the Second Empire. Cabarets, artisans and workers typified 1890s Belleville; colonised by artists in the 1990s, today Belleville is a trendy hangout.

On boulevard de Belleville, Chinese and Vietnamese shops rub shoulders with Muslim and kosher groceries, couscous and falafel eateries (*see p134* **Kosher quarter**), and a street market takes place on Tuesday and Friday mornings. Legend has it that Edith Piaf was born on the pavement outside no.72 rue de Belleville, as marked on the plaque: 'On the steps of this house was born on the 19 December 1915, in the greatest poverty, Edith Piaf, whose voice would later move the world.' Devotees run the nearby appointment-only **Musée Edith Piaf**, a modest two-room museum.

North of here, along avenue Simon-Bolivar, is the Parc des Buttes-Chaumont. This is the most desirable part of north-east Paris, with Haussmannian apartments overlooking the park: to the east, near place de Rhin-et-Danube, is a small area of tiny, hilly streets lined with small houses and gardens, known by locals as the Quartier Mouzaïa. The gallery space **Le Plateau**, a short walk south of the park, attracts contemporary art aficionados.

Up on the slopes of the Hauts de Belleville, there are views over the city from rue Piat and rue des Envierges, which lead to the modern but charming Parc de Belleville with its Maison des Vents devoted to birds and kites. Below the park, rue Ramponeau mixes new housing and relics of old Belleville. At no.23 an old smithy has been transformed into La Forge, an artists' squat, many of them members of La Bellevilloise association, which is trying to save the area from redevelopment.

'Mesnil-Montant' used to be a few houses on a hill with vines and fruit trees – then came the bistros, bordellos and workers' housing.

It became part of Paris in 1860 along with Belleville, and has a similar history. These days it's a thriving centre of alternative Paris, as artists and young professionals have moved in. Boulevard de Ménilmontant divides this trendy nightlife quarter from the cemetery of Père-Lachaise. While side streets still have male-only North African cafés, rue Oberkampf is home to some of the city's most humming bars, many following the runaway success of the pivotal **Café Charbon** (*see p232*).

The area mixes 1960s and '70s housing projects with older dwellings, some gentrified, some derelict. Just below rue des Pyrénées, which cuts through the 20th, you can rummage around the rustic Cité Leroy or Villa l'Ermitage, cobbled cul-de-sacs of little houses and gardens, and old craft workshops. Rue de l'Ermitage has a curious neo-Gothic house at no.19 – and a bird's eye view from the junction with rue de Ménilmontant, right down the hill to the Centre Pompidou and Tour St-Jacques. Across on rue Boyer, **La Maroquinerie** (*see p235* **12-bar booze**) puts on an eclectic mix of literary events, political debate and live music, and at 88 rue de Ménilmontant, graffiti-covered art squat La Miroiterie opens house for art shows and the *magasin gratuit*, a free swap shop.

East of Père-Lachaise on rue de Bagnolet, **La Flèche d'Or** (*see p318*), a converted station on the defunct Petite Ceinture railway line, is a landmark music venue. Beyond, the medieval **Eglise St-Germain-de-Charonne** is at the heart of what is left of the village of Charonne.

**Buttes-Chaumont.**

Sightseeing

Set at the top of steps next to its presbytery, below a hill once covered with vines, it is the only church in Paris, except St-Pierre-de-Montmartre, still to have its own graveyard.

Below here, centred on the old village high street of rue St-Blaise, is a prettified backwater of quiet tearooms and bistros, where old shops have been taken over by art classes. Place des Grès, once the location of the public pillory, and the nearby renovated houses and squares form a pristine, villagey bulwark against the housing estates encroaching along rue Vitruve.

Towards porte de Bagnolet, where rue de Bagnolet and rue des Balkans meet on the edge of a small park, the Pavillon de l'Hermitage is a small aristocratic relic built in the 1720s for Françoise-Marie de Bourbon, the daughter of Louis XIV, when it was in the grounds of the Château de Bagnolet. A little further south at porte de Montreuil, cross the Périphérique for the Puces de Montreuil flea market.

## Cimetière du Père-Lachaise

*Bd de Ménilmontant, 20th (01.55.25.82.10). M°*
*Père-Lachaise.* **Open** *6 Nov-15 Mar* 8am-5.30pm
Mon-Fri; 8.30am-5.30pm Sat; 9am-5.30pm Sun.
*16 Mar-5 Nov* 8am-6pm Mon-Fri; 8.30am-6pm Sat;
9am-6pm Sun & hols. **Map** p407 P5.

Père-Lachaise has as starry a line-up of illustrious corpses as anywhere in the world – it's the celebrity cemetery. Here lie Delacroix, Proust, Bizet – in fact, almost anyone French, talented and dead that you care to mention. Not even French, for that matter. Creed and nationality have never prevented entry: you just had to have lived or died in Paris or have an allotted space in a family tomb.

It was opened after the Terror of the 1790s, when the city's graveyards were full. The state passed a law to buy land for cemeteries and created the Cimetière de l'Est. Later named after the Jesuit Père de La Chaise, Louis XIV's confessor who lived on this estate, it was designed by Alexandre Brongniart as a public park and cemetery, a green and pleasant place in which Parisians could wander. Initially, people wanted to be buried in their native *quartiers*, and snubbed the new project. In a bid to gain popularity, the presumed remains of medieval lovers Abélard and Héloïse were moved here in 1817, along with those of Molière and La Fontaine. In next to no time, great ceremonial burials became the norm, and thousands of trees were cut down to make space for new graves: Sarah Bernhardt, Ingres, Balzac, Chopin, Colette, Edith Piaf and more. Since 2003, leases for ten, 30 and 50 years have been introduced, in addition to existing ones that are *temporaires* (about a century) and *perpétuelles* (until abandoned). Of the one million originally buried here, only 200,000 have enjoyed uninterrupted slumber. Finding a particular grave can be tricky. Requests for information from the entry guards will be met with a shrug, so buy a €2 map from the hawkers at the Père Lachaise métro entrance or from shops

nearby. Highlights include Chopin's medallion portrait and the muse of Music, famous neighbours La Fontaine and Molière, who knew each other in real life and now share the same fenced-off plot, and Victor Noir. This journalist, shot by Napoleon's cousin Prince Pierre, rests underneath a bronze likeness, its groin rubbed so often by women hoping to conceive that it gleams.

## Eglise St-Germain-de-Charonne

*Pl St-Blaise, 20th (01.43.71.42.04). M° Porte de*
*Bagnolet.* **Open** 9am-7pm.

The old village church of Charonne dates mainly from the 15th century, though one massive column and the bell tower remain from an earlier structure. The interior is almost square, with a triple nave and a simple organ loft. Two side altars have striking modern paintings (a crucifixion and a pietà) by Paul Rambié; a niche contains a wood statue of St Blaise.

## Musée Edith Piaf

*5 rue Crespin-du-Gast, 11th (01.43.55.52.72).*
*M° Ménilmontant.* **Open** by appointment 1-6pm
Mon-Thur (call 2 days ahead). Closed June, Sept.
**Admission** donation. **No credit cards**. **Map**
p403 N5.

Les Amis d'Edith Piaf runs this tiny two-room museum in the heart of the singer's old stomping ground. The Little Sparrow's little black dress and tiny shoes are touching, as are her letters and photos.

## Musée du Fumeur

*7 rue Pache, 11th (01.46.59.05.51/www.musee*
*dufumeur.net). M° Voltaire.* **Open** 2-7pm Tue-Sun.
**Admission** €4. **Map** p407 N6.

Here you'll find obscure smoking contraptions and their history, as well as different tobacco strains in the 'plantarium'. Relax at the end of your tour with a plant-based cocktail in the air-conditioned café.

## Parc des Buttes-Chaumont

*Rue Botzaris, rue Manin, rue de Crimée, 19th. M°*
*Buttes Chaumont.* **Open** *Oct-Apr* 7am-8.15pm daily.
*May, mid Aug-Sept* 7am-9.15pm daily. *June-mid Aug*
7am-10.15pm daily. **Map** p407 N2.

With its meandering paths and vertical cliffs, this lovely park – a former gypsum quarry, tip and public gibbet – was designed by Adolphe Alphand for Haussmann in the 1860s. Waterfalls now cascade out of a man-made cave. A bridge (cheerfully named the Pont des Suicides) crosses the lake to an island crowned by a mini-temple.

## Le Plateau

*33 rue des Alouettes, 19th (01.53.19.84.10/www.*
*fracidf-leplateau.com). M° Buttes Chaumont or*
*Jourdain.* **Open** 2-7pm Wed-Fri; noon-8pm Sat, Sun.
**Admission** free.

This modern art venue has become the low-budget challenger to the Palais de Tokyo. Born out of a campaign for an arts centre in north-east Paris, the small exhibition space addresses the diversity of current art practice with installations, painting, photography, experimental cinema, music and dance.

# The Latin Quarter

The intellectual tradition persists in this Left Bank *quartier*.

The section of the Left Bank east of boulevard St-Michel is said to have earned its name because the students here spoke Latin until the Revolution. Another theory is that the title alludes to the fact that this area was the heart of Roman Lutetia. Whatever the truth of the matter, the Latin Quarter is the site of the city's most important Roman remains: the Cluny baths, now part of the **Musée National du Moyen Age**, and the **Arènes de Lutèce** amphitheatre. The first two Roman streets were on the site of modern-day rue St-Jacques (later the pilgrims' route to Compostela) and rue Cujas. The forum was probably underneath what is now rue Soufflot. The area has been the university quarter since medieval times and, despite spiralling property prices, it still has a distinctly intellectual edge.

## Quartier de la Huchette

*In the 5th arrondissement.*
Boulevard St-Michel used to be synonymous with student rebellion; now it's a largely unprepossessing ribbon of fast-food joints and clothing chains, though Gibert Joseph and Gibert Jeune (for both, *see p243*) continue to furnish books and stationery to students. East of here, the semi-pedestrianised Quartier de la Huchette has retained much of its medieval street plan. Rue de la Huchette and rue de la Harpe are now best known for their kebabs and pizzas, though there are 18th-century wrought-iron balconies and carved masks in the latter street. At the tiny Théâtre de la Huchette (*see p344*), Ionesco's absurdist drama *La Cantatrice*

*Chauve* ('The Bald Soprano') has been playing continuously since 1957. Also of interest are rue du Chat-qui-Pêche, supposedly the city's narrowest street, and rue de la Parcheminerie, named after the parchment sellers and copyists who once lived here. Amid the tourist shops stands the city's most charming medieval church, the **Eglise St-Séverin**, with leering gargoyles, spiky gabled side chapels and an exuberantly vaulted Flamboyant Gothic interior.

Across ancient rue St-Jacques is the **Eglise St-Julien-le-Pauvre**, built as a resting place for 12th-century pilgrims. Nearby rue Galande has old houses and the Trois Mailletz cabaret at no.56 (5th, 01.43.54.00.79). The medieval cellars of the Caveau des Oubliettes jazz club (*see p322*) were used as a prison after the French Revolution (*oubliette* is the French word for a pit into which prisoners were thrown, then forgotten). At no.42, the Studio Galande (*see p297*) arts cinema still draws goths bearing rice and umbrellas for late screenings of the *Rocky Horror Picture Show* every Friday and Saturday. Just outside the church in square Viviani stands what is possibly the city's oldest tree, a false acacia planted in 1602, these days half-swamped by a vast thatch of ivy and propped up by some impressive concrete buttresses.

The little streets between here and the eastern stretch of boulevard St-Germain are among the city's oldest: streets like rue de Bièvre, which follows the course of the Bièvre river that flowed into the Seine in the Middle Ages, rue du Maître-Albert, and rue des Grands-Degrès, with traces of old shop signs painted on its buildings' façades. Remnants of the Collège des Bernardins, built for the Cistercian order, can be seen in rue de Poissy, where the 13th- to 14th-century Gothic monks' refectory is being restored after long service as firemen's barracks. Nearby stand the Eglise St-Nicolas-de-Chardonnet (23 rue Bernardins, 5th, 01.44.27.07.90), which is associated with the most reactionary part of the Catholic Church and still performs Mass in Latin, and the art deco Maison de la Mutualité (24 rue St-Victor, 5th, 01.40.46.12.00), whose uses range from trade unions' meetings to rock concerts.

At 47 quai de la Tournelle, the 17th-century Hôtel de Miramion now contains the **Musée de l'Assistance Publique**, devoted to the

*Sightseeing*

ory of Paris hospitals. You'll find food for budgets along quai de la Tournelle, starting ith Michelin-starred haute-cuisine restaurant a Tour d'Argent (*see p207* **Water with your meal?**), said to have been founded as an inn in 1582. After 60 years at the helm, owner Claude Terrail died in 2006, passing the restaurant on to his son André. Nearby is the populist Tintin shrine, *café-tabac* Le Rallye (no.11, 5th, 01.43.54.29.65). Place Maubert, now a breezy morning marketplace (Tue, Thur, Sat), witnessed the hanging of Protestants during the 16th-century Wars of Religion. Just behind the square, the modern police station is home to a curious array of grisly criminal evidence in the **Musée de la Préfecture de Police**.

On the corner of boulevard St-Germain and boulevard St-Michel stand the striking ruins of the late second-century Thermes de Cluny, the Romans' main baths complex; the adjoining Gothic Hôtel de Cluny provides a suitable setting for the **Musée National du Moyen Age**, the national collection of medieval art. Adjoining boulevard St-Germain, its garden has been replanted with species portrayed in medieval tapestries, paintings and treatises.

The neo-classical **Panthéon**. *See p153*.

### Eglise St-Julien-le-Pauvre

*Rue St-Julien-le-Pauvre, 5th (01.43.54.52.16). M° Cluny La Sorbonne*. **Open** 9.30am-1pm, 3-6.30pm daily. **Map** p408 J7.
A former sanctuary for pilgrims en route to Compostela, this much-mauled church dates from the late 12th century, on the cusp of Romanesque and Gothic, and has capitals richly decorated with vines, acanthus leaves and winged harpies. Once part of a priory, it became the university church when colleges migrated to the Left Bank, and was the site of riotous university assemblies. Since 1889 it has been used by the Greek Orthodox Church.

### Eglise St-Séverin

*3 rue des Prêtres-St-Séverin, 5th (01.42.34.93.50). M° Cluny La Sorbonne or St-Michel*. **Open** 11am-7.30pm daily. **Map** p408 J7.
Built on the site of the chapel of the hermit Séverin, itself on top of a much earlier Merovingian burial ground, this lovely Flamboyant Gothic edifice was long the parish church of the Left Bank. It was rebuilt on various occasions to repair damage after ransacking by Normans and to meet the needs of the growing population. The church dates from the 15th century, though the doorway, carved with foliage, was added in 1837 from the demolished Eglise St-Pierre-aux-Boeufs on Ile de la Cité. The double ambulatory is famed for its forest of 'palm tree' vaulting, which meets at the end in a unique spiral column that inspired a series of paintings by Robert Delaunay. The bell tower, a survivor from one of the earlier churches on the site, has the oldest bell in Paris (1412). Around the nave are stained-glass windows dating from the 14th and 15th centuries (most of those in the side chapels are by 19th-century Chartres master Emile Hersh), and the choir apse has striking stained glass designed by artist Jean René Bazaine in the 1960s. Next door, around the former cemetery, is the only remaining charnel house in Paris.

### Musée de l'Assistance Publique

*Hôtel de Miramion, 47 quai de la Tournelle, 5th (01.40.27.50.05/www.aphp.fr). M° Maubert Mutualité*. **Open** 10am-6pm Tue-Sun. Closed Aug. **Admission** €4; €2 reductions; free under-13s. PMP. **No credit cards. Map** p406 K7.
The history of Paris hospitals, from the days when they were receptacles for abandoned babies to the dawn of modern medicine with anaesthesia, is shown through paintings, prints, grisly medical devices and a mock ward and pharmacy.

### Musée National du Moyen Age – Thermes de Cluny

*6 pl Paul-Painlevé, 5th (01.53.73.78.00/www.musee-moyenage.fr). M° Cluny La Sorbonne*. **Open** 9.15am-5.45pm Mon, Wed-Sun. **Admission** €7.50; €5.50 18-25s, all on Sun; free under-18s, all on 1st Sun of mth. PMP. **Credit** Shop MC, V. **Map** p408 J7.
The national museum of medieval art is best known for the beautiful, allegorical *Lady and the Unicorn* tapestry cycle, but it also has important collections

of medieval sculpture and enamels. The building itself, commonly known as Cluny, is also a rare example of 15th-century secular Gothic architecture, with its foliate Gothic doorways, hexagonal staircase jutting out of the façade and vaulted chapel. It was built from 1485 to 1498 – atop a Gallo-Roman baths complex dating from the second and third centuries – to lodge priests, at the request of Jacques d'Amboise, abbot of the powerful Abbey of Cluny in Burgundy. The baths, built in characteristic Roman bands of stone and brick masonry, are the finest Roman remains in Paris. The vaulted frigidarium (cold bath), tepidarium (warm bath), caldarium (hot bath) and part of the hypocaust heating system are all still visible. A themed garden fronts the whole complex.

With its U-shaped residential building set behind an entrance courtyard, Cluny was a precursor of the Marais *hôtels particuliers* of the 16th and 17th centuries. After serving as a printworks and laundry, the *hôtel* was rented in the 1830s by the fervent medievalist Alexandre du Sommerand to house his collection, which laid the foundations for this museum created in 1844. Recent acquisitions include the illuminated manuscript *L'Ascension du Christ* from the Abbey of Cluny, dating back to the 12th century, and the 16th-century triptych *Assomption de la Vierge* by Adrien Isenbrant of Bruges. The mesmerising *Lady and the Unicorn* cycle depicts convoluted allegories of the five senses via six late 15th-century Flemish millefleurs tapestries, beautifully displayed in a special circular room. Other textiles include fragile Coptic embroidery, Edward III's emblazoned saddle cloth and a cycle of the life of St Stephen. The heads of the Kings of Judah from Notre-Dame cathedral, mutilated in the Revolution and rediscovered (minus their noses) in 1979, are considered the highlight of the sculpture collection.

### Musée de la Préfecture de Police

*4 rue de la Montagne-Ste-Geneviève, 5th (01.44.41.52.50/www.prefecture-police-paris. interieur.gouv.fr). Mº Maubert Mutualité.* **Open** 9am-5pm Mon-Fri; 10am-5pm Sat. **Admission** free. **No credit cards. Map** p406 J7.

Housed in a hideous police station, this museum looks at criminal Paris history since the establishment of the Paris police force in the 16th century. The eclectic collection includes prisoners' expenses from the Bastille (including those of dastardly jewel thief the Comtesse de la Motte), the crafty exploding flowerpot planted by Louis-Armand Matha in 1894, and the gory Epée de Justice, a 17th-century sword blunted by a succession of noble necks.

## The Sorbonne, Montagne Ste-Geneviève & Mouffetard

*In the 5th arrondissement.*
An influx of well-heeled residents in the 1980s put paid to the days of horn-rims, pipes and turtlenecks: accommodation here is now well beyond the reach of most students. The intellectual tradition persists, however, in the concentration of academic institutions around the Montagne Ste-Geneviève, and students throng the specialist bookstores and art cinemas on rue Champollion and rue des Ecoles.

The district's long association with learning began in about 1100, when a number of renowned scholars, including Pierre Abélard, began to reside and teach on the Montagne, independent of the established cathedral school of Notre-Dame. This loose association of scholars came to be referred to as a 'university'. The Paris schools attracted disciples from all over Europe, and the 'colleges' – in reality student residences dotted round the area (some still survive) – multiplied, until the University of Paris was eventually given official recognition with a charter from Pope Innocent III in 1215.

By the 16th century the university – named the **Sorbonne**, after the most famous of its colleges – had been co-opted by the Catholic Church. A century later, Cardinal Richelieu rebuilt it. Following the Revolution, when the university was forced to close, Napoleon revived the Sorbonne as the cornerstone of his new, centralised education system. The university participated enthusiastically in the uprisings of the 19th century, and was also a seedbed of the 1968 revolt, when it was occupied by protesting students. These days it is decidedly less turbulent. Also on rue des Ecoles, the independent **Collège de France** was founded in 1530 by a group of humanists led by Guillaume Budé under the patronage of François I. The neighbouring Brasserie Balzar (no.49, 5th, 01.43.54.13.67) has been fuelling amateur philosophy for years.

From here, climb rue St-Jacques to rue Soufflot for the most impressive introduction to place du Panthéon. Otherwise, follow rue des Carmes – with its baroque chapel, now used by the Syrian Church – and continue on rue Valette past the brick and stone entrance of the Collège Ste-Barbe, where Ignatius Loyola, Montgolfier and Eiffel studied. Alternatively, wend along the serpentine rue de la Montagne-Ste-Geneviève; at the junction of rue Descartes, cafés and eccentric wine bistros overlook the sculpted 19th-century entrance to what was formerly the elite Ecole Polytechnique (since moved to the suburbs) and is now the research ministry. There's a small park here too, and the popular bistro L'Ecurie (2 rue Laplace, 5th, 01.46.33.68.49) – an old stable burrowed into medieval cellars.

The huge, domed **Panthéon** was commissioned by Louis XV to honour Geneviève, the city's patron saint, but was

converted during the Revolution into a secular temple for France's *grands hommes*. The surrounding place du Panthéon, also conceived by Panthéon architect Jacques-Germain Soufflot, is one of the city's great set pieces: looking on to it are the elegant fifth arrondissement town hall and, opposite, the law faculty. On the north side, the Ste-Geneviève university library (no.10, 5th, 01.44.41.97.98), built by Labrouste with an iron-framed reading room, contains medieval manuscripts. On the other side you'll find the historic Hôtel des Grands Hommes (no.17, 5th, 01.46.34.19.60, www.hoteldesgrandshommes.com), where Surrealist mandarin André Breton invented 'automatic writing' in the 1920s.

Pascal, Racine and the remains of Sainte Geneviève are all interred within **Eglise St-Etienne-du-Mont**, on the north-east corner of the square. Just behind it, within the illustrious and elitist Lycée Henri IV, is the Gothic-Romanesque Tour de Clovis, part of the former Abbaye Ste-Geneviève. Take a look through the entrance (open during termtime) and you'll also catch glimpses of the cloister and other monastic structures. Further from place du Panthéon, along rue Clovis, is a chunk of Philippe-Auguste's 12th-century city wall. The exiled monarch James II once resided at 65 rue du Cardinal-Lemoine, in the severe buildings of the former Collège des Ecossais (now a school), founded in 1372 to house Scottish students; the king's brain was preserved here until carried off and lost during the French Revolution. Other well known ex-residents include Hemingway, who lived at 79 rue du Cardinal-Lemoine (note the plaque) and 39 rue Descartes in the 1920s, and James Joyce; the latter completed *Ulysses* while staying at 71 rue du Cardinal-Lemoine. Rimbaud lived in rue Descartes, while Descartes himself lived on nearby rue Rollin.

This area is still a mix of tourist picturesque and gentle village, where some of the buildings hide surprising courtyards and gardens. Pretty place de la Contrescarpe has been a famous rendezvous since the 1530s, when writers Rabelais, Ronsard and Du Bellay frequented the Cabaret de la Pomme de Pin at No.1; it still has some lively cafés. When George Orwell stayed at 6 rue du Pot-de-Fer in 1928 and 1929 (he described his time here and his work as a dishwasher in *Down and Out in Paris and London*), it was a place of astounding poverty; today the street is lined with bargain bars and restaurants, while the restored houses along rue Tournefort bear little relation to the garrets of Balzac's *Le Père Goriot*. Rue Mouffetard (*photo p152*), originally the road to Rome and one of the oldest streets in the city, winds southwards as a suite of cheap bistros, Greek and Lebanese

tavernas and knick-knack shops thronged with tourists; the vibe described by Hemingway – 'that wonderful narrow crowded market street, beloved of bohemians' – has somewhat faded. The busy street market (Tue-Sat, Sun morning) on the lower half seethes on weekends, when it spills on to the square and around the cafés in front of the **Eglise St-Médard**. There's another busy market, more frequented by locals, at **place Monge** (Wed, Fri, Sun morning).

Back to the west of the Panthéon, head south beyond rue Soufflot and you'll notice rue St-Jacques becomes prettier. Here you'll find several ancient buildings, including the elegant *hôtel* at no.151, good food shops, vintage bistro Perraudin (no.157, 5th, 01.46.33.15.75) and the Institut Océanographique (no.195, 5th, 01.44.32.10.70, www.oceano.org/io), which has well-stocked aquariums much loved by schoolkids. Rue d'Ulm contains the elite Ecole Normale Supérieure (no.45, 5th, 01.44.32.30.00, www.ens.fr), once occupied in protest by the unemployed in January 1998; in an echo of 1968, students also joined in.

Turn off up hilly rue des Fossés-St-Jacques to discover place de l'Estrapade; in the 17th century the *estrapade* was a tall wooden tower from which deserters were dropped repeatedly until they died. Nearby, in rue des Irlandais, the **Centre Culturel Irlandais** (*see p81*) hosts concerts, exhibitions, films, plays and spoken-word events promoting Irish culture. Back to the west of rue St-Jacques, rue Soufflot and broad rue Gay-Lussac (a hotspot of the May 1968 revolt), with their Haussmannian apartment buildings, lead to boulevard St-Michel and the Jardin du Luxembourg (*see p160*). Further south along rue St-Jacques, in the potters' quarter of Roman Lutetia, is the least altered and most ornate of the city's baroque churches, the landmark **Eglise du Val-de-Grâce**. Round the corner, at 6 rue du Val-de-Grâce, is the former home of Alfons Maria Mucha, the influential Moravian art nouveau artist, known for his posters of Sarah Bernhardt.

### Collège de France

*11 pl Marcelin-Berthelot, 5th (01.44.27.12.11/ 01.44.27.11.47/www.college-de-france.fr). M° Cluny La Sorbonne or Maubert Mutualité/RER Luxembourg.* **Open** 9am-5pm Mon-Fri. **Map** p408 J7. Founded in 1530 with the patronage of François I, the college is a place of learning and a research institute. The present building dates from the 16th and 17th centuries; there's also a later annexe. All lectures are free and open to the public; some have been given by such eminent figures as anthropologist Claude Lévi-Strauss, philosopher Maurice Merleau-Ponty and mathematician Jacques Tits.

**Sightseeing**

Path to perfection: the enchanting **Jardin des Plantes**. See p154.

## Eglise St-Etienne-du-Mont

*Pl Ste-Geneviève, 5th (01.43.54.11.79). Mº Cardinal Lemoine/RER Luxembourg.* **Open** 10am-7pm Tue-Sun. **Map** p408 J8.

Geneviève, patron saint of Paris, is credited with having miraculously saved the city from the ravages of Attila the Hun in 451, and her shrine has been a popular site of pilgrimage ever since. The present church was built in an amalgam of Gothic and Renaissance styles between 1492 and 1626, and once adjoined the abbey church of Ste-Geneviève. The façade mixes Gothic rose windows with rusticated roman columns and reliefs of classically draped figures. The interior is wonderfully tall and light, with soaring columns and a classical balustrade. The stunning Renaissance rood screen, with its double spiral staircase and ornate stone strapwork, is the only surviving one in Paris, and was possibly designed by Philibert Delorme. Also worth a look is the decorative canopied wooden pulpit by Germaine Pillon dating from 1651, adorned with figures of the Graces and supported by a muscular Samson sitting on the defeated lion. Sainte Geneviève's elaborate neo-Gothic brass-and-glass shrine (shielding the ancient tombstone) is located to the right of the choir, surrounded by an assorted collection of reliquaries and dozens of marble plaques bearing messages of thanks. At the back of the church (reached through the sacristy), the catechism chapel constructed by Baltard in the 1860s has a cycle of paintings relating the saint's life story.

## Eglise St-Médard

*141 rue Mouffetard, 5th (01.44.08.87.00). Mº Censier Daubenton.* **Open** 8am-noon, 2.30-7.30pm daily. **Map** p406 J9.

The original chapel here was a dependency of the Abbaye Ste-Geneviève. The rebuilding towards the end of the 15th century created a somewhat larger, late Gothic structure best known for its elaborate vaulted ambulatory.

## Eglise du Val-de-Grâce

*Pl Alphonse-Laveran, 5th (01.40.51.47.28). RER Luxembourg or Port-Royal.* **Open** noon-6pm Tue, Wed, Sat, Sun. **Admission** €5; €2.50 students, 6-12s; free under-6s. **No credit cards.** **Map** p406 H9.

Anne of Austria, the wife of Louis XIII, vowed to erect 'a magnificent temple' if God blessed her with a son. She got two. The resulting church and surrounding Benedictine monastery – these days a military hospital and the Musée du Service de Santé des Armées – were built by François Mansart and Jacques Lemercier. This is the most luxuriously baroque of the city's 17th-century domed churches, its ornate altar decorated with twisted barley-sugar columns. The swirling colours of the dome frescoes painted by Pierre Mignard in 1669 (which Molière himself once eulogised) are designed to give a foretaste of heaven. In contrast, the surrounding monastery offers the perfect example of François Mansart's classical restraint. Phone in advance if you're after a guided visit.

**Rue Mouffetard.** *See p150.*

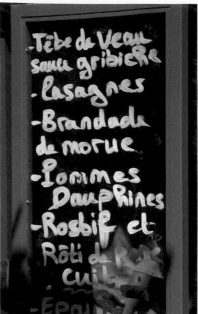

Sightseeing

## Musée du Service de Santé des Armées

*Val de Grâce, pl Alphonse-Laveran, 5th (01.40.51.51.94). RER Luxembourg or Port Royal.* **Open** noon-6pm Tue, Wed, Sat, Sun. **Admission** €5; €2.50 6-12s; free under-6s. **No credit cards.** **Map** p406 J9.

Housed in the royal convent designed by Mansart, next door to a military hospital, this museum traces the history of military medicine via replicas of field hospitals and ambulance trains, and antique medical instruments. The chilling section on World War I demonstrates how speedily the conflict propelled progress in medical science.

## Le Panthéon

*Pl du Panthéon, 5th (01.44.32.18.00). M° Cardinal Lemoine/RER Luxembourg.* **Open** 10am-6pm (until 6.30pm summer) daily. **Admission** €7.50; €4.50 18-25s; free under-18s (if accompanied by an adult). PMP. **Credit** MC, V. **Map** p408 J8.

Soufflot's neo-classical megastructure, with its huge dome, was the architectural *grand projet* of its day, commissioned by a grateful Louis XV to thank Sainte Geneviève for his recovery from illness. But by the time it was ready in 1790, a lot had changed; during the Revolution, the Panthéon was rededicated as a 'temple of reason' and the resting place of the nation's great men. The austere barrel-vaulted crypt now houses Voltaire, Rousseau, Hugo and Zola. New heroes are installed but rarely: Pierre and Marie Curie's remains were transferred here in 1995; André Malraux, writer, Resistance hero and de Gaulle's culture minister, arrived in 1996; Alexandre Dumas in 2002. Inside are Greek columns and domes, and 19th-century murals of Geneviève's life by Symbolist painter Puvis de Chavannes, a formative influence on Picasso during the latter's blue period.

Mount the steep spiral stairs to the colonnade encircling the dome for superb views. A replica of Foucault's Pendulum hangs here; the original proved that the earth does indeed spin on its axis, via a universal joint that lets the direction of the pendulum's swing rotate as the earth revolves. *Photo p148.*

## La Sorbonne

*17 rue de la Sorbonne, 5th (01.40.46.22.11/www. sorbonne.fr). M° Cluny La Sorbonne.* **Open** *Tours* by appointment. Closed July & Aug. **Map** p408 J7.

Founded in 1253 by Robert de Sorbon, the University of the Sorbonne was at the centre of the Latin Quarter's intellectual activity from the Middle Ages until 1968, when it was occupied by students and stormed by the riot police. The authorities then split the University of Paris into safer outposts, but the Sorbonne still houses the Faculté des Lettres. Rebuilt by Richelieu and reorganised by Napoleon, the present buildings date from the late 1800s, and have a labyrinth of classrooms and lecture theatres, as well as an observatory tower. The elegant dome of the 17th-century chapel dominates place de la Sorbonne; Cardinal Richelieu is buried inside. It's only open to the public for exhibitions or concerts.

# The Jardin des Plantes district

The quiet, easternmost part of the fifth arrondissement is home to yet more academic institutions, the Paris mosque and another Roman relic. Old-fashioned bistros on rue des Fossés-St-Bernard contrast with the forbidding 1960s architecture of the massive university campus of Paris VI and VII, the science faculty (known as Jussieu) built on what had been the site of the important Abbaye St-Victor. Between the Seine and Jussieu is the strikingly modern, glass-faced **Institut du Monde Arabe**, which has a programme of concerts and exhibitions and a restaurant with a great view. The **Jardin Tino Rossi**, by the river, contains the slightly dilapidated **Musée de la Sculpture en Plein Air**; in summer this is a spot for dancing and picnicking.

Hidden among the hotels of rue Monge is the entrance to the **Arènes de Lutèce**, a Roman amphitheatre. The remains of a circular arena and its tiers of stone seating were discovered in 1869, when the street was being built. Excavation started in 1883, thanks to lobbying by Victor Hugo. Nearby rise the white minaret and green pan-tiled roof of the **Mosquée de Paris**, built in 1922. Its beautiful Moorish tearoom is a student haunt.

The mosque looks over the **Jardin des Plantes** botanical garden. Opened in 1626 as a garden for medicinal plants, it features an 18th-century maze and a winter garden bristling with rare species. It also houses the Museum National d'Histoire Naturelle, with its brilliantly renovated **Grande Galerie de l'Evolution**, and a zoo, La Ménagerie, an unlikely by-product of the Revolution, when royal and noble collections of wild animals were impounded. Street names and the lovely animal-themed fountain on the corner of rue Cuvier pay homage to the many naturalists and other scientists who worked here. A short way away, at 11-13bis rue Geoffroy-St-Hilaire, the words 'Chevaux', 'Poneys' and 'Anes' are still visible on the façade of the old horse market.

## Arènes de Lutèce

*Rue Monge, rue de Navarre or rue des Arènes, 5th. M° Cardinal Lemoine or Place Monge.* **Open** *Summer* 8am-10pm daily. *Winter* 8am-5.30pm daily. **Admission** free. **Map** p406 K8.

This Roman arena, where wild beasts and gladiators fought, could seat 10,000 people. It was still visible during the reign of Philippe-Auguste in the 12th century, then disappeared under rubble. The site was rediscovered in 1869 and now incorporates a romantically planted garden. These days, it attracts skateboarders, footballers and boules players.

**Sightseeing**

## Grande Galerie de l'Evolution

*36 rue Geoffroy-St-Hilaire, 2 rue Bouffon or pl Valhubert, 5th (01.40.79.54.79/56.01). M° Gare d'Austerlitz or Jussieu.* **Open** *Grande Galerie* 10am-6pm Mon, Wed-Fri, Sun; 10am-8pm Sat. *Other galleries* 10am-5pm Mon, Wed-Fri; 10am-6pm Sat, Sun. **Admission** *Grande Galerie* €8; €7 4-18s; free under-4s. *Other galleries* (each) €6; €4 4-18s; free under-4s. **No credit cards. Map** p406 K9.

One of the city's most child-friendly attractions, this is guaranteed to bowl adults over too. Located within the Jardin des Plantes (*see below*), this beauty of a 19th-century iron-framed, glass-roofed structure has been modernised with lifts, galleries and false floors, and filled with life-size models of tentacle-waving squids, open-mawed sharks, tigers hanging off elephants and monkeys swarming down from the ceiling. The centrepiece is a procession of African wildlife across the first floor that resembles the procession into Noah's Ark. Glass-sided lifts take you up through suspended birds to the second floor, which deals with man's impact on nature and rewiring of evolution (crocodile into handbag). The third floor traces endangered and extinct species. The separate Galerie d'Anatomie Comparée et de Paléontologie contains over a million skeletons and a world-class fossil collection.

## Institut du Monde Arabe

*1 rue des Fossés-St-Bernard, 5th (01.40.51.38.38/ www.imarabe.org). M° Jussieu.* **Open** 10am-6pm Tue-Sun. *Library* 1-8pm Tue-Sat. *Café* noon-6pm Tue-Sun. *Tours* 3pm Tue-Fri; 3pm & 4.30pm Sat, Sun. **Admission** *Roof terrace, library* free. *Museum* €5; €4 reductions; free under-12s. PMP. *Exhibitions* varies. *Tours* €8. **Credit** MC, V. **Map** p406 K7.

A clever blend of high-tech and Arab influences, this Seine-side *grand projet* was constructed between 1980 and 1987 to a design by Jean Nouvel (whose latest triumph is the Musée du Quai Branly; *see p171* **Windows on the world**). Shuttered windows, inspired by the screens of Moorish palaces, act as camera apertures, contracting or expanding according to the amount of sunlight. A museum covering the history and archaeology of the Islamic Arab world occupies the upper floors: start at the seventh with Classical-era finds and work down via early Islamic dynasties to the present day. Unfortunately, the layout and arrangement are somewhat uninspired – objects in glass cases without much in the way of context. However, the Institut hosts several major crowd-pleasing exhibitions throughout the year. What's more, there's an excellent Middle East bookshop on the ground floor and the views from the roof terrace (to which access is free) are fabulous.

## Jardin des Plantes

*36 rue Geoffroy-St-Hilaire, 2 rue Bouffon, pl Valhubert or 57 rue Cuvier, 5th. M° Gare d'Austerlitz, Jussieu or Place Monge.* **Open** *Main garden* Winter 8am-dusk daily. Summer 7.30am-8pm daily. *Alpine garden* Apr-Sept 8am-4.30pm Mon-Fri; 1-5pm Sat, Sun. Closed Oct-Mar. *Ménagerie* Apr-Sept 9am-5pm daily. **Admission** *Alpine Garden* free

Mon-Fri; €1 Sat, Sun. *Jardin des Plantes* free. *Ménagerie* €7; €5 4-18s; free under-4s. **Credit** AmEx, MC, V. **Map** p406 L8.

Although small and slightly dishevelled, the Paris botanical garden – which contains more than 10,000 species and includes tropical greenhouses and rose, winter and Alpine gardens – is an enchanting place. Begun by Louis XIII's doctor as the royal medicinal plant garden in 1626, it opened to the public in 1640. The formal garden, which runs between two dead-straight avenues of trees parallel to rue Buffon, is like something out of *Alice in Wonderland*. There's also the Ménagerie (a small zoo) and the terrific Grande Galerie de l'Evolution (*see left*). Ancient trees on view include a false acacia planted in 1636 and a cedar from 1734. A plaque on the old laboratory declares that this is where Henri Becquerel discovered radioactivity in 1896. *Photo p151.*

## Jardin Tino Rossi (Musée de la Sculpture en Plein Air)

*Quai St-Bernard, 5th. M° Gare d'Austerlitz.* **Open** 8am-dusk Mon-Fri; 9am-dusk Sat, Sun. **Admission** free. **Map** p406 L8.

Despite recent replanting, this open-air sculpture museum by the Seine fights a constant battle against graffiti. Still, it's a pleasant enough, if traffic-loud, place for a stroll. Most of the works are second-rate, aside from Etienne Martin's bronze *Demeure I* and the Carrara marble *Fenêtre* by Cuban artist Careras.

## La Mosquée de Paris

*2 pl du Puits-de-l'Ermite, 5th (01.45.35.97.33/ tearoom 01.43.31.38.20/baths 01.43.31.18.14/ www.mosquee-de-paris.net). M° Monge.* **Open** *Tours* 9am-noon, 2-6pm Mon-Thur, Sat, Sun (closed Muslim hols). *Tearoom* 10am-11.30pm daily. *Restaurant* noon-2.30pm, 7.30-10.30pm daily. *Baths* (women) 10am-9pm Mon, Wed, Sat; 2-9pm Fri; (men) 2-9pm Tue, Sun. **Admission** €3; €2 7-25s, over-60s; free under-7s. *Tearoom* free. *Baths* €15-€35. **Credit** MC, V. **Map** p406 K9.

Some distance removed from the Arabic-speaking inner-city enclaves of Barbès Rochechouart and Belleville (*see p128* **Battle of Algiers**), this vast Hispano-Moorish construct is nevertheless the spiritual heart of France's Algerian-dominated Muslim population. Built from 1922 to 1926 with elements inspired by the Alhambra and the Bou Inania Medersa in Fès, the Paris mosque is dominated by a stunning green-and-white tiled square minaret. In plan and function it divides into three sections: religious (grand patio, prayer room and minaret, all for worshippers and not curious tourists); scholarly (Islamic school and library); and, via rue Geoffroy-St-Hilaire, commercial (café and domed hammam, *see p269*). La Mosquée café (open 9am-midnight daily) is delightful – a modest courtyard with blue-and-white mosaic-topped tables shaded beneath green foliage and scented with the sweet smell of sheesha (€6) smoke. Charming waiters distribute *thé à la menthe* (€2), along with syrupy, nutty North African pastries, sorbets and fruit salads.

# St-Germain-des-Prés & Odéon

Designer handbags now rule in the former stamping ground of the literary greats.

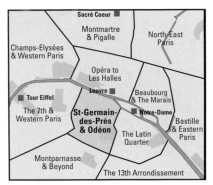

This stretch of the Left Bank used to be Paris's literary and intellectual powerhouse. Though still home to several major publishers, these days it's serious fashion territory, and boasts some of the most expensive property in the city.

For years, the lore of Paris café society and intellectual life was amply fed by the tales that leaked out of St-Germain-des-Prés. Verlaine and Rimbaud drank here; later, Sartre, Camus and de Beauvoir scribbled and squabbled, and musicians congregated around Boris Vian in the post-war jazz boom. Earnest types still pose with weighty tomes, and the literati continue to assemble on café terraces – to give interviews. With the local price hikes, the only writers living here these days are well-established ones.

In the 1990s a band of intellectuals founded 'SOS St-Germain' to battle against the tide of commercialism. The association's honorary president was bohemian singer Juliette Gréco, who performed in the local clubs in the 1950s, when she was living in a poky hotel room on rue de Seine. The campaigners' efforts have been largely in vain: St-Germain almost rivals avenue Montaigne for designer boutiques. Armani, Louis Vuitton, Dior, Cartier and Céline have all set up shop here, and **Karl Lagerfeld** (*see p247*) opened his photography gallery on rue de Seine. The jazz clubs and musicians, meanwhile, have mostly moved away.

## From the boulevard to the Seine

*In the 6th arrondissement.*
Hit by shortages of coal during World War II, Sartre shunned his cold flat on rue Bonaparte. 'The principal interest of the Café de Flore,' he noted at the time, 'was that it had a stove, a nearby métro and no Germans.' Although you can spend more on a few coffees here than on a week's heating these days, the **Café de Flore** (*see p236*) remains an arty favourite and hosts *café-philo* evenings in English. Its rival, **Les Deux Magots** (*see p237*), facing historic **Eglise St-Germain-des-Prés**, is frequented largely by tourists. Nearby is the celebrity favourite Brasserie Lipp (151 bd St-Germain, 6th, 01.45.48.53.91); art nouveau fans prefer Brasserie Vagenende (142 bd St-Germain, 6th, 01.43.26.68.18). The swish late-night bookshop **La Hune** (*see p243*) provides sustenance of a more intellectual kind.

St-Germain-des-Prés grew up around the medieval abbey, the oldest church in Paris and site of an annual fair that drew merchants from across Europe. There are traces of its cloister and part of the abbot's palace behind the church on rue de l'Abbaye. Constructed in 1586 in red brick with stone facing, the palace prefigured the architecture of **place des Vosges** (*see p135*). Charming place de Furstemberg (once the palace stables) is home to the house and studio where the elderly Delacroix lived when painting the murals in St-Sulpice; today it houses the **Musée National Delacroix**. Wagner, Ingres and Colette all lived on nearby rue Jacob; its elegant 17th-century *hôtels particuliers* now contain specialist book, design and antiques shops and a few pleasant hotels.

Further east, rue de Buci hosts a street market and upmarket food shops, and is home to cafés Les Etages (no.5, 6th, 01.46.34.26.26) and Bar du Marché (no.16, 6th, 01.43.26.55.15). Hôtel La Louisiane (60 rue de Seine, 6th, 01.44.32.17.17, www.hotellalouisiane.com) has hosted jazz stars Chet Baker and Miles Davis, and Existentialist lovers Sartre and de Beauvoir. Rue de Seine, rue

des Beaux-Arts and rue Bonaparte (Manet was born in the latter, at no.5, in 1832) are still packed with art galleries, mostly specialising in 20th-century abstraction, tribal art and art deco furniture. It was in rue des Beaux-Arts, at the Hôtel d'Alsace, that Oscar Wilde complained about the wallpaper and then checked out for good. Now fashionably renovated, it has rechristened itself L'Hôtel (*see p71*). La Palette (43 rue de Seine, 6th, 01.43.26.68.15) and Bistro Mazarin (42 rue Mazarine, 6th, 01.43.29.99.01) are good pitstops with enviable terraces; rue Mazarine, with shops selling lighting, vintage toys and jewellery, also has Terence Conran's brasserie **L'Alcazar** (no.62, 6th, 01.53.10.19.99, www.alcazar.fr) and hip club **Wagg** (*see p331*).

On quai de Conti stands the neo-classical Hôtel des Monnaies, built at the demand of Louis XV by architect Jacques-Denis Antoine; formerly the mint (1777-1973), it's now the **Musée de la Monnaie**, a coin museum. Next door stands the domed **Institut de France**, cleaned to within an inch of its crisp, classical life. Opposite, the iron Pont des Arts footbridge leads directly to the **Louvre** (*see pp93-100*). Further along, the city's main fine arts school, the **Ecole Nationale Supérieure des Beaux-Arts**, occupies an old monastery.

Coffee was first drunk in Paris in 1686 at Café Procope (13 rue de l'Ancienne-Comédie, 6th, 01.40.46.79.00), whose customers have included Voltaire, Rousseau, Verlaine – and, today, tourists. Look out for Voltaire's desk and a postcard from Marie-Antoinette. The back opens on to the twee, cobbled passage du Commerce-St-André, home to toy shops, jewellers and chintzy tearooms.

In the 18th century Dr Joseph-Ignace Guillotin first tested out his notorious device – designed, believe it or not, to make executions more humane – in the cellars of what is today the Pub St-Germain (17 rue de l'Ancienne-Comédie, 6th, 01.56.81.13.13); the first victim was, reputedly, a sheep. Jacobin regicide Billaud-Varenne was among those who felt the steel of Guillotin's gadget; his former home at 45 rue St-André-des-Arts was the site of the first girls' *lycée* in Paris, the Lycée Fénelon, founded in 1883. On quiet side streets such as rue des Grands-Augustins, rue de Savoie and rue Séguier, you'll find printers, bookshops and dignified 17th-century *hôtels particuliers*. On the corner of rue and quai des Grands-Augustins, **Lapérouse** restaurant (*see p214*) has a row of intimate private dining rooms, where gentlemen entertained their mistresses; Les Bouquinistes (53 quai des Grands-Augustins, 6th, 01.43.25. 45.94) is easier to peek into. Begun in 1292, the Hôtel de Fécamp, at 5 rue de Hautefeuille, was the townhouse of the abbots of Fécamp; nearby no.13 is the birthplace of poet Baudelaire. Another literary landmark is at 9 rue Gît-le-Coeur, where William Burroughs revised *Naked Lunch* at the Hôtel du Vieux Paris (6th, 01.44.32.15.90).

## Ecole Nationale Supérieure des Beaux-Arts (Ensb-a)

*14 rue Bonaparte, 6th (01.47.03.50.00/www. ensba.fr). M° St-Germain-des-Prés.* **Open** *Courtyard* 9am-5pm Mon-Fri. *Exhibitions* 1-5pm Tue-Sun. **Admission** €4; €2 reductions. *Exhibitions* prices vary. **Credit** V. **Map** p408 H6.

The city's most prestigious fine arts school resides in what remains of the 17th-century Couvent des Petits-Augustins, the 18th-century Hôtel de Chimay, some 19th-century additions and some chunks of assorted French châteaux moved here after the Revolution (when the buildings briefly served as a museum of French monuments, before becoming the art school in 1816). Exhibitions are often held here; the entrance is on quai Malaquais.

## Eglise St-Germain-des-Prés

*3 pl St-Germain-des-Prés, 6th (01.55.42.81.33/www. eglise-sgp.org). M° St-Germain-des-Prés.* **Open** 8am-7.45pm Mon-Sat; 9am-8pm Sun. **Map** p408 H7.

The oldest church in Paris. On the advice of Germain (later Bishop of Paris), Childebert, son of Clovis, had a basilica and monastery built here around 543. It was first dedicated to St Vincent, and came to be known as St-Germain-le-Doré ('the gilded') because of its copper roof, then later as St-Germain-des-Prés ('of the fields'). During the Revolution the abbey was burned and a saltpetre refinery installed; the spire was added in a clumsy 19th-century restoration. Still, most of the present structure is 12th century, and ornate carved capitals and the tower remain from the 11th. Tombs include those of Jean-Casimir, the deposed King of Poland who became Abbot of St-Germain in 1669, and of Scots nobleman William Douglas. Under the window in the second chapel is the funeral stone of philosopher-mathematician René Descartes; his ashes have been here since 1819.

## Institut de France

*23 quai de Conti, 6th (01.44.41.44.41/www.institut-de-france.fr). M° Louvre Rivoli or Pont Neuf.* **Open** *Guided tours* Sat, Sun (01.44.41.43.32/ www.monum.fr; call for times). **Admission** €8; €6 under-25s. **No credit cards. Map** p408 H6.

This elegant domed building with two sweeping curved wings was designed as a school (founded by Cardinal Mazarin for provincial children) by Louis Le Vau and opened in 1684. The five academies of the Institut (Académie Française, Académie des Inscriptions et Belles-Lettres, Académie des Beaux-Arts, Académie des Sciences, Académie des Sciences Morales et Politiques) moved here in 1805. Inside is Mazarin's ornate tomb by Hardouin-Mansart, and the Bibliothèque Mazarine (open to over-18s with ID and two photos; €15/year). The Académie Française, zealous guardian of the French language,

**Institut de France.**

was founded by Cardinal Richelieu in 1635 with the aim of preserving the purity of French from corrupting outside influences (such as English).

## Musée de la Monnaie de Paris

*11 quai de Conti, 6th (01.40.46.55.35/www.monnaie deparis.fr). M° Odéon or Pont Neuf.* **Open** 11am-5.30pm Tue-Fri; noon-5.30pm Sat, Sun. Closed Aug. **Admission** (incl audio guide) €8; free under-16s. **Credit** *Shop* AmEx, MC, V. **Map** p408 H6.

Housed in the handsome neo-classical mint built in the 1770s, this high-tech museum tells the tale of global and local coinage from its pre-Roman origins, using sophisticated displays and audio-visual presentations. The history of the franc, from its wartime debut in 1360, is outlined in detail.

## Musée National Delacroix

*6 pl de Furstemberg, 6th (01.44.41.86.50/www. musee-delacroix.fr). M° St-Germain-des-Prés.* **Open** 9.30am-4.30pm Mon, Wed-Sun. **Admission** €5; free under-18s, all on 1st Sun of mth. PMP. **Credit** MC, V. **Map** p408 H7.

Romantic painter Eugène Delacroix moved to this apartment and studio in 1857 in order to be near the Eglise St-Sulpice, where he was painting murals. The Louvre and the Musée d'Orsay house his major canvas works, but this collection includes small oil paintings (among them *Madeleine au Désert*), free pastel studies of skies, sketches and lithographs, as well as his palette. Exhibits include correspondence between Baudelaire and George Sand.

## St-Sulpice & the Luxembourg

*In the 6th arrondissement.*

Crammed with historic buildings and inviting shops, the quarter south of boulevard St-Germain between Odéon and Luxembourg epitomises civilised Paris. Just off the boulevard lies the covered market of St-Germain, now the

site of a shopping arcade, auditorium, food hall and underground swimming pool. There are bars and bistros along rue Guisarde, nicknamed rue de la Soif ('thirst street') thanks to its carousers; it contains the late-night Birdland bar (no.8, 6th, 01.43.26.97.59) and a couple of notable bistros: Mâchon d'Henri (no.8, 6th, 01.43.29.08.70) and Brasserie Fernand (no.13, 6th, 01.43.54.61.47). Rue Princesse and rue des Canettes are a mix of budget eateries and nocturnal haunts.

Pass the fashion boutiques, pâtisseries and antiquarian book and print shops and you come to **Eglise St-Sulpice**, a surprising 18th-century exercise in classical form with two unmatching turrets and a colonnaded façade. The square in front was designed in the 19th century by Visconti; it contains his imposing, lion-flanked Fontaine des Quatre Points Cardinaux (a pun on cardinal points and the statues of Bishops Bossuet, Fénelon, Massilon and Flechier, none of whom was actually a cardinal). It's now the centrepiece for the **Foire St-Germain**, a summer arts fair. The Café de la Mairie (8 pl St-Sulpice, 6th, 01.43.26.67.82) is a favourite with Left Bank intellectuals and students.

Amid shops of religious artefacts, the chic boutiques on place and rue St-Sulpice include **Yves Saint Laurent** (*see p250*), **Vanessa Bruno** (*see p250*) and milliner **Marie Mercié** (*see p257*). Prime shopping continues further west: clothes on rue Bonaparte and rue du Four, and accessory and fashion shops on rue du Dragon, rue de Grenelle and rue du Cherche-Midi. If you spot a queue in the latter, it's most likely for the bread at **Poilâne** (*see p260*). Across the street, at the junction of rue de Sèvres and rue du Cherche-Midi, César's bronze *Centaur* is the sculptor's tribute to Picasso.

# Paris promenade Literary lions

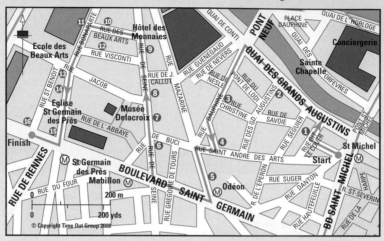

Nowhere on earth are there so many literary associations in so small an area as St-Germain-des-Prés. The myth of the struggling writer in a garret might have died now that Louis Vuitton has opened next to Les Deux Magots, but the ghosts, along with a dense concentration of bookshops, wholesalers and publishers, are still in evidence. So put on a pair of stout 'Gertrude Stein shoes', grab your 'Left Bank hat' (for Joycean dash) and set forth on a literary expedition.

Start at métro St-Michel, muttering 'when I was in Paris, boul' Mich', I used to...' (*Ulysses*), and take the rue de l'Hirondelle passageway to the right of the fountain. This will bring you out on rue Gît-le-Coeur. At no.9, on your right, is the **Relais Hôtel Vieux Paris** (**①**), also known as the Beat Hotel. It's been smartened up since a drug-addled William Burroughs wrote *Naked Lunch* here, but pictures of the Beats adorn the wall and Mme Odillard will show fans photos of those wild times in a signed copy of Brian Chapman's book *The Beat Hotel*. Walk on to join the quai des Grands-Augustins, opposite Les

Bouquinistes, where restaurant **Lapérouse** (**②**; *see p214*), at no.51, was a literary hot spot from 1870: its small salons – designed for dangerous liaisons – hosted the likes of Sand, Maupassant, Zola, Dumas and Hugo.

Next turn left down rue Dauphine, where Alain Fournier, author of *Le Grand Meaulnes*, lived at no.24 (**③**), and drop down rue Mazet. The restaurant **Magny**, where George Sand smoked cigars with Flaubert, Gautier and Turgenev at Sainte-Beuve's literary dinners, was at no.3; it's now called Azabu (**④**).

Crossing rue St-André-des-Arts, go through the archway at no.59 to find a charming covered passage and the back entrance of **Procope** (**⑤**). Dating from 1686, it's the city's oldest café and boasts Voltaire, Rousseau, the Marquis de Sade, Beaumarchais, Balzac, Verlaine, Hugo, La Fontaine and Anatole France among its former customers. The food, unfortunately, is mediocre, but upstairs you can see Voltaire's marble desk and a letter from the imprisoned Marie-Antoinette.

From here, turn right into boulevard St-Germain, and right again two roads up into

The early 17th-century chapel of St-Joseph-des-Carmes – once a Carmelite convent, now hidden within the Institut Catholique (21 rue d'Assas, 6th, 01.44.39.52.00, www.icp.fr) – was the scene of the murder of 115 priests during the Terror in 1792. To the east lies wide rue de

Tournon, lined by such grand 18th-century residences as the elegant Hôtel de Brancas (no.6), with figures of Justice and Prudence over the door. This street opens up to the **Palais du Luxembourg**, which now serves as the Senate, and the adjoining **Jardin du Luxembourg**.

rue de Seine, which is peppered with literary haunts. At no.60 is the modest **Hôtel La Louisiane** (**❻**). Cyril Connolly's *The Unquiet Grave* describes the ferrets wearing bells that were kept here during the war; Simone de Beauvoir and Sartre, along with many other Café Flore regulars, lodged here towards the end of the war. The only memorabilia on show is a newspaper interview with Juliette Greco, but the hotel has a living poet in situ: 95 year-old Albert Cossery, known as 'the last dandy', has lodged here for 62 years.

Further along at no.63 (**❼**), a plaque marks the house where Polish poet Adam Mickiewicz lived when his *Pan Tadeusz* was published in 1834. At no.57 (**❽**), its door crowned with the words 'Henri Diéval Maître Imprimeur', lived Baudelaire in the years when, stricken by debt, he only dared emerge at night. At no.31 (**❾**) a plaque attests to the fact that George Sand lived here in 1831. She arrived aged 26, having negotiated the right to spend half the year in Paris away from her philistine husband Casimir.

Take a left into rue des Beaux-Arts. At no.13 **L'Hôtel** (**❿**) was the scene of Oscar Wilde's death. The place has been opulently done up by Jacques Garcia, and Wilde's room contains a peacock print inspired by his London home. The Argentine writer Jorge Luis Borges was a frequent visitor to the hotel in the 1970s and '80s.

Turn left into rue Bonaparte. The corner building (**⓫**) is where William Cole stayed in 1765. His *Journal of My Journey to Paris* recounts an experience where a 'guide' exasperates him while he is mercilessly ripped off by his landlady.

Passing rue Visconti on the left, where Henry Miller taught his wife June to ride a bike, you'll see **Le Pré-aux-Clercs** (**⓬**) on the junction with rue Jacob. Still an unpretentious place, this art deco local was Hemingway's favourite restaurant when he lived at the Hôtel d'Angleterre. Miller's home when he arrived in Paris in 1930 was on the top floor of no.36 rue Bonaparte, the present-day **Hôtel St-Germain-des-Prés** (**⓭**). American lesbian columnist Janet Flanner, whose Letter from Paris appeared for almost 50 years in the *New Yorker*, was also a resident. Jean Cocteau smoked opium in room no.6, and Margaret Anderson, Jane Heap and Georgette Leblanc edited the last issue of *The Little Review* here, spilling green ink on the sheets. The present-day receptionists, however, know little about the literary aura of their workplace. **No.42 rue Bonaparte** (**⓮**), perhaps the most famous address on this road, remains unmarked. The 40-year-old Sartre moved into the fourth floor in 1945 with his mother and a piano, and stayed until 1962 when the apartment was bombed in protest at his stance against the war in Algeria. Were he resident today, the Marxist Sartre would doubtless look down with distaste on the Dior boutique below.

Only a few steps from here is café **Les Deux Magots** (**⓯**; *see p237*), a favourite hang-out of Sartre and de Beauvoir in the closing years of the war. Covert messages were exchanged between members of the Resistance in the café's toilets, over which a charming *dame pipi* still presides. The Deux Magots' literary associations are many – the walls are covered with photos of Hemingway and the Surrealists. While the terrace is filled with St Tropez types, the interior is still dignified and quiet enough to attract writers – even if they're just penning postcards.

To the right, along boulevard St-Germain, our tour ends with Les Deux Magots' Existentialist sister, **Café de Flore** (**⓰**; *see p236*), where Sartre and de Beauvoir virtually lived at the beginning of the war. Black American writers James Baldwin and Richard Wright also enjoyed the liberated spirit here; Baldwin completed *Go Tell It on the Mountain* in the Flore. These days the café awards its own writer's prize, and if you stay long enough you may see a famous face – Paul Auster or Paulo Coelho perhaps, both of whom have been known to drop in when they're in town.

Towards boulevard St-Germain is the neo-classical **Odéon, Théâtre de l'Europe** (*see p344*), built in 1779 and recently renovated. A house in the square in front was home to Revolutionary hero Camille Desmoulins, who incited the mob to attack the Bastille in 1789.

Now it's occupied by La Méditerranée (2 pl de l'Odéon, 6th, 01.43.26.02.30); an arty rendezvous in the 1940s, the restaurant's menus and plates were designed by Jean Cocteau. Joyce's *Ulysses* was first published in 1922 by Sylvia Beach at the iconic Shakespeare & Co at 12 rue de

l'Odéon (no relation to the current Latin Quarter bookshop, whose first owner was given permission to use the name). Next door is the venerable jukebox-blessed café **Le Bar Dix** (*see p236*).

Further along the street, at 12 rue de l'Ecole-de-Médecine, is the neo-classical Université René Descartes (Paris V) medical school, and the **Musée d'Histoire de la Médecine**. The Club des Cordeliers, set up by Danton in 1790, devised revolutionary plots across the street at the Couvent des Cordeliers (no.15); the 14th-century refectory, all that remains of the monastery founded by St Louis, houses modern art exhibitions. Marat, one of the club's leading lights, was stabbed to death in the bathtub at his home in the same street; David depicted the moment after the crime in his iconic painting, the *Death of Marat*. This was the surgeons' district: observe the sculpted doorway of the neighbouring *hôtel* and the domed building at no.5, once the barbers' and surgeons' guild. Climb rue André-Dubois to rue Monsieur-le-Prince to reach budget eaterie Polidor (no.41, 6th, 01.43.26.95.34), open since 1845.

### Eglise St-Sulpice

*Pl St-Sulpice, 6th (01.42.34.59.98/www.paroisse-saint-sulpice.org). M° St-Sulpice.* **Open** 7.30am-7.30pm daily. **Map** p408 H7.
It took 120 years (starting in 1646) and six architects to finish the church of St-Sulpice. The grandiose Italianate façade, with its two-tier colonnade, was designed by Jean-Baptiste Servandoni. He died in 1766 before the second tower was finished, leaving one tower a good five metres (16 feet) shorter than the other. The trio of murals by Delacroix in the first chapel – *Jacob's Fight with the Angel, Heliodorus Chased from the Temple* and *St Michael Killing the Dragon* – create a suitably sombre atmosphere.

### Jardin & Palais du Luxembourg

*Pl Auguste-Comte, pl Edmond-Rostand or rue de Vaugirard, 6th (01.42.34.23.89/www.senat.fr/visite). M° Odéon/RER Luxembourg.* **Open** *Jardin* summer 7.30am-dusk daily; winter 8am-dusk daily. **Map** p408 H8.
The palace was built in the 1620s for Marie de Médicis, widow of Henri IV, by Salomon de Brosse on the site of the former mansion of the Duke of Luxembourg. Its Italianate style, with Mannerist rusticated columns, was intended to remind her of the Pitti Palace in her native Florence. In 1621 she commissioned Rubens to produce the 24 huge paintings, now in the Louvre, celebrating her life. Reworked by Chalgrin in the 18th century, the palace now houses the French parliament's upper house, the Sénat (open only by guided visits or on the Journées du Patrimoine; *see p277*).
The mansion next door (l e Petit Luxembourg) is the residence of the Sénat's president. The gardens, though, are the real draw: part formal (terraces and

gravel paths), part 'English garden' (lawns and mature trees), they are the quintessential Paris park. The garden is almost crowded with sculptures: a looming Cyclops (on the 1624 Fontaine de Médicis), queens of France, a miniature Statue of Liberty, wild animals, busts of literary giants Flaubert and Baudelaire, and a monument to Delacroix. There are orchards (300 varieties of apples and pears) and an apiary. The Musée National du Luxembourg (*see below*) hosts prestigious art exhibitions, with lesser shows held in the former Orangerie. Most interesting, though, are the people: an international mixture of *flâneurs* and *dragueurs*, chess players and martial-arts practitioners, as well as children on ponies, in sandpits, on roundabouts and playing with the old-fashioned sailing boats on the pond (*see p284* **Playtime**). Then there are the tennis courts (*see p340*), *pétanque* pitches, and a bandstand.

### Musée d'Histoire de la Médecine

*Université René Descartes, 12 rue de l'Ecole-de-Médecine, 6th (01.40.46.16.93). M° Odéon or St-Michel.* **Open** *Mid July-Sept* 2-5.30pm Mon-Fri. *Oct-mid July* 2-5.30pm Mon-Wed, Fri, Sat. **Admission** €3.50; €2.50 students; free under-8s. **No credit cards**. **Map** p408 H7.
The history of medicine is the subject of the medical faculty collection. There are ancient Egyptian embalming tools, a 1960s electrocardiograph and a gruesome array of saws used for amputations. You'll also find the instruments of Dr Antommarchi, who performed the autopsy on Napoleon, and the scalpel of Dr Félix, who operated on Louis XIV.

### Musée des Lettres et Manuscrits

*8 rue de Nesle, 6th (01.40.51.02.25/www.museedeslettres.fr). M° Odéon.* **Open** 1-8pm Tue-Fri; 10am-6pm Sat-Sun. Closed Nov. **Admission** €6; €4.50 under-25s. **Credit** (€16 minimum) MC, V. **Map** p408 H7.
This intimate space in the heart of the Latin Quarter presents modern history as recorded in paper. More than 2,000 documents and letters give an insight into the lives of the great and the good, from Magritte to Mozart and Freud to François Mitterrand. Einstein arrives at the theory of relativity on notes scattered in authentic disorder, Baudelaire complains about his money problems in a letter to his mother and HMS *Northumberland*'s log-book records the day Napoleon boarded the ship to be taken to St Helena.

### Musée National du Luxembourg

*19 rue de Vaugirard, 6th (01.42.34.25.95/www.museeduluxembourg.fr). M° Cluny La Sorbonne or Odéon/RER Luxembourg.* **Open** 10.30am-10pm Mon, Fri, Sat; 10.30am-7pm Tue-Thur; 9am-7pm Sun. **Admission** €11; €9 students, 8-25s; free under-8s. **Credit** MC, V. **Map** p408 H7.
When it opened in 1750, this small museum was the first public gallery in France. Its current stewardship by the national museums and the French Senate has brought imaginative touches and some impressive coups. Until July 2008 there's an exhibition commemorating 50 years since the death of Fauvist Maurice de Vlaminck. Book ahead to avoid queues.

# Montparnasse & Beyond

Studios, skeletons and the city's first skyscraper.

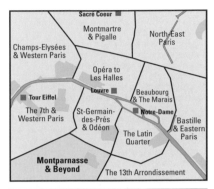

## Montparnasse

*In the 6th & 14th arrondissements.*
Artists Picasso, Léger and Soutine fled to 'Mount Parnassus' in the early 1900s to escape the rising rents of Montmartre. They were soon joined by Chagall, Zadkine and other refugees from the Russian Revolution, along with Americans such as Man Ray, Henry Miller, Ezra Pound and Gertrude Stein. Between the wars the neighbourhood was the epitome of modernity: studios with large windows were built by avant-garde architects; artists, writers and intellectuals drank and debated in the quarter's showy bars; and naughty pastimes – including the then risqué tango – flourished.

Sadly, the Montparnasse of today has lost much of its former soul, dominated as it is by the lofty **Tour Montparnasse** – the first skyscraper in central Paris. The dismay with which its construction was greeted prompted a change in building regulations in central Paris. At its foot are a shopping centre, the **Red Light** and **Club Mix** nightclubs (*see p330 and p331*) and an open-air ice rink in winter (*see p338*). For those with a head for heights, there are fabulous panoramic views to be had from the café on the 56th floor.

The old Montparnasse railway station witnessed two events of historic significance: in 1898 a runaway train burst through its façade (you've almost certainly seen the photograph),

and on 25 August 1944 the German forces surrendered Paris here. The station was rebuilt in the 1970s, a grey affair above which can be found the surprising **Jardin Atlantique**, the **Mémorial du Maréchal Leclerc** and the **Musée Jean Moulin**.

Rue du Montparnasse, appropriately enough for a street near the station that sends trains to Brittany, is dotted with crêperies. Nearby, strip joints have replaced most of the theatres on the ever-saucy rue de la Gaîté, but boulevard Edgar-Quinet has pleasant cafés and a street market (Wed, Sat), plus the entrance to the **Cimetière du Montparnasse**. Boulevard du Montparnasse still buzzes at night, thanks to its many cinemas and dining spots: giant art deco brasserie La Coupole (*see p216*); opposite, classic café Le Select (*see p238*); Le Dôme (no.108, 14th, 01.43.35.25.81), now a top-notch

**Fondation Cartier pour l'Art Contemporain.** *See p163.*

fish restaurant and bar; and restaurant La Rotonde (no.105, 6th, 01.43.26.48.26). All were popularised by the literati between the wars, and now use this heritage to their advantage; Le Select seems the most authentic. Nearby, on boulevard Raspail, stands Rodin's statue of Balzac, whose rugged rather than flattering appearance caused such a scandal that it was put in place only after the sculptor's death.

For a whiff of Montparnasse's artistic history, wander down rue de la Grande-Chaumière. Bourdelle and Friesz taught at the venerable Académie de la Grande-Chaumière (no.14), frequented by Calder, Giacometti and Pompon among others (it still offers drawing lessons); Modigliani died at no.8 in 1920, ruined by tuberculosis, drugs and alcohol; nearby **Musée Zadkine** occupies the sculptor's old house and studio. Rue Vavin and rue Bréa, leading to the Jardin du Luxembourg (*see p160*), have become an enclave of children's shops. Look out for no.6, the 1912 white-tiled apartment building where art nouveau architect Henri Sauvage lived.

Further east on boulevard du Montparnasse, literary café La Closerie des Lilas (no.171, 6th,

01.40.51.34.50) was a pre-war favourite with everyone from Lenin and Trotsky to Picasso and Hemingway; brass plaques on the tables indicate where each historic figure used to sit. Next to it is the lovely Fontaine de l'Observatoire, featuring bronze turtles and thrashing sea horses by Frémiet and figures of the four continents by Carpeaux.

From here, the Jardins de l'Observatoire form part of the green axis 1900 between the Palais du Luxembourg (*see p160*) and the original royal observatory, the **Observatoire de Paris**. A curiosity next door is the Maison des Fontainiers, built over an expansive (now dry-ish) underground reservoir originally commissioned by Marie de Médicis to supply water to fountains around the city.

A relatively recent addition to boulevard Raspail is the glass-and-steel **Fondation Cartier pour l'Art Contemporain**. Designed by architect Jean Nouvel, it houses the jewellers' head offices and an exhibition space dedicated to contemporary art and photography.

West of the train station, the redevelopment of Montparnasse is also evident in the circular place de Catalogne, a piece of 1980s postmodern

neo-classicism by Mitterrand's favourite
architect, Ricardo Bofill, and the housing
estates of rue Vercingétorix.

Traces of arty Montparnasse remain too:
in impasse Lebouis, an avant-garde studio
building has recently been converted into the
**Fondation Henri Cartier-Bresson**; at 21
avenue du Maine, an ivy-clad alleyway of
old studios contains the artist-run exhibition
space Immanence, as well as the **Musée du
Montparnasse**, housed in the former academy
and canteen of Russian painter Marie Vassilieff;
on rue Antoine-Bourdelle, the **Musée
Bourdelle** includes another old cluster of
studios, where sculptor Bourdelle, Symbolist
painter Eugène Carrière and, briefly, Marc
Chagall worked. Towards Les Invalides, on
rue Mayet, craft and restoration workshops
still hide in the old courtyards.

### Cimetière du Montparnasse

*3 bd Edgar-Quinet, 14th (01.44.10.86.50). M° Edgar
Quinet or Raspail.* **Open** *16 Mar-5 Nov* 8am-6pm
Mon-Fri; 8.30am-6pm Sat; 9am-6pm Sun. *6 Nov-
15 Mar* 8am-5.30pm Mon-Fri; 8.30am-5.30pm Sat;
9.30am-5.30pm Sun. **Admission** free. **Map** p405 G9.

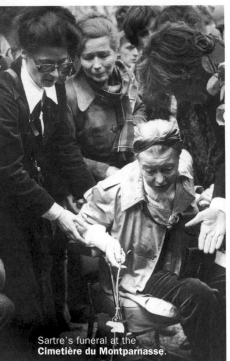

Sartre's funeral at the
**Cimetière du Montparnasse.**

This 1,800-acre cemetery was formed by con
deering three farms (you can still see the ruins
rural windmill by rue Froidevaux) in 1824. As w
much of the Left Bank, the Montparnasse cemeter
scores highly for literary credibility: Beckett,
Baudelaire, Sartre, de Beauvoir, Maupassant,
Ionesco and Tristan Tzara all rest here; the artists
include Brancusi, Henri Laurens, Frédéric Bartholdi
(sculptor of the Statue of Liberty) and Man Ray. The
celebrity roll-call continues with Serge Gainsbourg,
André Citroën (of automobile fame), comic Coluche
and actress Jean Seberg.

### Fondation Cartier pour l'Art Contemporain

*261 bd Raspail, 14th (01.42.18.56.72/recorded
information 01.42.18.56.51/www.fondation.
cartier.fr). M° Denfert-Rochereau or Raspail.*
**Open** 10am-10pm Tue; 10am-8pm Wed-Sun.
**Admission** €7.50; €5.50 reductions; free under-10s.
**Credit** AmEx, MC, V. **Map** p405 G9.
Jean Nouvel's glass-and-steel building, an exhibition
centre with Cartier's offices above, is as much a work
of art as the installations inside. Shows by artists
and photographers often have wide-ranging themes,
such as 'Birds' or 'Desert'. Live events around the
shows are called Nuits Nomades. *Photo p161.*

### Fondation Dubuffet

*137 rue de Sèvres, 6th (01.47.34.12.63/www.
dubuffetfondation.com). M° Duroc.* **Open** 2-6pm
Mon-Fri. Closed Aug. **Admission** €4; free under-10s.
**No credit cards**. **Map** p405 E8.
You have to walk up a winding garden path to get
to this museum housed in an old three-storey mansion. Founded by Jean Dubuffet, wine merchant and
master of *art brut,* a decade before his death in 1985,
the foundation ensures that a fair body of his works
is accessible to the public. There's a changing display of Dubuffet's lively drawings, paintings and
sculptures, plus models of the architectural sculptures from the *Hourloupe* cycle. The foundation
looks after the *Closerie Falbala*, the 3D masterpiece
of the cycle, housed at Périgny-sur-Yerres, east of
Paris (viewings by appointment only, €8).

### Fondation Henri Cartier-Bresson

*2 impasse Lebouis, 14th (01.56.80.27.00/www.
henricartierbresson.org). M° Gaîté.* **Open** 1-6.30pm
Tue-Fri, Sun; 1-8.30pm Wed; 11am-6.45pm Sat.
Closed Aug & between exhibitions. **Admission** €6;
€3 students, under-26s, over-60s, all 6.30-8.30pm
Wed. **No credit cards. Map** p405 F10.
Opened in 2003, this two-floor gallery is dedicated
to acclaimed photographer Henri Cartier-Bresson. It
consists of a tall, narrow *atelier* in a 1913 building,
with a minutely catalogued archive, open to
researchers, and a lounge on the fourth floor screening films. In the spirit of Cartier-Bresson, who assist-
ed on three Jean Renoir films and drew and painted
all his life (some drawings are also found on the
fourth floor), the Fondation opens its doors to other
disciplines with three annual shows. The convivial

**Sightseeing**

# Easy rider

Undeterred by the failure of similar enterprises in Amsterdam, Cambridge and Toronto, the mayor of Paris launched Vélib', the city's new free bicycle scheme, on 15 July 2007, with 10,000 gleaming grey bikes delivered in the dead of night to stands around the city. Parisians have been quick to adopt the new mode of transport (more than two million people took a test ride in the first 40 days), and they can be seen whizzing and wobbling along recently designated cycle paths.

As well as being a joy to ride, the bikes look pretty fantastic, with curvaceous handlebars and efficient dynamo lights. They were designed with the support of trendy hotel stylist Patrick Jouin, making them an instant hit with the fashionable crowd.

Bikes can be hired on a daily or weekly basis; payment is made directly at the regularly positioned *bornes* (parking meter stands). Choose English from the menu, then tap in your credit or debit card pin to authorise a default penalty payment (€150, like a deposit, in case you don't return the bike). The bicycles are easy to ride; despite being heavy, once you get one going it simply sails along.

A major pitfall in the system, however, soon becomes apparent should you choose to take your bike out to one of the popular nightlife areas such as Bastille or Oberkampf. With everyone going to the same place at the same time, all the *bornes* (like parking spaces) are likely to be full, and you could end up circling for hours or parking miles from your destination.

Although it is possible to 'identify' yourself to gain an extra 15 minutes' circling time and avoid an overtime penalty, in the worst case scenario you could arrive home in the small hours to find no spaces at the nearby *bornes*. The fine for keeping the bike longer than planned is steep: €1 for the first half hour, €2 for the second, and a hefty €4 for every half hour after that, which could mean losing up to €70 because you can't find a place to check it in at the end of the night. It can feel like playing Russian roulette with your credit card; holding on to the bike for good (€150 – the initial deposit) may seem a better option, except that they've been designed so only the management company can do repairs.

Nevertheless, Parisians seem to be enjoying the new sport of hovering, vulture-like, to snap up vacated *bornes*, or tossing coins to see who gets one. It's also worth remembering that the police have adopted a zero tolerance policy to Vélib' riders caught running red lights – particularly if they've had a few. The fine is €90, and you'll be expected to produce identification on the spot.

Hopefully Vélib' will have ironed out its teething troubles by the time this guide goes to press. By then a total of 20,000 bikes will be in action, and it is claimed that there will be 70 per cent more parking *bornes* than bikes. So if the lorries redistributing the bikes each night do their jobs properly, the system should function. One major oversight, though, is that they can't be used by Americans because they don't have chip and pin cards. *www.velib.paris.fr*

feel of the Fondation – and its Le Corbusier armchairs – foster relaxed discussion with staff and other visitors.

### Jardin Atlantique

*Gare Montparnasse or pl des Cinq-Martyrs-du-Lycée-Buffon, 15th. M° Gaîté or Montparnasse Bienvenüe.* **Open** 8am-dusk Mon-Fri; 9am-dusk Sat, Sun. **Map** p405 F9.
Perhaps the hardest of all the gardens in Paris to find, the Jardin Atlantique was opened in 1995. It's an engineering feat in itself: a modest oasis of granite paths, trees and bamboo is spread over the roof 18m (59ft) above the tracks of Montparnasse train station. Small openings allow you to peer down on the trains below; children seem to love the randomly triggered fountain jets.

### Mémorial du Maréchal Leclerc de Hauteclocque et de la Libération de Paris & Musée Jean Moulin

*Jardin Atlantique, 23 allée de la 2e DB (above Gare Montparnasse), 15th (01.40.64.39.44/www.ml-leclerc-moulin.paris.fr). M° Montparnasse Bienvenüe.* **Open** 10am-6pm Tue-Sun. **Admission** free. *Exhibitions* €4; €3 students, over-60s; €2 under-26s; free under-13s. **Credit** *Shop* MC, V. **Map** p405 F9.
This double museum retraces World War II and the Resistance through the Free French commander General Leclerc and left-wing hero Jean Moulin. Documentary material and film archives complement an impressive 270° slide show, complete with sound effects retelling the Liberation of Paris.

### Musée-Atelier Adzak

*3 rue Jonquoy, 14th (01.45.43.06.98). M° Plaisance.* **Open** usually 3-7pm Sat, Sun (call in advance). **Admission** free.
The eccentric house, studio and garden built by the late Roy Adzak harbour traces of the conceptual artist's plaster body columns and dehydrations. Now a registered British-run charity, it gives mostly foreign artists a chance to exhibit in Paris.

### Musée Bourdelle

*16-18 rue Antoine-Bourdelle, 15th (01.49.54.73.73/ www.bourdelle.paris.fr). M° Falguière or Montparnasse Bienvenüe.* **Open** 10am-6pm Tue-Sun. **Admission** free. *Exhibitions* prices vary. **Credit** MC, V. **Map** p405 F8.
The sculptor Antoine Bourdelle (1861-1929), pupil of Rodin, produced monumental works including the Modernist relief friezes at the Théâtre des Champs-Elysées (*see p316*), inspired by Isadora Duncan and Nijinsky. Set around a small garden, the museum includes the artist's apartment and studios, which were also used by Eugène Carrière, Dalou and Chagall. A 1950s extension tracks the evolution of Bourdelle's equestrian monument to General Alvear in Buenos Aires, and his masterful *Hercules the Archer*. A new wing by Christian de Portzamparc houses bronzes including various studies of Beethoven in different guises.

### Musée du Montparnasse

*21 av du Maine, 15th (01.42.22.91.96/www. museedumontparnasse.net). M° Montparnasse Bienvenüe.* **Open** 12.30-7pm Tue-Sun. **Admission** €6; €5 students, 12-18s; free under-12s. **No credit cards. Map** p403 F8.
Set in one of the last surviving alleys of studios, this was home to Marie Vassilieff, whose own academy and cheap canteen welcomed poor artists Picasso, Cocteau and Matisse. Trotsky and Lenin were also guests. Shows focus on the area's creative past and present-day artists.

### Musée Pasteur

*Institut Pasteur, 25 rue du Dr-Roux, 15th (01.45.68.82.83/www.pasteur.fr). M° Pasteur.* **Open** 2-5.30pm Mon-Fri. Closed Aug. **Admission** €3; €1.50 students. **Credit** MC, V. **Map** p405 E9.
The flat where the famous chemist and his wife lived at the end of his life (1888-95) has not been touched; you can see their furniture and possessions, photos and instruments. An extravagant mausoleum on the ground floor houses Pasteur's tomb, decorated with mosaics depicting his scientific achievements.

### Musée de la Poste

*34 bd de Vaugirard, 15th (01.42.79.23.45/www. museedelaposte.fr). M° Montparnasse Bienvenüe.* **Open** 10am-6pm Mon-Sat. **Admission** €5; €3.50 students under 26; free under-18s. PMP. *Permanent & temporary exhibitions* €6.50; €5 students under 26; free under-18s. **No credit cards. Map** p405 E9.
From among the uniforms, pistols, carriages, official decrees and fumigation tongs emerge snippets of history: during the 1871 Siege of Paris, hot-air balloons and carrier pigeons were used to get post out of the city, and *boules de Moulins*, balls crammed with hundreds of letters, were floated down the Seine in return, mostly never to arrive. The second section covers French and international philately.

### Musée Zadkine

*100bis rue d'Assas, 6th (01.55.42.77.20/www. zadkine.paris.fr). M° Notre-Dame-des-Champs/RER Port-Royal.* **Open** 10am-6pm Tue-Sun. **Admission** free. *Exhibitions* €4; €3 students, over-60s; €2 under-26s; free under-13s. **Credit** (€15 minimum) MC, V. **Map** p408 G8.
Works by the Russian-born Cubist sculptor Ossip Zadkine are displayed around this tiny house and garden near the Jardin du Luxembourg. Zadkine's works cover musical, mythological and religious subjects, and his style varies with his materials. Works are displayed at eye level, with drawings and poems by Zadkine and paintings by his wife, Valentine Prax.

### Observatoire de Paris

*61 av de l'Observatoire, 14th (www.obspm.fr). M° St-Jacques/RER Port-Royal.* **Open** *Tours* 1st Sat of mth (except Aug) by written reservation only to: Service de la Communication (service des visites), Observatoire de Paris, 61 av de l'Observatoire, 75014 Paris. **Map** p405 H10.

The Paris observatory was founded by Louis XIV's finance minister, Colbert, in 1667; it was designed by Claude Perrault (who also worked on the Louvre), with labs and an observation tower. The French meridian line drawn by François Arago in 1806 (which was used here before the Greenwich meridian was adopted as an international standard) runs north–south through the centre of the building. The dome on the observation tower was added in the 1840s, but what with urban light pollution, most stargazing is now carried out in Meudon and Provence. A visit entails a prior written appointment, but check the website for openings linked to astronomical happenings – or visit on the Journées du Patrimoine (*see p277*).

## Tour Montparnasse
*33 av du Maine, 15th (01.45.38.52.56/www.tour montparnasse56.com). M° Montparnasse Bienvenüe.* **Open** 1 Oct-31 Mar 9.30am-10.30pm daily. 1 Apr-30 Sept 9.30am-11.30pm daily. **Admission** €9.50; €6.80 students; €4 7-15s; free under-7s. **Credit** MC, V. **Map** p405 F9.

Built in 1974 on the site of the old station, this 209m (686ft) steel-and-glass monolith is shorter than the Eiffel Tower, but better placed for fabulous views of the city – including, of course, the Eiffel Tower itself. A lift whisks you up in 38 seconds to the 56th floor, where you'll find a display of aerial scenes of Paris, an upgraded café-lounge, a souvenir shop – and plenty of sky. On a clear day you can see up to 40km (25 miles). Another lift takes you up to the roof. Classical concerts are held on the terrace.

## Denfert-Rochereau & Montsouris

*In the 14th & 15th arrondissements.*
In the run-up to the 1789 Revolution, the bones of six million Parisians were taken from the handful of overcrowded city cemeteries and wheelbarrowed to the **Catacombes**, a vast subterranean network of tunnels that stretches under much of Paris. The sections under the 13th and 14th arrondissements are open to the public; the gloomy Denfert-Rochereau entrance is next to one of the toll gates of the Mur des Fermiers-Généraux, built by Ledoux in the 1780s.

The bronze *Lion de Belfort* dominates the traffic-laden place Denfert-Rochereau, a favourite starting point for the city's countless political demonstrations. The regal beast was sculpted by Bartholdi, of Statue of Liberty fame, and is a scaled-down replica of one in Belfort that commemorates the brave defence by Colonel Denfert-Rochereau of the town in 1870. Nearby, the southern half of rue Daguerre is a sociable, pedestrianised market street (Tuesday to Saturday, Sunday mornings) brimming with cafés and food stores.

One of the big draws here is the **Parc Montsouris**, with lovely lakes, dramatic cascades and an unusual history. Surrounding the western edge of the park are a number of modest, quiet streets – including rue du Parc Montsouris and rue Georges-Braque – that used to be lined in the 1920s and '30s with charming villas and artists' studios by avant-garde architects Le Corbusier and André Lurçat. On the southern edge of the park sprawls the **Cité Universitaire** complex, containing three dozen internationally themed halls of residence occupied by 6,000 students.

## Les Catacombes
*1 av Colonel Henri-Rol-Tanguy, 14th (01.43.22.47.63/www.catacombes.info). M°/RER Denfert Rochereau.* **Open** 9.30am-4pm Tue-Sun. **Admission** €5; €3.30 over-60s; €2.50 students, 14-26s; free under-14s. **Credit** (€15 minimum) MC, V. **Map** p407 H10.

This is the official entrance (there are numerous unofficial entrances in other arrondissements) to the extensive network of subterranean passages that runs under much of the city, particularly the 13th and 14th arrondissements. The 3,000km (1,864-mile) tunnel network started its life as a series of quarries, providing limestone for huge building projects such as Notre-Dame. By the late 18th century, when the city had extended this far south, many streets began to collapse. The authorities set about building tunnels and supports to prop up the earth. At the same time, with public burial pits overflowing in the era of the Revolutionary Terror, the bones of six million people were transferred to the *catacombes*. The bones of Marat, Robespierre and their cronies are tightly packed in with wall upon wall of their fellow citizens. It's an extraordinary sight, but it's not a journey for the faint-hearted: an 85-step spiral staircase takes visitors some 20m (66ft) below ground level to a mass of bones and carvings. Make sure you carry a torch with you – and don't try to take away one of the bones as a souvenir: your bags will be checked at the end.

## Cité Universitaire
*17 bd Jourdan, 14th (01.44.16.64.00/www.ciup.fr). RER Cité Universitaire.*
The Cité Internationale Universitaire de Paris is an odd mix. Created between the wars in a mood of internationalism and inspired by the model of Oxbridge colleges, the 37 halls of residence spread across landscaped gardens were designed in a variety of supposedly authentic national styles, some by architects of the appropriate nationality (Dutchman Willem Dudok, for instance, designed the De Stijl-style Collège Néerlandais); others, such as the Asie du Sud-Est building, with its Khmer sculptures and bird-beak roof, are merely exotic pastiches. The Brits get what looks like a minor public school; the Maison Internationale is based on Fontainebleau; the Swiss and Brazilians get Le Corbusier. You

Get your five a day on pedestrianised **Rue Daguerre**.

can visit the sculptural white Pavillon Suisse (01.44.16.10.16, www.fondationsuisse.fr), which has a Le Corbusier mural on the ground floor. The Cité's spacious landscaped gardens are open to the public, and the newly renovated theatre stages a mix of drama and modern dance. To apply to rent a room here, *see p378*.

### Parc Montsouris

*Bd Jourdan, 14th. RER Cité Universitaire.* **Open** 8am-dusk Mon-Fri; 9am-dusk Sat, Sun.
The most colourful of the capital's many parks, Montsouris was laid out for Baron Haussmann by Jean-Charles Adolphe Alphand. It includes a series of sweeping, gently sloping lawns, an artificial lake and cascades. On the opening day in 1878 the lake inexplicably emptied, and the engineer responsible committed suicide.

## The 15th arrondissement

Centred on the shopping streets of rue du Commerce and rue Lecourbe, the expansive 15th arrondissement has little to offer tourists, though as a largely residential district it has plenty of good restaurants and street markets. It's worth making a detour to visit **La Ruche** ('beehive'), designed by Eiffel as a wine pavilion for the 1900 Exposition Universelle and moved here to serve as artists' studios. Nearby is **Parc Georges Brassens**, opened in 1983, while at the porte de Versailles the sprawling **Paris-Expo** exhibition centre was created in 1923.

### Parc Georges Brassens

*Rue des Morillons, 15th. M° Porte de Vanves or Porte de Versailles.* **Open** 8am-dusk Mon-Fri; 9am-dusk Sat, Sun. **Map** p404 D10.
Built on the site of the old Abattoirs de Vaugirard, Parc Georges Brassens prefigured the industrial regeneration of Parc André Citroën and La Villette. The gateways, crowned by bronze bulls, have been kept, as have a series of iron meat-market pavilions, which house a second-hand book market at weekends. The Jardin des Senteurs is planted with aromatic species, and a small vineyard yields 200 bottles of Clos des Morillons every year.

### Paris-Expo

*1 pl de la Porte de Versailles, 15th (01.72.72.17.00/ www.paris-expo.fr). M° Porte de Versailles.* **Map** p404 B10.
This vast exhibition centre, spread over different halls, hosts all manner of trade and art fairs. Many, such as the Foire de Paris (*see p274*) and art fair FIAC (*see p300*), are open to the public.

### La Ruche

*Passage de Dantzig, 15th. M° Convention or Porte de Versailles.* **Map** p404 D10.
Take a peek through the fence or sneak in behind an unsuspecting resident to see the iron-framed former wine pavilion built by Eiffel for the 1900 Exposition Universelle, and rebuilt by philanthropic sculptor Alfred Boucher to be let as studios for struggling artists. Chagall, Soutine, Brancusi, Modigliani, Lipchitz and Archipenko spent periods here, and the 140 studios are still sought after by today's artists and designers.

# The 7th & Western Paris

To the east, elegant courtyards and exclusive shops. To the west, military history and monumental avenues.

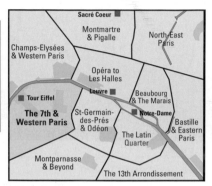

Townhouses spread west from St-Germain into the buttoned-up, establishment seventh arrondissement, with streetlife and café culture giving way to tranquil residential blocks and government offices. The seventh divides into the intimate Faubourg St-Germain, with its historic mansions and fine shops, and **Les Invalides**, with its wide windswept avenues and the **Eiffel Tower**.

## The Faubourg St-Germain

*In the 7th arrondissement.*

In the early 18th century, when the Marais went out of fashion, aristocrats built palatial new residences on the Faubourg St-Germain, the district developing around the site of the former city wall. It is still a well-bred part of the city, government ministries and foreign embassies colouring the area with flags and diplomatic number plates. Many fine *hôtels particuliers* survive; glimpse their stone gateways and elegant entrance courtyards on rues de Grenelle, St-Dominique, de l'Université and de Varenne.

Just west of St-Germain, the 'Carré Rive Gauche' or 'Carré des Antiquaires' – the quadrangle enclosed by quai Voltaire, rue des Sts-Pères, rue du Bac and rue de l'Université – is filled with antique shops. On rue des Sts-Pères, *chocolatier* Debauve &

Gallais (no.30, 7th, 01.45.48.54.67), with its period interior, has been making chocolates since 1800, originally for medicinal purposes. Rue du Pré-aux-Clercs, named after a field where students used to sort out their differences by duelling, is today a favourite with fashion insiders. There are still students to be found on adjoining rue St-Guillaume, home of the prestigious Fondation Nationale des Sciences-Politiques (no.27, 7th, 01.45.49.50.50), more commonly known as 'Sciences-Po'.

Rue de Montalembert is home to two of the Left Bank's most fashionable hotels: the **Hôtel Montalembert** (*see p75*) and the Hôtel du Pont-Royal, a gastronomic magnet ever since the addition of the trendy **Atelier de Joël Robuchon** (*see p217*). By the river, a Beaux-Arts train station – the towns once served still listed on the façade – houses the unmissable art collections of the **Musée d'Orsay**; outside on the esplanade are 19th-century bronze *animalier* sculptures. Next door is the lovely 1780s Hôtel de Salm, a mansion built for a German count, once the Swedish embassy and now the Musée National de la Légion d'Honneur et des Ordres de Chevalerie (2 rue de Bellechasse, 7th, 01.40.62.84.25), devoted to France's honours system since Louis XI. The Legion of Honour was established by Napoleon in 1802. Across the street, a modern footbridge, the Passerelle Solférino, crosses the Seine to the Tuileries. The fancy Hôtel Bouchardon today houses the **Musée Maillol**. Right beside its curved entrance, the Fontaine des Quatre Saisons by Edmé Bouchardon features statues of the seasons surrounding allegorical figures of Paris above the rivers Seine and Marne.

You'll have to wait for the open-house Journées du Patrimoine (*see p277*) to see the decorative interiors and private gardens of other *hôtels*, such as the Hôtel de Villeroy (Ministry of Agriculture; 78 rue de Varenne, 7th), Hôtel Boisgelin (Italian Embassy; 47 rue de Varenne, 7th), Hôtel d'Avaray (Dutch ambassador's residence; 85 rue de Grenelle, 7th), Hôtel d'Estrées (Russian ambassador's residence; 79 rue de Grenelle, 7th) or Hôtel de

Monaco (Polish Embassy; 57 rue St-Dominique, 7th). Among the most beautiful is the Hôtel Matignon (57 rue de Varenne, 7th), residence of the prime minister. Once used by French statesman Talleyrand for lavish receptions, it contains the biggest private garden in Paris. The Cité Varenne at no.51 is a lane of exclusive houses with private gardens.

Rue du Bac is home to the city's oldest and most elegant department store, **Le Bon Marché** ('the good bargain'; *see p240*), and to an unlikely pilgrimage spot, the **Chapelle de la Médaille Miraculeuse**. On nearby rue de Babylone, handy budget bistro Au Babylone (no.13, 7th, 01.45.48.72.13) has been serving up cheap lunches for decades, but the Théâtre de Babylone, where Beckett's *Waiting for Godot* was premiered in 1953, is long gone.

At the foot of boulevard St-Germain, facing place de la Concorde across the Seine, is the **Assemblée Nationale**, the lower house of the French parliament. Behind, elegant place du Palais-Bourbon leads into rue de Bourgogne, a rare commercial thoroughfare amid the official buildings, with some delectable pâtisseries and designer-furniture showrooms. Nearby, the mid 19th-century Eglise Ste-Clothilde (12 rue

Martignac, 7th, 01.44.18.62.60), with its skeletal twin spires, is an early example of Gothic Revival. Beside the Assemblée is the Foreign Ministry, often referred to by its address, 'quai d'Orsay'. Beyond it, a long, grassy esplanade leads up to golden-domed Les Invalides. The vast military hospital complex, with its Eglise du Dôme and St-Louis-des-Invalides churches, all built by Louis XIV, epitomises the official grandeur of the Sun King as expression of royal and military power. It now houses the **Musée de l'Armée**, as well as Napoleon's tomb inside the Eglise du Dôme. Stand with your back to the dome to survey the cherubim-laden Pont Alexandre III and the **Grand** and **Petit Palais** (*see p118*) over the river, all three put up for the 1900 Exposition Universelle.

Just beside Les Invalides is the **Musée National Rodin**, occupying the charming 18th-century Hôtel Biron and its romantic gardens. Rodin was invited here in 1908, on the understanding that he would give his work to the state. Many of his great sculptures, including the *Thinker*, the *Burghers of Calais* and the swarming *Gates of Hell*, are displayed in the building and around the gardens – as are those of his lesser known mistress, Camille Claudel.

**Les Invalides.** *See p170.*

## Assemblée Nationale

*33 quai d'Orsay, 7th (01.40.63.60.00/www.assemblee
-nationale.fr). M° Assemblée Nationale.* **Map** p405 F5.

Like the Sénat, the Assemblée Nationale (also known as the Palais Bourbon) is another royal building adapted for republicanism. It was built between 1722 and 1728 for the Duchesse de Bourbon, daughter of Louis XIV and Madame de Montespan, who also put up the neighbouring Hôtel de Lassay (now the official residence of the Assembly's president) for her lover, the Marquis de Lassay. The *palais* was modelled on the Grand Trianon at Versailles, with a colonnaded *cour d'honneur* opening on to rue de l'Université and gardens running down to the Seine. The Prince de Condé extended the palace, linked the two *hôtels* and laid out place du Palais-Bourbon. The Greek temple-style façade facing Pont de la Concorde (actually the rear of the building) was added in 1806 to mirror the Madeleine. Flanking this riverside façade are statues of four great statesmen: L'Hôpital, Sully, Colbert and Aguesseau. The Napoleonic frieze on the pediment was replaced by a monarchist one after the restoration: between 1838 and 1841, Cortot sculpted the figures of France, Power and Justice. After the Revolution, the palace became the meeting place for the Conseil des Cinq-Cents, the new legislative body. It was the forerunner of the parliament's lower house, which set up here for good in 1827. Visits are possible only by arrangement through a serving *député* (if you're French) – or, after long queuing, during the Journées du Patrimoine (*see p277*).

## Chapelle de la Médaille Miraculeuse

*Couvent des Soeurs de St-Vincent-de-Paul, 140 rue du Bac, 7th (01.49.54.78.88). M° Sèvres Babylone.* **Open** 7.45am-1pm, 2.30-7pm daily. **Map** p405 F7.

In 1830 saintly Catherine Labouré was said to have been visited by the Virgin, who gave her a medal that performed miracles. This kitsch chapel – murals, mosaics, statues and the embalmed bodies of Catherine and her mother superior – is one of France's most visited sites, attracting two million pilgrims every year. Reliefs in the courtyard tell the nun's story – and slot machines sell medals.

## Espace EDF Electra

*6 rue Récamier, 7th (01.53.63.23.45/www.edf.fr). M° Sèvres Babylone.* **Open** noon-7pm Tue-Sun. **Admission** free. **Map** p405 G7.

This former electricity substation, converted by Electricité de France for PR purposes, is now used for varied, well-presented exhibitions examining the likes of garden designer Gilles Clément.

## Les Invalides & Musée de l'Armée

*Esplanade des Invalides, 7th (01.44.42.40.69/ www.invalides.org). M° La Tour Maubourg or Les Invalides.* **Open** Apr-Sept 10am-6pm daily. Oct-Mar 10am-5pm daily. Closed 1st Mon of mth. **Admission** *Courtyard* free. *Musée de l'Armée & Eglise du Dôme* €7.50; €5.50 students under 26; free under-18s. PMP. **Credit** MC, V. **Map** p405 E6.

Its imposing gilded dome is misleading: the Hôtel des Invalides was (and in part still is) a hospital. Commissioned by Louis XIV for wounded soldiers, it once housed as many as 6,000 invalids. Designed by Libéral Bruand (the foundations were laid in 1671) and completed by Jules Hardouin-Mansart, it's a magnificent monument to Louis XIV and Napoleon. Behind lines of topiaried yews and cannons, the main (northern) façade has a relief of Louis XIV (Ludovicus Magnus) and the Sun King's sunburst. Wander through the main courtyard and you'll see grandiose two-storey arcades, sundials on three sides and a statue of Napoleon glaring out from the end; the dormer windows around the courtyards are sculpted in the form of suits of armour.

The complex contains two churches – or, rather, a sort of double church: the Eglise St-Louis was for the soldiers, the Eglise du Dôme for the king, and each had its own separate entrance. You'll find an opening behind the altar that connects the two. The long, barrel-vaulted nave of the church of St-Louis is hung with flags captured from enemy troops. Since 1840 the baroque Eglise du Dôme has been solely dedicated to the worship of Napoleon, whose body was supposedly brought here from St Helena (although this is now in doubt).

On the ground floor, under a dome painted by De la Fosse, Jouvenet and Coypel, are chapels featuring monuments to Vauban, Foch and Joseph Napoleon (Napoleon's older brother and King of Naples, Sicily and Spain). Napoleon II (King of Rome) is buried in the crypt with his father the emperor. Two dramatic black figures holding up the entrance to the crypt, the red porphyry tomb, the ring of giant figures, and the friezes and texts eulogising the emperor's heroic deeds give the measure of the cult of Napoleon, cherished in France for ruling large swaths of Europe and for creating an administrative and educational system that endures to this day.

The Invalides also houses the Musée de l'Ordre de la Libération and the Musée des Plans-Reliefs, the collection of scale models of cities begun by Vauban, and once used for military strategy. Also included in the entry price is the impressive Musée de l'Armée. For the military historian, the museum is a must, but even if cannons are not your thing, the building is a splendour. Besides military memorabilia, the rooms are filled with fine portraiture, such as Ingres' *Emperor Napoleon on his Throne*. The World War I rooms are moving, with the conflict brought into vivid focus by documents and photos. The Général de Gaulle wing deals with World War II, taking in not only the Résistance but also the Battle of Britain and the war in the Pacific, alternating artefacts with contemporary film footage. *Photo p169.*

## Musée Maillol

*59-61 rue de Grenelle, 7th (01.42.22.59.58/www. museemaillol.com). M° Rue du Bac.* **Open** 11am-6pm (last admission 5.15pm) Mon, Wed-Sun. **Admission** €8; €6 students; free under-16s. **Credit** *Shop* AmEx, MC, V. **Map** p405 G7.

# Windows on the world

The **Musée du Quai Branly** (*see p174*), the most significant recent addition to the city's roster of museums, was the pet project of former French president Jacques Chirac. Surrounded by trees on the banks of the Seine, the museum is a vast showcase for non-European cultures. Dedicated to the ethnic art of Africa, Oceania, Asia and the Americas, it joins together the collections of the Musée des Arts d'Afrique et d'Océanie and the Laboratoire d'Ethnologie du Musée de l'Homme, as well as contemporary indigenous art. Intended to 'recognise the rightful place of these civilisations, together with the heritage of peoples who are sometimes forgotten, in the present culture of the world', this is a museum with a mission.

It's not only the curatorial policy that reeks of ambition either: the museum is housed in an extraordinary building designed by Jean Nouvel, who was also responsible for the Institut du Monde Arabe (*see p154*) and the Fondation Cartier (*see p163*). Occupying a prime riverside site, Nouvel's creation, with its angular forms and coloured metal boxes, is a surprisingly baroque affair, a hotchpotch of visual metaphors: a bridge museum between Europe (not represented here) and the four other continents. It is also a pleasing addition to the quartier: the landscaped

gardens that take up half the site incorporate an open-air amphitheatre and extend to the building itself, with a 'vertical garden' of 15,000 plants scaling the façade.

Inside, dimly lit to create a shadowy, mysterious aura, the permanent collection is reached via a curving white ramp, a huge space divided into four zones for the four featured continents that also lets you wander from one to another along a central path or 'river'. Treasures include a tenth-century anthropomorphic Dogon statue from Mali, Vietnamese costumes, Gabonese masks, Aztec statues, Peruvian feather tunics, rare frescoes from Ethiopia, animal hide and bark cloth garments from the Americas, and the Harter bequest of masks and sculptures from Cameroon. A mezzanine gallery is used for pan-continental exhibitions.

Yet the museum's remit goes beyond merely presenting relics from the 300,000-strong collection. Music is a key feature of the interdisciplinary approach, with musical exhibits, a 500-seat auditorium for a full programme of theatre, music and dance, plus the opportunity to relay the oral tradition inherent to so many global cultures. A striking circular glass drum, or 'silo', rises up through the building to allow intriguing glimpses of the instruments in reserve.

Dina Vierny was 15 when she met Aristide Maillol (1861-1944) and became his principal model for the next decade, idealised in such sculptures as *Spring, Air* and *Harmony*. In 1995 she opened this delightful museum, exhibiting Maillol's drawings, engravings, pastels, tapestry panels, ceramics and early Nabis-related paintings, as well as the sculptures and terracottas that epitomise his calm, modern classicism. Vierny also set up a Maillol Museum in his Pyrenean village of Banyuls-sur-Mer. This Paris venue also has works by Picasso, Rodin, Gauguin, Degas and Cézanne, a whole room of Matisse drawings, rare Surrealist documents and works by naïve artists. Vierny has also championed Kandinsky and Ilya Kabakov, whose *Communal Kitchen* installation recreates the atmosphere of Soviet domesticity. Monographic exhibitions are devoted to modern and contemporary artists.

## Musée National Rodin

*Hôtel Biron, 79 rue de Varenne, 7th (01.44.18.61.10/www.musee-rodin.fr). Mº Varenne.* **Open** *Apr-Sept* 9.30am-5.45pm Tue-Sun (gardens until 6.45pm). *Oct-Mar* 9.30am-4.45pm (gardens until 5pm) Tue-Sun. **Admission** €6; €4 18-25s, all Sun; free under-18s, all 1st Sun of mth. PMP. *Exhibitions* €7; €5 18-25s. *Gardens* €1. **Credit** MC, V. **Map** p405 F6.

The Rodin museum occupies the *hôtel particulier* where the sculptor lived in the final years of his life. The *Kiss*, the *Cathedral*, the *Walking Man*, portrait busts and early terracottas are exhibited indoors, as are many of the individual figures or small groups that also appear on the *Gates of Hell*. Rodin's works are accompanied by several pieces by his mistress and pupil, Camille Claudel. The walls are hung with paintings by Van Gogh, Monet, Renoir, Carrière and Rodin himself. Most visitors have greatest affection for the gardens, spotted with trees and treasures: look out for the *Burghers of Calais*, the elaborate *Gates of Hell* (inspired by Dante's *Inferno*), the *Thinker*, *Orpheus* under shade, and unfinished nymphs emerging from their marble matrix. Fans can also visit the Villa des Brillants at Meudon (19 av Rodin, Meudon, 01.41.14.35.00, closed Mon-Thur & Oct-Apr), where Rodin worked from 1895.

## Musée d'Orsay

*1 rue de la Légion-d'Honneur, 7th (01.40.49.48.14/ recorded information 01.45.49.11.11/www.musee-orsay.fr). Mº Solférino/RER Musée d'Orsay.* **Open** 9.30am-6pm Tue, Wed, Fri-Sun; 9.30am-9.45pm Thur. **Admission** €7.50; €5.50 concessions; free under-18s, all 1st Sun of mth. PMP. **Credit** *Shop* MC, V. **Map** p405 G6.

The building was originally a train station, designed by Victor Laloux to coincide with the Exposition Universelle in 1900. The platforms proved too short for modern trains, and by the 1950s the station was threatened with demolition; it then became home to a theatre (the Renaud-Barrault), and scenes in Orson Welles' *The Trial* were filmed here. It was saved in the late 1970s when President Giscard d'Estaing decided to turn it into a museum spanning the fertile art period between 1848 and 1914. (The painter Edouard Détaille had said it looked like a palace of fine art when it was built.) Italian architect Gae Aulenti remodelled the interior, keeping the iron-framed coffered roof and creating galleries either side of a light-filled canyon. The arrangement has its drawbacks – upstairs, the Impressionists and post-Impressionists are knee-deep in tourists, while too much space is given downstairs to Couture's languid nudes and Meissonier's history paintings – but it somehow manages to keep its open-plan feel.

The museum follows a chronological route, from the ground floor to the upper level and then to the mezzanine, showing links between Impressionist painters and their forerunners. Running down the centre of the tracks, a central sculpture aisle takes in monuments and maidens by Rude, Barrye and Carrier-Belleuse, but the outstanding pieces are by Carpeaux, including his controversial *La Danse* for the façade of the Palais Garnier. The Lille side, on the right of the central aisle, is dedicated to the Romantics and history painters: Ingres and Amaury-Duval contrast with the Romantic passion of Delacroix's North African period, Couture's vast *Les Romains de la Décadence* and the cupids of Cabanel's *Birth of Venus*. Further on are early Degas canvases and works by Symbolists Moreau and Puvis de Chavannes; another gallery shows selections from the vast holdings of early photography.

The first rooms to the Seine side of the main aisle are given over to the Barbizon landscape painters: Corot, Daubigny and Millet. One room is dedicated to Courbet, with the *Artist and his Studio*, the monumental *Burial at Ornans* and the show-stopping *L'Origine du Monde*. This floor also covers pre-1870 works by the Impressionists, including Manet's provocative *Olympia*, and their precursor Boudin.

Upstairs are the Impressionists, Pissarro, Renoir and Caillebotte, Manet's *Déjeuner sur l'Herbe*, Monet's paintings of Rouen cathedral and works by Degas. Among the Van Goghs are *Church at Auvers* and *Wheat Field with Crows*. You'll also find the primitivist jungle of Le Douanier Rousseau, the gaudy lowlife of Toulouse-Lautrec, the colourful exoticism of Gauguin's Breton and Tahitian periods, and Cézanne's still lifes, landscapes and the *Card Players*, as well as works by Seurat and Signac, and the mystical pastel drawings of Odilon Redon.

On the mezzanine are works by the Nabis painters – Vallotton, Denis, Roussel, Bonnard and Vuillard. Several rooms are given over to art nouveau decorative arts, including furniture by Majorelle, and Gallé and Lalique ceramics. Paintings by Klimt and Burne-Jones reside here, and there are sections on architectural drawings and early photography. The sculpture terraces include busts by Rodin, heads by Rosso and bronzes by Bourdelle and Maillol.

Exhibitions scheduled for display in 2008 include a retrospective of the work of German artist Louis Corinth and a display of 19th-century English 'calotypes' (photographs).

UNESCO. *See p174.*

## West of Les Invalides

*The 7th & 15th arrondissements.*
South-west of the Invalides is the massive Ecole Militaire (av de La Motte-Picquet, 7th), the military academy built by Louis XV to educate the children of penniless officers; it would later train Napoleon. The severe neo-classical building was designed by Jacques Ange Gabriel. It's still used by the army and closed to the public. From the north-western side of the Ecole Militaire begins the vast Champ de Mars, a market garden converted into a military drilling ground in the 18th century. It has long been home to the most celebrated Paris monument of all, the **Eiffel Tower**. At the south-eastern end of the Champ de Mars stands the Mur pour la Paix ('wall for peace'), erected in 2000 to articulate hopes for peace. South-east of the Ecole are the Y-shaped **UNESCO** building, built in 1958, and the modernist Ministry of Labour. Fashionable apartments line broad avenues Bosquet and Suffren, though there's much architectural eclecticism in the area: look at the pseudo-Gothic and pseudo-Renaissance houses on avenue de Villars; Lavirotte's fabulous art nouveau doorway at 27 avenue Rapp; and the striking, box-shaped Notre Dame de l'Arche de l'Alliance church (81 rue d'Alleray, 15th, 01.56.56.62.56), which was completed in 1998. For signs of life, visit the Saxe-Breteuil street market, and the old-fashioned bistros Thoumieux (79 rue St-Dominique, 7th, 01.47.05.49.75) and, on an arcaded square next to a pretty fountain,

Fontaine de Mars (129 rue St-Dominique, 7th, 01.47.05.46.44). The upper reaches of rue Cler contain classy food shops.

### Les Egouts de Paris

*Entrance opposite 93 quai d'Orsay, by Pont de l'Alma, 7th (01.53.68.27.81). M° Alma Marceau/RER Pont de l'Alma.* **Open** 11am-4pm (until 5pm May-Sept) Wed-Sat. Closed 3wks Jan. **Admission** €3.80; €3.05 5-12s; free under-5s. **No credit cards. Map** p400 D5.
For centuries the main source of drinking water in Paris was the Seine, which was also the main sewer. Construction of an underground sewerage system began at the time of Napoleon. Today the Egouts de Paris constitutes a smelly museum; each sewer in the 2,100km (1,305-mile) system is marked with a replica of the street sign above. The Egouts can be closed after periods of heavy rain.

### Eiffel Tower

*Champ de Mars, 7th (01.44.11.23.45/recorded information 01.44.11.23.23/www.tour-eiffel.fr). M° Bir-Hakeim/RER Champ de Mars Tour Eiffel.* **Open** *15 June-9 Sept* 9am-12.45am daily. *10 Sept-14 June* 9.30am-11.45pm daily. **Admission** *By stairs* (1st & 2nd levels, 9am-12.30am) €4; €3.10 under-25s. *By lift* (1st level) €4.50; €2.30 3-12s; (2nd level) €7.80; €4.30 3-12s; (3rd level) €11.50; €6.30 3-12s; free under-3s. **Credit** AmEx, MC, V. **Map** p404 C6.
No building better symbolises Paris than the Tour Eiffel. Maupassant claimed he left Paris because of it, William Morris visited daily to avoid having to see it from afar – and it was originally meant to be a temporary structure. The radical cast-iron tower was built for the 1889 World Fair and the centenary of the 1789 Revolution by engineer Gustave Eiffel (whose construction company still exists today).

Eiffel made use of new technology that was already popular in iron-framed buildings. Construction took more than two years and used some 18,000 pieces of metal and 2,500,000 rivets. The 300m (984ft) tower stands on four massive concrete piles; it was the tallest structure in the world until overtaken by New York's Empire State Building in the 1930s. Vintage double-decker lifts ply their way up and down; you can walk as far as the second level. There are souvenir shops, an exhibition space, café and even a post office on the first and second levels. The smart Jules Verne restaurant, on the second level, has its own lift in the north tower. At the top (third level), there's Eiffel's cosy salon and a viewing platform with panels pointing out what to see in every direction. Views can reach over 65km (40 miles) on a good day, although the most fascinating perspectives are of the ironwork itself, whether gazing up from underneath or enjoying the changing vision as the lift rises. At night, for ten minutes on the hour, 20,000 flashbulbs attached to the tower provide a beautiful shimmering effect. The tower has some six million visitors a year; to avoid the queues, come late at night.

### UNESCO

*7 pl de Fontenoy, 7th (01.45.68.10.00/tours 01.45.68.16.42/www.unesco.org). M° Ecole Militaire.* **Open** 9.30am-6pm Mon-Fri. *Tours* 3pm Mon-Fri (in English on Tue). **Admission** free. **Map** p405 D7.

The Y-shaped UNESCO headquarters, built in 1958, is home to a swarm of international diplomats. It's worth visiting for the sculptures and paintings – by Picasso, Arp, Giacometti, Moore, Calder and Miró – and for the Japanese garden, with its contemplation cylinder by minimalist architect Tadao Ando. *Photos p173.*

### Village Suisse

*38-78 av de Suffren or 54 av de La Motte-Picquet, 15th (www.villagesuisseparis.com). M° La Motte Picquet Grenelle.* **Open** 10.30am-7pm Mon, Thur-Sun. **Map** p404 D7.

The mountains and waterfalls created for the Swiss Village at the 1900 Exposition Universelle are long gone, but the village lives on. Rebuilt with blocks of flats, the street level has been colonised by some 150 boutiques offering various high-quality, if pricey, antiques and collectibles.

## Along the Seine

Downstream from the Eiffel Tower is the **Musée du Quai Branly**, the Chirac-sponsored museum of primitive arts which opened in 2006 (*see p171* **Windows on the world**). A short way further on, the high-tech **Maison de la Culture du Japon** stands near Pont Bir-Hakeim on quai Branly. Beyond, the 15th arrondissement Fronts de Seine riverfront, with its tower-block developments, had some of

the worst architecture of the 1970s inflicted upon it. This would-be brave new world of walkways, suspended gardens and tower blocks has no easily discoverable means of access. The adjacent Beaugrenelle shopping centre is more straightforward to get into, but remains horribly dingy – although there are plans for an extensive redevelopment in the next few years. Further west, things look up: the sophisticated former headquarters of the Canal+ TV channel (2 rue des Cévennes, 15th), designed by American architect Richard Meier, is surrounded by fine modern housing; and the pleasant **Parc André Citroën**, created in the 1990s on the site of the former Citroën car works, runs all the way down to the Seine quayside, where you'll find the occasional cruise ship and summer party-goers.

### Maison de la Culture du Japon

*101bis quai Branly, 15th (01.44.37.95.00/ www.mcjp.asso.fr). M° Bir-Hakeim/RER Champ de Mars Tour Eiffel.* **Open** noon-7pm Tue, Wed, Fri, Sat; noon-8pm Thur. Closed Aug. **Admission** free. **Map** p404 C6.

Constructed in 1996 by the Anglo-Japanese architectural partnership of Kenneth Armstrong and Masayuki Yamanaka, this opalescent glass-fronted Japanese cultural centre screens films and puts on exhibitions and plays. It also contains a library, an authentic Japanese tea pavilion on the roof, where you can watch the tea ceremony, and a well-stocked book and gift shop.

### Musée du Quai Branly

*37-55 quai Branly, 7th (01.56.61.70.00/ www.quaibranly.fr). RER Pont de l'Alma.* **Open** 11am-7pm Tue, Wed, Sun; 11am-9pm Thur-Sat. **Admission** €8.50; €6 students; free under-18s. **Credit** AmEx, DC, MC, V. **Map** p404 C6.

This four-building collection of art and artefacts relating to non-European cultures opened to great fanfare in autumn 2006. An auditorium stages regular concerts – performances scheduled for 2008 include folk music from Rajasthan and the Cuban singer Martha Galarraga. *See also p171* **Windows on the world**.

### Parc André Citroën

*Rue Balard, rue St-Charles or quai Citroën, 15th. M° Balard or Javel.* **Open** 8am-dusk Mon-Fri; 9am-dusk Sat, Sun, public hols. **Map** p404 A9.

This park is a fun, postmodern version of a French formal garden, designed by Gilles Clément and Alain Prévost. It comprises glasshouses, computerised fountains, waterfalls, a wilderness and themed gardens featuring different coloured plants and even sounds. Stepping stones and water jets make it a garden for pleasure as well as philosophy. The tethered Eutelsat helium balloon takes visitors up for marvellous panoramic views over the city. If the weather looks unreliable, call 01.44.26.20.00 to check the day's programme.

# The 13th Arrondissement

This previously unremarkable Seine-side area is on the up.

It's all happening in the 13th – particularly in the new ZAC Rive Gauche development zone (*see p177* **In the zone**). This is where you'll find the newest bridge in Paris, the Passerelle Simone-de-Beauvoir, and next to it a floating swimming pool and sundeck, both inaugurated in 2006. Coming soon are the Cité de la Mode et du Design and a university complex that will eventually house 30,000 students and staff.

## Les Gobelins & La Salpêtrière

Its defining features might be 1960s tower blocks, but the 13th arrondissement is also historic, especially in the area bordering the fifth. The **Manufacture Nationale des Gobelins**, home to the state weaving companies, continues a tradition founded in the 15th century, when tanneries, dyers and weaving workshops lined the River Bièvre. This putrid waterway became notorious, and the slums that grew up around it were depicted in Victor Hugo's *Les Misérables*. The area was tidied up in the 1930s, when a small park, square René-Le-Gall, was laid out on the allotments used by tapestry workers. The river was built over, but local enthusiasts have since opened up a small stretch in the park. Nearby, through a gateway at 17 rue des Gobelins, you can spot the turret and first floor of a medieval house, recently renovated as apartments. The so-called Château de la Reine Blanche on rue

Gustave-Geffroy is named after Queen Blanche of Provence, who had a château here; it was probably rebuilt in the 1520s for the Gobelin family. Blanche was also associated with a nearby Franciscan monastery, of which a fragmentary couple of arches survive on the corner of rue Pascal and rue de Julienne.

In the northern corner of the 13th, next to Gare d'Austerlitz, sprawls the huge Hôpital de la Pitié-Salpêtrière founded in 1656, with its striking **Chapelle St-Louis**.

The busy intersection of place d'Italie has seen a number of developments in recent years. Opposite the 19th-century town hall stands the Centre Commercial Italie 2, a bizarre high-tech confection. It houses a shopping centre but, sadly, no longer the Gaumont Grand Ecran Italie cinema. You'll also find a food market on boulevard Auguste-Blanqui (Tue, Fri, Sun).

### Chapelle St-Louis-de-la-Salpêtrière
*47 bd de l'Hôpital, 13th (01.42.16.04.24). M° Gare d'Austerlitz.* **Open** 8.30am-6pm Mon-Fri, Sun; 11am-6pm Sat. **Admission** free. **Map** p406 L9.
This austerely beautiful chapel, designed by Libéral Bruand and completed in 1677, features an octagonal dome in the centre and eight naves in which they used to separate the sick from the insane, the destitute from the debauched. Around the chapel sprawls the vast Hôpital de la Pitié-Salpêtrière, founded on the site of a gunpowder factory (hence the name, derived from saltpetre) by Louis XIV to house rounded-up vagrant women. It became a centre for research into insanity in the 1790s, when renowned doctor Philippe Pinel began to treat some of the inmates as sick rather than criminal; Charcot later pioneered neuropsychology here, famously receiving a visit from Freud. Salpêtrière is today one of the city's main teaching hospitals, but the chapel is also used for contemporary art installations, notably during the Festival d'Automne (*see p277*), when its striking architecture provides a backdrop for artists such as Bill Viola, Anish Kapoor and Nan Goldin.

### Manufacture Nationale des Gobelins
*42 av des Gobelins, 13th (tours 01.43.13.46.46). M° Les Gobelins.* **Open** *Tours* 2pm, 3pm Tue-Thur. **Admission** €10; €6 7-24s; free under-7s. **No credit cards. Map** p406 K10.

The royal tapestry factory was founded by Colbert when he set up the Manufacture Royale des Meubles de la Couronne in 1662; it's named after Jean Gobelin, a dyer who owned the site. It reached the summit of its renown during the *ancien régime*, when Gobelins tapestries were produced for royal residences under artists such as Le Brun and Oudry. Tapestries are still made here (mainly for French embassies around the world), and visitors can watch weavers at work. The tour (in French) through the 1912 factory takes in the 18th-century chapel and the Beauvais workshops. Arrive 30 minutes before the tour starts.

## Chinatown & La Butte-aux-Cailles

South of rue de Tolbiac, the shop signs suddenly turn Chinese or Vietnamese, and even McDonald's is decked out *à la chinoise*. The city's main Chinatown runs along avenue d'Ivry, avenue de Choisy and into the 1960s tower blocks between. While much of the public housing in and around Paris is pretty bleak, here a distinctly eastern vibe reigns, with restaurants, Vietnamese *pho* noodle bars and Chinese pâtisseries, hairdressers and purveyors of exotic groceries; not to mention the expansive Tang Frères supermarket (48 av d'Ivry, 13th, 01.45.70.80.00), the main supplier for

Chinatown.

Chinatown. There's even a Buddhist temple hidden in a car park beneath the tallest tower (av d'Ivry, opposite rue Frères d'Astier-de-la-Vigerie, 13th). Lion and dragon dances, and martial arts demonstrations, take place on the streets at Chinese New Year (*see p278*).

In contrast to Chinatown, the villagey Butte-aux-Cailles, occupying the wedge between boulevard Auguste-Blanqui and rue Bobillot, is a neighbourhood of old houses, winding cobblestone streets, funky bars and restaurants. This workers' neighbourhood, home in the 19th century to many small factories, was one of the first to fight during the 1848 Revolution and the Paris Commune.

The Butte has preserved its rebellious character, with residents standing up to both urban planners and commercial developers. This predominantly *soixante-huitard* resistance is concentrated in the cobbled rue de la Butte-aux-Cailles and rue des Cinq-Diamants. Here you'll find relaxed, inexpensive bistros like the eccentric Le Temps des Cérises (18 rue Butte-aux-Cailles, 13th, 01.45.89.69.48), the co-operative, Chez Gladines (30 rue des Cinq-Diamants, 13th, 01.45.80.70.10) and the more upmarket **Chez Paul** (*see p210*). The cottages built in 1912 in a mock-Alsatian style around a central green at 10 rue Daviel were among the earliest public-housing schemes in Paris. Just across rue Bobillot, the **Piscine de la Butte-aux-Cailles** (*see p340*) is a charming Arts and Crafts-style swimming pool, fed by artesian wells. Further south, you can explore passage Vandrezanne, the little houses and gardens of square des Peupliers, rue des Peupliers and rue Dieulafoy, and the flower-named streets of the Cité Florale. By the Périphérique, the Stade Charléty (17 av Pierre-de-Coubertin, 13th, 01.44.16.60.60), designed by father and son Henri and Bruno Gaudin, is a superb piece of stadium architecture.

## The developing east

The construction in the mid-1990s of the **Bibliothèque Nationale de France** breathed life into the desolate area between Gare d'Austerlitz and the Périphérique, formerly a bleak expanse of goods yards, now known as the ZAC Rive Gauche (*see p177* **In the zone**). The ambitious, long-term ZAC project includes a new university quarter, an eastwards extension of the Latin Quarter, aided by the recent introduction of a footbridge capable of hosting exhibitions and a tramway providing links to the suburbs.

Further east, towards Porte d'Ivry, rue Watt is the lowest street in Paris (it runs below river level). At 12 rue Cantagrel you can see

# In the zone

The Zone d'Aménagement Concerté Rive Gauche, more simply known as 'Paris Rive Gauche', runs along the Left Bank of the Seine from the Gare d'Austerlitz to the boulevard Masséna. It came of age in 2006, with the opening of a new bridge (the Passerelle Simone-de-Beauvoir) and the extension of Paris-Plage, a popular summer feature previously reserved for the Right Bank.

Since the inauguration of the **Bibliothèque Nationale François Mitterrand** (*see below*) in 1996, this former industrial wasteland has undergone major changes, including the arrival of the high-tech, driverless métro line 14, a new RER station at the library and the opening of the 14-screen **MK2** cinema (*see p294*). As substantial as these changes have been, they're not the end of the story

The Paris VII Denis Diderot university has already moved into several of the renovated industrial buildings near the Seine, including the landmark Grands Moulins de Paris and the Halles aux Farines (Flour Hall). Like Les Frigos, an old warehouse converted into a ramshackle complex of artists' studios and rehearsal rooms, the university premises stand as a reminder of the area's heritage, and form a stark contrast to the surrounding glass-fronted offices and glitzy modern flats.

With more university departments set to migrate to the area in the next few years, Paris Rive Gauche is already being billed as the new Latin Quarter, an intellectual stronghold that will eventually house some 30,000 students and staff at four separate universities. Since June 2007, students and professors have been taking advantage of a new métro station, Olympiades.

Meanwhile, just south of Gare d'Austerlitz, a strip of run-down warehouses is soon to be reincarnated as the Docks de Seine. As well as shops, restaurants and a nightclub, the complex will house the new Cité de la Mode et du Design. By covering the warehouses with a grassed-over metal and wood structure and topping it with a panoramic garden terrace, architects Jakob & MacFarlane have created a suitably stylish new home for the Institut Français de la Mode (French Fashion Institute). A bridge, swimming pool, cinema, summer beach, city university and national institute of fashion: not bad for a site that was a sprawling mess of old railway tracks and abandoned buildings only a decade ago.

Le Corbusier's Cité de Réfuge de l'Armée de Salut hostel, a reinforced-concrete structure built from 1929 to 1933 to accommodate 1,500 homeless men, and a precursor of the architect's Cité Radieuse in Marseille.

## Bibliothèque Nationale de France François Mitterrand

*10 quai François-Mauriac, 13th (01.53.79.59.59/ www.bnf.fr). M° Bibliothèque François Mitterrand.* **Open** 2-7pm Mon; 9am-7pm Tue-Sat; 1-7pm Sun. **Admission** *1 day* €3.30. *2 weeks* €20. *1 year* €35; €18 students, 16-25s. **Credit** MC, V. **Map** p407 M10. Opened in 1996, the new national library was the last and costliest of Mitterrand's *grands projets*, the first stage in the redevelopment of the 13th arrondissement. Its architect, Dominique Perrault, was criticised for his curiously dated design, which hides readers underground and stores the books in four L-shaped glass towers. He also forgot to specify blinds to protect books from sunlight; they had to be added afterwards. In the central void is a garden (filled with 140 trees, which were transported from Fontainebleau at enormous expense). The library houses over ten million volumes and can accommodate 3,000 readers. The research section, just below the public reading rooms, opened in 1998. Much of the library is open to the public: books, newspapers and periodicals are accessible to anyone over 18, and you can browse through photographic, film and sound archives in the audiovisual section. There are regular classical music concerts and exhibitions too.

# Beyond the Périphérique

Paris's neglected suburbs are beginning to blossom.

Closing the social, cultural and economic divide between Paris and its suburbs is one of mayor Bertrand Delanoë's principal policies. So far, the most tangible evidence of this has been improved transport links (*see p36* **Delanoë's war on the car**). The recently inaugurated T3 tramway now runs alongside the southern edge of the Périphérique, which divides Paris and her *banlieue*. This eight-lane motorway has also succumbed to recent unifying initiatives which have seen sections of the road covered over and landscaped in an attempt to bring together city and *banlieue* (*see pp44-46*). Meanwhile, district councils of the outer boroughs are signing co-operation agreements with the *mairie*. One of the most recent, involving Ivry-sur-Seine, includes an ambitious plan for a local history museum to be built on a bridge across the river.

For many Parisians, though, the suburbs still evoke memories of the violent 2005 riots which saw an outpouring of long-suppressed anger from unemployed youths. Much of the *banlieue* (especially the undesirable northern and eastern suburbs) remains poor and neglected; venture here and you might as well be in another country – a land Parisians rarely enter, except to buy cheap supermarket petrol or to visit out-of-town DIY stores. For them, the *banlieue* (a term with predominantly negative connotations and rarely used to describe the upmarket suburbs of Neuilly, St-Cloud or Boulogne) is as much a mindset as a physical reality, encompassing as it does sink estates, high unemployment, drug crime and urban gangs.

Some of that negative reputation is deserved: on certain estates the fire brigade is attacked when ever it tries to extinguish blazes; attempts to reopen local shops are answered by chronic vandalism; and even the police are afraid to enter these areas without back-up. But there are also numerous respectable residential districts, with their own self-contained provincial atmosphere quite different from that of the city inside the Périphérique.

Other signs that things are beginning to change beyond the Périphérique include the opening of MAC/VAL (*see p180*), the first permanent collection of contemporary art to open in suburban Paris, and other art venues and galleries are following suit (for more on suburban cultural development, *see pp44-46*).

Rising property prices and high business rates in the city centre are making the suburbs increasingly popular with young families and small businesses alike. But for the many inner-city dwellers who would still never contemplate living outside Paris, the mistrust works both ways: there are *banlieusards* proud of belonging to the *neuf-trois* (slang for the 93 *département* of Seine St-Denis) rather than to the 'elitist' *soixante-quinze* (75) of Paris.

## St-Denis & the north

North of Paris, the *département* of Seine St-Denis (and part of adjoining Val d'Oise) is the one that best fulfils the negative stereotype of the *banlieue*. It's a victim of its own 19th-century industrial boom and the 20th-century housing shortage, when colossal estates went up in La Corneuve, Aulnay-sous-Bois and Sarcelles. It includes some of the poorest *communes* in all of France. Yet the *département* also boasts a buzzing theatre scene (*see p343* **All the world's a stage**), with the **MC93** in Bobigny (*see p341*), the **Théâtre Gérard-Philipe** (*see p342*) in St-Denis and the Théâtre de la Commune in Aubervilliers, as well as prestigious jazz and classical music festivals.

Amid the sprawl stands one of the treasures of Gothic architecture: the **Basilique St-Denis**, the final resting place for the majority of France's former monarchs. St-Denis also contains the atmospheric **Musée d'Art et d'Histoire de St-Denis**, located in a scrupulously preserved Carmelite convent, and a busy covered market. Its fine modern buildings include Oscar Niemeyer's head offices for Communist newspaper *L'Humanité* and Henri and Bruno Gaudin's extension to the town hall. Across the canal is the landmark **Stade de France** (*see p333*). Built to host the 1998 World Cup, it has provided a spur to the renewal of this long-run-down area characterised by small terraced houses, council flats, factories and wasteland.

Indeed, it could be said that the area of La Plaine St-Denis is on the up. The canal has been nicely landscaped with a footpath along the quay, the noisy motorway has been covered over by a series of garden squares and playgrounds, and smart canal-side apartments, a multiplex cinema, shopping centre and DIY superstore have all sprouted near the stadium, which is attracting more and more new businesses to the area. Over in nearby Aubervilliers, acres of 19th-century brick warehouses buzz with import-export businesses and recently arrived audio-visual companies.

Le Bourget, home to the city's first airport and still used for private business jets and an air fair, contains the **Musée de l'Air et de l'Espace** in its original passenger terminals and hangars. North-east of Paris, Pantin arrived on the cultural scene with the opening in 2004 of the **Centre National de la Danse** (*see p290*) in a cleverly rehabilitated office block. North-west of St-Denis, Ecouen, noted for its beautiful Renaissance château, now the **Musée National de la Renaissance**, allows for a glimpse of a more rural past.

## Basilique St-Denis

*1 rue de la Légion-d'Honneur, 93200 St-Denis (01.48.09.83.54). M° St-Denis Basilique/tram 1.*
**Open** *Apr-Sept* 10am-5.15pm Mon-Sat; noon-5.15pm Sun. *Oct-Mar* 10am-5.15pm Mon-Sat; noon-5.15pm Sun. *Tours* 10.30am, 3pm Mon-Sat; 12.15pm, 3pm Sun. **Admission** €6.50; €4.50 18-25s; free under-18s. PMP. **Credit** MC, V.
Legend has it that when St Denis was beheaded, he picked up his noggin and walked with it to Vicus Catulliacus (now St-Denis) to be buried. The first church, parts of which can be seen in the crypt, was built over his tomb in around 475. The present edifice was begun in the 1130s by Abbot Suger, the powerful minister of Louis VI and Louis VII. It is considered the first example of Gothic architecture, uniting the elements of pointed arches, ogival vaulting and flying buttresses. In the 13th century, master mason Pierre de Montreuil erected the spire and rebuilt the choir nave and transept. St-Denis was the burial place for all but three French monarchs between 996 and the end of the *ancien régime*, so the ambulatory is a museum of French funerary sculpture. It includes a fanciful Gothic tomb for Dagobert, the austere effigy of Charles V and the sculpted Renaissance tomb of Louis XII and his wife Anne de Bretagne. In 1792 these tombs were desecrated, and the royal remains thrown into a pit.

## Musée de l'Air et de l'Espace

*Aéroport de Paris-Le Bourget, 93352 Le Bourget Cedex (01.49.92.71.99/recorded information 01.49.92.70.62/www.mae.org). M° Gare du Nord, then bus 350/RER Le Bourget, then bus 152.*
**Open** *Apr-Sept* 10am-6pm Tue-Sun. *Oct-Mar* 10am-5pm Tue-Sun. **Admission** €7; €5 students; free under-18s. *With Concorde & Boeing 747* €9.50; €8 students; €3 children; free under-4s. PMP. **Credit** MC, V.
The impressive air and space museum is set in the former passenger terminal at Le Bourget airport. The collection begins with the pioneers, including fragile-looking biplanes, the contraption in which Romanian Vivia successfully flew 12m (40ft) in 1906, and the command cabin of a Zeppelin airship. On the runway are Mirage fighters, a US Thunderchief with painted shark-tooth grimace, and Ariane

**Basilique St-Denis.**

**Sightseeing**

launchers 1 and 5. A hangar houses the prototype Concorde 001 and wartime survivors. Other sections are devoted to hot air ballooning and space travel.

## Musée d'Art et d'Histoire de St-Denis

*22bis rue Gabriel-Péri, 93200 St-Denis (01.42. 43.05.10/www.musee-saint-denis.fr). M° St-Denis – Porte de Paris.* **Open** 10am-5.30pm Mon, Wed, Fri; 10am-8pm Thur; 2-6.30pm Sat, Sun. Closed public hols. **Admission** €4; €2 reductions; free under-16s. **No credit cards.**

This museum in St-Denis is set around the cloister of a former Carmelite convent, home to Louis XV's daughter, Louise de France, in the 1700s. Along with displays of archaeology, prints relating to the Paris Commune, post-Impressionist drawings and documents relating to local poet Paul Eluard, the most vivid part is the first floor, where items are displayed within the nuns' austere former cells.

## Musée National de la Renaissance

*Château d'Ecouen, 95440 Ecouen (01.34.38.38.50/ www.musee-renaissance.fr). Train Gare du Nord to Ecouen-Ezanville then bus 269 or walk.* **Open** 15 Apr-Sept 9.30am-12.45pm, 2-5.45pm Mon, Wed-Sun. Oct-14 Apr 9.30am-12.45pm, 2-5.15pm Mon, Wed-Sun. **Admission** €4.50; €3 18-25s, all on Sun; free under-18s, all on 1st Sun of mth. **Credit** MC, V.

The Renaissance château completed in 1555 for Royal Constable Anne de Montmorency and wife Margaret de Savoie is the setting for a collection of 16th-century decorative arts, arranged over three floors (some sections are open only at certain times – phone ahead). Best are the painted chimney pieces, decorated with biblical and mythological scenes.

## Musée Pierre Cardin

*33 bd Victor Hugo, 93400 St-Ouen (01.49.21. 08.20). M° Mairie de St-Ouen.* **Open** Wed, Sat. **Admission** €15.**No credit cards.**

In 2006, veteran French fashion designer Pierre Cardin opened his own museum in a specially converted former garage in the northern suburb of St-Ouen. Splendidly lit thanks to a vast glass roof, some 130 dummies model clothes and accessories from the main periods of Cardin's prolific career. There's the elegance of his debut working under Christian Dior, the revolutionary loose-strip miniskirts of the '60s, and the classic jumpsuits conceived for athletes at the 1972 Olympic Games, to name but a few. Also on display is a selection of Cardin-designed furniture.

## Vincennes & the east

The more upmarket residential districts in the east surround the Bois de Vincennes, such as Vincennes, with its royal château, St-Mandé and Charenton-le-Pont. Joinville-le-Pont and Champigny-sur-Marne draw weekenders for the riverside *guinguette* dancehalls.

## Château de Vincennes

*Av de Paris, 94300 Vincennes (01.48.08.31.20/ www.chateau-vincennes.fr). M° Château de Vincennes.* **Open** May-Aug 10am-noon, 1-6pm daily. Sept-Apr 10am-noon, 1-5pm daily. **Admission** Short visit €5; €3.50 18-25s, students; free under-18s. Long visit €6.50; €4.50 18-25s, students; free under-18s. **Credit** Shop MC, V.

An imposing curtain wall punctuated by towers encloses this medieval fortress, which is still home to an army garrison. The square keep was begun by Philippe VI and completed in the 14th century by Charles V, who added the curtain wall. Henry V died here in 1422, and Louis XIII used the château for hunting expeditions and had the Pavillon du Roi and Pavillon de la Reine built by Louis Le Vau, although any decorative elements disappeared when they became military barracks. Construction started on the soaring chapel in 1380, but it wasn't finished until the mid 16th century. *Photo p183.*

## MAC/VAL

*Pl de Libération, 94404 Vitry-sur-Seine (01.43. 91.64.20/www.macval.fr). M° Porte de Choisy then bus 183/RER C Gare de Vitry-sur-Seine then bus 180.* **Open** noon-7pm Tue, Wed, Fri-Sun; noon-9pm Thur. **Admission** €4; €2 reductions; free under-18s, students, all on 1st Sun of mth. **Credit** AmEx, V.

The MAC/VAL (Musée d'Art Contemporain du Val-de-Marne) opened in late 2005 and has proved a triumphant success, enticing Parisians from the city centre to the suburbs – no mean feat considering the notorious snootiness of the exclusive art crowd. Besides an enviable post-'50s permanent collection, it organises rotating temporary displays, and houses a resources centre, restaurant, garden and, of course, a bookshop. *See also pp44-46.*

## Musée de la Résistance Nationale

*Parc Vercors, 88 av Marx-Dormoy, 94500 Champigny-sur-Marne (01.48.81.53.36/www. musee-resistance.com). RER Champigny then bus 208.* **Open** 9am-12.30pm, 2-5.30pm Tue-Fri; 2-6pm Sat, Sun. Closed public hols, weekends in Aug, all Sept. **Admission** €5; €2.50 over-60s; free under-18s, students. **No credit cards.**

Occupying five floors of a 19th-century villa, the Resistance museum starts at the top with the prewar political background and works down, via defeat in 1940, through the Occupation and the rise of the Maquis, to victory. Hundreds of photographs aside, the material consists of newspaper files, three short archive films, a wall of machine guns and a railway saboteur's kit. Commendably, displays steer clear of Resistance hero tub-thumping.

## Pavillon Baltard

*12 av Victor-Hugo, 94130 Nogent-sur-Marne (01.43.24.76.76/www.pavillon-baltard.fr). RER Nogent-sur-Marne.* **Open** during exhibitions only.

When Les Halles was demolished, someone had the nous to save one of its Baltard-designed iron-and-glass market pavilions (no.8, eggs and poultry) and resurrect it for the benefit of the suburbs.

## Boulogne & the west

The capital's most desirable suburbs lie to the west. La Défense, Neuilly-sur-Seine, Boulogne-Billancourt, Levallois-Perret and, over the river, Issy-les-Moulineaux have become accepted business addresses for Parisians, notably in the advertising, media and service industries. Neuilly-sur-Seine is home to many of France's finance brains and captains of industry, and is where President Nicolas Sarkozy cut his political teeth as mayor in the early 1990s.

Boulogne-Billancourt is the main town and a lively centre in its own right. In 1320 the Gothic Eglise Notre-Dame was begun in tribute to a miraculous statue of the Virgin that washed up at Boulogne-sur-Mer. By the 18th century Boulogne was known for its wines and laundries, then, early in the 20th century, for its artist residents (Landowski, Lipchitz, Chagall, Gris), while Billancourt was known for car manufacturing, aviation and its film studios.

In the 1920s and '30s, Boulogne-Billancourt was proud of its modernity: Tony Garnier built the elegant new town hall on avenue André-Morizet; a new post office, apartments and schools all went up in the modern style; and private houses were built by the leading avant-garde architects of the day – Le Corbusier, Mallet-Stevens, Perret, Lurçat, Pingusson and Fischer – notably on rue Denfert-Rochereau, near the Bois de Boulogne, and rue du Belvedère. The **Musée des Années 30** focuses on artists and architects who lived or worked in the town at the time. The innovative glass-fronted apartment block by Le Corbusier – including the flat where he lived from 1933 to 1965 – can be visited each Wednesday morning at 24 rue Nungesser et Coli (reserve ahead on the Fondation Le Corbusier on 01.42.88.41.53, www.fondationlecorbusier.asso.fr).

The former Renault factory has sat in the Seine like a beached whale ever since it closed in 1992. In 2000 billionaire François Pinault decided to convert it, along with the Ile Seguin where it stands, into a contemporary art museum. Finally, in May 2005, frustrated by the inertia of the Boulogne-Billancourt local council and the lack of investment on the site, Pinault abandoned the idea. The Fondation François Pinault still went ahead – but in a very different location: a *palazzo* on the Grand Canal in Venice.

Across the Seine, villas in large gardens surround the Parc de St-Cloud, one of the loveliest areas of open space around Paris. South of St-Cloud is Sèvres, where the former royal porcelain manufacturer is now the **Musée National de la Céramique**.

In the 19th century, riverside towns like Chatou, Asnières and Argenteuil, accessible by train, became places of entertainment – for promenades, *guinguettes* and rowing on the Seine – as depicted in many Impressionist paintings. Ile de la Grande Jatte, between Neuilly and Courbevoie, was immortalised in Seurat's *La Grande Jatte*, and Renoir frequented the Ile de Chatou, where the old restaurant and dancehall, the Maison Fournaise, is now a small museum.

At Rueil-Malmaison, the romantic **Château de Malmaison** was loved by Napoleon and Josephine. Josephine had a second château, La Petite Malmaison (229bis av Napoléon-Bonaparte, 01.47.32.02.02, by appointment only), built nearby. The empress is buried in the Eglise St-Pierre-St-Paul in the old centre, as is her daughter Hortense de Beauharnais, Queen of Holland and mother of Napoleon III. At Port Marly, the fanciful Château de Monte-Cristo (01.39.16.49.49), built for Alexandre Dumas *fils*, has a tiled Moorish room; in its leafy grounds is the Château d'If, a folly inscribed with the names of Dumas' numerous works.

Suresnes, across the Seine from the Bois de Boulogne, has been a wine-producing village since Roman times, and still celebrates the Fête des Vendanges grape harvest every autumn. The 162-metre (532-foot) Mont Valérien was a place of pilgrimage; one of the nearby streets is still named rue du Calvaire. In 1841 a huge fortress was built here to defend Paris. It was occupied by the German army during World War II; French Résistants were brought here at night and shot. The fortress itself still belongs to the French army, and is the centre of its eavesdropping network. On the surrounding hill is the American Cemetery (190 bd de Washington), which contains the graves of American soldiers from World Wars I and II.

St-Germain-en-Laye is a smart suburb with a historic centre and a château, rebuilt by François I on the foundations of the fortress of Charles V. Here Henri II lived in style with his wife Catherine de Médicis and his mistress Diane de Poitiers; it was here also that Mary Queen of Scots grew up, Louis XIV was born and the deposed James II lived for 12 years. Napoléon III turned the château into the **Musée des Antiquités Nationales**.

### Château de Malmaison

*Av du Château, 92500 Rueil-Malmaison (01.41.29. 05.55/www.chateau-malmaison.fr). RER La Défense then bus 258.* **Open** *Apr-Sept* 10am-5pm Mon-Fri; 10am-5.30pm Sat, Sun. *Oct-Mar* 10am-4.30pm Mon, Wed-Fri; 10am-5pm Sat, Sun. **Admission** €5-€6.20; €3.50 18-25s, all on Sun; free under-18s, all on 1st Sun of mth. PMP. **Credit** AmEx, MC, V.

Napoleon and Josephine's love nest, bought by Josephine in 1799, was the emperor's favourite retreat during the Consulate (1800-03). After their divorce, Napoleon gave the château to his ex, who

died here in 1814. The couple redesigned the entrance as a military tent; you can see Napoleon's office, the billiard room and Josephine's tented bedroom. Today, the romantic château is often used for wedding receptions.

## Maison de Chateaubriand

*La Vallée aux Loups, 87 rue de Chateaubriand, 92290 Chatenay-Malabry (01.55.52.13.00/ www.maison-de-chateaubriand.fr). RER Robinson then walk.* **Open** (guided tours only except Sun) *Apr-Sept* 10am-noon, 2-6pm Tue-Sun. *Oct-Dec, Feb, Mar* 2-5pm Tue-Sun. **Admission** €4.50; €3 over-60s; free students, under-12s. **No credit cards.**

In 1807, attracted by the quiet Vallée aux Loups, René, Vicomte de Chateaubriand (1768-1848), set about turning a simple 18th-century country house into his own Romantic idyll, and planted the park with rare trees as a reminder of his travels. Most interesting is the double wooden staircase, based on a maritime design. Anyone familiar with David's *Portrait of Mme Récamier* hanging in the Louvre will find the original chaise longue awaiting the sitter, one of Chateaubriand's many lovers. After publishing an inflammatory work he was ruined, and in 1818 forced to sell up. The house offers free concerts in June, and literary evenings in spring and autumn.

## Mémorial de la France Combattante

*Rue du Professeur-Léon-Bernard, 92150 Suresnes (01.41.44.56.34/tour reservations 01.49.74.35.87). Train to Suresnes-Mont-Valérien/RER La Défense then bus 160, 360 or tram 2.* **Open** (by guided tour only) *Apr-Sept* 1.15pm, 4.30pm Sun. *Oct-Mar* 3pm Sun. By reservation Mon-Sat. **Admission** free.

Inaugurated in 1960 by Charles de Gaulle, and set against a massive Cross of Lorraine in pink granite from the Vosges, 16 bronze relief sculptures by 16 artists represent France's struggle for liberation – from a Gaullist perspective. Behind an eternal flame, the crypt contains tombs of 16 heroes from 16 French battles in World War II (a 17th is left empty for the last liberation hero). The memorial was built on the site where members of the Resistance were brought from prisons in Paris. A staircase from within the crypt leads visitors inside the curtain wall, then up around the hill to the chapel where prisoners were locked before execution, and down to the Clairière des Fusillés, the clearing where they were shot. The chapel walls were covered in the prisoners' last, desperate graffiti (of which only a small patch remains); it also contains five of the wooden firing posts against which the condemned were tied. Over 1,000 men were shot here (women were deported); no one is known to have escaped. A monument by artist Pascal Convert lists the names of the victims, including Communist politician Gabriel Péri.

## Musée des Années 30

*Espace Landowski, 28 av André-Morizet, 92100 Boulogne-Billancourt (01.55.18.46.42/www. annees30.com). M° Marcel Sembat.* **Open** 11am-6pm Tue-Sun. Closed 2wks Aug. **Admission**

(incl Musée-Jardin Paul Landowski) €4.30; €3.30 reductions; free under-16s. **Credit** MC, V.

The Musée des Années 30 shows how much second-rate art was produced in the 1930s, though there are decent modernist sculptures by the Martel brothers, graphic designs, and Juan Gris still lifes and drawings. The highlights are the designs by avant-garde architects Perret, Le Corbusier and Fischer. Exhibitions for 2008 include 'Les Objets du Design' (Feb-Apr) devoted to iconic 20th-century product design, and in the autumn a display of early costume and stage designs by Jenny Carré.

## Musée des Antiquités Nationales

*Château St-Germain, pl Charles-de-Gaulle, 78105 St-Germain-en-Laye (01.39.10.13.00/www.musee-antiquitesnationales.fr). RER St-Germain-en-Laye.* **Open** *May-Sept* 10am-6.15pm Mon, Wed-Sun. *Oct-Apr* 9am-5.15pm Mon, Wed-Sun. **Admission** €4.50; €3 students, 18-25s, all on Sun; free under-18s, all on 1st Sun of mth. **Credit** *Shop* MC, V.

Thousands of years spin by from one cabinet to the next in this awe-inspiring museum tracing France's rich archaeological heritage: some of the Paleolithic animal sculptures existed long before the Ancient Egyptians. The redesigned Neolithic galleries feature statue-menhirs, female figures and an ornate tombstone from Cys-la-Commune. Curiosities include the huge antlers from a prehistoric Irish deer and the 18th-century cork models of ancient sites.

## Musée Départemental Maurice Denis, 'Le Prieuré'

*2bis rue Maurice-Denis, 78175 St-Germain-en-Laye (01.39.73.77.87/www.musee-mauricedenis.fr). RER St-Germain-en-Laye.* **Open** 10am-5.30pm Tue-Fri; 10am-6.30pm Sat, Sun. **Admission** €3.80; €2.20 reductions; free under-12s. *Exhibitions* (with museum) €5.30; €3.80 reductions; free under-12s. **Credit** MC, V.

This former royal convent and hospital was bought to use as a home and studio by Nabi painter Maurice Denis; in 1915 he decorated the chapel in the garden. The remarkable collection comprises decorative objects, prints and paintings by the Nabis – the name, derived from Hebrew, means 'Prophets' – whose ranks included Sérusier, Bonnard, Vuillard, Roussel and Valloton. Seeking a renewed spirituality in painting, they took inspiration from Gauguin and Toulouse-Lautrec, whose paintings are also on show here.

## Musée-Jardin Paul Landowski

*14 rue Max-Blondat, 92100 Boulogne-Billancourt (01.46.05.82.69). M° Boulogne Jean Jaurès.* **Open** 10am-noon, 2-5pm Wed, Sat, Sun. Closed Aug. **Admission** €2.20; free under-16s. *With Musée des Années 30* €4.20; €3.20 reductions; free under-16s. **No credit cards.**

Sculptor Paul Landowski (1875-1961) won the Prix de Rome in 1900, and never lacked for state commissions, his work treating classical and modern themes on a monumental scale. One of his most intriguing creations is *Temple* – four sculpted walls depicting

the history of humanity. Some 100 sculptures are on show in this garden and studio.

## Musée National de la Céramique

*Pl de la Manufacture, 92310 Sèvres (01.41.14.
04.20). M° Pont de Sèvres.* **Open** 10am-5pm Mon,
Wed-Sun. Closed most public hols. **Admission**
€4.50; €3 18-25s; free under-18s, all on 1st Sun of
mth. *Exhibitions* €5.70; €4.20 CM. **Credit** MC, V.
Founded in 1738 as a private concern, the famous
porcelain factory moved to Sèvres from Vincennes
under the state in 1756. Finely painted, delicately
modelled pieces that epitomise French rococo style,
together with later Sèvres, adorned with copies of
Raphaels and Titians, demonstrat technical virtuos-
ity. The collection also includes Delftware, Meissen
and wonderful Ottoman plates.

## La Défense

The skyscrapers and walkways of La Défense –
named after a stand against the Prussians in
1870 – create a whole new world. The area has
been a showcase for French business since the
mid 1950s, when the CNIT hall was built to host
trade shows, but it was the arrival of the
**Grande Arche** that gave the district its most
dramatic monument. Today, more than 100,000
people work here, and another 35,000 live in the
blocks of flats on the southern edge, served by
the inevitable mall, an IMAX cinema, a huge
multiplex and a leisure complex. In summer
2007, Jean-Christophe Choblet, the creator of
**Paris-Plage** (*see p277*), created a series of
outdoor cultural events to encourage workers
to socialise in the neighbourhood rather than
take the usual commuter train home. On the
central esplanade are fountains and sculptures
by Miró and Serra. None of the skyscrapers
is especially distinguished architecturally,
although together they are an impressive sight,
and more building projects are in the pipeline.
*See also p42* **Reach for the sky?**.

## La Grande Arche de La Défense

*92044 Paris La Défense (01.49.07.27.27/www.
grandearche.com). M° La Défense.* **Open** *Apr-
Sept* 10am-8pm daily. *Oct-Mar* 10am-7pm daily.
**Admission** €9; €7.50 students, 6-18s; free under-6s.
**Credit** MC, V.
Completed for the bicentenary of the Revolution in
1989, the Grande Arche was designed by Danish
architect Johan Otto von Spreckelsen. Though it
lines up neatly on the Grand Axe – from the Louvre,
up the Champs-Elysées to the Arc de Triomphe –
the building itself is skewed. A vertigo-inducing
glass lift soars up through the 'clouds' to the roof,
for a fantastic view over Paris.

## Musée Mémorial Ivan Tourguéniev

*16 rue Ivan-Tourguéniev, 78380 Bougival
(01.45.77.87.12/www.tourgueniev.info). M° La
Défense then bus 258.* **Open** *Apr-Oct* 10am-6pm
Sun. Also by appointment for groups (weekdays).
**Admission** €4.60; €3.80 students, 12-25s; free
under-12s. **No credit cards**.
The dacha where novelist Ivan Turgenev lived until
his death in 1883 was a gathering spot for composers
Saint-Saëns and Fauré, divas Pauline Viardot and
Maria Malibran, and writers Henry James, Flaubert,
Zola and Maupassant. Letters and editions are on
the ground floor; above are the music room where
Viardot held court and the writer's deathbed.

**Château de Vincennes.** *See p180.*

Located in the heart of the LatinQuarter,
the Bouillon Racine combines art nouveau charm
and exceptionally tasty food.

Open daily noon-11pm (last order)
Live jazz 1st & 3rd Tuesdays of the month

3 rue Racine, 6th. M° Odéon.
Tel: 01.44.32.15.60
Email.bouillon.racine@wanadoo.fr
www.bouillonracine.com

# Eat, Drink, Shop

**Restaurant du Palais-Royal**. *See p189.*

# Restaurants

Star chefs and sublime ingredients are putting Paris back on the top table.

Joël Thiébault. Marie-Anne Cantin. Hugo Desnoyer. Vegetable producers, cheesemongers and butchers are stars in Paris, and you will see their names on the menus of the best restaurants. These days French cooking is increasingly about letting le produit shine with simple, fresh preparations. Technique remains important – no culture is more proud of its culinary heritage than the French – but superfluous flourishes are growing rare as chefs concentrate on bringing out the best in the main ingredients. Even haute cuisine chefs are not afraid to present pared-back dishes, such as Alain Passard at **Arpège** with his beetroot cooked in a salt crust.

Restaurant openings in the past year confirm this trend. At her Latin Quarter bistro **Toustem**, haute cuisine chef Hélène Darroze has moved away from mini-portions to serve rustic, country-style dishes in cast-iron pots, often highlighting products from her native Landes such as foie gras. Christian Constant again has his finger on the pulse of Paris dining with his new restaurant **Les Cocottes**, a kind of bistro-meets-diner where simple French dishes (oeufs sur le plat with mushrooms, salade niçoise, iced pea soup, sea bream with ratatouille) are served at a long counter that discourages lingering. Superchef Alain Ducasse has taken over the art deco seafood restaurant **Rech**, where the real star is not the chef himself but the freshest possible fish. At the 16-seat bistro **Spring**, chef Daniel Rose serves a no-choice menu that changes daily depending on what he finds at the market.

The fresh emphasis on ingredients is welcome news in a city that also has its share of tourist traps. It's not always easy to distinguish unscrupulous restaurateurs from hard-working chefs who start skimming their stocks at 7am, but a frequently changing menu, often handwritten on a blackboard, is a good sign. References to the meat's region of origin and whether fish is farmed or wild are even more encouraging, and you might see suppliers referred to by their first name (market gardener Joël being the most popular thanks to his dramatic pink-and-white-striped beetroot and yellow or red carrots). Restaurants with regional slants are often good bets, particularly if the chef is Basque or Breton. You don't always need to pay a lot to eat well, but it's

unlikely you'll have a memorable meal for less than €20 per person (not including drinks) at lunch and €30 at dinner.

Parisians are also eating differently, with less pressure to order a three-course meal. Chefs are designing their menus more flexibly, sometimes with whimsical categories that don't necessarily correspond to traditional starters, main courses and desserts, and Le Figaro's critic François Simon has been leading a one-man campaign to encourage the French to listen to their appetites rather than the waiter. Eating à la carte is often less of a bargain than ordering the three-course prix fixe, but if you are planning to spend several days in Paris it's wise to pace yourself. You might even opt to have a few of your meals at modern cafés serving fast, healthy food and freshly squeezed juices, such as **Rose Bakery**, **Scoop** and **Bioboa**.

Like any world capital, Paris has a dizzying number of international restaurants to choose from. Best among these are the North African restaurants – **Chez Omar** and the **404** are still classics – though you'll also find good Japanese, Chinese, Korean, Middle Eastern and Italian food if you're extremely selective.

Except for the very simplest restaurants, it's wise to book ahead. This can usually be done on the same day as your intended visit, although really top-notch establishments require bookings weeks in advance and confirmation the day before (remember that lunch can be much more affordable than dinner). If you've failed to get a reservation, you can try putting yourself on a waiting list a couple of days ahead, as last-minute cancellations are common.

All listings have been checked at time of going to press but are liable to change. Many venues close for their annual break in August, and some also close at Christmas. Restaurants in this chapter are presented by area, then by type: French or international. For more restaurant reviews, refer to Time Out Paris Eating & Drinking, available at www.timeout.com/shop.

---

❶ Purple numbers given in this chapter correspond to the location of each restaurant as marked on the street maps. See pp400-409.

---

## The Islands

### French

#### Brasserie de l'Ile St-Louis
*55 quai de Bourbon, 4th (01.43.54.02.59). M° Pont Marie.* **Open** noon-midnight Mon, Tue, Thur-Sun. Closed Aug. **Main courses** €20. **Credit** MC, V. **Map** p409 K7 **❶**
Happily, this old-fashioned brasserie soldiers on while exotic juice bars and fancy tea shops on the Ile St-Louis come and go. The terrace has one of the best summer views in Paris and is invariably packed; the dining room exudes shabby chic. Nicotined walls make for an agreeably authentic Paris mood, as does the slightly gruff waiter, though nothing here is gastronomically gripping: a well-dressed *frisée aux lardons*, a slab of fairly ordinary terrine, a greasy slice of *foie de veau* prepared *à l'anglaise* with a rasher of bacon, and a more successful pan of warming tripes. A dash more sophistication in the kitchen would transform this delightful place into something more exceptional.

#### Mon Vieil Ami
*69 rue St-Louis-en-l'Ile, 4th (01.40.46.01.35). M° Pont Marie.* **Open** noon-2.30pm, 7-11.30pm Wed-Sun. Closed 3wks Jan & 1st 3wks Aug. **Main courses** €22. **Prix fixe** €41. **Credit** AmEx, DC, MC, V. **Map** p409 K7 **❷**
Antoine Westermann from the Buerehiesel in Strasbourg has created a true foodie destination here. He may be one of Alsace's greatest chefs, but his modernised bistro cooking draws on all the regions of France – more unusually, he pays as much attention to vegetables as to meat and fish. Starters such as a tartare of finely diced raw vegetables with sautéed baby squid on top impress with their deft seasoning and accuracy of preparation. Typical of the mains is a cast-iron casserole of roast duck with caramelised turnips and couscous, or an updated bouillabaisse with red mullet fillets and artichoke. Desserts revisit bistro favourites – rum baba, chocolate tart or a light variation on the *café liègeois* in a cocktail glass. Even the classic high-ceilinged Ile St-Louis dining room has been successfully refreshed with black beams, white perspex panels between wall timbers, and a long, black *table d'hôte* down one side.

## The Louvre & Palais-Royal

### French

#### L'Ardoise
*28 rue du Mont-Thabor, 1st (01.42.96.28.18). M° Concorde or Tuileries.* **Open** noon-2.30pm, 6.30-11pm Tue-Sat; 6.30-11pm Sun. Closed 1st 3wks Aug. **Main courses** €19. **Prix fixe** €32. **Credit** MC, V. **Map** p401 G5 **❸**
One of the city's outstanding modern bistros, L'Ardoise is also one of the few to open on Sundays. The rather anonymous room is soon packed out with gourmets eager to sample Pierre Jay's reliably delicious cooking. A wise choice might be six oysters with warm chipolatas and a pungent shallot dressing, an unusual combination from Bordeaux;

**Eat, Drink, Shop**

Sit back and enjoy the view from the Seine-side **Brasserie de l'Ile St-Louis**.

equally attractive are a gamey hare pie with an escalope of foie gras nestling in its centre, or firm, shelled langoustines around a mousseline of celery and coated in a luscious chervil sauce. A lightly chilled, raspberry-scented Chinon, from a wine list sensibly arranged by price, provides a perfect complement.

### Chez La Vieille

*37 rue de l'Arbre-Sec, 1st (01.42.60.15.78). M°
Louvre Rivoli.* **Open** noon-2.30pm, 7.30-9.45pm
Mon, Tue, Thur, Fri; noon 2.30pm Wed. Closed Aug.
**Main courses** €25. **Prix fixe** *Lunch* €25. **Credit**
AmEx, MC, V. **Map** p406 J6 **❹**

The rustic ground floor of this bistro bursts with well-rounded regulars, while upstairs is plain and bright. A wondrous ad-lib selection of starters might include hot *chou farci* and home-made *terrine de foie gras*, both delivered by a smiling waitress. Equally impressive is *foie de veau*, coated in a pungent reduction of shallots and vinegar and served with potato purée. Puddings follow the same cornucopian principle as the starters, and the wine list includes a fine selection of wines from Corsica (birthplace of the eponymous *vieille* who now runs the dining room). Opening hours are limited and booking is essential, but the lunchtime prix fixe is a bargain.

### Le Grand Véfour

*17 rue de Beaujolais, 1st (01.42.96.56.27/www.
relaischateaux.com). M° Palais Royal Musée du
Louvre.* **Open** 12.30-1.30pm, 8-9.30pm Mon-Thur;
12.30-1.30pm Fri. Closed Aug. **Main courses** €74.
**Prix fixe** *Lunch* €88. **Credit** AmEx, DC, MC, V.
**Map** p402 H5 **❺**

Opened in 1784 (as the Café de Chartres), this is one of the oldest and most historic restaurants in Paris. Many of the greats of this world once feasted on this very spot, from Napoleon and his Josephine to the literary elite – André Malraux, Colette, Sartre, Simone de Beauvoir and Victor Hugo, who was a regular. Each member of staff is perfectly charming, particularly the knowledgeable sommeliers and the dashing maître d'hôtel, Christian David. An à la carte meal begins with a fantasia suite of delicacies: tiny frogs' legs, for example, artistically arranged within a circle of sage sauce; a first course of creamed Breton sea urchins served in their spiny shells with a quail's egg and topped with caviar; flash-fried langoustines with tangy mango sauce nestling inside a curled shell, with tiny girolles and a swirl of coriander juice. Fish dishes may be a touch overcooked, and the adventurous desserts are not always successful, but you'll forgive all after a glass of vintage armagnac.

### Le Meurice

*Hôtel Meurice, 228 rue de Rivoli, 1st
(01.44.58.10.10/www.meuricehotel.com). M°
Tuileries.* **Open** 12.30-2pm, 7.30-10pm Mon-Fri.
Closed 2wks Feb & Aug. **Main courses** €100.
**Prix fixe** *Lunch* €75. *Dinner* €190. **Credit** AmEx,
DC, MC, V. **Map** p401 G5 **❻**

Yannick Alléno, chef here since 2003, has really hit his stride and is doing some glorious, if rather understated, contemporary French luxury cooking. Few chefs working in Paris today exercise such restraint when it comes to letting superb produce star at the table, but Alléno has a light touch, teasing the flavour out of every leaf, frond, fin or fillet that passes through his hands. Turbot is sealed in clay before cooking and then sauced with celery cream and a coulis of flat parsley, while Bresse chicken stuffed with foie gras and served with truffled *sarladais* potatoes (cooked in the fat of the bird) is breathtakingly good. A fine cheese tray, with a stunning extra-aged comté, comes from Quatrehomme, and the pastry chef amazes with his signature millefeuille. The bemused complicity of the courtly but friendly waiters and sommeliers makes for a truly memorable meal.

### Restaurant du Palais-Royal

*110 galerie Valois, 1st (01.40.20.00.27/www.
restaurantdupalaisroyal.com). M° Palais Royal
Musée du Louvre or Bourse.* **Open** noon-2pm,
7-10pm Mon-Sat. Closed 19 Dec-10 Jan. **Main
courses** €28. **Prix fixe** €60. **Credit** AmEx,
DC, MC, V. **Map** p401 H5 **❼**

There can be few more magical places to dine on a summer evening, after the rest of this public garden has been shut off to the hoi polloi, than the terrace of this restaurant. Inside is memorable too: you sit in a quietly trendy red dining room alongside the commissars of arts and letters who work at the Ministry of Culture a few doors down. Risotto is a speciality and the Black, Black and Lobster is tremendous; rice simmered in rich squid ink is served al dente, topped with tender but fleshy pink lobster, sun-dried tomato and spring vegetables. The mains are slightly more restrained and might include roast sea bass with 'melted' leeks, or hare stew that is heartily countrified yet subtle and refined. Good quality wines are available by the half-litre carafe; and don't miss out on the *baba au rhum*, which comes with its very own pitcher of rum for extra dousing. *Photo p191.*

### Scoop

*154 rue St-Honoré, 1st (01.42.60.31.84/www.
scoopcafe.com). M° Palais Royal Musée du Louvre.*
**Open** 11.30am-6pm Mon-Wed; 11.30-10.30pm Thur,

**Eat, Drink, Shop**

# Price codes

With our reviews, we give the average price for a standard main course chosen from the à la carte menu. If 'Main courses' is not listed, only prix fixe options are available. 'Prix fixe' indicates the price of the venue's set menu at lunch and/or dinner. All bills include a service charge, but an additional tip of a few euros (for the whole table) is polite unless you're unhappy with the service.

## The best | Restaurants

### For confirmed carnivores
Atelier Maître Albert (see p209), Boucherie Roulière (see p213), Chez Toinette (see p200), Ribouldingue (see p212) and La Table de Lauriston (see p199).

### For dinner à deux
Astrance (see p194), La Gazzetta (see p206), Le Reminet (see p211), Le Souk (see p206) and Spring (see p200).

### For hearty appetites
L'Ambassade d'Auvergne (see p202), A la Biche au Bois (see p205), Chez Omar (see p204) and L'Opportun (see p216).

### For lunch on a budget
A la Bière (see p208), Bistrot Victoires (see p191), Les Cocottes (see p218), Kastoori (see p200) and Scoop (see p189).

### For oysters by the dozen
La Coupole (see p216), Huîtrerie Régis (see p214) and Rech (see p197).

### For star chefs at work
Alain Ducasse au Plaza Athénée (see p194), Le Chateaubriand (see p208), Le Meurice (see p189), Pierre Gagnaire (see p197) and Toustem (see p212).

### For terroir cuisine
L'Ami Jean (see p217), Breizh Café (see p202), La Cerisaie (see p216), Chez Michel (see p208) and Le Troquet (see p219).

### For vegetarians
L'Arpège (see p217), Bioboa (see p191), Rose Bakery (see p201) and La Taverna degli Amici (see p215).

Fri; 11.30am-6pm Sat, Sun. Closed 3wks Aug & 1wk Dec. **Main courses** €8-€15. **Prix fixe** €8-€14. **Credit** MC, V. **Map** p402 H5 **8**
What started out as an American-style ice-cream parlour has taken on a Paris personality suited to its fashionable surroundings behind the Louvre. For lunch, choose from healthy wraps, soups such as the delectable pumpkin concoction, savoury tarts and hot dishes. But be sure to save room for the main event – ice-creams in flavours such as chocolate espresso, toasted pecan or Vermont maple syrup. Service isn't ultra-speedy during peak times, so arrive early if you're rushed (later on, they run out of wraps and tarts). Delicious pancakes are served for Sunday brunch (noon-4.30pm), as well as hot dishes such as salmon and ratatouille.

Sidebar: **Eat, Drink, Shop**

## International

### Chez Vong
*10 rue de la Grande-Truanderie, 1st (01.40.26.09.36). M° Etienne Marcel or Les Halles.* **Open** noon-2.30pm, 7pm-10.30pm Mon-Sat. **Main courses** €20. Closed 3wks Aug **Prix fixe** *Lunch* €24. **Credit** AmEx, DC, MC, V. **Map** p402 J5 **9**
The staff at this intimate Chinese restaurant take pride in its excellent cooking, which covers the great dishes of Canton, Shanghai, Beijing and Sichuan. From the greeting at the door to the knowledgeable and trilingual service (Cantonese, Mandarin and French), each part of the experience is thoughtfully orchestrated to showcase China's diverse and delicious cuisines. Any doubts about authenticity are extinguished with the arrival of the beautifully presented dishes, which are placed on heated stands at the table. Expertly cooked spicy shrimp glistens in a smooth, characterful sauce of onions and ginger, while *Ma Po* tofu melts in the mouth, its spicy and peppery flavours melding with those of the fine pork mince.

### Kai
*18 rue du Louvre, 1st (01.40.15.01.99). M° Louvre Rivoli.* **Open** noon-2pm, 7-10.30pm Tue-Sat; 7-10.30pm Sun. Closed 1wk Apr & 3wks Aug. **Main courses** €27 **Prix fixe** *Lunch* €38. *Dinner* €65, €110. **Credit** AmEx, MC, V. **Map** p402 H5 **10**
This Japanese restaurant has rapidly developed a following among fashionable diners with discriminating tastes. Tall sprigs of cherry blossoms lend the only splash of colour to a room that manages to be both minimalist and warm. The 'Kai-style' sushi is a modern and zesty take on a classic: marinated and lightly grilled yellowtail is pressed on to a roll of *shiso*-scented rice. Seared tuna with avocado, miso and roasted pine nuts also delights, thanks to the ultra-fresh fish and erfect balance of flavours. Not to be outdone, the grilled aubergine with miso, seemingly simple, turns out to be a smoky, luscious experience, best enjoyed with a small spoon. A generous main of breaded pork lacks the finesse and refinement of the starters, but is nonetheless satisfying. Thoroughly French desserts come courtesy of celebrity pastry chef Pierre Hermé.

### Zen
*8 rue de l'Echelle, 1st (01.42.61.93.99). M° Louvre Rivoli.* **Open** noon-3pm, 7-10.30pm daily. Closed Aug. **Main courses** €12. **Prix fixe** €20-€50. **Credit** MC, V. **Map** p402 H5 **11**
There's no shortage of Japanese restaurants in this neighbourhood, but the recently opened Zen is refreshing in a couple of ways. First, there is no pale wood in sight – the colour scheme here is sharp white, green and yellow for a cheerful effect (helped by the giggling waitresses). Second, the menu has a lot to choose from – bowls of ramen, sushi and chirashi, hearty dishes such as chicken with egg on rice or tonkatsu – yet no detail is neglected, even in the careful making of the green tea. Everything here is

a notch above what you find in the nearby Japanese hub of rue Ste-Anne at the same price, and it's no wonder that 90 per cent of the clientele is Japanese. A perfect choice if you're spending a day at the Louvre – you can be in and out in 30 minutes.

## Opéra to Les Halles

## French

### Bioboa

*3 rue Danielle Casanova, 1st (01.42.61.17.67). Mᵒ Pyramides.* **Open** 10am-6pm Mon-Sat. **Main courses** €11.50. **Prix fixe** €12.70. **Credit** V. **Map** p401 G4 ⑫

The fact that this place describes itself as a 'food spa' shows how wholeheartedly it's embracing the organic ('bio' in French) revolution. There's a high-concept, if slightly sterile, air about the place: white designer chairs and tables; a weirdly beautiful bird fresco that winds through the eatery; and a mammoth fridge overflowing with ludicrously expensive mineral waters, exotic smoothies and colourful take-away salads for the fabulously busy. A healthy feast here might consist of soft-boiled eggs with sweet roasted autumn vegetables, or a generous juicy tofu burger complete with organic ketchup – one of Bioboa's staples. Non-smoking.

### Bistrot Victoires

*6 rue de la Vrillière, 1st (01.42.61.43.78). Mᵒ Bourse.* **Open** noon-3pm, 7-11pm daily. **Main courses** €11. **Credit** MC, V. **Map** p401 G5 ⑬

Bistros with vintage decor serving no-nonsense food at generous prices are growing thin on the ground in Paris, so it's no surprise that this gem is packed

to the gills with bargain-loving office workers and locals every day. The *steak-frites* are exemplary (*see p201* **Formidable frites**), featuring a slab of entrecôte topped with a smoking sprig of thyme, but *plats du jour* such as *blanquette de veau* (veal in cream sauce) are equally comforting and the giant salads and *tartines* provide welcome lighter alternatives. The tartare is under-seasoned and over-capered, and wines by the glass can be rough, but the authentic buzz should make up for any flaws.

### La Bourse ou la Vie

*12 rue Vivienne, 2nd (01.42.60.08.83). Mᵒ Bourse.* **Open** noon-10pm Mon-Fri. Closed 1wk Aug & 1wk Dec. **Main courses** €20. **Credit** AmEx, MC, V. **Map** p402 H4 ⑭

After a career as an architect, the round-spectacled owner of La Bourse ou la Vie has a new mission in life: to revive the dying art of the perfect *steak-frites* (*see p201* **Formidable frites**). His vivid yellow and red dining room is an unlikely setting for the daily meat fest that takes place here. The only decision you'll need to make is which cut of beef to order with your chips, unless you pick the cod. Choose between ultra-tender *coeur de filet* or a huge, surprisingly tender *bavette*. Rich, creamy pepper sauce is the speciality here, but the real surprise is the chips, which gain a distinctly animal flavour and inimitably crunchy texture from the suet in which they are cooked. Home-made desserts are temptingly displayed at the entrance.

### Drouant

*18 rue Gaillon, 2nd (01.42.65.15.16/www. drouant.com). Mᵒ Quatre Septembre or Pyramides.* **Open** noon-2.30pm, 7pm-midnight daily. **Main**

**Restaurant du Palais-Royal.** See p189.

courses €30. **Prix fixe** *Lunch & dinne*r €60. *Lunch*
€42. *Dinner* (10.30pm-midnight) €52. **Credit** AmEx,
DC, MC, V. **Map** p401 H4 ⑮
Star Alsatian chef Antoine Westermann, who runs
the successful Ile St-Louis bistro Mon Vieil Ami (*see
p187*), has whisked this landmark 1880 brasserie
into the 21st century with bronze-coloured ban
quettes and armchairs, a pale parquet floor and
rather incongruous butter-yellow paint and fabrics.
Black suits are de rigueur in a dining room heavy
with testosterone (at least at lunch). Westermann
has dedicated this restaurant to the art of the hors
d'oeuvre, served in themed sets of four ranging from
the global (a surprisingly successful Thai beef salad
with brightly coloured vegetables, coriander, and a
sweet and spicy sauce) to the nostalgic (silky leeks
in vinaigrette). The bite-sized surprises continue
with the main course accompaniments – four of
them for each dish, to be shared among diners – and
the multiple mini-desserts.

### Aux Lyonnais
*32 rue St-Marc, 2nd (01.42.96.65.04). M° Bourse or
Richelieu Drouot.* **Open** noon-1.45pm, 7.30-10.45pm
Tue-Fri; 7.30-10.45pm Sat. Closed Aug & 1wk Dec.
**Main courses** €21. **Prix fixe** €30. **Credit** AmEx,
MC, V. **Map** p402 H4 ⑯
This Ducasse-run bistro has perfectly preserved the
*bouchon* style and the pretty c1900 decor, keeping
the hearty spirit but revitalising the cuisine. As is
the wont of today's new-look, rustic-chic *terroir*
cooking, most things here arrive in cast-iron
casseroles or glass preserving jars, such as delicious
starters of poached egg in an exceptional frothy
sauce of morels and crayfish, and a little orange
*cocotte* packed with a roll-call of spring vegetables,
still just crunchy, in herb butter. Main courses featuring lots of simmering and stewing are a bit less
exciting. Veal Marengo – named after a Napoleonic
battle – proves to be a hefty veal shank braised in
wine with confit tomatoes, whole cloves of garlic and
tiny potatoes. It's back to preserving jars for dessert,
with a clever take on peach melba somewhere
between deconstructed trifle and ice-cream sundae.

### La Tour de Montlhéry
### (Chez Denise)
*5 rue des Prouvaires, 1st (01.42.36.21.82).
M° Les Halles/RER Châtelet Les Halles.* **Open**
noon-3pm, 7.30pm-5am Mon-Fri. Closed 14 July-
15 Aug. **Main courses** €24. **Credit** MC, V.
**Map** p402 J5 ⑰
At the stroke of midnight, the place is packed, jovial
and hungry. The busy, red-checked dining room is
intimate – you'll end up tasting a portion of your
neighbour's roasted lamb or chatting by the barrels
of wine stacked atop the bar. Savoury traditional
dishes, washed down by litres of the house Brouilly,
are the order of the day. Les Halles was the city's
wholesale meat market, and game, beef and offal
still rule here. Diners devour towering rib steaks
served with marrow and a heaped platter of fries,
home-made and among the best in town. Brave souls

can try *tripes au calvados*, grilled *andouillette* (lamb's
brain), or go for a stewed venison, served with succulent celery root and home-made jam.

### Un Jour à Peyrassol
*13 rue Vivienne, 2nd (01.42.60.12.92/www.
peyrassol.com). M° Bourse.* **Open** 12.30-2pm,
7.30-10pm Mon-Fri. Closed Aug & 1wk Dec. **Main
courses** €25. **Credit** MC, V. **Map** p402 H4 ⑱
As anyone who has travelled around Provence will
know, come winter the restaurants there go truffle-
crazy, putting the black tuber into everything from
soups to ice-cream. This casually chic little offshoot
of the Commanderie de Peyrassol, a picturesque
wine-producing castle in the Var, keeps up the game
with its blackboard menu, full of truffle treats. They
can be eaten on toast, atop a baked potato, in scram-
bled eggs or in a rich, creamy sauce enveloping
fluffy gnocchi. The natural complement is the
Commanderie's wine – white, red and rosé AOC
Côtes de Provence, which is also available at the
shop two doors down.

## International

### Higuma
*32bis rue Ste-Anne, 1st (01.47.03.38.59).
M° Pyramides.* **Open** 11.30am-10pm daily. **Main
courses** €8. **Prix fixe** €10.50-€12.50. **Credit** MC,
V. **Map** p401 H4 ⑲
On a street lined with small, authentic Japanese
eateries, Higuma's no-nonsense food and service
makes it one of the area's most popular destinations.
On entering, customers are greeted by plumes of aromatic steam emanating from the open kitchen-cum-
bar, where a small team of chefs ladle out giant
bowls of noodle soup piled high with meat, vegetables or seafood. You can slurp a meal at the counter
or sit at a Formica table in the front or back room.
Best value are the set menus at around €10, which
generally start with a plate of *gyoza* – seven hot and
succulent dumplings – and continue with a hearty
bowl of ramen. If you don't feel like splattering yourself with broth, the *yakitori* is also very good and the
tempura passable.

### Liza
*14 rue de la Banque, 2nd (01.55.35.00.66).
M° Bourse.* **Open** 12.30-2pm, 8-10.30pm Mon-Thur;
12.30-2pm, 8-11pm Fri, Sat; noon-4pm Sun. **Main
courses** €25. **Prix fixe** *Dinner* €42. **Credit** AmEx,
MC, V. **Map** p402 H4 ⑳
Liza Soughayar's restaurant showcases the style
and superb food of contemporary Beirut. All of the
furniture and table settings come from Lebanon, and
impress with their edgy design. The menu is also
unexpected, with plenty of meze that even fans of
Lebanese cooking won't know. Lentil, fried onion
and orange salad is delicious, as are the *kebbe*
(minced seasoned raw lamb) and grilled halloumi
cheese with home-made apricot preserve. Main
courses such as minced lamb with coriander-spiced
spinach and rice or a mixed grill of Mediterranean

fish are light, flavoursome and well presented. Try one of the excellent Lebanese wines, and finish up with the halva ice-cream with carob molasses. This place packs out with a young crowd nightly, so be sure to book. Although there's no prix fixe menu at lunchtime, prices are cheaper at €17-€32.

## Champs-Elysées & western Paris

## French

### Alain Ducasse au Plaza Athénée
*Hôtel Plaza Athénée, 25 av Montaigne, 8th (01.53.67.65.00/www.alain-ducasse.com). M° Alma Marceau.* **Open** 7.45-10.15pm Mon-Wed; 12.45-2.15pm, 7.45-10.15pm Thur, Fri. Closed mid July-mid Aug & 2wks Dec. **Prix fixe** €220-€320. **Credit** AmEx, DC, MC, V. **Map** p400 D5 **㉑**
The sheer glamour factor would be enough to recommend this restaurant, Alain Ducasse's most lofty Paris undertaking (though Christophe Moret runs the kitchen day to day). The dining room has a cheerful clementine-and-white colour scheme, while the ceiling drips with 10,000 crystals. The dining room's layout makes the waiters conspicuous, but they're personable, with none of the stiffness sometimes encountered in this style of restaurant. An *amuse-bouche* of a single langoustine in a lemon cream with a touch of Iranian caviar starts the meal off beautifully, but other dishes can be inconsistent: a part-raw/part-cooked salad of autumn fruit and veg in a red, Chinese-style sweet-and-sour dressing; Breton lobster in an overwhelming sauce of apple, quince and spiced wine. Cheese is predictably delicious, as is the *rum baba comme à Monte-Carlo*, with the finest rums for dousing.

### Les Ambassadeurs
*Hôtel de Crillon, 10 pl de la Concorde, 8th (01.44.71.16.17/www.crillon.com). M° Concorde.* **Open** 7-10.30am Mon; 7-10.30am, 12.30-1.45pm, 7.30-9.45pm Tue-Sat; noon-3pm Sun. Closed 1st wk Jan & Aug. **Main courses** €90. **Prix fixe** *Lunch* (Tue-Sat) €75. *Dinner* €200. *Brunch* (Sun) €66-€72. **Credit** AmEx, DC, V. **Map** p401 F4 **㉒**
The 18th-century butterscotch marble decor by Jacques-Ange Gabriel is unlikely to put anyone at ease (and the tables are miles apart), but the service is so enthusiastic, warm and polished that even before you've ordered you'll feel very, very special (though still not entirely at ease). Since the arrival of chef Jean-François Piège, the experience of eating at Les Ambassadeurs has become sublime. At €70 per person it may sound absurd to say that the lunch menu is excellent value, but compared to almost anywhere serving haute cuisine this is value indeed. In a main of Rossini-style bluefin tuna, a tube of foie gras is magically embedded in the tuna's raw centre, while crunchy-soft veal sweetbreads come with fresh morel mushrooms and tiny roasted potatoes. A succession of bright ideas makes the meal memorable: bite-sized ice-creams arrive straight after the mains, followed by tiny citrus-flavoured *madeleines* and pineapple macaroons. This could have been our dessert, but it was just a prelude to the chocolate, banana and lime gateau, and *gariguette* strawberries and basil enveloped in a feather-light meringue cage studded with gold leaf.

### Astrance
*4 rue Beethoven, 16th (01.40.50.84.40). M° Passy.* **Open** 12.15-1.30pm, 8-9.30pm Tue-Fri. Closed 1wk Feb, 4wks Aug, 1wk Oct & 1wk Dec. **Prix fixe** *Lunch* €70. *Dinner* €170. **Credit** AmEx, DC, MC, V. **Map** p404 B6 **㉓**
When Pascal Barbot opened Astrance, he was praised for creating a new style of Paris restaurant – refined, yet casual and affordable. A few years later, this small, slate-grey dining room feels just like a haute cuisine restaurant, with seemingly as many staff as diners and prices comparable to Taillevent's (*see p199*). Most customers, having secured their reservations at least a month ahead, give free rein to the chef with their 'Menu Astrance' (€170). Barbot has an indisputably original touch, combining foie gras with thin slices of white mushrooms and a lemon condiment, or sweet lobster with candied grapefruit peel, a grapefruit and rosemary sorbet, and raw baby spinach. Beautiful as this is, it won't necessarily send you into ecstasies; rather, the experience is quietly pleasurable. Wines by the glass are reasonably priced but not always elegant enough to stand up to the food.

### Le Bistrot d'à Côté Flaubert
*10 rue Gustave-Flaubert, 17th (01.42.67.05.81/ www.michelrostang.com). M° Courcelles.* **Open** 12.30-2pm, 7.30-11pm Tue-Fri; 7.30-11pm Sat. Closed 3wks Aug. **Main courses** €25. **Prix fixe** *Lunch* €29. **Credit** AmEx, MC, V. **Map** p400 D2 **㉔**
Star chef Michel Rostang took over this old *épicerie*, kept the pretty period interior and began serving up what he thought genuine bistro food should be. Starters, though, have a degree of sophistication that reflects haute cuisine roots. They include a wonderfully complex *pressé* of asparagus, sundried tomatoes and *coppa* ham accompanied by a raw artichoke and parmesan salad, and marinated *lisette* (small mackerel) with mushrooms, carrots and mesclun. Main courses are simpler but equally well prepared, with the emphasis on fine-quality meat (there's always a beef offering of the day) and a varied choice of accompaniments. Lamb from the Pyrenees is served up in a crumble crust with garlic shortbread biscuit and a bowl of smooth purée, while *dos de lieu* (pollack) comes with spicebread crust and jus, served with perfectly cooked vegetables.

### Le Cou de la Girafe
*7 rue Paul-Baudry, 8th (01.56.88.29.55). M° St-Philippe-du-Roule.* **Open** 12.30-2.30pm, 7.30-11pm Mon-Fri; 7.30-11pm Sat. Closed Aug & 1wk Dec. **Main courses** €25. **Prix fixe** *Lunch* €30. **Credit** AmEx, MC, V. **Map** p401 E4 **㉕**

Eat, Drink, Shop

At first there seems to be something slightly banal about this beige and brown restaurant, which is far enough from the Champs-Elysées to attract more locals than tourists through the door. Its freshly revamped dining room has a vaguely safari feel, thanks to the discreet leopard-print decor. Though the menu doesn't make a particularly original read, the food is impeccable. The *assiette de saumon* presents salmon in all its guises – smoked, raw and cooked. Thin, crunchy slices of red onion and plenty of fresh herbs make herring with potato salad seem a modern dish rather than a bistro classic, while a little black casserole bursts with chunks of juicy rabbit and tiny spring vegetables with perfectly preserved colour and texture. Desserts don't make any waves, but this is an address to keep in mind for its decent combination of style and substance. Prices are lower at lunchtimes, coming in at around €24-€35.

## Goupil le Bistro

*4 rue Claude-Debussy, 17th (01.45.74.83.25). Mᵒ Porte de Champerret.* **Open** noon-2pm, 8-11.30pm Mon-Fri. Closed Aug. **Main courses** €23. **Credit** AmEx, V. **Map** p400 C1 ㉖

On the outer edge of the 17th, Goupil is everything you imagine a traditional French bistro to be, with its burgundy-and-cream colour scheme, wooden tables and chairs, bunches of flowers and scribbled blackboard menu. You may picture an owner with a curly moustache – yet the driving force behind the bistro is a young chef who toils in an open kitchen that wouldn't look out of place in a space shuttle. The menu is seasonal and short. A *tarte fine aux maquereaux* makes the most of the fish, layering the mackerel fillets on buttery puff pastry topped with tastebud-tingling mustard sauce. Beetroot carpaccio with *mâche* (lamb's lettuce) and egg mimosa again employs humble ingredients to great effect,

Bistro fare gets an upmarket twist at Michel Rostang's **Bistrot d'à Côté Flaubert**.

# Back to school

If maman thought frozen dinners were the best thing since sliced bread, all is not lost. Midday cookery classes in Paris can now help you acquire the skills needed to host dazzling Gallic dinner parties. Classes start at €15 and are mostly conducted in French, though many of the chefs speak a little English.

**L'Atelier des Chefs** (10 rue Penthièvre, 8th, 01.53.30.05.82, www.atelierchefs.com) was the first school to turn the thirst for culinary knowledge into lunch-hour classes. Its simple formula has been a wild success: students pay €15 to learn a single dish, then gather at the table to enjoy the fruit of their labours with extras such as dessert, wine and coffee costing €2 to €3 each.

Near the Bastille, the friendly **Atelier des Sens** (40 rue Sedaine, 11th, 01.40.21.08.50, www.atelier-des-sens.com) has followed in the footsteps of L'Atelier des Chefs, offering hour-long classes specially designed for the 'gourmet in a hurry'. For €34, you can learn to put together a sophisticated feast such as veal tartare with yoghurt sauce, soy caramel and mesclun followed by raspberry and tomato gazpacho with almond *tuiles*.

Upstairs from the Guy Degrenne tableware shop near place de la Madeleine, the **Académie Cinq Sens** (Village Royal, 25 rue Royale, 8th, 01.47.42.14.10, www.academie cinqsens.com) has also got in on the act with its 'midday cookery' lesson for €20. You might learn how to make a *bavette* (beef flank steak) with shallot sauce, but the classes

more often put a modern spin on French dishes: quail with chorizo or rabbit piccata with beaufort cheese is typical.

To combat a decline in the consumption of fresh fruit and vegetables, the French government sponsors **Cuisine Fraîch'Attitude** (60 rue du Faubourg Poissonnière, 10th, 01.49.49.15.15, www.cuisinefraich attitude.com) in the tenth arrondissement. Among the guest instructors and consultants are some of the best chefs in town: Pascal Barbot of Astrance (*see p194*), William Ledeuil of Ze Kitchen Galerie, and Bruno Viala of hip Montmartre restaurant La Famille. You might learn to improvise with courgettes and broccoli or play with soups or tapas. At just €12, these classes fill up particularly quickly.

Long a bastion of culinary instruction, the **Ecole Ritz Escoffier** (38 rue Cambon, 1st, 01.43.16.30.50, www.ritzparis.com) has introduced hour-long Ritzy Breaks for €45 on Tuesdays, Wednesdays and Thursdays. If a majority of English speakers sign up, the class may be held in English. As you might expect, the Ritz doesn't skimp on luxury ingredients, and you could sit down to saffron risotto with Dublin Bay prawns or sole fillet with ginger and curry spices.

So how do these schools keep their lunchtime classes affordable? With the exception of Cuisine Fraich'Attitude, which is publicly funded, they all offer a range of extended programmes alongside the lunchtime courses.

thanks to elegant presentation and a perfectly balanced dressing. Just as impressive is a more luxurious monkfish meunière (cooked in butter) with sautéed artichokes and chanterelles. Finish with a classic dessert such as *île flottante*.

### Granterroirs

*30 rue de Miromesnil, 8th (01.47.42.18.18/www.* *granterroirs.com). M° Miromesnil.* **Open** 9am-8pm Mon-Fri. *Food served* noon-3pm. Closed 3wks Aug. **Main courses** €21. **Prix fixe** €31. **Credit** MC, V. **Map** p401 F3 ㉗

This *épicerie* with a difference is the perfect remedy for anyone for whom the word *'terroir'* conjures up visions of big, indigestible helpings of grease-soaked peasant food. Here, the walls heave with more than 600 enticing specialities from southern France, including Périgord foie gras, tapenade from Provence, charcuterie from Aubrac and a fine selection of wines straight from the domaines. Great gift ideas – but why not sample some of the goodies on display before you buy by enjoying the midday *table d'hôte* feast? Come in early to ensure that you can choose from the five succulent *plats du jour* on offer (such as a piece of marinated salmon with dill on a bed of warm potatoes). Plonk yourself at one of the massive communal tables, make your order and soak up the laid-back, convivial ambience.

### Pierre Gagnaire

*6 rue Balzac, 8th (01.58.36.12.50/www.pierre-* *gagnaire.com). M° George V or Charles de Gaulle Etoile.* **Open** noon-1.30pm, 7.30-9.30pm Mon-Fri, Sun. Closed 1wk Apr & Aug. **Main courses** €105. **Prix fixe** *Lunch* €95, €245. *Dinner* €245. **Credit** AmEx, MC, V. **Map** p400 D3 ㉘

At Pierre Gagnaire most starters alone cost over €90, which seems to be the price of culinary experimentation – Gagnaire is something of a scientist, often working with molecular gastronomy specialist Hervé This. The more accessibly priced €90 lunch menu is far from the experience of the *carte*: the former is conventionally presented in three courses, while the latter involves four or five plates for each course. Even the *amuse-bouches* fill the table: an egg 'raviole' (interesting technically but jarring to the palate), crisp-like waffled potatoes with chilli, ricotta with apple, fish in a cauliflower jelly, and glazed monkfish. The best thing about the lunch menu is that it includes four very indulgent desserts (half of 'le grand dessert'): clementine, raspberry and vanilla, chocolate, and passion fruit. Coffee is priced at €8.50, but at least if you don't finish your wine the staff will let you take it home.

### Rech

*62 av des Ternes, 17th (01.45.72.29.47). M° Ternes.* **Open** noon-2pm, 6.30-10pm. Closed 3wks Aug. **Main courses** €28. **Prix fixe** *Lunch* €28. *Dinner* €53. **Credit** AmEx, MC, V. **Map** p400 C2 ㉙

Say what you like about star chef Alain Ducasse spreading himself too thin, he is not a man to overlook details. His personal touches are everywhere in this art deco seafood restaurant, which he took over

in spring 2007, from the Japanese fish prints on the walls of the upstairs dining room to the blown glass candleholders on the main floor tables. Otherwise, the restaurant has preserved much of its original character: the seafood shucker outside has been on staff here since 1982. The kitchen turns out the kind of precise, Mediterranean-inspired cooking you would expect from Ducasse: glistening sardine fillets marinated with preserved lemon, silky lobster ravioli, octopus carpaccio painted with pesto, steamed Scottish salmon sprinkled with fleur de sel. As the fish dishes are light, you can justify indulging in a perfectly aged camembert (the restaurant's only cheese) and the XL éclair, an event in itself.

### Restaurant L'Entredgeu

*83 rue Laugier, 17th (01.40.54.97.24). M° Porte de Champerret.* **Open** noon-2pm, 7.30-11pm Tue-Sat. Closed 1wk Apr, 1st 3wks Aug & 1wk Dec. **Prix fixe** *Lunch* €22, €30. *Dinner* €30. **Credit** DC, MC, V. **Map** p400 C2 ㉚

Warning. Reading the menu here will make you seriously doubt your capacity for pudding, and choosing between the robust dishes will have you wishing you'd gone elasticised. Have no fear. The heartiness belies refined, perfectly gauged cooking, served in civilised portions. The place is brisk, well lit and full of chattering locals rejoicing in what Paris does best. Table turnover is fast, but this is not a place to linger smoochily in any case – you'll be too busy marvelling at the sharp *gribiche* sauce cutting through the milky crisp-battered oysters, the depth and aroma of the saffron-infused fish soup, the perfect layered execution of the caramelised pork belly, and the delicate desserts. The wine list is creative and assured: before the food arrives (and you won't wait for long), try the Alain Renardat Cerdon du Bugey, a sparkling rosé with hints of raspberry.

### Senderens

*9 pl de la Madeleine, 8th (01.42.65.22.90/www.* *senderens.fr). M° Madeleine.* **Open** noon-3pm, 7.30-11.30pm daily. Closed 3wks Aug. **Main courses** €35. **Prix fixe** €110-€150 (with wine). **Credit** AmEx, DC, MC, V. **Map** p401 G4 ㉛

Long live Alain Senderens. The veteran chef has reinvented his art nouveau institution (formerly Lucas Carton) with a *Star Trek* interior and a truly mind-boggling fusion menu. Now, instead of his famed *canard à l'Apicius*, Senderens serves roast duck foie gras with a warm salad of black figs and liquorice powder, or monkfish steak with Spanish mussels and green curry sauce. Each dish comes with a suggested wine, whisky, sherry or punch (to accompany a rum-doused *savarin* with slivers of ten-flavour pear), and while these are perfectly matched, the mix of flavours and alcohols can be a tad overwhelming by the end of a meal. The chef seems to be getting to grips with his new style – a sole tempura was not as crisp as it might have been – but even a faintly flawed meal here is an event, as much for the eclectic clientele as the food. The bar Le Passage upstairs serves tapas, perfect for a snack after the opera.

Eat, Drink, Shop

## Stella Maris

*4 rue Arsène-Houssaye, 8th (01.42.89.16.22/www. stellamarisparis.com). M° Charles de Gaulle-Etoile.* **Open** noon-2.30pm, 7.30-10.30pm Mon-Fri; 7.30-10.30pm Sat. Closed 2wks Aug. **Main courses** €50. **Prix fixe** *Lunch* €43, €99. *Dinner* €99, €130. **Credit** AmEx, DC, MC, V. **Map** p400 D3 ③②

Tateru Yoshino has divided his life between Paris and Tokyo for many years. Trained by Robuchon and Troisgros, he turns out food that is resolutely French. A certain Japanese understatement and demureness pervade, however. The service is at times faltering, but charmingly so, and the newly designed space beautiful. You might float your way through foie gras with carrots, truffles and pistachio oil, pan-fried sea bass with saffron risotto, and a perfectly lopsided Grand Marnier soufflé that instantly disappears on the tongue in a sugary breeze. The exquisite powdery blandness of the tasting-menu-going-home-present *cake aux marrons glacés* brings it all softly, dreamily, back next morning at breakfast. Expensive (a bonsai's throw from the place de l'Etoile, after all) but wonderful.

## La Table de Lauriston

*129 rue de Lauriston, 16th (01.47.27.00.07). M° Trocadéro.* **Open** noon-2.30pm, 7-10.30pm Mon-Fri; 7-10.30pm Sat. Closed 3wks Aug & 1wk Dec. **Main courses** €23. **Prix fixe** *Lunch* €25. **Credit** AmEx, MC, V. **Map** p400 B5 ③③

Serge Barbey's dining room has a refreshingly feminine touch: stripes of pink, orange and silver paint, with velvety chairs in indigo and gold, patterned banquettes and whimsical paintings. In spring, stalks of asparagus from the Landes are expertly trimmed to avoid any stringiness and served with the simplest *vinaigrette d'herbes*. More extravagant is the *foie gras cuit au torchon*, in which the duck liver is wrapped in a cloth and poached in a bouillon. Entrecôte (rib steak) is always on the menu and comes with *gratin dauphinois* or sautéed *ratte* potatoes. Skip the crème brûlée and the *moelleux au chocolat*, which you could have anywhere, and order a dessert with attitude: the giant *baba au rhum*.

## Taillevent

*15 rue Lamennais, 8th (01.44.95.15.01/www. taillevent.com). M° George V.* **Open** 12.15-1.30pm, 7.15-9.30pm Mon-Fri. Closed Aug. **Main courses** €75. **Prix fixe** *Lunch* €70, €140, €190. *Dinner* €140, €190. **Credit** AmEx, DC, MC, V. **Map** p400 D3 ③④

Taillevent owes much of its ongoing success to the personality of its owner, Jean-Claude Vrinat, whose decision to hire young chefs with character is testament to his own expertise. Past the spacious and rather subdued front room is a livelier, almost brasserie-like second salon. Prices here are not as shocking as in some restaurants at this level; there's a €70 lunch menu, though you might have to make a point of asking for it. *Rémoulade de coquilles St-Jacques* is a technical feat, with slices of raw, marinated scallop wrapped in a tube shape around a finely diced apple filling, encircled by a mayonnaise-like

*rémoulade* sauce. An earthier and lip-smacking dish is the trademark *épeautre* – an ancient wheat – cooked 'like a risotto' with bone marrow, black truffle, whipped cream and parmesan, and topped with sautéed frogs' legs. *Ravioli au chocolat araguani* is a surprising and wonderful dessert: pillowy pockets of soft chocolate pasta explode in the mouth, releasing liquid bitter chocolate.

# International

## Le Bistrot Napolitain

*18 av Franklin D. Roosevelt, 8th (01.45.62.08.37). M° St-Philippe-du-Roule.* **Open** noon-2.30pm, 7.15-10.30pm Mon-Fri. Closed 1wk July, Aug & 1wk Dec. **Main courses** €25. **Credit** MC, V. **Map** p401 E4 ③⑤

This chic Italian bistro off the Champs-Elysées is as far from a tourist joint as it is possible to be. On weekday lunchtimes (it doesn't open on Saturday night or Sunday) it is full of suave Italianate businessmen in modish pinstripes. The decor is plain, the tablecloths starched white, and the kitchen open, with the *pizzaiolo* shoving fluffy pizzas in and out of the oven while orders are shouted over the heads of diners. Generosity defines the food – not just big plates, but lashings of the ingredients that others skimp on, such as the slices of tangy parmesan piled high over rocket on the fresh and tender beef carpaccio. The pizzas are as good as they say they are: the Enzo comes with milky, almost raw *mozzarella di bufala* and tasty tomatoes, which prove how good the crust is as it doesn't become a soggy mush. For pasta you can choose between dried and fresh, with variations such as fresh saffron tagliatelle.

# Montmartre & Pigalle

# French

## A. Beauvilliers

*52 rue Lamarck, 18th (01.42.55.05.42). M° Lamarck-Caulaincourt.* **Open** 12.15-2.30pm, 8-10.30pm Tue-Sat. Closed 2wks Aug & 1wk Dec. **Main courses** €35. **Prix fixe** *Lunch* €35, €68. *Dinner* €45, €68. **Credit** AmEx, DC, MC, V. **Map** p402 J1 ③⑥

Named after Marie-Antoinette's cook, this chandelier-bedecked restaurant behind the butte Montmartre once attracted *le tout Paris* thanks to its charismatic owner. Now run by young chef Yohan Paran, it has acquired a more provincial air that contrasts pleasantly with the inventive French cooking. For a romantic experience – aim for the terrace, weather permitting – it's worth splurging on the €63 tasting menu, which makes abundant use of luxury ingredients such as foie gras, scallops, farm-raised pigeon, truffles and rare argania oil from Morocco. Typical of Paran's style are pancetta-wrapped scallops served with a creamy purée of vitelotte potatoes, a blue variety. The good-value €35 prix fixe at lunch is well worth the climb to this lesser-known part of Montmartre.

## Chez Toinette

*20 rue Germain-Pilon, 18th (01.42.54.44.36). M°
Abbesses or Pigalle.* **Open** 7.30-11.30pm Mon-Sat.
Closed last 3wks Aug. **Main courses** €17. **Credit**
MC, V. **Map** p401 H2 **⑰**

This stalwart purveyor of bistro fare behind the
Théâtre de Montmartre has steadily upped its prices
in line with its burgeoning success. However, the
blackboard menu is still good value in an area
known for rip-offs. As you squeeze into the seats,
the amiable waiter describes each dish with pride,
then presents an appetiser of olives, ripe cherry
tomatoes and crisp radishes. Of the starters, try the
red-blooded wild boar terrine, the gloriously creamy
*chèvre chaud* or the soufflé-like asparagus quiche.
Carnivorous mains include *mignon de porc*, spring
lamb and assorted steaks – the lamb seared in rosemary is a deliciously lean morsel. Round it all off on
a high note with Armagnac-steeped prunes.

## Georgette

*29 rue St-Georges, 9th (01.42.80.39.13). M° Notre-
Dame-de-Lorette.* **Open** noon-2.45pm, 7.30-11pm Tue-
Fri. Closed 1wk Apr, Aug & 1wk Nov. **Main courses**
€15. **Credit** AmEx, MC, V. **Map** p402 H3 **㊳**

A mix of 1950s Formica tables (with matching bar)
and ancient wooden beams provides the external
charm, but what has won Georgette a loyal following since it opened three years ago is the chef's lov-
ing use of seasonal ingredients. Hearty meat dishes
satisfy the local business crowd, while lighter
options might include slightly bony sea bream with
provençal vegetables, or a charlotte of juicy lamb
chunks and aubergine. For calorie counters there's
an unsweetened prune and pear compote – though
the creamy, cloud-like fontainebleau cheese with
raspberry coulis is worth abandoning any diet for.

## Le Moulin de la Galette

*83 rue Lepic, 18th (01.46.06.84.77). M° Notre-
Dame-de-Lorette.* **Open** noon-2.45pm, 7.30-11pm
Tue-Fri. Closed Aug. **Main courses** €30. **Credit**
AmEx, MC, V. **Map** p402 H3 **㊴**

The butte Montmartre was once dotted with windmills, and this one survives, housing a chic restaurant with a few romantic tables in the cobbled
courtyard outside. It's hard to imagine a more picturesque setting in Montmartre, but the kitchen
makes an effort nonetheless with updated dishes
such as foie gras with melting beetroot cooked in
lemon balm and juniper or suckling pig alongside
potato purée. Desserts, such as figs caramelised with
muscovado sugar, look like a painter's tableau.
Overall a meal here is worth the price, though if
you're on a budget it's best to stick to one of the set
menus and order carefully from the wine list.

## Pétrelle

*34 rue Pétrelle, 9th (01.42.82 11.02). M° Anvers.*
**Open** 8-9.30pm Tue-Sat. Closed 4wks July/Aug &
1wk Dec. **Main courses** €25. **Prix fixe** €29.
**Credit** MC, V. **Map** p402 J2 **㊵**

Jean-Luc André is as inspired a decorator as he is a
cook, and the quirky charm of his dining room has
made it popular with fashion designers and film
stars alike. A faded series of early 20th-century
tableaux is one recent flea market find, but behind
the style is some serious substance. André seeks out
the very best ingredients from local producers, and
the quality shines through. The €29 no-choice menu
is huge value for money (on our last visit, marinated
sardines with tomato relish, rosemary-scented rabbit with roasted vegetables, deep purple poached
figs); or you can splash out with luxurious à la carte
dishes such as tournedos Rossini. If you're looking
for a quick and delicious lunch near Montmartre,
visit André's annexe, Les Vivres, next door.

## Spring

*28 rue de la Tour d'Auvergne, 9th (01.45.96.05.72).
M° Anvers or Cadet.* **Open** 8.30pm Tue, Wed;
1pm & 8.30pm Thur, Fri. Closed Aug & 1wk Dec.
**Prix fixe** *Lunch* €33. *Dinner* €39. **Credit** MC, V.
**Map** p402 J1 **㊶**

Where do Michelin inspectors go on their day off?
To Spring, where 30-year-old American chef Daniel
Rose has wowed the critics since opening this sleek
16-seat bistro in 2006. After an apprenticeship that
took him to Guatemala, Italy, the US and the
kitchens of Le Meurice, he decided to keep things
simple by serving a no-choice four-course menu that
changes every day according to what he finds at the
place des Fêtes market. On a late spring day this
might result in a velvety cauliflower soup (made
without cream), chunky octopus salad with potatoes,
radishes and herbs, poached guinea hen with root
vegetables, and baked apple with French toast. A
meal feels like a big dinner party, with Rose the affa-
ble host. Reservations obligatory.

## International

### Kastoori

*4 pl Gustave-Toudouze, 9th (01.44.53.06.10). M° St-
Georges.* **Open** 11.30am-2.30pm, 7-11.30pm daily.
**Main courses** €13. **Prix fixe** *Lunch* (Mon-Fri) €8,
€10. *Dinner* €15. **Credit** MC, V. **Map** p401 H2 **㊷**

It's no surprise that Kastoori's terrace, on a delightful 19th-century square, is often full: this friendly,
family-run Indian restaurant is one of the few good-
value eateries in the area. We're not talking ubiquitous mass-produced buffets: each dish on the lunch
and dinner set menus is prepared with care and
home-mixed spices, and you can taste the difference.
Amid dangling lanterns, Indian fabrics and (perhaps
too much) incense inside, or under hot lamps outside, order some popadoms to taste the home-made
chutneys served in an ornate metal boat, and choose
from tangy *raita* and *kaleji* (coriander-sprinkled, cur-
ried lamb liver) as starters, followed by a choice of
tandoori chicken, chicken curry, *saag paneer* or the
dish of the day, selected from the à la carte menu.
You can bring your own wine for no corkage fee, and
don't miss the delicious lassis or *kulfis* for afters.

# Formidable frites

Since the *vache folle* (mad cow) crisis, the quality of meat in Paris restaurants has never been better. Unfortunately, the same can't be said for *frites*, the accompaniment that, at its best, can elevate a simple steak to sublime heights. Since fantastic fries are a labour of love, most restaurateurs opt for the convenience of the frozen variety. Only a few purists continue to carve their chips from fresh potatoes.

Aficionados may argue over the merits of skinny versus chunky, but what really counts is the fat used to fry the *frites*. At **La Bourse ou la Vie** (*see p191*), a bistro run by garrulous former architect Patrice Porte, the thin *frites* served alongside the signature *steak au poivre* get their distinctive meaty flavour from suet. As in all the finest *steak-frites* restaurants there is little else on the menu here, allowing the kitchen to concentrate on what it does best.

Also from the skinny school of *frite*-frying is **L'Ami Louis** (32 rue du Vertbois, 3rd, 01.48.87.77.48), whose roast chicken accompanied by heaps of *frites* cooked in goose fat is renowned the world over, attracting the likes of Bill Clinton to this 1920s time-warp dining room. Just as good,

and not quite as pricey, are the shoestring *frites* sizzled in peanut oil at **Savy** (23 rue Bayard, 8th, 01.47.23.46.98), a vintage 1930s bistro off the Champs-Elysées devoted to the hearty cuisine of the Aveyron in central France. The best way to eat them is alongside the gargantuan shoulder of lamb for two people, which arrives beautifully charred and crisp, and a bottle of Mercurey from the well-stocked cellar. *Frite* heaven.

At 11.30am and 7pm every day, *frite* fans queue up for a table in the original branch of Le Relais de Venise, **L'Entrecôte** (271 bd Pereire, 17th, 01.45.74.27.97) on the outskirts of the 17th arrondissement, for its secret steak sauce and shoestring *frites*, also called *allumettes* (matchsticks). The restaurant has two other, less busy, branches in Paris and opened a London outpost in 2005. According to Jean-Claude Ribaut, food writer at *Le Monde*, chicken liver, thyme, cream and mustard are among the key ingredients of the mysterious sauce. As for *frites*, their signature light crisp texture comes from the peanut oil they're fried in.

Chunkier *frites* have their supporters too, and one reliable source of these is the **Bistrot Victoires** (*see p191*), where an entrecôte served with a smoking branch of thyme and a pile of rough-textured golden *frites* costs a modest €11. Though it could be argued that *pommes Pont Neuf* are technically not *frites*, it's hard to overlook the symmetrical stack of thick-cut potato chips served alongside the *filet de boeuf du Limousin* at the **Restaurant du Palais-Royal** (*see p189*). It costs €32, but as a Paris experience this dish is hard to beat. The key to the *frites* at both these restaurants? Palm oil, which, like the dish itself, is probably not something you want to indulge in every day.

## Rose Bakery

*46 rue des Martyrs, 9th (01.42.82.12.80). M° Notre-Dame-de-Lorette.* **Open** 9am-7pm Tue-Fri; 10am-5pm Sat, Sun. Closed 2wks Aug & 1wk Dec. **Main courses** €14. **Credit** AmEx, MC, V. **Map** p402 H2 ❹
This English-themed café run by a Franco-British couple stands out for the quality of its ingredients – organic or from small producers – as well as the too-good-to-be-true puddings: carrot cake, sticky toffee pudding and, in winter, a chocolate-chestnut tart.

The DIY salad plate is crunchily satisfying, but the thin-crusted *pizzettes*, daily soups and occasional risottos are equally good choices. Don't expect much beyond scones in the morning except at weekends, when brunch is served to a packed-out house. Popular with health-conscious locals who love the smoke-free atmosphere and expats who can't believe their luck, the dining room – which looks as if it might have once been a garage – is minimalist but welcoming. The service is friendly. *Photo p202.*

Rose Bakery. *See p201.*

# Beaubourg & the Marais

## French

### L'Ambassade d'Auvergne

*22 rue du Grenier-St-Lazare, 3rd (01.42.72.31.22/ www.ambassade-auvergne.com). M° Arts et Métiers.* **Open** noon-2pm, 7.30-10pm daily. **Main courses** €18. **Prix fixe** *Lunch* €20, €28. *Dinner* €28. **Credit** AmEx, MC, V. **Map** p409 K5 **44**

This rustic *auberge* is a fitting embassy for the hearty fare of central France. Go easy on the complimentary pâté and thick-sliced country bread while you look at the menu – you're going to need your appetite later. An order of cured ham comes as two hefty, plate-filling slices, while the salad bowl is chock-full of green lentils cooked in goose fat, studded with bacon and shallots. The *rôti d'agneau* arrives as a pot of melting chunks of lamb in a rich, meaty sauce with a helping of tender white beans. Dishes arrive with the flagship *aligot*, served with pomp as the waiter lifts great strands of the creamy, elastic mash-and-cheese concoction into the air and lets it plop on to the plates with a dramatic flourish. Of the regional wines (Chanturgue, Boudes, Madargues), the rather fruity AOC Marcillac makes a worthy partner for a successful meal.

### Breizh Café

*109 rue Vieille-du-Temple, 3rd (01.42.72.13.77). M° Filles du Calvaire.* **Open** noon-11pm Wed-Sun. Closed 3wks Aug. **Main courses** €10. **Credit** MC, V. **Map** p409 L5 **45**

With its modern interior of pale wood and its choice of 15 artisanal ciders,the recently opened Breizh Café is a world away from the average crêperie. For the complete faux-seaside experience, you might

start with a plate of oysters before indulging in an inventive buckwheat *galette* such as the Cancalaise, made with potato, smoked herring from Brittany and herring roe. The choice of fillings is fairly limited, often relying on some combination of ham or andouille (tripe sausage), cheese and eggs, but the ingredients are high-quality – including the use of Valrhona chocolate with 70 per cent cocoa solids in the dessert crêpes.

### Le Dôme du Marais

*53bis rue des Francs-Bourgeois, 4th (01.42.74.54.17). M° Rambuteau.* **Open** noon-2.30pm, 7-10.30pm Tue-Sat. Closed 1wk Jan & 3wks Aug. **Main courses** €23. **Prix fixe** *Lunch* €25, €36, €48, €70. *Dinner* €36, €48, €70. **Credit** AmEx, MC, V. **Map** p409 K6 **46**

Lying somewhere between casual and formal, bistro and haute cuisine, Le Dôme du Marais seems to have got it just about right. The staff won't turn a hair if you show up in jeans, but should you feel the urge to mark the occasion with finery, the octagonal, domed dining room would provide a fitting backdrop. The pre-Revolutionary building once served as the auction room for state-owned pawnbrokers; today it has been done up in burgundy and gilt, with tables dressed in sparkling white linen. Owner-chef Pierre Lecoutre loves to work with seasonal produce, serving, say, *filet de courbine*, a white fish available only for three weeks of the year, in a chorizo cream sauce next to fresh little broad beans that also have a brief season. *Monceau de chocolat* and strawberry *dacquoise* live up to their stunning good looks.

### Le Hangar

*12 impasse Berthaud, 3rd (01.42.74.55.44). M° Rambuteau.* **Open** noon-2.30pm, 7.30-11pm Tue-Sat. Closed Aug. **Main courses** €17. **No credit cards. Map** p409 K5 **47**

**Le Petit Marché.**

It's worth making the effort to find this bistro by the Centre Pompidou, with its terrace tucked away in a hidden impasse and excellent cooking. The exposed stone walls and smartly set tables are immediately welcoming, and the long, airy room fills with locals and slightly baffled tourists. A bowl of tapenade and toast is supplied to keep you going while choosing from the comprehensive *carte*. It yields, for starters, tasty and grease-free *rillettes de lapereau* (rabbit) alongside perfectly balanced pumpkin and chestnut soup. Main courses include a well-seasoned steak tartare, served with a crisp salad and *pommes dauphines*, and superb pan-fried foie gras on a smooth potato purée made with olive oil. Puddings such as chocolate soufflé and warm white-wine tart with cinnamon are also tempting – but if you're going to splurge, remember that payment is in cash only.

### Le Petit Marché

*9 rue de Béarn, 3rd (01.42.72.06.67). M° Chemin Vert.* **Open** noon-3pm, 7.30pm-midnight Mon-Fri; noon-4pm Sat, Sun. **Main courses** €17. **Prix fixe** *Lunch* €20.50. **Credit** AmEx, MC, V. **Map** 409 L6 **48**

Just a step away from place des Vosges, Petit Marché attracts a fashion-conscious crowd. The woody interior is warm and welcoming, while the heated terrace offers a view of the *gendarmerie*. The menu is short and modern with Asian touches. Raw tuna is flash-fried in sesame seeds and served with a Thai sauce, making for an original and refreshing starter; crispy-coated deep-fried king prawns have a similar oriental lightness. The main vegetarian risotto is rich in basil, coriander, cream and al dente green beans, contrasting winningly with the unctuous rice. Pan-fried scallops with lime are precision-cooked to avoid any hint of rubberiness, and

accompanied by a good purée and more beans. There's a short wine list; the carafe of house red is unusually good.

## International

### 404

*69 rue des Gravilliers, 3rd (01.42.74.57.81). M° Arts et Métiers.* **Open** noon-2.30pm, 8pm-midnight Mon-Fri; noon-4pm (brunch), 8pm-midnight Sat, Sun. **Main courses** €19. **Prix fixe** *Brunch* €21. *Lunch* €17. **Credit** AmEx, DC, MC, V. **Map** p409 K5 **49**

However much others try to copy Algerian-born Momo's formula, they can't replicate the unique atmosphere of his Paris and London restaurants. It might be the fact that the exquisite lamps are antiques and there's real *tadelakt* in the bathroom, or that celeb friends like Ozwald Boateng might drop in; most likely it's because the staff in their tastefully decorated T-shirts just can't wait for the party to kick off. Book for the late sitting if you like to dance on the tables: before you've finished your mint cocktails the waiters will already be gyrating on the bar. Starters include *salade méchouia* (a refreshing combination of diced tomato, red peppers and garlic), *zalouk* (aubergine and garlic) or stuffed sardines. Of the mouthwatering tagines the chicken with pear is a winner, but the real revelation is the fish tagine absolutely bursting with flavour. The fruit salads and pistachio pastries are more of an afterthought as the soundtrack brings everyone to their feet.

### Anahi

*49 rue Volta, 3rd (01.48.87.88.24). M° Arts et Métiers, Temple or République.* **Open** 8pm-midnight daily. **Main courses** €28. **Credit** MC, V. **Map** p402 K5 **50**

A rickety old building in a narrow and ill-lit street deep in the Marais houses this trendy Argentinian restaurant. Slabs of grilled beef fresh (well, vacuum-packed) from the pampas pull in the crowds, cheerily welcomed by Carmina and Pilat, the sisters who started up in this old charcuterie some 20 years ago. The original white-tiled walls feature black-and-white photos of the pair, and the art deco ceiling was painted by Albert Camus' brother. Tuck into *torta pascualina*, a sweetish spinach tart with onions, or try the standout ceviche made with sea bass. Mains of skewered chicken breast marinated in lemon and served with apple and pineapple salsa and sweet potato purée, and *cururú de camarao* (grilled *gambas* with peanuts and okra) are satisfying, but the *bif angosto* – a juicy fillet served with a green salad – is the star. Match it with a choice Chilean red.

### Chez Omar

*47 rue de Bretagne, 3rd (01.42.72.36.26). Mº Temple or Arts et Métiers.* **Open** noon-2.30pm, 7-10.30pm Mon-Sat; 7-10.30pm Sun. **Main courses** €16. **No credit cards. Map** p409 L5 🐼

Keeping it simple: no-nonsense nosh at **Le Bistrot Paul Bert**.

The once-fashionable Omar doesn't take reservations, and the queue can stretch the length of the zinc bar and through the door. Everyone is waiting for the same thing: couscous. Prices range from €11 (vegetarian) to €24 (*royale*); there are no tagines or other traditional Maghreb mains, only a handful of French classics (duck, fish, steak). Overstretched waiters slip through the crowds with mounds of semolina, steaming vats of vegetable-laden broth and steel platters heaving with meat and more meat, including the stellar *merguez*. Even on packed nights there's an offer of seconds – gratis, of course – to encourage you to stay; big appetites might find room for the giant platter of Algerian pastries the waiter leaves at your table. Non-smokers beware: the proximity of your neighbours means you'll share more than just their conversation.
**Other locations**: Café Moderne, 19 rue Keller, 11th (01.47.00.53.62).

## Bastille & eastern Paris

### French

#### A la Biche au Bois

*45 av Ledru-Rollin, 12th (01.43.43.34.38). M° Gare de Lyon.* **Open** 7-11pm Mon; noon-2pm, 7-11pm Tue-Fri. Closed 4wks July-Aug & Christmas wk. **Main courses** €15. **Prix fixe** €24.90. **Credit** AmEx, DC, MC, V. **Map** p407 M8 ➎➋
However crowded it gets here, it doesn't matter because everyone always seems so happy with the food and the convivial atmosphere. It's impossible not to be enthusiastic about the more than generous portions offered with the €24.90 prix fixe menu, one of the very few in town to include a selection of game in season, including Scottish grouse. Salade niçoise and a hearty slab of game terrine with the requisite jar of gherkins are both virtually a meal in themselves. Mains might include tasty portions of wild duck in blackcurrant sauce, partridge with cabbage or wild venison stew which, like the coq au vin and the boeuf bourguignon, is served in the Biche's signature cast-iron casserole dishes. Lingering too long over your choice of the many perfectly ripe cheeses incurs the risk of getting served half a dozen of them. If you can still do dessert, go for one of the home-made tarts laden with seasonal fruits or, for something lighter, one of the sorbets liberally drenched in vodka, Calvados or liqueur. The wine list also has a reputation as one of the best-value selections in town, particularly the Rhône section. Book in advance, but expect to wait anyway – it's a small price to pay for a blissful if unsophisticated experience.

#### Le Bistrot Paul Bert

*18 rue Paul-Bert, 11th (01.43.72.24.01). M° Charonne.* **Open** noon-2pm, 7.30-11pm Tue-Thur; noon-2pm, 7.30-11.30pm Fri, Sat. Closed Aug. **Main courses** €21. **Prix fixe** *Lunch* €16. *Dinner* €32. **Credit** MC, V. **Map** p407 N7 ➎➌

This heart-warming bistro gets it right almost down to the last crumb, and is a popular haunt of local businessmen and artisans. No-nonsense, pared-down cooking is its forte: expect high-quality seasonal produce, very simply prepared. A starter salad of *ris de veau* illustrates the point, with lightly browned veal sweetbreads perched on a bed of green beans and baby carrots and lightly nipped with a sauce of sherry vinegar and deglazed cooking juices. Though this approach is appealing, there are times when it can be too plain. Cod steak with a fan of roasted carrots and white asparagus is perfectly cooked, but could do with a sprinkling of grey sea salt and a squirt of lemon juice. Carnivores seem to fare better under the minimalist regime; a roast shoulder of suckling pig and a thick steak with a raft of golden, clearly home-made, thick-cut *frites* look inviting indeed. This is one of the rare bistros that still offer a help-yourself cheese tray, and it's an unfailingly pleasant selection of nicely aged, seasonal cheeses. Desserts are superb too, including what may be the best *île flottante* in Paris and a truly top-notch *Paris Brest* (choux pastry filled with mocha-hazelnut cream). If you're in the area at lunchtime, the prix fixe menu is remarkable value.

#### Bofinger

*5-7 rue de la Bastille, 4th (01.42.72.87.82/www. bofingerparis.com). M° Bastille.* **Open** noon-3pm, 6.30pm-12.30am Mon-Fri; noon-12.30am Sat, Sun. **Prix fixe** €30.50. **Credit** AmEx, DC, MC, V. **Map** p409 L7 ➎➍
Opposite the Bastille opera house, Bofinger is a post-show haunt that draws big crowds at other times for its authentic art nouveau setting and brasserie atmosphere. Downstairs is the prettiest place to eat, but upstairs is air-conditioned. As at many Flo group restaurants, the food is always adequate but rarely aspires to great culinary heights. An à la carte choice might start with plump, garlicky escargots or a well-made langoustine terrine, followed by an intensely seasoned salmon tartare, a generous (if unremarkable) cod steak, or calf's liver accompanied by cooked melon. Alternatively, you could go for the foolproof brasserie meal of oysters and fillet steak, followed by a rabidly pungent plate of munster cheese and accompanying bowl of cumin, washed down by the fine Gigondas at €35.50 a bottle.

#### L'Encrier

*55 rue Traversière, 12th (01.44.68.08.16). M° Ledru-Rollin or Gare de Lyon.* **Open** noon-2.15pm, 7.30-11pm Mon-Fri; 7.30-11pm Sat. Closed Aug & Christmas wk. **Main courses** €14. **Prix fixe** *Lunch* €14. *Dinner* €19, €23. **Credit** MC, V. **Map** p407 M7 ➎➎
Through the door and past the velvet curtain, you find yourself face to face with the kitchen – and a crowd of locals, many of whom seem to know the charming boss personally. Start with fried rabbit kidneys on a bed of salad dressed with raspberry vinegar, an original and wholly successful combination, and follow with goose *magret* with honey – a

**Eat, Drink, Shop**

welcome change from the usual duck version and served with crunchy, thinly sliced sautéed potatoes. To end, share a chocolate cake, or try the popular profiteroles. The fruity Chinon is a classy red at a rather steep €24, but worth every cent.

### La Gazzetta

*29 rue de Cotte, 12th (01.43.47.47.05). M° Ledru-Rollin.* **Open** 11.30am-3pm, 6.30pm-1am Tue-Sun. Closed Aug. **Main courses** €25. **Prix fixe** *Lunch* €14, €16. *Dinner* €34, €45. **Credit** AmEx, DC, MC, V. **Map** p407 M7 ⑤⑥

Opened by the team behind the bar Le Fumoir, La Gazzetta has a similarly moody feel, with dim lighting, a long zinc bar and retro decor. Chef Petter Nilssen is Swedish but made his name in the south of France, and his food shows a Scandinavian influence in dishes such as bonito in a sweet-salty marinade with caraway, borage leaves, radish and pomelo or new potatoes from the island of Noirmoutier off the Atlantic coast with seaweed butter and dill. Unusual fish such as *sar royal* (a relative of sea bream) come with vegetables puréed with almonds or pistachios. The €32 menu is a good bet with four courses and not too many decisions to make. It's worth meeting early for a drink at the bar, where you can choose from Italian or southern French wines by the glass or savour the cocktail of the day.

### Le Temps au Temps

*13 rue Paul-Bert, 11th (01.43.79.63.40). M° Faidherbe Chaligny.* **Open** noon-2.30pm, 8-10.30pm Tue-Sat. Closed Aug & 1wk Dec. **Main courses** €20. **Prix fixe** *Lunch* €18, €30. *Dinner* €30. **Credit** AmEx, MC, V. **Map** p407 N7 ⑤⑦

This bistro's friendly new owners have retained its original name, but replaced the former riot of broken timepieces with just two or three clocks, opening up the room with a clear glass frontage. The €27 menu might begin with a home-made *fromage de tête*, well worth the three days it took in the making, or a cleverly balanced dish of warm *ratte* potatoes and sundried tomatoes topped with anchovies. The quality of the main courses doesn't flag, with, for instance, a delicate fillet of verbena-steamed John Dory on a bed of cauliflower 'couscous'. Ice-creams are home-made, and include an exquisite violet sorbet.

### Le Train Bleu

*Gare de Lyon, pl Louis-Armand, 12th (01.43.43.09.06/www.le-train-bleu.com). M° Gare de Lyon.* **Open** 11.30am-3pm, 7-11pm daily. **Main courses** €26. **Prix fixe** *Lunch* €48. *Dinner* €48, €95. **Credit** AmEx, DC, MC, V. **Map** p407 M8 ⑤⑧

This listed dining room – with vintage frescoes of the alluring destinations of the Paris-Lyon-Marseille railway and big oak benches with shiny brass coat racks – exudes a pleasant air of expectation. Don't expect cutting-edge cooking, but rather fine renderings of French classics using first-rate produce. Lobster served on walnut oil-dressed salad leaves is a generous, beautifully prepared starter, as is the

pistachio-studded *saucisson de Lyon* with a warm salad of small *ratte* potatoes. Mains of veal chop topped with a cap of cheese, and *sandre* (pike-perch) with a 'risotto' of *crozettes* are also pleasant, although given the size of the starters and the superb cheese tray, you could have a satisfying meal even if you forgo a main course. A few reasonably priced wines would be a welcome addition.

### Au Vieux Chêne

*7 rue du Dahomey, 11th (01.43.71.67.69). M° Faidherbe Chaligny.* **Open** noon-2pm, 8-10.30pm Mon-Fri; 8-10.30pm Sat. Closed 1wk July & 2wks Aug. **Main courses** €35. **Prix fixe** *Dinner* €29. **Credit** MC, V. **Map** p407 N7 ⑤⑨

While everyone loves the fly-in-amber atmosphere of old enamelled advertisements, the zinc-capped bar by the door when you come in, and the tiled floor, what makes this bistro so special is the earnestness of their desire to please – everyone here wants you to eat and drink to your heart's content. And you will indeed, as chef Stéphane Chevassus just gets better and better. A starter of langoustines encased in fine crunchy angel hair and garnished with slices of fresh mango is delicious and refreshing, while chilled tomato soup is garnished with mint, a ball of tomato sorbet and a drizzle of olive oil. Chevassus is a gifted game cook too, as proved by the tender roast pigeon sautéed with Chinese cabbage and its accompaniment of mushrooms cooked with galangal root, which brings out the sweetness of the bird. Puddings too live up to the high standards, with a moreish *moelleux d'abricots*, and a chocolate ganache layered between buttery shortbread with a silky praline ice-cream. The Faugères goes down a treat with a plate of perfectly ripened cheeses from Alléosse.

## International

### Le Souk

*1 rue Keller, 11th (01.49.29.05.08). M° Ledru-Rollin or Bastille.* **Open** 7.30-11.30pm Tue-Fri; 11.30am-2.30pm, 7.30pm-12.30am Sat; 11.30am-2.30pm, 7.30pm-11.30am Sun. **Main courses** €18. **Prix fixe** €27. **Credit** DC, MC, V. **Map** p407 N7 ⑥⓪

Potted olive trees mark the entrance to this lively den of Moroccan cuisine. Start with savoury *b'stilla*, a pasty stuffed with duck, raisins and nuts, flavoured with orange-blossom water and sprinkled with cinnamon and powdered sugar, or creamy aubergine dip scooped up with fluffy Moroccan bread, made on the premises. Don't fill up, though, as the first-rate tagines and couscous are enormous. The *tagine canette* (duckling stewed with honey, onions, apricots, figs and cinnamon then showered with toasted almonds) is terrific; *couscous bidaoui* arrives in handsome earthenware, a hefty shank of lamb on the side. Cold beer goes down well, but you might prefer a bottle of Algerian or Moroccan red wine. For dessert try the excellent millefeuille with fresh figs, while sweet mint tea is poured in a long stream by a *djellaba*-clad waiter.

# Water with your meal?

Paris is not short of magical settings, but nothing can beat dining with a view of the river. Along the quays of the Seine, traffic can sometimes intrude on the experience, so it's also worth venturing up to the relatively peaceful banks of the Canal St-Martin.

Perhaps the ultimate Seine view is from **La Tour d'Argent** (15-17 quai de la Tournelle, 5th, 01.43.54.23.31, www.tourdargent.com), whose glassed-in top floor is far removed from the fumes below. The restaurant continues to serve its famous numbered duck, which is carved and pressed with great ceremony on a little platform in the dining room. Given the splendid surroundings and solicitous service, the set lunch menu is pretty good value at €130.

A privileged view of the Seine can also be had at **Lapérouse** (*see p214*), a 17th-century townhouse famous for the hanky-panky that once took place in its private salons between politicians and their mistresses. You can still reserve these salons, but the best view of the river is from the wood-beamed and candlelit main dining room. There is a €45 prix fixe at lunch, though the dining room is at its most romantic in the evening.

Popular bistro **Les Bouquinistes** (53 quai des Grands-Augustins, 6th, 01.43.25.45.94, www.lesbouquinistes.com) overlooks the frenetic quai des Grand-Augustins, but it's worth putting up with a bit of traffic noise to taste the cooking of Magdala de Beaulieu-Caussimon. There is a limited-choice *retour du marché* menu, though it's hard to resist à la carte creations such as pan-fried foie gras with apple and celeriac purée.

On the slightly quieter quai de la Tournelle, La Tour d'Argent's down-to-earth bistro annexe **La Rôtisserie du Beaujolais** (19 quai de la Tournelle, 5th, 01.43.54.17.47) serves high-quality spit-rosted meats at wooden tables laid with check cloths.

Just across the bridge from here, the Ile St-Louis feels comparatively serene. The best vantage point for admiring the back of Notre-Dame and the Seine is undoubtedly the terrace of the **Brasserie de l'Ile St-Louis** (*see p187*), which is covered and heated in winter. One of the few remaining independent brasseries in Paris, this tavern-like restaurant serves hearty Alsatian-inspired cuisine. More subdued is the Japanese restaurant **Isami** (4 quai d'Orléans, 4th, 01.40.46.06.97), which serves great sushi.

Along the Canal St-Martin in the tenth arrondissement it's a more bohemian scene, with the area's creative types filling the café terraces at the first hint of sunshine. **Chez Prune** (*see p232*) was the original *bobo* (bohemian bourgeois) haunt along the canal and remains as popular as ever. The food, when it makes it to your table, is hearty and delicious. A little less frantic but just as much fun is **La Marine** (55 Quai de Valmy, 10th, 01.42.39.69.81), a long-established bistro serving good-value dishes such as red mullet millefeuille or fish in crisp brik pastry.

**Eat, Drink, Shop**

# North-east Paris

## French

### A la Bière

*104 av Simon-Bolivar, 19th (01.42.39.83.25). M°
Colonel Fabien.* **Open** noon-3pm, 7pm-1.30am daily.
**Main courses** €11. **Prix fixe** €13.40. **Credit** V.
**Map** p403 M2

A la Bière looks like one of those nondescript corner
brasseries with noisy pop music and lots of smoke,
but what makes it stand out is an amazingly good-
value €13.40 prix fixe full of fine bistro favourites,
all served with a smile. White tablecloths and finely
balanced kirs set the tone; starters of thinly sliced
pig's cheek with a nice French dressing on the salad,
and a home-made rabbit terrine exceed expectations.
The mains live up to what's served before: charcoal-
grilled entrecôte with hand-cut chips, and juicy
Lyonnais sausages with potatoes drenched in olive
oil, garlic and parsley. The staff know their wine and
never hurry the diners; there's usually jolly banter
going on at the bar. This is one of the few bargains
left in Paris – let's hope it stays that way.

### Le Chateaubriand

*129 av Parmentier, 11th (01.43.57.45.95). M°
Goncourt.* **Open** noon-2pm, 8-11pm Tue-Fri; 8-11pm
Sat. Closed 3wks Aug, 1wk Dec. **Prix fixe** *Lunch* €19
*Dinner* €40. **Credit** AmEx, MC, V. **Map** p403 M4

After a hit debut at La Famille in Montmartre, self-
taught Basque chef Iñaki Aizpitarte has taken over
this very stylish bistro. His menu displays the same
gastronomic daring that made La Famille a hit –
come at dinner to try the cooking at its most adventurous, as a much simpler (albeit cheaper) menu is
served at lunch. Dishes have been deconstructed
down to their very essence and put back together
again. You'll understand immediately if you try

starters such as chunky steak tartare garnished with
a quail's egg, Vietnamese-style dipping sauce with
whole peanuts, or asparagus with tahini foam and
little splinters of sesame-seed brittle. The cooking's
not always so cerebral – Aizpitarte's Spanish goat's
cheese with stewed apple jam is brilliant, as is his
chocolate custard with Espelette pepper. Be sure to
book a few days ahead.

### Chez Michel

*10 rue de Belzunce, 10th (01.44.53.06.20). M° Gare
du Nord.* **Open** 6.45pm-midnight Mon; noon-2pm,
7pm-midnight Tue-Fri. Closed 2wks Aug. **Prix fixe**
€30. **Credit** MC, V. **Map** p402 K2

Chez Michel is just behind the imposing St-Vincent-
de-Paul church and a few minutes' walk from Gare
du Nord – and while the area isn't particularly
classy, the food is. Thierry Breton is from Brittany,
and so proud of his origins that he sports the Breton
flag on his chef's whites. His menu is stacked with
hearty offerings from said hearty region. Marinated
salmon with purple potatoes served in a preserving
jar, pickled herring-style, is succulently tender; so,
too, is the fresh abalone. As for the rabbit, braised
with rosemary and Swiss chard, it might just be the
best bunny in town. Blackboard specials, which
carry a €5-€25 supplement, follow the seasons:
game-lovers are spoilt in the cooler months with
wood pigeon, wild boar and venison, and there are
usually some juicy, fat, fresh scallops on offer too.

## International

### Le Cambodge

*10 av Richerand, 10th (01.44.84.37.70/www.
lecambodge.fr). M° Goncourt or République.* **Open**
noon-2.30pm, 8-11.30pm Mon-Sat. **Closed** 1 Aug-
15 Sept, 24 Dec-1 Jan. **Main courses** €16. **Credit**
MC, V. **Map** p402 L4

Chez Michel.

They don't take bookings, they are always full and the tables are so close together you can practically see your neighbour's tonsils. However, with over ten years in business to show for it, the food, service and low prices make up for what Le Cambodge lacks in convenience and comfort. The system here is simple: you write your order on a piece of paper, including preferences such as 'no coriander', 'no peanuts' or 'extra rice', and after a short wait the dishes appear. Two favourites are the *bobun spécial*, a hot and cold mix of sautéed beef, noodles, salad, bean sprouts and imperial rolls, and *banhoy*, a selection of the same ingredients to be wrapped in lettuce and mint leaves and dipped in a sauce. They also serve soups, salads and curries including the house speciality *natin*, stewed pork in a fragrant coconut sauce.

### Dong Huong

*14 rue Louis-Bonnet, 11th (01.43.57.18.88). Mº Belleville.* **Open** noon-10.30pm Mon, Wed-Sun. Closed 2wks Jan & 3wks Aug. **Main courses** €7. **Credit** MC, V. **Map** p403 N4 ⑥⑤

The excellent food attracts a buzzy crowd, but this is also, significantly, one of the few Paris restaurants to banish smokers to a separate room (on the lower floor). Dishes arrive promptly and in most generous portions. The delicious *bành cuôn*, steamed Vietnamese ravioli stuffed with minced meat, mushrooms, bean sprouts, spring onions and deep-fried onion, are served piping hot. *Com ga lui*, chicken kebabs with tasty lemongrass, though not as delicate, come with tasty rice. *Bò bùn chà giò* (noodles with beef and small *nem* topped with onion strips, spring onion and crushed peanuts) makes a meal in itself. For dessert, the mandarin, lychee and mango sorbets are tasty and authentic – and don't miss out on the dark, sickly sweet iced lotus-flower tea, with lotus seeds, lychees and seaweed jelly.

### Ile de Gorée

*70 rue Jean-Pierre-Timbaud, 11th (01.43.38.97.69). Mº Parmentier.* **Open** 7pm-midnight daily. **Main courses** €15. **Credit** MC, V. **Map** p403 M4 ⑥⑥

Gorée Island is a 15-minute ferry ride off the Senegal coast. As for its namesake in the most happening bar quarter of Paris, mango and peach punch and live kora music set the mood. Simple but very well-prepared *boudin créole* (black pudding with cinnamon) and *aloco* (sautéed plantains) with sweet tomato relish can be followed with a hearty *dem farci* (stuffed mullet) in brown sauce or *thiou poisson* (whole fish) with tomatoes, bell peppers, carrots, potatoes and basmati rice, richly marinated with a sauce that tingles with flavour. Muomuo, the friendly house cat, will happily lap up the rest of your rum-raisin ice-cream from the bowl, but disdains the exotic selection of coconut, mango and pistachio sorbets. The cooks wave goodbye – an enchanted isle indeed.

### Kazaphani

*122 av Parmentier, 11th (01.48.07.20.19). Mº Parmentier or Goncourt.* **Open** noon-3pm, 7pm-midnight Tue-Fri, Sun; 7pm-midnight Sat.

Closed 2wks Aug. **Main courses** €16. **Prix Lunch** €18, €29, €35. **Credit** MC, V. **Map** p403 M5 ⑥⑦

The atmosphere at this family-run Cypriot restaurant is so relaxed that you might feel you've walked into someone's home. The room is pleasantly decorated with rhododendron boughs and paintings of Cyprus. The €32 meze menu brings dish after dish of food; highlights include the octopus in olive oil, lemon and garlic; wonderfully lemony mushrooms; a tasty paste of broad beans; and a taramasalata so pale and creamy it's a world away from the usual lurid pink concoction that dares to bear the same name. Next arrive plates of calamares, deep-fried whitebait and huge, aniseed-flavoured *gambas*. Meat dishes are excellent quality too, particularly the crisp meatballs and stuffed pork. You can match the food with any of the good red wines on offer – Hatzimichalis, say, or Nemea.

### La Madonnina

*10 rue Marie-et-Louise, 10th (01.42.01.25.26). Mº Goncourt or Jacques Bonsergent.* **Open** noon-2.30pm, 8-10.30pm Mon-Thur; noon-2.30pm, 8-11pm Fri; 8-11pm Sat. Closed 2wks Aug. **Main courses** €14. **Prix fixe Lunch** €12. **Credit** MC, V. **Map** p402 L4 ⑥⑧

La Madonnina flirts with kitsch so skilfully that it ends up coming off as cool. With its candles, mustard yellow walls and a smattering of red-checked tablecloths, this is the perfect place for a romantic night out or dinner with a group of friends. La Madonnina describes itself as a *trattoria napoletana*, but it would be fair to say that most of the dishes are pan-southern Italian. The extremely short menu changes monthly; don't miss the home-made pastas, such as artichoke and ricotta ravioli. The *cassata*, an extremely sweet Sicilian version of cheesecake, is authentic and unusual to see on menus outside Italy. Come early or be sure to reserve.

## The Latin Quarter & the 13th

## French

### Atelier Maître Albert

*1 rue Maître-Albert, 5th (01.56.81.30.01/www.atelier maitrealbert.com). Mº St-Michel or Maubert Mutualité.* **Open** noon-2.30pm, 6.30-11.30pm Mon-Wed; noon-2.30pm, 6.30pm-1am Thur, Fri; 6.30pm-1am Sat; 6.30-11.30pm Sun. **Main courses** €25. **Prix fixe Lunch** €29. **Credit** AmEx, DC, MC, V. **Map** p406 J7 ⑥⑨

This Guy Savoy outpost in the 5th has slick decor by Jean-Michel Wilmotte, who designed Savoy's eponymous restaurant. The indigo-painted, grey marble-floored dining room with open kitchen and rôtisseries on view is attractive but very noisy at night – book a table in the quieter bar area if you want to be able to chat over dinner without shouting. The short menu lets you have a Savoy classic or two to start with, including oysters in seawater *gelée* or more inventive dishes such as the ballotine of chicken, foie gras and celery root in a chicken-liver

**Eat, Drink, Shop**

sauce. Next up, perhaps, a chunk of tuna served with tiny iron casseroles of dauphinois potatoes, and cauliflower in béchamel sauce. *Photo p215.*

## L'Avant-Goût

*26 rue Bobillot, 13th (01.53.80.24.00). M° Place d'Italie.* **Open** noon-2pm, 7.45-10.45pm Tue-Sat. Closed 3wks Aug. **Main courses** €16.50. **Prix fixe** €31. **Credit** MC, V.

Self-taught chef Christophe Beaufront has turned this nondescript street on the edge of the villagey Butte-aux-Cailles into a foodie destination. Typical of Beaufront's cooking is his *pot-au-feu de cochon aux épices*, a much-written-about dish that has been on his menu for years. He now presents the pork, sweet potato and fennel garnished with deep-fried ginger on a plate with a glass of bouillon to drink on the side. It's good, if not earth-shaking – however, a starter of piquillo pepper stuffed with smoked haddock rillettes illustrates his talent. Reluctant cooks will be interested to know that Beaufront's food is available to take away at the *épicerie* across the street, complete with cast-iron cooking pots (to be returned).

## Le Buisson Ardent

*25 rue Jussieu, 5th (01.43.54.93.02). M° Jussieu.* **Open** noon-2pm, 7.45-10pm Mon-Fri; 7.45-10pm Sat. Closed Aug. **Main courses** €19. **Prix fixe** *Lunch* €16, €31. *Dinner* €31. **Credit** MC, V. **Map** p406 K8 ⑦

This bistro's square front dining room with its red banquettes and painted glass panels dating from 1923 has a quintessentially Paris charm, especially when compared to the surrounding kebab shops (just across from Jussieu campus, this restaurant caters to professors rather than students). There is plenty for adventurous eaters on chef Stéphane Maubuit's menu, such as pan-fried squid with chorizo and quinoa or white bean and pig's ear salad with pan-fried foie gras, but he also does conventional dishes (chestnut velouté with spice bread croûtons) very well. Desserts are slightly less remarkable, but this is one of the area's best finds for the price.

## Chez Paul

*22 rue Butte-aux-Cailles, 13th (01.45.89.22.11). M° Place d'Italie.* **Open** noon-2.30pm, 7.30-11.30pm daily. **Main courses** €17. **Credit** DC, MC, V.

Chez Paul's wood and white drapery provide a chic alternative to other places along this street. Tradition takes pride of place – *pot-au-feu*, beef knuckle, bone marrow – and you can eat your way from one end of a beast to the other. Seafood makes an appearance on the blackboard menu in the shape of oysters, whelks, an excellent starter of pan-fried mullet fillets with olive tapenade, and a main of monkfish nuggets in a creamy garlic sauce served with gleaming spinach. Liquorice ice-cream and carafes of chilled Brouilly also go down well. Book ahead.

# Menu lexicon

## Meals (repas)

**petit déjeuner** breakfast. **déjeuner** lunch. **dîner** dinner. **souper** late dinner, supper.

## Preparation (la préparation)

**en croûte** in a pastry case. **désossé** deboned. **farci** stuffed. **au four** baked. **flambé** flamed in alcohol. **forestière** with mushrooms. **fricassé** fried and simmered in stock, usually with creamy sauce. **fumé** smoked. **garni** garnished. **glacé** frozen or iced. **gratiné** topped with breadcrumbs or cheese and grilled. **à la grècque** vegetables served cold in the cooking liquid with oil and lemon juice. **grillé** grilled. **haché** minced. **julienne** (vegetables) cut into matchsticks. **lamelle** very thin slice. **mariné** marinated. **pané** breaded. **en papillote** cooked in a packet. **parmentier** with potato. **pressé** squeezed. **râpé** grated. **salé** salted.

## Cooking type (la cuisson)

**cru** raw. **bleu** practically raw. **saignant** rare. **rosé** (of lamb, duck, liver, kidneys) pink. **à point** medium rare. **bien cuit** well done.

## Basics (essentiels)

**ballotine** stuffed, rolled-up piece of meat or fish. **crème fraîche** thick, slightly soured cream. **épices** spices. **feuilleté** 'leaves' of (puff) pastry. **fromage** cheese. **fruits de mer** shellfish. **galette** round flat cake of flaky pastry, potato pancake or buckwheat savoury crêpe. **gelée** aspic. **gibier** game. **gras** fat. **légume** vegetable. **maison** of the house. **marmite** small cooking pot. **miel** honey. **noisette** hazelnut; small, round portion of meat. **noix** walnut. **noix de coco** coconut. **nouilles** noodles. **oeuf** egg; – **en cocotte** baked egg; – **en meurette** egg poached in red wine; – **à la neige** *see île flottante.* **parfait** sweet or savoury mousse-like mixture. **paupiette** slice of meat or fish, stuffed and rolled. **timbale** dome-shaped mould, or food cooked in one. **tisane** herbal tea. **tourte** covered pie or tart, usually savoury.

## Meat (viande)

**agneau** lamb. **aloyau** beef loin. **andouillette** sausage made from pig's offal. **bavette** beef flank steak. **biche** venison. **bifteck** steak. **boudin noir/blanc** black (blood)/white

## L'Ourcine

*92 rue Broca, 13th (01.47.07.13.65). Mº Les Gobelins or Glacière.* **Open** noon-2pm, 7-10.30pm Tue-Thur; noon-2.30pm, 7-11pm Fri, Sat. Closed 4wks July-Aug. **Prix fixe** *Lunch* (Tue-Fri) €22. *Dinner* €22, €30. **Credit** MC, V. **Map** p406 J10 **71**
This cream-and-red restaurant near Gobelins is a wonderful destination for anyone who really loves Basque and Béarnais cooking, since the kitchen sends out comforting, delicious and impeccably prepared regional classics. Start with *pipérade*, succulent chorizo or a spread of sliced beef tongue with piquillo peppers; then try the sautéed baby squid with parsley, garlic and Espelette peppers, or the *piquillos* stuffed with puréed cod and potato. Service is friendly, and an appealing atmosphere is generated by a growing band of regulars. The wine list is quite short but does offer several pleasant Southwestern bottles (the Madiran is a better buy than the Irouleguey). The homely desserts include *gâteau basque* and ewe's milk cheese with black cherry preserve.

## Le Pré Verre

*8 rue Thénard, 5th (01.43.54.59.47). Mº Maubert Mutualité.* **Open** noon-2pm, 7.30-10.30pm Tue-Sat. Closed 3wks Aug & 2wks Dec. **Prix fixe** *Lunch* €13. *Dinner* €26.50. **Credit** MC, V. **Map** p408 J7 **72**

Philippe Delacourcelle knows how to handle spices like few other French chefs, having lived in Asia for long enough to master ingredients like cassia bark and tamarind. He also trained with the late Bernard Loiseau, and learned the art of French pastry at Fauchon. Salt cod with cassia bark and smoked potato purée is a classic: what the fish lacks in size it makes up for in rich, cinnamon-like flavour and crunchy texture, while smooth potato cooked in a smoker makes a startling accompaniment. Spices have a way of making desserts seem esoteric rather than decadent, but the roast figs with olives are an exception to the rule. The main floor is non-smoking.

## Le Reminet

*3 rue des Grands-Degrés, 5th (01.44.07.04.24). Mº Maubert Mutualité or St-Michel.* **Open** noon-2.30pm, 7.30-1.30pm Tue, Thur-Sun. Closed 3wks Jan & 3wks Aug. **Main courses** €22. **Prix fixe** *Lunch* (Mon, Thur, Fri) €13, €55; (Sat) €18, €55. *Dinner* €55. **Credit** MC, V. **Map** p406 J7 **73**
This reliable, open-on-Sunday bistro, tucked beside Notre Dame, recently changed hands. Although the cooking may lack a little of its former sparkle, some oysters and a melting Camembert tart are both up to standard. A chunky steak, rare yet piping hot, comes with potato wedges fried in goose fat, and a moist chicken breast stuffed with wild mushrooms is served on top of a comforting *fricassée* of root

pudding. **boeuf** beef; – **bourguignon** beef cooked Burgundy style, with red wine, onions and mushrooms; – **gros sel** boiled beef with vegetables. **carbonnade** beef stew with onions and stout or beer. **carré d'agneau** rack of lamb. **cassoulet** stew of white haricot beans, sausage and preserved duck. **cervelle** brains. **châteaubriand** thick fillet steak. **chevreuil** young roe deer. **civet** game stew. **cochon de lait** suckling pig. **contre-filet** sirloin steak. **côte** chop; – **de boeuf** beef rib. **croque-madame** sandwich of toasted cheese and ham topped with an egg. **croque-monsieur** sandwich of toasted cheese and ham. **cuisses de grenouille** frogs' legs. **daube** meat braised in red wine. **entrecôte** beef rib steak. **escargot** snail. **estouffade** meat that's been marinated, fried and braised. **faux-filet** sirloin steak. **filet mignon** tenderloin. **foie** liver; – **de veau** calf's liver. **gigot d'agneau** leg of lamb. **hachis parmentier** shepherd's pie. **jambon** ham; – **cru** cured raw ham. **jarret** ham shin or knuckle. **langue** tongue. **lapin** rabbit. **lard** bacon. **lardon** small cube of bacon. **lièvre** hare. **marcassin** wild boar. **merguez** spicy lamb/beef sausage. **mignon** small meat fillet.

**moelle** bone marrow; **os à la** – marrowbone. **navarin** lamb and vegetable stew. **onglet** cut of beef, similar to *bavette*. **pavé** thick steak. **petit salé** salt pork. **pied** foot (trotter). **porc** pork. **porcelet** suckling pig. **pot-au-feu** boiled beef with vegetables. **queue de boeuf** oxtail. **ragoût** meat stew. **rillettes** potted pork or tuna. **ris de veau** veal sweetbreads. **rognons** kidneys. **rôti** roast. **sang** blood. **sanglier** wild boar. **saucisse** sausage. **saucisson sec** small dried sausage. **selle** (*d'agneau*) saddle of lamb). **souris d'agneau** lamb knuckle. **tagine** slow-cooked North African stew. **tartare** raw minced steak (also tuna or salmon). **tournedos** small slices of beef fillet, sautéed or grilled. **travers de porc** pork spare ribs. **tripes** tripe. **tripoux** dish of sheep's offal and sheep's feet. **veau** veal.

### Poultry (volaille)

**aiguillettes** (*de canard*) thin slices (of duck breast). **blanc** breast. **caille** quail. **canard** duck; **confit de** – preserved duck. **coquelet** baby rooster. **dinde** turkey. **faisan** pheasant. **foie gras** fattened goose or duck liver. **gésiers** gizzards. **magret** duck breast. **oie** goose. ▶

# Menu Lexicon (continued)

**perdrix** partridge. **pintade/pintadeau** guinea fowl. **poulet** chicken. **suprême** (*de poulet*) fillets (of chicken) in a cream sauce.

## Fish & seafood (poissons & fruits de mer)

**anguille** eel. **bar** sea bass. **belon** smooth, flat oyster. **bisque** shellfish soup. **bouillabaisse** Mediterranean fish soup. **bourride** bouillabaisse-like soup, without shellfish. **brochet** pike. **bulot** whelk. **cabillaud** fresh cod. **carrelet** plaice. **colin** hake. **coquille** shell. **coquilles St-Jacques** scallops. **crevettes** prawns (UK), shrimp (US). **crustacé** shellfish. **daurade** sea bream. **eglefin** haddock. **escabèche** sautéed and marinated fish, served cold. **espadon** swordfish. **fines de claire** crinkle-shelled oysters. **flétan** halibut. **goujon** breaded, fried strip of fish; also a small catfish. **hareng** herring. **homard** lobster. **huître** oyster. **langoustine** Dublin Bay prawns, scampi. **limande** lemon sole. **lotte** monkfish. **maquereau** mackerel. **merlan** whiting. **merlu** hake. **meunière** fish floured and sautéed in butter. **moules** mussels; – **à la marinière** cooked with white wine and shallots. **morue**

dried, salted cod; **brandade de** – cod puréed with potato. **oursin** sea urchin. **palourde** type of clam. **poulpe** octopus. **quenelle** light, poached fish (or poultry) dumpling. **raie** skate. **rascasse** scorpion fish. **rouget** red mullet. **St-Pierre** John Dory. **sandre** pike-perch. **saumon** salmon. **seiche** squid. **truite** trout.

## Vegetables (légumes)

**aligot** mashed potatoes with melted cheese and garlic. **asperge** asparagus. **céleri** celery. **céleri rave** celeriac. **cèpe** cep mushroom. **champignon** mushroom; – **de Paris** button mushroom. **chanterelle** small, trumpet-like mushroom. **choucroute** sauerkraut; – **garnie** with cured ham and sausages. **ciboulette** chive. **citronelle** lemongrass. **coco** large white bean. **cresson** watercress. **crudités** assorted raw vegetables. **duxelles** chopped, sautéed mushrooms. **échalote** shallot. **endive** chicory (UK), Belgian endive (US). **épinards** spinach. **frisée** curly endive. **frites** chips (UK), fries (US). **gingembre** ginger. **girolle** small, trumpet-like mushroom. **gratin dauphinois** sliced potatoes baked with milk, cheese and garlic. **haricot** bean; – **vert** green bean. **mâche**

---

vegetables. A creamy combination of berries, chocolate and pears makes the perfect autumn dessert. The charming new team has a tough act to follow in this pocket-sized restaurant, but with a bottle of excellent Bordeaux and a bill of just over €100 for two, it remains a useful address.

### Ribouldingue

*10 rue St-Julien-le-Pauvre, 5th (01.46.33.98.80). M° St-Michel.* **Open** noon-2pm, 7-11pm Mon-Sat. **Prix fixe** €27. **Credit** MC, V. **Map** p408 J7 ❼
This bistro facing St-Julien-le-Pauvre church is the creation of Nadège Varigny, who spent ten years working with Yves Camdeborde before opening a restaurant inspired by the food of her childhood in Grenoble. It's full of people, including critics and chefs, who love simple, honest bistro fare, such as *daube de boeuf* (a winey beef stew with macaroni) or seared tuna on a bed of melting aubergine. If you have an appetite for offal, go for the gently sautéed brains with divine new potatoes or veal kidneys with a perfectly prepared potato gratin. For dessert, try the fresh ewe's cheese with bitter honey

### Toustem

*12 rue de l'Hôtel Colbert, 5th (01.40.51.99.87). M° St-Michel or Maubert-Mutualité.* **Open** noon-2.30pm, 7-11pm Mon-Sat. **Main courses** €24. **Prix fixe** Lunch €24. **Credit** MC, V. **Map** p406 J7 ❼

Opened in summer 2007, this oddly decorated outpost of Hélène Darroze's restaurant empire is contributing to the gastronomic revival of the Latin Quarter. Darroze is from southwest France, and this little bistro, with heavy wood beams and gothic doors, is where you'll find her cooking at its most generous. Foie gras features prominently on the menu, perhaps in a strongly seasoned terrine or in big, pan-fried chunks with penne in a creamy mushroom-studded sauce – high cholesterol heaven. Vegetables such as multicoloured tomatoes come from star market gardener Joël Thiébault, and desserts such as a strawberry *vacherin* (fresh strawberries, vanilla ice cream and meringue) come in big glass *coupes*.

## International

### Rouammit & Huong Lan

*103 av d'Ivry, 13th (01.53.60.00.34). M° Corvisart.* **Open** noon-3pm, 7-11pm Tue-Fri; noon-4pm Sat, Sun. Closed 1wk Aug. **Main courses** €8. **Credit** MC, V. **Prix fixe** (Tue-Fri) €8.90, €10.80, €11.90.
Fans of South-east Asian food eventually learn to seek out Laotian holes-in-the-wall in Paris rather than splurge on flashier Thai restaurants. A perfect example is this plainly decorated Chinatown joint, easy to spot thanks to the queue that stretches outside the door; show up early or be prepared to wait.

lamb's lettuce. **morille** morel mushroom.
**navet** turnip. **oignon** onion. **oseille** sorrel.
**persil** parsley. **pignon** pine kernel. **poivre**
pepper. **poivron** red or green (bell) pepper.
**pomme de terre** potato. **pommes lyonnaises**
potatoes fried with onions. **potiron** pumpkin.
**riz** rice. **tapenade provençal** olive and caper
paste. **truffes** truffles.

### Fruit (fruits)

**ananas** pineapple. **cassis** blackcurrants;
blackcurrant liqueur. **citron** lemon; – **vert**
lime. **fraise** strawberry. **framboise** raspberry.
**groseille** redcurrant; – **à maquereau**
gooseberry. **mirabelle** tiny yellow plum.
**myrtille** bilberry, blueberry. **pamplemousse**
grapefruit. **pomme** apple. **prune** plum.
**pruneau** prune. **quetsche** damson.

### Desserts & cheese (desserts & fromage)

**bavarois** moulded cream dessert. **beignet**
fritter or doughnut. **chèvre** goat; goat's
cheese. **clafoutis** batter filled with fruit.
**crème brûlée** creamy custard dessert with
caramel glaze. **crème chantilly** sweetened
whipped cream. **fromage blanc** smooth cream
cheese. **glace** ice-cream. **ile flottante**
whipped egg white floating in vanilla custard.
**marquise** mousse-like cake. **réglisse**
liquorice. **tarte aux pommes** apple tart. **tarte
Tatin** warm, caramelised apple tart cooked
upside down. **vacherin** cake of layered
meringue, cream, fruit and ice-cream; a soft,
cow's milk cheese.

### Herbs, spices, soups & sauces (herbes, épices, soupes & sauces)

**aïoli** garlic mayonnaise. **anchoïade** spicy
anchovy and olive paste. **béarnaise** sauce
of butter and egg yolk. **blanquette** 'white'
stew made with eggs and cream. **cannelle**
cinnamon. **potage** soup. **velouté** stock-based
white sauce; creamy soup. **vichyssoise** cold
leek and potato soup.

### Drinks

**bière** beer. **eau** water; – **de robinet** tap water;
– **gazeuse/pétillante** sparkling mineral water;
– **plate** still mineral water. **eau de vie** fruit
spirit or liqueur. **vin** wine; – **blanc** white wine;
– **rouge** red wine.

The food here is cheap and delicious, and the service
super-efficient and friendly. To try the full span of
flavours – hot, sour, aromatic, sweet – it's best to go
in a group and order compendiously. Among the
highlights are *lap neua*, a tongue-tickling, chilli-
spiked salad made with slivers of beef and tripe; lac-
quered duck in curry sauce; *khao nom kroc*, Laotian
ravioli filled with shrimp; and sweet, juicy prawns
stir-fried with Thai basil. Even the sticky rice is
exceptional. If you're in the mood for an adventurous dessert, try the assortment of gelatins, all worm-
like shapes and fluorescent colours.

## St-Germain-des-Prés & Odéon

### French

#### Boucherie Roulière

*24 rue des Canettes, 6th (01.43.26.25.70). M° St-
Sulpice, Mabillon or St-Germain-des-Prés.* **Open**
noon-2.30pm, 7-11.30pm Tue-Thur, Sun; noon-
2.30pm, 7pm-midnight Fri, Sat. **Main courses**
€18.50. **Credit** MC, V. **Map** p408 H7 **76**
This is not somewhere to take your vegetarian
friends, as Boucherie Roulière glorifies the art of
meat preparation. The blackboard menu offers a
simple collection of grilled meat and fish, accompanied by traditional bistro favourites to begin and end
your meal. *Ravioles aux truffes* make an irresistible
first course, with a real perfume of earthy luxury.
Main courses include a perfectly grilled *rognon de
veau* (veal kidney) with a separate pot of sauce and
some seriously good mash. Thick tuna steak is pink
and moist; the fishmonger's art is taken seriously
too. Desserts and the single house cheese – perhaps
a perfectly ripe camembert – keep up the standard.
Service is of the boisterous, macho Paris style, but
friendly enough, and a growing flock of regulars
crowds in for the marrowbones. *Photo p216.*

#### Le Comptoir

*Hôtel Le Relais Saint-Germain, 9 carrefour de
l'Odéon, 6th (01.44.27.07.50). M° Odéon.* **Open**
noon-6pm, 8.30-midnight (last orders 9pm) Mon-Fri;
noon-11pm Sat, Sun. Closed 3wks Aug. **Main
courses** €15. **Prix fixe** *Dinner* (Mon-Fri) €45.
**Credit** AmEx, DC, MC, V. **Map** p408 H7 **77**
Yves Camdeborde was one of the first chefs to introduce the accessibly priced, market-inspired menu at
La Régalade in the early 1990s. He now runs the bijou
17th-century Hôtel Le Relais Saint-Germain, whose
art deco dining room, modestly dubbed Le Comptoir,
serves brasserie fare from noon to 6pm and on weekend nights – salads and a hot *plat du jour*, such as
duck confit with smooth mashed potatoes – and a

**Eat, Drink, Shop**

five-course *prix fixe* feast on weekday evenings. The single dinner sitting lets the chef take real pleasure in his work. On the daily menu, you might find dishes like an iced cream of chicken soup spiked with *vin jaune du Jura* and dotted with chanterelle mushrooms, or rolled saddle of lamb with vegetable-stuffed 'Basque ravioli' – Camdeborde is from southwest France. In summer, the handful of pavement tables makes for fine people-watching. The catch? The prix fixe dinner is booked up as much as six months in advance.

## La Ferrandaise
*8 rue de Vaugirard, 6th (01.43.26.36.36). M° Odéon/ RER Luxembourg.* **Open** noon-2.30pm, 7-10.30pm Tue-Thur; noon-2.30pm, 7pm-midnight Fri; 7pm-midnight Sat. **Main courses** €24. **Prix fixe** *Lunch* €24, €33. *Dinner* €33. **Credit** MC, V. **Map** p408 H7 ⑩
This bistro with stone walls, a giant chandelier and portraits of cows on the walls has quickly established a faithful clientele, seemingly dominated by local business people. In the modern bistro tradition, the young, northern French chef serves solid, classic food with a twist. A platter of excellent ham, sausage and terrine arrives as you study the blackboard menu, and the bread is crisp-crusted, thickly sliced sourdough. Almost every dish is a variation on standards: two specialities are the potato stuffed with escargots in a camembert sauce, and a wonderfully flavoured, slightly rosé slice of veal. Desserts might include intense chocolate with rum-soaked bananas and a layered glass of mango and meringue. Wines start at €14.

## Huîtrerie Régis
*3 rue de Montfaucon, 6th (01.44.41.10.07). M° Mabillon.* **Open** 11am-midnight Tue-Sun. Closed mid July-Sept. **Main courses** €35. **Prix fixe** €21.50, €30. **Credit** MC, V. **Map** p408 H7 ⑰
Paris oyster fans are often obliged to use one of the city's big brasseries to get their fix of shellfish, but what if you just want to eat a reasonably priced platter of oysters? Enter Régis and his 14-seat oyster bar in the heart of St-Germain. The tiny white room feels pristine, the tables are properly laid, and it's non-smoking. Here you can enjoy the freshest oysters from the Marenne for around €25 a dozen. The bread and butter is fresh and wines are well-chosen. Régis attracts an enviable crowd of fans who have discovered that oysters make a sexy prelude or postlude to an evening at the cinema. Hungry souls can supplement their feast with a rather ordinary scallop terrine or more happily enjoy a slice of rustic, homemade apple tart or the cheese of the day. Régis waxes lyrical about his oysters and the welcome could not be warmer.

## Josephine 'Chez Dumonet'
*117 rue du Cherche-Midi, 6th (01.45.48.52.40). M° Duroc.* **Open** 12.30-2.30pm, 7.30-10.30pm Mon-Fri. **Main courses** €22. **Credit** AmEx, MC, V. **Map** p405 F8 ⑳

At this bastion of bistro cooking, luxury ingredients bring a touch of glamour and attract a well-heeled, loyal clientele. The dining room is comfortingly old-fashioned. Dishes can come as half-portions, letting you try some classy numbers without breaking the bank. In truffle season, the salad of lamb's lettuce, warm potatoes and truffle shavings is €31 in its half-portion version. Delicious sautéed potatoes, rich in goose fat and garlic, accompany both the tournedos and steak tartare, which is one of the best in town. Puddings are sumptuous too.

## Lapérouse
*51 quai des Grands-Augustins, 6th (01.43.26.68.04). M° St-Michel.* **Open** noon-2.30pm, 7.30-10pm Mon-Fri; 7.30-10pm Sat. Closed 1wk Jan & Aug. **Main courses** €40. **Prix fixe** *Lunch* €45, €105. *Dinner* €105. **Credit** AmEx, DC, MC, V. **Map** p408 J6 ㉛
One of the most romantic spots in Paris, Lapérouse was formerly a clandestine rendezvous for French politicians and their mistresses; the tiny private dining rooms upstairs used to lock from the inside. Chef Alain Hacquard does a modern take on classic French cooking: his beef fillet is smoked for a more complex flavour; a tender saddle of rabbit is cooked in a clay crust, flavoured with lavender and rosemary and served with ravioli of onions. The only snag is the cost, especially of the wine – a half-bottle of Pouilly-Fuissé is nearly €35. The lunch menu is limited, but frankly, the seductive Seine-side dining room has always been best savoured at night.

## Le Restaurant
*L'Hôtel, 13 rue des Beaux-Arts, 6th (01.44.41.99.01/ www.l-hotel.com). M° St-Germain-des-Prés.* **Open** 12.30-2pm, 7.30pm-10pm Tue-Sat. **Main courses** €35. **Prix fixe** *Lunch* €42, €75. *Dinner* €75. **Credit** AmEx, DC, MC, V. **Map** p408 H6 ㉜
Since being taken over by Oxford-based Cowley Manor, L'Hôtel has rechristened its restaurant (formerly Le Belier) and put the talented Philippe Bélisse in charge of the kitchen. The place is designed in luxurious and decadent style by Jacques Garcia, but it's Bélisse's cooking that really mark it out. You can choose from a short seasonal menu with dishes such as pan-fried tuna, John Dory or suckling pig. But for the same price you can also enjoy the marvellous four-course *menu dégustation* (€74), or, even better, the *menu surprise* at €125, which includes unusual wines whose identity you're expected to guess. Dishes change with the seasons, but highlights of the autumn menu were the wild Breton crab stuffed with fennel, avocado and *huile d'Argan*, and a memorable main course of pigeon on a bed of beetroot. Be sure to start your meal with the house cocktail, a combination of champagne, violette and lime.

## Le Timbre
*3 rue Ste-Beuve, 6th (01.45.49.10.40). M° Vavin.* **Open** noon-1.30pm, 7.30-10.30pm Tue-Sat. Closed Aug & 1wk Dec. **Main courses** €17. **Prix fixe** *Lunch* €26. *Dinner* (Sat) €30. **Credit** MC, V. **Map** p405 G8 ㉝

**Atelier Maître Albert.** *See p209.*

Chris Wright's restaurant, open kitchen included, might be the size of the average student garret, but this Mancunian aims high. His menu of three to four starters, main courses and desserts changes every week, and he uses the same suppliers as the city's top chefs. Typical of his cooking is a spring-like plate of fresh green asparagus elegantly cut in half lengthwise and served with dabs of anise-spiked sauce and balsamic vinegar, and a little crumbled parmesan. Main courses are also pure in presentation and flavour – a thick slab of pork, pan-fried but not the least bit dry, comes with petals of red onion that retain a light crunch, while juicy guinea fowl is served on a bed of tomato and pineapple chutney. Should you opt for cheese, you'll have a choice between '*le vrai*' (British cheddar) and '*le faux*' (perhaps a goat's cheese from the Ardèche).

## International

### Bread & Roses

*7 rue de Fleurus, 6th (01.42.22.06.06). M° St-Placide.* **Open** 8am-8pm Mon-Sat. Closed Aug & 1wk Dec. **Main courses** €18. **Credit** AmEx, MC, V. **Map** p405 G8 ❽

Come for a morning croissant and you might find yourself staying on for lunch, so tempting are the wares at this Anglo-influenced *boulangerie/épicerie/* café. Giant wedges of cheesecake sit alongside French pastries, while huge savoury puff-pastry tarts are perched on the counter. Attention to detail shows even in the authentically pale taramasalata, which is matched with buckwheat-and-seaweed bread. Prices reflect the quality of the often-organic

ingredients, but that doesn't seem to deter any of the moneyed locals, who order towering birthday cakes here for their snappily dressed offspring.

### La Taverna degli Amici

*16 rue du Bac, 6th (01.42.60.37.74). M° Assemblée Nationale or Solférino.* **Open** noon-2.30pm, 7.30-11pm Mon-Fri; 7.30-11pm Sat. Closed Aug & 1wk Dec. **Main courses** €16. **Prix fixe** *Lunch* €18. **Credit** MC, V. **Map** p401 G6 ❽

La Taverna degli Amici is the ideal spot for a quick business lunch or a big, rumbustious dinner with friends. Divided over two floors, the yellow-walled rooms are well lit and airy. Run by the exceptionally friendly Notaro family, who own, manage and cook, the restaurant is constantly bustling. Don't miss the mixed bruschette, which includes three different outstanding vegetable toppings, such as grilled courgettes marinated in olive oil, lemon and parsley. Pastas feature fresh, tasty toppings, such as their most popular dish, penne with *caccioricotta* (made with ewe's milk) and rocket. Most of the regulars finish off with home-made tiramisu.

## Montparnasse & beyond

### French

#### Apollo

*3 pl Denfert-Rochereau, 14th (01.45.38.76.77). M°/RER Denfert Rochereau.* **Open** noon-3pm, 7pm-11pm daily. **Main courses** €18. **Prix fixe** *Lunch* €15, €18, €30. *Dinner* €30. **Credit** AmEx, MC, V. **Map** p405 H10 ❽

**Boucherie Roulière.** *See p213.*

From the same team that conceived Quai Ouest, this high-design restaurant in the former RER offices at Denfert Rochereau brings a breath of novelty into a staid part of Paris. The decor fits nicely with the original design, but the menu is firmly in the 21st century. Modern takes on classic comfort food include herring caviar and potatoes, *blanquette de coquilles St-Jacques* and braised beef with carrots. The food is generally good and generously served, as are desserts such as pineapple and bananas sautéed in vanilla-flavoured rum.

### La Cerisaie
*70 bd Edgar Quinet, 14th (01.43.20.98.98). Mº Edgar Quinet or Montparnasse.* **Open** noon-2pm, 7-10pm Mon-Fri. Closed Aug & 1wk Dec. **Main courses** €15. **Credit** MC, V. **Map** p405 G9 **⑥⑦**
Nothing about La Cerisaie's unprepossessing red façade in the shadow of the Montparnasse Tower hints at the talent that lurks inside. The chef's wife quickly makes you feel welcome in the minuscule ochre-and-red room. With a simple starter of white asparagus served with preserved lemon and drizzled with bright green parsley oil, chef Cyril Lalanne proves his ability to select and prepare the finest produce. On the daily changing blackboard menu you might find *bourride de maquereau*, a thrifty take on the garlicky southern French fish stew, or *cochon noir de Bigorre*, an ancient breed of pig that puts ordinary pork to shame. *Baba à l'armagnac*, a variation on the usual rum cake, comes with stunningly good chantilly. There is a

good selection of wines from small producers, many of them at affordable prices – look for armagnacs and other alcohols from the south-west.

### La Coupole
*102 bd du Montparnasse, 14th (01.43.20.14.20). Mº Vavin.* **Open** 8am-1am Mon-Fri; 8.30am-1am Sat, Sun. **Main courses** €40. **Prix fixe** €19.90, €30.50. **Credit** AmEx, DC, MC, V. **Map** p405 G9 **⑥⑧**
Though Montparnasse today is a far cry from its avant-garde heyday when this restaurant opened in 1927 – as a *bar américain* with cocktails and dancing, where you could savour the indecency of the tango – La Coupole still glows with some of the old glamour. The people-watching remains superb, inside and out, while the long ranks of linen-covered tables, professional waiters, 32 art deco columns painted by different artists of the epoch, mosaic floor and sheer scale of the operation still make coming here an event. What's more, it continues to be a favourite with Parisians of all ages, as well as out-of-towners and tourists. The set menu offers unremarkable steaks, foie gras, fish and autumn game stews, but the real treat is the shellfish, displayed along a massive counter. Take your pick from the *claires*, *spéciales* and *belons*, or go for a platter brimming with crabs, oysters, prawns, periwinkles and clams.

### L'Opportun
*64 bd Edgar Quinet, 14th (01.43.20.26.89). Mº Edgar Quinet.* **Open** noon-3pm, 7-11.30pm Mon-Sat. **Main courses** €19. **Prix fixe** €21 (until 10pm). **Credit** AmEx, DC, MC, V. **Map** p405 G9 **⑥⑨**

Corpulent owner-chef Serge Alzérat is passionate about Beaujolais, dubbing his convivial cream and yellow restaurant a centre of 'beaujolaistherapy' and a place for 'the prevention of thirst'. He's also an advocate for good, honest Lyonnais food. Thus his menu is littered with the likes of *sabodet* (thick pork sausage) with a purée of split peas, duck skin salad, *tête de veau* (a favourite of ex-president Chirac, whose photo graces the walls) and meat – lots of it. There's a lightweight 250g veal or beef onglet or, if you need a heftier protein fix, a 400g version, both served with mounds of savoury cabbage dotted with bacon and crusty, baked potatoes. Starters are just as generous: salad of dandelion leaves with roasted tomatoes, bacon chunks and a runny poached egg, and rounds of lightly toasted chèvre, accompanied by thick slices of ham and apple. *Fromage* fans should skip dessert and try the st-marcellin by Roanne's master cheesemaker Hervé Mons.

## The 7th & western Paris

### French

### Le 144 Petrossian
*18 bd de La Tour-Maubourg, 7th (01.44.11.32.32/ www.petrossian.fr). M° La Tour Maubourg.* **Open** noon-2.30pm, 7.30-10.30pm Tue-Sat. **Main courses** €40. **Prix fixe** *Lunch* €35, €90. *Dinner* €45, €90. **Credit** AmEx, DC, MC, V. **Map** p401 E5 ⑳
Young Senegalese-French chef Rougui Dia now directs the kitchen in which she worked for several years, with intriguing results. As before, you'll find Russian specialities such as blinis, salmon and caviar (at €39 an ounce) from the Petrossian boutique downstairs, but Dia has added preparations and spices from all over the world. You might start with the Tsar's cup of three different slices of marinated salmon on a bed of artichoke hearts with cumin, or a divine risotto made with carnaroli rice, codfish caviar and crisp parmesan. In a similar Med-meets-Russia vein are main courses of lamb 'cooked for eleven hours' on a raisin-filled blini, and roast sea bream with a terrific lemon-vodka sauce, accompanied by tasty *kasha*. A cool, runny-centred chocolate cake with ice-cream and jellied quince finishes things off in modern French style. A caution: whereas at lunch glasses of wine are offered for €5, at dinner bottles start at €40.

### L'Agassin
*8 rue Malar, 7th (01.47.05.94.27). M° Ecole Militaire.* **Open** noon-2.30pm, 7-11pm Tue-Sat. **Closed** Aug. **Prix fixe** *Lunch* €23, €34. *Dinner* €34. **Credit** AmEx, DC, MC, V. **Map** p405 D6 ㉛
André Le Letty left Anacréon – a bistro on a busy boulevard in the 13th – to open this cream-and-brown restaurant in the heart of aristocratic Paris, a few steps from L'Ami Jean. It's a curious mix of contemporary and classic, with occasional old-fashioned touches in the cooking (skate in butter and caper

sauce served with steamed potatoes) but a modern spirit, thanks to the use of unexpected spices. Several dishes come with supplements of €2 to €10, but these are often worth the extra cost – the *girolle* mushrooms in season are beautifully firm and juicy, served in a light cream sauce. The chef's take on prune *clafoutis* is unusually light, with armagnac ice-cream the perfect accompaniment.

### L'Ami Jean
*27 rue Malar, 7th (01.47.05.86.89). M° Ecole Militaire.* **Open** noon-2pm, 7pm-midnight Tue-Sat. **Closed** Aug. **Main courses** €27. **Prix fixe** €32. **Credit** MC, V. **Map** p405 D6 ㉜
This long-running Basque address has become a hit since the arrival of chef Stéphane Jégo. Excellent bread from Poujauran is a perfect nibble when slathered with a tangy, herby *fromage blanc* – as are starters of sautéed baby squid on a bed of ratatouille, and little rolls of aubergine stuffed with perfectly seasoned braised lamb. Tender veal shank comes de-boned with a lovely side of baby onions and broad beans with tiny cubes of ham, while house-salted cod is soaked, sautéed and doused with an elegant vinaigrette. There's a great wine list, and some lovely Brana *eau de vie* should you decide to linger; a party spirit sets in as the night grows long.

### L'Arpège
*84 rue de Varenne, 7th (01.45.51.47.33/www.alain-passard.com). M° Varenne.* **Open** noon-2.30pm, 8-10.30pm Mon-Fri. **Main courses** €70. **Credit** AmEx, DC, MC, V. **Map** p405 F6 ㉝
Assuming you can swallow an exceptionally high bill – we're talking €42 for a potato starter – and forsake the normal full-dress drill of an haute cuisine meal, the chances are you'll have a spectacular time at chef Alain Passard's Left Bank establishment. His attempt to plane down and simplify the haute experience – the chrome-armed chairs in the already minimalist dining room look like something from the former DDR – seems a bit of a misstep; but then something edible comes to the table, such as tiny smoked potatoes served with a horseradish mousseline. Delicate vegetable-stuffed ravioli in lobster bouillon are classy and quietly sexy, but nowhere near as satisfying, especially at €58. A main course of sautéed free-range chicken garnished with a roasted shallot, an onion, potato *mousseline* and pan juices is the apotheosis of comfort food. Desserts are elegant and edgy, and service is impeccable. The one terrible drawback to eating out here is the sky-high pricing of the wine list.

### L'Atelier de Joël Robuchon
*5 rue de Montalembert, 7th (01.42.22.56.56/ www.robuchon.com). M° Rue du Bac.* **Open** 11.30am-3.30pm, 6.30pm-midnight daily. **Main courses** €30. **Prix fixe** €110. **Credit** MC, V. **Map** p405 G6 ㉞
This is star chef Joël Robuchon's Paris take on a New York coffee-shop-cum-sushi-and-tapas-bar. The lacquer interior and two U-shaped bars – you sit on

**Eat, Drink, Shop**

stools at a wenge-wood counter by Pierre-Yves Rochon – are the epitome of sassy Left Bank chic, and the food is fine, with inspiration from Astrance (*see p194*) and Spain's El Bulli. The menu is split into three different *formules*: start with caviar, Spanish ham, a large seasonal salad or maybe an assortment of little tasting plates, perhaps bearing veal sweetbreads skewered with a bay leaf twig and served with Swiss chard in cream. Then go classic (a steak), fanciful (*vitello tonnato*, veal in tuna and anchovy sauce) or lush (sublime cannelloni of roast Bresse chicken, stuffed with foie gras and served with wild mushrooms). Desserts are less inspired, the fluffy, melting passionfruit soufflé with pistachio ice-cream being the best.

### Chez les Anges

*54 bd de La Tour-Maubourg, 7th (01.47.05.89.86/ www.chezlesanges.com). Mº La Tour Maubourg.* **Open** noon-3pm, 7.30-11pm Mon-Fri. **Main courses** €28. **Prix fixe** €34. **Map** p401 E6 **95**
Jacques Lacipière of the bistro Au Bon Accueil is behind the revival of this restaurant, which was known for its superb Burgundian cooking back in the 1960s and '70s (hence the dated decor). You can order à la carte, with main dishes priced at around €20 to €30, or alternatively opt for the good-value 'Menu Surprise'. This takes a tapas-style approach, with each course arriving in sets of two or three tiny portions. These change from day to day, but might include creations such as cauliflower bavarois and little frogs' legs fritters. Though the cooking isn't on the level of, say, Joël Robuchon, the chef is clearly making a real effort and the friendly waiters are full of goodwill.

### Les Cocottes

*135 rue St-Dominique, 7th (no reservations). Mº Ecole Militaire/RER Pont de l'Alma.* **Open** 8am-10pm Mon-Fri. **Main courses** €15. **Credit** MC, V. **Map** p400 D6 **96**
Christian Constant has found the perfect recipe for pleasing Parisians at his new bistro: non-stop service and a flexible menu of salads, soups, *verrines* (light dishes served in jars) and *cocottes* (served in cast-iron pots), all at bargain prices – for this neighbourhood. Within weeks of opening there were queues outside the door for the high (and not particularly comfortable) seats along the long counter and at a few tables. Service is swift and the food satisfying, though the *vraie salade César Ritz* contains inauthentic hardboiled egg. Soups such as an iced pea velouté are spot-on, and *cocottes* range from sea bream with ratatouille to potatoes stuffed with pig's trotter.

### Gaya Rive Gauche

*44 rue du Bac, 7th (01.45.44.73.73). Mº Rue du Bac.* **Open** 12.15-2.30pm, 7.15-11pm Mon-Sat; Closed Aug & 1wk Dec. **Main courses** €40-€45. **Credit** AmEx, MC, V. **Map** p405 G6 **97**
Pierre Gagnaire, a chef known for his individuality, runs this Left Bank seafood restaurant, redecorating with a fish-scale wall and cloth-less white tables.

Dated decor but decent tapas-style treats at **Chez les Anges**.

The line is blurred between starters and mains, with menu titles such as *'insolites'* (unexpected) and *'essentiel'*. Given Gagnaire's reknown, it's a relief to see starters at around €20 and main courses at less than €50, even if the great man himself is not in the kitchen. Typical of his style is a seafood jelly with neatly arranged *coco de Paimpol* white beans and Spanish ham, followed by strips of wild sea bass simply sautéed and deglazed with manzanilla sherry. As so often happens with Gagnaire, not everything works; nonetheless, it's exciting to experience his unique take on French cuisine. Gaya is particularly refreshing in a city where many seafood restaurants have fallen into a minimalist rut.

### Le Gorille Blanc

*11bis rue Chomel, 7th (01.45.49.04.54). M° Sèvres-Babylone.* **Open** noon-2.30pm, 7-10.30pm Mon-Fri; 7-10.30pm Sat. **Main courses** €18. **Prix fixe** *Lunch* €19.50. **Credit** AmEx, MC, V. **Map** p405 G6 ❾❽

There are not many inspiring places to eat in the area around the Bon Marché department store, so this quiet side-street bistro is quite a find. The moustachioed chef is from southwest France, which is always a good sign, and the little dining room is decorated with framed black-and-white photographs of – what else? – gorillas. Crisp-skinned duck confit with sautéed potatoes is a sure bet here, but the kitchen also turns out sprightly fish dishes such as tapenade-coated sea bream fillet wrapped in filo pastry and served with tomato and aubergine confit. Desserts are simple but tasty – think tropical fruit crumble or chocolate tart.

### Les Ombres

*27 quai Branly, 7th (01.47.53.68.00). M° Alma-Marceau.* **Open** noon-2.30pm, 7-10.30pm daily. **Main courses** €30. **Prix fixe** *Lunch* €37. *Dinner* €95. **Credit** AmEx, MC, V. **Map** p404 D5 ❾❾

The full-on view of the glittering Eiffel Tower at night would be reason enough to come to this glass-and-iron restaurant on the top floor of the Musée du Quai Branly, but young chef Arnaud Busquet's food also demands that you sit up and take notice. The influence of Joël Robuchon – a mentor to Busquet's mentor – shows in dishes such as thin green asparagus curved into a nest with tiny *lardons* and topped with a breaded poached egg, ribbons of parmesan and meat *jus*, or red mullet fillets with the tiniest diced courgette and beautifully dressed mesclun. There is a reasonable prix fixe at lunch, but the view isn't quite as dramatic by day.

### Restaurant Thierry Burlot

*8 rue Nicolas-Charlet, 15th (01.42.19.08.59). M° Pasteur.* **Open** noon-2pm, 7.30-10pm Mon-Fri. Closed 2wks July, 2wks Aug & 1wk Dec. **Main courses** €21. **Credit** AmEx, MC, V. **Map** p405 E9 ❿❶❶

Thierry Burlot's modern bistro continues to draw crowds with an enticing menu of artistically prepared food served in stylish and upbeat surroundings. Produced with fresh ingredients, the offerings vary from earthy, truffle-laden dishes to lighter fish

and seafood numbers, including the quite exquisite langoustines grilled with vanilla, served as a starter or main course. A meal might start with excellent lightly poached egg topped with shards of truffles and framed by fresh leeks, followed by oven-cooked sea bass in a delightful herb and mushroom sauce. Original desserts include intricate chocolate creations and home-made caramel ice-cream. Service is undertaken by an efficient (if rather charmless) coterie of black-clad Paris twentysomethings.

### Le Troquet

*21 rue François-Bonvin, 15th (01.45.66.89.00). M° Sèvres Lecourbe.* **Open** noon-2pm, 7.30-11pm Tue-Sat. Closed 1wk May, Aug & 1wk Dec. **Prix fixe** *Lunch* €28, €40. *Dinner* €30, €40. **Credit** MC, V. **Map** p405 D8 ❶❶❶

Decorated with 1930s light fixtures and a proud Crillon certificate, this restaurant feels deceptively old-fashioned. Christian Etchebest's Basque-inspired cooking may have rustic touches, but his style is modern, with portions sometimes on the small side. From a brief but tempting lunch menu, start with fresh goat's cheese on crisp pastry, sprinkled with Espelette pepper and served with just-cooked red cabbage. Vegetable soup turns out to be a creamy, cardamom-scented blend, which you ladle yourself on to foie gras and a spoonful of crème fraîche. The mains are stunning: a thick tuna steak wrapped in cured ham and served with a rich squash purée or plump farm chicken breast stuffed with tapenade, and cabbage cooked with juniper, pork and olive oil. Desserts are simple but satisfying, including a towering soufflé.

### Le Violon d'Ingres

*135 rue St-Dominique, 7th (01.45.55.15.05). M° Ecole Militaire/RER Pont de l'Alma.* **Open** noon-2.30pm, 7-10.30pm Tue-Sat. **Main courses** €26. **Prix fixe** €70, €90. **Credit** MC, V. **Map** p400 D6 ❶❶❷

Chef Christian Constant has done away with the plush carpet and outsized vases in this once-staid dining room, in favour of a stylish cream-and-brown colour scheme with a long, high table up front and a bar at the back. Acknowledging the importance of value to today's diner, he has also slashed prices by more than half. Since the change, the dining room has been packed with a mix of smartly dressed locals and American gourmands, who have always appreciated Constant's take on classic French cooking. Fluffy blinis made with ratte potatoes (a small, yellow variety) and served with two kinds of fish roe, dill, chives, crème fraîche, and chopped hard-boiled egg show that the kitchen is not cutting corners. Much of Constant's cooking is unabashedly rich, as in scallops with generous lashings of herb butter and almond-crusted sea bass in a buttery caper sauce, but he also serves a mean avocado-and-crab salad. Bistro-style desserts are outstanding, including an intense chocolate tart with vanilla ice-cream and roasted fig, and three *pots de crèmes* (chocolate, coffee and vanilla).

**Eat, Drink, Shop**

# Cafés & Bars

From old-school haunts to edgy music bars, the capital's café culture is alive and kicking.

Café culture is a slippery concept in today's Paris. Anyone picturing Robert Doisneau's classic Paris café – all red banquettes and fortified zinc counter – should check out Philippe Starck's slick haute-design or a host of other trendy joints that compare favourably with those in, say, Berlin or New York.

If it's nostalgic Paris you're after, then try classics such **Les Deux Magots**, **Le Café de Flore**, or **La Palette**, with its art-deco tiles, sturdy zinc counter and leafy terrace, and **Le Cochon à l'Oreille**, a remnant of Les Halles' heyday as the city's food market.

Quintessential cafés aside, the city's new bar scene is thriving. The most exciting recent additions are to be found east of Oberkampf in the traditionally working-class neighbourhoods of Ménilmontant and Belleville. A number of converted spaces have done away with traditional boundaries between bar, club, restaurant and dancehall (*see p235* **12-bar booze**). The **Bellevilloise** (a former Parisian co-operative) and the **Maroquinerie** (previously a leather factory) house restaurant, bar, terrace, music venue and exhibition space all under one roof. The daddy of them all, **La Flèche d'Or**, lodged in a disused railway station, is more popular than ever thanks to free admission and live electro or indie nights.

Despite these attractions further east, the Oberkampf area in the 11th arrondissement is still a night-time hub where revellers are spoilt for choice. Other hotspots include the Marais (and its north-west overspill around Etienne Marcel and Arts et Métiers métro stations) – home to fashionable bars and satisfying brunch spots – and the Canal St-Martin in the 10th, not forgetting the picturesque, village-like area around Abbesses in Montmartre. The Left Bank and Montparnasse boast a proud, if overplayed literary heritage (*see p158* **Paris promenade**), while the west still has swank and glitz.

France has now joined its European neighbours in banning smoking in public places.

➊ Pink numbers in this chapter correspond to the location of each café/bar as marked on the street maps. *See pp400-409.*

It's cheaper to drink at the counter than be served at a table, cheaper inside than on the terrace, and cheaper before 10pm, when a *tarif de nuit* might be imposed. Wine in three colours is ubiquitous, and coffee comes as a strong espresso unless otherwise requested. The sturdy brasserie and noble bistro provide food with formality akin to a restaurant, so if you're just there for a drink, you'll pay more for the social nicety of aproned-and-waistcoated service. You can usually run a tab, and tipping is optional; just a few small coins left in the silver dish will suffice.

## The Louvre & Palais-Royal

### Angelina
*226 rue de Rivoli, 1st (01.42.60.82.00). M° Tuileries.* **Open** 8am-7pm daily. **Credit** MC, V. **Map** 408 G5 ➊
Angelina is home to some of the most voluptuous desserts and decadent hot chocolates Paris has to offer. Get your sugar fix in the faded grandeur of a belle époque salon conveniently situated just steps from the Louvre. A house speciality is the so-thick-it-could-be-solid 'African' hot chocolate and delicious Mont Blanc dessert – a ball of meringue covered in a generous layer of whipped cream and sweet chestnut. There is no shortage of epicurean delights to accompany your hot chocolate, notably the mille-feuille, the *vendome* or the *Paris brest*. It tends to be very popular at weekends, so be prepared to queue.

### Le Café des Initiés
*3 pl des Deux-Ecus, 1st (01.42.33.78.29). M° Louvre Rivoli or Les Halles.* **Open** 7.30am-1am Mon-Sat. **Credit** AmEx, MC, V. **Map** p402 H5 ➋
Once a crumbling corner café, now a designer hangout, the Café des Initiés is a top spot for a trendy tipple. The main room is lined with ergonomic red banquettes, a long zinc bar provides character, and sleek black articulated lamps peer down from the ceiling. The friendly staff and central location have helped put this place firmly on the aperitif map.

### Café Marly
*93 rue de Rivoli, cour Napoléon du Louvre, 1st (01.49.26.06.60). M° Palais Royal Musée du Louvre.* **Open** 8am-2am daily. **Credit** AmEx, DC, MC, V. **Map** p401 H5 ➌
A class act, this, as you might expect of a Costes café whose lofty arcaded terrace overlooks the Louvre's glass pyramid. Accessed through the passage Richelieu (the entrance for advance Louvre ticket

holders), the prime location comes at a price: it's €6 for a Heineken – so you might as well splash out €12 on a Chocolate Martini or a Shark of vodka, lemonade and grenadine. Most wines are under €10 a glass and everything is impeccably served by razor-sharp staff. Brasserie fare and sandwiches are on offer too.

## Entr'acte
*47 rue de Montpensier, 1st (01.42.97.57.76). M° Pyramides or Palais Royal.* **Open** noonmidnight daily. **Credit** MC, V. **Map** p402 H5 ❹
There's something happening around the Palais-Royal – and it's not just Marc Jacobs and the fashion crowd moving in. A little detour off avenue de l'Opéra, down a staircase, and you find an unexpected congregation of imbibers and diners spread over a corner of pavement, half here for this little bar near the Comédie Française, half for the adjoining Sicilian pizzeria. There's food to be had at Entr'acte too – €10 plates of cheese and charcuterie, standard pastas and so on – but most customers come to enjoy an early evening glass of house Bourgueil. If it's raining, though, you may be out of luck: the interior is tiny, with an equally poky basement. Free Wi-Fi and even laptop-lending are offered.

## Le Fumoir
*6 rue de l'Amiral-de-Coligny, 1st (01.42.92.00.24/ www.lefumoir.fr). M° Louvre Rivoli.* **Open** 11am-2am daily. Closed 2wks Aug. **Credit** AmEx, MC, V. **Map** p402 H6 ❺

This elegant bar facing the Louvre has become a local institution: neo-colonial fans whirr lazily, oil paintings adorn the walls and even the bar staff seem to have sprung from the interior decorator's sketches. A sleek crowd sips Martinis or reads papers at the long mahogany bar (originally from a Chicago speakeasy), giving way to young professionals in the restaurant and pretty things in the library. It can feel a touch too try-hard and well-behaved, but expertly mixed cocktails should help take the edge off any evening.

## Kong
*1 rue du Pont-Neuf, 1st (01.40.39.09.00). M° Pont Neuf.* **Open** noon-2am Mon-Thur, Sun; noon-3am Fri, Sat. **Credit** AmEx, MC, V. **Map** p408 J6 ❻
Set on the top two floors of the Kenzo building overlooking the Pont Neuf, this Philippe Starck-designed bar is one of the city's hottest places for cocktails. The bright, mishmash interior is manga-inspired, with lots of neon, Hello Kitty knick-knacks, grey leather sofas and (wisely avoided after a few too many *coupes*) rocking chairs in the main dining area. The best bet is to perch yourself at the long bar, flirt with the too-beautiful-to-bartend staff and order an excellent Vodkatini or three. After dark you can make a music suggestion with each order; at weekends they carve out a tiny dancing space for the designer-bedecked crowd to strut their stuff into the small hours.

Pull up a chair and sup a glass of Bourgueil at **Entr'acte**.

**Eat, Drink, Shop**

## The best Cafés/Bars

### For nostalgia

**Angelina** (*see p220*), **Café de Flore** (*see p236*), **Le Cochon à L'Oreille** (*see p222*), **Les Deux Magots** (*see p237*) and **La Palette** (*see p237*).

### For fine wines

**Le Baromètre** (*see p227*), **Le Baron Rouge** (*see p230*), **Le Cinquante** (*see p232*) and **Le Verre Volé** (*see p235*).

### For beer lovers

**L'Alimentation Générale** (*see p231*), **Le Baron Rouge** (*see p230*), **Le Brébant** (*see p222*) and **Le Sancerre** (*see p227*).

### For creative cocktails

**L'Alimentation Générale** (*see p231*), **Ave Maria** (*see p231*), **Café Chéri(e)** (*see p232*), **Le Crocodile** (*see p235*), **Impala Lounge** (*see p225*), **La Jungle** (*see p223*) and **Palais de Tokyo** (*see p225*).

### For wallet-friendly tipples

**Au Rendez-vous des Amis** (*see p227*), **Le Baromètre** (*see p227*), **Le Cinquante** (*see p232*), **Entr'acte** (*see p221*), **Le Fanfaron** (*see p234*) and **Le Tournesol** (*see p238*).

### For drinking into the small hours

**Le Bar** (*see p236*), **Le Brébant** (*see p222*), **Le N'Importe Quoi** (*see p223*), **Le Tambour** (*see p225*) and **Le Truskel** (*see p225*).

### For music

**Bar Ourcq** (*see p231*), **La Bellevilloise** (*see p231*), **Le Café des Sports** (*see p232*), **Le Fanfaron** (*see p230*), **La Flèche d'Or** (*see p233*), **La Fourmi** (*see p226*), **La Jungle** (*see p223*), **Le Mange Disque** (*see p233*), **Le Motel** (*see p230*) and **Le N'Importe Quoi** (*see p223*).

## Opéra to Les Halles

### Le Brébant

*32 bd Poissonnière, 9th (01.47.70.01.02). M° Grands Boulevards.* **Open** 7.30am-6am daily. **Credit** MC, V. **Map** p402 J4 **7**
If anything points to a new broom sweeping the Grand Boulevards, it's this prominent, round-the-clock bar-bistro. There's a permanently busy terrace below a colourful, stripy awning, while playful, orange-shirted waiters rush around the cavernous,

split-level, arty interior of bare bulbs and wrought iron. Prices are steep, even by Paris standards, so push the boat out and opt for an expertly made fruit Daiquiri, or a Bonne Nouvelle of Bombay Sapphire gin and Pisang Ambon. There are rarer bottled beers too – Monaco, Picon and sundry brews from Brabant. A board advertises a decent range of proper eats: steak tartare (€14) and so on.

### Le Café de l'Olympia

*2 bd de la Madeleine, 9th (01.42.65.10.62). M° Madeleine or Opéra.* **Open** 6.30am-2am daily. **Credit** V. **Map** p401 G4 **8**
A couple of steps from the famed music venue of the same name (*see p320*), the Olympia feels as timeless as the stars to whom it once served pre-show drinks. The street-level interior is decked out in musical instruments, while downstairs Piaf and Gainsbourg posters reign – only the terrace, proclaiming €16 brunches and English breakfasts, exudes 21st-century excess. Nonetheless, it's a perfect place for a passing drink.

### Le Café Noir

*65 rue Montmartre, 2nd (01.40.39.07.36). M° Sentier.* **Open** 8am-2am Mon-Fri; 4pm-2am Sat. **Credit** DC, MC, V. **Map** p402 J4 **9**
This buzzing and enticingly kitsch corner bar is Noir in name but scarlet in tone – and brash in attitude. A framed Gainsbourg portrait and quotation exhort 'Music Above All', although they're fighting for your attention with leopard-spotted bicycles, reindeer-antlered fish heads, dinky hanging baskets and papier-mâché lightshades, offset by a tiled bar counter – and all of it the size of a swimming pool changing cubicle. The regulars make the place nice, naughty, bitchy and boho, forever picking up on the giggling at the next banquette or prized pavement table. There's a modest lunchtime menu too.

### Café de la Paix

*12 bd des Capucines, 9th (01.40.07.36.36). M° Opéra.* **Open** 7am-midnight daily. **Credit** AmEx, DC, MC, V. **Map** p401 G4 **10**
The sumptuous terrace café-restaurant of the InterContinental Paris Le Grand (*see p64*) exudes history. Your table, beneath the ornate, stucco ceiling or overlooking Garnier's opera house, may have been patronised by Oscar Wilde, Josephine Baker, Emile Zola – or Bartholdi and the Franco-American Union as they sketched out the Statue of Liberty. You'll be treated as one of their equals by the immaculate staff, and presented with little bowls of crisps, nuts and olives to accompany your €10 kir or €8 glass of draught Grimbergen. They mix a classy cocktail too, from a range of ten standards, although your €19 could be just as enjoyably spent on a flute of Moët & Chandon. Lap it up – this is once-in-a-holiday stuff.

### Le Cochon à l'Oreille

*15 rue Montmartre, 1st (01.42.36.07.56). M° Les Halles.* **Open** 11am-2am Mon-Sat. **No credit cards. Map** p402 J5 **11**

This impeccably preserved *bistrot à vins* is a relic from Les Halles' heyday as the city's legendary food market. Its ornate wooden doors with misty glass panelling open onto a café with its original features fully intact. The antique public telephone in the corner, the imposing zinc counter and the intimate wooden booths are charming reminders of the days when Les Halles enlivened the whole *quartier*. Most impressive, however, are the tiles that show vivid scenes of the market in all its chaotic splendour. Le Cochon is obviously proud of its heritage and guests are encouraged to record their impressions in notebooks tucked away in little nooks. Join the locals for a glass of wine or sample from a concise menu of meat-oriented dishes.

### De la Ville Café

*34 bd Bonne-Nouvelle, 10th (01.48.24.48.09). M°Bonne Nouvelle.* **Open** 11am-2am daily. **Credit** MC, V. **Map** p402 J4 ⑫

Opened by the Café Charbon (*see p232*) crew and other Ménilmontant movers, De la Ville has brought good news to Bonne-Nouvelle. A major expansion and refurb have upped the ante, bringing the Marais in-crowd to this otherwise ignored quarter. Inside, the distressed walls and hippie feel remain, but the curvy club section at the back has become über-cool. A grand staircase leads to a first-floor lounge and exhibition space, where the interior is ambitious and arty, with a fashion edge. Having elevated the 11th to bar legend, can the crew transform the 10th, and bring a café boom back to the boulevards?

### Harry's New York Bar

*5 rue Daunou, 2nd (01.42.61.71.14/www.harrys-bar.fr). M° Opéra.* **Open** 10.30am-4am daily. **Credit** AmEx, DC, MC, V. **Map** p401 G4 ⑬

The city's quintessential American bar is still an institution beloved of expats, visitors and hard-drinking Parisians. The white-coated bartenders mix some of the most lethal cocktails in town, from the trademark Bloody Mary (invented here, so they say) to the Pétrifiant, an aptly-named elixir of half a dozen spirits splashed into a beer mug. They can whip up personalised creations: we remember (patchily) a string of delicious concoctions that had us swooning in the downstairs piano bar.

### La Jungle

*56 rue d'Argout, 2nd (01.40.41.03.45/www.la-jungle.com). M° Sentier.* **Open** 10am-2am Mon-Fri; 4pm-2am Sat, Sun. **Credit** AmEx, MC, V. **Map** p402 J5 ⑭

The Jungle rocks with easy sociability and a sense of unaffected fun – despite its morose collection of scruffy animal skins. There's a programme of live Afro-jazz on Wednesdays and Fridays (€2 extra on drinks), some of it half decent – but really you're here for exotic cocktails (€6) such as 'Ti Georges, Zoulou and the vodka-soaked Gazelle Allumée, plus ethnic dishes with a Cameroonian bent. Hearty n'dolé soup, chicken *yassa* and *boudin créole* can be washed down with Flag beer from Senegal. A branch at 15 rue d'Aboukir nearby is run in the same vein.

### Le N'Importe Quoi

*16 rue du Roule, 1st (01.40.26.29.71/www.nimportequoi.fr). M° Châtelet.* **Open** 6pm-4am Wed; 6pm-5am Thur-Sat. **Credit** MC, V. **Map** p402 J5 ⑮

A young clientele, much of it female, frequents this low-ceilinged downtown den, filling the multi-coloured space with post-work natter – many of the regulars work in the nearby offices of respected

Le Brébant.

**Eat, Drink, Shop**

music magazine *Les Inrockuptibles*. A cellar of similar decor and intimacy opens up at weekends and for private parties.

### Somo

*168 rue Montmartre, 2nd (01.40.13.08.80/www.hipbars.com). Mº Sentier or Grands Boulevards.* **Open** noon-2am Mon-Fri; 6pm-4am Sat. **Credit** AmEx, MC, V. **Map** p402 J4 ⑯

Somo is a sleeker, more grown-up expat-owned offering than the Lizard Lounge (*see p229*), Stolly's (*see p229*) and the Bottle Shop (5 rue Trousseau, 11th, 01.43.14.28.04). Popular with suits from the nearby Bourse after work, it chills out later in the evening and at weekends, when bright young things arrive to party amid the fairy lights, aided and abetted by well-mixed €9 Absolut-based cocktails. There's a full menu on offer too: the €13.90 dinner's a snip, the €9 bar snacks are not. Weekend DJ spots here have become a solid fixture on the Saturday night circuit.

### Le Tambour

*41 rue Montmartre, 2nd (01.42.33.06.90). Mº Sentier.* **Open** 6pm-6am daily. **Credit** MC, V. **Map** p402 J5 ⑰

The Tambour is a classic nighthawks' bar, decked out with vintage transport chic, its slatted wooden banquettes and bus-stop-sign bar stools occupied by chatty regulars who give the 24-hour clock their best shot. Neither tatty nor threatening, there's a long dining room memorable for its métro map from Stalingrad station.

### Le Truskel

*10 rue Feydeau, 2nd (01.40.26.59.97/www.truskel. com). Mº Bourse.* **Open** 8pm-3am Tue, Wed; 8pm-5am Thur-Sat. Closed Aug. **Credit** MC, V. **Map** p402 H4 ⑱

The formula is quite simple at this pub-cum-disco: an excellent selection of beers, fruity Belgian and quality Czech included, attends to your thirst while an extensive repertoire of Britpop assaults your ears. The back area is set aside for dancing; malcontent expats love it, but not as much as the French boys who can't hold their Murphy's. As a cheeky touch, a bar bell rings for no reason whatsoever, causing first-time UK-visitors to down their drinks in one and dive for the bar.

## Champs-Elysées & western Paris

### Le Dada

*12 av des Ternes, 17th (01.43.80.60.12). Mº Ternes.* **Open** 6am-2am Mon-Sat; 6am-10pm Sun. **Credit** AmEx, MC, V. **Map** p400 C3 ⑲

Perhaps the hippest café on this classy avenue in a stuffy part of town, Le Dada is best known for its well-placed, sunny terrace. Inside, the wood-block carved tables and red walls provide a warm atmosphere for a crowd that tends towards the well-heeled,

well-spoken and, well, loaded. That said, the atmosphere is friendly; if terracing is your thing, you could happily spend a summer's day here. *Photo p226.*

### Impala Lounge

*2 rue de Berri, 8th (01.43.59.12.66). Mº George V.* **Open** noon-2am Mon-Thur, Sun; noon-4am Fri, Sat. **Credit** AmEx, MC, V. **Map** p400 D4 ⑳

Dubbed the 'African Bar' by regulars, this wannabe-hip spot hams up the colonial with zebra skins, masks and a throne hewn from a tree trunk. Beer, wine, tea and standard favourites can all be had, but best are the cocktails, one of which claims to boost a waning libido with its mystery mix of herbs and spices. DJs rock Sunday afternoon away, and the snack-and-mains menu includes ostrich.

### Ladurée

*75 av des Champs-Elysées, 8th (01.40.75.08.75/www. laduree.fr). Mº George V or Franklin D. Roosevelt.* **Open** 7.30am-midnight daily. **Credit** AmEx, DC, MC, V. **Map** p400 D4 ㉑

Everything in this elegant tearoom suggests decadence, from the 19th century-style interior and service to the labyrinthine corridors that lead to the toilets. While you bask in the warm glow of bygone wealth, indulge in tea, pastries and, above all, the hot chocolate. It's a rich, bitter, velvety tar that will leave you in the requisite stupor for any lazy afternoon. The original branch at 16 rue Royale (8th, 01.42.60.21.79) is also known for its macaroons.

### Libresens

*33 rue Marbeuf, 8th (01.53.96.00.72). Mº Franklin D. Roosevelt.* **Open** 9am-3am daily. **Credit** MC, V. **Map** p401 D4 ㉒

Unusually for this part of town, the Libresens is reasonably priced, down to earth and frequented by a nicely turned-out crowd who are not too self-obsessed or posy. Design is slick, with low lighting and comfortable seating which accommodates groups and couples alike. Particularly attractive are the large booths and a section of seating arranged in a square, cocooned from the rest of the bar thanks to strategically placed tassels. The crowd is made up mostly of Parisians here for a drink after work, and rightly so – the happy hour, between 6.30pm and 8.30pm, includes flutes of champagne for €5 and cocktails for €7.

### Palais de Tokyo

*13 av du Président-Wilson, 16th (01.47.20.00.29). Mº Iéna.* **Open** noon-midnight Tue-Sun. **Credit** AmEx, MC, V. **Map** p400 C5 ㉓

The Palais de Tokyo is one of the hippest destinations in the otherwise staid 16th. The majestic neo-classical building has a stripped-back interior and stunning outdoor terrace overlooking the Seine. The Palais has hosted everything from contemporary art exhibits to haute couture fashion shows, but its bar still manages to put together quirky cocktails for €9. Strawberry margaritas and the Brazilian-inspired Rio Bamako with cachaça, lime and ginger juice are particularly tempting. DJs play an eclectic mix daily

**Le Dada** – if the sun's out, head for the terrace. *See p225.*

from 10pm, but it really packs a crowd at weekends. In summer, when the bar moves outside, the terrace throngs with beautiful people.

### Petit Défi de Passy
*18 av du Président-Kennedy, 16th (01.42.15.06.76). M° Passy/RER Avenue du Pdt Kennedy.* **Open** 10am-midnight daily. **Credit** AmEx, DC, MC, V. **Map** p404 B6 ㉔
In permanent rebellion against its posh postcode, this refreshingly no-fuss bar-restaurant challenges the local chi-chi rule, jollying along friendly students and English teachers through happy hour. It's bursting with toff totty, and the best bit is, it's cheap.

### Le Rival
*20 av George V, 8th (01.47.23.40.99). M° George V.* **Open** 7am-2am daily. **Credit** MC, V. **Map** p400 D4 ㉕
Stylish but low key, this four-star contemporary bar makes a mean martini: fresh fruit, Polish or Detroit, with a wellyful of Zubrowka or Krupnik chucked in and served with pzazz. Other highlights of the €12 cocktail range are a Saigon Extra Mule with Poire Williams, lemon and ginger beer, and a Spiced Swizzle of rum and amaretto. A decent glass of Brouilly or Chablis sets you back €7, par for the course – but heaven knows how they can charge €18 for a cheeseburger and hash browns. Still, the shopaholic and business clientele seem happy to stump up.

### Sir Winston
*5 rue de Presbourg, 16th (01.40.67.17.37). M° Charles de Gaulle Etoile.* **Open** 9am-3am Mon-Wed, Sun; 9am-4am Thur-Sat. **Credit** AmEx, V. **Map** p400 C4 ㉖

A bit of an anomaly, this. Grand and imperial, and located within sight of high-end glitz, Sir Winston does a nice line in jazz and gospel brunches on a Sunday. Colonial knick-knacks, chesterfields and chandeliers make up the decor, with Winnie himself framed behind a sturdy bar counter. A battalion of whiskies stands guard beside him, and the wine list is equally *recherché*. Where this place falters is in its girly cocktail menu. A Sir Winston Breezer of Bacardi, melon liqueur, pineapple and banana juice? Harrumph!

## Montmartre & Pigalle

### La Divette de Montmartre
*136 rue Marcadet, 18th (01.46.06.19.64). M° Lamarck Caulaincourt.* **Open** 5pm-1am Mon-Sat; 5-11pm Sun. **Credit** MC, V.
Tucked away among Montmartre's hilly backstreets, this cavern of colourful nostalgia is run by Serge and serves as his *Recherche du temps perdu* in album-cover, poster and table-football form. Beatles albums line up over the bar, Rolling Stones under it and an Elvis clock ticks in between; this decorative trinity is interrupted by *yé-yé* pop tat, the occasional green of St-Etienne football iconography and an old red telephone box. On tap are Wieckse Witte, Afflighem, Pelforth and gossip about the days when Manu Chao were regulars.

### La Fourmi
*74 rue des Martyrs, 18th (01.42.64.70.35). M° Pigalle.* **Open** 8.30am-2am Mon-Thur; 8.30am-4am Fri, Sat; 10am-2am Sun. **Credit** MC, V. **Map** p402 H2 ㉗

Set on the cusp of the 9th and 18th arrondissements, La Fourmi is retro-industrial at its best. It's an old bistro that has been converted for today's tastes, with picture windows giving light and visual bustle to the spacious, roughshod, sand-coloured main interior, whose prime seats are on the podiums at the back. The classic zinc bar counter is crowned by industrial lights, and an excellent music policy and cool clientele – although they'd have to go some to beat the bar staff – ensure a pile of flyers. As good a place as any to find out what's happening in town.

### Au Rendez-vous des Amis

*23 rue Gabrielle, 18th (01.46.06.01.60). M°*
*Abbesses.* **Open** 8.30am-2am daily. **Credit** MC, V.
**Map** p402 J1 ㉘
Considering its proximity to a tourist hub, this café/bar is still cheap, making it popular with locals, foreign students and the odd tourist as well. It has a happy hour between 8pm and 10pm, during which a glass of wine or a kir will set you back a very reasonable €2. Grab a cosy nook around the back; it's been recently refurbished, and there are plenty of upholstered spots to choose from.

### Le Sancerre

*35 rue des Abbesses, 18th (01.42.58.08.20).*
*M° Abbesses.* **Open** 7am-2am Mon-Thur; 7am-4am Fri, Sat; 9am-2am Sun. **Credit** MC, V. **Map** p402 H1 ㉙
Of the many choices on rue des Abbesses, this is the most popular, its terrace full, its large, dark-wood interior an attractive mix of cool and cosy. Taps of Paulaner, Grimbergen and Record accompany bottled Belgians Kriek and Mort Subite; standard cocktails (€5.50 on Mondays) are presented with the same care as the couple of *plats du jour* and a good range of mains and salads. However, the service can be teeth-grindingly slow.

## Beaubourg & the Marais

### Andy Whaloo

*69 rue des Gravilliers, 3rd (01.42.71.20.38). M° Arts et Métiers.* **Open** 4pm-2am Mon-Sat. **Credit** AmEx, MC, V. **Map** p409 K5 ㉚
Andy Whaloo – created by the people behind its neighbour 404 and London's Momo and Sketch – is Arabic for 'I have nothing'. Bijou? The place brings new meaning to the word. A formidably fashionable set crowds in here and fights for a coveted place on an upturned paint can; from head to toe, it's a beautifully designed venue, crammed with Moroccan artefacts and a spice-rack of colours. It's quiet early on with a surge around 9pm, and the atmosphere heats up as the night gets longer.

### L'Apparemment Café

*18 rue des Coutures St-Gervais, 3rd (01.48.87.12.22).*
*M° St-Sébastien Froissart.* **Open** noon-2am Mon-Fri; 4pm-2am Sat; 12.30pm-midnight Sun. **Credit** MC, V. **Map** p409 L6 ㉛

On a narrow street flanking the Picasso museum, the 'Apparently' looks more like a communal living room than a café. Low lighting, cosy nooks and entertainment in the form of *Trivial Pursuit* or *Cranium* (both in French) make for an excellent place to while away an afternoon. The location is perfect for dedicated shoppers too, being just off the rue Vieille-du-Temple, with its established boutiques and new designers. Lunches come in the form of a simple DIY platter of meats, cheeses, breads and salads, but at €14 for the basic version, they're a bit rudimentary. Eating is obligatory during busy periods, when it is definitely advisable to book.

### Le Baromètre

*17 rue Charlot, 3rd (01.48.87.04.54). M° Arts et Métiers.* **Open** 8am-11pm Mon-Sat. **Credit** MC, V.
**Map** p409 L5 ㉜
Unpretentious but serious wine bar and eaterie, favoured by the craftsmen and artisans native to this now sought-after street before the fashionistas and designers moved in. Lunchtimes tend to be heaving, so unless you're after a €12 sit-down *menu du jour* in green banquettes at the back, you're better off passing through on a lazy afternoon, ordering up a *tartine* thickly spread with pâté, or a plate of cheese, and choosing from a 20-strong selection of wines by the glass, most for under €2.

### L'Estaminet d'Arômes et Cépages

*39 rue de Bretagne, 3rd (01.42.72.34.85). M° Temple.* **Open** 9am-8pm Tue-Sun. **Credit** MC, V.
**Map** p409 L5 ㉝
L'Estaminet d'Aromes et Cépages is tucked away in the Marché des Enfants rouge, a charming neighbourhood market and one of the city's oldest (*see p261* **Market forces**). The café has a warm provençal interior, a grandfather clock counting time in the corner and guests eating €12 *plats du jour* off Limoges porcelain. The wine distributors Aromes et Cépages, who have a shop around the corner, own L'Estaminet, which is technically their *bar à vins* (wines around €4 a glass); but it's a café in all but name, and a distinctive one at that.

### L'Etoile Manquante

*34 rue Vieille-du-Temple, 4th (01.42.72.48.34/*
*www.cafeine.com). M° Hôtel de Ville or St-Paul.*
**Open** 9am-2am daily. **Credit** MC, V. **Map** p409 K6 ㉞
The hippest of Xavier Denamur's merry Marais bars. The cocktails are punchy, the traditional tipples just as good, the salads and cold snacks reasonably priced and tasty – but it's the design and buzz that are the draws here. The decor is trendy and comfortable, embellished with multicoloured lighting and interesting art. As ever with Denamur's places, no visit is complete without a trip to the toilets: here, an electric train shuttles between cubicles, starlight beams down from the ceiling, and a hidden camera films you washing your hands. Just watch the small screen on the wall behind you.

**Eat, Drink, Shop**

# Raising the bar

Hôtel Raphaël.

Some exclusive, others legendary, most tucked away from the outside world, Paris hotel bars make for some of the best and most mythical drinking dens in the city.

The daddy of them all, the **Hemingway Bar at the Ritz** (15 pl Vendôme, 1st, 01.43.16.33.65) is a wonderfully civilised place in which to get smashed. Bartender Colin dispenses fabulous cocktails – among them the 'Sidecar' costing a jaw-dropping €400 – plus compliments and flowers for the ladies, all in a gloriously suave manner. **Bar Cambon** opposite (entrance at 38 rue Cambon, 1st, 01.43.16.30.90) is a good spot for posh partying, while the **Bar Vendôme** (01.43.16.33.63) at the front of the hotel has a perfect summer terrace.

If it hasn't been reserved for VIPs for the night, stunning sundowners can also be had on the seventh-floor roof terrace of the **Hôtel Raphaël** (17 av Kléber, 16th, 01.53.64.32.00). Downstairs, the **Bar Anglais**, while staid, is the stuff of history: Eisenhower toasted liberation here, and contemporaries Ava Gardner, Marlon Brando and Cary Grant all popped in for a *verre* at some point. Serge Gainsbourg wrote several of his songs while propping up the bar.

**Le Dokhan's** (Hôtel Trocadéro Dokhan's, 117 rue Lauriston, 16th, 01.53.65.66.99) is the perfect choice for amorous encounters. Think high ceilings, ornate gilt, decorative panelling and service so discreet it's practically invisible. It is also a champagne bar par excellence, with over 80 bottles of bubbly on its expertly compiled menu.

Those looking for something just a little less subtle should head to the **V** (Four Seasons George V, 31 av George-V, 8th, 01.49.52.70.00) for a glitzy beverage or three. Champagne at €25 a glass, €33 for a club sandwich – it's sure swank at the Cinq. Higher on the see-and-be-seen scale is **Le Bar du Plaza** (Hôtel Plaza Athénée, 25 av Montaigne, 8th, 01.53.67.66.00), a cocktail bunny's most outré fantasy, with flattering lighting, high chairs offering maximum leg-crossing opportunities, and ridiculous drinks. Avoid the savoury concoctions and instead go for an old-fashioned but expertly mixed standard, or join the PR crowd and indulge in a Fashion Ice: alcoholic ice lollies that offer maximum flirting potential.

Traditionalist trendies still make a beeline for the **Costes** (239 rue St-Honoré, 1st, 01.42.44.49.80), all champers and air kisses, or the **Murano** (13 bd du Temple, 3rd, 01.42.71.20.00), with its inventive interior, sassy staff and creative vodka-based *boissons* – go for the Red Fruits and Love combo, vodka and summer fruits artfully served up in test tubes.

In a departure from the glitz of the other establishments, the **Hotel Eldorado** (18 rue des Dames, 17th, 01.45.22.13.42) off the place de Clichy, is a modest and not especially popular hotel. However, its excellent **Bistrot des Dames** is frequented by everyone from models to mortals, and rightly so since it's set in a gob-smackingly lovely high-walled courtyard, that comes complete with sky-high trees, fairy lights and a down-to-earth menu offering €7.50 cocktails and a home-cooked main courses for €16.

These days, hotels can make a name for themselves purely through the buzz around the bar alone. A classic example is the **Hôtel Amour** (*see p57*), whose slightly retro brasserie (with leafy garden) has wowed the in-crowd as much as did the arty guest rooms.

### Lizard Lounge

*18 rue du Bourg-Tibourg, 4th (01.42.72.08.11/
www.cheapblonde.com). M° Hôtel de Ville.* **Open**
noon-2am daily. **Credit** MC, V. **Map** p409 K6 ⑤
An anglophone/-phile favourite deep in the Marais,
this loud and lively (hetero) pick-up joint provides
lager in pints (€6), strong, well-mixed cocktails (€7)
and a viewing platform from which the beer-gog-
gled can ogle their prey. Bare brick and polished
woodwork are offset by the occasional lizard, but
the main backdrop is provided by a housey soundtrack. Bargain boozing kicks off at 5pm; at 8pm
another happy hour begins down in the sweaty cellar bar, ending at 10pm. Mercifully, given the five
straight hours of cheap drinks, the downstairs
dancefloor is minuscule. Show off your catch at the
popular weekend brunch.

### Le Loir dans la Théière

*3 rue des Rosiers, 4th (01 42 72 90 61). M° St-Paul.*
**Open** 11.30am-7pm Mon-Fri; 10am-7pm Sat, Sun.
**Credit** V. **Map** p409 L6 ㊱
Named after the unfortunate dormouse who is mercilessly dunked in the pot at the Mad Hatter's tea
party, Le Loir has plenty of squishy sofas to complement its comfort food. Specialising in baked
goods, its famed lemon meringue and chocolate fon-
dant are divine. Lunches are inevitably oversha-
owed by the decadent desserts, though the *tartes
salées* usually score well. But be warned: this place
is packed at weekends, when brunch tourists scour
the Marais for tables. Long lines of people looking
enviously at your plate, together with occasionally
patchy service, can sometimes compromise your eating experience. Come early or be prepared to queue.

### La Perle

*78 rue Vieille-du-Temple, 3rd (01.42.72.69.93). M°
Chemin Vert or St-Paul.* **Open** 6am-2am Mon-Fri;
8am-2am Sat, Sun. **Credit** MC, V. **Map** p409 L6 ㊲
This recent Marais hit is commendably simple. Cool
little touches – arty dabblings on the walls, the old
locomotive over the bar – meet sleek rows of grey
chairs spread on the quiet corner of rue de la Perle
and rue Vieille-du-Temple, and patterned banquettes within. The Pearl's real triumph is its all-day
and late-night hetero/homo mix: it feels like a neighbourhood bar, with labourers and cravatted screen-
writers rubbing elbows at the counter. There's
unpretentious and inexpensive attention to detail,
and the menu runs from hearty omelettes to a delicate *salade marine*. Expect a DJ later on. *Photo p230.*

### Le Petit Fer à Cheval

*30 rue Vieille-du-Temple, 4th (01.42.72.47.47).
M° St-Paul.* **Open** 9am-2am daily. **Credit** MC, V.
**Map** p409 K6 ㊳
If Glasgow's Horseshoe boasts the UK's longest bar
counter, its Paris near-namesake must contain one
of France's smallest. It may be tiny, but it's charming: a marble ring surrounded by old film and promotional posters and headed by a vintage clock and
an ornate mirror backdrop. Behind the glassy façade

hides a friendly dining room lined with old métro
benches, offering space, but not scenery – for that,
try the tables out front looking over rue Vieille-du-
Temple's bustle. In business since 1903, the Little
Horseshoe enjoyed a retro makeover by Xavier
Denamur and his team in the 1990s.

### Stolly's

*16 rue Cloche-Perce, 4th (01.42.76.06.76/www.
cheapblonde.com). M° Hôtel de Ville or St-Paul.*
**Open** 4.30pm-2am daily. **Credit** MC, V. **Map**
p409 K6 ㊴
This seen-it-all drinking den has been serving a
mainly anglophone crowd expert vodka tonics and
old Velvets tunes for nights immemorial. The staff
make the place what it is, smoothing the passage
from arriving sober to sinking them relentlessly
until you're rotten. A summer terrace eases libation,
as do long happy hours, but don't expect anyone to
faff about with food. There's football on TV and a
plastic shark to compensate.

### Les Templiers

*18 rue Caffarelli, 3rd (01.42.76.03.22). M° Temple.*
**Open** 9am-2am Mon-Sat. **Credit** V. **Map** p409 L5 ㊵
Les Templiers has earned a reputation as the ideal
pre-club venue but is equally busy at lunchtimes,
when its long room and terrace of red-checked tables
fill with diners eagerly tucking into €10.50 bacon
cheeseburgers or €11 house salads of chicken and
Charlotte potatoes. Its motto, 'good food, people and
sound' (sound what?), doesn't do the place justice:
it's a rather funky space with a merry-go-round
horse, cool music (often electro) and liberal mix of
clientele. Food is served until midnight.

### Wini June

*16 rue Dupetit-Thoars, 3rd (01.44.61.76.41).
M° Temple.* **Open** 6pm-2am daily. **Credit** MC, V.
**Map** p409 L5 ㊶
Wini June's virtual living room has become a
favourite haunt of Paris fashionistas and designers.
It's tiny, but what it lacks in size it makes up for in
fastidious attention to detail. Guests sit on Empire-
style or contemporary furnishings, the wine is served
in crystal glasses, the attentive staff bring attractive
nibbles with your drink, and the soundtrack stays
just the right side of soft rock. The pint-sized terrace
is a particularly welcoming spot: flimsy plastic
chairs have been shunned in favour of an outdoor
version of the interior, flanked with bamboo.

## Bastille & eastern Paris

### L'Antenne Bastille

*32ter bd de la Bastille, 12th (01.43.43.34.92).
M° Bastille.* **Open** 8am-2am Mon-Fri; noon-2am
Sat; 2-9pm Sun. **Credit** AmEx, DC, MC, V.
**Map** p409 M7 ㊷
A great little retro bar just minutes from the Bastille
opera, L'Antenne has a terrace overlooking the
Port de l'Arsenal marina and a simple interior that's
light and airy. You can get a humble *jambon-beurre*

**Eat, Drink, Shop**

Happy hours: **La Perle**'s simple style is a hit with the Marais crowd. *See p229.*

sandwich for under €3 or a Toblerone from the rows arranged in sweet-shop fashion under the Maurice Chevalier posters. There's more substantial (and equally cheap) food too: a *plat du jour* at €8.50 and an €11.50 daily *formule*. A thirtysomething clientele banters quietly, leaving hedonism to the younger mob in nearby rue de la Roquette and rue de Lappe.

## Le Baron Rouge

*1 rue Théophile-Roussel, 12th (01.43.43.14.32).*
*M° Ledru-Rollin.* **Open** 10am-3pm, 5-10pm Tue-Thur; 10am-10pm Fri, Sat; 10am-3pm Sun. **Credit** AmEx, MC, V. **Map** p407 N7 ⓭
Calling this simply a wine bar might give the wrong impression. It sells wine, certainly – bloody great barrels of the stuff, piled high and sold at very reasonable prices by the glass. But there are draught beers too, the ever more present St-Omer and far rarer Jenlain and Corsican Pietra. But overall, the Red Baron is best described as a chat room. Regulars congregate here to yak while they sip, perhaps with a plate of sausages or a few oysters. It's a popular pre-dinner spot, so don't expect much elbow room; guests often spill out onto the pavement.

## Le Fanfaron

*6 rue de la Main-d'Or, 11th (01.49.23.41.14).*
*M° Ledru-Rollin.* **Open** 6pm-2am Mon-Sat. Closed 2wks Aug. **No credit cards. Map** p407 N7 ⓮
On a small backstreet, Le Fanfaron (named after Dino Risi's 1962 cult movie) is the favoured haunt for musically inclined retro dudes. Owner Xavier's enviable collection of rare film soundtracks, the cheap (€2.30) beer and sound of needle against crackly vinyl pack them in. The decor is kitsch-cool,

with Stones and Iggy memorabilia, second-hand furniture and '60s movie posters. There are reasonably priced goat's cheese and *saucisson* bar snacks too.

## La Liberté

*196 rue du Fbg-St-Antoine, 12th (01.43.72.11.18).*
*M° Faidherbe Chaligny.* **Open** 9am-2am Mon-Fri; 11am-2am Sat, Sun. **Credit** AmEx, MC, V. **Map** p407 N7 ⓯
By day this is a relaxed spot; the decor is a little primitive and rubbing elbows is inevitable, but it's pleasantly convivial with good, reasonably priced food. By night, though, the pace is manic and the drinks flow. La Lib comprises a small terrace and a narrow bar area dangling with knick-knacks and invariably packed; a back room is for those who actually want to talk to each other. The rest are happy to guzzle (house punch or decent bottled Belgian brews), guffaw and cop off. The music's always right: African beats, Burning Spear or Little Richard howling *Lucille.*

## Le Motel

*8 passage Josset 11th, (01.58.30.88.52). M°*
*Ledru-Rolin.* **Open** 6pm-2am Tue-Sun. Closed Aug. **Credit** MC, V. **Map** p407 M7 ⓰
Le Motel is the latest addition to the city's growing indie scene. It follows a simple formula: cheap drinks and excellent music. During happy hour (6pm to 9pm) a pint of *blonde* costs €3.50 and cocktails – the mojito is particularly good – €3. With DJs almost every night, the music ranges from cutting-edge indie to contemporary neo-folk and rock classics, with the odd Mowtown hit thrown in for good measure. Friendly twentysomethings cluster around

faux Louis XVI armchairs or try their luck in the Sunday pop quiz. Although this place is new, it already boasts an army of regulars.

## L'Opa
*9 rue Biscornet, 12th (01.46.28.12.90/www.opa-paris.com). M° Bastille.* **Open** 8pm-2am Tue-Thur; 9pm-6am Fri, Sat. **Credit** V. **Map** p409 M7 **47**
Late opening hours and Eric Perier's diverse nightly range of entertainment (DJs, videos, live acts and the odd open mic night) are the attractions here, along with free admission and reasonable drinks prices. It's all set in a sturdy, two-storey building near the Bastille opera, with a couple of comfortable sofas to take the edge off the institutional appearance, a modest stage in one corner and an upstairs chill-out space and separate bar.

## Pause Café
*41 rue de Charonne, 11th (01.48.06.80.33). M° Ledru-Rollin.* **Open** 8am-2am Mon-Sat; 9am-8pm Sun. **Credit** MC, V. **Map** p407 M7 **48**
Featured in Cedric Klapisch's 1996 film *Chacun Cherche son Chat*, which was shot on location in the *quartier*, the Pause Café has managed to prolong its hour of glory thanks to its large terrace on the corner of rues Charonne and Keller. Inside, the modern salons benefit from a smattering of primary colours with ornately plastered ceilings and lots of light. Having been immortalised on celluloid, the friendly staff occasionally let fame go to their heads – service can be excruciatingly slow. The food – French café fare – is not bad, but you might be waiting for a while; best to opt for a well-mixed cocktail at €7.50 or a demi for €4 instead.

## North-east Paris

### L'Alimentation Générale
*64 rue Jean-Pierre-Timbaud, 11th (01.43.55.42.50). M° Parmentier.* **Open** 5pm-2am Mon-Sat. **Credit** AmEx, MC, V. **Map** p403 M4 **49**
The 'Grocery Store' is rue Jean-Pierre-Timbaud's answer to La Mercerie (*see p234*): it, too, is a big old space filled with junk. Cupboards of kitsch china or plastic peppers face the long bar counter, while elsewhere lampshades made from kitchen sponges are a particularly inspired touch. The beer is equally well chosen – Flag, Sagres, Picon and Orval by the bottle – and the €8 house speciality involves obscure combinations of fruit, spices and alcohol, throwing basil and figs into the mix. Salads are just as imaginative. Professional sounds emerge from a DJ booth the size of a small airport terminal: expect a €5 cover price for big names or live bands. Oh yes – and the most brazen toilet walls on this side of town.

### L'Atmosphère
*49 rue Lucien-Sampaix, 10th (01.40.38.09.21). M° Gare de l'Est or Jacques Bonsergent.* **Open** 9.30am-1.45am Mon-Sat; 9.30am-midnight Sun. **No credit cards. Map** p402 L3 **50**

L'Atmosphère remains at the centre of the Canal St-Martin renaissance and sums up the spirit of the area. Parisians of all kinds chat, read and gaze from the waterside terrace; within, the simple, tasteful interior, animated conversation and cheapish drinks provide entertainment enough. It's always packed, but brave the crowds on Sundays for early-evening world and experimental music slots.

### Ave Maria
*1 rue Jacquard, 11th (01.47.00.61.73). M° Parmentier.* **Open** 6.30pm-2am daily. **No credit cards. Map** p403 M5 **51**
Unlike some places that eschew good food for alcohol and a funky interior, colourful Ave Maria does all three very well. In a paean to all things kitsch, Virgin Marys are in abundance, a canopy of chinoiserie parasols hangs near the entrance, and a vast collection of Hindu gods takes pride of place near the bar. The music, a combination of reggae, funk, soul and dub, is carefully chosen but unobtrusive. Strangers sharing wooden benches discuss curiosities on the menu; main meals, which are a combination of meat, spices, lentils, rice and fruit, are as interesting as their description – one signature dish is called '*le destin terrifiant d'Amélie Poulet*'. The cocktails are equally exotic; a jug of quirky Agua Borabora – mango, kiwi, rose, vodka and champagne for two – will set you back €14.

### Bar Ourcq
*68 quai de la Loire, 19th (01.42.40.12.26). M° Laumière.* **Open** *Winter* 5pm-midnight Wed, Thur, Sun; 3pm-2am Fri, Sat. *Summer* 5-9.30pm Wed-Fri, Sun; 3pm-2am Sat. **No credit cards. Map** p403 N1 **52**
The Ourcq is set along a canal embankment broad enough to accommodate *pétanque* games (ask at the bar) and a cluster of deckchairs. It's a completely different scene from the crowded bustle along Canal St-Martin: more discerning and less self-satisfied. The cabin-like interior has a cosy raised area at the back and has recently become smoke-free. Drinks are listed in a hit parade of prices, starting with €2 for a *demi* or glass of red wine, €3 for a Pelforth or Kir, and €4 for a lively Mojito. Pastas at €7, exhibitions and a regular DJ spot keep the cool clientele sated. Closed on rainy weekdays in summer.

### La Bellevilloise
*19 rue Boyer, 20th (01.46.36.07.07). M° Gambetta.* **Open** 6pm-1am Wed-Fri; 11am-2am; 11am-11pm. **Credit** V. **Map** p403 P4 **53**
The Bellevilloise is the latest incarnation of a space that once housed the capital's very first workers' co-operative. This vestige of Ménilmontant's political past multi-tasks as a bar, restaurant, club and exhibition space (*see p235* **12-bar booze**). It also has a charming terrace where you can enjoy some decent views of the *quartier* with your wine and tapas. The quality of food is variable – you're best off drinking from the fine range of cocktails at €7 or trying one of the exotic coffees. *Photos p232.*

## Café Charbon

*109 rue Oberkampf, 11th (01.43.57.55.13/www. nouveaucasino.net). M° Parmentier or Ménilmontant.* **Open** 9am-2am Mon-Thur, Sun; 9am-4am Fri, Sat. **Credit** MC, V. **Map** p403 N5 ❺❹

This beautifully restored belle époque building sparked the Oberkampf nightlife boom. Its booths, mirrors, chandeliers and adventurous music policy put trendy locals at ease, capturing the essence of café culture spanning each end of the 20th century. After 15 years or more, the formula still works, copied by scores of nearby bars. The management opened the equally popular Nouveau Casino nightclub next door (*see p329*) and has continued the empire-building with the groovified De la Ville Café (*see p223*) in the 10th.

## Café Chéri(e)

*44 bd de la Villette, 19th (01.42.02.02.05). M° Belleville.* **Open** 8am-2am daily. **Credit** MC, V. **Map** p403 M3 ❺❺

This splendid DJ bar (*see also p325*) has expanded its brief and its opening hours to become an all-day café – without watering down any of the funky chic that keeps it well ahead of the pack after dark. Large jars on the bar pack all kinds of punches, such as the €5 Chéri(e) of dark rum; fruit vodkas are another speciality. DJ nights are conceived with equal craft. The interior sparkles with wit and invention – note the marvellous mural alluding to the personal sacrifices made for a life of coupledom. There's a front terrace if you need conversational respite from the BPM.

## Le Café des Sports

*94 rue de Ménilmontant, 20th (01.46.36.07.07). M° Gambetta.* **Open** 9am-1.30am daily. Closed Aug. **Credit** MC, V. **Map** p403 P4 ❺❻

The recent inundation of the rue Boyer by excellent bars has upped the ante. In order to compete, Le Café des Sports has a fine and consistently eclectic music programme: Saturdays are dedicated to electro, Tuesdays to pop or *chanson*, and Thursdays to world dub. Beer and wine are fabulously cheap (€1.50 from 6 to 8pm). Unlike its sprawling neighbours, Le Café des Sports has just one room to call home. DJs play in the space around the back, and the bar – which is central to the operation – takes pride of place amongst the bright yellow tables.

## Chez Prune

*36 rue Beaurepaire, 10th (01.42.41.30.47). M° Jacques Bonsergent.* **Open** 8am-2am Mon-Sat; 10am-2am Sun. **Credit** AmEx, MC,V. **Map** p402 L4 ❺❼

Chez Prune is still one of the best places to spend an evening along the Canal St-Martin. The local bourgeois-bohemian HQ, this traditional café, with high ceilings and low lighting, sticks to a simple formula: groups of friends crowd around the cosily ordered banquettes, picking at moderately priced cheese or meat platters. Mostly, though, they come for a few leisurely drinks or an *apéro* before heading on to one of the late night venues around the canal.

## Le Cinquante

*50 rue de Lancry, 10th (01.42.02.36.83). M° Jacques Bonsergent.* **Open** Sept-July 5.30pm-2am daily. *Aug* 5.30pm-2am Tue-Sun. **No credit cards**. **Map** p402 L4 ❺❽

Spunky little place, this, just down from the Canal St-Martin. Bare brick, formica and framed '50s ads form the decor, although ambience comes with the inner circle of regulars: boho types in on the scene. These days it's established enough to produce its own T-shirts and customised bar stools. Reasonable

prices – 50cl pitchers of sauvignon, Brouilly and Chablis in the €10 range, or by the glass – attract a mixed bag of tastes and generations. The two rooms behind the main bar are set aside for dining (affordable classics) and performances (generally acoustic). Last orders are at 1.20am – no arguments there, then.

## La Flèche d'Or

*102bis rue de Bagnolet, 20th (01.44.64.01.02/ www.flechedor.fr). M° Alexandre Dumas or Gambetta.* **Open** 8pm-2am Mon-Thur, Sun; 8pm-6am Fri, Sat. **Credit** MC, V. **Map** p407 Q6 **❺❾**

The Flèche, housed in a disused station hall, straddles the abandoned *petite ceinture* railway that encircles Paris. Closer in style to urban venues in Berlin and New York, it welcomes indie or electro acts every night, with free admission. You can get yourself a €5 *demi* from the bar that snakes its way around the centre, or a €14.50 cheeseburger from the restaurant – which has brilliant views of the afore-mentioned railway, not to mention a Greek god suspended overhead.

## La Gouttière

*96 av Parmentier, 11th (01.43.55.46.42). M° Parmentier.* **Open** 8am-2am Mon-Fri; 3pm-2am Sat. **Credit** V. **Map** p403 M4 **❻⓿**

Far enough (five minutes) from rue Oberkampf to feel off the beaten track, the Gutter is not out and out libertine, but you're on the right lines. Certainly, a come-what-may approach to music, drinking and eye contact abounds, in a crowded room. Inside, assuming you can see it, decor consists of a few LP covers and the kind of colour scheme often put to good use in adventure playgrounds. Reasonably priced lunches and animated seduction techniques complete the picture.

## L'Ile Enchantée

*65 bd de la Villette, 10th (01.42.01.67.99). M° Colonel Fabien.* **Open** 8am-2am Mon-Fri; 5pm-2am Sat. **Credit** MC, V. **Map** p403 M3 **❻❶**

The latest DJ bar on the burgeoning scene north-west of Belleville, the Enchanted Island's minimal house/electro sounds allow the focus to stay firmly on conversation. The high ceilings and French windows let in acres of Belleville skyline, and the studded banquettes add to the chic but retro vibe. The wine list is formidable and sturdy cocktails come in at €6.50 a hit. A slightly older crowd ensures a buzz without any need to be the next best thing in town.

## Le Mange Disque

*58 rue de la Fontaine, 11th (01.58.30.87.07). M° Goncourt.* **Open** 5pm-2am Tue-Sat. Closed Aug. **No credit cards**. **Map** p403 M4 **❻❷**

This remarkably cool bar shows just what you can do with a little art, a fine taste in music, the most mundane of furniture and the right connections. If you want to launch a CD, introduce a DJ or simply imbue your bash with cool, then do it here. There are other factors, of course. Savvy owner Hubert has brought in choice wines from little-known producers in south-west France but only charges €2-€3 a glass for them. Likewise, the smallish snacks cost under €10. Stacks of vinyl are left out for browsing and with the constant traffic of events and launches, no two evenings are the same. A good name to drop.

## Le Maroquinerie

*23 rue Boyer, 20th (01.40.33.35.05). M° Gambetta.* **Open** 6pm-2am daily. Closed Aug. **Credit** MC, V. **Map** p403 P4 **❻❸**

La Maroquinerie's former life as a leather factory is little in evidence these days. Transformed into a bright café and bar, it also hosts the occasional

**La Bellevilloise.** *See p231.*

literary debate and live act (*see p235* **12-bar booze**). You can eat your way through a reasonably priced menu or sip a €3 glass of wine from a list sourced from across France. This neat little café – all exposed brick and enamel posters drilled into the walls – is a particularly atmospheric spot.

## La Mercerie
*98 rue Oberkampf, 11th (01.43.38.81.30). M°  Parmentier.* **Open** 7pm-2am daily. **Credit** MC, V. **Map** p403 N5 🄬
Opposite the landmark Charbon (*see p232*) and infinitely more grungy, the spacious Mercerie features bare walls – bare everything, in fact – allowing room for the usual Oberkampf shenanigans of death-wish drinking against a loud, eclectic musical backdrop. A DJ programme is lipsticked on to the back-bar mirror. Happy hour stretches to 9pm, so you can cane the house vodkas (apricot, mango, honey) and still have enough euros to finish the job after dusk. The back area, with its tea lights, provides intimacy if that's where your evening's headed.

## Mon Chien Stupide
*1 rue Boyer, 20th (01.46.36.25.49). M° Gambetta.* **Open** 6pm-2am Tue-Sun. **Credit** MC, V. **Map** p403 P4 🄬
As the action moves relentlessly eastwards from Oberkampf, the once-distant outposts of Gambetta and Bagnolet appear on the radar of the discerning bar-hopper. Colourful and humorous, a bar for grown-ups rather than the kids' hangouts the other side of rue Sorbier, My Stupid Dog calls itself (with some justification) a 'Bar Expo': the portraits of black musicians are striking, while the swirling lightshades unusual and the strings of pretty lights a talking point. An undercurrent of jazzy sounds drifts along nicely. Commendably unsympathetic to canines – note the 'Dog Paste' sign by the bar. *Photo p236.*

## L'Ogre à Plumes
*49-51 rue Jean-Pierre-Timbaud, 11th (01.48.06.64.39). M° Parmentier.* **Open** noon-3pm; 6pm-2am Tue-Sun. Closed Aug. **Credit** MC, V. **Map** p403 M4 🄬
A café and bar which calls itself a 'space for creation', the Ogre welcomes spoken-word artists, authors and playwrights to address its public in a cosy little downstairs den, comprising a stage and a few rows of red velvet cinema seats. Diners in the cosy café upstairs can enjoy simple pickings (a *plat du soir* can be had for €12) and perhaps the occasional rendition by the staff of a verse or two from Rimbaud or Baudelaire.

## Le Panier
*32 rue Ste-Marthe, 10th (01.42.01.38.18). M° Belleville.* **Open** 10am-2am daily. **No credit cards.** **Map** p403 M3 🄬
The cobbled rue Ste-Marthe buzzes with the energy of ateliers, restaurants and bars. Le Panier enjoys a prominent position on a blissfully shaded square and has at its centre a vast terrace. So much space is a rarity in Paris, and this is a choice spot

in summer. The food (served all day) is hit or miss, and service can be as relaxed as the atmosphere. Best just to opt for a cheese plate and a glass of wine.

## Au Passage
*1bis passage St-Sébastien, 11th (01.43.55.07.52). M° St-Sébastien Froissart.* **Open** 9am-11pm daily. **Credit** MC, V. **Map** p409 M5 🄬
A strange find, this, tucked down a long, narrow alleyway off rue Amelot, opposite the back entrance of Pop In – look out for the green Stella sign. Inside is red and black and Bohemian all over. Artists cluster around the corner bar, passing over the €2 bottles of Tsingtao beer for glasses of teeth-staining *vin rouge*, perhaps dipping into a plate of meat or cheese nibbles (€5/€8). There's art on the far wall, some retro cookbooks and a feeling that entire decades could pass without anyone really noticing.

## Au P'tit Garage
*63 rue Jean-Pierre-Timbaud, 11th (01.48.07.08.12). M° Parmentier.* **Open** 6pm-2am daily. **Credit** AmEx, MC, V. **Map** p403 M4 🄬
As sweetly tuned as Chuck Berry's cherry-red '53, this quite marvellous rock 'n' roll bar is the pick of the bunch on rue J-P-T. Not that the owners have fitted it with Americana or waitresses on roller-skates; the L'il Garage is as basic as the real car-fit business a few doors down the road. The stuffing bursts out of some of the bar stools and skip-salvage chairs accompany wobbly tables of ill-matched colours. Regulars cluster around the twin decks at the bar, while music-savvy Frenchettes giggle and gossip at the back, dancing and downing drinks with equal enthusiasm.

## Le Phénix
*18 rue des Panoyaux, 20th (no phone). M° Ménilmontant.* **Open** noon-1am daily. **No credit cards.** **Map** p403 P5 🄬
Of the cluster of bars near the junction of Panoyaux and Ménilmontant, this is the brightest and wittiest, with a neat back garden to boot. The main front bar area, beneath a ceiling of erotic tiles, is dominated by a table football over which a scarf exclaims: 'FC Ferraille – Death To The Referee'. Belgian Maes runs at an affordable €2 a *demi*, while McEwan's is a baffling €3. Shouldn't someone tell them?

## Le Pure Café
*14 rue Jean-Macé, 11th (01.43.71.47.22). M° Ledru-Rollin.* **Open** 7.30am-2am daily. **Credit** MC, V. **Map** p407 N7 🄬
A place that should satisfy film buffs and foodies, Le Pure Café was the setting for a rendez-vous between Julie Delpy and Ethan Hawke in the movie *Before Sunset*. Trivia aside, it's a local favourite; the bright interior is a world away from the sombre style of some traditional bistros, and it manages to revive traditional food equally well by using quality ingredients assembled with a twist. A main course will set you back around €18, a glass of wine €4.

# 12-bar booze

Up the hill from métro Ménilmontant, too steep for the drunken hordes of Oberkampf to ever make it, is a village of music and bonhomie that could just make your Paris night to remember. **Studio de l'Ermitage** (8 rue de l'Ermitage, 20th, 01.44.63.03.86) is a live music and dancing venue hidden behind a graffitied industrial exterior. Its eclectic programming includes the cult once-a-month Cumbia Ya!, where a Columbian 8-piece band electrifies a dance-crazy crowd (this is nothing like the salsa, and you don't need to know any steps, just let rip). Down some steep steps from here you reach **Les 3 Châpeaux** (48 rue des Cascades, 20th, 01.46.36.90.06, www.les3chapeaux.com), a tagine and couscous restaurant where local personality Makhtouf invites live talent every night of the week (except Mondays and Tuesdays). The music might be anything from Polish gypsy to French reggae and rock, with members of the audience often getting up to jam and the whole room dancing by the end of the evening. The *chapeau* goes round for the musicians three times a night.

If you cross rue de Ménilmontant you'll reach rue Boyer, where you'll find the well-established **La Maroquinerie** (*see p233*) with indie rock, *chanson* and world music acts, and a 'literary café' that hosts intellectual debates. With the Momboye African dance school and an Afro-Cuban arts association on the same street, Boyer's got rhythm. Newcomer **La Bellevilloise** (*see p231*) proved a real hit in the summer of 2007, with its delicious roof terrace bar and Latin-inspired cocktails, not to mention its glass-roofed bar-restaurant – complete with olive trees growing inside – a popular brunch rendezvous. Cocktail hour music in the restaurant is free, while the downstairs concert venue hosts a varied programme of world music.

If electronic music is more your scene, on the corner of rues Boyer and de Ménilmontant the trad working-class **Café des Sports** (*see p232*) has become a trend-setter to rival La Perle in the Marais, attracting a hip crowd to groove on its tiny dance floor during free DJ sessions most nights of the week. Afterwards you can cool off in the bar of **Le Colimaçon** restaurant opposite (107 rue de Ménilmontant, 20th, 01.40.33.10.40), where guitars are often propped, and sometimes played, in a friendly neighbourhood atmosphere.

## Le Verre Volé

*67 rue de Lancry, 10th (01.48.03.17.34)* $M^o$ *Jacques Bonsergent.* **Open** 10.30am-2.30pm, 7pm-2am Tue-Sun. Closed Aug. **Credit** MC, V. **Map** p402 L4 ⑫

Twice a day this *cave à vins* doubles up as a wine bar and eatery. Diners sit around a handful of battered old tables and sample vintages described to them with any number of sparkling adjectives. Although the wine (which comes at around €4 per glass) is the focus at Le Verre Volé, you are obliged to eat – which is no bad thing, since a hearty Toulouse sausage and mash will set you back an altogether humble €11.50. Purists who would prefer a simple snack to complement their *bon vin* should opt for a plate of charcuterie and cheese at €11. The small dimensions, chatter and slightly hyperactive service give the place an energy that is charming, though some people might find it a little boisterous.

## The Latin Quarter

### Le Crocodile

*6 rue Royer-Collard, 5th (01.43.54.32.37). RER Luxembourg.* **Open** 10pm-late Mon-Sat. Closed Aug. **Credit** MC, V. **Map** p408 J8 ⑬

Ignore the apparently boarded-up windows at Le Crocodile – if you're here late, it's open. Young friendly regulars line the sides of this small, narrow bar and try to decide on a drink: not easy, given the length and complexity of the cocktail list. At last count there were 311 choices (the number increases on a yearly basis), each one more potent than the last. Pen and paper are provided to note your decision; the pen comes in handy for point-and-choose decisions when it all gets hazy. Given the €6-per-cocktail happy hour (Mon-Thur before midnight; €9 other times), this can be rather soon. We think we can recommend an *accroche-coeur*, a supremely '70s mix of champagne and Goldschläger, served with extra gold leaf; after that, we had to start pointing.

### Le Pantalon

*7 rue Royer-Collard, 5th (no phone). RER Luxembourg.* **Open** 5.30pm-2am Mon-Sat. **No credit cards. Map** p408 J8 ⑭

Le Pantalon is a local café that seems familiar yet is utterly surreal. It has the standard fixtures and fittings, including the old soaks at the bar – plus a strange vacuum-cleaner sculpture, disco-light toilets and the world's most prosaic proposal of marriage. Offbeat decor aside, the regulars and staff are enough to tip the balance firmly into eccentricity.

**Eat, Drink, Shop**

Friendly and very funny French grown-ups and foreign students chat in a mishmash of languages; drinks are always cheap enough to make you tipsy without the worry of a cash-crisis hangover.

## Pop Corner

*16 rue des Bernadins, 5th (01.44.07.12.47). M°
Maubert-Mutualité.* **Open** 6pm-2am Tue-Thur; 6pm-4am Fri, Sat. **Credit** MC, V. **Map** p406 K7 **75**
A smoky and successful marriage of music bar and Brit pub, set between St-Germain and the river. The clientele is a mix of with-it young professional Parisiennes and anglophone expats unloosening their ties – post-work, pre-shag stuff (there's even a bed in the corner). Abstract art on bare brick and €5 Poptions Magiques cocktails (Indi Pop: vodka and honey) add alternative touches – but both sexes are here to sink pints and peruse the possibilities.

# St-Germain-des-Prés & Odéon

## Le Bar

*27 rue de Condé, 6th (01.43.29.06.61). M° Odéon.*
**Open** 8pm-late Mon-Sat. **No credit cards.**
**Map** p408 H7 **76**
Le Bar is one of those places that you only ever visit when it's very, very late and you're very, very drunk. It'll all come back to you: it's almost completely pitch black, has a shrine-type affair at the back of the bar and gravel on the floor; and everyone talks in whispers – and the drinks are exceedingly strong. Once you've been here, you'll find yourself strangely drawn back at inappropriate times when you really should be going home to bed, and at least one member of the party is guaranteed to fall asleep on the comfy black leather banquettes. There's a strange echo effect in the corridor leading down to the toilet, so if Le Bar is your last chance to pull before the sun comes up, don't discuss your strategy too loudly.

## Le Bar Dix

*10 rue de l'Odéon, 6th (01.43.26.66.83). M° Odéon.*
**Open** 6pm-2am daily. **No credit cards.** **Map**
p408 H7 **77**
It's been here forever, this homely cavern of a bar. Generations of students have glugged back jugs of the celebrated home-made sangría while squeezed into the cramped upper bar, tattily authentic with its Jacques Brel record sleeves, Yves Montand handbills and pre-war light fittings. The jukebox sadly no longer runs on vinyl, but the CDs weep suitably nostalgic pop nectar. Spelunkers and hopeless romantics negotiate the hazardous stone staircase to drink in the cellar bar, with its candlelight and century-old advertising murals. Can someone please come and slap a preservation order on the place?

## Le Bar du Marché

*75 rue de Seine, 6th (01.43.26.55.15). M° Mabillon
or Odéon.* **Open** 8am-2am daily. **Credit** MC, V.
**Map** p408 H7 **78**

The market in question is the Cours des Halles, the bar a convivial corner café opening out on to a pleasing bustle of St-Germain-des-Prés. It's all wonderfully simple, with easy dishes like a ham omelette or a plate of herring in the €7 range, half-decent Brouilly or muscadet at €4-€5 a glass, a few retro posters – Campari, Piaf, the Frères Jacques – and the regular passing of a beret-topped waiter. It couldn't be anywhere else in the world. Locals easily outnumber tourists, confirming Rod Stewart's unusually astute observation that Paris gives the impression that no one is ever working. Recommended.

## Café de Flore

*172 bd St-Germain, 6th (01.45.48.55.26/www.cafe-de-flore.com). M° St-Germain-des-Prés.* **Open** 7.30am-1.30am daily. **Credit** AmEx, DC, MC, V.
**Map** p408 H7 **79**
Bourgeois locals crowd the terrace tables at lunch, eating club sandwiches with knives and forks, as anxious waiters frown at couples with pushchairs or single diners occupying tables for four. This historic café, former HQ of the Lost Generation intelligentsia, attracts tourists, and, yes, celebs have been known to alight here from time to time. But a *café crème* is €4.60, a Perrier €5 and the omelettes and *croque-monsieurs* are best passed over for better dishes on the menu (€15-€25). Upstairs, play readings are held on Mondays and philosophy discussions on the first Wednesday of the month, both at 8pm, in English.

## Chez Georges

*11 rue des Canettes, 6th (01.43.26.79.15). M° Mabillon.* **Open** noon-2am Tue-Sat. Closed Aug.
**Credit** MC, V. **Map** p408 H7 **80**
Belonging to a dying breed of *cave-bars* associated with the Latin Quarter, Chez Georges is beloved of students, professionals and neighbourhood eccentrics alike. Regulars pass by during the day to

sip wine over a game of chess or sink an *apéro* come early evening. At night, the *cave* fills up with people dancing to *chanson*, pop classics and even the odd Bar Mitzvah track. The tropical heat generated is mascara-melting, and it's not for the claustrophobic.

### Les Deux Magots

*6 pl St Germain-des-Prés, 6th (01.45.48.55.25/ www.lesdeuxmagots.com). M° St-Germain-des-Prés.* **Open** 7.30am-1am daily. Closed 1wk Jan. **Credit** AmEx, DC, MC, V. **Map** p408 H7 ③

If you stand outside Les Deux Magots you've got to be prepared to photograph tourists wanting proof of their encounter with French philosophy. The former haunt of Sartre, de Beauvoir et al now draws a less pensive crowd that can be all too '*m'as-tu vu*', particularly on weekends. The hot chocolate is still good (and the only item served in generous portions) – but, like everything else, it's pricey. Visit on a weekday afternoon when the editors return, manuscripts in hand, to the inside tables, leaving enough elbow room to engage in some serious discussion.

### Les Editeurs

*4 carrefour de l'Odéon, 6th (01.43.26.67.76). M° Odéon.* **Open** 8am-2am daily. **Credit** AmEx, MC, V. **Map** p408 H7 ③

It's no surprise to see row upon row of books in the bright, modern interior of Les Editeurs. A café with literary leanings, it sits on the lovely carrefour de l'Odéon, a crossroads that leads to the Luxembourg gardens. Bask in the glory of literary greats, as portraits of authors and their editors look down on you. Breakfast is extremely good value at €12; in the evening, main courses come in at €18.

### La Palette

*43 rue de Seine, 6th (01.43.26.68.15). M° Odéon.* **Open** 9am-2am Mon-Sat. Closed Aug. **Credit** MC, V. **Map** p408 H6 ③

La Palette is the café-bar of choice for the very beau Beaux-Arts students who study at the venerable institution around the corner. Its prime location and majestic bar have attracted such luminaries as Jim Morrison, Picasso and, predictably perhaps, Ernest Hemingway. With such an illustrious heritage, La Palette certainly has personality. The back room, which is decorated with wonderfully preserved art-deco illustrations, is usually packed. Or you can get a Chablis for €6 or a *demi* at €4.50 and grab a spot on the leafy terrace – but again, be prepared for formidable competition for seats. The staff can be warm or grumpy, but are mostly just entertaining.

### Au Petit Suisse

*16 rue de Vaugirard, 6th (01.43.26.03.81). M° Odéon.* **Open** 7am-midnight Mon-Sat; 7am-10.30pm Sun. **Credit** DC, MC, V. **Map** p408 H7 ③

Named after Marie de Médicis' Swiss Guards, the compact Au Petit Suisse has an enviable location next to the Jardin du Luxembourg and so pulls in a range of posh locals, harassed au pairs and Gauloise-puffing Sorbonne students. The formal waiters excel in French snottiness, but at least it's authentic and blissfully tourist-free. Brave the haughty stares for one of the handful of tables, order a kir with a side of sneer and lap up a genuine sixth arrondissement café experience.

### Le Rostand

*6 pl Edmond-Rostand, 6th (01.43.54.61.58). RER Luxembourg.* **Open** 8am-2am daily. **Credit** MC, V. **Map** p408 H6 ③

Le Rostand has a truly wonderful view of the Jardin du Luxembourg from its classy interior, decked out with oriental paintings, a long mahogany bar and wall-length mirrors. It's a terribly well-behaved place – consider arriving draped in furs or sporting the latest designer eyewear if you want to fit in with the

**Mon Chien Stupide.** *See p234.*

**Eat, Drink, Shop**

well-heeled clientele. Whiskies and cocktails are pricey, but not as steep as the brasserie menu. Perfect for a civilised drink after a spin round the gardens.

## Montparnasse

### Le Select

*99 bd du Montparnasse, 6th (01.42.22.65.27). M°* *Vavin.* **Open** 7am-2am Mon-Thur, Sun; 7am-4am Fri, Sat. **Credit** MC, V. **Map** p405 G8 ⑧⑥
For a decade between the wars, the junction of boulevards Raspail and du Montparnasse was where Man Ray, Cocteau and Lost Generation Americans hung out in the vast glass-fronted cafés. Eight decades on, Le Select is the best of these inevitable tourist haunts. Sure, its pricey menu is big on historical detail and short on authenticity, but by and large Le Select manages to hold on to its heyday with dignity.

### Le Tournesol

*9 rue de la Gaîté, 14th (01.43.27.65.72). M° Gaîté.* **Open** 8.30am-1.30am Mon-Sat; 9.30am-1.30am Sun. **Credit** AmEx, MC, V. **Map** p405 F9 ⑧⑦
Off the beaten track, the Tournesol is young and vibrant. There is outdoor seating in the shadow of the Tour Montparnasse and an exposed brick interior, with a soul, funk and electro soundtrack. A *croque-monsieur* will set you back €5.40, a steak €10.50 and a *demi* of Stella €2.70. A well organised back space is presided over by an abstract tableau and leaves plenty of seating for groups.

## The 7th & western Paris

### Le Café du Marché

*38 rue Cler, 7th (01.47.05.51.27). M° Ecole Militaire.* **Open** 7am-midnight Mon-Sat; 7am-5pm Sun. **Credit** MC, V. **Map** p405 D6 ⑧⑧
This well-loved address is frequented by trendy locals, shoppers hunting down a particular type of cheese and tourists who've managed to make it this far from the Eiffel Tower. Le Café du Marché really is a hub of neighbourhood activity. Its *pichets* of decent house plonk go down a treat, and mention must be made of the food – such as the huge house salad featuring lashings of foie gras and Parma ham.

### Café Thoumieux

*4 rue de la Comète, 7th (01.45.51.50.40/www.* *thoumieux.com). M° La Tour Maubourg.* **Open** noon-2am Mon-Fri; 5pm-2am Sat. Closed 3wks Aug. **Credit** AmEx, MC, V. **Map** p405 E6 ⑧⑨
Café Thoumieux is a laid-back destination for cocktails, tapas or big-screen sport. Banquettes snake around the room and spiky Aztec-pattern lamps light up the faces of the pretty young locals who have made this place their own. The flavoured vodkas are delicious and include vanilla, caramel and banana; just watch out for the treacherous, extra-high bar stools (the banquettes are definitely the safest option) and the monstrous, pebble-dashed sink in the toilets – it's real.

**Le Rostand** – the perfect spot for a drink after a trip to the Jardin du Luxembourg. *See p237.*

Eat, Drink, Shop

# Shops & Services

Pick your shopping area, then splurge.

In an increasingly globalised world, Paris still hangs on to the pleasure of shopping in small boutiques. Even though its department stores stock big name brands, they bear little resemblance to the shining temples of luxury that are found in London or New York. This is all because Parisians love to swish through the golden doors of high-end brands on Avenue Montaigne (8th), to be seated while being served in the shoe shops of rue de Grenelle (7th), and to seek out original pieces in the growing number of concept stores and multi-label boutiques, where an expert buyer's eye has already sorted the wheat from the chaff. Except in chain stores, which are the same the world over, you are still expected to say 'bonjour madame' when you enter a store; this ice-breaker opens the door to a more personalised form of shopping which is far more enjoyable than simply browsing the racks.

Paris has five key fashion shopping areas. Avenue Montaigne is still the bastion of the big names in couture, with Dior, Prada, Dolce & Gabbana and the LVMH headquarters, but the **Golden Triangle** around the Champs-Elysées now also features multi-label store Montaigne Market, and more youthful fashion in the form of Paul & Joe, Chrome Hearts jewellery and Zadig & Voltaire De Luxe, as well as Louis Vuitton's new concept store with its 'bag bar' and video art.

Paul Smith's new store and Roberto Cavalli's flagship have injected new life into the luxury heartland of **rue du Fbg-St-Honoré**, while Miu Miu, Manoush and Paule Ka have moved in to be near Colette on **rue St-Honoré**, whose fashion vibe runs all the way to the Palais Royal, where the twin American beacons of Marc Jacobs and Rick Owens have made the hallowed cloisters hip.

On the Left Bank, the Bon Marché department store is the apex of **St-Germain**'s shopping area, where you'll find all the top-end French and international names, including Yves Saint Laurent and Sonya Rykiel, as well as smaller fashion houses. Rue du Four has seen a cluster of new openings, rue de Seine has a concentration of gorgeous lingerie shops, and rue de Grenelle is the place for shoes and bags.

Urban and streetwear is concentrated around **rue Etienne Marcel**, near the fashion manufacturing district of the Sentier where

Going up: **Le Bon Marché**. *See p240.*

porters pushing rolls of fabric and wheeling cellophane-wrapped garments still stop traffic.

The **Marais** continues to surprise and delight. Away from the established rue des Rosiers, where L'Eclaireur's stores draw fashionistas, the rue Charlot area, dubbed 'haut Marais' (*see p249* **Marais à la mode**), is the hippest place in which to shop, and has also attracted a cluster of superlative vintage shops. More quirky, small-label design can be found around Abbesses métro (18th) or near Canal St-Martin (10th).

Family-run food shops have thankfully not been eroded by supermarket culture, and tend to cluster in 'market streets' such as rue des Martyrs and rue Mouffetard, as well as around the many covered and open-air food markets (*see p261* **Market forces**). Here everything from a vintage bottle of armagnac to a single praline chocolate is lovingly served, wrapped and presented. Informed discussion is still very much part of the purchasing process, and the beautiful, old-style shops, unchanged for decades, add to the pleasure.

Different areas have different specialities (*see p266* **Shopping by area**). There are clusters of antiques shops in the seventh arrondissement and second-hand and rare book outlets in the fifth; crystal and porcelain manufacturers still dot rue de Paradis in the tenth; furniture craftsmen as well as children's clothes shops inhabit rue du Fbg-St-Antoine; bikes and cameras are clustered on boulevard Beaumarchais; and the world's top jewellers can be found on place Vendôme. The historic covered passages in the second and ninth are also fun to shop in, where chic contemporary stores like cosmetics line By Terry are mixed in with philatelists and booksellers.

Finally, no shopping trip to the capital would be complete without a visit to a flea market (*see p271* **Bargain hunt**), where haggling is still de rigueur and cash is the payment of choice.

### SALES AND OPENING HOURS

Shops are generally open from 10am to 7pm Monday to Saturday, with specialist boutiques closing for an hour at lunch. Some are closed on Monday mornings. Sunday opening is found in the Marais, on the Champs-Elysées, at Bercy Village and in the Carrousel du Louvre. Many shops on the Champs-Elysées stay open till midnight, and Thursday is late-night closing at department stores. Small corner grocery stores open late for essentials. Many family-run concerns close in August. Twice a year, in January and July, boutiques sell off seasonal stock at reduced prices to make way for incoming collections. The nationwide dates for the sales (*soldes*) are imposed by the state-run consumer office; call 01.40.27.16.00 for more details.

# General

## Department stores

The revamped *grands magasins* have brought in trendy designers and luxury spaces in a concerted attempt to lure shoppers away from independent boutiques.

### BHV (Bazar de l'Hôtel de Ville)

*52-64 rue de Rivoli, 4th (01.42.74.90.00/ DIY hire 01.42.74.97.23/www.bhv.fr). M° Hôtel de Ville.* **Open** 9.30am-7.30pm Mon, Tue, Thur-Sat; 9.30am-9pm Wed. **Credit** AmEx, MC, V. **Map** p406 J6.

Hardware heaven: there's even a Bricolage Café with internet access. Upper floors have a good range of men's outdoor wear, upmarket bed linen, toys, books, household appliances – and a large space devoted to every type of storage utility.

Printemps.

### Le Bon Marché

*24 rue de Sèvres, 7th (01.44.39.80.00/www. bonmarche.fr). M° Sèvres Babylone.* **Open** 9.30am-7pm Mon-Wed, Fri; 10am-9pm Thur; 9.30am-8pm Sat. **Credit** AmEx, DC, MC, V. **Map** p405 G7.

The city's oldest department store, opened in 1848, is also its most swish and user-friendly, thanks to an extensive redesign by LVMH. Luxury boutiques, Dior and Chanel among them, take pride of place on the ground floor; escalators designed by Andrée Putman take you up to the fashion floor, which has an excellent selection of global designer labels, from Lanvin to APC. Designer names also abound in Balthazar, the prestigious men's section, while VIP services include personal shopping stylists for men and women. The adjoining Grande Epicerie food hall (01.44.39.81.00, www.lagrandeepicerie.fr, 8.30am-9pm Mon-Sat) has a café and restaurant. *Photo p239.*

### Galeries Lafayette

*40 bd Haussmann, 9th (01.42.82.34.56/ fashion shows 01.42.82.30.25/fashion advice 01.42.82.35.50/www.galerieslafayette.com). M° Chaussée d'Antin/RER Auber.* **Open** 9.30am-7.30pm Mon-Wed, Fri, Sat; 9.30am-9pm Thur. **Credit** AmEx, DC, MC, V. **Map** p401 H3.

The store has revamped its fashion, beauty and accessories sections and, in hot competition with Printemps (*see p241*), opened a third-floor lingerie department. More than 90 designers are represented on the first and second floors, including Cavalli, Lacroix and Givenchy. There are five fashion and beauty consultants to guide you through the sartorial maze, and the men's fashion space on the third floor, Lafayette Homme, has natty designer corners and a 'Club' area with internet access. On the first

floor, Lafayette Gourmet has exotic foods galore, and a vast wine cellar. The domed ceiling is eminently photogenic, and there's a rooftop café. Over the road, Lafayette Maison (www.lafayettemaison.com) offers five floors of design for the home.
**Other locations** Centre Commercial Montparnasse, 14 rue du Départ, 14th (01.45.38.52.87).

### Printemps

*64 bd Haussmann, 9th (01.42.82.50.00/www.*
*printemps.com). M° Havre Caumartin/RER*
*Auber.* **Open** 9.35am-7pm Mon-Wed, Fri, Sat;
9.35am-10pm Thur. **Credit** AmEx, DC, MC, V.
**Map** p401 G3.

Printemps is the home of superlatives: its shoe department (on the fifth floor of Printemps de la Mode) and beauty department are the largest in the world, the latter stocking some 200 brands. The lingerie department is the stuff of fantasy, with gorgeous smalls from Erès, Gaultier, Pucci and the like. In all, there are six floors of fashion in the men's and women's stores. On the second floor of Printemps de la Mode, French designers APC and Zadig et Voltaire sit side by side with Moschino and Dolce & Gabbana; Miss Code, on the fifth floor, targets the teens. Along with furnishings, Printemps de la Maison contains the more conceptual 'function floor', with saucepans and coffee machines neatly organised on steel shelving. The ninth-floor terrace restaurant sports an art nouveau cupola.

### Tati

*4 bd de Rochechouart, 18th (01.55.29.52.50/*
*www.tati.fr). M° Barbès Rochechouart.* **Open**
10am-7pm Mon-Sat. **Credit** MC, V. **Map** p402 J2.
Expect to find anything from T-shirts to wedding dresses, as well as bargain children's clothes and household goods at this discount heaven. It's unbeatably cheap, but don't expect high quality.
**Other locations** throughout the city.

## Shopping malls

### Bercy Village

*Cour St Emilion, 12th (www.bercyvillage.com).*
*M° Cour St Emilion.* **Open** 11am-9pm daily.
**Credit** AmEx, DC, MC, V. **Map** p407 P10.
A shopping and leisure development housed in old wine warehouses, Bercy is a relaxed place to shop in, with the advantage of late and Sunday opening. Squarely aimed at tourists and out-of-towners, the shops include Agnès b, Nature et Découvertes and a Fnac for children, Andaska and Pacific Adventure sports shops, L'Occitane, Oliviers & Co and Résonances for gifts, and Omnisens spa and Sephora for beauty. There are cafés, restaurants, a park and cinema complex.

### Drugstore Publicis

*133 av des Champs-Elysées, 8th (01.44.43.79.00/*
*www.publicisdrugstore.com). M° Charles de Gaulle*
*Etoile.* **Open** 8am-2am Mon-Fri; 10am-2am Sat, Sun.
**Credit** MC, V. **Map** p400 D4.

A 1960s legend, Drugstore Publicis has been clad with neon swirls by architect Michele Saee following a long renovation in 2004; a glass-and-steel café oozes on to the pavement. On the ground floor there's a newsagent, pharmacy, bookshop and upmarket deli full of quality olive oils and elegant biscuits; a video screen reminds you that Publicis is an advertising agency. The basement is a macho take on Colette (*see p250*), keeping selected design items and lifestyle mags, but replacing high fashion with wines and a cigar cellar.

### La Galerie du Carrousel du Louvre

*99 rue de Rivoli, 1st (01.43.16.47.10/www.*
*lecarrouseldulouvre.com). M° Palais Royal Musée*
*du Louvre.* **Open** 10am-8pm daily. **Credit** AmEx,
MC, V. **Map** p406 J6.
This massive underground centre – open every day of the year – is home to more than 35 shops, mostly big-name chains vying for your attention and cash. The Petit Prince boutique and Réunion des Musées Nationaux shops are great for last-minute gifts.

# Specialist

## Books & magazines

### Artazart

*83 quai de Valmy, 10th (01.40.40.24.00/www.*
*artazart.com). M° Jacques Bonsergent.* **Open**
10.30am-7.30pm Mon-Fri; 2-8pm Sat, Sun. **Credit**
AmEx, MC, V. **Map** p402 L4.
A bright yellow beacon on trendy Canal St-Martin, this bookshop and gallery stocks cutting-edge publications on fashion, art, architecture and design.

### Assouline

*35 rue Bonaparte, 6th (01.43.29.23.20/www.*
*assoulinefrance.com). M° St-Germain-des-Prés.*
**Open** noon-7pm Mon; 10.30am-7.30pm Tue-Sat.
**Credit** AmEx, DC, MC, V. **Map** p408 H7.
The chic showcase for French publisher Assouline displays its gorgeous tomes on art, design and philosophy, along with exquisite stationary and candles scented with a smell of old books for biblio-fetishists.

### Bouquinistes

*Along the quais, especially quai de Montebello & quai*
*St-Michel, 5th. M° St-Michel.* **Open** times vary from
stall to stall, generally Tue-Sun. **No credit cards**.
**Map** p406 J7.
The green, open-air boxes along the *quais* are one of the city's oldest institutions. Most sell second-hand books – ignore the nasty postcards and rummage through boxes packed with ancient paperbacks for something Existential. Feel free to haggle.

### Brentano's

*37 av de l'Opéra, 2nd (01.42.61.52.50/www.*
*brentanos.fr). M° Opéra or Pyramides.* **Open** 10am-
7.30pm Mon-Sat. **Credit** (€45 minimum) AmEx,
DC; (€17 minimum) MC, V. **Map** p401 G4.

**Eat, Drink, Shop**

PRINTEMPS
DEPARTMENT STORE PARIS

CATCH THE FRENCH FASHION TOUCH

Publicis EtNous

# PRINTEMPS
**64, BOULEVARD HAUSSMANN - 75009 PARIS**
**OPEN MONDAY TO SATURDAY FROM 9:35 AM TO 7 PM - THURSDAY UNTIL 10 PM**
**OUVERT DU LUNDI AU SAMEDI DE 9H35 À 19H - NOCTURNE LE JEUDI JUSQU'À 22H**
**WWW.PRINTEMPS.COM/INTERNATIONAL**

**GRAND MAGASIN PRINTEMPS - CAPTUREZ L'ESPRIT MODE DE PARIS**

Brentano's is good for American classics, modern fiction and bestsellers, plus business titles. The children's section is in the basement.

### Galignani
*224 rue de Rivoli, 1st (01.42.60.76.07). Mº Tuileries.* **Open** 10am-7pm Mon-Sat. **Credit** MC, V. **Map** p401 G5.
Opened in 1802, this was the first English-language bookshop in Europe. Today it stocks fine arts books, French and English literature, and magazines.

### Gibert Joseph
*26 bd St-Michel, 6th (01.44.41.88.88/www.gibert joseph.com). Mº St-Michel.* **Open** 10am-7.30pm Mon-Sat. **Credit** MC, V. **Map** p408 J7.
Formed back in 1929, this string of bookshops is normally packed out with students. Stationery, CDs, DVDs and art supply branches can be found further up the boulevard.
**Other locations** 30, 32 & 34 bd St-Michel, 6th.

### La Hune
*170 bd St-Germain, 6th (01.45.48.35.85). Mº St-Germain-des-Prés.* **Open** 10am-11.45pm Mon-Sat; 11am-7.45pm Sun. **Credit** AmEx, MC, V. **Map** p405 G7.
This Left Bank institution boasts a global selection of art and design books, and a magnificent collection of French literature and theory. *Photo p244.*

### Librairie Flammarion
*Centre Pompidou, 19 rue Beaubourg, 4th (01.44.78.43.22/www.flammarioncentre.com). Mº Rambuteau.* **Open** 11am-10pm Mon, Wed-Sun. Closed 2wks Sept. **Credit** AmEx, MC, V. **Map** p402 K5.
A pleasant place in which to peruse first-rate art, design, photography and cinema titles, this shop also stocks children's books, postcards (the post office next door is the quietest in town) and arty magazines.

### Librairie 7L
*7 rue de Lille, 7th (01.42.92.03.58). Mº Rue du Bac or Solférino.* **Open** 10.30am-7pm Tue-Sat. **Credit** AmEx, DC, MC, V. **Map** p405 G6.
Karl Lagerfeld's love of books gets street frontage in this shop, with fashion, art, design and poetry titles – and every magazine worth reading.

### Mode... Information
*22 rue Pierre-Lescot, 1st (01.40.13.81.50/www.modeinfo.com). Mº Etienne Marcel.* **Open** 9am-7pm Mon-Fri; 11am-6pm Sat. **Credit** AmEx, DC, MC, V. **Map** p402 J5.
A first for Paris, this specialised fashion bookshop allows members of the public access to all the trade secrets, with fashion and design tomes, look books, trend forecasting, Pantone cards and magazines.

### The Red Wheelbarrow
*22 rue St-Paul, 4th (01.48.04.75.08/www.thered wheelbarrow.com). Mº St Paul.* **Open** 10am-6pm Mon; 10am-7pm Tue-Sat; 2-6pm Sun. **Credit** MC, V. **Map** p407 L7.

Canadian Penelope Fletcher Le Masson and American Abigail Altman run this friendly literary bookshop in the Marais, which also has an excellent children's section.

## English-language

### Village Voice
*6 rue Princesse, 6th (01.46.33.36.47/www.village voicebookshop.com). Mº Mabillon.* **Open** 2-7.30pm Mon; 10am-7.30pm Tue-Sat; noon-6pm Sun. **Credit** AmEx, DC, MC, V. **Map** p405 H7.
New fiction, non-fiction and literary magazines in English, plus literary events and poetry readings.

### WH Smith
*248 rue de Rivoli, 1st (01.44.77.88.99/www.whsmith. fr). Mº Concorde.* **Open** 9am-7.30pm Mon-Sat; 1-7.30pm Sun. **Credit** AmEx, MC, V. **Map** p401 G5.
Some 70,000 English-language titles and a near impenetrable crush around the magazine section; the first floor has books, DVDs and audiobooks.

## Children

## Fashion
Children's fashion is clustered on rue Bréa (6th), rue Vavin (6th) and rue du Fbg-St-Antoine (12th). **Monoprix** (www.monoprix.fr) is a good source of inexpensive children's clothes, with some branches stocking Petit Bateau basics. For chic at a snip, try the **Bonpoint** (42 rue de l'Université, 7th, 01.40.20.10.55) and **Cacharel** (114 rue d'Alésia, 14th, 01.45.42.53.04) stock shops; it may be last season's stuff, but no-one is going to know?

### Bonton
*82 rue de Grenelle, 7th (01.44.39.09.20/www. bonton.fr). Mº Rue du Bac.* **Open** 10am-7pm Mon-Sat. Closed 2wks Aug. **Credit** AmEx, DC, MC, V. **Map** p405 F6.
At this concept store for kids and trendy parents, T-shirts and trousers come in rainbow colours, and at pretty steep prices. Furniture and accessories are also available, plus a children's hairdresser. Check out, too, the new Bonton Bazar store on rue du Bac, with cute kids' merchandise for every room in the house: bedroom, bathroom, kitchen and 'library'.
**Other locations** 122 rue du Bac, 7th (01.42.22.77.69); 118 rue Vielle-du-Temple, 3rd (01.42.72.34.69).

### Jacadi
*116 rue d'Alésia, 14th (01.40.44.51.87/www.jacadi. fr). Mº Alésia.* **Open** 11am-7pm Mon; 10am-7pm Tue-Sat. **Credit** MC, V.
Jacadi's well-made clothes for babies and children – pleated skirts, smocked dresses, dungarees and Fair Isle knits – are a hit with well-to-do parents. The rue d'Alésia store is the largest, and also stocks Véronique Delachaux's youthful maternity clothes.
**Other locations** throughout the city.

La Hune. *See p243.*

### Du Pareil au Même

*120-122 rue du Fbg-St-Antoine, 12th (01.43.
44.67.46/www.dpam.com). M° Ledru-Rollin.*
**Open** 10am-7pm Mon-Sat. **Credit** AmEx,
MC, V. **Map** p407 N7.
Bright, cleverly designed basics for children aged
three months to 14 years, at low prices. The Bébé
branch, with fashionable accessories and clothing
for kids up to two years, is a good source of gifts.
**Other locations** throughout the city.

### Petit Bateau

*26 rue Vavin, 6th (01.55.42.02.53/www.petit-
bateau.com). M° Vavin.* **Open** 10am-7pm Mon-Sat.
**Credit** AmEx, MC, V. **Map** p405 G8.
Renowned for its comfortable, well-made cotton
T-shirts, vests and other separates, Petit Bateau car-
ries an equally coveted teen range.
**Other locations** throughout the city.

### Six Pieds Trois Pouces

*222 bd St-Germain, 7th (01.45.44.03.72). M°
Solférino.* **Open** 10.30am-7pm Mon-Sat. **Credit**
AmEx, DC, MC, V. **Map** p405 F6.
The excellent array of children's and teens' shoes
runs from Start-rite and Aster to Timberland and
New Balance, plus the shop's own-label series.
**Other locations** 19 rue de la Monnaie, 1st
(01.40.41.07.79); 85 rue de Longchamp, 16th
(01.45.53.64.21); 78 av de Wagram, 17th
(01.46.22.81.64).

### Zef

*15 rue Debelleyme, 3rd (01.42.76.09.65/www.zef.eu).
M° St Sébastien Froissart.* **Open** 11am-7.30pm Mon-
Sat. **Credit** AmEx, DC, MC, V. **Map** p409 L5.
Zef's designer is the daughter of famous Italian fash-
ion photographer Paolo Reversi. The trendy chil-
dren's separates have a very Italian look, in soft

muted colours with adorable details like elbow
patches on the jackets. Boots and sheepskin gilets
and hats are also part of the look.
**Other locations** 32 rue de Richelieu, 1st
(01.42.60.61.04); 55bis rue des Saints-Pères,
6th (01.42.22.45.22).

## Toys & books

Traditional toyshops abound. Department
stores (*see p240*) go overboard at Christmas.
For children's books in English, try **WH Smith**
(*see p243*) or **Brentano's** (*see p241*).

### Arche de Noé

*70 rue St-Louis-en-l'Ile, 4th (01.46.34.61.60).
M° Pont Marie.* **Open** 10.30am-7pm daily. **Credit**
AmEx, MC, V. **Map** p409 K7.
'Noah's Ark' is a great place for Christmas shopping,
with traditional wooden toys from eastern Europe,
games and jigsaws, and finger puppets.

### Fnac Junior

*19 rue Vavin, 6th (01.56.24.03.46/www.eveiletjeux.
com). M° Vavin.* **Open** 10am-7.30pm Mon-Sat.
**Credit** AmEx, MC, V. **Map** p405 G8.
Fnac carries books, toys, DVDs, CDs and CD-Roms
for the under-12s. Storytelling and other activities
(Wed, Sat) take place for three-year-olds and up.
**Other locations** throughout the city.

### Au Nain Bleu

*5 bd Malesherbes, 8th (01.42.65.20.00/www.aunain
bleu.com). M° Madeleine.* **Open** 2-7pm Mon; 10am-
7pm Tue-Sat. **Credit** AmEx, MC, V. **Map** p401 F4.
The city's best toyshop, decorated like a circus tent,
draws gasps of wonder from children and parents.
Wooden doll's houses, pirate ships and gorgeous
dolls are made to last more than one generation.

### Village Joué Club
*3-5 bd des Italiens, 2nd (01.53.45.41.41/www.joue club.fr). M° Richelieu Drouot.* **Open** 10am-8pm Mon-Sat. **Credit** AmEx, MC, V. **Map** p402 H4.
The largest toy store in Paris is spread out on ground level in and around passage des Princes.

## Fashion

All big-name international designers have their own shops in Paris. **Marc Jacobs'** recent opening has helped make the Palais-Royal a shopping destination, away from the heavyweight names in the Golden Triangle between the Champs-Elysées, George-V and avenue Montaigne. Avenue Montaigne itself is enjoying a trendy upgrade. Elsewhere across the city, the label-filled boutiques are a fashionista's dream. Concept stores, where fashion, art, music and design all collide under one roof, are an ever-growing trend, with **Paul Smith**'s new shop, the huge streetwise **LE66** and underground **Base One** joining **Colette**, **Surface to Air** and **Spree**.

In addition to pan-European brands like Mango, H&M and Zara, the high street has its fair share of Gallic cheapies: think **Etam**, Jennyfer and Pimkie. The highest density is in the Forum des Halles (1st), on nearby rue de Rivoli, between the métro stations of Châtelet and Louvre Rivoli, and around Galeries Lafayette and Printemps (8th).

## Designer

### Antik Batik
*18 rue de Turenne, 4th (01.44.78.02.00/www.antik batik.fr). M° Chemin Vert.* **Open** 11am-7.30pm Mon-Sat; 2-7pm Sun. **Credit** MC, V. **Map** p409 L6.
Christophe Sauvat and Gabriella Cortese's filmy, lusciously printed silk gowns and kaftans are pretty irresistible. Shame they can't put a mirror in the changing rooms, though – parading around the boutique in what are sometimes wholly transparent garments can prove embarrassing.
**Other locations** 42 av Montaigne, 8th (01.47.23.74.12).

### A-poc
*47 rue des Francs-Bourgeois, 4th (01.44.54.07.05). M° Rambuteau or St-Paul.* **Open** 11am-7pm Mon-Sat. Closed 3wks Aug. **Credit** AmEx, DC, MC, V. **Map** p409 L6.
The unusual name is an acronym for 'A Piece of Cloth', and Issey Miyake's lab-style boutique takes a conceptual approach to fashion. Alongside ready-to-wear cotton Lycra clothes are rolls of wool jersey cut *sur mesure*; Miyake's assistants will be happy to advise. His original shop (3 pl des Vosges, 4th, 01.48.87.01.86) today houses the creations of Naoki Takizawa, protégé to the old master. *Photo p246.*

### Azzedine Alaïa
*7 rue de Moussy, 4th (01.42.72.19.19). M° Hôtel de Ville.* **Open** 10am-7pm Mon-Sat. **Credit** AmEx, DC, MC, V. **Map** p409 K6.
Ringing the doorbell gains you entry to the factory-style showroom in the same building as Alaïa's headquarters and apartment, where the 72-year-old Tunisian creator continues to astound with his originality. Stunning haute couture creations are in the back room, and sexy shoes bordering on fetish are scattered among the mannequins and rails.

### Balenciaga
*10 av George-V, 8th (01.47.20.21.11/www. balenciaga.com). M° Alma Marceau or George V.* **Open** 10am-7pm Mon-Sat. **Credit** AmEx, DC, MC, V. **Map** p400 D5.
With Nicolas Ghesquière at the helm, the Spanish fashion house is ahead of Japanese and Belgian designers in the hip stakes. Floating fabrics contrast with dramatic cuts, producing a sophisticated urban style that the fashion *haut monde* can't wait to slip into. Bags and shoes are also available.

### Chanel
*31 rue Cambon, 1st (01.42.86.28.00/www.chanel. com). M° Concorde or Madeleine.* **Open** 10am-7pm Mon-Sat. **Credit** AmEx, DC, MC, V. **Map** p401 G4.
Fashion legend Chanel has managed to stay relevant, thanks to Karl Lagerfeld. Coco opened her first boutique in this street, at no.21, in 1910, and the tradition continues in this elegant space. Lagerfeld has been designing for Chanel since 1983 and keeps on rehashing the classics, like the little black dress and the Chanel suit, with great success.
**Other locations** 42 av Montaigne, 8th (01.47.23.74.12).

### Comme des Garçons
*54 rue du Fbg-St-Honoré, 8th (01.53.30.27.27). M° Concorde or Madeleine.* **Open** 11am-7pm Mon-Sat. **Credit** AmEx, DC, MC, V. **Map** p401 F4.
Rei Kawakubo's design ideas and revolutionary mix of materials have influenced fashions for the past two decades, and are showcased in this fire engine-red, fibreglass store. Exclusive perfume lines get a futuristic setting at Comme des Garçons Parfums (23 pl du Marché-St-Honoré, 1st, 01.47.03.15.03).

### Costume National
*5 rue Cambon, 1st (01.40.15.04.36/www.costume national.com). M° Concorde.* **Open** 11.30am-7pm Mon; 10.30am-7pm Tue-Sat. **Credit** AmEx, MC, V. **Map** p401 G4.
This Milan-based label produces young, sexy clothes for men and women. Designer Ennio Capasa used to work for Yohji Yamamoto, and is as keen on black as he is on giving women hourglass figures.

### Dior
*26-30 av Montaigne, 8th (01.40.73.73.73/www.dior. com). M° Franklin D. Roosevelt.* **Open** 10am-7pm Mon-Sat. **Credit** AmEx, DC, MC, V. **Map** p400 D5.

**A-poc.**
*See p245.*

The whole Dior universe is here on avenue Montaigne, from the main prêt-à-porter store through jewellery, menswear and eyewear to Baby Dior, where impossibly rich babes-in-arms are coochy-cooed by drooling assistants. **Other locations** throughout the city.

### Gaspard Yurkievich
*43 rue Charlot, 3rd (01.42.77.55.48/www. gaspardyurkievich.com). Mº Filles du Calvaire.* **Open** 11am-7pm Tue-Sat. **Credit** MC, V. **Map** p402 L5.
The first boutique of this native Parisian fashion missile. Hot men's and women's designs and a dangerous line of shoes are all on display.

### Hermès
*24 rue du Fbg-St-Honoré, 8th (01.40.17.46.00/ www.hermes.com). Mº Concorde or Madeleine.* **Open** 10.30am-6.30pm Mon-Sat. **Credit** AmEx, DC, MC, V. **Map** p401 F4.
The fifth generation of the family directs the Hermès empire from this venerable 1930s building. Originally – and still – a saddler, it is no also-ran in the fashion stakes with Jean-Paul Gaultier at the reins. Most of its clients, however, are wealthy tourists after a horsey scarf or tie.

### Isabel Marant
*16 rue de Charonne, 11th (01.49.29.71.55/ www.isabelmarant.tm.fr). Mº Ledru-Rollin.* **Open** 10.30am-7.30pm Mon-Sat. **Credit** AmEx, MC, V. **Map** p407 M7.
Marant's style is easily recognisable in her ethno-babe brocades, blanket-like coats and decorated sweaters. It's a favourite among young trendies and artsy *parisiennes*. **Other locations** 47 rue de Saintonge, 3rd (01.42.78.19.24); 1 rue Jacob, 6th (01.43.26.04.12).

### Jack Henry
*25 rue Charlot, 3rd (01.42.78.93.51/www.jack henry.fr). Mº Filles du Calvaire.* **Open** 11am-7.30pm Tue-Sun. **Credit** AmEx, MC, V. **Map** p409 L5.

The work of this Paris-trained American designer has real intellectual heft to it, but you only have to touch the soft-as-stockings cotton and wool jersey from Japan to want his finely crafted, beautifully conceived tunics, skirts and jackets. Luxurious leather bags and jewellery from selected designers including Théodora Gabrielli, alias Dorothée, who patiently creates new pieces while serving in the shop, are also on display. **Other locations** 1 rue Montmartre, 1st (01.42.21.46.01).

### Jean-Paul Gaultier
*6 rue Vivienne, 2nd (01.42.86.05.05/www.jeanpaul gaultier.com). Mº Bourse.* **Open** 10.30am-7pm Mon-Fri; 11am-7pm Sat. **Credit** AmEx, DC, MC, V. **Map** p402 H4.
Having celebrated his 30th year in the fashion business, Gaultier is still going strong. His boudoir boutique with its peach taffeta walls stocks men's and women's ready-to-wear and the reasonably priced JPG Jeans lines, with the haute couture department upstairs (01.42.97.48.12, by appointment only). **Other locations** 44 av George-V, 8th (01.44.43.00.44).

### John Galliano
*384-386 rue St-Honoré, 1st (01.55.35.40.40/ www.johngalliano.com). Mº Concorde or Madeleine.* **Open** 11am-7pm Mon-Sat. **Credit** AmEx, DC, MC, V. **Map** p401 G4.
It's hard to imagine how he manages it all, but Dior chief Galliano still has his own range and a reputation as one of the UK's most original designers. You can view the small but diverse collection of flamboyant and feminine delights through the showcase window, or from the Louis XVI-style leather chairs inside.

### Kenzo
*1 rue du Pont Neuf, 1st (01.73.04.20.03/www. kozen.com). Mº Pont Neuf.* **Open** 10am-7pm Mon-Sat. **Credit** AmEx, DC, MC, V. **Map** p402 J6.

Eat, Drink, Shop

Kenzo has long been a friend of Paris, having dressed the city itself in its various flamboyant publicity campaigns. The flagship store has three floors of men's and women's fashion and is crowned with the Bulle Kenzo spa and Philippe Starck-designed Kong restaurant on the fifth floor. **Other locations** throughout the city.

## Lagerfeld Gallery

*40 rue de Seine, 6th (01.55.42.75.50/www. karllagerfeld.com). M° Odéon.* **Open** 11am-7pm Tue-Sat. Closed Aug. **Credit** AmEx, DC, MC, V. **Map** p408 H6.

Andrée Putman helped create this shrine to King Karl's brand of stylish minimalism: Lagerfeld's fashion creations and photography are both on display. You could sneak in just to browse the latest fashion, beauty and art publications, scattered over a handsome round table at the front of the gallery.

## Louis Vuitton

*101 av des Champs-Elysées, 8th (08.10.81.00.10/ www.vuitton.com). M° George V.* **Open** 10am-8pm Mon-Sat. **Credit** AmEx, DC, MC, V. **Map** p400 D4.

The 'Promenade' flagship sets the tone for Vuitton's global image, from the 'bag bar', bookstore and new jewellery department to the women's and men's ready-to-wear. Contemporary art, videos by Tim White Sobieski and a pitch-black elevator by Olafur Eliasson complete the picture. Accessed by lift, the Espace Vuitton hosts temporary art exhibits – but the star of the show is the view over Paris. **Other locations** 6 pl St-Germain-des-Prés, 6th; 22 av Montaigne, 8th.

## Manoush

*217 rue St Honoré, 1st (01.40.20.04.44/www. manoush.com). M° Tuileries.* **Open** 10am-7pm Mon-Sat. **Credit** AmEx, DC, MC, V. **Map** p400 D4.

Manoush, meaning 'gypsy' in French slang, has proved more than a flash-in-the-pan favourite during the gypsy skirt craze and now boasts four boutiques touting designer Frédérique Trou-Roy's kitsch and kooky vision. **Other locations** 12 rue du Jour, 2nd (01.44.88.28.08); 75 rue Vielle-du-Temple, 3rd (01.44.54.54.59); 52 rue du Four, 6th (01.42.22.78.45).

## Marc Jacobs

*34 galerie de Montpensier, 1st (01.55.35.02.60/ www.marcjacobs.com). M° Palais Royal Musée du Louvre.* **Open** 11am-8pm Mon-Sat. **Credit** AmEx, DC, MC, V. **Map** p402 H5.

By choosing the Palais-Royal for his first signature boutique in Europe, Marc Jacobs brought new life, and an influx of fashionistas, to these elegant cloisters. Stocking womenswear, menswear, accessories and shoes, it's already become a place of pilgrimage for the designer's legion of admirers, who are snapping up his downtown New York style.

## Martin Grant

*10 rue Charlot, 3rd (01.42.71.39.49/www.martin grantparis.com). M° Temple.* **Open** 10am-6pm Mon-Fri. Closed 3wks Aug. **Credit** MC, V. **Map** p406 K6.

Grant's shop is now tucked away on a second-floor Marais apartment. This is couture as interpreted by Australian designer Martin Grant. If you're a stickler for steady cuts, pure textiles and unfussy designs, pay him a visit.

## Martin Margiela

*23 & 25bis rue de Montpensier, 1st (01.40.15.07.55/ www.maisonmartinmargiela.com). M° Palais Royal Musée du Louvre.* **Open** 11am-7pm Mon-Sat. **Credit** AmEx, DC, MC, V. **Map** p402 H5.

The first Paris outlet for the JD Salinger of fashion is a pristine, white, unlabelled space. His collection for women (Line 1) has a blank label but is recognisable by external white stitching. You'll also find Line 6 (women's basics) and Line 10 (menswear), plus accessories for men and women and shoes. **Other locations** 13 rue de Grenelle, 7th (01.45.49.06.45).

## Miu Miu

*219 rue St Honoré, 1st (01.58.62.53.20/www. miumiu.com). M° Tuileries.* **Open** 11am-7pm Mon; 10am-7pm Tue-Sat. **Credit** AmEx, DC, MC, V. **Map** p401 G5.

Prada's younger sister now has the rue St Honoré branch as its main boutique, selling its reckless men's and women's fashions, shoes and bags. **Other locations** 16 rue de Grenelle, 7th (01.53.63.20.30).

## Paul & Joe

*64 rue des Sts-Pères, 7th (01.42.22.47.01/www. paulandjoe.com). M° Rue du Bac or St-Germain-des-Prés.* **Open** 10am-7pm Mon-Sat. **Credit** AmEx, MC, V. **Map** p405 G6.

Fashionistas have taken a shine to Sophie Albou's retro-styled creations. The latest collection dresses leggy young things and their intellectual paramours in what look like pristine 1960s couture pieces from the back of *maman*'s and *papa*'s wardrobe. **Other locations** 56 rue Vieille-du-Temple, 3rd (01.42.72.42.06); 62 rue des Sts-Pères, 7th (01.42.22.47.01); 46 rue Etienne-Marcel, 2nd (01.40.28.03.34); 2 av Montaigne, 8th (01.47.20.57.50); 123 rue de la Pompe, 16th (01.45.53.01.08).

## Paule Ka

*233 rue St-Honoré, 1st (01.42.97.57 06/www. pauleka.com). M° Tuileries.* **Open** 11am-7pm Mon; 10am-7pm Tue-Sat. **Credit** AmEx, DC, MC, V. **Map** p401 G4.

Serge Cajfinger's '60s couture-influenced collections continue to gather a loyal following. With the opening of his St Honoré boutique he now has a foot in each of the city's fashion districts. **Other locations** 20 rue Malher, 4th (01.40.29.96.03); 192 bd St-Germain, 6th (01.45.44.92.60); 45 rue François 1er, 8th (01.47.20.76.10).

## Paul Smith

*3 rue du Fbg-St-Honoré, 8th (01.42.68.27.10/ www.paulsmith.co.uk). M° Concorde.* **Open** 11am-7pm Mon; 10am-7pm Tue-Sat. **Credit** AmEx, DC, MC, V. **Map** p401 F4.

**Eat, Drink, Shop**

Ban Thaï Spa

**The largest Thai Spas in Paris**
**The most Famous**
**Visit us with or without appointment**
**Open everyday from 11am - 9pm**

**2 Traditional Thai Massage Areas**
**Aroma Oil Massage**
**Bangkok-style Foot Massage**
**And Over 500 m² for you to use**

**Paris - Montorgueil**
Contemporary Asian Spa
5 rue Mandar
75002 Paris
**Tel: 01.40.28.00.80**
**www.massage-thai-paris.fr**

**Paris - Marais**
Contemporary Asian Spa
Thai Home Spa
68 rue de la Verrerie, 75004 Paris
**Tel: 01.42.77.28.28**
**www.thai-spa.fr**

# Marais à la mode

You can always tell an area has achieved hip status: it acquires a name. Until recently the 'haut Marais' was just a quiet corner of the third arrondissement, where most commercial activity occurred behind closed doors. In the last couple of years, however, it has seen an explosion of boutique openings that has made it the city's hottest fashion *quartier*. It even has its own blog (http://hautmarais. blogspot.com) to keep you in the loop.

The adventurous multi-label boutique **Shine** (*see p253*) has been credited with starting the trend, moving here at the end of 2005 from rue de Charonne, while **Gaspard Yurkievich** (*see p246*) was one of the first designers to open up here. Now established fashion names are fighting to get a place next to avant-garde upstarts in the new golden triangle delineated by rues Charlot, Poitou and Turenne. **Isabel Marant** (*see p246*) arrived in April 2007, along with purveyor of rock-chic **Corinne Cobson** (66 rue Charlot, 3rd, 01.42.60.51.31, www.corinnecobson.com), and the following month concept shop **Surface 2 Air** (*see p253*) beamed in from its old premises on rue de l'Arbre Sec.

First stop for anyone wanting a one-off fashion statement must be **Galerie Simone** (*see p251*), exhibiting the limited-edition creations of designers on mannequins, plus some original jewellery. Two new names to conjure with are **Swildens** (22 rue de Poitou, 3rd, 01.42.71.19.12) – youthful casuals in linen and cotton from former maternity-wear designer Juliette Swildens – and **Anikalena Karlström** (16 rue du Pont-aux-Choux, 3rd, 01.44.59.32.85, www.anikalena.com), who uses tailoring, soft fabrics, silk and leather to create a collection with a strong story each season. **Emilie Casiez**, formerly of Surface 2

Air, now has her own shop selling T-shirts and tunics with original graphics (57 rue Charlot, 3rd, 01.42.74.59.89, www.emiliecasiez.com), and **m.ppaccard** (20 rue du Pont-aux-Choux, 3rd, 01.42.93.43.06) is another designer elevating the T-shirt into a statement. Dainty two-tone ballerinas and pumps that are oh-so-French can be found at **Estelle Yomeda** (4 rue de Normandie, 3rd, 01.44.59.80.33, www.estelleyomeda.com), and **Hoses** (41 rue de Poitou, 3rd, 01.42.78.80.62, www.hoses-imited.com) has a gorgeous shoe collection chosen by stylist Valery Duboucheron.

Men are catered for too, notably by **Jacenko** (*see p254*), with a sharp eye for metrosexual style. Newcomer **Christophe Lemaire** (*see p254*) is causing a storm with his rock-dandy look, while at **Le Bouclard** (15 rue Charlot, 3rd, 01.42.36.14.66, www.le-bouclard.com) you'll find streetwear from the likes of Adidas Heritage, Artsym, Zucca and Final Home. The cult embroidered T-shirts of Baron Y are at **Matières à Réflexion** (19 rue de Poitou, 3rd, 01.42.72.16.31, www.matieresareflexion. com), where you can also get a bag custom-made on site from your '80s leather jacket.

In tune with the off-beat look cultivated here, the haut Marais is fast becoming the vintage centre of Paris. Couture pieces can be found at exquisite **Studio W** (*see p257*) and **La Belle Epoque** (*see p256*), while **Le Bazar de Julie** (19 rue de Poitou, 3rd, 01.42.72.74.24) is piled high with '60s and '70s boots and separates. **Pretty Box** (46 rue de Saintonge, 3rd, 01.48.04.81.71) also concentrates on recent vintage from the '70s and '80s, and **Esprit Vinyle** (57 rue de Saintonge, 3rd, 01.42.71.55.95, www.esprit-vinyle.com) mixes vintage with new by Stella Cadente, Ysasu, Luna Bosoca and Zaza Factory.

Interiors magazine editors are mad about Paul Smith's new concept store, with its 'so British' atmosphere cultivated with '40s wallpaper, antiques, old books and bric-a-brac, much of which is for sale. His collections for men, women and children, along with eyewear and accessories, are all gathered in this elegant Haussmann apartment.
**Other locations** *22-24 bd Raspail, 7th (01.42.84.15.30).*

### Prada
*10 av Montaigne, 8th (01.53.23.99.40/www. prada.com). M° Alma Marceau.* **Open** 11am-7pm Mon; 10am-7pm Tue-Sat. **Credit** AmEx, DC, MC, V. **Map** p400 D5.

Fashionistas just can't seem to get enough of Miuccia Prada's elegant designs. Handbags of choice are complemented by a ready-to-wear line.
**Other locations** 5 rue de Grenelle, 6th (01.45.48.53.14); 6 rue du Fbg-St-Honoré, 8th (01.58.18.63.30).

### Rick Owens
*130 galerie de Valois, 1st (01.40.20.42.52/www. owenscorp.com). M° Palais Royal Musée du Louvre.* **Open** noon-7pm Mon; 10am-7pm Tue-Sat. **Credit** AmEx, DC, MC, V. **Map** p402 H5.
The LA designer and rock star favourite brings his glamour-meets-grunge style to the Palais-Royal, with hoods, zips and asymmetrical wrappings.

## Sonia Rykiel

*175 bd St-Germain, 6th (01.49.54.60.60/www.
soniarykiel.com). M° St-Germain-des-Prés or Sèvres
Babylone.* **Open** 10.30am-7pm Mon-Sat. **Credit**
AmEx, DC, MC, V. **Map** p405 G6.
The queen of stripes produces skinny rib knitwear
evoking the Left Bank babes of yore. Menswear is
across the street, while two newer boutiques stock
the younger, more affordable Sonia by Sonia Rykiel
range (59 rue des Sts-Pères, 6th, 01.49.54.61.00) and
kids' togs (4 rue de Grenelle, 6th, 01.49.54.61.10).
Also on rue de Grenelle, on the site of Sonia's original 1966 shop, the Rykiel Woman store at no.6
(01.49.54.66.21) stocks a range of designer sex toys.
**Other locations** throughout the city.

## Tsumori Chisato

*20 rue Barbette, 3rd (01.42.78.18.88). M° Hôtel de
Ville or St-Paul.* **Open** 11am-7pm Mon-Sat. Closed
2wks Aug. **Credit** AmEx, MC, V. **Map** p409 L6.
Known for her inventive use of colour and wispy
fabrics, this designer has a cult following thanks to
poetic, romantic designs big on ingenious detail.

## Vanessa Bruno

*25 rue St-Sulpice, 6th (01.43.54.41.04/www.vanessa
bruno.com). M° Odéon.* **Open** 10.30am-7.30pm Mon-
Sat. **Credit** AmEx, DC, MC, V. **Map** p408 H7.
Mercerised cotton tanks, flattering trousers and feminine tops have a Zen-like quality that stems from
Bruno's stay in Japan, and they look good on any
figure. She also makes great bags; the ample Lune
was created to mark ten years in the business.
**Other locations** 12 rue de Castiglione, 1st
(01.42.61.44.60); 100 rue Vieille-du-Temple, 3rd
(01.42.77.19.41).

## Yohji Yamamoto

*25 rue du Louvre, 1st (01.42.21.42.93/www.
yohjiyamamoto.co.jp). M° Les Halles or Sentier.*
**Open** 10.30am-7pm Mon-Sat. **Credit** AmEx, DC,
MC, V. **Map** p405 G7.
One of the few true pioneers working in fashion
today, Yamamoto is a master of cut and finish, both
strongly inspired by the kimono and traditional
Tibetan costume. His dexterity with form makes for
unique shapes and styles, largely black, but when
he does colour, it's a blast of brilliance. You can find
the men's boutique at 47 rue Etienne-Marcel (1st,
01.45.08.82.45).

## Yves Saint Laurent

*6 pl St-Sulpice, 6th (01.43.29.43.00/www.ysl.com).
M° St-Sulpice.* **Open** 11am-7pm Mon; 10.30am-7pm
Tue-Sat. **Credit** AmEx, DC, MC, V. **Map** p408 H7.
Yves Saint Laurent retired in 2002 after a 40-year
career that began at Dior and continued with the
androgynous revolution he fomented in the 1960s
under his own name, getting women into dinner and
jump suits. This is the main women's store; you'll
find menswear at no.12 (01.43.26.84.40).
**Other locations** Men 32 rue du Fbg-St-Honoré,
8th (01.53.05.80.80). Women 38 rue du Fbg-St-Honoré,
8th (01.42.65.74.59).

# Boutique & concept

## AB33 and N°60

*33 & 60 rue Charlot, 3rd (01.42.71.02.82/
01.44.78.91.90). M° Filles du Calvaire.* **Open** 11am-
8pm Tue-Sun. **Credit** AmEx, MC, V. **Map** p409 L5.
In under two years, AB33, the original boutique run
by fashion addict Agathe Buchotte, has become a
must in every like-minded woman's address book
for its eclectic mix of pieces from smaller brands like
Odd Molly and Laundry Industry. The newer N°60
revels in a more rock 'n' roll attitude, courtesy of
labels like McQ, Chalayan and April 77.

## Base One

*47bis rue d'Orsel, 18th (01.53.28.04.52/www.
baseoneshop.com). M° Anvers.* **Open** 12.30-8pm Tue-
Sat; 3.30-8pm Sun. Closed 2wks Aug. **Credit** MC, V.
**Map** p402 J2.
The dynamic clubland duo Princesse Léa and Jean-
Louis Faverole squeeze items from little known local
and international designers (Shai Wear, Li-Lei,
Drolaic, 0K47), plus small, established brands
(Fenchurch, Motel, Consortium) into their sitting-
room style boutique. Calling it an underground
Colette would be somewhere near the mark.

## Les Belles Images

*74 rue Charlot, 3rd (01.42.76.93.61/www.les
bellesimages.com). M° Filles du Calvaire.* **Open**
11am-7.30pm Tue-Sat. **Credit** MC, V. **Map** p402 L5.
A serious retro '60s vibe reigns at this chic boutique,
where owner Sandy Bontout showcases items from
current collections of obscure and big-name French
and international labels, such as Ambali separates,
Walk that Walk shoes and editor's picks from
Veronique Leroy and Vivienne Westwood. A men's
section was added in autumn 2006.

## Colette

*213 rue St-Honoré, 1st (01.55.35.33.90/
www.colette.fr). M° Pyramides or Tuileries.* **Open**
11am-7pm Mon-Sat. **Credit** AmEx, DC, MC, V.
**Map** p401 G4.
Renowned and much-imitated one-stop concept and
lifestyle store Colette is still influential. This shrine
to the limited edition displays must-have accessories
inside clinical glass cases away from sticky fingers.
Books, media, shiny new gadgets, and the hair and
beauty brands själ, Kiehl's and uslu airlines are scattered amid the magazines and photo albums on the
ground floor and mezzanine. Upstairs has a selection of 'in' clothes and accessories. Lunch, with a
global selection of mineral water, can be nibbled in
the chic basement Water Bar.

## L'Eclaireur

*3ter rue des Rosiers, 4th (01.48.87.10.22/www.
leclaireur.com). M° St-Paul.* **Open** 11am-7pm Mon-
Sat. **Credit** AmEx, DC, MC, V. **Map** p409 L6.
Housed in a dandified warehouse, L'Eclaireur stocks
uncompromising designs by Comme des Garçons,
Martin Margiela, Dries van Noten, Carpe Diem and

# Stocking up

One of the keys to Paris style on a budget is the 'stock shop'. Stock shops are discount boutiques for various brands selling end-of-line, prototypes or excess stock at reduced prices. They will not be advertised on brands' websites so you need to be in the know. They also account for the fact that Paris sales are nowhere near as exciting as the London ones: excess merchandise tends to end up in the stock shops rather than on the racks of department stores.

The largest concentration of stock shops is on rue d'Alésia (M° Alésia). Sonia Rykiel's **SR Store** (64 rue d'Alésia, 14th, 01.43.95.06.13) is as well laid out as a genuine Rykiel boutique, but with none of the attitude you'll find on bd St-Germain. While the clothes are marked down 20 to 30 per cent, the shoe department yields some fabulous bargains. It also has childrenswear.

**Cacharel Stock** (114 rue d'Alésia, 14th, 01.45.42.53.04) offers up to 40 per cent off last season's stock in all the brand's ranges and is particularly beloved of chic *mamans*. If you're looking for a special gift for friends who have just had a baby, this is the place. E-bay mums used to kitting out their progeny in style will also love the **Bonpoint** end-of-series shop at 42 rue de l'Université (7th, M° Rue du Bac, 01.40.20.10.55), where the chic brand's collections can be bought at about 40 per cent off.

In the Marais (M° St Paul and St Sébastien Froissart), **Zadig et Voltaire** (22 rue du Bourg Tibourg, 4th, 01 44 59 39 62), **Lolita Lempicka** (Studio Lolita, 2bis rue des Rosiers, 4th, 01.48.87.09.67) and **Alaïa** (18 rue de la Verrerie, 4th, 01.42.72.19.19) all have stock shops, while **L'Habilleur** (44 rue de Poitou, 3rd, 01.48.87.77.12) in the newly christened

'haut Marais' (*see p249* **Marais à la mode**) has an ever-changing selection of *dégriffés* (designer wear with the label cut out). Urbanites use this slick store for its menswear and womenswear by the likes of Roberto Collina, Paul & Joe and Stefano Mortari, at up to 60 per cent off original prices. For men looking for classic style, **Stock B**'s large warehouse (114 rue de Turenne, 3rd, 01.53.01.56.35) has great bargains on last season's suits, shirts and coats from Kenzo, Assaro, Cerruti and Givenchy.

High-end labels including Chanel and Lagerfeld, and vintage in mint condition, can be sought out at **Le Mouton à Cinq Pattes** (138 bd St-Germain, 6th, 01.43.26.49.25, M° Odéon) but you have to know what you're buying as this shop is *dégriffé* too. For true Ab Fab style – it's the ideal place to find a gown for the red carpet at Cannes – don't miss a scout around **L'Annexe des Créateurs** (19 rue Godet de Mauroy, 9th, 01.42.65.46.40, www.annexedescreateurs.com, M° Madeleine), where seasoned fashion queen Edwige Meister stocks Prada, Moschino, Lacroix, Marc Jacobs and a selection of vintage Chanel suits. At the other end of the scale, **Stock Kookaï** (82 rue Réaumur, 2nd, 01.45.08.93.69, M° Réaumur Sébastopol) has current season wear and end-of-line offers at up to 70 per cent discount.

Finally, if you're willing to spend a day out of Paris, get the RER to **La Vallée** shopping village (3 Cours de la Garonne, 77700 Serris, 01.60.42.35.00, www.lavalleevillage.com). With more than 80 well-known men's and women's brands – from Paul Smith to Kenzo via Diesel and Agnès b – and mark-downs from 30 to 70 per cent, you're bound to find something to make the trip worthwhile.

Junya Watanabe. Among its exclusive finds, check out ethereal smocks by Finnish designer Jasmin Santanen. At the secretive rue Hérold branch you have to ring the doorbell to enter. A new space in rue Boissy d'Anglas, near Concorde, sells chic fashions for men and women, and has its own café-restaurant with an accent on Fornasetti.
**Other locations** 10 rue Hérold, 1st (01.40.41.09.89); 8 rue Boissy d'Anglas, 8th (01.53.43.03.70).

### Espace Créateurs Forum des Halles
*Level -1, Porte Berger & Grand Balcon, Forum des Halles, 1st (www.forumdeshalles.com). M° Les Halles.* **Open** 10am-7.30pm Mon-Sat. **Credit** AmEx, DC, MC, V. **Map** p402 J5.

Situated on level -1 of Forum des Halles, this space dedicated to young designers is worth visiting despite the location. Isabel Marant and Erotokritos both started out here. Among the eight boutiques' multi-label selections, check out trendy Senegalese designer Xuly Bët, theatrical flair from TT WIP and Zike's bags made from recycled car interiors.

### Galerie Simone
*124 rue Vieille-du-Temple, 3rd (01.42.74.21.28). M° St Sébastien Froissart.* **Open** noon-7pm Tue-Sat. **Credit** AmEx, DC, MC, V. **Map** p409 L5.

Simone Gaubatz sources and cultivates talented young designers from around the world, displaying their most eye-catching creations on mannequins in

**Kabuki Femme.**

## Kabuki Femme

*25 rue Etienne-Marcel, 1st (01.42.33.55.65/*
*www.babarabui.com). M° Etienne Marcel.* **Open**
10.30am-7.30pm Mon-Sat. Closed 29 July-22 Aug.
**Credit** AmEx, DC, MC, V. **Map** p402 J5.
On the ground floor there's intrepid footwear and
bags by Costume National, Miu Miu and Prada, plus
Fendi's cult creations; Burberry belts and Miu Miu
sunglasses are also stocked. Upstairs are outfits by
Véronique Leroy, Prada and Costume National.
**Other locations** Kabuki Homme, 21 rue Etienne-
Marcel, 1st (01.42.33.13.44).

## Kokon To Zai

*48 rue Tiquetonne, 2nd (01.42.36.92.41/www.*
*kokontozai.co.uk). M° Etienne Marcel.* **Open**
11.30am-7.30pm Mon-Sat. **Credit** AmEx, DC, MC, V.
**Map** p402 J5.
Always a spot-on spotter of the latest creations, this
tiny style emporium is sister to the Kokon To Zai in
London. The neon club feel of the mirrored interior
matches the dark glamour of the designs. Unique
pieces straight off the catwalk share space with creations by Marjan Peijoski, Noki, Raf Simons, Two
Tom, Ziad Ghanem and new Norwegian designers.

## LE66

*66 av des Champs-Elysées, 8th (01.53.53.33.80/*
*www.le66.fr). M° George V.* **Open** 11am-8pm daily.
**Credit** AmEx, DC, MC, V. **Map** p400 D4.
This new bohemoth of a concept store offers just
about every hip brand going. Prime location is given
to the 66 products of the moment, with a personality
choosing their favourites each month, and the entire
Puma Sport fashion line, together with bags by Urban
Mobility and products by the American street artist
OBEY. On the ground floor are books and magazines,
plus a space devoted to Potemkin, the DVD specialist found on Canal St-Martin, before you encounter
the 100 men's and women's designers (American
Retro, Majestic, nocollection, Zoe Tees, etc) and 400
models of shoes on the lower ground floor.

## Maria Luisa

*40 rue du Mont-Thabor, 1st (01.47.03.48.08).*
*M° Concorde.* **Open** 10.30am-7pm Mon-Sat.
**Credit** AmEx, DC, MC, V. **Map** p401 G4.
Venezuelan Maria Luisa Poumaillou was one of the
city's first stockists of Galliano, McQueen and the
Belgians, and has an eye for rising stars such as
Bernhard Willhelm, Eley Kishimoto, Undercover
and Emma Cook. Nearby branches cover up-and-
coming young designers (no.38, 01.42.96.47.81),
menswear (no.19bis, 01.42.60.89.83) and shoes and
accessories (2 rue Cambon, 01.47.03.96.15).

## Me

*29 rue du Dragon, 6th (01.53.63.02.52). M° St-*
*Germain-des-Prés.* **Open** 10am-7pm Mon-Sat.
**Credit** AmEx, MC, V. **Map** p405 G7.
Oversized dolls are the mannequins at Me, the most
youthful division of Issey Miyake, created by his disciples as an offshoot of Pleats Please. Washable,
pleated stretch tops make up 80% of the collection.

this gallery-style space. This is the place to find
something truly original, from Feral Flair's hand-
printed wool in acid colours and Yohji Yamamoto-
style coats to Monica's sequinned '50s-style skirts.
There is also an emphasis on ethical clothes, including Hagamainty jackets from Madagascar and
Deborah Lindquist's recycled cashmere. Hand-made
jewellery around the €90 mark includes An Van
Hove's avant-garde necklaces made from electrical
connectors and Strelitziasunsun's crystalline beads.

## Jay Ahr

*2-4 rue du 29-Juillet, 1st (01.42.96.95.23/www.*
*jayahr.com). M° Tuileries.* **Open** 11am-7pm Mon-Sat.
**Credit** AmEx, MC, V. **Map** p401 G5.
Former jewellery designer Jonathan Riss opened this
shop as a fashion stylist in 2004, and struck gold
with simple, figure-flaunting '60s inspired dresses.
Think plunging necklines and Bianca Jagger in her
heyday, with Ali McGraw and Anita Pallenberg in
the mix. There are no price tags on the dresses, so
you have to ask; prices start at around €500.

## Joseph

*147 bd St-Germain, 6th (01.55.42.77.56). M° St-*
*Germain-des-Prés.* **Open** 11am-7pm Mon, Sat;
10.30am-7pm Tue-Fri. **Credit** AmEx, DC, MC, V.
**Map** p405 G6.
Taking a cue from its London store, Joseph has
opened a multi-brand shop in place of Onward. Still
here are pieces by Ann Demeulemeester, Dries van
Noten and Bruno Pieters, plus accessories by Bijoux
de Sophie and handbags by Jérôme Dreyfuss.

### Mona

*17 rue Bonaparte, 6th (01.44.07.07.27). M° St-Germain des-Prés.* **Open** 11am-1.30pm, 2.30-7pm Mon-Fri; 11am-7pm Sat. **Credit** AmEx, MC, V. **Map** p408 H6.

This concept boutique features tightly edited selections and sales assistants who double as stylists, not to mention a red carpet (ideal for practice runs). The eponymous owner used to run a shoe boutique; designers often customise models to her wishes.

### Shine

*15 rue de Poitou, 3rd (01.48.05.80.10). M° Filles du Calvaire.* **Open** 11am-7.30pm Mon-Sat. **Credit** AmEx, MC, V. **Map** p407 M7.

For funkier clothes than Maria Luisa (*see p252*), Vinci d'Helia has what you need: sexy T-shirts with unusual detailing, Luella's chunky knits, and Earl Jeans trousers and jackets.

### Spree

*16 rue de La Vieuville, 18th (01.42.23.41.40). M° Abbesses.* **Open** 2-7pm Mon; 11am-7.30pm Tue-Sat. Closed 1wk Aug. **Credit** AmEx, MC, V. **Map** p402 H1.

Artistic director Bruno Hadjadj and fashion designer Roberta Oprandi offer fashion, design and art with a Montmartre vibe – 1960s chairs draped in the latest fashions by Preen and Isabel Marant. **Other locations** 1 rue St-Simon, 7th (01.42.22.05.04).

### Surface 2 Air

*68 rue Charlot, 3rd (www.surface2air.com). M° St-Sébastien Froissart.* **Open** 11am-7.30pm Mon-Sat. **Credit** MC, V. **Map** p409 L5.

This non-concept concept store also acts as a gallery and graphic design agency. The cult clothing selection takes in Alice McCall's sassy frocks, Fifth Avenue Shoe Repair jeans and printed dresses by Wood Wood. For men, labels include Marios, Wendy & Jim and F-Troupe.

## Womenswear

### Agnès b

*2, 3, 6 & 19 rue du Jour, 1st (men 01.42.33.04.13/women 01.45.08.56.56/www.agnesb.com). M° Les Halles.* **Open** *Oct-Apr* 10am-7pm Mon-Sat. *May-Sept* 10am-7.30pm Mon-Sat. **Credit** AmEx, MC, V. **Map** p402 J5.

Agnès b rarely wavers from her design vision: pure lines in fine quality cotton, merino wool and silk. Best buys are shirts, pullovers and cardigans that keep their shape for years. Her mini-empire of men's, women's, children's, travel and sportswear shops is compact; see the website for details. **Other locations** throughout the city.

### American Apparel

*31 pl du Marché-St-Honoré, 1st (01.42.60.03.72/www.americanapparel.net). M° Opéra, Pyramides or Tuileries.* **Open** 10.30am-7.30pm Mon-Sat. **Credit** AmEx, DC, MC, V. **Map** p401 G4.

Paris has acquired a taste for American Apparel's ethically spotless, colourful cotton basics, which are now being seen customised around town. After setting up base here in 2005, the LA brand now has five Paris stores. **Other locations** 123 rue Vieille-du-Temple, 3rd (01.44.54.33.44); 41 rue du Temple, 4th (01.42.74.71.03); 7 rue Gozlin, 6th (01.40.46.02.00); 10 rue Beaurepaire, 10th (01.42.49.50.01).

### Antoine et Lili

*95 quai de Valmy, 10th (01.40.37.41.55/www.antoineetlili.com). M° Jacques Bonsergent.* **Open** 11am-7pm Mon, Sun; 11am-8pm Tue-Fri; 10am-8pm Sat. **Credit** AmEx, DC, MC, V. **Map** p402 L3.

Antoine and Lili's fuchsia-pink, custard-yellow and apple-green shopfronts, reflected in the Canal St-Martin, are a colour therapist's dream. The bobo designer's clothes, often in wraparound styles, adapt to all sizes and shapes. The Canal St-Martin 'village' comprises womenswear, a kitsch home decoration boutique and childrenswear, which has replaced the former Antoine et Lili café. **Other locations** 11 rue Montmartre, 1st (01.40.13.08.22); 51 rue des Francs-Bourgeois, 4th (01.42.72.26.60); 87 rue de Seine, 6th (01.56.24.35.81); 90 rue des Martyrs, 18th (01.42.58.10.22).

### Bali Barret

*36 rue du Mont-Thabor, 1st (01.49.26.01.75/www.balibarret.com). M° Concorde.* **Open** 2-7pm Mon; 10.30am-7pm Tue-Sat. **Credit** AmEx, MC, V. **Map** p401 G5.

Stocking four different colours each season, this French label offers an androgynous take on classic styles with a sexy twist. Look out for funky belts and bags and the matching stripy knickers, stockings and cotton polo-necks.

### Barbara Bui

*23 rue Etienne-Marcel, 1st (01.40.26.43.65/www.barbarabui.fr). M° Etienne Marcel.* **Open** 10.30am-7.30pm Mon-Sat. **Credit** AmEx, DC, MC, V. **Map** p402 J5.

Businesswomen who like to cut to the chase have a sartorial ally in Bui: lean, finely cut trousers, figure-hugging shirts and jackets, and dagger heels. Bui has branched out into loungey CDs, and there's a café two doors up (no.27, 01.45.08.04.04). **Other locations** throughout the city.

### Firmaman

*200 bd Pereire, 17th (01.44.09.71.32/www.bonton.fr). M° Porte Maillot.* **Open** 11am-7pm Tue-Sat. **Credit** AmEx, DC, MC, V. **Map** p400 B2.

Realising that pregnant women have long been scouring regular boutiques for a more fashionable maternity look, Marguerite Pineau Valencienne has chosen appropriate clothes from the likes of Isabel Marant, Bash and Citizens of Humanity, which are displayed alongside maternity wear by Blossom, Pietro Brunelli and Virginie Castaway. The first maternity concept store, it also has lingerie, well-being products and gifts for mums, dads and babies.

**Eat, Drink, Shop**

## Formes

*10 pl des Victoires, 2nd (01.40.15.63.81/www.
formes.com). Mᵒ Sentier.* **Open** 10.30am-7pm Mon-
Sat. **Credit** AmEx, DC, MC, V. **Map** p402 H5.
The most glamorous maternity wear is to be found
at this well-known French brand, including fabulous
chiffon cocktail dresses designed to flatter, not to
hide that bump.
**Other locations** throughout the city.

## Marithé et François Girbaud

*38 rue Etienne-Marcel, 2nd (01.53.40.74.20/
www.girbaud.com). Mᵒ Etienne Marcel.* **Open**
11.30am-7.30pm Mon; 10.30am-7.30pm Tue-Sat.
**Credit** AmEx, DC, MC, V. **Map** p405 J5.
The pioneering *soixante-huitard* Girbaud pair came
up with streetwear in high-tech fabrics using laser
cutting and welding. This flagship store has four
floors and a garden.
**Other locations** throughout the city.

## Zadig & Voltaire

*42 rue des Francs-Bourgeois, 3rd (01.44.54.00.60/
www.zadig-et-voltaire.com). Mᵒ Hôtel de Ville or St-
Paul.* **Open** 1.30-7.30pm Mon, Sun; 10.30am-7.30pm
Tue-Sat. **Credit** AmEx, DC, MC, V. **Map** p409 K6.
Z&V's relaxed, urban collection is a winner. Popular
separates include cotton tops, shirts and faded jeans;
its winter range of cashmere jumpers is superb. The
more upmarket Zadig & Voltaire De Luxe is at 18
rue François 1er (01.40.70.97.89).
**Other locations** throughout the city.

# Menswear

Shops in **Streetwear & clubwear** (*see p255*)
stock more casual clothes; many of the brands
listed in **Designer** (*see p245*) also cater for
chaps. For details of more menswear shops in
the Marais, *see p249* **Marais à la mode**.

## APC

*4 rue de Fleurus, 6th (01.42.22.12.77/www.apc.fr).
Mᵒ St-Placide.* **Open** 11am-7.30pm Mon-Sat. **Credit**
AmEx, MC, V. **Map** p405 G8.
The look here is simple but stylish; think perfectly
cut basics in muted tones. Hip without being remote-
ly try-hard, its jeans are a big hit with denim aficionados – the skinny version caused a stampede
when they came out. Womenswear is at no.3.

## Christophe Lemaire

*28 rue de Poitou, 3rd (01.44.78.00.09/www.
lemaireonline.com). Mᵒ St-Sébastien Froissart.*
**Open** 11am-7.30pm Mon-Sat. **Credit** AmEx, DC,
MC, V. **Map** p409 L6.
Creative director for Lacoste for seven years,
Lemaire has now opened his own boutique in an old
pharmacy. It's decorated like a fantasy apartment:
the salon, in '70s gold and glitz, stocks his own label
menswear and womenswear in high-tech Japanese
textiles, and leads into a soundproofed music
room with a wall of old speakers where you can buy
collectable Lacoste and Lemaire's own fave CDs.

Next door the seductive 'Japanese salon' holds the
jeans range. You can also buy the vintage lighting
on display here.

## L'Eclaireur Homme

*12 rue Malher, 4th (01.44.54.22.11/www.
leclaireur.com). Mᵒ St-Paul.* **Open** 11am-7pm Mon-
Sat. **Credit** AmEx, DC, MC, V. **Map** p409 L6.
Amid the exposed ducts of this old printworks you'll
find items by Prada, Comme des Garçons, Dries van
Noten and Martin Margiela. The star is Italian Stone
Island, whose radical clothing features parkas with
a steel shell to counteract pollution.
**Other locations** 26 av des Champs-Elysées, 8th
(01.45.62.12.32).

## Eglé Bespoke

*26 rue du Mont-Thabor, 1st (01.44.15.98.31). Mᵒ
Concorde.* **Open** 11am-7pm Mon-Sat. **Credit** MC, V.
**Map** p401 G5.
Two young entrepreneurs are reviving bespoke for
a new generation in this tiny shop. Custom shirts
start from €119 and can be delivered in a week or
so; they will also make or copy shirts for women and
produce made-to-order jeans for both sexes. Laser-
printed buttons from South America are perfect for
stamping your beloved's shirt with a secret message.

## Jacenko

*38 rue de Poitou, 3rd (01.42.71.80.38). Mᵒ St-
Sébastien Froissart.* **Open** 11am-7.30pm Tue-Sat;
2-7pm Sun. **Credit** MC, V. **Map** p402 J5.
A tasteful little boutique whose owner has a faultless eye for shirts, jackets, pullovers and accessories
that are dandy but not downright gay. McQ, Viktor
& Rolf, Givenchy and John Smedley are all stocked.

## Kanabeach

*78 rue Jean-Jacques-Rousseau, 1st (01.40.26.41.66/
www.kanabeach.com). Mᵒ Etienne Marcel.* **Open**
11am-7.30pm Mon-Sat. **Credit** MC, V. **Map** p402 J5.
With its mini waterfall, astroturf garden, mini cara-
van and changing rooms resembling beach cabins,
this French store has a campsite vibe. The
autumn/winter men's and women's collections
include Jacquard check red-and-apricot coats, navy
and cream trousers, and colourful separates.

## Madelios

*23 bd de la Madeleine, 1st (01.53.45.00.00/www.
madelios.com). Mᵒ Madeleine.* **Open** 10am-7pm Mon-
Sat. **Credit** AmEx, DC, MC, V. **Map** p401 G4.
A one-stop shop for men's fashion, with two floors
and more than 100 labels. Suits by Kenzo, Paul
Smith and Givenchy, plus shoes and accessories.

## Nodus

*22 rue Vieille-du-Temple, 4th (01.42.77.07.96/
www.nodus-boutique.fr). Mᵒ Hôtel de Ville or St-Paul.*
**Open** 10.45am-2pm, 3-7.30pm Mon-Sat; 1-7.30pm
Sun. **Credit** AmEx, DC, MC, V. **Map** p409 K6.
Under the wooden beams of this cosy men's shirt
specialist are neat rows of striped, checked and plain
dress shirts, stylish silk ties with subtle graphic
designs, and silver-plated crystal cufflinks.

Other locations 107 rue de Rennes, 6th (01.45.44.97.48); 191 rue du Fbg-St-Honoré, 8th (01.56.88.22.02); galerie du Claridge, 74 av des Champs-Elysées, 8th (01.43.59.32.53); 26 rue des Mathurins, 9th (01.40.06.08.74); 46 rue de Passy, 16th (01.42.24.15.03); 97 rue de Longchamp, 16th (01.47.27.31.80).

### Pull-In Underwear

*8 rue Française, 2nd (01.42.36.91.06/www.pull-in.com). M° Etienne Marcel.* **Open** 10am-7.30pm Mon-Sat. **Credit** AmEx, MC, V. **Map** p402 H5.
Hailing from South-West France, Pull-In is the official underwear supplier to the French rugby team. The ultra-trendy brand makes swimwear, but its boxers in wacko surfer patterns have now supplanted Calvin Kleins as *the* visible waistband for Gallic hip hoppers. They are also said to be wonderfully soft and comfy.

## Streetwear & clubwear

### Adidas

*150 rue de Rivoli, 1st (01.58.62.51.60/www.adidas.com). M° Louvre Rivoli.* **Open** 10am-7.30pm Mon-Sat. **Credit** AmEx, MC, V. **Map** p402 H5.
Three shiny floors of hard-to-find Adidas models; look out for re-issues of 1970s models nestling up with the entire Yamamoto-designed range.

### Boutique M Dia

*5-7 rue des Innocents, 1st (01.40.26.03.31/www.mdiawear.com). M° Châtelet/RER Châtelet Les Halles.* **Open** 1-8pm Mon; 11am-8pm Tue-Sat. **Credit** DC, MC, V. **Map** p406 J6.

Mohammed Dia, a rebel from the Sarcelles *banlieue*, went to America and came back with an idea to get him out of the ghetto: fashion design. Some €20 million later, he has his own line of men's and women's urban sports clothes, plus shoe line Tariq, worn by the NBA's Dallas Mavericks. His first boutique is a shrine to his vision, offering all from the Dia range.

### Clery Brice

*11 rue Pierre-Lescot, 1st (01.45.08.58.70). M° Les Halles/RER Châtelet Les Halles.* **Open** 11am-12.30pm, 1.30-8pm Mon-Sat. **Credit** MC, V. **Map** p402 J5.
Here you pay lofty prices to get limited editions of the coolest trainers six months before the rest of the world even finds out they should be wearing them.

### Ekivok

*39 bd de Sébastopol, 1st (01.42.21.98.71/www.ekivok.com). M° Les Halles/RER Châtelet Les Halles.* **Open** 11am-7.30pm Mon-Sat. **Credit** MC, V. **Map** p402 J5.
In Ekivok's graffiti-covered boutique you'll find major brands Bullrot, Carhartt, Hardcore Session and Juicy Jazz for men, and Golddigga, Punky Fish, Skunk Funk, Emilie the Strange and Hardcore Session for women, plus Eastpak accessories.

### Kiliwatch

*64 rue Tiquetonne, 2nd (01.42.21.17.37/www.kiliwatch.com). M° Etienne Marcel.* **Open** 2-7pm Mon; 11am-7.30pm Tue-Sat. **Credit** AmEx, MC, V. **Map** p402 J5.
The trailblazer of the rue Etienne-Marcel revival is filled with hoodies, casual shirts and washed-out jeans. Brands such as Gas, Edwin and Pepe Jeans accompany pricy, good-condition second-hand garb.

### The Lazy Dog

*2 passage Thiéré, 11th (01.58.30.94.76/www.thelazydog.fr). M° Ledru-Rollin.* **Open** noon-7pm Mon; 11am-7.30pm Tue-Sat. **Credit** MC, V. **Map** p407 M7.
Upstairs, this trendy store stocks graphic design-related objects and books, plus manga-style toys and clothes. There's a basement gallery too.

### Puma Store

*22 bd de Sébastopol, 4th (01.44.59.88.02/www.puma.com). M° Rambuteau.* **Open** 10.30am-7.30pm Mon-Sat. **Credit** AmEx, MC, V. **Map** p402 J5.
Puma offers its brand of sport, lifestyle and fashion at this flashy, two-floor flagship store. Speciality fixtures show off Christy Turlington's yoga clothes, and obscure versions of the popular Mostro trainer.

### Royal Cheese

*24 rue Tiquetonne, 2nd (01.40.28.06.56/www.royalcheese.com). M° Etienne Marcel.* **Open** 11am-1pm, 2-8pm Mon-Sat. **Credit** AmEx, DC, MC, V. **Map** p402 J5.
Clubbers hit Royal Cheese to snaffle up hard-to-find imports: Stüssy, Cheap Monday and Lee for the boys; Insight, Sessun, Edwin and Lazy Oaf for the girls. Prices are hefty: its Japanese jeans cost €200. **Other locations** 3 rue Mandar, 2nd (01.44.82.04.85).

**Eat, Drink, Shop**

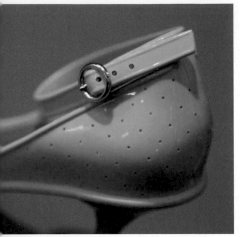

Killer heels: **Le Vestibule** is a foot fashionista's heaven.

### Le Vestibule

*3 pl Ste-Opportune, 1st (01.42.33.21.89). M°
Châtelet.* **Open** 10.30am-8pm Mon-Sat. **Credit**
AmEx, MC, V. **Map** p402 J5.
No longer doing vintage street and clubwear, Le
Vestibule still has a juicy selection of insider labels
and footwear.

## Used & vintage

*See also p269* **Antiques & flea markets.**

### Adrenaline

*30 rue Racine, 6th (01.44.27.09.05). M° Odéon.*
**Open** 11am-7pm Mon-Sat. **Credit** AmEx, MC, V.
**Map** p408 H7.
This *dépôt-vente* specialises in vintage luggage and
handbags. Iconic Vuitton suitcases and Kelly and
Birkin bags command enormous prices, but there
are some slightly more affordable pieces and a small
collection of '60s couture.

### La Belle Epoque

*10 rue de Poitou, 3rd (06.80.77.71.32). M° St
Sébastien Froissart.* **Open** 1.30-6.30pm Tue-Sat.
**Credit** MC, V. **Map** p409 L5.
Ex-model and theatrical costumier Philippe will
happily spend many hours rhapsodising about the
joys of vintage. In the shop you'll find everything
from the blue velours Grace Jones ensemble by
Yves Saint Laurent to a selection of inexpensive '70s
shirts and fake fur coats.

### Come On Eline

*16-18 rue des Taillandiers, 11th (01.43.38.12.11).
M° Ledru-Rollin.* **Open** *Sept-July* 11.30am-8.30pm
Mon-Thur; 11.30am-7.30pm Fri; 4-8pm Sun.
*Aug* 2-8pm Mon-Fri. **Credit** DC, MC, V.
**Map** p407 M7.

The owners of this three-floor vintage wonderland
have an eye for what's funky, from cowboy gear to
1960s debutantes frocks. They can afford to charge
high prices (Hermès scarves cost around €100), but
the stock is well sourced and in good condition.

### Didier Ludot

*20-24 galerie de Montpensier, 1st (01.42.96.06.56/
www.didierludot.com). M° Palais Royal Musée du
Louvre.* **Open** 11am-7pm Mon-Sat. **Credit** AmEx,
DC, MC, V. **Map** p402 H5.
Didier Ludot's temples to vintage haute couture
today appear in Printemps, London's Harrods and
New York's Barneys, stocking his own line of little
black dresses – also available at aptly named La
Petite Robe Noire (125 galerie de Valois, 1st,
01.40.15.01.04). The prices are steep, but the pieces
are stunning: Dior, Molyneux, Balenciaga, Pucci,
Féraud and, of course, Chanel, from the 1920s
onwards. Ludot also curates exhibits, using the
exclusive shop windows around the Palais-Royal
as a gallery.

### Free 'P' Star

*8 rue Ste-Croix-de-la-Bretonnerie, 4th
(01.42.76.03.72). M° St-Paul.* **Open** noon-11pm
Mon-Sat; 2-10pm Sun. **Credit** MC, V. **Map** p409 K6.
Late-night shopping is fun at this Aladdin's cave of
retro glitz, ex-army wear and glad rags that provides
many a cross-dresser with fancy dress partywear.

### Rag

*83-85 rue St-Martin, 4th (01.48.87.34.64). M°
Rambuteau.* **Open** 10am-8pm Mon-Sat; noon-8pm
Sun. **No credit cards. Map** p402 K5.
One half of Rag focuses on pilots' navy jumpers and
1970s shirts at €15, colourful puffer jackets and '70s
heels; the other may yield a vintage Hermès scarf,
1960s Paco Rabanne dress or Gucci accessory.

### Studio W

*6 rue du Pont-aux-Choux, 3rd (01.44.78.05.02). M°
St-Sébastien Froissart.* **Open** 2-7.30pm Tue-Sat (Mon
during fashion weeks). **Credit** MC, V. **Map** p409 L5.
Aesthete William Moricet's tiny shop is simply
exquisite, from the vintage Courrèges and Yves
Saint Laurent couture on mannequins to the glossy
golden retriever who lounges among crocodile and
patent leather shoes and bags. There's some fabulous jewellery for sale too.

### Wochdom

*72 rue Condorcet, 9th (01.53.21.09.72). M° Anvers
or Pigalle.* **Open** noon-8pm Mon-Sat. **Credit** DC,
MC, V. **Map** p402 J2.
This temple to vintage stocks a mainly female collection, inclined towards the spotty and stripy 1980s.
There are copies of *Interview*, *Elle* and *Vogue*, and
old vinyl too.

## Fashion accessories & services

### Eyewear

Get an eye test at an *ophtalmologiste*, then take
along your prescription for cool French specs.

### Alain Mikli

*74 rue des Sts-Pères, 7th (01.45.49.40.00/
www.mikli.fr). M° Sèvres Babylone or St-Sulpice.*
**Open** 10am-7pm Mon-Sat. **Credit** AmEx, DC, MC,
V. **Map** p405 G7.
Cult French designer Mikli, the first to inject vroom
into prescription peepers, uses cellulose acetate, a
blend of wood and cotton sliced from blocks. At his
flagship Starck-designed boutique, frames are laid
out in a glass counter like designer sweeties.
**Other locations** 4 rue Bachaumont, 2nd
(01.42.82.08.42); 1 rue des Rosiers, 4th
(01.42.71.01.56).

### Anne et Valentin

*4 rue Ste-Croix-de-la-Bretonnerie, 4th
(01.40.29.93.01/www.anneetvalentin.com). M° Hôtel
de Ville or St-Paul.* **Open** noon-8pm Tue-Sat. Closed
12-22 Aug. **Credit** AmEx, DC, MC, V. **Map** p409 K6.
This modish French eyewear firm occupies a cosy
three-floor Marais boutique. A&V design chic uni-
sex frames: light titanium models have names like
Tarzan and Truman; coloured acetate frames have
inventive details and colour combinations.

### Hats

### Maison Michel

*65 rue Ste-Anne, 2nd (01.42.96.89.77/www.michel-
paris.com). M° Pyramides.* **Open** By appointment.
**Credit** MC, V. **Map** p401 H4.
One of the specialist businesses saved from extinc-
tion by Chanel, Maison Michel has been making hats
since 1936 and supplies haute couture designers and
the Paris opera. They can create the perfect panama
or a flamboyant creation for the races, and also
launched a prêt-à-porter range in 2006 with a range
of sexy, shiny, '60s-inspired cloches and caps.

### Marie Mercié

*23 rue St-Sulpice, 6th (01.43.26.45.83). M° Odéon.*
**Open** 11am-7pm Mon-Sat. **Credit** AmEx, MC, V.
**Map** p408 H7.
Mercié's creations make you wish you lived in an
era when hats were de rigueur. Step out in one
shaped like curved fingers (complete with shocking-
pink nail varnish and pink diamond ring) or a beret
like a face with red lips and turquoise eyes. Ready-
to-wear starts at €30; *sur mesure* takes ten days.

### Jewellery

Dotted in and around place Vendôme, the key
*joailliers* define the luxurious spirit of Paris.
Many fun and costume jewellery boutiques are
found in the Marais. *See also p251* **Galerie
Simone** and *p246* **Jack Henry**.

### Boucheron

*26 pl Vendôme, 1st (01.42.61.58.16/www.
boucheron.com). M° Opéra.* **Open** 10.30am-7pm
Mon-Sat. **Credit** AmEx, DC, MC, V. **Map** p401 G4.
Boucheron was the first to set up on place Vendôme,
eager for celebrity custom from the nearby Ritz
hotel. Owned by Gucci, the grand jeweller still manages to produce stunning pieces, using traditional
motifs with new accents: witness, for example, its
fabulous chocolate-coloured gold watch.
**Other locations** 78 rue Sts-Pères, 7th
(01.44.39.10.29).

### Cartier

*3 rue de la Paix, 2nd (01.42.18.53.70/www.cartier.
com). M° Opéra.* **Open** 10.30am-7pm Mon-Sat.
**Credit** AmEx, DC, MC, V. **Map** p401 G4.
This mythic French jeweller and watchmaker has
recently renovated and reopened its impressive
landmark headquarters. Downstairs, pearls, pan-
thers and the Trinity ring jostle for attention among
historic pieces commissioned by crowned heads; the
upper salons house perfumer Mathilde Laurent's
bespoke scents, starting at €60,000.
**Other locations** 3 rue de la Paix, 2nd
(01.42.18.53.70); 10 cité du Retiro, 8th (01.58.18.18.18).

### Casoar

*29 galerie de Montpensier, 1st (01.42.96.39.54/
www.cartier.com). M° Opéra.* **Open** 10.30am-7pm
Mon-Sat. **Credit** AmEx, DC, MC, V. **Map** p401 G4.
This elegant outpost of the fashion editors' favourite
jewellery shop displays intricate re-editions of
Napoléon III, belle époque and art deco jewellery
such as intaglio rings and earrings in *pâte de verre*.

### Chanel Joaillerie

*18 pl Vendôme, 1st (01.55.35.50.05/www.
chanel.com). M° Opéra or Tuileries.* **Open** 11am-7pm
Mon-Sat. **Credit** AmEx, DC, MC, V. **Map** p401 G4.

**Eat, Drink, Shop**

Chanel launched its fine jewellery in the 1990s, reissuing the single collection – big on platinum and diamonds – that Coco had designed some 60 years previously. The current line reinterprets Coco's motifs – camellias, stars and comets – in a modern way.

### Dior Joaillerie

*8 pl Vendôme, 1st (01.42.96.30.84/www.dior.com). M° Opéra or Tuileries.* **Open** 11am-7pm Mon, Sat; 10.30am-7pm Tue-Fri. **Credit** AmEx, DC, MC, V. **Map** p401 G4.

The unabashed bling of Victoire de Castellane's designs is responsible for the fad of semi-precious coloured stones and runaway success of the 'Mimi Oui', a ring with a tiny diamond on a slim chain. **Other locations** 28 av Montaigne, 8th (01.47.23.52.39).

### KarryO'

*62 rue des Sts-Pères, 6th (01.45.48.94.67/www. karryo.com). M° St-Germain-des-Prés.* **Open** 11am-7pm Mon-Sat. **Credit** MC, V. **Map** p405 G7.

Paris socialites come here to source their vintage jewellery, as well as modern creations by owner Karine Berrebi. Her adjacent gallery, Unique, features one-of-a-kind finds, from jewellery and decorative objects to Hermès bags and the occasional Schiaparelli fur.

### 4me

*115 rue Vieille-du-Temple, 3rd (01.42.77.30.06/ www.4meby.com). M° St-Sébastien-Froissart.* **Open** noon-7pm Tue-Sat; 2-7pm Sun. **Credit** MC, V. **Map** p409 L5.

Julie Bernardin's tiny boutique is dedicated to the accessory's accessory. Here you will find one-off jewels for personalising jeans, handbags, iPods and mobiles, including the sweet 'Oh Oui' marriage-themed jewel strung with lace and champagne cork.

### Viveka Bergström

*23 rue de la Grange aux Belles, 10th (01.40.03.04.92/www.viveka-bergstrom.com). M° Colonel Fabien.* **Open** 1-7pm Tue-Fri; noon-7pm Sat. **Credit** AmEx, MC, V. **Map** p402 L3.

The daughter of Saab's aeroplane designer in the 1950s, Viveka Bergström makes slinky tassel necklaces, oversized beaten gold rings and brooches and conversation starters like the angel-wing bracelet and a necklace featuring the Paris map.

## Lingerie & swimwear

The greater part of the third floor of **Galeries Lafayette** (*see p240*) is accounted for by underwear; for swimwear, *see also p272* **Sport & fitness**.

### Alice Cadolle

*4 rue Cambon, 1st (01.42.60.94.22/www.cadolle. com). M° Concorde or Madeleine.* **Open** 10am-1pm, 2-7pm Mon-Sat. Closed Aug. **Credit** AmEx, MC, V. **Map** p401 G4.

Five generations of lingerie-makers are behind this boutique, founded by Hermine Cadolle, who claims to be the inventor of the bra. Great-great-granddaughter Poupie Cadolle continues the tradition in a cosy space devoted to a luxury ready-to-wear line of bras, panties and corsets. Cadolle Couture, by appointment only, is at 255 rue St-Honoré, 1st (01.42.60.94.94).

### Erès

*2 rue Tronchet, 8th (01.47.42.28.82/www.eres.fr). M° Madeleine.* **Open** 10am-7pm Mon-Sat. **Credit** AmEx, DC, MC, V. **Map** p401 G4.

Erès' beautifully cut swimwear has embraced a sexy '60s look complete with buttons on the low-cut briefs. One advantage for the natural woman is that the top and bottom can be purchased in different sizes, or you can buy just one piece of a bikini. **Other locations** 4bis rue du Cherche-Midi, 6th (01.45.44.95.54); 40 av Montaigne, 8th (01.47.23.07.26); 6 rue Guichard, 16th (01.46.47.45.21).

### Fifi Chachnil

*231 rue St-Honoré, 1st (01.42.61.21.83/www. fifichachnil.com). M° Tuileries.* **Open** 11am-7pm Mon-Sat. **Credit** AmEx, MC, V. **Map** p401 G4.

Chachnil has a new approach to frou-frou underwear in the pin-up tradition. Her chic mixes – deep red silk bras with boudoir pink bows, and pale turquoise girdles with orange trim – will have you and your admirer purring in delight. Check the transparent black babydoll negligées with an Empire-line bust. **Other locations** 68 rue Jean-Jacques-Rousseau, 1st (01.42.21.19.98).

### Marlies Dekkers

*10 rue du Cherche-Midi, 6th (01.42.84.02.40/ www.marliesdekkers.com). M° Sèvres Babylone.* **Open** 11am-7pm Mon; 10am-7pm Tue-Sat. **Credit** AmEx, DC, MC, V. **Map** p405 G7.

This Dutch lingerie designer, winner of the 2007 Veuve Clicquot Businesswoman of the Year, has a growing celebrity following for her daring, but far from frou-frou, underwear. The new Paris store is high-tech with just a touch of the red light about it.

### Princesse Tam-Tam

*52 bd St-Michel, 6th (01.42.34.99.31/www. princessetam-tam.com). M° Cluny La Sorbonne.* **Open** 1.30-7pm Mon; 10am-7pm Tue-Sat. **Credit** AmEx, MC, V. **Map** p408 J7.

This inexpensive underwear and swimwear brand now has traffic-stopping promotions. Bright colours and sexily transparent and sporty gear are in. **Other locations** throughout the city.

### Sabbia Rosa

*73 rue des Sts-Pères, 6th (01.45.48.88.37). M° St-Germain-des-Prés.* **Open** 10am-7pm Mon-Sat. **Credit** AmEx, MC, V. **Map** p405 G7.

Let Moana Moatti tempt you with feather-trimmed satin mules or spread out satin, silk and chiffon negligées in fine shades of tangerine, lemon, mocha and pistachio. All sizes are medium, others are made *sur mesure*; prices are just the right side of stratospheric.

### Vannina Vesperini

*4 rue de Tournon, 6th (01.56.24.32.72/www.*
*vanninavesperini.com). M° Odéon.* **Open** 11am-7pm
Mon-Sat. **Credit** AmEx, MC, V. **Map** p408 J7.
Only the finest silk satin is used for this prize-
winning designer's underwear, camisoles and
sophisticated nightwear. The new boutique has a
made-to-measure atelier by appointment.

### Yoba

*11 rue du Marché-St-Honoré, 1st (01.40.41.04.06/*
*www.yobaparis.com). M° Tuileries.* **Open** 11am-8pm
Mon-Wed, Fri; 11am-9pm Thur; noon-8pm Sat.
**Credit** MC, V. **Map** p401 G5.
One for the liberated woman, this smart boutique
stocks items from wispy lingerie to cheeky sex toys.

## Shoes & bags

The luxury floor at **Printemps** (*see p241*) is a
good source of designer footwear labels. Rue du
Dragon, rue de Grenelle and rue du Cherche-
Midi form an axis lined with numerous shoe
and accessory shops.

### Bruno Frisoni

*34 rue de Grenelle, 6th (01.42.84.12.30/www.*
*brunofrisoni.fr). M° Rue du Bac.* **Open** 10.30am-7pm
Tue-Sat. **Credit** AmEx, V. **Map** p405 G7.
Innovative Frisoni's shoes have a cinematic, pop
edge: modern theatrics not for the conventional.

### Christian Louboutin

*19 rue Jean-Jacques-Rousseau, 1st (01.42.36.05.31).*
*M° Palais Royal Musée du Louvre.* **Open** 10.30am-
7pm Mon-Sat. Closed 3wks Aug. **Credit** AmEx,
MC, V. **Map** p402 J5.
It's no longer Manolos, but Louboutin's red-soled
glamour shoes that are top of the tree in New York.

Each of his creations (with hallmark red soles) is
displayed in an individual frame. There is now a
made-to-measure service.
**Other locations** 38 rue de Grenelle, 7th
(01.42.22.33.07).

### Hervé Chapelier

*1bis rue du Vieux-Colombier, 6th (01.44.07.06.50/*
*www.hervechapelier.fr). M° St-Germain-des-Prés or*
*St-Sulpice.* **Open** 10.15am-7pm Mon-Sat. **Credit**
AmEx, MC, V. **Map** p407 G7.
Tops for chic, hard-wearing, bicoloured totes. Often
copied, never equalled. Sizes and prices range from
a dinky purse at €22 to a weekend bag at €130.
**Other locations** 390 rue St-Honoré, 1st
(01.42.96.38.04); 45 av Georges-V, 8th (01.47.23.85.60);
55 bd de Courcelles, 8th (01.47.54.91.27).

### Iris

*28 rue de Grenelle, 7th (01.42.22.89.81). M° Rue du*
*Bac or St-Sulpice.* **Open** 10.30am-7pm Mon-Sat.
**Credit** AmEx, MC, V. **Map** p405 F7.
This white boutique stocks shoes by Marc Jacobs,
John Galliano, Proenza-Schouler and Viktor & Rolf.

### Jamin Puech

*61 rue de Hauteville, 10th (01.40.22.08.32/www.*
*jamin-puech.com). M° Poissonnière.* **Open** 11am-7pm
Mon-Fri; noon-7pm Sat. **Credit** AmEx, DC, MC, V.
**Map** p402 K3.
The complete collection of Isabelle Puech and Benoît
Jamin's dazzling handbags is on show in a bohemian
setting complete with antler-horn chairs.
**Other locations** 68 rue Vieille-du-Temple, 3rd
(01.48.87.84.83); 43 rue Madame, 6th (01.45.48.14.85).

### Moss

*22 rue de Grenelle, 7th (01.42.22.01.42). M° Rue*
*du Bac or St-Sulpice.* **Open** 10.30am-7pm Mon-Sat.
**Credit** AmEx, MC, V. **Map** p405 F7.

**Peggy Huyn Kinh.** *See p260.*

The three sisters who run this boutique pride themselves on sourcing cutting-edge couture shoes hard to find elsewhere, such as creations by former Celine stylist Avril Gau and signature styles by Laurence Dacade, Duccio del Duca and Hartian Bourdin. You'll also find scarves by Octavio Pizzaro and jewellery by Karry O', the fourth sister.

### Patrick Cox

*62 rue Tiquetonne, 2nd (01.40.26.66.55/ www.patrickcox.co.uk). Mᵒ Etienne Marcel.* **Open** 10.30am-7.30pm Mon-Sat. **Credit** AmEx, MC, V. **Map** p402 J5.

Elegance off the catwalk is Cox's forte, with ultra-feminine designs and fabrics. His stiletto boots and kitten heels make your feet feel like a million euros. **Other locations** 21 rue de Grenelle, 7th (01.45.49.24.28).

### Peggy Huyn Kinh

*9-11 rue Coëtlogon, 6th (01.42.84.83.83/ www.phk.fr). Mᵒ St-Sulpice.* **Open** 10am-7pm Mon-Sat. **Credit** AmEx, MC, V. **Map** p405 G7.

Once creative director at Cartier, Peggy Huyn Kinh now makes bags of boar skin and python, plus silver jewellery. *Photo p259.*

### Pierre Hardy

*156 galerie de Valois, 1st (01.42.60.59.75/ www.pierrehardy.com). Mᵒ Palais Royal Musée du Louvre.* **Open** 11am-7pm Mon-Sat. **Credit** AmEx, DC, MC, V. **Map** p402 H5.

This classy black-and-white shoebox is home to Hardy's range of superbly conceived footwear – with a price tag to match – for men and women.

### Repetto

*22 rue de la Paix, 2nd (01.44.71.83.20/www. repetto.com). Mᵒ Opéra.* **Open** 10.30am-7.30pm Mon-Sat. **Credit** AmEx, MC, V. **Map** p401 G4.

This ballet shoe-maker struck gold when it decided to reissue its dance shoes with pavement soles. The full range of prowly *ballerines* and showbiz dance boots in black, metallic and spangly finishes is sold alongside actual balletwear, and you can try out your *pointes* on a red carpet with a *barre* if you want to show off.

### Rodolphe Menudier

*14 rue de Castiglione, 1st (01.42.60.86.27/www. rodolphemenudier.com). Mᵒ Concorde or Tuileries.* **Open** 11am-7.30pm Mon; 10.30am-7.30pm Tue-Sat. **Credit** AmEx, MC, V. **Map** p401 G5.

This silver-and-black boutique makes the perfect backdrop for Menudier's racy designs. Open, silver-handled drawers display his stilettos in profile, plus outrageous thigh-high boots with Plexiglass soles; more demure customers can opt for a pair of sweet ballerina pumps.

### Roger Vivier

*29 rue du Fbg-St-Honoré, 8th (01.53.43.00.00/ www.rogervivier.com). Mᵒ Concorde or Madeleine.* **Open** 11am-7pm Mon-Sat. **Credit** AmEx, DC, MC, V. **Map** p401 F4.

Vivier is credited with inventing the stiletto. His legend lives on at this boutique with vintage models and new designs by Bruno Frisoni (*see p259*).

## Food & drink

You could spend a lifetime sampling the breads, pastries, chocolate and cheeses available in Paris. Open-air markets continue to beckon with their fresh, seasonal goods, and both **Galeries Lafayette** and **Bon Marché** (for both, *see p240*) have luxury food halls.

## Bakeries

### Arnaud Delmontel

*39 rue des Martyrs, 9th (01.48.78.29.33/www. arnaud-delmontel.com). Mᵒ St-Georges.* **Open** 7am-8.30pm Mon, Wed-Sun. **No credit cards. Map** p402 H2.

With its crisp crust and chewy crumb shot through with irregular holes, Delmontel's Renaissance bread is one of the finest in Paris. He puts the same skill into his unsurpassable almond croissants and *tarte au citron à l'ancienne*, available in individual portions. **Other locations** 57 rue Damrémont, 18th (01.42.64.59.63).

### L'Autre Boulange

*43 rue de Montreuil, 11th (01.43.72.86.04). Mᵒ Faidherbe Chaligny or Nation.* **Open** 7.30am-1.30pm, 3.30-7.30pm Tue-Sat. Closed Aug. **Credit** MC, V. **Map** p407 P7.

Michel Cousin bakes up to 23 kinds of organic loaves in his wood-fired oven – types like the *flutiot* (rye bread with raisins, walnuts and hazelnuts), the *sarment de Bourgogne* (sourdough and a little rye) and a spiced cornmeal bread ideal with foie gras.

### Le Boulanger de Monge

*123 rue Monge, 5th (01.43.37.54.20/www. leboulangerdemonge.com). Mᵒ Censier Daubenton.* **Open** 7am-8.30pm Tue-Sun. **Credit** MC, V. **Map** p406 K9.

Dominique Saibron uses spices to give inimitable flavour to his organic sourdough *boule*. Every day about 2,000 bread-lovers visit his boutique, which also produces one of the city's best baguettes.

### Moisan

*5 pl d'Aligre, 12th (01.43.45.46.60). Mᵒ Ledru-Rollin.* **Open** 7am-8pm Tue-Sat; 7am-2pm Sun. **No credit cards. Map** p407 N7.

Moisan's organic bread, *viennoiseries* and rustic tarts are outstanding. At this branch, by the market, there's always a queue snaking out the door. **Other locations** 4 av du Général-Leclerc, 14th (01.43.22.34.13).

### Poilâne

*8 rue du Cherche-Midi, 6th (01.45.48.42.59/ www.poilane.com). Mᵒ Sèvres Babylone or St-Sulpice.* **Open** 7.15am-8.15pm Mon-Sat. **Credit** (€20 minimum) AmEx, DC, MC, V. **Map** p405 G7.

# Market forces

With their brightly coloured awnings and vocal merchants, open-air food markets are hard to overlook in Paris. But there is another kind of market known more to locals than visitors, who might easily walk past their discreet entrances without noticing them. The 13 *marchés couverts*, or covered food halls, are among the oldest and most atmospheric markets in Paris. Best of all they are open every day except Monday, with most stalls selling their wares from 8.30am to 1pm and 4pm to 7.30pm Tuesday to Saturday, and 8.30am to 1.30pm Sunday.

The **Marché des Enfants Rouges** (39 rue de Bretagne, 3rd, Mº Filles du Calvaire or Temple), which reopened several years ago after a period of neglect in the 1990s, is named after the orphanage that stood here in the 16th century. The orphans were dressed in red, and the nickname stuck when the building became a covered market in 1777. Reviving a covered market is never easy and it took some time for the Enfants Rouges to develop a loyal clientele. Part of its current success is due to the variety of *traiteurs*, who sell ready-made Japanese, Moroccan and Italian dishes and provide seating. There is also a very good wine bar, Arômes et Cépages, which serves cheese and charcuterie plates as well as oysters on weekends. The market is at its busiest and best on Saturdays and Sundays.

Another market to have been restored in recent years is the **Marché St-Germain** (4/6 rue Lobineau, 6th, Mº Mabillon), which has to compete with the nearby street market on rue de Seine and the popular Raspail open-air market. Despite this, the covered market is gradually carving out a niche with unusual stalls such as juice and soup bar Litchi and Japanese pâtisserie Colombia. Bacchus & Ariane is a friendly wine shop that recently began serving charcuterie from the market's best butcher, Serge Caillaud. The lucky children who go to the crèche in the same building eat vegetables and fruit from the market's well-stocked stands.

Probably the most entertaining covered market in Paris is the working-class-meets-bobo **Marché Beauvau** (pl d'Aligre, 12th, Mº Ledru-Rollin), which takes place alongside the rue d'Aligre open-air market and dates from 1779. Busy every day of the week but particularly at weekends, when locals congregate outside the nearby wine bar Le Baron Rouge to slurp oysters and wine, it houses high-quality stalls such as renowned butcher Michel Brunon, fromager Philippe Langlet, olive oil and condiment specialist Sur les Quais, an impressive fishmonger and the best fruit and vegetable specialist in the area. There is even a stall dedicated to unusual beers, a rarity in Paris. This is one of the city's friendliest markets and when regular clients spot a newcomer they dish out tips such as 'Goûtez le comté, c'est excellent!'

Other covered markets worth visiting include **Marché couvert St-Quentin** (85bis, bd Magenta, 10th, Mº Gare de l'Est); **Marché couvert de Passy**, (pl de Passy, 16th, Mº Muette); and **Marché couvert Secrétan** (33 av Secrétan, 19th, Mº Bolivar).

Apollonia Poilâne runs the family shop, where locals queue for fresh country *miches*, flaky-crusted apple tarts and buttery shortbread biscuits. **Other locations** 49 rue de Grenelle, 15th (01.45.79.11.49).

## Cheese

The sign *maître fromager affineur* denotes merchants who buy young cheeses from farms and age them on their premises; *fromage fermier* and *fromage au lait cru* signify farm-produced and raw milk cheeses respectively.

### Alléosse
*13 rue Poncelet, 17th (01.46.22.50.45/www.fromage-alleosse.com). Mº Ternes.* **Open** 9am-1pm, 4-7pm Tue-Thur; 9am-1pm, 4.30-7pm Fri, Sat. **Credit** MC, V. **Map** p400 C2.
People cross town for these cheeses – wonderful farmhouse camemberts, delicate st-marcellins, a choice of *chèvres* and several rarities.

### Fromagerie Dubois et Fils
*80 rue de Tocqueville, 17th (01.42.27.11.38). Mº Malesherbes or Villiers.* **Open** 9am-1pm, 4-8pm Tue-Fri; 8.30am-7.45pm Sat; 9am-1pm Sun. Closed 1st 3wks Aug. **Credit** AmEx, MC, V. **Map** p401 E2.
Superchef darling Dubois stocks 80 types of goat's cheese, plus prized, aged st-félicien.

### Fromagerie Quatrehomme
*62 rue de Sèvres, 7th (01.47.34.33.45). Mº Duroc or Vaneau.* **Open** 8.45am-1pm, 4-7.45pm Tue-Thur; 8.45am-7.45pm Fri, Sat. **Credit** MC, V. **Map** p405 F8.
The award-winning Marie Quatrehomme runs this inviting *fromagerie*. Justly famous for her comté fruité, beaufort and squishy st-marcellin, she also sells specialities such as goat's cheese with pesto. **Other locations** 9 rue du Poteau, 18th (01.46.06.26.03).

### Marie-Anne Cantin
*12 rue du Champ-de-Mars, 7th (01.45.50.43.94/www.cantin.fr). Mº Ecole Militaire or Latour Maubourg.* **Open** 8.30am-7.30pm Mon-Sat. **Credit** AmEx, MC, V. **Map** p404 D6.
Cantin, a defender of unpasteurised cheese and supplier to many posh Paris restaurants, offers aged *chèvres* and amazing morbier, mont d'or and comté.

## Chocolate

### Cacao et Chocolat
*29 rue de Buci, 6th (01.46.33.77.63). Mº Mabillon.* **Open** 10.30am-2pm, 3-7.30pm daily. **Credit** AmEx, DC, MC, V. **Map** p405 H7.
This shop, decorated in burned orange and ochre, recalls chocolate's ancient Aztec origins, with its choice of spicy fillings (honey and chilli, nutmeg, clove and citrus), chocolate masks and pyramids. **Other locations** 63 rue St-Louis-en-l'Ile, 4th (01.46.33.33.33); 36 rue Vieille-du-Temple, 4th (01.42.71.50.06).

### Christian Constant
*37 rue d'Assas, 6th (01.53.63.15.15). Mº Rennes or St-Placide.* **Open** 8.30am-9pm Mon-Fri; 8.30am-8pm Sat, Sun. **Credit** MC, V. **Map** p405 G8.
A master chocolate-maker and *traiteur*, Constant scours the globe for new ideas. His *ganaches* are subtly flavoured with verbena, jasmine or cardamom.

### Jean-Paul Hévin
*3 rue Vavin, 6th (01.43.54.09.85/www.jphevin.com). Mº Notre-Dame-des-Champs or Vavin.* **Open** 10am-7pm Tue-Sat. Closed Aug. **Credit** AmEx, MC, V. **Map** p405 G8.
Hévin fills his chocolates with potent cheeses, and loyal customers serve them with wine as an aperitif. Aphrodisiac chocolates are another favourite. **Other locations** 231 rue St-Honoré, 1st (01.55.35.35.96); 16 av de La Motte-Picquet, 7th (01.45.51.77.48).

### La Maison du Chocolat
*89 av Raymond-Poincaré, 16th (01.40.67.77.83/www.lamaisonduchocolat.com). Mº Victor Hugo.* **Open** 10am-7pm Mon-Sat. **Credit** AmEx, MC, V. **Map** p400 B4.
Robert Linxe opened his first Paris shop in 1977 and has been inventing new chocolates ever since, using Asian spices, fresh fruits and herbal infusions. **Other locations** throughout the city.

### Patrick Roger
*108 bd St-Germain, 6th (01.43.29.38.42/www.patrickroger.com). Mº Odéon.* **Open** 10.30am-7.30pm Tue-Sat. **Credit** MC, V. **Map** p408 H7.
Sceaux-based Roger is shaking up the art of chocolate-making. While other *chocolatiers* aim for gloss, Roger may create a brushed effect on hens so realistic you almost expect them to lay (chocolate) eggs.

### Richart
*258 bd St-Germain, 7th (01.45.55.66.00/www.richart.com). Mº Solférino.* **Open** 10am-7pm Mon-Sat. **Credit** AmEx, MC, V. **Map** p405 F6.
Each chocolate *ganache* has an intricate design, packages look like jewel boxes, and each purchase comes with a tract on how best to savour the stuff.

## Drinks

### Les Caves Augé
*116 bd Haussmann, 8th (01.45.22.16.97). Mº St-Augustin.* **Open** 1-7.30pm Mon; 9am-7.30pm Tue-Sat. Closed Mon in Aug. **Credit** AmEx, MC, V. **Map** p401 E3.
The oldest wine shop in Paris – Marcel Proust was a regular customer – is serious and professional.

### Les Caves Taillevent
*199 rue du Fbg-St-Honoré, 8th (01.45.61.14.09/www.taillevent.com). Mº Charles de Gaulle Etoile or Ternes.* **Open** 9am-7.30pm Tue-Sat. Closed 1st 3wks Aug. **Credit** AmEx, DC, MC, V. **Map** p400 D3.
Choose from half a million wines here to go with your meal at the nearby Taillevent restaurant (*see p199*).

Les Caves Augé.

## Julien, Caviste

*50 rue Charlot, 3rd (01.42.72.00.94). M° Filles du Calvaire.* **Open** 9am-1.30pm, 3.30-7.30pm Tue-Sat; 10.30am-1.30pm Sun. Closed 3rd wk Aug. **Credit** AmEx, MC, V. **Map** p402 L5.

Julien promotes the small producers he has discovered, and often holds wine tastings on Saturdays.

## Lavinia

*3 bd de la Madeleine, 1st (01.42.97.20.20/ www.lavinia.fr). M° Madeleine.* **Open** 10am-8pm Mon-Fri; 9am-8pm Sat. **Credit** AmEx, DC, MC, V. **Map** p401 G4.

This modern wine emporium is great fun, with its *dégustation* machines on the ground floor (you buy a card for €10 and can taste up to ten different wines of the week by swiping it). It stocks many non-French wines, and the glassed-in cave has everything from a 1945 Mouton-Rothschild at €22,000 to trendy and 'fragile' wines under €10.

## Legrand Filles et Fils

*1 rue de la Banque, 2nd (01.42.60.07.12). M° Bourse.* **Open** 11am-7pm Mon-Sat. Closed Mon in July & Aug. **Credit** AmEx, MC, V. **Map** p402 H4.

Fine wines and brandies, teas and *bonbons,* plus a showroom for regular wine tastings.

## Ryst Dupeyron

*79 rue du Bac, 7th (01.45.48.80.93/www. dupeyron.com). M° Rue du Bac.* **Open** 12.30-7.30pm Mon; 10.30am-7.30pm Tue-Sat. Closed 2wks Aug. **Credit** AmEx, MC, V. **Map** p405 F7.

The Dupeyrons have been selling armagnac for four generations, and still have bottles from 1868. Treasures here include 200 fine Bordeaux wines and an extensive range of vintage port.

## Global

### Les Délices d'Orient

*52 av Emile-Zola, 15th (01.45.79.10.00). M° Charles Michels.* **Open** 8.30am-9pm Tue-Sun. **Credit** MC, V. **Map** p404 B8

Shelves groan under stuffed aubergines, halva, falafel and all manner of Middle Eastern delicacies. **Other locations** 14 rue des Quatre-Frères-Peignot, 15th (01.45.77.82.93).

### Izraël

*30 rue François-Miron, 4th (01.42.72.66.23). M° Hôtel de Ville.* **Open** 9.30am-1pm, 2.30-7pm Tue-Fri; 9.30am-7pm Sat. Closed Aug. **Credit** MC, V. **Map** p409 K6.

A Marais fixture, this narrow shop stocks spices and other delights from Mexico, Turkey and India.

### Jabugo Ibérico & Co

*11 rue Clément-Marot, 8th (01.47.20.03.13). M° Alma Marceau or Franklin D. Roosevelt.* **Open** 10am-9pm Mon-Fri; 10am-8pm Sat. **Credit** AmEx, DC, MC, V. **Map** p400 D4.

Spanish hams here have the Bellota-Bellota label, meaning that the pigs have been allowed to feast on acorns. Manager Philippe Poulachon compares his cured hams (€98 a kilo) to the delicacy of truffles. They also sell hams at the *épicerie* attached to restaurant Bellota-Bellota (18 rue Jean-Nicot, 7th, 01.53.59.96.96).

## Markets

*See p261* **Market forces**.

## Pâtisseries

### Arnaud Lahrer

*53 rue Caulaincourt, 18th (01.42.57.68.08). M° Lamarck Caulaincourt.* **Open** 10am-7.30pm Tue-Sat. **Credit** MC, V. **Map** p401 H1.

Look out for the strawberry-and-lychee flavoured *bonheur* and the chocolate-and-thyme *récif.*

### Finkelsztajn

*27 rue des Rosiers, 4th (01.42.72.78.91/www. laboutiquejaune.com). M° St-Paul.* **Open** 10am-7pm Mon, Wed-Sun. Closed 15 July-15 Aug. **Credit** (€20 minimum) AmEx, MC, V. **Map** p409 L6.

This motherly, yellow-fronted shop, in business since 1946, stocks dense Jewish cakes filled with poppy seeds, apples or cream cheese.

### Gérard Mulot

*76 rue de Seine, 6th (01.43.26.85.77). M° Odéon.* **Open** 6.45am-8pm Mon, Tue, Thur-Sun. Closed Easter & Aug. **Credit** V. **Map** p408 H7.

Gérard Mulot rustles up truly stunning pastries. A popular example is the *mabillon*: caramel mousse with apricot marmalade. **Other locations** 93 rue de la Glacière, 13th (01.45.81.39.09).

**Eat, Drink, Shop**

## Pierre Hermé

*72 rue Bonaparte, 6th (01.43.54.47.77). M°
Mabillon, St-Germain-des-Prés or St-Sulpice.* **Open**
10am-7pm Tue-Fri, Sun; 10am-7.30pm Sat. Closed 1st
3wks Aug. **Credit** AmEx, DC, MC, V. **Map** p405 G7.
Pastry superstar Hermé attracts connoisseurs from
St-Germain and afar with his seasonal collections.
**Other locations** 185 rue de Vaugirard, 15th
(01.47.83.89.96).

## Treats & *traiteurs*

### Da Rosa

*62 rue de Seine, 6th (01.40.51.00.09/www.darosa.fr).
M° Odéon.* **Open** 10am-11pm daily. **Credit** AmEx,
MC, V. **Map** p408 H7.
José Da Rosa sourced ingredients for top restaurants
before filling his own shop with Spanish hams,
Olivier Roellinger spices and Luberon truffles.

### Fauchon

*26 & 30 pl de la Madeleine, 8th (01.70.39.38.00/
www.fauchon.com). M° Madeleine.* **Open** No.26
8am-9pm Mon-Sat. No.30 9am-8pm Mon-Sat.
**Credit** AmEx, MC, V. **Map** p401 F4.
The city's most famous food shop is worth a visit,
particularly for the beautifully packaged gift items.

### Hédiard

*21 pl de la Madeleine, 8th (01.43.12.88.88/
www.hediard.fr). M° Madeleine.* **Open** 8.30am-9pm
Mon-Sat. **Credit** AmEx, DC, MC, V. **Map** p401 F4.
The first to introduce exotic foods to Paris, Hédiard
specialises in rare teas and coffees, spices, jams and
candied fruits. The original shop, dating from 1880,
has a posh tearoom upstairs, La Table d'Hédiard.
**Other locations** throughout the city.

### Huilerie Artisanale Leblanc

*6 rue Jacob, 6th (01.46.34.61.55/www.huile-leblanc.
com). M° St-Germain-des-Prés.* **Open** noon-7pm
Tue-Fri; 10am-7pm Sat. Closed 2wks Aug. **No
credit cards. Map** p405 H6.
The Leblanc family started out making walnut oil
from its family tree in Burgundy before branching
out to press pure oils from hazelnuts, almonds, pine
nuts, grilled peanuts, pistachios and olives.

### La Maison de la Truffe

*19 pl de la Madeleine, 8th (01.42.65.53.22/
www.maison-de-la-truffe.com). M° Madeleine.* **Open**
9.30am-9pm Mon-Sat. **Credit** AmEx, DC, MC, V.
**Map** p401 F4.
Truffles worth more than gold, more affordable (artificial) truffle oils, sauces and vinegars, truffle-
enhanced foie gras – Guy Monier offers them all.

### Torréfacteur Verlet

*256 rue St-Honoré, 1st (01.42.60.67.39). M° Palais
Royal Musée du Louvre.* **Open** 9.30am-6.30pm Mon-
Sat. **Credit** MC, V. **Map** p401 G5.
Eric Duchaussoy roasts rare beans to perfection
– sip a cup here or take home some of the finest
fresh coffee in Paris.

## Gifts

## Florists

### Le Bar Fleur's

*3 rue des Tournelles, 4th (01.42.71.04.51/http://
fleuretvodka.free.fr). M° Bastille.* **Open** noon-2am
Tue-Sun. **Credit** AmEx, MC, V. **Map** p409 L6.
Ideal if you are suddenly smitten by the urge to give
flowers and need Dutch courage in order to present
them: this florist doubles as a champagne and vodka
bar and is open till 2am.

### Monceau Fleurs

*92 bd Malesherbes, 8th (01.53.77.61.77/www.
monceaufleurs.com). M° Villiers.* **Open** 8.30am-
9pm Mon-Sat; 9am-7.30pm Sun. **Credit** MC, V.
**Map** p401 E2.
The citywide branches sell an affordable range of
fresh *fleurs*. Order and pay for bouquets online too.
**Other locations** throughout the city.

### Au Nom de la Rose

*87 rue St-Antoine, 4th (01.42.71.34.24/www.
aunomdelarose.fr). M° St-Paul.* **Open** Sept-July 10am-
9pm daily. *Aug* 10am-9pm Mon-Sat. **Credit** AmEx,
DC, MC, V. **Map** p409 L7.
Specialising in roses, Au Nom can supply a bouquet,
as well as rose-based beauty products and candles.
**Other locations** throughout the city.

## Souvenirs & eccentricities

*See also p241* **Shopping malls**.

### Le Boudoir et sa Philosophie

*18 rue Charlot, 3rd (01.48.04.89.79/www.le
boudoiretsaphilosophie.fr). M° St-Sébastien
Froissart.* **Open** 2-7pm Tue-Sat. **Credit** MC, V.
**Map** p405 G6.
Carla Vizzi's boutique is not just full of pretty things;
it's also faithful to the 18th-century philosophy of
the boudoir – a place for collecting your thoughts in
private, preparing yourself for public view, and
receiving intimate friends. The cabinet of curiosities
section includes portraits of dogs in human garb,
and you can also commission your own pet portrait
if you bring in a photograph.

### Diptyque

*34 bd St-Germain, 5th (01.43.26.45.27/www.
diptyqueparis.com). M° Maubert Mutualité.* **Open**
10am-7pm Mon-Sat. **Credit** V. **Map** p405 G6.
Don't miss Diptyque's divinely scented candles.
They come in 48 different varieties and are probably
the best you'll ever find.

### Galeries Laffitte

*27 rue Laffitte, 9th (01.47.70.38.83). M° Notre-
Dame-de-Lorette.* **Open** 9am-7pm Mon-Fri; 10am-
6.30pm Sat. **Credit** MC, V. **Map** p402 H3.
The basement houses a regular *papeterie* filled with
pens and notebooks, while the ground floor has art
supplies and a wonderful selection of gifts, from

quality leather bags to Italian pastel-coloured diary covers and hand-bound notebooks. There's a good children's toy section too.

### Paris-Musées

*29bis rue des Francs-Bourgeois, 4th (01.42.74.13.02). M° St-Paul.* **Open** 2-7pm Mon; 11am-1pm, 2-7pm Tue-Fri; 11am-7pm Sat; noon-7.30pm Sun. **Credit** AmEx, DC, MC, V. **Map** p409 L6.

Run by the museum federation, this shop sells lamps and ceramics from local museums.

### Sennelier

*3 quai Voltaire, 7th (01.42.60.72.15/www. magasinsennelier.fr). M° St-Germain-des-Prés.* **Open** 2-6.30pm Mon; 10am-12.45pm, 2-6.30pm Tue-Sat. **Credit** AmEx, DC, MC, V. **Map** p405 G6.

Old-fashioned colour merchant Sennelier sells oil paints, watercolours and pastels, including rare pigments, plus primered boards, varnishes and paper. **Other locations** 4bis rue de la Grande-Chaumière, 6th (same phone).

## Health & beauty

## Cosmetics

### L'Artisan Parfumeur

*24 bd Raspail, 7th (01.42.22.23.32). M° Rue du Bac.* **Open** 10.30am-7.30pm Mon-Sat. **Credit** AmEx, DC, MC, V. **Map** p405 G7.

Among scented candles, potpourri and charms, you'll find the best vanilla perfume Paris can offer – Mûres et Musc, a bestseller for two decades. **Other locations** throughout the city.

### By Terry

*36 galerie Véro-Dodat, 1st (01.44.76.00.76/ www.byterry.com). M° Palais Royal Musée du Louvre.* **Open** 10.30am-7pm Mon-Sat. **Credit** AmEx, MC, V. **Map** p402 H5.

Terry de Gunzburg, who earned her reputation at Yves Saint Laurent, offers made-to-measure 'haute couleur' make-up by skilled chemists and colourists combining high-tech treatments and handmade precision. There's prêt-à-porter, too. **Other locations** 1 rue Jacob, 6th (01.46.34.00.36); 10 av Victor-Hugo, 16th (01.55.73.00.73).

### Conceptual Scent

*48-50 rue de l'Université, 7th (01.45.44.50.14). M° Rue du Bac.* **Open** 10am-7pm Mon-Sat. **Credit** AmEx, MC, V. **Map** p405 G6.

Invisible from the street, this minimal space is a temple to fragrance, selling its own delicious lines of perfumes, gels and candles. Sniff out the Eau Interdite, a curious, absinthe-scented eau de cologne.

### Détaille 1905

*10 rue St-Lazare, 9th (01.48.78.68.50/www. detaille.com). M° Notre-Dame-de-Lorette.* **Open** 3-7pm Mon; 10am-7pm Tue-Fri; 11am-4pm Sat. **Credit** MC, V. **Map** p401 H3.

Step back in time at this shop, opened, as the name suggests, in 1905 by war artist Edouard Détaille. Six fragrances (three for men and three for women) are made from century-old recipes.

### Editions de Parfums Frédéric Malle

*37 rue de Grenelle, 7th (01.42.22.77.22/ www.editionsdeparfums.com). M° Rue du Bac or St-Sulpice.* **Open** 1-7pm Mon; 11am-7pm Tue-Sat. **Credit** AmEx, DC, MC, V. **Map** p405 F6.

Choose from a range of eight perfumes by Frédéric Malle, former consultant to Hermès and Lacroix. Carnal Flower by Dominique Ropion is seduction in a bottle. **Other locations** 21 rue du Mont-Thabor, 1st (01.42.22.77.22); 140 av Victor-Hugo, 16th (01.45.05.39.02).

### Galerie Noémie

*92 av des Champs-Elysées, 8th (01.44.76.06.26/ www.galerienoemie.com). M° George V.* **Open** 11am-7pm Mon-Thur; 11am-9pm Fri, Sat. **Credit** AmEx, DC, MC, V. **Map** p402 J5.

You can tell owner Noémie is a painter by the way all the make-up is set out in palettes. Little pots of gloss (starting from €7.50) in myriad colours triple as lip gloss, eyeshadow or blusher. Check out Noemie's blog at http://blog.galerie-noemie.com/. **Other locations** Galeries Lafayette, 40 bd Haussmann, 9th (01.42.82.34.56).

### Guerlain

*68 av des Champs-Elysées, 8th (01.45.62.52.57/ www.guerlain.com). M° Franklin D. Roosevelt.* **Open** 10.30am-8pm Mon-Sat; 3-7pm Sun. **Credit** AmEx, DC, MC, V. **Map** p401 E4.

Perfume's great golden oldie recently had a facelift and is looking more ravishing than ever. Head to the first floor to get the full measure of the history behind the house that created the mythic Samsara, Mitsouko and L'Heure Bleue.

### L'Occitane

*55 rue St-Louis-en-l'Ile, 4th (01.40.46.81.71/ www.loccitane.com). M° Pont Marie.* **Open** 11am-7pm Mon; 10am-7pm Tue; 10am-7.30pm Wed-Fri; 10am-8pm Sat, Sun. **Credit** AmEx, DC, MC, V. **Map** p409 K7.

The many branches of this popular Provençal chain proffer natural beauty products in neat packaging. Soap rules, along with essential oils and perfumes. **Other locations** *throughout the city.*

### Salons du Palais-Royal Shiseido

*Jardins du Palais-Royal, 142 galerie de Valois, 1st (01.49.27.09.09/www.salons-shiseido.com). M° Palais Royal Musée du Louvre.* **Open** 10am-7pm Mon-Sat. **Credit** AmEx, DC, MC, V. **Map** p401 H5.

Under the arcades of the Palais-Royal, Shiseido's perfumer Serge Lutens practises his aromatic arts. A former photographer at Paris *Vogue* and artistic director of make-up at Christian Dior, Lutens is a maestro of rare taste. Bottles of his concoctions – Tubéreuse Criminelle, Rahat Loukoum and Ambre Sultan – can be sampled by visitors. Look out for

# Shopping by area

## Châtelet & Les Halles

The unlovely, underground **Forum des Halles** shopping centre, currently being revamped is the commercial heart of Paris. As well as the numerous chain stores and an enormous **Fnac** (*p272*), it has the **Espace Créateurs** (*p251*) for young designers. The surrounding streets are a good bet for streetwear, with shops like **Clery Brice** (*p255*), **Ekivok** (*p255*) and **Le Vestibule** (*p256*). High-street fashion names crowd along **rue de Rivoli** – including **Adidas** (*see p255*). More upmarket names here range from the classic **Agnès b** (*p253*) to new French success story **Manoush** (*p247*), both on rue du Jour. For beauty buffs, there's the chic **Spa Nuxe** (*p269*), **La Bulle Kenzo** (*p246*) salon or the no-frills **L'Esthétique de Demain** (*p269*), as well as make-up at **By Terry** (*p265*).

## Rue Etienne-Marcel & environs

When Rei Kawakubo set up the first **Comme des Garçons** (*p245*) Paris boutique in this grungy area just north of Les Halles, he kickstarted the transformation of this locality into the rebellious but chic neighbour of stuffy place des Victoires. Designer togs abound at **Jean-Paul Gaultier** (*p246*), **Kabuki Femme** (*p252*), **Yohji Yamamoto** (*p250*) and **Kokon To Zai** (*p252*), while nearby streetwear shops attract a younger clientele. Typical of the mix is rue Tiquetonne, with **Patrick Cox**'s elegant, expensive shoes (*p260*) at No.62 and hoodies and denim at **Kiliwatch** (*p255*).

## Rue St-Honoré & environs

The poshest part of the first arrondissement spreads out from rue St-Honoré and encompasses the glamorous, diamond-studded place Vendôme, where the city's jewellers reside. It's a roll-call of fashion's most powerful players, from **Chanel** (*p245*) to **Colette** (*p250*). If you prefer your haute couture vintage, try **Didier Ludot** (*p256*) in the 18th-century Palais-Royal, a new fashion draw with the arrival of **Marc Jacobs** (*p247*) and **Rick Owens** (*p249*). **Christian Louboutin** (*p259*), **Pierre Hardy** (*p260*) and **Rodolphe Menudier** (*p260*) offer show-stopping shoes, while **Alice Cadolle** (*p258*), **Fifi Chachnil** (*p258*) and **Yoba** (*p259*) create sumptuous undies. Smart specialist food shops include **Fauchon** (*p264*), **Hédiard** (*p264*) and **La Maison de la Truffe** (*p264*). High street

chains and gift shops occupy **La Galerie du Carrousel du Louvre** (*p241*); for rarer finds, pay a visit to the **Louvre des Antiquaires** (*p269*).

## Rue du Fbg-St-Honoré & the Champs-Elysées

When St-Honoré crosses into the 8th and becomes **rue du Fbg-St-Honoré**, it takes on an air of exclusivity. The area covers the lovely shops around **Madeleine**, the A-grade fashion strip of **avenue Montaigne** – home to **Christian Dior** (*p245*) and **Prada** (*p249*) – and the **Champs-Elysées,** which has sprouted a new mega-concept store, **LE66** (*p252*). For failsafe gourmet goodies, try **Alléosse** (*p262*), **Jabugo Ibérico & Co** (*p263*) or **La Maison du Chocolat** (*p262*). Beauty salons and stores include **Anne Sémonin** (*p268*) and **Guerlain** (*p265*). Big stores on the Champs-Elysées such as cosmetics giant **Sephora** (*p268*), **Fnac** (*p272*) and **Virgin Megastore** (*p272*) are open until midnight, and **Drugstore Publicis** (*p241*) is handy for late-night buys.

## Opéra & Grands Boulevards

Department stores **Printemps** (*p241*) and **Galeries Lafayette** (*p240*) provide the commercial heartbeat to this busy *quartier*, surrounded by chains such as Zara and Mango. Here, too, are children's shops **Du Pareil au Même** (*p244*) and **Village Joué Club** (*p245*); books at **Brentano's** (*p241*); plus sports and games equipment at **Citadium** (*p272*) and **René Pierre** (*p272*). The historic **Cartier** (*p257*) store and cult ballet-shoe maker **Repetto** (*p260*) are on rue de la Paix; wine shop **Les Caves Augé** (*p262*) is another old-timer.

## Montmartre

Funky, independent designers cluster around the winding streets by Sacré-Coeur. **Boulevard de Rochechouart** is known for its discount shops – the bargain basement **Tati** is at no.4 (*see p241*). Fashionable types gravitate towards **Spree** (*p253*) or vintage store **Wochdom** (*p257*). If you need a reviving cake or two, **Arnaud Delmontel** (*p260*) and **Arnaud Lahrer** (*p263*) are on hand. Just north is the biggest flea market in Paris, the **Marché aux Puces de Clignancourt** (*p269*).

## Canal St-Martin

This mini *quartier* provides the perfect canal-side esplanade for relaxed browsing; **Antoine**

Didier Ludot.

**et Lili** (*p253*) sells riotously colourful clothing, and many smaller, off-beat fashion stores are on rue Beaurepaire, while design-focused bookshop **Artazart** (*p241*) stocks impressive coffee table tomes.

### Bastille

Traditionally home to fine furniture craftsmen, **rue du Fbg-St-Antoine**, **rue de Charonne** and **rue Keller** are peppered with designer fashion and interiors shops, such as **Caravane Chambre 19** (*p270*), **Galerie Patrick Seguin** (*p270*) and **Silvera** (*p270*). Children's clothes shops run east along rue du Fbg-St Antoine from Mº Ledru-Rollin. Of particular note for clothes are vintage shop **Come on Eline** (*p256*) and **Isabel Marant** (*p246*), though many designers have deserted this area in favour of the 'haut Marais'. Local food and wine shops include **L'Autre Boulange** (*p260*) and **Moisan** (*p260*).

### The Marais

**Rue des Rosiers**, **rue des Francs-Bourgeois** and offshoots house designer boutiques and interiors shops. Label-lovers should look out for **Les Belles Images** (*p250*) and **L'Eclaireur** (*p250*). Men are well catered for, with **L'Eclaireur Homme** (*p254*), **Jacenko** (*p254*) and **Nodus** (*p254*). The 'haut Marais' area around rues Charlot and Poitou is the hottest centre for avant-garde and young designers, and vintage, with **Galerie Simone** (*p251*), **Shine** (*p253*), **AB33** (*p250*) and hip concept store **Surface 2 Air** (*p253*). Jewish bakeries

include the famous **Finkelsztajn** (*p263*). For everything else, there's the landmark **BHV** department store (*p240*).

### St-Germain-des-Prés & Odéon

Stores line up on **boulevard St-Germain**, by **St-Sulpice church** and along **rue de Buci**. There's a fashionable name around every corner: **Miu Miu** (*p247*), **Sonia Rykiel** (*p250*), **Yves Saint Laurent** (*p250*) and more; **Le Bon Marché** department store (*see p240*) also stocks designer labels. Hip **APC** (*p254*), **Hervé Chapelier** (*p259*) and **Vanessa Bruno** (*p250*) provide head-to-toe garb – as do seconds store **Le Mouton à Cinq Pattes** (*see p251* **Stocking up**) and lingerie shop **Princesse Tam Tam** (*p258*). Interspersed are the children's clothes shops of rue Vavin and plenty of bookshops: **Fnac Junior** (*p244*), **La Hune** (*p243*), **Librairie 7L** (*p243*), and **Village Voice** (*p243*). The area also houses seven master chocolate-makers (*see p262*). For more savoury edibles, head for **Da Rosa** (*p264*), **Huilerie Artisanale Leblanc** (*p264*) and the famous **Poilâne** (*p260*).

### St-Michel & the 5th

St-Germain's bookish cousin is the hub of publishing: stock up on reading material at **Gibert Joseph** (*p243*) and the **bouquinistes** (*p241*). Here, too, are the fragrant **Diptyque** (*p264*) and the **Hammam de la Grande Mosquée** (*p269*).

Spa Nuxe.

Fleurs d'Oranger, which the great man defines as the smell of happiness. Many of the perfumes are exclusive to the Salons; prices start at around €100. **Other locations** *2 pl Vendôme, 1st (01.42.60.68.61); 29 rue de Sèvres, 6th (01.42.22.46.60); 66 bd Montparnasse, 15th (01.43.20.95.40).*

### Sephora
*70 av des Champs-Elysées, 8th (01.53.93.22.50/ www.sephora.fr). M° Franklin D. Roosevelt.* **Open** *Sept-June* 10am-midnight daily. *July, Aug* 10am-1.30am. **Credit** AmEx, DC, MC, V. **Map** p401 E4.
The flagship of the cosmetic supermarket chain houses 12,000 brands of scent and slap. Sephora Blanc (14 cour St-Emilion, 12th, 01.40.02.97.79) features beauty products in a minimalist interior. **Other locations** throughout the city.

## Salons & spas

### Anne Sémonin
*Le Bristol, 108 rue du Fbg-St-Honoré, 8th (01.42.66.24.22/www.lebristolparis.com). M° Champs-Elysées Clemenceau or Miromesnil.* **Open** 10am-7pm Tue-Sat. **Credit** AmEx, DC, MC, V. **Map** p401 E3.
Facials involve delicious concoctions of basil, lavender, lemongrass, ginger and plant essences. Also on offer are reflexology and a selection of massage styles, from Thai to ayurvedic. Body treatments cost from €70 to €210. Sémonin's renowned seaweed skincare products and essential oils are also on sale. **Other locations** *2 rue des Petits-Champs, 2nd (01.42.60.94.66).*

### Appartement 217
*217 rue St-Honoré, 1st (01.42.96.00.96/www. lappartement217.com). M° Tuileries.* **Open** 10am-7pm Tue-Sat. **Credit** AmEx, DC, MC, V. **Map** p401 G5.

Opened by Colette's former beauty director Stéphane Jaulin, a feng-shuied Haussmannian apartment is the setting for facials using organic beauty guru Dr Hauschka's products and ayurvedic or deep tissue massages. The water's been decalcified, electrical currents are insulated, and the silky-soft kimonos are made from organic wood pulp.

### Les Bains du Marais
*31-33 rue des Blancs-Manteaux, 4th (01.44.61.02.02/www.lesbainsdumarais.com). M° St-Paul.* **Open** *Men* 11am-11pm Thur; 10am-8pm Fri. *Women* 11am-8pm Mon; 11am-11pm Tue; 10am-7pm Wed. *Mixed* 7-11pm Wed; 10am-8pm Sat; 11am-11pm Sun. Closed Aug. **Credit** AmEx, MC, V. **Map** p409 K6.
This hammam and spa mixes the modern and traditional (lounging beds and mint tea). Facials, waxing and essential oil massages (€60) are also available. The hammam and standard massage are each €30.

### La Bulle Kenzo
*1 rue du Pont-Neuf, 1st (01.73.04.20.04/www. labullekenzo.com). M° Pont Neuf.* **Open** 10am-8pm Mon-Sat. **Credit** AmEx, DC, MC, V. **Map** p406 J6.
Kenzo's flagship store houses a chic, high-concept beauty salon. The two massage rooms offer two rather different vibes: the Pétillante room has a disco ball, while the Japanese Zen cocoon room provides calmer pleasures.

### L'Espace Payot
*62 rue Pierre-Charon, 8th (01.45.61.42.08). M° George V.* **Open** 7am-10pm Mon-Fri; 9am-7pm Sat; 10am-5pm Sun. **Credit** AmEx, MC, V. **Map** p400 D4.
Opened in 2006 by Dr Nadia Payot, one of the leading ladies in French skincare, this institute offers the entire gamut of luxurious face and body treatments.

One of the largest spas in Paris, it has a gym, pool, sauna and steam bath, and health food bar. Prices range from €40 to €80, while a day pass is €150.

## L'Esthétique de Demain

*15 rue de la Grande-Truanderie, 1st (01.40.26.53.10). M° Châtelet or Etienne Marcel.* **Open** 2-7pm Mon; 10am-8.30pm Tue-Fri; 10am-7pm Sat. **Credit** MC, V. **Map** p402 J5.
If you're looking to get the job done without a lot of hoopla, this low-key, low-cost salon specialising in hair removal is for you. Waxing for men and women starts at €9, facials from €28. Massages 'per minute' are also on offer (it's €10 for ten minutes) along with reflexology, Reiki and more.

## Hammam de la Grande Mosquée

*1 rue Puits-de-l'Ermite, 5th (01.43.31.18.14). M° Censier Daubenton.* **Open** *Men* 2-9pm Tue; 10am-9pm Sun. *Women* 10am-9pm Mon, Wed, Sat; 2-9pm Fri. **Credit** MC, V. **Map** p406 K9.
The authentic hammam experience in this beautiful 1920s mosque has become very popular with *parisiennes*, so avoid weekends when the volume of traffic makes it less relaxing than it should be. Follow a steam session with a *gommage* (exfoliation with a rough mitt), then a massage. The hammam is €15, *gommage* €10 and massage €10. Swimwear is compulsory. Towel and gown hire is also available.

## Hammam Med Centre

*43-45 rue Petit, 19th (01.42.02.31.05/www. hammammed.com). M° Ourcq.* **Open** *Women* 11am-10pm Mon-Fri; 9am-7pm Sun. *Mixed* 10am-9pm Sat. **Credit** MC, V. **Map** p403 N5.
This hammam is hard to beat – spotless mosaic-tiled surroundings, flowered sarongs and a relaxing pool. The exotic 'Forfait florale' option (€139) will have you enveloped in rose petals and massaged with *huile d'Argan* from Morocco, while the more simple hammam and *gommage* followed by mint tea and pastries is €39. Plan to spend a few hours here as the soft-voiced staff take things at their own pace.

## Spa Nuxe

*32 rue Montorgueil, 1st (01.55.80.71.40/www. nuxe.com). M° Les Halles.* **Open** 9am-9pm Mon-Fri; 9am-7.30pm Sat. **Credit** AmEx, MC, V. **Map** p402 J4.
This luxurious day spa housed in stone vaults with wooden cabins and safari-style tents offers massages and skin treatments using Nuxe's gentle, plant-based products. The facials, where you undress completely, begin with a short foot, tummy and neck message for total relaxation; from €70.

## House & home

### Antiques & flea markets

Knowing who specialises in what is essential for antiques buying in Paris. Classy traditional antiques can be found in the **Louvre des**

**Antiquaires, Carré Rive Gauche** (6th), **Village Suisse** and rue du Fbg-St-Honoré (1st). You'll find art deco in St-Germain-des-Prés (7th) and retro by rue de Charonne (11th). For books, look in the **bouquinistes** (*see p241*) and at Parc Georges Brassens (15th).
As well as flea markets (*see p271* **Bargain hunt**), there are also plenty of *brocantes*, *braderies* and *vide greniers* – antiques' and collectors' markets and the French equivalent of the car boot sale, advertised by street banners and posters.

## Louvre des Antiquaires

*2 pl du Palais-Royal, 1st (01.42.97.27.27/www. louvre-antiquaires.com). M° Palais Royal Musée du Louvre.* **Open** 11am-7pm Tue-Sun. Closed Sun in July & Aug. **Credit** varies. **Map** p406 H5.
This upmarket antiques centre houses 250 antiques dealers: perfect for Louis XV furniture, tapestries, porcelain, jewellery, model ships and tin soldiers.

## Marché aux Puces d'Aligre

*Pl d'Aligre, rue d'Aligre, 12th. M° Ledru-Rollin.* **Open** 7.30am-1.30pm Tue-Sun. **Map** p407 N7.
The only flea market in central Paris, Aligre stays true to its junk tradition with a handful of *brocanteurs* peddling books, phone cards, kitchenware and oddities at what seem to be optimistic prices.

## Marché aux Puces de Clignancourt

*Av de la Porte de Clignancourt, 18th. M° Porte de Clignancourt.* **Open** 7am-7.30pm Mon, Sat, Sun.
The mother of all flea markets is home to some 2,500 dealers at ten main markets. Don't bother to arrive early for bargains – most stalls don't open till 9am. *See also p271* **Bargain hunt**.

## Marché aux Puces de Vanves

*Av Georges-Lafenestre & av Marc-Sangnier, 14th. M° Porte de Vanves.* **Open** 7am-7.30pm Sun.
Vanves is the smallest and friendliest of the Paris flea markets. If you get there early enough, there are decent second-hand clothes, dolls, costume jewellery and silverware. *See also p271* **Bargain hunt**.

## Le Village St-Paul

*Rue St-Paul, rue Charlemagne & quai des Célestins, 4th. M° St-Paul.* **Open** 10am-7pm Mon-Sat. **No credit cards. Map** p409 L7.
This colony of antiques sellers, spread across small linking courtyards, is a source of retro furniture, kitchenware and wine gadgets.

## Design & interiors

The vast **Lafayette Maison** (*see p240*) offers a selection of current design and homewares.

## Astier de Villatte

*173 rue St-Honoré, 1st (01.42.60.74.13/www. astierdevillatte.com). M° Palais Royal Musée du Louvre.* **Open** 11am-7.30pm Mon-Sat. Closed 3wks Aug. **Credit** AmEx, MC, V. **Map** p401 G4.

Once home to Napoleon's silversmith, this ancient warren now houses ceramics inspired by 17th- and 18th-century designs, handmade by the Astier de Villatte siblings in their Bastille workshop.

### Caravane Chambre 19
*19 rue St-Nicolas, 12th (01.53.02.96.96/www. caravane.fr). M° Ledru-Rollin.* **Open** 11am-7pm Tue-Sat. Closed 2wks Aug. **Credit** AmEx, MC, V. **Map** p407 M7.
This offshoot of Françoise Dorget's original Marais shop has goodies such as exquisite hand-sewn quilts from west Bengal, crisp cotton and organdie tunics, Berber scarves, lounging sofas and daybeds. **Other locations** 22 rue St-Nicolas, 12th (01.53.17.18.55); 6 rue Pavée, 4th (01.44.61.04.20).

### Christian Liaigre
*42 rue du Bac, 7th (01.53.63.33.66/www.christianliaigre.fr). M° Rue du Bac.* **Open** 10am-7pm Mon-Sat. Closed 3wks Aug. **Credit** AmEx, MC, V. **Map** p405 G6.
This French interior decorator fitted out Marc Jacobs' boutiques. His showroom displays his elegant lighting and furniture designs. **Other locations** 61 rue de Varenne, 7th (01.47.53.78.76).

### Christophe Delcourt
*39 rue Lucien Sampaix, 10th (01.42.71.34.84/ www.christophedelcourt.com). M° Jacques Bonsergent.* **Open** 9am-noon, 1-6pm Mon-Fri. Closed Aug. **Credit** AmEx, DC, MC, V. **Map** p401 G4.
Delcourt's art deco-influenced, geometrical lights and furniture are given a contemporary spin by their combination of stained wood and black steel.

### CSAO
*9 rue Elzévir, 3rd (01.44.54.55.88/www.csao.fr). M° St-Paul.* **Open** 11am-7pm Mon-Sat; 2-7pm Sun. **Credit** AmEx, DC, MC, V. **Map** p409 L6.
This boutique offers African craftwork created according to fair trade principles. The artisans often fashion their objects out of recycled materials, such as funky furniture constructed from tins.

### FR 66
*25 rue de Renard, 4th (01.44.54.35.36/www. fr66.com). M° Hôtel de Ville.* **Open** 10am-7pm Mon-Sat. Closed 2-3wks Aug. **Credit** AmEx, MC, V. **Map** p406 K6.
Somewhere between a gallery and a shop, this two-level experimental space accommodates contemporary artists and designers who produce exciting and original products for the home – not only furniture, but electrical fittings, and floor and wall coverings.

### Galerie Patrick Seguin
*5 rue des Taillandiers, 11th (01.47.00.32.35/ www.patrickseguin.com). M° Bastille or Ledru-Rollin.* **Open** 10am-7pm Tue-Sat. Closed 2wks Aug. **Credit** AmEx, DC, MC, V. **Map** p407 M7.
Seguin specialises in French design from the 1950s: items by Jean Prouvé and Charlotte Perriand are on display in a showroom designed by Jean Nouvel.

### Sentou Galerie
*24 rue du Pont-Louis-Philippe, 4th (01.42.77.44.79/ 01.42.71.00.01/www.sentou.fr). M° Pont Marie.* **Open** 10am-7pm Tue-Sat. **Credit** AmEx, MC, V. **Map** p409 K7.
A trend-setting shop for colourful tableware and furniture: painted Chinese flasks, vases and so on. **Other locations** 29 rue François-Miron, 4th (01.42.78.50.60); 26 bd Raspail, 7th (01.45.49.00.05).

### Silvera
*41 rue du Fbg-St-Antoine, 11th (01.43.43.06.75/ www.silvera.fr). M° Bastille or Ledru-Rollin.* **Open** 10am-7pm Mon-Sat. Closed 2wks Aug. **Credit** AmEx, MC, V. **Map** p407 M7.
The former Le Bihan was taken over by Silvera in 2005 and is now a three-floor showcase for modern design. Look out for furniture and lighting from Perriand, Pesce, Pillet, Morrison, Arad and others. **Other locations** 58 av Kléber, 16th (01.53.65.78.78).

## Kitchen & bathroom

### Bains Plus
*51 rue des Francs-Bourgeois, 4th (01.48.87.83.07). M° Hôtel de Ville.* **Open** 2-7pm Mon, Sun; 11am-7.30pm Tue-Sat. **Credit** AmEx, MC, V. **Map** p409 K6.
This is the ultimate gentlemen's shaving shop: stock includes duck-shaped loofahs, seductive dressing gowns, chrome mirrors, bath oils and soaps.

### E Dehillerin
*18 rue Coquillière, 1st (01.42.36.53.13/www.e-dehillerin.fr). M° Les Halles.* **Open** 9am-12.30pm, 2-6pm Mon; 9am-6pm Tue-Sat. **Credit** MC, V. **Map** p402 J5.
Suppliers to great chefs since 1820, this no-nonsense warehouse stocks just about every kitchen utensil ever invented. A saucepan from Dehillerin for life.

### Laguiole Galerie
*1 pl Ste-Opportune, 1st (01.40.28.09.42/www.forge-de-laguiole.com). M° Châtelet.* **Open** 10.30am-1pm, 2-7pm Mon-Sat. **Credit** MC, V. **Map** p406 J6.
Philippe Starck designed this chic boutique, a showcase for France's classic knife, the Laguiole.

## Music & entertainment

### CDs & DVDs

**Gibert Joseph** (*see p243*) also stocks CDs and DVDs; **WH Smith** (*see p243*) stocks British DVDs. For new and second-hand vinyl, head over to rue Keller in the 11th for electronica and rue de Navarre (5th) for jazz.

### Crocodisc
*40-42 rue des Ecoles, 5th (01.43.54.47.95/ www.crocodisc.com). M° Maubert Mutualité.* **Open** 11am-7pm Tue-Sat. Closed 2wks Aug. **Credit** MC, V. **Map** p408 J7.

*Eat, Drink, Shop*

# Bargain hunt

Paris flea markets are chock full of curiosities. Bargain hunters and serious collectors can peruse an impressive number of markets for objects as diverse as medieval stained glass windows, vintage Philippe Starck pieces and 3m (12-foot) clock faces. Key stops on the flea market trail are the sprawling Marché aux Puces de Clignancourt, the smaller, tree-lined Marché de Vanves and the contemporary design market 'Les Puces du Design'.

**The Marché aux Puces de Clignancourt** (*see p269*), also known as the Marché aux Puces de St Ouen (in the north of Paris), is the biggest in Europe. Open from 9am to 7pm daily except Sunday, its size and organisation may overwhelm the first-time visitor. Understanding how this Byzantine emporium is ordered is key to making the most of your time here. There are 15 to 20 distinct markets under the Clignancourt umbrella, amounting to around 2,000 stalls. Skip past vendors trying to flog cheap imports off the back of a lorry and head straight for the rue des Rosiers, the main artery of the market.

Each market has at least one speciality, and while some are indoors in American mall-like constructions, others are outdoors in a more rustic setting. Such is the quality of Clignancourt's wares these days that you can substitute a visit to the Musée des Arts Décoratifs for a jaunt to the market. Make sure you pop into Paul Bert and La Serpette, for antique and contemporary furniture. For jewellery, glassware and knick-knacks, head for the warren-like Vernaison

market. The Biron is well ordered with upmarket stalls selling curiosities, fans and furniture. The Dauphine has a preponderance of booksellers and antique dealers, but is decidedly unattractive and prices are high.

Infinitely more tranquil than Clignancourt and a favourite with serious collectors, the **Marché de Vanves** (*see p269*) is set along two streets (avenue Marc-Sangnier and avenue Georges-Lafenestre) in the 14th arrondissement each Saturday and Sunday. Expect to find anything from vintage dolls to hairdressing manuals, although little furniture is sold. There are far fewer tourists at Vanves than Clignancourt, and since it attracts connoisseurs and dealers, it is best to arrive at 7am when the market opens.

Lastly, the term 'flea market' can only be loosely applied when it comes to **Les Puces du Design** (quai de la Loire, 19th, www.pucesdudesign.info), which stocks haute design furniture no older than the last century. The likes of Joe Colombo, Verner Panton and Saarinen are represented among the 60-odd stalls hosted by some of the foremost design boutiques in Paris.

Contemporary design has only taken off relatively recently, since Parisians have traditionally preferred their homes to look like those of their forefathers. But even in the eternal capital things change, and this bi-annual three-day event takes place during June and October. If your budget does not stretch to an Eames chair, you can purchase the work of unknown designers or just enjoy the spectacle.

**Eat, Drink, Shop**

The excellent, if expensive, range includes rock, funk, African, country and classical, in the form of new and second-hand vinyl and CDs. For jazz and blues, try sister shop Crocojazz.
**Other locations** Crocojazz, *64 rue de la Montagne-Ste-Geneviève, 5th (01.46.34.78.38).*

### Fnac
*Levels -1 to -3, Porte Lescot, Forum des Halles, 1st (01.40.41.40.00/ticket office 08.92.68.36.22/ www.fnac.com). M° Les Halles.* **Open** 10am-7.30pm Mon-Sat. **Credit** AmEx, MC, V. **Map** p402 J5.
Fnac is a supermarket of culture: books, DVDs, CDs, audio kit, computers and photographic equipment. Most branches – notably the vast Forum des Halles one – stock everything; others specialise, such as Fnac Music at 4 place de la Bastille. All branches operate as a concert box office. If you plan on a large purchase, save by signing up for Fnac membership.
**Other locations** throughout the city.

### Monster Melodies
*9 rue des Déchargeurs, 1st (01.40.28.09.39). M° Les Halles.* **Open** noon-7pm Mon-Sat. **Credit** MC, V. **Map** p402 J5.
The owners are prepared to help you on a treasure hunt – and with more than 10,000 second-hand CDs of every variety, that's just as well.

### Virgin Megastore
*52-60 av des Champs-Elysées, 8th (01.49.53.50.00/ www.virginmega.fr). M° Franklin D. Roosevelt.* **Open** 10am-midnight Mon-Sat; noon-midnight Sun. **Credit** AmEx, DC, MC, V. **Map** p401 E4.
The luxury of perusing CDs and DVDs till midnight makes this a choice spot, and the listening posts let you sample any CD by scanning its barcode. Tickets for concerts and sports events are available here too. This main branch has the best selection of books.
**Other locations** Carrousel du Louvre, 99 rue de Rivoli, 1st (01.44.50.03.10); 5 bd Montmartre, 2nd (01.40.13.72.13); 15 bd Barbès, 18th (01.56.55.53.70).

## Musical instruments

### Paris Accordéon
*80 rue Daguerre, 14th (01.43.22.13.48/www. parisaccordeon.com). M° Denfert Rochereau or Gaîté.* **Open** 9am-noon, 1-7pm Tue-Fri; 9am-noon, 1-6pm Sat. **Credit** AmEx, MC, V. **Map** p405 G10.
Accordions, from simple squeezeboxes to beautiful tortoiseshell models, both second-hand and new.

## Sport & fitness

Unless you need specialised equipment, you'll find what you want at **Go Sport** (www.go-sport.com) or **Décathlon** (www.decathlon.fr).

### Citadium
*50-56 rue de Caumartin, 9th (01.55.31.74.00/ www.citadium.com). M° Havre Caumartin.* **Open** 9am-8pm Mon, Tue, Fri, Sat; 10am-8pm Wed; 9am-9pm Thur. **Credit** AmEx, DC, MC, V. **Map** p401 G3.

Cultish emporium of sporting goods, from hip watches to cross-country skis, on four themed floors.

### Nauti Store
*40 av de la Grande-Armée, 17th (01.43.80.28.28/ www.nautistore.fr). M° Argentine.* **Open** 11am-7pm Mon; 10.30am-7pm Tue-Sat. **Credit** DC, MC, V. **Map** p400 C3.
This shop stocks a vast range of sailing clothes and shoes from labels such as Helly Hansen and Sebago.

### René Pierre
*35 rue de Maubeuge, 9th (01.44.91.91.21/www. rene-pierre.fr). M° Poissonnière.* **Open** 10am-1pm, 2-6.30pm Mon-Sat. **Credit** MC, V. **Map** p402 H3.
France's finest table-football tables, ready for free delivery as far as Calais to UK buyers.

### Subchandlers – Plongespace
*80 rue Balard, 15th (01.45.57.01.01/www. subchandlers.com). M° Balard.* **Open** 10.30am-7.30pm Tue-Sat. **Credit** AmEx, MC, V. **Map** p404 A9.
This diving specialist stocks all apparatus, plus underwater cameras. Monthly soirées on diving too.

## Tickets

The easiest way to reserve and buy tickets for concerts, plays and matches is from a **Fnac** store. You can also reserve on www.fnac.com or by phone (08.92.68.36.22; 9am-8pm Mon-Sat) and pick them up at one of their *points de vente* (see site for full list) – or pay with your credit card and have them sent to your home. **Virgin** has teamed up with Ticketnet to create an online ticket office (www.virginmega.fr). Tickets can also be purchased by phone (08.25.12.91.39) and sent to your home for a €5.50 fee.

### Fnac Forum
*Levels -1 to -3, Porte Lescot, Forum des Halles, 1st 08.25.02.00.20/www.fnac.com). M° Les Halles/RER Châtelet Les Halles.* **Open** 10am-7.30pm Mon-Sat. **Credit** AmEx, MC, V. **Map** p402 J5.

### Virgin Megastore
*52-60 av des Champs-Elysées, 8th (01.49.53.50.00/ www.virginmega.fr). M° Franklin D. Roosevelt.* **Open** 10am-midnight Mon-Sat; noon-midnight Sun. **Credit** AmEx, MC, V. **Map** p401 E4.

## Travel agents

### Nouvelles Frontières
*13 av de l'Opéra, 1st (08.25.00.07.47/www.nouvelles-frontieres.fr). M° Pyramides.* **Open** 9am-7pm Mon-Sat. **Credit** V.
Agent with 16 branches in Paris.

### Thomas Cook
*17 rue du Colisée, 8th (08.26.82.67.77/www. thomascook.fr). M° Opéra.* **Open** 10am-7pm Mon-Sat. **Credit** AmEx, DC, MC, V.
Travel agent with more than 30 branches in Paris.

*Eat, Drink, Shop*

# Arts & Entertainment

**Jardin du Luxembourg**. *See p284.*

# Festivals & Events

Capital celebrations all year long.

As well as hosting a panoply of cultural events throughout the year, Paris celebrates innumerable anniversaries and religious festivals. Indeed, the city seems to turn every commemoration into a serious, state-funded event – and mayor Bertrand Delanoë has been energetic in his attempts to refresh the capital's diary. **Paris-Plage**, an urban beach set up by the Seine for the summer, and **Nuit Blanche**, an autumnal, all-night culture fest, have been high-profile successes (*see p276* **Up all night**).

The cultural season starts in October, keeping busy until the beginning of summer, when most companies head south. Many summer events are free, such as Paris-Plage, the **Fête de la Musique** and **Bastille Day**.

## PUBLIC HOLIDAYS

On *jours feriés*, banks, many museums, most businesses and a number of restaurants close (those remaining open may charge a premium); public transport runs a Sunday service. Bastille Day, New Year's Day, May Day and Christmas Day are the most widely observed holidays.

The bank holiday calendar runs as follows: New Year's Day (*Jour de l'An*); Easter Monday (*Pâques*); May Day (*Fête du Travail*); VE Day (*Victoire 1945*), 8 May; Ascension Day (*Jour de l'Ascension*); Whit Monday (*Pentecôte*); Bastille Day (*Quatorze Juillet*), 14 July; Feast of the Assumption (*Fête de l'Assomption*), 15 August; All Saints' Day (*Toussaint*), 1 November; Remembrance Day (*L'Armistice 1918*), 11 November; Christmas Day (*Noël*).

## Spring

### Six Nations

*Stade de France, 93210 St-Denis (08.92.70.09.00/ www.stadedefrance.fr). RER B La Plaine Stade de France or RER D Stade de France St-Denis.* **Admission** varies. **Date** Feb-Mar.
Paris is invaded by Brits and Celts for three big rugby weekends in winter. Tickets are hard to come by – log on to www.rbs6nations.com at least three months in advance.

### Fashion Week

*Various venues (www.modeaparis.com).* **Date** Mar & Oct.
Paris presents its haute couture and prêt-à-porter collections to invited guests only. Everyone who's anyone shows here, from Valentino to Viktor & Rolf. The better hotels fill up, as do the trendier bistros.

### Le Printemps des Poètes

*Various venues (01.53.80.08.00/www.printemps despoetes.com).* **Date** Mar.
Celebrating the centenary of poet René Char's birth, the 2008 edition of this popular national poetry festival has 'L'Eloge de l'Autre' as its theme.

### Printemps du Cinéma

*Various venues (www.printempsducinema.com).* **Date** Mar.
Film tickets all across the city are cut to a bargain €3.50 for this popular three-day film event.

### Banlieues Bleues

*Various venues in Seine-St-Denis (01.49.22.10.10/ www.banlieuesbleues.org).* **Admission** €14-€20. **Date** Mar-Apr.
Five weeks of quality French and international jazz, blues, R&B, soul, funk, flamenco and world music.

### Le Chemin de la Croix

*Square Willette, 18th (01.53.41.89.00). M° Abbesses or Anvers.* **Date** Good Friday.
Mini-pilgrimage as crowds follow the Archbishop of Paris from the bottom of Montmartre up to Sacré-Coeur as he performs the Stations of the Cross.

### Foire du Trône

*Pelouse de Reuilly, 12th (www.foiredutrone.com). M° Porte Dorée.* **Admission** free; rides €1.50-€4. **Date** late Mar-May.
France's biggest funfair: stomach-churning rides, bungee jumping and *barbe à papa* (candyfloss).

### Marathon de Paris

*Av des Champs-Elysées, 8th, to av Foch, 16th (01.41.33.15.68/www.parismarathon.com).* **Date** 6 Apr.
From the Champs-Elysées all along the Right Bank to the Bois de Vincennes and back along the Left Bank to the Bois de Boulogne, 35,000 runners take in the sights for the 32nd staging of this event in 2008.

### Foire de Paris

*Paris-Expo, pl de la Porte de Versailles (01.49.09.60.00/www.foiredeparis.fr). M° Porte de Versailles.* **Admission** €12; €10 concessions; €7 under-7s. **Date** 30 Apr-12 May 2008.
This enormous lifestyle fair includes world crafts and foods, plus the latest health and house gizmos.

### Fête du Travail

**Date** 1 May.
May Day is strictly observed. Key sights (the Eiffel Tower aside) close, and unions march in eastern Paris via Bastille. Vendors sell sweet-smelling posies of lily of the valley (*muguet*) on every street corner.

## La Nuit des Musées

*All over France (www.nuitdesmusees.culture.fr).*
**Admission** free. **Date** mid May.
For one night, landmark museums across Paris open late and organise various special entertainments.

## Quinzaine des Réalisateurs

*Forum des Images, Porte St-Eustache, Forum des Halles, 1st (01.44.89.99.99/www.quinzaine-realisateurs.com). M° Les Halles.* **Admission** €5.50.
**Date** May, June.
As soon as the dust has settled at Cannes, the Directors' Fortnight programme comes to Paris.

## French Tennis Open

*Stade Roland-Garros, 2 av Gordon-Bennett, 16th (01.47.43.48.00/www.frenchopen.org). M° Porte d'Auteuil.* **Admission** €21-€75.
**Date** 25 May-8 June.
The glitzy Grand Slam tennis tournament is always well attended by showbiz stars. The tricky clay courts have been the downfall of many a champion.

## Festival de St-Denis

*Various venues in St-Denis (01.48.13.12.10/ www.festival-saint-denis.fr). M° St-Denis Basilique.* **Admission** €9-€55. **Date** 29 May-2 July.

The Gothic St-Denis basilica and other historic buildings in the neighbourhood host four weeks of quality classical concerts through the month of June.

## Summer

## Le Printemps des Rues

*(01.47.97.36.06/www.leprintempsdesrues.com.*
**Admission** free. **Date** late May or early June.
Despite financial worries, this annual two-day street-theatre festival is all set to continue in 2008.

## Prix de Diane Hermès

*Hippodrome de Chantilly, 16 av du Général-Leclerc, 90209 Chantilly (03.44.62.41.00/www.france-galop.com).* **Admission** €8; €4 concessions; free under-18s. **Date** 8 June 2008.
The French Derby draws the crème de la crème of high society to the races at Chantilly, sporting silly hats and keen to take a flutter. *See p339* **A day at the races**.

## Fête de la Musique

*All over France (01.40.03.94.70/www.fetedela musique.fr).* **Admission** free. **Date** 21 June.
Concerts are held all over the city – and indeed nationwide – for this free music festival.

**Six Nations**: France vs England at the Stade de France.

**Arts & Entertainment**

# Up all night

The first **Nuit Blanche** (*see p277*), conceived by artistic impresario Jean Blaise with the financial and logistical support of then newly elected mayor Bertrand Delanoë, took place in the autumn of 2002. Blaise's nocturnal festival of art, in which familiar parts of the city were turned into galleries, succeeded on a scale neither he nor the mayor could have imagined, with more than 500,000 people thronging the streets of Paris from dusk until dawn. It probably helped that many cafés and bars decided to stay open unusually late.

Since that auspicious beginning, Nuit Blanche has gone from strength to strength, growing exponentially and colonising new areas of the city each year. Indeed, the event is as much about Paris as it is about the cutting-edge art it showcases: the organisers envisage it as a way of tracing a 'new map of the city', opening up corners of the cityscape usually off-limits to solitary night-time urban explorers. Nuit Blanche transforms the lonely vigil of the nocturnal *flâneur* into something that is experienced collectively.

In 2007, the festival was concentrated in the following areas: Batignolles and St-Lazare in the north-west; Madeleine and the Louvre; Les Halles, Marais and the Bastille (traditionally the busiest part of town during Nuit Blanche); Bercy; and Les Olympiades in the burgeoning 13th arrondissement (*see p177* **In the zone**). True to Delanoë's vision of Paris as a city of the avant-garde, the emphasis was on innovative work in digital video art and street art. Guillaume Plisson, for example, covered the 13th in luminous

graffiti tags, while a production of an opera by Rossini was projected on a giant screen erected on the *parvis* of the Hôtel de Ville. And in the Marais, the walls of the mobile Pleinmuseum, by day opaque and impenetrable, were transformed into screens showing the work of leading video artists – as good a metaphor as any, you might say, for what happens to Paris on a single night in October each year.

## Gay Pride March
*Information: Centre Gai et Lesbien (01.43.57.21.47/ www.inter-lgbt.org).* **Date** 28 June.
Outrageous floats and flamboyant costumes parade towards Bastille, followed by an official fête and various club events.

## Foire St-Germain
*Pl St-Sulpice and venues in St-Germain-des-Prés, 6th (01.43.29.61.04/www.foiresaintgermain.org). M° St-Sulpice.* **Admission** free. **Date** June, July.
St-Germain-des-Prés lets its hair down for a month of concerts, theatre and workshops.

## Paris Jazz Festival
*Parc Floral de Paris, Bois de Vincennes (39.75/www. parcfloraldeparis.com/www.paris.fr). M° Château de Vincennes.* **Admission** *Park* €3. **Date** June, July.
Free jazz weekends at the lovely Parc Floral.

## Festival Chopin à Paris
*Orangerie de Bagatelle, Parc de Bagatelle, Bois de Boulogne, 16th (01.45.00.22.19/www.frederic-chopin.com). M° Porte Maillot, then bus 244.* **Admission** €16-€31. **Date** June, July.
Candlelit evening recitals in the Bagatelle gardens.

## La Goutte d'Or en Fête
*Eglise St-Bernard, square St-Bernard, 18th (06.62.08.83.99/www.gouttedorenfete.org). M° Barbès Rochechouart.* **Admission** free. **Date** late June-early July.
Established and local artists play reggae, raï and rap.

## Paris Cinéma
*Various venues (01.55.25.55.25/www.paris cinema.org).* **Admission** varies. **Date** early July.
Premieres, tributes and restored films make up the programme of the city's summer film-going initiative.

## Solidays

*Longchamp Hippodrome (01.53.10.22.22/ www.solidays.com). M° Porte Maillot.* **Admission** *Day* €20. *Weekend* €35. **Date** 4-6 July.
A three-day music festival, all for the benefit of AIDS charities. *See also p317.*

## Miss Guinguette

*41 quai Victor Hugo, Ile du Martin-Pêcheur, 94500 Champigny-sur-Marne (information 01.49.83.03.02/ www.guinguette.fr). RER Champigny-sur-Marne.* **Admission** €7. **Date** 14 July.
A quest to find the light-footed queen of the open-air dancehall scene at this river-island venue.

## Le Quatorze Juillet (Bastille Day)

*All over France.* **Date** 14 July.
France's national holiday commemorates the events of 1789. On the eve, Parisians dance at place de la Bastille. At 10am on the 14th, crowds line up down the Champs-Elysées as the President reviews a full military parade. By night, the Champ de Mars fills for the fireworks display.

## Le Tour de France

*Av des Champs-Elysées, 8th (01.41.33.15.00/ www.letour.fr).* **Date** July.
The ultimate endurance test climaxes after some 3,500km (2,175 miles). Blink and you'll miss the winner as the event ends on the Champs-Elysées.

## Le Cinéma en Plein Air

*Parc de la Villette, 19th (01.40.03.75.75/ www.villette.com). M° Porte de Pantin.* **Admission** free. **Date** mid July-end Aug.
A themed season of films screened under the stars on Europe's largest inflatable screen.

## Paris, Quartier d'Eté

*Various venues (01.44.94.98.00/www.quartierdete. com).* **Admission** free-€15. **Date** mid July-mid Aug.
A series of classical and jazz concerts, dance and theatre performances in outdoor venues.

## Paris-Plage

*Pont des Arts to Pont de Sully (08.20.00.75.75/ www.paris.fr). M° Châtelet, Hôtel de Ville, Louvre Rivoli, Pont Marie, Sully Morland.* **Admission** free. **Date** mid July-mid Aug.
Palm trees, hammocks and 2,000 tonnes of fine sand bring a seaside atmosphere to the Seine. *Photo p278.*

## Fête de l'Assomption

*Cathédrale Notre-Dame de Paris, pl du Parvis Notre-Dame, 4th (01.42.34.56.10). M° Cité/RER St-Michel Notre-Dame.* **Admission** free. **Date** 15 Aug.
A national holiday. Notre-Dame again becomes a place of religious pilgrimage for Assumption Day.

## Rock en Seine

*Domaine National de St-Cloud (08.92.68.08.92/ www.rockenseine.com). M° Porte de Ste-Cloud.* **Admission** *Day* €42. *3 days* €98. **Date** end Aug.
Three days, three stages, and one world-class line-up of rock and indie groups. *See also p317.*

# Autumn

## Jazz à la Villette

*Parc de la Villette, 211 av Jean-Jaurès, 19th (01.44.84.44.84/www.jazzalavillette.com). M° Porte de Pantin.* **Admission** €12-€30. **Date** early Sept.
One of the best local jazz fests.

## Techno Parade

*www.technoparade.fr.* **Date** 13 Sept.
This parade (finishing at Bastille) marks the start of electronic music festival Rendez-vous Electroniques.

## Journées du Patrimoine

*Across France (08.20.20.25.02/www.jp.culture.fr).* **Date** 20-21 Sept.
Embassies, ministries, scientific establishments and corporate headquarters open their doors. The festive Soirée du Patrimoine takes place on the first Journée. Get *Le Monde* or *Le Parisien* for a full programme.

## Festival d'Automne

*Various venues. Information: 156 rue de Rivoli, 1st (01.53.45.17.17/www.festival-automne.com).* **Admission** €3-€60. **Date** mid Sept-mid Dec.
Major annual festival of challenging contemporary theatre, dance and modern opera, intent on bringing non-Western culture into the French consciousness. 'Autumn Festival' is a bit of a misnomer, as some exhibitions run over the new year into January.

## Nuit Blanche

*Various venues (39.75/www.paris.fr).* **Admission** free. **Date** early Oct.
Culture by moonlight: galleries and museums host one-off installations, while swimming pools, bars and clubs stay open till very late.

## Prix de l'Arc de Triomphe

*Hippodrome de Longchamp, Bois de Boulogne, 16th (01.49.10.20.30/www.france-galop.com). M° Porte d'Auteuil, then free shuttle bus.* **Admission** €8; €4 concessions; free under-18s. **Date** 5 Oct.
France's richest flat race attracts the elite of horse racing amid much pomp and ceremony. *See p339* **A day at the races.**

## Mondial de l'Automobile

*Paris-Expo, pl de la Porte de Versailles (01.56.88.22.40/www.mondial-automobile.com). M° Porte de Versailles.* **Admission** €12; €10 reductions; €7 under-7s. **Date** 4-9 Oct.
The largest and most visited automobile exhibition showcases cutting-edge cars from all over the world.

## Fête des Vendanges à Montmartre

*Rue des Saules, 18th (01.30.21.48.62/www. fetedesvendangesdemontmartre.com). M° Lamarck Caulaincourt.* **Date** 10-12 Oct.
Folk music, speeches, locals in costume and a parade celebrate the 800-bottle Montmartre grape harvest. *Chansons* accompany the village-fête atmosphere, with produce stands in Montmartre all weekend.

**Arts & Entertainment**

## FIAC

*01.47.56.64.20/www.fiacparis.com.* **Admission** €25; €12.50 reductions. **Date** 23-27 Oct.

Now held at the Louvre and the Grand Palais, this respected international art fair gives France a chance to strut its contemporary stuff.

## Les Puces du Design

*Quai de la Loire, 19th (01.53.40.78.77/www. pucesdudesign.com). M° Jaurès.* **Admission** free. **Date** Oct & June.

Having recently moved to the up-and-coming end of the canal, this modern design market draws specialist retailers from all over France.

## Festival Inrockuptibles

*Various venues (01.42.44.16.16/www.lesinrocks. com).* **Admission** varies. **Date** early Nov.

Once indie-centred, this festival curated by popular rock magazine *Les Inrockuptibles* today champions trance, techno and trip hop.

## Armistice Day

*Arc de Triomphe, 8th. M° Charles de Gaulle Etoile.* **Date** 11 Nov.

To commemorate French combatants who served in the World Wars, the President lays wreaths at the Tomb of the Unknown Soldier under the Arc de Triomphe. The *bleuet* (a cornflower) is worn.

## Fête du Beaujolais Nouveau

*www.beaujolaisgourmand.com.* **Date** mid Nov.

The third Thursday in November sees cafés and wine bars buzz as patrons assess the new vintage.

## Winter

## Africolor

*Various venues in the suburbs, including Montreuil, St-Denis and St-Ouen (01.47.97.69.99/ www.africolor.com).* **Admission** €5-€15. **Date** late Nov-late Dec.

A month-long African music festival, held at a handful of venues in the *banlieue*.

## Paris sur Glace

*Pl de l'Hôtel de Ville, 4th; M° Hôtel de Ville. Pl Raoul Dautry, 15th; M° Montparnasse Bienvenüe. Pl de la Bataille de Stalingrad, 19th; M° Stalingrad. Information: 39.75/www.paris.fr.* **Admission** free (skate hire €6). **Date** Dec-Mar.

Totter around the edges of these outdoor rinks while fearless five-year-olds zoom past.

## Noël (Christmas)

**Date** 24, 25 Dec.

Christmas is a family affair in France, with a dinner on Christmas Eve (*le réveillon*), normally after mass. Notre-Dame cathedral fills for the 11pm service. Usually the only bars and restaurants open are the ones in the city's main hotels.

## New Year's Eve/New Year's Day

**Date** 31 Dec, 1 Jan.

Crowds running into the tens of thousands swarm along the Champs-Elysées and let off bangers. Nightclubs and restaurants hold expensive soirées. On New Year's Day the Grande Parade de Paris brings floats, bands and dancers.

## Fête des Rois (Epiphany)

**Date** 6 Jan.

Pâtisseries sell *galettes des rois*, cakes with a frangipane filling in which a *fève*, or tiny charm, is hidden.

## Mass for Louis XVI

*Chapelle Expiatoire, 29 rue Pasquier, 8th (01.42.65.35.80). M° St-Augustin.* **Date** Jan.

On the Sunday closest to 21 January – the anniversary of the beheading of Louis XVI in 1793 – royalists and right-wing crackpots mourn the end of the monarchy.

## Nouvel An Chinois

*Around av d'Ivry & av de Choisy, 13th. M° Porte de Choisy or Porte d'Ivry. Also av des Champs Elysées, 8th.* **Date** Jan.

Lion and dragon dances, and lively martial arts demonstrations, celebrate the Chinese New Year.

**Paris-Plage.** *See p277.*

# Cabaret, Circus & Comedy

Get your kicks with sequins, satire and acrobatic antics galore.

Provocative dancing is still alive and well in the city's traditional cabarets, where synchronised boob-bouncing and glam girls in garters cast their sparkly spell over coachloads of tourists. Media mogul Gérard Louvin has also added to the fun with **Bobin'O**, the first new cabaret to hit town since the 1980s.

For a Gallic giggle, satire is kept alive in old-fashioned *café-théâtres*, where songs and sketches accompany dinner and a bottle of plonk. If French isn't your forte, veteran Anglo venue **Laughing Matters**, at La Java, is the sole provider of belly laughs in English, with comedy acts from across the Channel, the US and Australia. As for circus, Paris laps it up with performances from traditional ringmaster acts to avant-garde acrobatics and horse shows.

## Cabaret & café-théâtre

The year the Eiffel Tower raised its final girders (1889), the **Moulin Rouge** was raising something of its own: skirts. The risqué, frock-lifting dance called *quadrille réaliste* (later dubbed the cancan) became such a trademark that, nearly 120 years later, busty babes are still slinking across the cabaret stages of Paris. These days, cabaret is an all-evening, smart-dress extravaganza, complete with pre-show gourmet meal and champagne. It may be touristy and expensive (you won't get much change from €100), but it is an unrivalled spectacle. Male dancers, acrobats and magicians complement the foxy foxtrots; the dancing is perfectly synchronised, the costumes beautiful, and the whole caboodle now perfectly respectable.

## Cabaret

### Bobin'O

*14-20 rue de la Gaîté, 14th (01.43.27.24.24/ 08.20.00.90.00/www.bobino.fr). M° Edgar Quinet or Gaîté.* **Dinner** 7.30pm Tue-Sat. **Shows** 9.30pm Tue-Sat. **Nightclub** 11pm-2am Tue-Sat. **Admission** *Show* (incl champagne) €70. *Dinner & show* €125-€195. **Credit** AmEx, MC, V. **Map** p405 F9.
Brace yourself for drag acts, transsexual usherettes, bare bottoms, dancing waiters, sequin-clad performers and posh nosh. Then look beyond the glitter

(and the grey hair – most punters are middle-aged) and decide whether the city's first ever 'Cabaret-Restaurant-Lounge-Club' is more than a just a moneyspinner. The sleek silver and mauve decor certainly looks the part; the young performers mime, sing and dance wholeheartedly; and when the curtain falls the music kicks in until the wee hours. But you can't help feeling the Bobin'O is like a big-budget Butlins holiday show – sparkly, but lacking imagination.

### Crazy Horse Saloon

*12 av George-V, 8th (01.47.23.32.32/www. crazyhorse.fr). M° Alma Marceau or George V.* **Shows** 8.30pm, 11pm Mon-Fri, Sun; 7.30pm, 9.45pm, 11.50pm Sat. **Admission** *Show* (incl 2 drinks) €50. *Show* (incl champagne) €100-€120; €50-€60 students. **Credit** AmEx, DC, MC, V. **Map** p400 D4.
More risqué than the other cabarets, the Horse, whose *art du nu* was invented in 1951 by Alain Bernadin, is an ode to feminine beauty: 13 lookalike dancers, with identical body statistics (when standing, the girls' nipples and hips are all the same height), move around the stage, clad only in rainbow light and strategic strips of black tape. The girls put on some tantalising numbers, with titles such as *God Save Our Bare Skin* (a sexy take on the Changing of the Guards) and *Va Va Voom*. Dinner prior to the show can be arranged from 135€ per person (show included) at nearby Fouquet's, Findi, Devez, Chez Francis or Bateaux Parisiens.

### Le Lido

*116bis av des Champs-Elysées, 8th (01.40.76.56.10/ www.lido.fr). M° Franklin D. Roosevelt or George V.* **Lunch** 1pm. **Matinée** 3pm Tue, Sun (once a mth, dates vary). **Dinner** 7pm. **Shows** 9.30pm, 11.30pm daily. **Admission** *Matinée show* (incl champagne) €85. *Lunch & matinée show* (incl champagne) €125. *9.30pm show* (incl champagne) €100; €20 under-12s. *11.30pm show* (incl champagne) €90; free under-12s. *Dinner & show* €140-€250; €30 under-12s. **Credit** AmEx, DC, MC, V. **Map** p400 D4.
This is the largest, priciest cabaret of the lot: high-tech touches (check out the descending balcony and disappearing lamps) optimise visibility, and chef Philippe Lacroix, who trained under Alain Ducasse, provides fabulous gourmet nosh. On stage, 60 Bluebell Girls slink around, shaking their boobs with sequinned panache and donning wild and wacky costumes.

© Bal du Moulin Rouge 2003/2008 - Moulin Rouge®

Kis Gautier

# Discover the Show of the Moulin Rouge !

*1000 costumes of feathers, rhinestones and sequins,*
*sumptuous settings, the expected return of the giant Aquarium,*
*the world famous French Cancan and … the 60 Doriss Girls !*

Dinner & Show at 7pm from €145 • Show at 9pm : €99, 11pm : €89

Montmartre - 82, boulevard de Clichy - 75018 Paris
Reservations : 33 (0)1 53 09 82 82 • www.moulin-rouge.com

## Moulin Rouge

*82 bd de Clichy, 18th (01.53.09.82.82/www.moulin-rouge.com). M° Blanche.* **Dinner** 7pm. **Shows** 9pm, 11pm daily. **Admission** *9pm show* (incl champagne) €99. *11pm show* €89 (incl champagne). *Dinner & show* €145-€175. **Credit** AmEx, DC, MC, V. **Map** p401 G2.

Toulouse-Lautrec posters, glittery lampposts and fake trees lend tacky charm to this most traditional of glamour revues, while 60 Doriss dancers cavort with faultless synchronisation. Costumes are flamboyant, the *entr'acte* acts funny and the sets seamlessly changed before your eyes. The downer is the space: with tables packed in like sardines, rubbing elbows with perfect strangers is an inevitable hazard. But if you can bear intimacy with international businessmen, the Moulin Rouge won't disappoint.

## Café-théâtre

### Au Bec Fin

*6 rue Thérèse, 1st (01.42.96.29.35). M° Pyramides.* **Shows** 7pm, 8.15pm, 9.45pm Mon-Sat. *Matinées for children* 2.30pm, 4.30pm Wed, Sat, Sun. *Show for 3-6s* 11am Wed, Sat, Sun. Closed Aug. **Admission** *Show* €16; €9-€12 concessions. *Dinner & show* €30-€36. **Credit** AmEx, MC, V. **Map** p401 H5.

With a 300-year-old pedigree, the smallest *café-théâtre* in Paris offers wholesome family entertainment. After dining downstairs, head up the rickety staircase to see anything from Oscar Wilde in French to stand-up comedy or a cheesy version of *Cendrillon* for the little 'uns.

### Les Blancs Manteaux

*15 rue des Blancs-Manteaux, 4th (01.48.87.15.84/ www.blancsmanteaux.fr). M° Hôtel de Ville.* **Shows** from 7pm daily (phone for details). **Admission** *Show* €35. *Dinner & show* €99 (2 courses incl drink). **No credit cards. Map** p409 K6.

This Marais institution has two theatres, multiple weekly performances and new stand-up several times a month. With a dinner-and-show ticket (reserve and pay at the theatre), you can dine on Moroccan cuisine at nearby L'Arganier.

### Chez Michou

*80 rue des Martyrs, 18th (01.46.06.16.04/www. michou.com). M° Pigalle.* **Dinner** 8.15pm daily. **Shows** 10.30pm approx. **Admission** *Show* €35. *Dinner & show* €99 (incl wine). **Credit** MC, V. **Map** p402 H2.

Drag, sparkling costumes, good food and wine: Michou's show is not as 'blue' as his azure-attire suggests. Come here for larger-than-life impersonations of Brigitte Bardot and Tina Turner, and book ahead if you want to dine.

### Au Lapin Agile

*22 rue des Saules, 18th (01.46.06.85.87/www.au-lapin-agile.com). M° Lamarck Caulaincourt.* **Shows** 9pm-2am Tue-Sun. **Admission** *Show* (incl 1 drink) €24; €17 students (except Sat & public hols). **No credit cards. Map** p402 H1.

The prices have gone up and they sell their own compilation CDs, but that's all that seems to have changed since this quaint, pink bar first opened in 1860. Tourists now outnumber the locals, but the Lapin harbours an echo of old Montmartre.

### Le Petit Casino

*17 rue Chapon, 3rd (01.42.78.36.50/www.lepetit casino.fr). M° Arts et Métiers or Rambuteau.* **Dinner** 8pm. **Shows** 9pm, 10.30pm daily (times may vary). **Admission** *Show* (2 acts) €18. *Dinner* €15 (€21 Sat & public hols). **Credit** MC, V. **Map** p406 K5.

Up-and-coming talents find precious stage space in this traditional *café-théâtre* devoted to one-man shows and cheap 'n' tasty nosh. If your French is up to scratch, two nightly acts ensure you'll crack a smile without breaking the bank.

## Comedy & fringe theatre

### Le Bout

*6 rue Frochot, 9th (01.42.85.11.88/www.lebout.com). M° Pigalle.* **Shows** daily, times vary. **Admission** €15; €10 concessions. *2 shows* €20. **No credit cards. Map** p402 H2.

In the heart of Pigalle, this *café-théâtre* school has been cramming them into its 40-seater venue since 1999. The emphasis is on newcomers but not necessarily amateurs. The annual Festival du Rire plays here each summer too.

### Café de la Gare

*41 rue du Temple, 4th (01.42.78.52.51/www. cdlg.org). M° Hôtel de Ville.* **Shows** 9pm Mon, Tue; 7pm, 8.30pm, 10pm Wed-Sat; 9pm Sun. **Admission** €24; €20 over-60s; €15 students and under-25s. **Credit** MC, V. **Map** p406 K6.

Up and running since the revolutionary days of 1968, the most famous fringe theatre in Paris has 300 stage-hugging seats and hosts quality French stand-up and raucous, irreverent comedies.

### Caveau de la République

*1 bd St-Martin, 3rd (01.42.78.44.45/www.caveau.fr). M° République.* **Shows** 8.30pm Thur-Sat; 3.30pm Sun. Closed Aug. **Admission** €30 Thur; €37 Fri-Sun; €24.50 over-60s; €15 under-26s (except Sat). **Credit** MC, V. **Map** p402 L4.

This traditional *chansonnier* has been churning out political-satirical songs and sketches for more than a century. Nowadays stand-up comedy is the main draw and the laughs are mostly wrung from current scandals.

### Le Point Virgule

*7 rue Ste-Croix-de-la-Bretonnerie, 4th (01.42.78.67.03/www.lepointvirgule.com). M° Hôtel de Ville.* **Shows** 9pm Mon-Tue; 7pm, 8pm, 9.15pm, 10.35pm Wed-Fri; 4pm, 5.15pm, 7pm, 8pm, 9.15pm, 10.15pm Sat; 2.15pm (children's show), 5.30pm, 8pm, 9.15pm, 10.30pm Sun. **Admission** €18; €14 reductions. *Children's show* €12; €10 children. **No credit cards. Map** p409 K6.

Cirque d'Hiver Bouglione.

This small Marais theatre has become the ultimate launch pad for up-and-coming comedians, with daily shows, a *café-théâtre* school and an annual comedy festival in September. On Wednesday and Sunday afternoons there's a children's show.

### Le Zèbre

*63 bd de Belleville, 11th (01.43.55.55.55/www. lezebre.com). M° Belleville.* **Shows** days vary. **Dinner & show** 8pm Fri-Sat. **Admission** €12; €10 children. *Dinner & show* €78; €35 children. **Credit** MC, V. **Map** p403 N4.

After forays in all directions, the art deco Z is as eclectic as ever, with everything from satirical stand-up and chirruping *chanson* to circus ateliers, children's shows and a circus-cum-cabaret *diner-spectacle*.

## Comedy in English

### Laughing Matters

*La Java, 105 rue du Fbg-du-Temple, 10th (01.53.19.98.88/www.anythingmatters.com). M° Goncourt.* **Shows** days vary. **Admission** €20; €17 students. **No credit cards. Map** p403 M4.

Promoter Karel Beer is seemingly the only man Anglophone mirthsters will cross the sea for. He's recently added music concerts to his repertoire too.

## Circus

Whether it's with animals, acrobats or both, circus in Paris is a year-round fixture and involves a lot more than just plain old clowning around. See *Cirque* in the children's section of *Pariscope* for listings and also *pp283-289* **Children**.

### Cirque d'Hiver Bouglione

*110 rue Amelot, 11th (01.47.00.28.81/www.cirque dhiver.com). M° Filles du Calvaire.* **Shows** *Late Oct-late Feb* days vary. **Admission** €23.50-€39. **Credit** AmEx, MC, V. **Map** p409 L5.

Inaugurated in 1852, this traditional circus has been in the same family for seven decades. After an eight-month facelift, it has reopened its doors with a twice-yearly extravaganza, cabaret and performances by international artists.

### Cirque Pinder

*Pelouse de Reuilly, Bois de Vincennes, 12th (01.45.90.21.25/www.cirquepinder.com). M° Porte de Charenton or Porte Dorée.* **Shows** *Mid Nov-mid Jan* 2.30pm, 5.30pm, 8.30pm daily. **Admission** €13-€50; free under-2s. **Credit** AmEx, DC, MC, V.

With horses, lions, elephants and monkeys, Pinder is the oldest and most traditional travelling circus in France. The final leg of its annual tour is the Christmas show at the Pelouse de Reuilly.

### Espace Chapiteaux

*Parc De La Villette, 19th (01.42.09.01.09/www. villette.com). M° Porte de la Villette.* **Shows** days vary. **Admission** varies. **Credit** MC, V. **Map** p403 inset.

This big top hosts companies such as Cirque Plume, Centre National des Arts du Cirque and aerialists Les Arts Saut.

### Grand Céleste Cirque

*22 rue Paul Meurice, 20th (01.53.19.99.13/ www.grandceleste.com). M° Porte des Lilas.* **Shows** *Nov-end Feb* 8.30pm Thur, Fri, Sat; 4pm Sun (days may vary). *Matinées* Wed, Fri, Sat, Sun (times vary). **Admission** €14-€27; €11 students (Thur). **No credit cards.**

Three blue tents host this circus of traditional acts. If you fancy tightrope walking or learning to juggle, courses are on offer.

### Théâtre Equestre Zingaro

*176 av Jean-Jaurès, 93300 Aubervilliers (01.48.39.18.03/www.zingaro.fr). M° Fort d'Aubervilliers.* **Shows** 8.30pm Tue-Sat; 5.30pm Sun. **Admission** €20-€38. **Credit** MC, V.

This nomadic and poetic equestrian circus is based in Aubervilliers. Each year brings a new show.

# Children

Paradise for *les p'tits.*

**Parc Floral de Paris.** *See p285.*

One thing that makes Paris a great place to visit with children is that there's no deserted centre; kids are everywhere. Add to that the fact that most Parisians live in apartments without gardens, and you'll find a capital positively bursting with playgrounds.

Most of the famous sights on any child's wish list can be ticked off without undue stress, although it may be wise to head for the **Eiffel Tower** (*see p173*) early in the morning, when the queues are less daunting. For a relaxing overview of the heart of the city, a boat trip down the Seine is hard to beat. The waterborne **Batobus** links eight prime sights, including the Eiffel Tower, the Louvre and Notre-Dame. *See p90* **Sightseeing from the Seine.**

Paris has become much more cycle- and skate-friendly in recent years, so you can take a spin *en famille* along the cycle lanes by the Seine and the Canal St-Martin. The RATP rents out hard-to-steal blue and white bikes, plus junior bikes and child seats, at a number of locations across the city (www.rouelibre.fr). For a day out in beautiful surroundings, the **Bois de Vincennes** (*see p139*) in the east and the **Bois de Boulogne** (*see p124*) in the west provide woodlands, picnic areas, boating lakes and cycle rental.

Gaps in the academic schedule (Wednesday, weekends and school holidays) are filled with all kinds of organised children's activities, ranging from museum workshops to special film screenings and theatre productions.

Listings weeklies *Pariscope, L'Officiel des Spectacles, Figaroscope* (with Wednesday's *Le Figaro*) and *Télérama*'s *Sortir* supplement all have children's sections. Look out, too, for the bi-monthly free magazine *Paris-Mômes,* distributed with daily newspaper *Libération* or found in toy shops and public libraries.

## GETTING AROUND

Paris drivers can be fast and furious, so only cross at a zebra crossing or traffic lights – and stay alert even then. Turning traffic should give priority to pedestrians, but often doesn't. Keep an eye out for skaters, scooter-riders and cyclists speeding down narrow pavements.

Turnstiles, stairs and crowded carriages make negotiating the métro tricky with a pushchair, so travel with a kangaroo pouch for babies or lightweight folding pushchair if possible. Travel between 10.30am and 4pm to avoid the crowds. The driverless line 14 (Gare St-Lazare to Bibliothèque François Mitterrand) is a big hit with kids, who can sit at the front and peer down the tunnel as the train advances; the mostly overground lines 6 (Nation to Charles de Gaulle Étoile) and 2 (Nation to Porte Dauphine) offer attractive city views; and a number of RER stations have lifts.

It's often better, though, to take the bus. Some, such as nos.24 and 63 (www.ratp.fr), pass numerous sights, and all have priority seats near the front for those travelling with under-fours, who go free on public transport. Four- to

# Playtime

The first thing that stands out about children's playgrounds in Paris is just how many there are. Even the tiniest square or park will have a small climbing structure and bouncy animals, sometimes with a sandpit and ping-pong tables as well.

Some merit a special trip. For all its royal origins and proximity to the Louvre and smart rue St-Honoré, the **Jardin des Tuileries** (*see p105*) boasts a playground and trampoline park, plus pony rides, toy sailing boats to rent and a full-scale commercial funfair along the rue de Rivoli terrace in summer.

The **Jardin du Luxembourg** (*see p160*) offers all sorts of urban entertainment with its pony rides, puppet shows, pedal karts,

sandpits in a quiet fenced-off garden near the Orangerie, old-fashioned metal swingboats and merry-go-round. The playground has an entrance fee but is more imaginative than most, with plenty of high slides for bigger kids and a challenging spider's web.

Amid the fairground rides, bears and farm animals of the **Jardin d'Acclimatation** (*see p288*) are two playgrounds (free) and a big paddling area with sprinklers for cooling off. For small kids, ingenious sand-digging machines and funky seesaws with long insect antennae are a treat, while bigger children can fly through the air, Tarzan-like, on pulley swings or slide through tunnels.

In the **Parc de la Villette** (*see p144*), there is a succession of gardens and playgrounds to explore. Kids love the Chinese dragon slide as they climb up its tail and zoom out of its fire-breathing mouth, the Jardin des Voltiges has climbing ropes and unusual balancing games, and the slinkily modern Jardin des Dunes et Vents, with different zones for all ages from nought to 12, has pedal windmills, waves of bouncy tubes and giant hamster wheels.

The **Jardin des Enfants aux Halles**, also known as the Jardin des Eléphants after the two ivy-covered elephants by the entrance, is an imaginative oasis lurking in the midst of Les Halles (*see p112*), designed in the 1980s by sculptor Claude Lalanne. Seven-to 11-year-olds can roam through a bamboo forest, an antique city and a maze, and cross streams by rope bridges and stepping stones. Unfortunately it's become a political football in the battle over the redevelopment of Les Halles and the Mairie seems reluctant to maintain it, so make sure you get there quick; no parents allowed.

ten-year-olds qualify for a half-price *carnet* (a book of ten tickets) for all transport, including the Montmartrobus minibus and Montmartre funicular. Taxi drivers will usually take a family of four, as under-tens count as half; they charge €1 to carry a pushchair. If you're stuck miles from anywhere, try G7 taxis (01.41.27.66.99), which has an English-speaking booking line.

## EATING OUT

Eating out is an essential part of life for most Parisians, and French children start going to cafés and bistros at an early age. Bring crayons: paper tablecloths have satisfied generations

of would-be artists. Children's menus, when available, usually follow an unimaginative formula of burger and chips or chicken and chips, followed by ice-cream, but for something more imaginative children can often order just a starter and dessert, or a half-portion from the main menu.

Fun places to go to with children include the big *belle époque* dining room at affordable **Chartier** (7 rue du Fbg-Montmartre, 9th, 01.47.70.86.29, www.restaurant-chartier.com); **Tokyo Eat** at the Palais de Tokyo (13 av du Président-Wilson, 16th, 01 01.47.20.00.29,

www.palaisdetokyo.com), with its big round
tables that are good for families; the tables
above the cars in the high-tech **Atelier
Renault** (53 av des Champs-Elysées, 8th,
08.11.88.28.11, www.atelier.renault.com); and
**Apollo** (3 pl Denfert-Rochereau, 14th,
01.45.38.76.77, www.restaurant-apollo.com),
with its jungly terrace and neo-Pop interior.
**Vinéa Café** (01.44.74.09.09, www.vinea-
café.com) and the **Frog at Bercy Village**
(01.43.40.70.71, www.frogpubs.com), on
the Cour St-Emilion near Parc de Bercy,
are good for traffic-free outdoor eating. On
Sundays, fashionable nightclub **Showcase**
(01.45.61.25.43, www.showcase.fr) puts
on a family brunch, where children are
entertained with games and make-up.

**SEASONAL EVENTS**
A series of funfairs punctuate the year, the best
being **La Fête à Neu-Neu** (Bois de Boulogne,
autumn) and the **Foire du Trône** (Pelouse de
Reuilly, Bois de Vincennes, spring). In summer,
**La Fête des Tuileries** offers views from the
big wheel, along with other rides. Christmas
means cute window displays at the city's
department stores, free carousels, and
outdoor skating rinks at the Hôtel de Ville,
Montparnasse and La Villette; Hôtel de Ville is
best for kids, with a special rink and toboggan
run. Other family-friendly events include the
**Chinese New Year** parade (February), while
the gigantic **Salon de l'Agriculture** (March)
provides farm animals galore. In summer,
events move outdoors: the **Fête de la
Musique** (21 June) is one of the highlights.
**Bastille Day** (14 July) brings a military parade
and air force fly-past, and a fireworks display
in the evening. In July and August, **Paris,
Quartier d'Eté** (www.quartierdete.com)
brings eclectic world music, dance and
performance to Paris parks, much of it free;
in the **Parc Floral de Paris** (*photo p283*), the
**Pestacles** programme (www.pestacles.fr) each
Wednesday from June to September offers free
workshops, storytellers, clowns and concerts.
**Paris-Plage** offers a child's feast of sandy
beaches, sprinklers, paddling pools and activity
workshops on the quais of the Seine. *See also
pp274-278* **Festivals & Events**.

## Babies & toddlers

The English-speaking support group Message
(01.58.60.00.53, www.messageparis.org, annual
membership €79) aims to provide a social
network for anglophone parents and parents-
to-be, and publishes the handy *ABCs of
Motherhood in Paris* (€25 for non-members,
€20 for members).

Nappy-changing facilities are few and far
between, so always pack a portable changing
mat. A spot worth remembering is the WC
chalet in the **Jardin du Luxembourg**, where
€0.40 gives you access to loos with a padded
changing table; the **Galeries Lafayette** and
**Printemps** (*for both, see p241*) department
stores have clean, well-equipped nappy
changing facilities.
Breastfeeding in public places is often
frowned upon in France, so you may have
to feed *en plein air*, or in a quiet corner of a
museum or restaurant. Take a scarf for places
where modesty is essential.
A city break with tots in tow doesn't have
to mean missing out on the city's galleries and
museums. Almost all of the main attractions
have child-friendly activities or green spaces
nearby – handy as a reward for good behaviour,
or if you're prepared to split into two groups.
There's a carefully tended garden by **Notre-
Dame** (*see p89*), and even the quiet and
dignified **Musée Rodin** (*see p172*) has its
outdoor distractions, with a sandpit to dig in
and sculpture-filled gardens to explore. And if
the heady heights of the Eiffel Tower prove too
daunting, more down-to-earth amusements can
be found at the adjacent Champ de Mars, with
its play areas and donkey rides; or there are old-
style merry-go-rounds by the river.

# Babysitting

## The American Church in Paris
*65 quai d'Orsay, 7th (01.40.62.05.00/www.
acparis.org). M° Invalides or Pont de l'Alma.* **Open**
9am-10.30pm Mon-Sat; 3-7pm Sun. **Map** p405 E5.
The free noticeboard inside the main entrance has
'situations wanted' ads from recommended English-
speaking babysitters and au pairs.

## Baby Sitting Services
*01.46.21.33.16/www.babysittingservices.com.* **Open**
24hrs daily. *Office* 7am-9pm daily. **Rates** 8am-10pm
€6.80/hr Mon-Sat; 10pm-8am €7.50/hr. €8/hr +
€11.90 fee Sun & bank hols. €1/hr/child supplement
for 3 or more children. **Credit** MC, V.
Babysitting can be organised at two hours' notice.
School pick-up, outings, children's parties and long-
term babysitting can also be arranged.

# Museums & sightseeing

Egyptian mummies at the **Louvre** (*see p93-99*);
suits of armour at **Les Invalides** (*see p170*);
Picasso's sculptures, paintings and collages at
**Musée Picasso** (*see p135*); dinosaur skeletons
at the Galeries de Paléontologie et d'Anatomie
Comparée at the **Muséum National
d'Histoire Naturelle**; theatrically lit tribal
masks, totems and American Indian cowhides

**Arts & Entertainment**

at the **Musée du Quai Branly** (*see p174*);
early flying machines, rockets and the chance
to go inside Concorde at the **Musée de l'Air
et de l'Espace** at Le Bourget (*see p179*);
model boats at the **Musée National de la
Marine** (*see below*); the Argonaut submarine
at **La Cité des Sciences et de l'Industrie**
(*see p289* **The appliance of science**); or
fashion and jewellery at the **Musée de la
Mode et du Textile**: there's plenty to feed a
child's imagination. Under-18s also get in free
to the national museums, including the Louvre,
Orsay, Centre Pompidou, Quai Branly, Rodin
and Picasso museums.

Most museums offer children's workshops
(in French) on Wednesday afternoons, at
weekends and in the holidays. At the Louvre
the programme for kids varies from painting
and mosaics to chivalry or learning to write in
hieroglyphics. Next door, the **Museé des Arts
Décoratifs** (*see p105*) offers hands-on art
workshops for ages four to 12, as well as special
tours tailored to different age groups. The
**Palais de Tokyo** (*see p120*) has inventive
'Tok Tok' workshops, often led by notable
contemporary artists, and the Musée Rodin
and **Musée Bourdelle** (*see p165*) both run
children's clay-modelling workshops.

### Centre Pompidou – Galerie des Enfants

*Rue St-Martin, 4th (01.44.78.49.13/www.
centrepompidou.fr/enfants). M° Hôtel de Ville or
Rambuteau/RER Châtelet Les Halles.* **Open** *Museum*
11am-9pm Mon, Wed-Sun. *Workshops* most Wed &
Sat afternoons & school hols. **Admission** *Museum*
€10; free under-18s. *Workshops* €10. **Credit** MC, V.
**Map** p402 K5.

In the ground-floor gallery, imaginative exhibitions
specially conceived by top artists and designers
introduce children to aspects of modern art, design
and architecture, often with interactive elements and
the opportunity to touch. There are also hands-on
workshops for six- to 12-year-olds, and family workshops one Sunday afternoon a month. Outside, look
for the colourful Stravinsky fountain on the south
side, designed by Niki de Saint Phalle and Jean
Tinguely, and the animated clock in the Quartier de
l'Horloge on the piazza's north side: every hour, its
man-size automaton Le Défenseur du Temps
('Defender of Time') valiantly fights off a crab, a
dragon or a cockerel (and all three at noon and 6pm).
*See also p131.*

### Cité de l'Architecture

*Palais de Chaillot, 17 pl du Trocadéro, 16th
(01.58.51.52.00/www.citechaillot.fr).* **Admission** €7;
€5 concessions; free under-18s. **No credit cards.**
**Map** p400 B5.

Colourful mini building sites created by designer
Matali Crasset are dotted around the permanent
display of life-size architectural mouldings at the

Musée des Monuments Français, letting children try
their hand at architecture and learn the concepts of
Romanesque and Gothic as they create fantastical
animal heads, design stained-glass windows or build
a Romanesque arch.

### Etoiles du Rex

*1 bd Poissonnière, 2nd (01.45.08.93.58/www.
legrandrex.com). M° Bonne Nouvelle.* **Open**
10am-7pm Wed-Sun (tours leave every 5mins).
**Admission** €9.50; €8 under-12s. **Credit** AmEx,
MC, V. **Map** p402 J4.

The slick, 50-minute backstage tour of the glorious
art deco Grand Rex cinema is a great way to entertain any kids with acting aspirations. Be prepared to
ham your heart out when, propelled by automatic
doors, lifts and mystery voices, you visit the projec-
tion room, climb behind the giant screen and are
thrust into a whirlwind of sound dubbing, special
effects and an audition for *King Kong*.

### Grévin

*10 bd Montmartre, 9th (01.47.70.85.05/www.musee-
grevin.com). M° Grands Boulevards.* **Open** 10am-
6.30pm (last admission 5.30pm) Mon-Fri; 10am-7pm
(last admission 6pm) Sat, Sun & hols. **Admission**
€17.50; €15.50 students; €11 6-14s; free under-6s.
**Credit** AmEx, DC, MC, V. **Map** p402 H4.

The Paris waxworks has now cheerfully removed
any mention of museum from its name and whittled
the historical component down to a few colourful
tableaux (Louis XIV at Versailles, the French
Revolution) in favour of a panoply of sporting and
showbiz stars and personalities. Bring a camera so
that children can pose for photos alongside Naomi
Campbell, Zinédine Zidane, Pablo Picasso, Brigitte
Bardot, the Queen or Laurel and Hardy. A small
gallery at the top of a spiral staircase near the end
shows how waxworks are made, from the initial
sculpture to fixing real hair strand by strand and
choosing the right colour of eyeballs.

### Musée de la Magie

*11 rue St-Paul, 4th (01.42.72.13.26/www.musee
delamagie.com). M° St-Paul or Sully-Morland.* **Open**
2-7pm Wed, Sat, Sun (extra hours & days in school
hols). **Admission** €9; €7 under-12s. **No credit
cards. Map** p409 L7.

A small museum of magic and curiosities housed in
vaulted cellars. Small kids love the distorting mirrors and putting their hands in the lion's mouth. A
short magic show is included in the visit – it's in
French, but rabbits out of hats translate pretty well.

### Musée National de la Marine

*Palais de Chaillot, 17 pl du Trocadéro, 16th
(01.53.65.69.69/www.musee-marine.fr). M°
Trocadéro.* **Open** 10am-6pm Mon, Wed-Sun.
**Admission** €8; €4 6-18s; free under-6s. **Credit**
*Shop* MC, V. **Map** p400 B5.

If your children dream of adventure on the high seas,
this maritime museum is for them. Highlights are a
model of the *Océan*, a 19th-century sailing vessel
equipped with an impressive 120 cannons; a gilded

barge built for Napoleon; and some extravagant, larger-than-life figureheads, from serene-faced angels to leaping seahorses. There are also dozens of model boats, dating from the 18th to the 20th century, and a window through which you can watch the in-house restoration team at work. *See also p119.*

### Muséum National d'Histoire Naturelle
*36 rue Geoffroy-St-Hilaire, 2 rue Bouffon, 57 rue Cuvier, 5th (01.40.79.54.79/www.mnhn.fr). M° Gare d'Austerlitz or Jussieu.* **Open** *Nov-Mar* 10am-5pm Mon, Wed-Sun (10am-6pm Grande Galerie de l'Evolution). *Apr-Oct* 10am-6pm Mon, Wed-Sun. Last admission 45mins before closing. **Admission** *Grande Galerie de l'Evolution* €8; €6 students & 4-13s; free under-4s. *Galeries de Paléontologie et d'Anatomie Comparée* or *Galerie de Minéralogie et de Géologie* €6; €4 4-13s; free under-4s. **Credit** MC, V. **Map** p406 K9.

The Grande Galerie de l'Evolution houses stuffed creatures shown to great effect in the artily lit, lofty central forum, creating a Noah's Ark-like parade through different habitats. The Salle de Découverte has temporary exhibitions, microscopes and interactive games. Also in the Jardin des Plantes complex are the small Ménagerie zoo (*see p154*), separate pavilions containing hunks of meteorites and crystals in the Galerie de Minéralogie et de Géologie, and the bony remains of fish, birds, monkeys, dinosaurs and humans in the Galerie de Paléontologie et d'Anatomie Comparée.

### Musée de la Poupée
*Impasse Berthaud, 3rd (01.42.72.73.11/www.musee delapoupeeparis.com). M° Rambuteau.* **Open** 10am-6pm Tue-Sun. **Admission** €7; €5 12-25s; €3 3-11s; free under-3s. **No credit cards. Map** p406 L7.

This small private museum displays some 400 dolls (mostly of French origin) with their accompanying accessories and pets, arranged in thematic tableaux. Temporary exhibits, covering topics such as Barbie or dolls in regional costumes, are presented in the last three rooms. A shop and doll's hospital share the premises.

### Stade de France
*Guided visits via entrance Porte H, Stade de France, 16th (01.55.93.00.00/tour reservations 08.92.70.09.00/www.stadefrance.fr). M° St-Denis Porte de Paris/RER Stade de France St-Denis.* **Tours** every hr 10am-5pm daily. **Admission** €10; €8 reductions; free under-6s. **Credit** AmEx, DC, MC, V.

Football-crazy kids love the behind-the-scenes tours of France's national sports stadium. After a quick scan of the museum (photos, football shirts, electric guitars from the rock stars who also play here), the tour begins by sitting in the stands and ends with a runout through the tunnel to the sound of applause. On the way, you can visit the changing and shower rooms and learn about the on-site hospital and prison cells.

## Aquaria, menageries & zoos

### Cinéaqua
*2 av des Nations Unies, 16th (01.40.69.23.23/ www.cineaqua.com). M° Trocadéro.* **Open** 10am-8pm daily. **Admission** €19.50; €15 students; €12 under-12s; free under-3s. **Credit** MC, V. **Map** p400 B5.

This superb new aquarium contains 500 species of fish and invertebrates, sharks and coral aplenty, plus a three-screen cinema. The problem is the price. There are kids' clubs from 1pm to 4pm on Wednesdays, Saturdays and Sundays, a touch pool and set feeding times: 4pm is the sharks' tea party.

### Ménagerie du Jardin des Plantes
*57 rue Cuvier, 5th (01.40.79.37.94/www.mnhn.fr). M° Gare d'Austerlitz, Jussieu or Place Monge.* **Open** 9am-6pm Mon-Sat; 9am-6.30pm Sun. **Admission** €7; €5 4-13s; free under-4s. **Credit** AmEx, MC, V. **Map** p406 K8.

This small zoo was founded in 1794, when the royal Ménagerie was moved here from Versailles. Its inhabitants include vultures, monkeys, orang-utans, ostriches, flamingoes, a century-old turtle, a lovely red panda, and lots of satisfyingly scary spiders and snakes. There's a petting zoo with farm animals for small kids, while older ones can zoom in on microscopic species in the Microzoo.

### Palais de la Porte Dorée Aquarium Tropical
*293 av Daumesnil, 12th (01.44.74.84.80/www.palais-portedoree.org). M° Porte Dorée.* **Open** 10am-5.15pm Tue-Sun. **Admission** €4.50-€5.70; €6-€8 1 adult with 1 or 2 children under 12; €3-€4.20 4-25s; free under-4s. **No credit cards.**

The basement of this art deco palace, built for the colonial exhibition in 1931 (now home to the new museum of immigration), contains the much-loved city aquarium and its colonial crocodiles, brought over from Dakar in 1948; other watery residents include cuttlefish, clownfish and sharks, and dark galleries of luminous deep-water species.

### Parc de Thoiry
*78770 Thoiry-en-Yvelines (01.34.87.53.76/www. thoiry.tm.fr). 45km (28 miles) west of Paris; by car A13, A12, then N12 direction Dreux until Thoiry.* **Open** *July, Aug* 10am-6pm daily. *Sept-June* 10am-5pm Mon-Sat; 10am-6pm Sun. **Admission** Free under-3s. *Safari park, park & château* €22.90; €15.90 3-14s. *Park & château* €18; €13 3-14s. **Credit** MC, V.

As well as a château, the Parc de Thoiry houses one of Europe's first animal reserves. In the safari park, accessible only by car, zebras rub their noses over your windscreen, lions stretch out in the shade, and bears amble down tracks. In the adjoining zoo, rarities include Siberian lynx and Tonkean macaques. The ticket is valid for the zoo, maze and gardens.

### Parc Zoologique de Paris
*53 av de St-Maurice, 12th (01.44.75.20.00/ www.mnhn.fr). M° Porte Dorée.* **Open** *Summer* 9am-6pm Mon-Sat; 9am-6.30pm Sun & bank hols.

**Arts & Entertainment**

*Winter* 9am-5pm Mon-Sat; 9am-5.30pm Sun & bank hols. **Admission** €5; free under-4s. **Credit** MC, V.

Located on the edge of the Bois de Vincennes, the main Paris zoo was founded in the 1930s and laid out with fake mountains, lakes and ditches to avoid the use of cages where possible. Today it is in the midst of a huge transformation that will create a series of 'biozones' representing different ecosystems. In the meantime the Grand Rocher is out of bounds and some of the animals have been moved, but there are still plenty of acrobatic gibbons, macaques and baboons to keep children amused, as well as a giraffe house and the Nocturama, where you can see lemurs in night-time conditions.

## Performing arts & sports

Numerous traditional circuses (*see p282*), complete with big cats and liberty horses, pitch tent each winter on the Pelouse de Reuilly or Bois de Boulogne, and the Cirque Bouglione occupies the gorgeous Cirque d'Hiver. All-year round the **Cirque du Grand Céleste** (*see p282*) puts on an entertaining, modern, family-oriented circus show, without animals; it also runs a circus school, initiating children into trapeze, tightrope, juggling and acrobatic skills on Wednesdays.

Fables, fairy tales and folk stories are favourites at children's shows at the city's theatres and *café-théâtres* on Wednesday afternoons, at weekends and in the holidays. The varied programme of theatre, dance and musical creations at the **Théâtre Dunois** (7 rue Louise-Weiss, 13th, 01.45.84.72.00, www.theatredunois.org) is specifically geared towards children, including the Glitterbird, Art for the Very Young Festival in October. Aimed at one- to five-year-olds, it brings in companies from all over Europe.

Children's films are generally dubbed into French, but you can see VO (*version originale*) screenings of the latest Hollywood hits at dozens of cinemas across town (*see p293-298*). Keep a lookout for children's showings on Wednesdays and Saturday afternoons at the **Cinémathèque Française** (*see p295* **A sanctuary for cinephiles**) and **L'Ecran des Enfants** (Oct-June 2.30pm Wed) at the **Centre Pompidou**, and the **Pochette Surprise!** on the second Sunday morning of the month at Le Balzac (www.cinemabalzac.com), a programme of mainly silent films (Chaplin, Harold Lloyd, Buster Keaton, etc) with piano accompaniment. The IMAX cinema in La Villette's **Géode** (*see p294*) will keep kids enthralled.

Paris is good for watery entertainment too. The 35 public pools (www.paris.fr) include the new **Piscine Josephine-Baker** (*see p340*), moored on the Seine and filled with purified water pumped from the river; the art nouveau **Piscine de la Butte-aux-Cailles**, with indoor and outdoor pools fed by artesian wells; and the recently restored **Espace Sportif Pailleron**, near Buttes-Chaumont, which has two pools and an ice rink (rollerskating in summer). At the indoor **Aquaboulevard** (*see p340*), over-threes can splash down different slides and ride the waves.

## Theme parks

### Disneyland Paris/Walt Disney Studios Park

*Marne-la-Vallée (08.25.30.60.30/from UK 0870 503 0303/www.disneylandparis.com). 32km E of Paris. RER A or TGV Marne-la-Vallée-Chessy. By car A4 exit 14.* **Open** *Disneyland Paris* Sept-mid July 10am-8pm Mon-Fri; 9am-8pm Sat, Sun. Mid July-Aug 9am-11pm daily. *Studios Park* Winter 10am-6pm Mon-Fri; 9am-6pm Sat, Sun. Summer 9am-6pm daily. **Admission** 1 park €43; €35 3-11s; free under-3s. 1-day hopper (both parks) €53; €45 3-11s; free under-3s. **Credit** AmEx, MC, V.

Now 15 years old, the once-controversial theme park is a familiar part of the flat Ile de France landscape, drawing some 12 million visitors a year. Radiating out from sugary Main Street USA, with its shops and Disney character parade, are Fantasyland, Adventureland, Frontierland and Discoveryland, all liberally scattered with souvenir shops and theme restaurants. Fantasyland, with its Alice maze, Sleeping Beauty's castle and teacup and Dumbo rides, is most suitable for small children; the splashy Pirates of the Caribbean and Phantom Manor provide spooky fun; and daredevils can experience the bone-shaking Indiana Jones et le Temple de Péril and Space Mountain. Various seasonal entertainments punctuate the year: fireworks in summer and Halloween treats in autumn. The adjacent Studios Park takes you into animation studios and on a special effects tram tour through a film set.

### Jardin d'Acclimatation

*Bois de Boulogne, 16th (01.40.67.90.82/www. jardindacclimatation.fr). M° Les Sablons.* **Open** *May-Sept* 10am-7pm daily. *Oct-Apr* 10am-6pm daily. **Admission** €2.70; €1.35 concessions; free under-3s. **Credit** (€15 minimum) MC, V.

Founded in 1860, this amusement park and garden has bears, a Normandy-style farm and an aviary, as well as boat rides, a funfair with Chinese dragon rollercoaster, flying chairs and the Enchanted House for children aged two to four. Older kids can visit the Explor@dome (*see p289* **The appliance of science**), steer radio-controlled boats or try out the mini automobile circuit and mini golf. Many of the attractions cost €2.70 (€32 for 15); others are free, including the playgrounds, puppet shows and distorting mirrors. A miniature train (€5.40/€4.05 including entrance fee) runs from Porte Maillot through the Bois de Boulogne to the park entrance.

# The appliance of science

From the minutiae of ant colonies to understanding gears or the mysteries of tornadoes, the city's science museums offer plenty of opportunity for hands-on activities.

The **Cité des Enfants**, a unique children's science museum within the huge, high-tech Cité des Sciences et de l'Industrie at La Villette, is in the process of a major expansion programme. Although aimed at children up to 12 years old, those near the upper age limit may well find there's too much play and not enough science, and prefer the more technical approach of Explora, the main museum display up on levels one and two.

'It is forbidden to not touch' is the slogan of the **Exploradome**, located inside the Jardin d'Acclimatation. Although much smaller than La Villette, it's notable for its excellent *animateurs* who demonstrate and explain (in French, but they're happy to try to summarise in English) the different pieces

of equipment, taking in such phenomena as movement, optical illusions and the formation of sand dunes.

Although it's the most old-fashioned of the capital's science museums, the **Musée des Arts et Métiers** is the one that makes most effort for English-speaking children. The emphasis is on engineering and the history of inventions, and there's an English audio guide for seven to 12-year-olds. Elsewhere you'll find crank handles to turn, touch-screen film footage and staff explaining the principles of Foucault's pendulum.

## Cité des Enfants

*Niveau 0, Cité des Sciences et de l'Industrie, 30 av Corentin-Cariou, 19th (01.40.05.80.00/www.cite-sciences.fr). Mº Porte de la Villette.* **Open** (90min sessions, reservation recommended) 10.30am, 12.30pm, 2.30pm, 4.30pm Tue-Sun. **Admission** €6; children must be accompanied by an adult. **Credit** AmEx, MC, V. **Map** p403 inset.

## Exploradome

*Jardin d'Acclimatation, Bois de Boulogne, 16th (01.53.64.90.40/www.exploradome. com). Mº Les Sablons.* **Open** 10am-6pm daily. **Admission** €5. **Credit** MC, V.

## Musée des Arts et Métiers

*60 rue Réaumur, 3rd (01.53.01.82.00/ www.arts-et-metiers.net). Mº Arts et Métiers.* **Open** 10am-6pm Tue, Wed, Fri-Sun; 10am-9.30pm Thur. **Admission** €6.50; free under-18s; audio guide €2.50. **Credit** V. **Map** p402 K4/K5.

## La Mer de Sable

*Ermenonville (03.44.54.18.44/www.merdesable.fr). By coach from RER Roissy-Charles de Gaulle 1 (check website for times). By car A1 exit 7, direction Ermenonville.* **Open** *Apr-Sept* days & times vary. **Admission** €18; €15 3-11s; free under-3s. **Credit** MC, V.

Complete with a bison and camel farm, the Wild West-themed Mer de Sable ('Sea of Sand'), France's oldest theme park, owes its desert-like sandy setting to a strange natural phenomenon in the middle of the Ermonenville forest. The park is now under the same ownership as Grévin, Parc Astérix and France Miniature, and a clutch of new rides, live shows and eateries has been added to the popular Cheyenne river water ride, big wheel, miniature train and carousels.

## Parc Astérix

*60128 Plailly (08.26.30.10.40/www.parcasterix.fr). 36km N of Paris. By coach from the Louvre or RER Roissy-Charles de Gaulle 1 (check website for times). By car A1 exit Parc Astérix.* **Open** *Apr-June* 10am-6pm daily. *July, Aug* 9.30am-7pm daily. *Sept-mid Nov* 10am-6pm Wed, Sat, Sun. Closed mid Nov-Mar except during Christmas hols. **Admission** €37; €27 3-11s; free under-3s. **Credit** MC, V.

Wittily laid out with Ancient Greece, the Roman Empire and the indomitable Gaulish village, just like Goscinny and Uderzo's comic-book creation, the native rival to Disney is very popular with Paris children, especially those who feel too grown up for princess parades. Attractions include a splashy water ride on a menhir and Goudurix, Europe's largest rollercoaster with seven loop-the-loops.

# Dance

Capital choreography, from ballet to belly dancing.

Dance is thriving in Paris, with an accomplished, avant-garde scene and a visiting battalion of renowned international companies: 2008 sees the return of Anne Teresa De Keersmaeker, Pina Bausch, Angelin Preljocaj and William Forsythe to the well-established **Théâtre de la Ville** and **Théâtre de Chaillot**. There is also no shortage of ballet productions at the **Théâtre du Châtelet** and **Palais Garnier**, where the Bolshoi will be leading the programme in January, followed by Carolyn Carlson later in the year. And once again the **Festival d'Automne** features an impressive line-up of established dance innovators.

Now in its fourth year as HQ for over 600 regional companies, the **Centre National de la Danse** outside the city centre in Pantin reaches out to its audience with a well-devised series of performances, while smaller dance 'laboratories' such as **Ménagerie de Verre, Point Ephémère** and **Regard du Cygne** showcase new work by smaller companies.

Dance centres and festivals outside Paris are determined to draw audiences to their suburban locations too, with a distinct mix of styles and cultures. Hip hop and other urban dance forms now enjoy well-deserved recognition with festivals such as **Suresnes Cité Danse** and **Rencontres de la Villette**.

Dance classes are available to suit all tastes and levels in Paris, for adults and children alike, and those who fancy swirling under the stars will relish the open-air salsa and tango dancing on the Left Bank throughout summer.

## INFORMATION AND RESOURCES

For listings, see *Pariscope* and *L'Officiel des Spectacles*. For events coverage, look out for two monthlies: *La Terrasse* (distributed free at major dance venues) and the glossy *Danser*.

For shoes and equipment, **Sansha** (52 rue de Clichy, 9th, 01.45.26.01.38) has a good reputation, and **Repetto** (22 rue de la Paix, 2nd, 01.44.71.83.06) supplies the Opéra with pointes and slippers; **Menkes** (12 rue Rambuteau, 3rd, 01.40.27.91.81) sells serious flamenco gear as well as outsize glam-rock boots.

## Festivals

Every season sees some kind of contemporary dance festival in or near Paris. The year starts with **Faits d'Hiver** (www.faitsdhiver.com),

and hip hop festival **Suresnes Cité Danse** (www.theatre-suresnes.fr), both in January. May and June welcome the **Rencontres Chorégraphiques de Seine-St-Denis** (www.rencontreschoregraphiques.com), the **IRCAM Agora festival** (www.ircam.fr) and **Onze Bouge** (www.festivalonze.org). The street-dance **Rencontres de la Villette** (www.rencontresvillette.com) takes place at various surburban locations every October. You will also find smaller dance festivals at the **Maison des Arts de Créteil**, as well as the **Ménagerie de Verre** in the 11th. *See also pp274-278* **Festivals & Events**.

### Les Etés de la Danse
*Grand Palais, av Winston Churchill, 8th (www. lesetesdeladanse.com). M° Champs-Elysées Clemenceau.* Date *July.*
Founded in 2005, this festival puts the spotlight on one company or choreographer, with a month of performances in the atmospheric setting of the Grand Palais. The shows are accompanied by workshops and activities to ensure a festival spirit.

### Paris quartier d'été
*01.44.94.98.00/www.quartierdete.com.*
Date *July, Aug.*
With 60,000 visitors in 2007, this popular festival features eclectic programmes and free outdoor performances in Paris and its outskirts. Public rehearsals and talks give audiences the chance to meet prestigious international choreographers.

### Festival d'Automne
*01.53.45.17.00/www.festival-automne.com.*
Date *Sept-Dec.*
For 35 years, the Festival d'Automne has shown the way forward in the performing arts. With a focus on leading French experimental companies, the festival also invites big-name choreographers from around the world.

## Major dance venues

### Centre National de la Danse
*1 rue Victor-Hugo, 93507 Pantin (01.41.83.27.27/ box office 01.41.83.98.98/www.cnd.fr). M° Hoche/ RER Pantin.* **Open** *Box office* 10am-7pm Mon-Fri. **Admission** €6-€14. **Credit** AmEx, MC, V.
Since opening in 2004, the aim of this impressive centre has been to break down the barriers between dancers and the audience. As well as an expertly curated selection of performances in the studios, the *'Grandes leçons de danse'* invite the audience to

**Théâtre du Châtelet.**

watch contemporary dance masterclasses four times a year. There are also exhibitions, a phenomenal archive of films and choreographic material available to the public.

### Maison des Arts de Créteil

*Pl Salvador-Allende, 94000 Créteil (01.45.13.19.19/ www.maccreteil.com). M° Créteil-Préfecture.* **Open** *Box office* 1-7pm Tue-Sat. Closed mid July-Aug. **Admission** €8-€30. **Credit** MC, V.

This suburban arts centre has an eclectic programme of contemporary performances by Ballet de Lorraine and Lotte van den Berg, as well as ballet classics by Serge Lifar, Roland Petit and Maurice Béjart presented by the Ballet de l'Opéra National de Paris. Don't miss the Festival International Exit in the spring.

### Palais Garnier

*Pl de l'Opéra, 9th (08.92.89.90.90/www.opera-de-paris.fr). M° Opéra.* **Open** *Box office* 11am-6pm Mon-Sat. *Telephone bookings* 9am-6pm Mon-Sat. Closed 15 July-end Aug. **Admission** €7-€160. *Concessions* 1hr before show. **Credit** AmEx, MC, V. **Map** p401 G4.

The Ballet de l'Opéra National de Paris manages to tread successfully between tutu classics and new productions, between the Opéra Bastille and lavish Palais Garnier, where the renovated grand foyer is a must-see. The Bolshoi will be guest company in early 2008, followed by Mats Ek and Carolyn Carlson later in the summer. The ballet school's yearly performance in April embodies the spirit of this revered institution.

### Théâtre du Châtelet

*1 pl du Châtelet, 1st (01.40.28.28.00/www. chatelettheatre.com). M° Châtelet.* **Open** *Box office* July, Aug 1-6pm daily. Sept-June 11am-7pm daily. **Admission** from €10. **Credit** AmEx, MC, V. **Map** p402 J6.

Across the square from the Théâtre de la Ville, this classical music institution continues to open up its programme to other live artistic disciplines. The new dance season will take the audience on a journey with great European acts such as Ballet Preljocaj, Compañia Nacional de Danza and John Neumeier's Hamburg Ballett in April.

### Théâtre National de Chaillot

*1 pl du Trocadéro, 16th (01.53.65.30.00/ www.theatre-chaillot.fr). M° Trocadéro.* **Open** *Box office* 11am-7pm Mon-Sat; 1-5pm Sun. *Telephone bookings* 11am-7pm Mon-Sat. Closed July, Aug. **Admission** €27-€33; €12-€27 concessions. **Credit** MC, V. **Map** p400 C5.

Tango fanatic Ariel Goldenberg always pulls together an exciting international dance programme at Chaillot. Frédéric Flamand's *Silent Collision*, Saburo Teshigawara's *Glass Tooth* and Buenos Aires Tango4 are among the attractions in 2008, with William Forsythe closing the season.

### Théâtre de la Ville – Les Abbesses

*2 pl du Châtelet, 4th (01.42.74.22.77/www.theatre delaville-paris.com). M° Châtelet.* **Open** *Box office* 11am-8pm Mon-Sat. *Telephone bookings* 11am-7pm Mon-Sat. Closed July, Aug. **Admission** €12-€23; €12 under-28s. **Credit** MC, V. **Map** p406 J6.

This leading contemporary dance venue has nurtured long-standing collaborations with international choreographers. This year will see the return of Anne Teresa De Keersmaeker, Sankai Juku and Pina Bausch; other highlights include the irreverent *Ha Ha!* by Maguy Marin, *Spiegel* by Wim Vandekeybus and his Ultima Ves, and Akram Khan Company's new creation *Bridge*. Book early – most shows sell out well before opening night. The smaller auditorium of sister venue Théâtre des Abbesses will welcome Les Ballets C de la B and Sidi Larbi Cherkaoui. **Other locations:** Théâtre des Abbesses, 31 rue des Abbesses, 18th (01.42.74.22.77).

**Arts & Entertainment**

# Other dance venues

### L'Etoile du Nord
*16 rue Georgette-Agutte, 18th (01.42.26.47.47).*
*M° Guy Môquet.* **Open** *Box office* 1-6pm Mon-Fri.
Closed July, Aug. **Admission** €19; €10-€14
concessions. **Credit** V.
This smaller venue splits its programme between
theatre and contemporary multimedia dance. The
Avis de Turbulences festival (end May-mid June)
has a number of mixed bills. There is also a friendly
bar, open before and after performances.

### Ménagerie de Verre
*12-14 rue Léchevin, 11th (01.43.38.33.44/www.*
*menagerie-de-verre.org). M° Parmentier.* **Open**
*Box office* 1-7pm Mon-Fri. Closed July, Aug.
**Admission** €13; €10 concessions. **No credit**
**cards. Map** p403 N5.
This multidisciplinary hothouse is rooted in the
avant-garde, with contemporary dance and classes
given by rotating guest teachers. It also hosts bi-
annual festival Les Inaccoutumés.

### Point Ephémère
*200 quai de Valmy, 10th (01.40.34.02.48/www.*
*pointephemere.org). M° Jaurès or Louis Blanc.*
**Open** noon-2am Mon-Sat; 1-9pm Sun. **Admission**
free. **Map** p402 M2.
This dynamic art centre showcases music, visual
arts and dance. Facilities include studios, exhibition
and performance spaces, a 300-seat auditorium, a
bar and a traditional French restaurant. A variety
of dance classes are available too. Admission to performances in the dance studio is free.

### Regard du Cygne
*210 rue de Belleville, 20th (01.43.58.55.93/redcygne.*
*free.fr). M° Télégraphe.* **Open** *Box office* 1hr before
show. Closed Aug. **Admission** €6-€15. **No credit**
**cards. Map** p403 Q3.
This pared-down studio in Belleville is a great place
to get a taste of the alternative contemporary dance
scene. Pieces are original and often experimental,
and its Spectacles Sauvages nights allow unknowns
to show a ten-minute piece to the public.

### Théâtre de la Bastille
*76 rue de la Roquette, 11th (01.43.57.42.14/*
*www.theatre-bastille.com). M° Bastille or Voltaire.*
**Open** *Box office* 10am-6pm Mon-Fri; 2-6pm Sat.
Closed July, Aug. **Admission** €13-€20. **Credit**
MC, V. **Map** p407 M6.
Small theatre showcasing innovative contemporary
dance and drama pieces. Highlights for 2008 include
Raimund Hogue's emotional tribute to Maria Callas,
*36, Avenue Georges Mandel*, in March.

### Théâtre de la Cité Internationale
*17 bd Jourdan, 14th (01.43.13.50.50/www.*
*theatredelacite.com). RER Cité Universitaire.* **Open**
*Box office* 2-7pm Mon-Fri. *Telephone bookings* 2-7pm
Mon-Sat. Closed July, Aug. **Admission** €21; €7.50-
€12.50 concessions; €14 for all Mon. **Credit** MC, V.

A well-established contemporary dance venue at the
Cité Universitaire, hosting shows, workshops and
other festive events.

# Dance classes & events

### Canal Central
*12 rue Lucien Sampaix, 10th (01.78.01.07.30/*
*www.canalcentral.fr). M° Gare de l'Est, Jacques*
*Bonsergent or République.* **Open** 9.30am-8pm
Mon-Fri. **Classes** €20. **Map** p402 L4.
The perfect place for a spot of relaxation and well-
being. Canal Central offers classes in Feldenkrais
and Alexander technique, as well as yoga, pilates
and other disciplines, all in an airy studio. The
'sounder sleep système' courses help to improve
physical and mental relaxation.

### Centre de Danse du Marais
*41 rue du Temple, 4th (01.42.72.15.42/08.92.*
*68.68.70/www.parisdanse.com). M° Hôtel de Ville or*
*Rambuteau.* **Open** 9am-9pm Mon-Fri; 9am-8pm Sat;
9am-7pm Sun. **Classes** €18. **Map** p402 K5.
There's a huge choice of classes here, with big-name
teachers such as belly dance star Leila Haddad and
ballet's Casati-Lazzarelli team. The five-class 'sam-
pler' pass is a good deal at €68.

### Centre Momboye
*25 rue Boyer, 20th (01.43.58.85.01/www.*
*momboye.com). M° Gambetta.* **Open** 9am-10.30pm
daily. **Classes** €14-€15. **Map** p403 P4.
This is the only centre devoted entirely to African
dance, taught to live drumming. There's hip hop too.

### Dance on the banks of the Seine
*Jardins Tino Rossi, 5th. M° Austerlitz.* **Open** *May-
Sept* from 7pm daily. **Classes** free. **Map** p406 L8.
In summer, the amphitheatres of this Seine-side park
fill up with salsa, rock, tango, Irish, hip hop and just
about any other dance form you can think of.
Informal classes are held around 7pm or 8pm, then
the *bal* begins.

### Studio Harmonic
*5 passage des Taillandiers, 11th (01.48.07.13.39/*
*www.studioharmonic.fr). M° Bastille.* **Open** *Office*
10am-5pm Mon-Fri. **Classes** 9.30am-10pm Mon-Fri;
9am-7.30pm Sat. Closed 3wks Aug. **Classes** €15.
**Map** p407 M7.
The rising star among Paris's dance schools,
Studio Harmonic's claim to fame is teacher Laure
Courtellemont and her trademark raggajam, a blend
of hip hop and Afro-Caribbean dance.

### White Cloud
*16 passage de la Main d'Or, 11th (01 47 00 02 13/*
*www.whitecloudparis.com). M° Bastille or Ledru*
*Rollin.* **Open** 9am-8pm Mon-Fri; 9am-6pm Sat.
**Classes** €55. **Map** p407 N7.
This relaxed and friendly centre invites you to
stretch and strengthen with the help of the Gyrotonic
Expansion System, which draws from swimming,
dance and yoga.

# Film

Cinephiles will never feel short-changed in the city of silver screens.

Accattone. See p296.

Accattone. See p296.

Cinema-going is a serious pastime in Paris. More tickets per capita are bought here than anywhere else in Europe and, in any given week, there's a choice of around 350 movies – not counting festivals. Although the city's cinematic landscape is constantly evolving, the overall picture remains healthy. Last year, a hard-fought battle between the city's three multiplex groups ultimately worked out in favour of the cinema-goer. After **MK2** lost its Beaugrenelle multiplex lease to the **Europalace** group, it struck back by severing its season ticket partnership with Europalace, and forming an alliance with the city's other major multiplex player, **UGC** – meaning the fused Illimité pass now gives access to over 230 MK2 and UGC screens around Paris. Europalace's response was to offer its own pass holders' reductions for friends and family. Meanwhile, MK2 confirmed its ambition by announcing the construction of a 14-screen complex in the 19th arrondissement, due to open in 2012.

The rise of the multiplex doesn't mean a reduction in the choice and variety of films on offer – far from it. In Paris, multiplexes regularly show films from Eastern Europe, Asia and South America, while countless independent cinemas continue to screen a hugely eclectic assortment of cult, classic and just plain obscure films. As well as retrospectives and cut-price promotions, there are often visits from a major director or star.

The city's enduring passion for cinema is reciprocated by the film industry, with some 730 short and feature films shot here in 2006, including Hollywood blockbusters such as *The Bourne Ultimatum*. Maverick director Luc Besson recently announced the founding of a Cité Européenne du Cinéma in the northern suburb of St-Denis. The complex, which will house nine studios, will give the national film industry a massive boost when it's completed in a couple of years' time.

Local interest is large enough to sustain a small avalanche of monthly movie magazines and there's an entire book fair, the **Salon du Livre, des Revues et du DVD de Cinéma**, devoted to writing on film. Launched in 2007, the **Salon du Cinéma** gives film buffs a chance to visit mocked-up movie sets and meet world-renowned directors and actors. Meanwhile, French DVD labels produce some of the most expertly curated discs in the world. Take a look at the extensive film sections of **Fnac** or **Virgin Megastore** (for both, *see*

*p272*) and you're more than likely to find American and British titles otherwise unavailable in the US or UK.

### INFORMATION AND TICKETS
New releases hit the screens on Wednesdays. Hollywood is well represented, of course, but Paris audiences have a balanced cinematic diet that satisfies their appetite for international films as well as shorts and documentaries. On top of this there are the 150-plus annual releases funded or part-funded with French money (the French film industry is still the world's third largest, after the US and India).

For venues, times and prices, consult one of the city's two main weekly listings magazines: *L'Officiel des Spectacles* and *Pariscope*. *Films nouveaux* are new releases, *Exclusivités* are the also-showing titles, and *Reprises* means rep. For non-francophone flicks, look out for two letters somewhere near the title: VO (*version originale*) means a screening in the original language with French subtitles; VF (*version française*) means that it has been dubbed into French.

Buy tickets in the usual way at the cinema – for new blockbusters, especially at multiplexes, it pays to buy tickets at least one screening in advance. You can also phone **AlloCiné** (08.92.89.28.92, www.allocine.fr). Online booking may entail a booking fee. Seats are often discounted by 20 to 30 per cent at Monday or Wednesday screenings, and the Mairie sponsors cut-price promotions at cinemas throughout the year.

All multiplex chains offer *cartes illimitées,* season tickets that allow unlimited access.

## Cinemas

### Giant screens & multiplexes

### La Géode
*26 av Corentin-Cariou, 19th (08.92.68.45.40/www. lageode.fr). Mº Porte de la Villette.* **Admission** €9; €7 under-25s. **Credit** MC, V. **Map** p403 inset.
The IMAX cinema at the Cité des Sciences occupies a shiny geodesic sphere. The 1,000sq m (10,800sq ft) hemispheric screen lets you experience 3D plunges through natural scenery, and animated adventures where figures zoom out to grab you.

### Le Grand Rex
*1 bd Poissonnière, 2nd (08.92.68.05.96/www. legrandrex.com). Mº Bonne Nouvelle.* **Admission** €7-€8.50; €5.50-€6.90 students, over-60s, under-12s. *Les Etoiles du Rex tour* €9.50; €8 under-12s. **Credit** MC, V. **Map** p402 J4.
With its wedding-cake exterior, fairy-tale interior and the largest auditorium in Europe (2,750 seats), this is one of the few cinemas to upstage whatever it screens: no wonder it's a listed historic monument.

Its blockbuster programming (usually in French) is suited to its vast, roll-down screen; it also hosts concerts and rowdy all-night compilation events. There are six smaller screens too. The Etoiles du Rex tour is a 50-minute, SFX-laden taste of movie magic.

### Max Linder Panorama
*24 bd Poissonnière, 9th (08.92.68.00.31/ www.maxlinder.com). Mº Grands Boulevards.* **Admission** €8.50; €6.50 Mon, Wed, Fri, students (except weekends), under-12s. **Credit** MC, V. **Map** p402 J4.
This state-of-the-art cinema, with THX surround sound and an 18m (60ft) screen, is named after the dapper French silent comedian who owned it between 1914 and 1925. The walls and 700 seats are all black to prevent even the tiniest twinkle of reflected light distracting the audience from what's happening on the screen. Look for all-nighters and one-off showings of rare vintage films or piano-accompanied silents.

### MK2 Bibliothèque
*128-162 av de France, 13th (08.92.69.84.84/ www.mk2.com). Mº Bibliothèque François Mitterrand or Quai de la Gare.* **Admission** €9.80; €6.80 students and over-60s (except weekends); €5.90 under-18s; €19.80 monthly pass. **Credit** MC, V. **Map** p407 M10.
The MK2 chain's flagship offers an all-in-one night out: 14 screens, three restaurants, a bar open until 5am at weekends and two-person 'love seats'. A paragon of imaginative programming, MK2 is growing all the time; it has added ten more venues in town, including two along the Bassin de la Villette with waterside cafés. For details of the Illimité season ticket, *see below* UGC Ciné Cité Bercy.

### UGC Ciné Cité Bercy
*2 cour St-Emilion, 12th (08.92.70.00.00/www.ugc. fr). Mº Cour St-Emilion.* **Admission** €9.90; €6.50 students, over-60s (except Sat and Sun before 7pm); €5.90 under-18s; €19.80 monthly pass. **Credit** MC, V. **Map** p407 P10.
This ambitious 18-screen development screens art movies and mainstream fodder, and hosts regular meet-the-director events. The 19-screen UGC Ciné Cité Les Halles (7 pl de la Rotonde, Nouveau Forum des Halles, 1st, 08.92.70.00.00) serves the same mix. For €19.80 a month, the UGC/MK2 Illimité card offers film buffs unlimited screenings at any UGC or MK2 venue, as well as some independents. Also now available, at €35 a month, is the Illimité 2 card, which is valid for two people.

## Showcases

### Auditorium du Louvre
*Musée du Louvre, 99 rue de Rivoli, 1st (01.40.20.55.55/www.louvre.fr). Mº Palais Royal Musée du Louvre.* **Admission** €9; €4 under-26s; free under-18s. **Credit** MC, V. **Map** p402 H5.

# A sanctuary for cinephiles

On the edge of the leafy Parc de Bercy in the 12th arrondissement, a stylish, curvaceous Frank Gehry building houses France's national film institute, the **Cinémathèque Française** (*see p296*). While the daring of Gehry's architecture affirms the modernist ambitions of today's Cinémathèque, it shouldn't obscure the institute's pivotal role in shaping the cinematic landscape of France.

Founded in 1936, the Cinémathèque quickly assumed a place at the heart of French film culture. Not only did it conserve and restore films, it also allowed new generations to discover little-screened or classic works. A 60-seat cinema inaugurated in 1948 near the Champs-Elysées would be the meeting place of budding film buffs François Truffaut, Jean-Luc Godard, Jacques

Rivette and Eric Rohmer. As directors, this group went on to form the *nouvelle vague*, a cinematic avant-garde that redefined the language of film in the '50s and '60s.

Under the visionary directorship of Henri Langlois, the Cinémathèque went from strength to strength, opening a Musée du Cinéma and relocating to the prestigious Palais de Chaillot at Trocadéro. Langlois himself was at the heart of one of the more colourful episodes in the institution's history when, in 1968, he was sacked due to budget cuts. The backlash was immediate and the country's top directors published a letter of protest in *Le Monde*, while the cinema-going public organised daily protests outside the Cinémathèque's headquarters. In the face of such pressure, the Ministry of Culture had no option but to reinstate Langlois, whose work was later recognised with a lifetime achievement Oscar in 1974.

Today, the Cinémathèque continues to uphold Langlois' vision, organising a programme of rarities, oddities and classics on its four screens. Recent seasons have included a Michael Caine retrospective and a '30s/'40s Shanghai cinema cycle. Thanks to its work as a literary publisher, the Cinémathèque was also a driving force in the elevation of film studies to academic respectability. It continues to perform a pedagogical role today, publishing books and DVDs.

The site at Bercy is also home to the Musée du Cinéma, which displays highlights from the Cinémathèque's extensive collection of film equipment, costumes and photographs. Exhibits include the robot from Fritz Lang's *Metropolis* and Vivien Leigh's dress from *Gone with the Wind*. Bercy also boasts the country's best-endowed *médiathèque*, where students, researchers and cinephiles can consult films, videos and other movie-related documents. Heaven, indeed, for film buffs.

This 420-seat auditorium was designed by IM Pei, as part of the Mitterand-inspired renovation of the Louvre (*see p86* **Who built the Louvre?**). Film screenings are often related to the exhibitions; silent movies with live music are regulars.

### Centre Pompidou
*Rue St-Martin, 4th (01.44.78.12.33/www. centrepompidou.fr). M° Hôtel de Ville or Rambuteau.* **Admission** €5.50; €3.50 students. **Credit** MC, V. **Map** p406 K6.

The varied programme here features themed series, experimental and artists' films, and a weekly documentary session. This is also the venue for the Cinéma du Réel festival; held in March, it champions documentary films (www.cinereel.com).

### Le Cinéma des Cinéastes
*7 av de Clichy, 17th (01.53.42.40.20). M° Place de Clichy.* **Admission** €8.50; €6.80 students, under-12s, over-60s. **Credit** MC, V. **Map** p401 G2.

Done out to evoke the studios of old, this three-screen showcase of world cinema holds meet-the-director sessions and festivals of classic, foreign, gay and documentary films. Also offers a monthly pass.

## La Cinémathèque Française

*51 rue de Bercy, 12th (01.71.19.33.33/www. cinematheque.fr). M° Bercy.* **Admission** *Permanent exhibitions* €2.50-€3. *Temporary exhibitions* €7-€9; €6 under-12s. *Films* €6; €5 students, 13s-18s; €3 under-12s; free for members. *Membership* €10/month. **Credit** MC, V. **Map** p407 N9.

Relocated to Frank Gehry's striking, spacious cubist building, the Cinémathèque Française now boasts four screens, a bookshop, a restaurant, a temporary exhibition space and the Musée du Cinéma, where it displays a fraction of its prolific collection of movie memorabilia. In the spirit of its founder Henri Langlois, the Cinémathèque hosts major retrospectives, cult movies, classics, experimental cinema and Q&A sessions with directors. *See also p295* **A sanctuary for cinephiles**.

## Forum des Images

*2 Grande Galerie, Porte St-Eustache, Forum des Halles, 1st (01.44.76.63.00/www.forumdesimages. net). M° Les Halles.* **Open** 1-9pm Tue-Sun. Closed 2wks Aug. **Admission** (per day) €5.50; €4.50 students, under-26s. Membership available. **Credit** AmEx, MC, V. **Map** p402 J5.

Following a major facelift, the hyperactive Forum des Images is due to reopen towards the end of 2008. The new, open layout will make it easier to move between spaces: a film archive dedicated to Paris on celluloid, a photo library and four auditoriums

screening a thought-provoking, entertaining programme of films grouped around such themes as 'Gangsters' or 'Death'. A new addition is the François Truffaut library, where users will be able to consult books and DVDs. The Forum hosts Les Rencontres, the trash treats of L'Etrange Festival, films from the critics' favourites at Cannes, and Pocket Films, a festival of films shot entirely on mobile phones.

# Arthouses

## Accattone

*20 rue Cujas, 5th (01.46.33.86.86). M° Cluny La Sorbonne/RER Luxembourg.* **Admission** €7; €6 Wed, students, under-20s (except Fri nights and weekends). **No credit cards. Map** p408 J8.

Named after Pasolini's first film, this tiny Latin Quarter cinema has a clear preference for old Italian arthouse. That said, there's still plenty of room on the rolling weekly programme of around 30 films for the likes of Buñuel, Oshima, Roeg and Ken Russell. In the 1960s the cinema was managed by none other than François Truffaut.

## Action

**Action Christine** *4 rue Christine, 6th (01.43. 29.11.30/www.actioncinemas.com). M° Odéon or St-Michel.* **Admission** €7.50; €6 students, under-20s. **No credit cards. Map** p408 J7.

**Action Ecoles** *23 rue des Ecoles, 5th (01.43.29.79.89). M° Maubert Mutualité.* **Admission** €7.50; €6 students, under-20s. **No credit cards. Map** p408 J8.

Seven decades of arthouse action at **Le Champo**. *See p297.*

**Grand Action** *5 rue des Ecoles, 5th (01.43.
54.47.62/www.legrandaction.com). M° Cardinal
Lemoine.* **Admission** €8; €6.50 students, under-20s.
**No credit cards. Map** p406 K8.
A Left Bank stalwart, the Action group is renowned
for screening new prints of old movies. It's heaven
for anyone who's nostalgic for Tinseltown classics
and quality US independents.

## Le Balzac
*1 rue Balzac, 8th (01.45.61.10.60/www.cinema
balzac.com). M° George V.* **Admission** €9; €7 Mon,
Wed, students, under-18s, over-60s; €5 under-12s.
**No credit cards. Map** p400 D4.
Built in 1935 and boasting a mock ocean-liner foyer,
Le Balzac scores highly for design and programming. Jean-Jacques Schpoliansky, the ever-genial
manager, is often found welcoming punters in person at the start of each screening. The Balzac
recently acquired a digital projector, and awards
prizes according to audience votes. It now accepts
the UGC/MK2 Illimité card.

## Le Champo
*51 rue des Ecoles, 5th (01.43.54.51.60/
www.lechampo.com). M° Cluny La Sorbonne or
Odéon.* **Admission** €7.50; €6 Wed, last screening
Sun, lunchtime matinées, students, under-20s. **No
credit cards. Map** p408 J7.
The two-screen Champo has been in operation for
nearly seven decades, a venerable past recognised
in 2000 when it was given historic monument status. In the 1960s it was a favourite haunt of *nouvelle
vague* directors such as Claude Chabrol.

## Le Cinéma du Panthéon
*13 rue Victor-Cousin, 5th (01.40.46.01.21/
www.cinemapantheon.com). RER Luxembourg.*
**Admission** €7; €5.50 Mon, Wed, students, 13-18s;
€4 under-13s. **Credit** MC, V. **Map** p408 J8.
To celebrate its centenary in 2007, the city's oldest
surviving movie house opened a tea room with interior design by Catherine Deneuve. It continues to
screen new, often obscure international films and
hosts meet-the-director nights and discussions.

## Le Denfert
*24 pl Denfert-Rochereau, 14th (01.43.21.41.01/
www.allocine.fr). M° Denfert Rochereau/RER
Denfert Rochereau.* **Admission** €6.50; €5 Mon,
Wed, students, over-60s; €4.60 under-15s. **No credit
cards. Map** p405 H10.
This charming little cinema offers a nicely eclectic
repertory selection that ranges from François Ozon
and Hayao Miyazaki to shorts and animation, as
well as new-release foreign films.

## L'Entrepôt
*7-9 rue Francis-de-Pressensé, 14th (01.45.40.07.50/
www.lentrepot.fr). M° Pernety or Plaisance.*
**Admission** €7; €5.60 students, over-60s; €4
under-12s. **No credit cards. Map** p405 F10.
A diverse array of documentaries, shorts, gay
cinema and productions from developing nations are
more common here than mainstream stuff.

## Images d'Ailleurs
*21 rue de la Clef, 5th (01.45.87.18.09). M° Censier
Daubenton.* **Admission** €6; €5.50 concessions;
€4.70 under-12s, for all Mon. **No credit cards.
Map** 406 K9.
Opened in 1990, this cinema focuses on films from
Africa and other rare movie treats.

## Le Latina
*20 rue du Temple, 4th (01.42.78.47.86/www.
lelatina.com). M° Hôtel de Ville.* **Admission** €7.50;
€6 Mon, Tue, students, under-20s. **No credit cards.
Map** p406 K6.
The programming at this flag-bearer for Latin cultures runs from Argentinian to Romanian films.
Latin dance features at the €17 film-dinner-dancing
deals on Monday and Wednesday evenings.

## Le Mac Mahon
*5 av Mac-Mahon, 17th (01.43.80.24.81/www.
cinemamacmahon.com). M° Charles de Gaulle Etoile.*
**Admission** €6.50; €4.50 students. **No credit
cards. Map** p400 C3.
This single-screen, 1930s-era cinema has changed
little since its 1960s heyday (tickets are still, delightfully, of the tear-off variety), when its all-American
programming fostered the label '*mac-mahonisme*'
among the buffs who haunted the place. Americana
still makes up the bulk of what's on the screen.

## La Pagode
*57bis rue de Babylone, 7th (01.45.55.48.48).
M° St-François-Xavier.* **Admission** €8; €6.50
Mon, Wed, students, under-21s. **No credit cards.
Map** p405 F7.
This glorious edifice is not, as local legend might
have it, a block-by-block import, but a 19th-century
replica of a pagoda by a French architect. Renovated
in the late 1990s, this is one of the loveliest cinemas
in the world.

## Studio 28
*10 rue Tholozé, 18th (01.46.06.36.07/www.
cinemastudio28.com). M° Abbesses or Blanche.*
**Admission** €7.50; €6.30 students, under-18s.
**No credit cards. Map** p401 H1.
The venue for the first screening of Buñuel's scandalous *L'Age d'Or*, this historic cinema also features
in the more heartwarming *Amélie*. It offers a decent
repertory mixture of classics and recent movies,
complete with Dolby sound and a civilised bar for a
pre- or post-screening tipple.

## Studio Galande
*42 rue Galande, 5th (01.43.54.72.71). M° Cluny La
Sorbonne or St-Michel.* **Admission** €7.80; €6. Wed,
students. **No credit cards. Map** p408 J7.
Some 20 different films are screened in subtitled versions at this venerable Latin Quarter venue every
week: international arthouse fare, combined with the
occasional instalment from the *Matrix* series. On
Fridays and Saturdays, fans of *The Rocky Horror
Picture Show* turn up in drag, equipped with rice and
water pistols.

**Arts & Entertainment**

## Festivals & special events

The city plays host to a range of film festivals, some of them free, some taking place outdoors. See also pp274-278 **Festivals & Events**.

### Salon du Cinéma

*Parc des expos, Porte de Versailles, 15th (www.salonducinema.com). Mº Porte de Versailles.* **Date** Jan.

This popular new event features behind-the-scenes reconstructions of movie sets, allowing the public to watch the work of make-up artists, cameramen and stuntmen. Visitors can also attend conferences and debates with international directors.

### Festival International de Films de Femmes

*Maison des Arts, pl Salvador-Allende, 94040 Créteil (01.49.80.38.98/www.filmsdefemmes.com). Mº Créteil – Préfecture.* **Date** Mar.

A selection of retrospectives and new international films by female directors. The festival celebrates its 30th birthday in 2008.

### Printemps du Cinéma

*Various venues (www.printempsducinema.com).* **Date** Mar.

Three days of bargain €3.50-entry films at cinemas all across Paris.

### Côté Court

*Ciné 104, 104 av Jean-Lolive, 93500 Pantin (01.48.46.95.08/www.cotecourt.org). Mº Eglise de Pantin.* **Date** Mar-Apr.

A great selection of new and old short films shown at Ciné 104 and a handful of neighbouring venues.

### Paris Cinéma

*Various venues (01.55.25.55.25/www. pariscinema.org).* **Date** July.

A programme of shorts and documentaries sponsored by the mairie.

### Cinéma au Clair de Lune

*Various venues (01.44.76.63.00/www.forum desimages.net).* **Date** Aug.

Night-time films on giant open-air screens in squares and public gardens around town: a party atmosphere is guaranteed.

### 3 Jours/3 Euros

*All cinemas throughout Paris (www.paris.fr/fr/ culture/missioncinema).* **Date** Aug.

This Mairie-sponsored promotion is timed to start getting kids into cinemas before the schools go back. For three days, every screening costs just €3.

### L'Etrange Festival

*Forum des Images (see p296/www.etrange festival.com).* **Date** Sept. **Map** p404 J5.

Explicit sex, gore and weirdness in the screenings and 'happenings' at this annual feast of all things unconventional draw large crowds.

### Salon du Livre, des Revues et du DVD de Cinéma

*Cinémathèque Française, 51 rue de Bercy, 12th (www.cinemathequefrançaise.com). Mº Bercy.* **Date** Oct. **Map** p407 N9.

European publishers of cinema-related books sell their wares; there are also round-table discussions and a chance to meet filmmakers. After a three-year hiatus, this (usually) annual event returns in 2008.

### Les Rencontres

*Forum des Images (see p296).* **Date** Nov, Dec. **Map** p404 J5.

A global choice of new independent features, documentaries and short films, usually screened in the presence of the director.

## Bookshops

Paris is well supplied with film bookshops. **Virgin Megastore** (*see p272*) also stocks a range of English-language movie books.

### Cinédoc

*45-53 passage Jouffroy, 9th (01.48.24.71.36/ www.cine-doc.fr). Mº Grands Boulevards.* **Open** 10am-7pm Mon-Sat. **Credit** V. **Map** p402 J4.

Finding what you're looking for isn't easy in this narrow, tobacco-scented bookshop. Ask the staff or take pot luck among the old photos, film magazines and books about special effects in *Star Wars*.

### Ciné Reflet

*14 rue Monsieur le Prince, 6th (01.40.46.02.72). Mº Odéon.* **Open** 1-8pm Mon-Sat; 3-7pm Sun. **Credit** MC, V. **Map** p408 H7.

This sprawling shop is well stocked with old photos, posters, and new and second-hand books. The strong English-language selection includes the *Time Out Film Guide* and magazines like *Sight & Sound*. Current and back issues of *Les Cahiers du Cinéma* and *Première* fill shelf after shelf.

### Contacts

*24 rue du Colisée, 8th (01.43.59.17.71/www. medialibrairie.com). Mº Franklin D Roosevelt or St-Philippe-du-Roule.* **Open** 10am-7pm Mon-Fri; 2-7pm Sat. **Credit** MC, V. **Map** p401 E4.

Truffaut's favourite *librairie* has been selling books on film for over 40 years. The stock is well organised, with a large and up-to-date selection of English-language titles. You'll also find *Film Comment* and *American Cinematographer*, plus a few videos.

### Scaramouche

*161 rue St-Martin, 3rd (01.48.87.78.58). Mº Rambuteau.* **Open** 11.30am-1pm, 2-8pm Mon-Sat. **Credit** MC, V. **Map** p402 K5.

This large-ish shop covers cinema and *gestuelle* (mime and puppetry). The film section includes a wide range of titles in English, plus a huge collection of publicity photos and portraits filed by film, actor or director. Wim Wenders and Alain Renais have been known to pop in.

# Galleries

The Marais continues to rule the roost.

Commercial art galleries in Paris provide an impressively international coverage, but the sheer profusion can be bewildering. To make your way through the rich offerings, pick up the **Galeries Mode d'Emploi** leaflet (also available online at www.fondation-entreprise-ricard.com) or check out **www.paris-art.com** to find out what shows are on and hit the galleries at *vernissage* time, usually Saturday evenings, when the city's artists, collectors, critics and curators do the rounds of what's opening. The art hub is in the Marais, where essential stops include **Galerie Emmanuel Perrotin** for immaculate presentations on a SoHo scale, **Yvon Lambert** for international names, **Chantal Crousel** for cutting-edge installations and video art, and **Chez Valentin** for challenging conceptual projects.

Interesting new galleries continue to open, nosing out old workshops and industrial spaces, hidden gardens and courtyards among the historic mansions, drawing fashion and style followers in their wake. Across the river, **Kamel Mennour** heads a revitalised St-Germain-des-Prés scene, amid more traditional modern art and design galleries, while the rue Louise-Weiss enclave has rather run out of steam but continues to show an eclectic range of often experimental work.

The **Navette de l'Art** ('art bus'; 01.47.00. 90.85, www.art-process.com) gives an insider's tour of selected new galleries, private collections and alternative spaces once a month. The outfit behind it also holds 'Dining with…' art dinners at **Point Ephémère** (*see p330*), as well as organising tailor-made tours.

Note that most galleries close on Sundays, Mondays, from mid July to the end of August, and at Christmas. Admission is free.

## ART FAIRS IN MUTATION

Being in the right place at the right time is an essential part of the international art circuit, and Paris has its place in the art calendar as collectors arrive in town to be in on the art fair buzz and the associated parties, special events and exhibition openings. While it fails to rival market leader Art Basel or the trendiness of Art Miami or London's Frieze, long-standing art fair **FIAC** (www.fiacparis.com) is looking happier now it's left the anonymity of Paris-Expo to return to central Paris, with exhibitors split between the Grand Palais and the Cour Carrée

The spirit of St-Germain still flickers at **Galerie Lara Vincy**. *See p304.*

Arts & Entertainment

of the Louvre. Covering both historic 20th-century modern art and the latest contemporary trends, it remains a good way to keep track of the local scene. During the same dates, spin-off **Show Off** (www.showoffparis.com) at Espace Pierre Cardin features around 35 young galleries from across Europe, plus a performance programme and even children's workshops, while **Slick** (www.slick-paris.com) goes for a grungier style at La Bellevilloise but has so far disappointed on quality.

Another fair that has made its international mark is **Paris Photo** (www.parisphoto.fr) in the Carrousel du Louvre in mid-November, gathering a worldwide selection of top-name galleries and spanning the medium from 19th-century pioneers to contemporary art photography. Newcomer **DiVA** (www.divafair.com) also takes place in November, and is devoted to video art and digital media.

A second batch of art fairs hits Paris in springtime. Held in a marquee in the Tuileries, the **Salon des Arts et Design** has undergone a mutation from antiques fair to focus on sought-after 20th-century design. A week later, **Art Paris** in the Grand Palais is geared to a more domestic market than FIAC. But the most interesting arrival in 2007 was the **Salon de Dessin Contemporain**, where 35 galleries were each given a room in a 19th-century *hôtel particulier* – a niche rendezvous for the sort of drawings loved by aficionados but rarely given space at the big art fairs or gallery shows.

## Beaubourg & the Marais

### La B.A.N.K.

*42 rue Volta, 3rd (01.42.72.06.90/www.bankgalerie.com). Mº Arts et Métiers.* **Open** 11am-7pm Mon-Sat. **Map** p402 K4.

# Arty undertaking

Rising from the dead in north-east Paris, the conversion of the old Pompes Funèbres on the rue d'Aubervilliers is an ambitious project to bring contemporary creativity to the former home of the municipal undertakers. Where once this 19th-century colossus housed barns, workshops, horses and hearses, shops for mourning wear and storage for 6,000 coffins, from summer 2008 **104** will become a home for artists, photographers, choreographers, musicians, filmmakers and writers 'sharing the creative process with the widest possible public'.

Municipal initiatives to bring art to the people are all too often well-meaning but patronising (a hip hop concert here, an urban dance festival there), but joint directors Robert Cantarella and Frédéric Fisbach insist that there will be no dumbing down or compromise at 104. The only requirement will be that the artists in residence regularly present their work in progress to the public. 'We will not adapt the works to the *quartier*. In opening the doors of the studio, an artist can do a difficult work yet still be a bridge to creation,' says Cantarella.

And opening up to the neighbourhood – in one of the poorest parts of Paris, dominated by massive housing estates – means just that. The broad, glass-roofed central nave will function like a public street running right through the complex; in addition to a café, where locals and visitors can mingle with resident artists and performers, amenities will include a newsagent, sports shop, grocer and interior garden.

Something else that will distinguish it from other art venues in the capital is that it is intended principally as 'a place of production and not a place of distribution'. Although there are two auditoria, the raison d'être of 104 is the making of art on site. Each year, 35 artists in residence from all over the world will be selected on the basis of proposals for specific projects, for which 104 will provide not only the workspace, but also the technical wherewithal, as well as production and administrative services. Indeed the final artwork or performance may well only be seen for a couple of performances here before, the directors hope, it goes on tour elsewhere.

In the run-up to the opening in September 2008, staff have moved into an old butcher's shop next door at 11bis rue Curial. There are public site visits on the first Friday of the month (reservation essential) and a pre-programme of projects by artists, including Stéphane Couturier, Maï Lucas, writer Olivia Rosenthal, and Alain Bernardini, whose photos of the building workers have been pasted on the site hoardings.

### 104

*104 rue d'Aubervilliers, 19th (01.40.05.51.71/www.104.fr/pre-opening website www.11bis.fr). Mº Riquet.*

Adventurous young gallery B.A.N.K. is making a name for itself with shows by young artists such as Mounir Fatmi and Zoulikha Bouabdellah, often with a political/socially committed edge.

## g module

*15 rue Debelleyme, 3rd (01.42.71.14.75/www. g-module.com). Mº Filles du Calvaire or St-Sébastien Froissart.* **Open** 2-7pm Tue-Sat. **Map** p409 L5.

American Jeff Gleich left SoHo for the Marais in 2000, on a mission to introduce Paris art lovers to American artists not previously seen in Europe. Artists such as fellow New Yorkers Gordon Terry and Peggy Preheim exemplify his dual tastes for psychedelia and intricate draughtsmanship.

## Galerie Alain Gutharc

*7 rue St-Claude, 3rd (01.47.00.32.10/www.alain gutharc.com). Mº St-Sébastien Froissart.* **Open** 2-7pm Tue-Sat; 11am-1pm, 2-7pm Sat. **Map** p409 L6.

The last of the Bastille galleries has now moved to the Marais, opening with an atmospheric installation by Emmanuel Lagarrigue. Gutharc talent-spots young French artists, mostly working in installation or photography.

## Galerie Almine Rech

*19 rue de Saintonge, 3rd (01.45.83.71.90/www. galeriealminerech.com). Mº Filles du Calvaire.* **Open** 11am-7pm Tue-Sat. **Map** p409 L5.

Continuing the Louise Weiss exodus, Almine Rech has returned to the Marais. Spread over two floors, her new gallery has more of an apartment feel in which to show off big international names. As well as regulars James Turrell and Ugo Rondinone, look out for powerful films by French artist Ange Leccia.

## Galerie Anne de Villepoix

*43 rue de Montmorency, 3rd (01.42.78.32.24/www. annedevillepoix.com). Mº Rambuteau.* **Open** 10am-7pm Mon-Sat. **Map** p402 K5.

Along with pieces by international names such as Chris Burden and Erwin Wurm, the gallery features distinctive and varied talents on the French scene, such as the bravura monochrome paintings of Ming and the witty conceptual work of Franck Scurti.

## Galerie Chantal Crousel

*10 rue Charlot, 3rd (01.42.77.38.87/www.crousel. com). Mº Filles du Calvaire.* **Open** 11am-1pm, 2-7pm Tue-Sat. **Map** p409 L5.

Crousel celebrated the 25th anniversary of her gallery in 2005 with a move to a new space in rue Charlot's burgeoning design and fashion scene. She was the first in France to show work by Mona Hatoum and Tony Cragg. Hot younger talents include Rikrit Tiravanija and Thomas Hirschhorn, as well as Anri Sala and Melik Ohanian, two of France's most exciting video artists.

## Galerie Chez Valentin

*9 rue St-Gilles, 3rd (01.48.87.42.55/www.galerie chezvalentin.com). Mº Chemin Vert.* **Open** 2-7pm Tue-Fri; 11am-7pm Sat. **Map** p409 L6.

A gallery at the experimental cutting edge. Shows here tend to be radically conceptual but often fun: look for pseudo-documentaries by video-maker Laurent Grasso, photos by Nicolas Moulin, installations by Pierre Ardouin and projects by 2003 Prix Duchamp winner Mathieu Mercier.

## Galerie Daniel Templon

*30 rue Beaubourg, 3rd (01.42.72.14.10/www.daniel templon.com). Mº Rambuteau.* **Open** 10am-7pm Mon-Sat. **Map** p402 K5.

A Paris institution since the '60s and conveniently located opposite the Centre Pompidou, Galerie T is a favourite with the French art establishment. It mainly shows paintings – in other words, items private collectors might want to put on their walls. Jean-Michel Alberola, Gérard Garouste, Philippe Cognée and Vincent Corpet all feature on the list, along with the American David Salle and Jonathan Meese, currently at the forefront of new German expressionism.

## Galerie Dominique Fiat

*16 rue des Coutures-St-Gervais, 3rd (01.40.29.98.80/ www.galeriefiat.com). Mº St-Sébastien Froissart.* **Open** 11am-7pm Tue-Sat. **Map** p409 L6.

Fiat is part of the dynamic new generation of galleries. Shows have included the word games and art world parodies of novelist and artist Thomas Lélu (who renamed the gallery Galerie Dominique Fiat Panda for the occasion) and crossover shows by designers Christian Biecher and Robert Stadler.

## Galerie Emmanuel Perrotin

*76 rue de Turenne, 3rd (01.42.16.79.79/www. galerieperrotin.com). Mº St-Sébastien Froissart.* **Open** 11am-7pm Tue-Sat. **Map** p409 L5.

Perrotin is one of the sharpest figures around town: not content with owning a gallery in Miami and a glossy magazine, he added a spacious new annexe in 2007 around the corner from his elegant Paris HQ. As well as the quirky Japanese set of Takashi Murakami, Mariko Mori et al, and big French names like Sophie Calle, Xavier Veilhan and Bernard Frize, he also features the radical Austrian collective Gelatin, and young talents like Jim Myerson, Kolkoz and Leandro Erlich.

## Galerie Jean Brolly

*16 rue de Montmorency, 3rd (01.42.78.88.02/www. jeanbrolly.com). Mº Rambuteau.* **Open** 11am-7pm Tue-Sat. **Map** p409 K5.

Jean Brolly was a collector long before leaving industry to open his own gallery in 2002. The focus here is on painters, including Adam Adach, Daniel Schlier, Tatjana Doll and Frédéric Bruly-Bouabré.

## Galerie Karsten Greve

*5 rue Debelleyme, 3rd (01.42.77.19.37/www.galerie-karsten-greve.com). Mº St-Sébastien Froissart.* **Open** 11am-7pm Tue-Sat. **Map** p409 L5.

The Cologne gallery's smart Paris outpost is the venue for retrospective displays of top-ranking artists: think big names rather than any serious risk

taking. Jannis Kounellis, Louise Bourgeois, Pierre Soulages, John Chamberlain and Dubuffet have all featured here.

## Galerie Laurent Godin

*5 rue du Grenier-St-Lazare, 3rd (01.42.71.10.66/ www.laurentgodin.com). M° Rambuteau.* **Open** 11am-7pm Tue-Sat. **Map** p402 K5.

After running a public space in Lyon, Laurent Godin has quickly made a name with his Paris gallery, which features a cross-generational mix from New York neo-Pop artist Haim Steinbach and waste-paper expert Wang Du to promising installations by young French artist Vincent Olinet.

## Galerie Magda Danysz

*78 rue Amelot, 11th (01.45.83.38.51/www.magda-gallery.com). M° Filles du Calvaire.* **Open** 11am-7pm Tue-Fri; 2-7pm Sat. **Map** p402 L5.

Magda Danysz has moved into a three-storey space on the fringes of the Marais near the Cirque d'Hiver, aiming to make contemporary art accessible. She has a taste for artists with graffiti- and cartoon-influenced styles.

## Galerie Maisonneuve

*22 rue de Poitou, 3rd (01.43.66.23.99/www.galerie-maisonneuve.com). M° Filles du Calvaire.* **Open** 11am-7pm Tue-Sat. **Map** p409 L5.

After starting in a flat in a Belleville tower block, Maisonneuve has now joined the burgeoning haut-Marais set, but continues to take an original approach to its displays: the initial output was devoted to an evolving project by Mathieu Briand.

Other artists represented include Jan Kopp, Alexandre Périgot and Caecilia Tripp.

## Galerie Marian Goodman

*79 rue du Temple, 3rd (01.48.04.70.52/www.marian goodman.com). M° Rambuteau.* **Open** 11am-7pm Tue-Sat. **Map** p409 K6.

This New York gallery owner has an impressive Paris presence in a beautiful 17th-century mansion. Artists include Chantal Akerman, Pierre Huyghe, Tacita Dean and Eija-Liisa Ahtila.

## Galerie des Multiples

*17 rue St-Gilles, 3rd (01.48.87.21.77/www.galerie desmultiples.com). M° Chemin Vert.* **Open** 2-7pm Tue-Sat. **Map** p409 L6.

Artist Mathieu Mercier was one of the founders of this gallery, where shows can take the form of any-thing from posters to soup ladles or rock music-inspired pieces by Saâdane Afif.

## Galerie Nathalie Obadia

*3 rue du Cloître-St-Merri, 4th (01.42.74.67.68/www. galerie-obadia.com). M° Rambuteau.* **Open** 11am-7pm Mon-Sat. **Map** p406 K6.

You'll find all media represented here (with a predilection for painting), including the likes of Mañuel Ocampo, Fiona Rae, Carole Benzaken and Jessica Stockholder.

## Galerie Nelson-Freeman

*59 rue Quincampoix, 4th (01.42.71.74.56/www. galerienelsonfreeman.com). M° Hôtel de Ville or Rambuteau.* **Open** 11am-1pm, 2-7pm Tue-Sat. **Map** p406 J6.

La Bellevilloise. *See p304.*

Now associated with the New York dealer Peter Freeman, Galerie Nelson-Freeman was the first venue in France to show Thomas Ruff and Rodney Graham. It also features rising French artists such as Stéphane Calais, and represents the late Fluxus maverick Robert Filliou.

## Galerie Polaris

*15 rue des Arquebusiers, 3rd (01.42.72.21.27/ www.galeriepolaris.com). M° St-Sébastien Froissart.* **Open** 1-7pm Tue-Fri; 11am-1pm, 2-7pm Sat. **Map** p409 L6.

Polaris has moved into new premises in an old gym converted by architect Odile Decq, who created the opening installation. Stéphane Couturier, known for his stunning flattened perspective building site images, heads a selection of artists mainly working in photo and video.

## Galerie Schleicher + Lange

*12 rue de Picardie, 3rd (01.42.77.02.77/www. schleicherlange.com). M° Filles du Calvaire.* **Open** 2-7pm Tue-Sat. **Map** p409 L5.

Shows put on by these two young Germans focus on artists yet to exhibit in Paris, alternating between upcoming London-based talents, such as Zoe Mendelson, and discoveries from eastern Europe. They also host Vidéo Surveillance, an occasional programme of video screenings.

## Galerie Thaddaeus Ropac

*7 rue Debelleyme, 3rd (01.42.72.99.00/www. ropac.net). M° Filles du Calvaire.* **Open** 10am-7pm Tue-Sat. **Map** p409 L5.

Ropac's main base is in Salzburg, but he also runs this attractive Paris gallery, featuring American Pop and neo-Pop by Warhol, Tom Sachs and Alex Katz, along with European artists such as Ilya Kabakov, Sylvie Fleury and Gilbert & George.

## Galerie Yvon Lambert

*108 rue Vieille-du-Temple, 3rd (01.42.71.09.33/ www.yvon-lambert.com). M° Filles du Calvaire.* **Open** 10am-1pm, 2.30-7pm Tue-Fri; 10am-7pm Sat. **Map** p409 L5.

Lambert celebrated 30 years in the business in 2006 and remains a powerhouse of the French scene, with plenty of big-name stuff, a New York offshoot and a personal collection given museum status in Avignon. The gallery has been restructured to include a dedicated video space. While the main gallery shows leading international names – American bigwigs Sol LeWitt, Nan Goldin and Jenny Holzer, plus next-generation Douglas Gordon, Jonathan Monk and France's Claude Levêque – the street-front art bookshop has a window showcase and basement gallery for younger artists.

## Galerie Zurcher

*56 rue Chapon, 3rd (01.42.72.82.20/www.galerie zurcher.com). M° Arts et Métiers.* **Open** noon-7pm Tue-Sat. **Map** p402 K5.

Amid the Chinese wholesalers north of Beaubourg, Zurcher shows emerging artists with a fresh take on painting and video: Marc Desgrandschamps, Camille Vivier and Elisa Sighicelli. Mathilde Rosier and Eléonore de Montesquiou are also featured.

# Champs-Elysées

## Galerie Jérôme de Noirmont

*38 av Matignon, 8th (01.42.89.89.00/www. denoirmont.com). M° Miromesnil.* **Open** 11am-7pm Mon-Sat. **Map** p401 E4.

Its location could arouse suspicions that de Noirmont sells purely business art. Not so. He puts on eye-catching shows of, among others, AR Penck, Jeff Koons, Shirin Neshat, Bettina Rheims and Fabrice Hyber, along with the glossily kitsch duo Pierre et Gilles, and art-world personalities Eva and Adèle.

## Galerie Lelong

*13 rue de Téhéran, 8th (01.45.63.13.19/www.galerie-lelong.com). M° Miromesnil.* **Open** 10.30am-6pm Tue-Fri; 2-6.30pm Sat. **Map** p401 E3.

If you hanker after Miró, Tapies, Bacon or Kounellis, then Lelong is a safe bet with its selection of bankable, post-war international names. The gallery also has plush branches in New York and Zurich.

# St-Germain-des-Prés

## Galerie Denise René

*196 bd St-Germain, 7th (01.42.22.77.57/ www.deniserene.com). M° Rue du Bac or St-Germain-des-Prés.* **Open** 10am-1pm, 2-7pm Tue-Sat. **Map** p406 G6.

Denise René has remained committed to kinetic art, Op art and geometrical abstraction by Soto et al, ever since Tinguely first presented his machines here in the 1950s.

**Other locations** 22 rue Charlot, 3rd (01.48.87.73.94).

## Galerie G-P et N Vallois

*36 rue de Seine, 6th (01.46.34.61.07/www.galerie-vallois.com). Mº Mabillon or Odéon.* **Open** 10.30am-1pm, 2-7pm Mon-Sat. **Map** p408 H7.

Interesting conceptual work in all media includes the likes of American provocateur Paul McCarthy, Turner Prize winner Keith Tyson and a clutch of French thirty- and fortysomethings, including Alain Bublex and Gilles Barbier, as well as veteran *affichiste* Jacques Villeglé.

## Galerie Kamel Mennour

*47 rue St-André-des-Arts, 6th (01.56.24.03.63/ www.galeriemennour.com). Mº Odéon or St-Michel.* **Open** 11am-7.30pm Tue-Sat. **Map** p408 H7.

After bursting on to the St-Germain scene with chic, often provocative shows by fashion photography crossovers David LaChapelle and Ellen von Unwerth and filmmaker Larry Clark, Mennour has been responsible for introducing talented emerging artists Kader Attia and Adel Abdessemed, who reflect France's multicultural society, and showing ever-energetic Daniel Buren. The gallery recently moved into larger premises.

## Galerie Lara Vincy

*47 rue de Seine, 6th (01.43.26.72.51/www.lara-vincy. com). Mº Mabillon, Odéon or St-Germain-des-Prés.* **Open** 2.30-7pm Mon; 11am-1pm, 2.30-7pm Tue-Sat. **Map** p408 H7.

Liliane Vincy, daughter of the founder, is one of the few characters to retain something of the old St-Germain spirit and a sense of 1970s Fluxus-style happenings. Interesting theme and solo shows include master of the epigram Ben, as well as text-, music- and performance-related pieces. *Photo p299.*

## Galerie Loevenbruck

*40 rue de Seine, 6th (01.53.10.85.68/www. loevenbruck.com). Mº Mabillon or Odéon.* **Open** 2-7pm Tue-Sat. **Map** p408 H6.

Funky Loevenbruck injected a dose of humour into St-Germain with a bunch of artists – Virginie Barré, Bruno Peinado and Olivier Blankaert, and Philippe Mayeux – who treat conceptual concerns with a light touch.

## in situ Fabienne Leclerc

*6 rue du Pont-de-Lodi, 6th (01.53.79.06.12/ www.insituparis.fr). Mº Odéon or St-Michel.* **Open** 11am-7pm Tue-Sat. **Map** p408 H6.

A recent arrival in St-Germain, Fabienne Leclerc consistently impresses with the quality of installations from a set of highly individual artists, including Mark Dion, known for his interest in zoology and scientific history, Indian star Subodh Gupta and video maestro Gary Hill.

## Air de Paris

*32 rue Louise-Weiss, 13th (01.44.23.02.77/www.air deparis.com). Mº Chevaleret.* **Open** 11am-7pm Tue-Sat. **Map** p407 M10.

This gallery shows experimental, neo-conceptual and chaotic material. A hip international stable of artists includes Liam Gillick, Carsten Höller and Philippe Parreno. Don't miss the 'Random Gallery' – displays in the shop window between Air de Paris and neighbour Praz-Delavallade.

## Art:Concept

*16 rue Duchefdelaville, 13th (01.53.60.90.30/ www.galerieartconcept.com). Mº Bibliothèque François Mitterrand or Chevaleret.* **Open** 11am-7pm Tue-Sat. **Map** p407 M10.

Despite the cramped conditions, Art:Concept presents some interesting, electic work: installations by artists Michel Blazy, Richard Fauguet and Martine Aballéa, the photoworks or happenings of Roman Signer and Vidya Gadalston's intricate drawings.

## Galerie Kréo

*22 rue Duchefdelaville, 13th (01.53.60.18.42/www. galeriekreo.com). Mº Chevaleret.* **Open** 10am-6pm Tue-Fri; 11am-7pm Sat. **Map** p407 M10.

Occupying the area between design as function and design as art, Kréo commissions limited-edition pieces by leading contemporary designers. Look out for Marc Newson, Jasper Conran, Ron Arad and native talent such as the Bouroullec brothers.

## gb agency

*20 rue Louise-Weiss, 13th (01.53.79.07.13/ www.gbagency.fr). Mº Chevaleret.* **Open** 11am-7pm Tue-Sat. **Map** p407 M10.

The gb agency brought young artists Loris Gréaud and Elina Brotherus to the fore. Shows group several artists together in an exploration of temporality and the exhibition concept itself.

## Jousse Entreprise

*24 & 34 rue Louise-Weiss, 13th (01.53.82.10.18/ www.jousse-entreprise.com). Mº Bibliothèque François Mitterrand or Chevaleret.* **Open** 11am-7pm Tue-Sat. **Map** p407 M10.

Philippe Jousse presents contemporary artists – such as Matthieu Laurette, Frank Perrin and challenging young video artist Clarisse Hahn – alongside 1950s avant-garde furniture by Jean Prouvé, lights by Serge Mouille and ceramics by Georges Jouve.

## La Bellevilloise

*21 rue Boyer, 20th (01.53.27.35.77/www. labellevilloise.com). Mº Gambetta.* **Open** hours vary. **Map** p403 P4.

The focus here is firmly on artistic innovation and experimentation, with exhibitions, concerts, debates, recording studios and a café. *Photos p302.*

# Gay & Lesbian

Bonjour, monsieur.

Paris is one of the most gay-friendly cities in Europe, if not the world. Gays and lesbians live in every part of the city and are visibly involved in every walk of life, but the centre of the gay and lesbian community is concentrated in Beaubourg and the 'Gay Marais'.

Have a cocktail or light lunch, collect your thoughts and flirt with the waiter at any of the cafés located near the intersection of rue des Archives and rue Ste-Croix de la Bretonnerie, located just a short walk from Hôtel de Ville and the Centre Pompidou. Then amble idly through the nearby streets to discover shops catering to every fetish, as well as funky fashion boutiques, and peruse the international gay and lesbian press or pick up free monthly magazines listing the hottest events at bookstores like **Les Mots à la Bouche**.

In the evening the cafés and restaurants are popular spots at which to start the merriment before moving on to bars and clubs, such as the red-hot **Raidd Bar** or the venerable **Bains-Douches** (*see p331*). Lesbians can find a few nice bars of their own on rue Roi de Sicile, but sadly the trailblazing club Pulp has closed its doors. **Queen** on the Champs-Elysées, though now a dowager, remains a clubbing institution, while **La Scène Bastille** (*see p330*) is a trend-setter, and the small but always fun **L'Insolite** still draws a great crowd.

Paris comes out on the last Sunday in June during the annual **Gay Pride March**, which always has a strong social and political focus. For the last few years, it has been led by the openly gay mayor, Bertrand Delanoë, who came out two years before running for office, then won by a large margin and is now one of France's most respected politicians. Although most Paris gays and lesbians say that they encounter very little, if any, discrimination in their day-to-day lives, and by and large feel integrated into mainstream society, the march is a powerful reminder of what the gay rights movements have accomplished over the last 30 years, and of what they have yet to achieve.

### INFORMATION AND RESOURCES

Both *Têtu* (www.tetu.com) and *Préf* magazines (www.preferencesmag.com) report on goings-on in gay life and have text in English; *La Dixième Muse* (www.ladixiememuse.com) provides similar information for lesbians. There are also several free bi-weekly publications, distributed in gay bookshops, bars and clubs; the most useful are *2 Weeks-Paris* (www.2xparis.fr), *Tribumove* (www.tribumove.com) and *AgendaQ*. For the girls, there is *Barbi(e)turix* (http://barbieturix.hautefort.com). Two excellent and informative websites provide regularly updated listings (in English) of all things gay and lesbian in the city: check out www.paris-gay.com or www.gayvox.com.

### Centre Gai et Lesbien

*3 rue Keller, 11th (01.43.57.21.47/www.cglparis.org). Mº Bastille or Ledru-Rollin.* **Open** *4-8pm Mon-Sat. Library 2-6pm Fri, Sat.* **Map** *p407 M7.*
In addition to providing information on topics ranging from the socio-political (if you don't know what rights gays and lesbians have or don't have in France, you can learn about them here) to the bio-medical (find out where to get tested for free, or about the latest developments in the treatment of HIV, for example), this multifunctional centre and library also hosts meetings for a variety of support groups and associations.

Popular rendezvous **Café Cox**. *See p306.*

### Inter-LGBT

*c/o Maison des Associations du l'Ile, boîte 8, 5 rue Perrée, 75003 Paris (01.72.70.39.22/www.inter-lgbt.org).* **Map** p409 L5.
The Interassociative Lesbienne, Gaie, Bi & Trans is an umbrella group of 50 French LGBT associations. It organises the Printemps des Assoces in the Espace des Blancs Manteaux (48 rue Vieille-du-Temple, 4th) every April and the annual Pride march.

### SOS Homophobie

*01.48.06.42.41/www.sos-homophobie.org.* **Open** 6pm-10pm Mon, Fri; 8pm-10pm Tues, Wed, Thur, Sun; 2pm-4pm Sat.
Victims and witnesses of homophobic crimes and discrimination can report them to this confidential service, which offers support and publishes an annual report on homophobia.

# Gay Paris

## Bars & cafés

### Le Bear's Den

*6 rue des Lombards, 4th (01.42.71.08.20/ www.bearsden.fr). Mᵒ Châtelet or Hôtel de Ville.*

**Open** 4pm-2am Mon-Thur, Sun; 4pm-4am Fri, Sat. **Credit** MC, V. **Map** p406 J6.
A friendly local for bears, muscle bears, chubbies and their admirers. Visit the website for details on comically named theme nights such as 'Charcuterie'. Bears, wolves and the men who love hairy men also gather at the nearby Wolf Bar (37 rue des Lombards, 1st, 01.40.28.02.52, www.wolfparis.com).

### Le Café Arena

*29 rue St-Denis, 1st (01.45.08.15.16). Mᵒ Châtelet.* **Open** 9am-6am daily. **Credit** MC, V. **Map** p406 J5.
This new bar-restaurant, with a great terrace for people-watching and friendly staff, has quickly become the hottest rendezvous in Les Halles.

### Café Cox

*15 rue des Archives, 4th (01.42.72.08.00/www. cox.fr). Mᵒ Hôtel de Ville.* **Open** 11pm-2am daily. **No credit cards.** **Map** p409 K6.
Beefy, hairy, shaven-headed folk congregate along the pavement in front of Café Cox for post-work drinks, before moving on to more intimate surroundings. *Photo p305.*

### Le Duplex

*25 rue Michel-le-Comte, 3rd (01.42.72.80.86). Mᵒ Hôtel de Ville or Rambuteau.* **Open** 8am-2am daily. **Credit** V. **Map** p409 K5.

# Get (your kit) off

In the last few years a major trend on Paris's gay scene has been the *soirée naturiste* – an evening for nudists. The trend started when one bar began organising a few theme nights every month in conjunction with a nudist social club, but the evenings proved so popular that the inevitable next step was the all-naked cruising bar, the granddaddy of which is **L'Impact** (*see p308*). These days, in any given month, there are more than 70 *soirées naturistes* in more than a half dozen bars and clubs across the capital. If you've ever picked up someone in a bar and couldn't wait to get home to get your kit off, well, now you don't have to – your kit's already off.

L'Impact was the first bar to become 100% nudist. When you enter, you receive a sack to put your clothes in (it will be safely kept in the cloakroom; some bars have lockers instead), but keep your shoes on for safety reasons. The bar upstairs is brightly lit, so if you are shy about your body you might want to head downstairs to the dimly lit basement. This is where most of the action takes place.

Following L'Impact's lead, soon other bars started having *soirées naturistes*, including **Le Bunker** (150 rue St-Maur, 11th, Tue &

Thur), the **Banque Club** (23 rue Penthièvre, 8th, Sun), **Le Transfert** (3 rue de la Soudiere, 2nd, Sun), **Next** (87 rue St-Honoré, 1st, Thur), and **Le QG** (12 rue Simon le Franc, 4th, Sat & Sun afternoons), to name just a few. Given their success, it was only natural that a second all-naked cruising bar should open. **Bar Entre Deux Eaux** (45 rue de la Folie-Méricourt, 11th) opened in early 2005 and has been enjoying considerable success ever since. Complete listings for the *soirées naturistes* can be found in free monthly magazines such as *2X* and *AgendaQ*.

Not many of these bars have showering facilities, so if you prefer to be clean when you've finished getting dirty, you might want to check out one of the many saunas in Paris. One of the best is **IDM** (*see p308*). Manager Stephane and his team offer a friendly welcome, a clean towel and a pleasant environment. Head downstairs for the wet and dry saunas, or upstairs for cruising and fetish rooms. The place gets busy during after-work hours, and the clientele is varied. IDM also has a small but well-equipped gym, a snack bar and a small relaxation pool, and frequently organises cabaret nights.

This small, unpretentious bar just round the corner from the Centre Pompidou caters to a thirtysomething crowd. It's a popular meeting place for various gay associations, with friendly staff and works by local artists hanging on the walls.

### L'Interface Bar

*34 rue Keller, 11th (01.47.0067.15). M° Bastille, Ledru-Rollin or Voltaire.* **Open** 3pm-2am Mon-Thur, Sun; 3pm-4am Fri, Sat. **No credit cards.** **Map** p407 M6.

The small, unpretentious Interface is on the trendy and *très* gay rue Keller. The very friendly staff cater mostly to thirtysomethings, making this a great place to start the evening before heading off to the Scène nightclub around the corner or the hardcore Keller leather bar down the street.

### Les Marronniers

*18 rue des Archives, 4th (01.40.27.87.72). M° Hôtel de Ville.* **Open** 9am-2am Mon-Sat; noon-4pm Sun. **Credit** MC, V. **Map** p409 K6.

An excellent place for people-watching, this bar with a prime location is central in every sense of the word. Stop in for a drink or a light meal, then linger for a while on the crowded terrace to get a real insight into the workings of the city's gay scene.

### Le Mixer

*23 rue Ste Croix de la Bretonnerie, 4th (01.48.87. 55.44/www.mixerbar.com). M° Hôtel de Ville.* **Open** 5pm-2am daily. **Credit** AmEx, MC, V. **Map** p409 K6.

A mixed, young and happy crowd gathers at this watering hole for cocktails before heading off to the clubs. DJs spin the latest techno and house to energise the crowd. Some nights are strictly for the girls.

### Open Café

*17 rue des Archives, 4th (01.42.72.26.18/www. opencafe.fr). M° Hôtel de Ville or Rambuteau.* **Open** 10am-2am Mon-Thur, Sun; 10am-4am Fri, Sat. **Credit** MC, V. **Map** p409 K6.

Cruise and be cruised in the café everybody passes through at some point in the evening. Great staff and prompt service help. A small terrace allows for excellent people-watching at any time of the day or night.

### Le Quetzal

*10 rue de la Verrerie, 4th (01.48.87.99.07). M° Hôtel de Ville.* **Open** 5pm-5am daily. **Credit** MC, V. **Map** p409 K6.

This popular bar is considered one of the 'musts' of the Marais, as it is often filled with hot men and a few drag queens who help to keep things lively. You might be able to find some action in the small dark space upstairs.

### Raidd Bar

*23 rue du Temple, 4th (01.48.87.80.25/www. raiddbar.com). M° Hôtel de Ville.* **Open** 6.30pm-5am daily. **Credit** (minimum €10) MC, V. **Map** p406 K6.

The Raidd is standing room only at street level, with another bar and red velvet couches down below. The hot, herculean bartenders take turns in the wall-mounted shower for nightly shows, a DJ spins and

the dancefloor is jam-packed with buff, shirtless, sweaty men, especially after other bars close between 1am and 2am.

## Restaurants

### Le Gai Moulin

*10 rue St Merri, 4th (01.48.87.06.00). M° Hôtel de Ville.* **Open** 7pm-midnight daily. **Credit** MC, V. **Map** p406 K6.

A long-time favourite in the Marais. The tables are close together and you'll rub elbows with your neighbours, but it makes for a pleasant and convival ambience. On Tuesdays there's an open-mic cabaret in the basement.

### Le Kofi du Marais

*54 rue Ste-Croix-de-la-Bretonnerie, 4th (01.48.87. 48.71). M° Hôtel de Ville.* **Open** noon-11pm daily. **Credit** AmEx, MC, V. **Map** p406 K6.

Modern, simple cooking with an American twist is the speciality here. Club sandwiches, burgers and salads are menu staples. Prices are reasonable and the service is good.

### Aux Trois Petits Cochons

*31 rue Tiquetonne, 2nd (01.42.33.39.62/www. auxtroispetitscochons.fr). M° Etienne Marcel.* **Open** 8pm-1am. **Credit** MC, V. **Map** p406 J5.

This gay-owned, gay-run restaurant offers traditional French cuisine with a contemporary twist. The three-course menu (€33) changes daily and is based on the freshest ingredients available. It's very popular, so reservations are recommended. A second restaurant, Pig'z, has opened at 5 rue Marie Stuart in the 2nd (01.42.33.05.89).

### Ze Restoo

*41 rue des Blancs-Manteaux, 3rd (01.42.74.10.29). M° Rambuteau.* **Open** 7pm-1am Mon-Sat. **Credit** AmEx, MC, V. **Map** p409 K6.

This new restaurant has become a popular place to eat with friends before heading out for a fun-filled evening. There's a very relaxed atmosphere, with good service and dishes that have been spiced up with island flavours.

## Clubs

As well as the venues listed below, a mixed but increasingly gay crowd mingles at **Les Bains Douches** (*see p331*), **Nouveau Casino** (*see p229*) and **La Scène Bastille** (*see p330*). Most gay clubs are very hetero-friendly.

### C.U.D.

*12 rue des Haudriettes, 3rd (01.42.71.56.60/ www.cud-bar.com). M° Rambuteau.* **Open** 4pm-7am daily. **Credit** MC, V. **Map** p409 K5.

Upstairs is a laidback bar, but downstairs in the old cellar is a dancefloor that can get very crowded, especially after 2am. The patrons are a mixed bunch, and it's popular with the bears.

## Les Follivores & les Crazyvores

*Bataclan, 50 bd Voltaire, 11th (01.43.14.00.30/ www.le-bataclan.com/http://follivore.free.fr). M° St-Ambroise.* **Admission** (incl 1 drink) €17. **Credit** V. **Map** p407 M5.

Twice a month, the Bataclan concert hall transforms itself into a club to host these two legendary parties. Crazyvores features music from the 1970s and '80s, while at Follivores the DJs spin gay classics from all eras mixed with cutting-edge techno. These are big events with exuberant crowds – the drag queens put on their best ballgowns and biggest wigs, and the men sport their tightest T-shirts. Great fun.

## Queen

*102 av des Champs-Elysées, 8th (01.53.89.08.90/ www.queen.fr). M° George V.* **Open** midnight-7am Mon-Thur, Sun; midnight-8am Fri, Sat. **Admission** €15 Mon-Thur, Sun; €20 Fri, Sat. **Drinks** €10. **Credit** *Bar* AmEx, MC, V. **Map** p400 D4.

One of the oldest and largest clubs, Queen's main gay nights are Saturday@Queen and Overkitsch on Sundays in the summer months, but every night is a little gay, especially during fashion week. Big-name DJs often spin here to a crowd sprinkled with VIPs.

## Le Tango (aka La Boite à Frissons)

*13 rue au Maire, 3rd (01.42.72.17.78/www.boite-a-frissons.fr). M° Arts et Métiers.* **Open** 8pm-2am Thur; 10.30pm-5am Fri, Sat; 6-11pm Sun. **Admission** €7; free Thur. **Credit** V. **Map** p409 K5.

Wacky crowd, Madonna songs and accordion tunes. At the Friday and Saturday Bal de la Boite à Frissons, couples dance the foxtrot, tango, madison or *guinguette* in the early part of the evening, followed after midnight by music of every variety except techno. This unusual old dance hall never fails to entertain.

# Sex clubs & saunas

## Le Bunker

*150 rue St-Maur, 11th (01.53.36.01.16/www. bunker-cruising.com). M° Goncourt.* **Open** 4pm-2am Mon-Thur; 4pm-3.30am Fri; 4pm-4.30am Sat; 4pm-1am Sun. **Admission** €7. **Map** p403 M4.

Formerly known as the Docks, this cruising club is one of the hottest in Paris. Located not far from the Oberkampf bar district in a remote corner of the 11th, it features all-naked and underwear-only nights during the week, and hardcore themes on the weekend. Friday is a very popular night, as is the first Saturday of the month, when Le Bunker hosts its S&M-themed 'Red and Black Night' – not for the faint-hearted.

## Le Deep

*80 quai de l'Hôtel de Ville, 4th (01.42.78.88.49). M° Hôtel de Ville.* **Open** 4pm-5am daily. **Admission** €5.70-€7.70 (incl 1 drink). **Credit** MC, V. **Map** p409 K6.

The Deep is located right on the river just behind the Hôtel de Ville. The ground floor features a bar and occasional strippers; the other two floors are for cruising and offer a number of private cubicles for

when you find Mr Right Now. Each night has a theme – the military-themed 'Uniformes' night on Wednesdays has been pretty hot recently.

## Le Dépot

*10 rue aux Ours, 3rd (01.44.54.96.96/www. ledepot.com). M° Etienne Marcel.* **Open** midnight-dawn daily. **Admission** €7.50 before 11pm, €10 after 11pm Mon-Thur, Sun; €12 (incl 1 drink) Fri, Sat. **Credit** MC, V. **Map** p402 K5.

A very busy dance club upstairs with a labyrinthine maze of cubicles, glory holes and darkrooms downstairs. The clients have a lot of attitude and pick-pockets work the darkroom, so be careful.

## IDM

*4 rue du Fbg-Montmartre, 9th (01.45.23.10.03). M° Grands Boulevards.* **Open** noon-1am Mon-Thur, Sun; noon-2am Fri, Sat. **Admission** €15 Mon-Fri; €17 Sat, Sun; €10 under-30s. **Credit** MC, V. **Map** p402 J4.

The city's largest and best gay sauna is split over three levels and has plenty of cabins and corridors to prowl. The wet sauna is on two levels and the small relaxation pool and showers are always the perfect temperature. A few times a month there are also performances by drag queens and other singers. *See also p306* **Get (your kit) off.**

## L'Impact

*18 rue Greneta, 2nd (01.42.21.94.24/www.impact-bar.com). M° Châtelet.* **Open** 8pm-3am Mon-Thur; 10pm-6am Fri, Sat; 3pm-3am Sun. **Admission** €11. **Credit** MC, V. **Map** p402 K5.

The city's first all-naked cruising club offers various theme nights, a plentiful supply of condoms and lube, and a 2am-3am happy hour. €12 gets you a plastic bag for all your clothes (keep your shoes on), plus a drink. Most of the action happens downstairs in the cubicles, sling, labyrinth and giant bed. Tuesdays are Horse Man Naked nights, where interested parties can be measured up. Should they pass the 20cm (eight-in) stipulation, they're granted free admission. The all-naked cruising bar idea has proved very successful, and there are several imitators in the capital. *See p306* **Get (your kit) off.**

## Sun City

*62 bd de Sébastopol, 3rd (01.42.74.31.41/www. ledepot.com). M° Etienne Marcel.* **Open** midnight-6am daily. **Admission** €18 Mon-Fri; €19.50 Sat, Sun; €11under-26s. **Credit** MC, V. **Map** p402 J5.

A Bollywood-themed sauna where very pretty boys stand around and look uninterested. Owned and operated by the Dépot team (*see p308*), it features dry saunas, jacuzzi, hammams, video rooms, a pool, a gym and a bar. The decor is lovely, if a bit kitsch, and the atmosphere very relaxing.

## Univers Gym Paris-Sauna Hammam Musculation

*20-22 rue des Bons-Enfants, 1st (01.42.61.24.83/ 08.25.70.04.29/www.universgym.fr). M° Les Halles or Palais-Royal Musée du Louvre.* **Open** noon-2am

Mon-Sat; 6pm-2am Sun. **Admission** €13 before 2pm, €17.50 after; €9 after 10pm. *Under-26s* €7 before 2pm, €9 after; €6 after 10pm; €5 Tue after 8pm. **Credit** AmEx, DC, MC, V. **Map** p402 H5.
Although this is more sauna than gym, complete work-out facilities are available. A towel must be worn in the bar and gym areas; do as you please everywhere else. In late 2006 the gym closed for renovation after a fire caused extensive damage. The much-missed Univers is due to reopen in early 2008, but check the website before visiting as a series of bureaucratic problems has slowed the renovations.

## Shops & services

### Boy'z Ba'zaar
*5 rue Ste Croix de la Bretonnerie, 4th (01.42.71. 34.00). Mº Hôtel de Ville or St-Paul.* **Open** 2-10pm daily. **Credit** AmEx, MC, V. **Map** p409 K6.
The trendiest clothes for nightclubbers, fashionistas and urban hipsters in the heart of the gaybourhood.

### Les Dessous d'Apollon
*17 rue du Bourg-Tibourg, 4th (01.42.71.87.37/ www.lesdessousdapollon.com). Mº Hôtel de Ville or St-Paul.* **Open** noon-7.30pm Mon-Sat; 3-7pm Sun. **Credit** AmEx, DC, MC, V. **Map** p409 K6.
The most extensive selection of underwear – ranging from functional to sexy and downright eccentric – that you'll ever encounter. Also sells T-shirts, jeans and accessories.

### iEM
*16 rue Ste-Croix-de-la-Bretonnerie, 4th (01.42.74. 01.61/www.iem.fr). Mº Hotel de Ville.* **Open** 1pm-8pm Mon-Thur; 1pm-10pm Fri, Sat; 3pm-7pm Sun. **Credit** AmEx, MC, V. **Map** p403 M4.
This sex hypermarket emphasises the harder side of gay life. Videos, clothes and gadgets can all be found, with leather and rubber upstairs.
**Other locations**: 43 rue de l'Arbre Sec, 1st, 01.42.96.05.74.

### Legay Choc
*45 rue Ste-Croix-de-la-Bretonnerie, 4th (01.48.87. 56.88/www.legaychoc.fr). Mº Hôtel de Ville.* **Open** 8am-8pm Mon, Tue, Thur-Sun. **No credit cards.** **Map** p409 K6.
Run by two brothers (one gay, one straight) whose surname just happens to be Legay, this Marais *boulangerie* and pâtisserie is very popular. The pastries are delightful, and the lunch-hour sandwiches are generous, so expect lengthy queues. For special occasions, a penis-shaped loaf can be made to order. A satellite store, serving only sandwiches, opened nearby at 17 rue des Archives (01.48.87.24.61).

### Les Mots à la Bouche
*6 rue Ste-Croix-de-la-Bretonnerie, 4th (01.42.78.88.30/www.motsbouche.com). Mº Hôtel de Ville or St-Paul.* **Open** 11am-11pm Mon-Sat; 1-9pm Sun. **Credit** AmEx, MC, V. **Map** p409 K6.
Something of an institution in the Marais, this bookshop has a large selection of gay-interest fiction, non-fiction and magazines, plus a good English-language section.

### Nickel
*48 rue des Francs-Bourgeois, 4th (01.42.77.41.10/ www.nickel.fr). Mº Hôtel de Ville or Rambuteau.* **Open** 11am-7.30pm Mon, Tue, Fri, Sat; 11am-9pm Wed, Thur. **Credit** AmEx, MC, V. **Map** p406 L6.
Nickel offers body and skincare treatments, strictly for men. A one-hour facial is €45-€55, a manicure €13 and an hour-long relaxing massage €45. Staff are adept, but speak to manager Franck Tainier for any truly complicated epidermal needs.

### Plus Que Parfait
*23 rue des Blancs-Manteaux, 4th (01.42.71.09.05). Mº Hôtel de Ville or St-Paul.* **Open** 3-8pm Mon; noon-8pm Tue-Sat; 3-7pm Sun. Clothes deposit Mon-Fri. **Credit** MC, V. **Map** p409 K6.
This *dépôt vente*, where pristine condition, second-hand designer clothing is sold on commission, is a veritable treasure trove of men's fashion finds.

iEM.

## Space Hair

*10 rue Rambuteau, 3rd (01.48.87.28.51). M°
Rambuteau.* **Open** noon-10pm Mon; 10am-11pm Tue-
Fri; 9am-10pm Sat. **Credit** MC, V. **Map** p409 K6.
Space Hair is divided into two salons, Cosmic and
Classic, with a 1980s kitsch feel, late opening hours
and cute stylists; it's best to book ahead.

## Where to stay

### Hôtel Central Marais

*2 rue Ste-Croix-de-la-Bretonnerie, 4th (01.48.87.
56.08/www.hotelcentralmarais.com). M° Hôtel de
Ville or St-Paul.* **Rates** €87 single or double; €107
triple; €7 breakfast. **Credit** MC, V. **Map** p409 K6.
If location and affordable rates are more important
to you than plush surroundings, then this aptly
named hotel is a good choice. The barmen of the
Central bar (located below the hotel) act as receptionists from 5pm until 2am daily, and can keep you
updated on the local nightlife.

### Hôtel Duo

*11 rue du Temple, 4th (01.42.72.72.22/www.
duoparis.com). M° Hôtel de Ville.* **Rates** €135-€155
single; €200-€300 double; €350-430 suite; €14
breakfast. **Credit** AmEx, DC, MC, V. **Map** p406 K6
The mixed but very gay-friendly Duo is a stylish
place to rest your head. What's more, it has helpful
staff at the reception – a rarity in this trendy area.

# Lesbian Paris

Things have changed in the last year or so –
both Pulp nightclub and Bliss Kfé lounge have
closed – but the girly scene still continues to
flourish, especially near the corner of rue Roi de
Sicile and rue des Ecouffes in the Marais. Most
of the bars welcome men who are accompanied
by women, but a few are ladies only. And some
girl-only parties are organised at clubs like **Le
Tango** (*see p308*); look for the free monthly
magazine *Barbi(e)turix* for details.

### Le 3W Kafe

*8 rue des Ecouffes, 4th (01.48.87.39.26/www.3w-
kafe.com) M° St-Paul.* **Open** 6pm-2am daily. **Credit**
MC, V. **Map** p409 K6.
A convivial place where beautiful, chic women go to
have a drink, meet other women and listen to good
music. There's a small dance space in the basement,
and a number of theme nights every month. The
three Ws stand for 'women with women'.

### La Champmeslé

*4 rue Chabanais, 2nd (01.42.96.85.20). M° Bourse
or Pyramides.* **Open** 3pm-early morning Mon-Sat.
**Credit** MC, V. **Map** p402 H4.
This veteran girl bar remains a popular hangout for
lesbian locals and visitors. Beer is the drink of choice
– pull up a seat and enjoy the regular cabaret nights.

### Chez Moune

*54 rue Pigalle, 9th (01.45.26.64.64). M° Pigalle.*
**Open** 10.30pm Tue-Sat . **Credit** MC, V. **Map** p401 H2.
Probably the oldest lesbian cabaret in Paris, Chez
Moune opened in 1936 and still has nightly shows.
Saturdays are women only.

### Le Day Off

*10 rue de l'Isly, 8th (01.45.22.87.90). M° Gare St-
Lazare.* **Open** 11am-3am Mon-Fri. **Credit** MC, V.
**Map** p401 G3.
Apt name for this weekday-only pub-restaurant –
heavy drinking enjoyed by work-weary lesbians.
Crowded in the early evening.

### The Dollhouse

*24 rue du Roi de Sicile, 4th (01.40.27.09.21). M° St-
Paul.* **Open** 1-8pm Tue-Sat;2pm-8pm Sun, Mon.
**Credit** MC, V. **Map** p409 L6.
This store, located close to 3W, specialises in lingerie
and gadgets for girls. Upstairs you'll find a selection
of sophisticated and sexy underwear; head downstairs for the sexcessories.

### Le Nyx Café

*30 rue du Roi de Sicile, 4th (no phone). M° St-Paul.*
**Open** 6pm-2am daily. **Credit** MC, V. **Map** p409 L6.
The Bliss Kfe may have closed but the Nyx has
recently opened in its place. It is still mostly a girl
bar, but is open to everyone as it seeks to establish
itself. Recent theme nights have included live rock
and drag queens.

### O'Kubi Caffé

*219 rue St-Maur, 10th (01.42.01.35.08/www.
okubicaffe.com). M° Goncourt.* **Open** 6pm-2am daily.
**Credit** MC, V. **Map** p403 M3.
O'Kubi recently celebrated its first anniversary and
continues to grow in popularity. It is now a bar as
well and serves a light menu.

### Le Rive Gauche

*1 rue du Sabot, 6th (01.42.22.51.70). M° St-
Germain-des-Prés.* **Open** 11pm-dawn Fri, Sat. **No
credit cards**. **Map** p405 G7.
This weekend women-only nightclub is one of the
hottest places on the lesbian scene. The decor is very
'70s and the music very eclectic.

### Le Troisième Lieu

*62 rue Quincampoix, 4th (01.48.04.85.64/
www.letroisiemelieu.com). M° Rambuteau.* **Open**
6pm-2am Mon-Sat. **Credit** MC, V. **Map** p406 K5.
Elaborate *tartines*, delicious desserts and strong
drinks are the fare at this lesbian-run bar and restaurant. Despite its militant subtitle ('Cantine des
Ginettes Armées'), the vibe is jovial. There are also
areas devoted to music and dancing. *See also p326.*

### Unity Bar

*176-178 rue St-Martin, 3rd (01.42.72.70.59/
http://unity.bar.free.fr). M° Rambuteau.* **Open** 4pm-
2am daily. **No credit cards**. **Map** p402 K5.
This ladies-only bar is more butch than lipstick, with
pool tables and a good beer selection.

# Music

From opera to electro, Paris is back on the world stage.

## Classical & Opera

Alongside plans for a new purpose-built concert hall (*see p313* **Music hall**), the most exciting development on the current classical music scene is the enterprising season at the **Opéra Comique**. This outstandingly beautiful miniature opera house, which saw the premiere of Bizet's *Carmen*, has been under-funded for half a century, but can now look forward to financial security thanks to its promotion to National Theatre status. Director Jérôme Deschamps may be better known in France for television satire than opera, but his genuine passion for promoting the French repertoire in the house is obvious. His first season has all the right ingredients, kicking off with Chabrier's *L'Etoile* conducted by John Eliot Gardiner, then continuing with a revival of Lully's *Cadmus et Hermione*. Next comes the forgotten French 19th-century masterpiece *Zampa*, conducted by Early Music champion William Christie, and to finish the season, the Paris premiere of Pascal Dusapin's *Roméo et Juliette* and Gershwin's *Porgy and Bess*.

Director Jean-Luc Choplin is responsible for a similarly eclectic but arguably more daring mix of productions at the **Châtelet**. Operatic programming opens with the Chinese mythological pop opera *Monkey: Journey to the West* by Damon Albarn and Jamie Hewlett, and goes on to stage the world premieres of the first African Opera, *Bintou Wéré* by Zé Manel Fortes, and David Cronenberg's *The Fly* with music by Howard Shore, conducted by tenor superstar Placido Domingo.

At the **Opéra National de Paris**, Gérard Mortier continues his uncompromising directorship with fun and fireworks sidelined in favour of worthy contemporary production values. Krzysztof Warlikowski's new production of *Parsifal* will no doubt ruffle some Wagnerian feathers, but Luigi Dallapiccola's *Il Prigoniere* and a new commission by Georg Friederich Haas entitled *Melancholia* may well send some listeners back to their Puccini CDs, a composer whom Mortier persists in describing as second rate. Mortier's successor in the top job will be Nicolas Joël, currently the director of the Opéra de Toulouse. This may appear something of a musical and dramatic retreat, but the return to a safe, less controversial, pair of hands may well benefit the national house.

Meanwhile at Radio France, Thierry Beauvert has now added the overall command of music to his position as head of the France Musique radio station, and thankfully brought more music and less chat to the airwaves. Radio France is responsible for two of the city's main orchestras: the **Orchestre Philharmonique de Radio France**, whose musical director is Myung-Whun Chung, and the **Orchestre National de France**, led by the venerable Kurt Masur. Both are challenged and outpaced in terms of publicity and tight programming by the **Orchestre de Paris**, now back home in the newly restored Salle Pleyel, before it moves into the new concert hall under the baton of Paavo Järvi, who takes over from Christoph Eschenbach in 2010.

Contemporary creations remain a strong suit in the city's musical make-up, thanks to the work of **IRCAM**, the **Ensemble Intercontemporain** and the still active Pierre Boulez. Important names to watch out for among the current generation of composers include Dusapin, Fénélon and Eötvös.

The Early Music scene is still led by William Christie's **Les Arts Florissants**, but the new toast of the record companies is French conductor Emmanuelle Haïm, whose eagerness to use top singers from outside the Early Music ghetto, such as Mexican tenor Rolando Villazón, has injected glamour into the earnest world of the specialists led by Christophe Rousset and Jean-Claude Malgoire.

There's plenty going on in the churches too. The **Festival d'Art Sacré** (01.44.70. 64.10) presents church music in authentic settings in the run-up to Christmas; **Les Grands Concerts Sacrés** (01.48.24.16.97) and **Musique et Patrimoine** (01.42.50. 96.18) also offer concerts at various churches; and music in Notre-Dame cathedral is taken care of by **Musique Sacrée Notre-Dame** (01.44.41.49.99, tickets 01.42.34.56.10).

The main musical provider in summer is the **Paris Quartier d'Eté** festival (www.quartierdete.com), with concerts in gardens across the city. The **Festival de Saint-Denis** (www.festival-saint-denis.fr) also offers top names in a spectacular setting. (*See also pp274-278* **Festivals & Events**.)

Arts & Entertainment

## INFORMATION AND TICKETS

For listings, see *L'Officiel des Spectacles* or *Pariscope*. Monthly magazines *Le Monde de la Musique* and *Diapason* also list classical concerts, while *Opéra Magazine* provides good coverage of all things vocal. Look out too for *Cadences* and *La Terrasse*, two free monthlies distributed outside concerts.

Many venues and orchestras offer cut-rate tickets to students under 26 an hour before curtain-up. Be wary of smooth-talking ticket touts around the Opéra and at big-name concerts. For the **Fête de la Musique** (21 June) all events are free, and year-round freebies crop up at the **Maison de Radio France** and the **Conservatoire de Paris**, as well as in certain churches.

## Orchestras & ensembles

### Les Arts Florissants

*01.43.87.98.88/www.arts-florissants.com.*
William Christie's 'Arts Flo' are France's leading Early Music group, and their worldwide reputation has blossomed. This year the musicians will travel the world with *Il Sant'Alessio* by Stefano Landi starring rising French counter tenor Philippe Jaroussky. A departure will be the group's performances of Hérold's *Zampa* at the Opéra Comique, a 19th-century *opéra comique* rather than a baroque rediscovery.

### Ensemble Intercontemporain

*01.44.84.44.50/www.ensembleinter.com.*
Glamorous Finnish conductor Susanna Mälkki is the musical director of this prestigious bastion of contemporary music founded by Pierre Boulez. The exacting standard of the 31 soloists is beyond reproach, and the ensemble regularly commissions new work as well as participating in valuable educational work at the Cité de la Musique and IRCAM.

### Ensemble Orchestral de Paris

*08.00.42.67.57/www.ensemble-orchestral-paris.com.*
John Nelson remains one of the finest conductors in France. While his orchestra doesn't have the best players in Paris, it nonetheless provides a stimulating addition to the city's musical life. Highlights this season include performances in the pit of the Théâtre des Champs-Elysées for Stravinsky's *The Rake's Progress*, and, in the same theatre, versions of the Mozart late symphonies.

### Orchestre Colonne

*01.42.33.72.89/www.orchestrecolonne.fr.*
Led by composer Laurent Petitgirard, the musical and artistic director, this orchestra is beginning to regain some of its former prestige. Each concert teams a contemporary work with more popular pieces, and the band has attracted a recording contract with the first CD dedicated to the music of Gabriel Pierné, successor to Edouard Colonne, the orchestra's founder.

### Orchestre Lamoureux

*01.58.39.30.30/www.orchestrelamoureux.com.*
This worthy orchestra still suffers from insufficient funding, and its concert appearances in the capital are sparse, but musical director Yutaka Sado encourages diverse programming. This season the focus is on contemporary composer Piotr Moss, who will have one of his pieces performed in each of the orchestra's Paris concerts.

### Orchestre National de France

*01.56.40.15.16/www.radiofrance.fr.*
Kurt Masur celebrated his 80th birthday last year, and under his firm direction the orchestra's performances of the German symphonic repertoire now rank alongside the best in the world. In the summer of 2008 the maestro will embark on a Beethoven cycle culminating with the *Ninth Symphony* at the Théâtre des Champs Elysées on 12 July.

### Orchestre de Paris

*01.56.35.12.00/www.orchestredeparis.com.*
Christoph Eschenbach made it known last year that he would not be prolonging his contract with the orchestra after 2010, and his successor has been named as Paavo Järvi. Eschenbach does fine work with the orchestra and was instrumental in promoting the project for the new concert hall (*see p313* **Music hall**). This year Dvořák and the Russians receive special attention with visits from conductors Valery Gergiev and Sir Andrew Davis.

### Orchestre Pasdeloup

*01.42.78.10.00/www.concertspasdeloup.com.*
The Pasdeloup is the oldest orchestra in Paris, but the time when it premiered works by major composers (Ravel and Bizet, among others, had work performed here for the first time) has long gone. Programming now concentrates on a light repertoire of popular easy-listening classics, enlivened by the occasional interesting soloist.

### Orchestre Philharmonique de Radio France

*www.radiofrance.fr.*
Highly respected musical director Myung-Whun Chung and his orchestra play to a high standard, but in 2008 the musical director is not a strong guiding presence in the orchestra's 50 or so concerts. The repertoire remains varied and the flexibility of the band seems to guarantee its ongoing success, finishing the season in the pit of the Châtelet for the world premiere of *The Fly*.

## Venues

### Auditorium du Louvre

*Entrance through Pyramid, Cour Napoléon, Musée du Louvre, rue de Rivoli, 1st (01.40.20. 55.55/reservations 01.40.20.55.00/www.louvre.fr).* $M^o$ Palais Royal Musée du Louvre. **Box office** 9am-7pm Mon, Wed-Fri. Closed July, Aug. **Admission** €6-€30. **Credit** MC, V. **Map** p401 H5.

# Music hall

The case for a new concert hall in Paris has been the subject of a decidedly inharmonious debate ever since the reconstruction of the city after World War II. The Salle Pleyel was always an inadequate building to house the great symphony orchestras of the capital, and despite a major refit, troublesome acoustics remain a problem. Its reopening in 2006 only served to encourage calls for a brand new concert hall.

Christophe Eschenbach, the musical director of the Orchestre de Paris, declared that he would resign unless plans for a new venue went through; at the time his orchestra was camping out in the wholly inappropriate Théâtre Mogador, while Pleyel was being renovated. A new development has finally been given the go-ahead, though the bad news for Eschenbach is that it won't open until 2012 – two years after he's due to give up his leadership of the orchestra.

The success of the new building will be dependent on programming, which must be attractive enough to fill the 2,000-seater on a regular basis. At present, symphonic concerts in Paris are shared between the Salle Pleyel, the Maison de la Radio, the Théâtre des Champs Elysées and the Châtelet. These last two venues were designed as theatres and host a broad range of cultural events including ballet and opera. Currently only high-profile concerts with a star soloist or an iconic conductor are guaranteed sell-outs, while less prestigious names or more challenging repertoires regularly play to half-empty houses. For what is to be grandly named the Philharmonie de Paris, marketing,

as well as depth of musical quality and innovative programming, will be crucial.

The site designated for the new hall is the Parc de la Villette on the edge of the 19th arrondissement, adjacent to the Cité de la Musique, in an area previously occupied by the city's abattoir. Well-heeled residents will no doubt find the journey across town tedious, but music students and suburban residents will benefit from the area's continuing regeneration. With hindsight it was short-sighted of the Mitterand government not to construct a full-sized concert hall as part of the Cité de la Musique, instead of the undersized hall housed inside Christian de Portzamparc's complex. Portzamparc was one of the shortlisted architects for the new project, but eventually the commission went to Jean Nouvel, the architect responsible for several remarkable buildings in the capital, notably the Institut du Monde Arabe (*see p154*) and the new Musée du quai Branly (*see p171* **Windows on the world**).

Nouvel's brief is to design a hall with excellent acoustics, close contact between public and platform, and which has is able to host jazz and world music as well as symphony orchestras. Despite technological advances, acoustics and atmosphere remain an inexact science, and judgement will have to be reserved on the project until the doors open in 2012. It is to be hoped, however, that the architect's promise that the space will be a 'metaphor for music' will fulfil the long held dream of a world-class concert hall that Parisians can call their own.

The Auditorium du Louvre packs a full season with chamber music, lunchtime concerts and music on film. This year the chamber music has a distinctly Germanic flavour designed to coincide with exhibitions by Kiefer and Biedermeier, including a very tempting Beethoven series.

## Châtelet – Théâtre Musical de Paris

*1 pl du Châtelet, 1st (01.40.28.28.40/www.chatelet-theatre.com). M° Châtelet.* **Box office** 11am-7pm daily. *By phone* 10am-7pm Mon-Sat. Closed July, Aug. **Admission** €10-€125. **Credit** AmEx, DC, MC, V. **Map** p408 J6.

New director Jean-Luc Choplin's attempts to create a more popular cultural experience than that provided by the esoteric programming at the Opéra National have so far proved inconclusive. Alongside

the adventurous operatic offerings, it's good to find Albert Roussel's *Pâdmavatî* and a taste of Spanish zarzuela before the world premiere of Howard Shore's *The Fly*, staged by David Cronenberg and conducted by Placido Domingo in June and July 2008. The concert programming is more traditional, with an excellent series of piano recitals planned.

## Cité de la Musique

*221 av Jean-Jaurès, 19th (01.44.84.45.00/www.cite-musique.fr). M° Porte de Pantin.* **Box office** noon-6pm Tue-Sun. *By phone* 11am-7pm Mon-Sat; 10am-6pm Sun. **Admission** €5.60-€33. **Credit** MC, V. **Map** p403 (inset).

The energetic programming here features a vast non-classical repertoire that includes ethnic music and jazz. Concerts are frequently split up into series with a pedagogic aim; the theme for 2008 is 'the

**Arts & Entertainment**

IRCAM.

sacred and the profane'. Watch out for the Domaine Privé series, in which musicians reveal their private musical passions. The museum has a smaller concert space, while the Conservatoire (01.40.40.45.45) is host to world-class performers and professors, and features many free concerts. *Photo p323.*

## IRCAM

*1 pl Igor-Stravinsky, 4th (01.44.78.48.43/www.
ircam.fr). M° Hôtel de Ville.* **Box office** 10am-1pm, 2-6pm Mon-Fri. **Admission** €5-€14. **Credit** AmEx, DC, MC, V. **Map** p406 K6.

The bunker set up in 1969 by the avant-garde composer Pierre Boulez to create electronic microtonal music for the new century is looking rather less redundant nowadays, thanks largely to its full programme of conferences and courses, and the showcase IRCAM Festival (5-20 June 2008). Current director Frank Madlener has succeeded in raising the profile of the institution; particularly interesting are the Concerts Cursus, a series that presents new electronic work by young composers from different cultural backgrounds. IRCAM's concerts are performed here, in the main hall of the neighbouring Centre Pompidou (*see p131*) and at the Théâtre des Bouffes du Nord (*see p344*).

## Maison de Radio France

*116 av du Président-Kennedy, 16th (01.56.40.
15.16/information 01.42.30.15.16/www.radio
france.fr). M° Passy/RER Avenue du Pdt Kennedy.* **Box office** 11am-6pm Mon-Sat. **Admission** €5-€55. **Credit** AmEx, DC, MC, V. **Map** p404 A7.

State-owned radio station France Musique broadcasts a superb range of classical concerts, operas and ethnic music from here. The main stage (the Salle Olivier Messiaen) may be charmless, but the quality of music-making from the Orchestre National de France and the Orchestre Philharmonique de Radio France makes up for it. The Passe Musique offers under-26s admission to four concerts for €18, or a year of concerts for €99. Occasional free events are spread over themed weekends, but the Présences contemporary music festival is now going to be spread across four cities, with the Paris events limited to three days in May at the Cité de la Musique.

## Musée National du Moyen Age

*6 pl Paul-Painlevé, 5th (01.53.73.78.16/www.musee-
moyenage.fr). M° Cluny La Sorbonne.* **Admission** €16; €13 students, under-18s. **Credit** AmEx, MC, V. **Map** p408 J7.

The museum presents a worthy programme of medieval concerts in which troubadours and the use of polyphony reflect the museum's collection.

## Musée d'Orsay

*62 rue de Lille, 7th (01.40.49.47.57/www.
musee-orsay.fr). M° Solférino/RER Musée
d'Orsay.* **Admission** €11-€30; €6-€20 under-26s. **Credit** MC, V. **Map** p405 G6.

The museum runs a full and enterprising series of lunchtime and evening concerts. The lunchtime concerts at 12.30pm concentrate on promising young artists. In 2008, there will be particular emphasis on the music of Switzerland and Russia.

## Opéra National de Paris, Bastille

*Pl de la Bastille, 12th (08.36.69.78.68/www.opera deparis.fr). M° Bastille.* **Box office** (130 rue de Lyon, 12th) 10.30am-6.30pm Mon-Sat. *By phone* 9am-6pm Mon-Fri; 9am-1pm Sat. **Admission** €5-€300. **Credit** AmEx, MC, V. **Map** p409 M7.

The modern building everyone (except the skateboarders outside) loves to hate: even the exterior of the house is decaying, with netting protecting passers-by from falling fascia tiles. If you want to make the administration squirm, just mention the unfinished *salle modulable* or the unflattering acoustics of the theatre. Director Gerard Mortier has introduced cutting-edge dramatic values, but disappointed those who enjoy spectacular singing and lavish period costume. However detractors who have henceforth been critical of the casts' lack of superstars will be happy to see Russian Anna Netrebko making her house début in Bellini's *I Capuleti e i Montecchi*, along with a strong revival of Verdi's *Don Carlos* in summer 2008.

## Opéra National de Paris, Palais Garnier

*Pl de l'Opéra, 9th (08.36.69.78.68/www.opera deparis.fr). M° Opéra.* **Box office** 10.30am-6.30pm Mon-Sat. *By phone* 9am-6pm Mon-Sat. **Admission** €7-€160. **Credit** AmEx, MC, V. **Map** p401 G4.

The restored Palais Garnier, with its ornate, extravagant decor and ceiling by Marc Chagall, is the jewel in the crown of Paris music-making, although the Opéra National often favours the high-tech Bastille

for new productions. The traditional 19th-century glamour contrasts with director Gerard Mortier's rejection of opera as a museum art form, and the house has been chosen for the premiere of this year's new commission, *Melancholia* by Haas, in June 2008.

## Péniche Opéra

*Facing 46 quai de la Loire, 19th (01.53.35.07.76/ reservations 01.53.35.07.77/www.penicheopera.com). M° Jaurès or Laumière.* **Box office** 10am-7pm Mon-Fri; 2-7pm Sat. **Admission** €11-€24. **Credit** MC, V. **Map** p403 M1.

The Péniche Opéra is an enterprising, boat-based company that produces a programme of chamber-scale shows and concerts. They are directed by the indefatigable Mireille Larroche, and range from baroque rarities to contemporary creations via charming revue-style shows concentrating on forgotten French comic opera and operetta.

## Salle Cortot

*78 rue Cardinet, 17th (01.47.63.85.72). M° Malesherbes.* **No box office. Admission** phone for details. **Map** p401 E2.

This intimate concert hall in the Ecole Normale de Musique has excellent acoustics for chamber music events and masterclasses.

## Salle Gaveau

*45 rue La Boétie, 8th (01.49.53.05.07/www.salle gaveau.com). M° Miromesnil.* **Box office** 10am-6pm Mon-Fri. **Admission** €10-€75. **Credit** MC, V. **Map** p401 E3.

Many of the smaller underachieving Paris orchestras have found refuge in the Salle Gaveau, but the programming for 2008 lacks the top-quality chamber music that used to be the hall's core repertoire.

## Salle Pleyel

*252 rue du Fbg-St-Honoré, 8th (01.42.56.13.13/ www.sallepleyel.fr). Mº Ternes.* **Box office** noon-7pm Mon-Sat. *By phone* 11am-7pm Mon-Sat; 11am-5pm Sun. **Admission** €10-€85. **Credit** MC, V. **Map** p400 D3.

Home to the Orchestre de Paris, the newly restored concert hall looks splendid, but the improved acoustics are only partially successful. The London Symphony Orchestra and the Leipzig Gewandhaus are visiting in June 2008, and the hall has regained its prestigious status as the only venue dedicated to large-scale symphonic concerts in the capital, at least until the completion of the city's new concert hall in 2012 (*see p313* **Music hall**).

## La Sorbonne

*Amphitheatre Richelieu, 17 rue de la Sorbonne, 5th (01.42.62.71.71/www.musique-en-sorbonne.org). Mº Cluny La Sorbonne or Odéon.* **Box office** by phone or at the door. **Admission** €18-€40. **Credit** MC, V. **Map** p408 J7.

The lecture theatres of the university make a prestigious setting for a seriously presented series of concerts featuring the orchestra and chorus of Paris Sorbonne, as well as smaller-scale chamber music.

## Théâtre des Bouffes du Nord

*37bis bd de la Chapelle, 10th (01.46.07.34.50/www. bouffesdunord.com) Mº La Chapelle.* **Box office** by phone or in person 11am-6pm Mon-Sat. **Admission** €8-€20. **Credit** MC, V. **Map** p402 K1.

This elegant theatre boasts one of the best programmes of chamber music in the capital, directed by Micheline Rozan and Peter Brook. A contemporary collaboration with IRCAM brings a visit from the Klangforum Wien under Sylvain Cambreling in June 2008, alongside an impressive line-up of top chamber ensembles including the Vermeer and Prazák quartets.

## Théâtre des Champs-Elysées

*15 av Montaigne, 8th (01.49.52.50.50/www. theatrechampselysees.fr). Mº Alma Marceau.* **Box office** 1-7pm Mon-Sat. *By phone* 10am-noon, 2-6pm Mon-Fri. **Admission** €5-€156. **Credit** AmEx, MC, V. **Map** p400 D5.

This beautiful art nouveau theatre, with bas-reliefs by Bourdelle, hosted the scandalous premiere of Stravinsky's *Le Sacre du Printemps* in 1913. Director Dominique Meyer, recently announced as the future intendant of the Vienna Opera, is rightly proud of the theatre's unsubsidised status, and maintains its tradition of quality programming. It remains the favourite venue for visiting foreign orchestras, including the Vienna Philharmonic and the Dresden Staaskapelle. The prestigious line-up of conductors includes Riccardo Muti, Valery Gergiev, Seiji Ozawa and Christian Thielemann. A new production of

Verdi's *Falstaff* in June 2008, along with a joint recital by tenors Rolando Villazón and Juan Diego Florez in July, are the operatic highlights of the season, while the exciting list of recitalists includes top pianists Nikolai Lugansky and Piotr Anderszewski.

## Théâtre National de l'Opéra Comique

*Pl Boieldieu, 2nd (01.42.44.45.40/www.opera-comique.com). Mº Richelieu Drouot.* **Box office** 9am-9pm Mon-Sat. *By phone* 11am-6pm Mon-Sat. **Admission** €7-€100. **Credit** AmEx, DC, MC, V. **Map** p402 H4.

Jérôme Deschamps' first season at this previously underachieving theatre looks more than promising. The repertoire ranges from Lully to the contemporary work of Pascal Dusapin, and the public look set to welcome this jewel box of a theatre back to the centre of the Parisian music scene.

## Théâtre du Tambour-Royal

*94 rue du Fbg-du-Temple, 11th (01.48.06.72.34/ tambour.royal.monsite.wanadoo.fr). Mº Belleville or Goncourt.* **Box office** 6.30-8pm Tue-Fri; 3-8pm Sat, Sun. *By phone* 10am-8pm Mon-Sat. **Admission** €16-€21. **Credit** MC, V. **Map** p403 M4.

This charming venue is where Maurice Chevalier launched his career. Its programming includes occasional chamber music concerts and revue-style shows, including the popular *Mozart en français*.

## Théâtre de la Ville

*2 pl du Châtelet, 4th (01.42.74.22.77/www.theatre delaville-paris.com). Mº Châtelet.* **Box office** 11am-7pm Mon-Sat. **Admission** €12-€30. **Credit** MC, V. **Map** p408 J6.

Programming in this vertiginous concrete amphitheatre features hip chamber music outfits such as the Kronos Quartet and Early Music pioneer Fabio Biondi, along with soloists such as French pianist Alexandre Tharaud and tenor Werner Güra. The musical season spills over to performances at Les Abbesses (31 rue des Abbesses, 18th), which shares the same phone number and box office hours. *See also p344.*

# Rock, Roots & Jazz

The result of the 1980s government decree which stipulated that at least 40 per cent of music broadcast in France must be French seems to have been a preponderance over the airwaves of Gallic oldies and dubious cover versions. As far as pop and rock are concerned, American and British groups are seen as *'décomplexé'* (meaning without hang-ups or complexes), whereas France is stuck with a more cerebral tradition, attested to by the enduring popularity of *chanson* and jazz.

Both these genres are well represented at the larger Paris venues, which also play host to blues and a diverse range of Arab and

African acts. Some, like Malian duo Amadou and Mariam – whose global hit *Diamanché à Bamako* was produced by Franco-Spanish music guru Manu Chao – come to Paris to record.

But the contemporary music scene has more to offer than just world music and *chanson*. Indeed there are a number of Paris-based music makers who could justifiably be described as *décomplexé*. They create genre-bending party music that combines the disposability of pop with left-field credibility – something that can't really be said of the young French rockers, hopelessly lost in nostalgic pop classicism, who you'll find onstage at **Olympia** or the new **Mécanique Ondulatoire**.

The real innovation and excitement comes from labels like Ed Banger, purveyors of fine French electronica (*see p321* **In the name of Justice**), and artists such as Kavinsky, Para One, young female provocateurs Yelle, Miami-born rapper Uffie, glam rockers Fancy (remixed by Ed Banger boss Pedro Winter) and Teki Latex from rap group TTC. These acts offer a boundary-breaking mix of hip hop, dance and experimental new music.

This up-and-coming Paris music community is tightly-knit and based in a handful of ultra hip venues, notably **Le ParisParis**, which is the place in which to catch the Ed Banger crew facing off against rivals Fancy and TTC in an iPod battle.

### INFORMATION AND RESOURCES

If you're intending to spend any length of time in Paris, or even just planning ahead, one of the best resources is the free, daily *Les InrocksParis* e-newsletter, which you can subscribe to via www.lesinrocks.com. In addition, www.infoconcert.com is well worth a look. Otherwise, there's the *Les Inrockuptibles* magazine or the reliable, bi-monthly gig bible *Lylo*, which is available free in bars and branches of **Fnac** (*see p272*). The Fnac and **Virgin Megastore** ticket offices also display details of upcoming concerts. Depending on your tastes (and comprehension of French) radio can be useful for tip-offs; Nova (101.5 FM) does electro, lounge and world; TSF (89.9FM) and FIP (105.1FM) cover jazz; and Le Mouv' (92.1FM) and OuiFM (102.3 FM) are for rock fans.

Box offices are usually closed during the day, and most venues take a break for some or all of August. Prices for gigs vary more according to a group or artist's pulling power, but several excellent venues, such as **La Flèche d'Or**, host regular free nights. For concerts, it's best to turn up at the time stated on the ticket – strictly enforced noise curfews mean that timings are closely adhered to.

## Festivals

### Sous la Plage
*Parc André-Citroën, 15th (www.souslaplage.com). M° Javel.* **Date** Early July-mid September.
The best bet for decent free music over the summer is down on the beach. Head to Paris-Plage for a connoisseurs' selection of pop, rock and electro.

### Solidays
*Hippodrome de Longchamp, 16th (www.solidays. com). M° La Muette.* **Date** mid July.
For a stronger French bias than Rock en Seine, and more focus on electronic and dub styles, this is the one – 2007 saw popular native talents (Diam's, Joeystarr, Grand Corps Malade) play alongside Lily Allen and Lauryn Hill.

### Rock en Seine
*Parc de St-Cloud, 16th (www.rockenseine.com). M° Pont de St-Cloud.* **Date** late Aug.
This riverside festival is the capital's alternative rock mecca: Björk, Arcade Fire, the Jesus and Mary Chain and French New Wave legends Les Rita Mitsouko topped the bill in 2007.

## Further Afield

### Les Eurockéennes
*www.eurockeennes.com. Gare de Lyon or Gare de l'Est to Belfort (4hrs).* **Date** early July.
For the full in-tents experience, try France's answer to Glastonbury or Benicassim: 2007's typically impressive bill included Marilyn Manson, Wu-Tang Clan and Queens of the Stone Age.

### La Route du Rock
*www.laroutedurock.com. Gare Montparnasse to St-Malo (3hrs 30mins).* **Date** mid Aug.
In the port town of St-Malo, you can take in the salty air and check out a consistently impressive, rock-orientated line-up. The 2007 line up included Sonic Youth, LCD Soundsytem and Justice.

### Les Transmusicales
*www.lestrans.com. Gare Montparnasse to Rennes (2hrs 30mins).* **Date** early Dec.
The main festival takes place in giant aircraft hangars just outside Rennes, but virtually every bar in the city hosts up-and-coming French talent. The hippest event of its size in France.

## Stadium venues

### Palais Omnisports de Paris-Bercy
*8 bd de Bercy, 12th (08.92.69.23.00/www.bercy.fr). M° Bercy.* **Open** *Box office* 11am-6pm Mon-Sat. **Credit** AmEx, DC, MC, V. **Map** p407 N9.
Only the biggest stars in the pop firmament get to appear at this mega-venue – Gwen Stefani and Rod Stewart were among the big draws last year, and Céline Dion will be playing 19-27 May 2008.

**Arts & Entertainment**

## Zénith

*211 av Jean-Jaurès, 19th (www.le-zenith.com). Mº Porte de Pantin.* **No credit cards. Map** p403 inset. State-of-the-art sound and credible bands make this the large venue of choice. The Arctic Monkeys, White Stripes and Beastie Boys brought the noise last year. Tickets available from Fnac and Virgin.

## Rock venues

### Le Bataclan

*50 bd Voltaire, 11th (01.43.14.00.30/www.le-bataclan.com). Mº Oberkampf.* **Open** times vary. **No credit cards. Map** p403 M5.
Established in 1864, this highly distinctive venue is still standing after the odd facelift and remains discerning in its booking of major rock, world, jazz and hip hop acts.

### Bus Palladium

*6 rue Fontaine, 9th (01.45.26.80.35/01.42.23.18.62/ www.lebuspalladium.com). Mº Pigalle or St Georges.* **Open** 8.30pm-dawn Wed-Sat; 3pm-dawn Sun. **No credit cards. Map** p401 G2.
This mythical 1960s venue managed to re-establish itself in recent years as a vital locale, attracting rock acts along with electro and hip hop.

### Café de la Danse

*5 passage Louis-Phillipe, 11th (01.47.00.57.59/ www.chez.com/cafedeladanse).* **Open** times vary. Closed July, Aug. **No credit cards. Map** p407 M7.
Pristine sound and a rarefied ideal of pop and rock perfection typify this former dancehall. It's mostly seated, but there's room to shake a tailfeather down at the front.

### La Cigale/La Boule Noire

*120 bd de Rochechouart,18th (01.49.25.81.75/ www.lacigale.fr). Mº Anvers or Pigalle.* **Open** times vary. **Credit** MC, V. **Map** p402 J2.
One of the city's finest venues, the lovely, horseshoe-shaped Cigale is linked to the more intimate Boule Noire, good for catching cult visiting acts.

### Le Divan du Monde

*75 rue des Martyrs, 18th (01.42.52.02.46/www. divandumonde.com). Mº Anvers or Pigalle.* **Open** times vary. **Credit** MC, V. **Map** p402 H2.
It's come a long way since the days when Toulouse-Lautrec used to sup absinthe here, but the decadent spirit of this old Montmartre haunt has just about survived. Indie, hip hop and electro groups share space with DJs, artists and photographers.

### Elysée Montmartre

*72 bd de Rochechouart, 18th (01.44.92.45.36/www. elyseemontmartre.com). Mº Anvers.* **Open** *Bar* 11am-midnight daily. *Concerts* times vary. **Credit** *Bar* MC, V. **Map** p402 J2.
A reliable, spacious venue in Montmartre. Dancing girls once lifted their skirts here on a regular basis, but these days you're more likely to catch De La Soul

or Ojos de Brujo throwing down some grooves. Also hosts the enduring Le Bal party night and the monthly Open House (*see p329*).

### La Flèche d'Or

*102bis rue de Bagnolet, 20th (01.44.64.01.02/www. flechedor.fr). Mº Alexandre Dumas.* **Open** 8pm-2am Mon, Sun; 8pm-5am Wed-Sat. *Concerts* times vary. Tickets free. **Credit** MC, V. **Map** p403 Q5.
This revitalised indie and electro venue, with credible French and foreign names, and a comfy restaurant area, is definitely worth a look for its frequent free nights.

### Mains d'Oeuvres

*1 rue Charles-Garnier, 93400 St-Ouen (01.40.11. 25.25/www.mainsdoeuvres.org). Mº Garibaldi or Porte de Clignancourt.* **Open** *Bar* 9.30am-midnight daily. *Concerts* 8.30pm, days vary. **Admission** €10. **Credit** *Bar* MC, V.
A hub for fringe musical and performance activity in Paris, this former leisure centre for car factory workers specialises in left-field electro, rock mavericks and multimedia artists.

### La Maroquinerie

*23 rue Boyer, 20th (01.40.33.35.05/www. lamaroquinerie.fr). Mº Gambetta.* **Open** *Box office* (in person only) 2.30-6.30pm Mon-Fri. *Concerts* 8pm Mon-Fri. Closed Aug. **Credit** MC, V. **Map** p403 P4.
Literary discussion and rock 'n' roll co-exist contentedly at this happening hangout. Home to the Inrocks Indie Club nights, featuring up-and-coming Anglo and French rock acts.

### La Mécanique Ondulatoire

*8 passage Thière, 11th (www.lamecond.com). Mº Bastille or Ledru Rollin.* **Open** 6pm-2am Mon-Sat. *Concerts* from 8pm Tue-Sat. **Admission** €3-€6. **Credit** MC, V. **Map** p407 M7.
Cementing Bastille's status as the city's prime hangout for rockers, this exciting new arrival has three levels and mixes scuzzy live acts with eclectic DJs, plus jazz on Tuesday nights.

### Nouveau Casino

*109 rue Oberkampf, 11th (01.43.57.57.40/www. nouveaucasino.net). Mº Ménilmontant, Parmentier or St-Maur.* **Open** *Concerts* times vary. **Credit** *Bar* MC, V. **Map** p403 N5.
Loveable if rather commercial venue run by the adjacent Café Charbon (*see p232*), with great acoustics, gigs and club nights featuring rock, dub and garage, plus reasonable drinks prices. Get sweaty down on the floor or survey the action from the balcony.

### Olympia

*28 bd des Capucines, 9th (08.92.68.33.68/www. olympiahall.com). Mº Opéra.* **Open** *Box office* 10am-9pm Mon-Sat; 10am-7pm Sun. *Concerts* times vary. **Credit** AmEx, DC, MC, V. **Map** p401 G4.
The Beatles, Sinatra, Hendrix and, of course, Piaf all performed here. Now it's mainly a nostalgia shop, but Coco Rosie and Rachid Taha brought some more contemporary sounds in 2007.

**Point Ephémère**. *See p320.*

## Le ParisParis

*5 av de l'Opéra, 1st (01.42.60.64.45/www.*
*leparisparis.com). M° Pyramides.* **Open** 11pm-
6am Tue-Sun. *Concerts* times vary. **Admission**
free. **Drinks** €10. **Credit** MC, V. **Map** p401 H5.
This small, sweaty venue is the one of the newest
additions to Paris nightlife, where many of the capital's most fashional musical figures can be found
hanging out or engaging in iPod battles.

## Point Ephémère

*200 quai de Valmy, 10th (01.40.34.02.48/www.*
*point.org). M° Jaurès or Louis Blanc.* **Open** noon-
2am daily. *Concerts* 8.30pm daily. **Credit** AmEx,
DC, MC, V. **Map** p403 Q5.
Sister venue to Mains d'Oeuvres (*see p318*), this converted warehouse brings together up-and-coming
local rock, jazz and world gigs with a restaurant,
recording studio and exhibitions. *Photos p319.*

## La Scène Bastille

*2bis rue des Taillandiers, 11th (01.48.06.50.70/www.*
*la-scene.com). M° Bastille.* **Open** midnight-6am Wed-
Sun. *Concerts* 7.30pm-10.45pm Mon-Fri. Closed Aug.
**Credit** MC, V. **Map** p407 M7.
This beautifully designed bar and restaurant offers
the option of chilling out in alcoves or joining the
kids to groove to hip hop, funk and jazz.

## Le Trabendo

*211 av Jean-Jaurès, 19th (01.42.01.12.12/www.*
*trabendo.fr). M° Porte de Pantin.* **Open** times
vary. **Credit** MC, V. **Map** p403 inset.
This quirky, futuristic spot in Cité de la Musique has
carved out a niche for all things alternative, anything from post-rock to drum 'n' bass, avant-garde
hip hop to modern jazz.

## Le Triptyque

*142 rue Montmartre, 2nd (01.40.28.05.55/www.*
*letriptyque.com). M° Bourse or Grands Boulevards.*
**Open** 9.30pm-4am Mon-Wed; 9pm-6am Thur-Sat;
8pm-2am Sun. *Concerts* times vary. **Credit** AmEx,
MC, V. **Map** p402 J4.
A focal point for Paris rock, the Triptyque is one of
the hippest places in town, with eclectic programming and a fantastically sweaty moshpit-cum-
dancehall area.

## Rock in bars

### Le Cavern

*21 rue Dauphine, 6th (01.43.54.53.82/www.*
*lecavern.com). M° Odéon.* **Open** 7pm-2am Tue-
Thur, Sun; 7pm-5am Fri, Sat. *Concerts* 10.30pm
Fri, Sat. **Admission** free. **Credit** MC, V.
**Map** p408 H6.
This atmospheric cellar in the heart of St-Germain
pulls in lively crowds for rock and funk groups and
hosts jam sessions on Wednesday nights.

### Le Gambetta

*104 rue de Bagnolet, 20th (01.43.70.52.01/*
*legambetta.free.fr). M° Gambetta.* **Open** 10am-

2am daily. *Concerts* 9pm. **Admission** free-€5.
**Credit** AmEx, DC, MC, V. **Map** p407 Q6.
Small, smoky joint which hosts DJs and local bands
thumping away at their guitars. Despite the official
opening hours, weekend parties have been known
to last all night.

## O'Sullivans by the Mill

*92 bd de Clichy, 18th (01.42.52.24.94/www.*
*osullivans-pubs.com). M° Blanche.* **Open** noon-
5am Mon-Thur, Sun; noon-6am Fri, Sat. *Concerts*
times vary. **Credit** MC, V. **Map** p401 G2.
This Irish chain bar hosts live acts, weekend rock
nights which last until the early hours and salsa sessions on Sundays.

## Le Reservoir

*16 rue de la Forge-Royal, 11th (01.43.56.39.60/*
*www.reservoirclub.com). M° Faidherbe Chaligny or*
*Ledru-Rollin.* **Open** 8pm-2am Mon-Thur; 8pm-5am
Fri, Sat; noon-5pm Sun. **Credit** AmEx, DC, MC, V.
**Map** p407 N7.
This classy, Anglo-inspired venue hosts regular
club nights, stand-up comedy and live indie acts, as
well as low-key performances from larger acts. Also
serves up a jazz brunch on Sundays.

## Chanson

### Chez Adel

*10 rue de la Grange-aux-Belles, 10th (01.42.*
*08.24.61). M° Jacques Bonsergent.* **Open**
noon-midnight Tue-Sun. *Concerts* 5pm Tue-
Sun. **Credit** MC, V. **Map** p402 L3.
Boss Adel is probably the most renowned *chanson*-
café owner in Paris, and this fine address attracts
countless devotees with its repertoire of *chanson* and
eastern European sounds.

### Le Limonaire

*18 cité Bergère, 9th (01.45.23.33.33/limonaire.*
*free.fr). M° Grands Boulevards.* **Open** *Concerts*
10pm Mon-Sat; 7pm Sun. Closed Mon & Sun July,
Aug. **Credit** MC, V. **Map** p402 J4.
A *bistrot à vins* where serious *chanson* takes the
limelight. Performances vary from acoustic, piano-
led *chansonniers* to cabarets.

### Au Magique

*42 rue de Gergovie, 14th (01.45.42.26.10/*
*www.aumagique.com). M° Pernéty.* **Open**
9.30pm Wed, Thur; 10pm Fri, Sat. **No credit
cards.** **Map** p405 F10.
Artiste-in-residence Marc Havet serenades punters
with politically incorrect *chanson* at the weekend.
Expect poetry events and exhibitions too.

### Sentier des Halles

*50 rue d'Aboukir, 2nd (01.42.61.89.96/www.*
*sentierdeshalles.fr). M° Sentier.* **Open** *Concerts*
8-10pm Tue-Sat. **No credit cards.** **Map** p402 J4.
Closer to a concert venue than a music bar, Le
Sentier has developed beyond its traditional *chanson* base to embrace a variety of modern styles.

Arts & Entertainment

# In the name of Justice

Much has been made in the French music press of the new wave of Paris rock acts. But give or take the odd article in the UK, their impact outside France has been minimal. It's a different matter with dance music and electro, however, with Paris regularly being annointed the centre of the clubbing universe.

This happened in the mid-1990s with French Touch, and again last year when Ed Banger became the hippest record label on the planet, just ahead of other Paris prime movers such as Institubes and Record Makers. The label's success is intimately linked with the rise of its flagship group, Justice, comprising former graphic designers Gaspar Augé and Xavier de Rosnay. Back in 2003 Justice entered a radio remix competition with 'Never Be Alone', their take on a song by dreamy British rockers Simian. This effortless hybrid of pop, dance and rock caught the attention of then newly established Ed Banger, who immediately signed the group and made the track their second release. The remix gathered a cult following and went on to win the Best Video award at the 2006 MTV Europe Music Awards. By the time Justice's debut album, *Cross*, was released last year, anticipation

was at fever pitch. And in the meantime, Ed Banger had also been assiduously building up an enviable roster of artists – SebastiAn, Feadz, DJ Medhi, Mr Flash – all of whom were churning out party-starting productions of their own.

Though Ed Banger's current status is the result principally of chutzpah and good fortune, the shrewdness of the enterprise shouldn't be underestimated. After all, label boss Pedro Winter is also the manager of dance pioneers Daft Punk. Justice have, understandably, resisted the 'new Daft Punk' tag, but the parallels are irresistible. While Augé and de Rosnay's look (vintage rock T-shirts, leather, sideburns) is less radical than Daft Punk's robot/helmet guise, they've nevertheless shown a canny grasp of iconography in their use of the cross motif which adorns their album cover and takes centre stage at their live shows.

Justice's recordings, meanwhile, are liberally strewn with the kind of descending, arpeggiated chord sequences that Daft Punk have made their own, though their gritty, overloaded production style and studied trash aesthetic aligns them with rock as well as dance. Perhaps France has got to grips with the language of rock after all?

### Le Vieux Belleville

*12 rue des Envierges, 20th (01.44.62.92.66/www.le-vieux-belleville.com) M° Pyrénées.* **Open** 8pm Thur-Sat. **Credit** MC, V. **Map** p403 N4.
If you desire an authentic Belleville rendezvous, there's no better location than Joseph Pantaleo's old-style café with terrace, where the traditions of accordion music and croaky-voiced *chanson* endure. There's also the occasional exhibition of paintings by local artists.

## Floating venues

### Batofar

*Opposite 11 quai François-Mauriac, 13th (01.53.60.17.30/www.batofar.org). M° Bibliothèque François Mitterrand or Quai de la Gare.* **Open** 9pm-late Wed-Sat. **Admission** €5-€20. **Credit** MC, V. **Map** p407 N10.
Distinctively red, enduringly hip party boat moored by the banks of the Seine in the 13th arrondissement, laying on DJs, rappers and underground noise-merchants for an up-for-it crowd. It comes into its own in the summer, when the terrace opens from 7pm. *See also p332* **The city that never sleeps.**

### Le Cabaret Pirate

*Opposite 11 quai François-Mauriac, 13th (01.44.06.96.45/www.guinguettepirate.com). M° Bibliothèque François Mitterrand or Quai de la Gare.* **Open** 7pm-2am Tue-Thur; 7pm-late Fri-Mon. **Admission** €5-€10. **Credit** MC, V. **Map** p407 N10.
Formerly the Guinguette Pirate, this Chinese junk has drifted away from the cult indie performers of yore and now ploughs a rootsier furrow.

## World & traditional music

### Cité de la Musique

*221 av Jean-Jaurès, 19th (01.44.84.44.84/www.cite-musique.fr). M° Porte de Pantin.* **Open** Tue-Sat (times vary). **Admission** €17-€38. **Credit** MC, V. **Map** p403 inset.
This Villette venue welcomes prestigious names from the four corners of the globe, and also does a fine line in avant-jazz and electronica. *Photo p323.*

### Institut du Monde Arabe

*1 rue des Fossés-St-Bernard, 5th (01.40.51.38.38/www.imarabe.org). M° Jussieu.* **Open** *Concerts* 8.30pm Fri, Sat. **Admission** varies. **Credit** MC, V. **Map** p409 K7.

This huge, plush auditorium attracts some of the biggest names in Arab music. In 2008, there'll be an emphasis on the music of the Mediterranean.

## Le Kibélé

*12 rue de l'Echiquier, 10th (01.48.24.57.74/www. kibele.fr). M° Bonne Nouvelle.* **Open** *Concerts* 9pm Mon-Sat. **Admission** free-€5. **Credit** AmEx, MC, V. **Map** p402 K4.

Music from across the Mediterranean and beyond, with a Turkish restaurant in the same building.

## Satellit' Café

*44 rue de la Folie-Méricourt, 11th (01.47.00.48.87/ www.satellit-cafe.com). M° Oberkampf, Parmentier or St-Ambroise.* **Open** *Bar* 8pm-1am Tue, Wed; 8pm-3am or 5am Thur; 10pm-6am Fri, Sat. *Club* 11pm-6am Thur-Sat. *Concerts* 9pm Tue-Thur (except July, Aug).* **Admission** €10; €8 students. **Credit** *Bar* MC, V. **Map** p403 M5.

This spacious bar lends its sound system to all things global, but the focus is on traditional African music. Great late-night bar too.

## Théâtre de la Ville

*2 pl du Châtelet, 4th (01.42.74.22.77/www.theatre delaville-paris.com). M° Châtelet.* **Open** *Box office* 11am-7pm Mon-Sat. *Concerts* 8.30pm Mon-Fri; 5pm Sun. **Admission** €17; €12 students. **Credit** MC, V. **Map** p408 J6.

Music and dance of the highest order can be found at both sites, with jazz and music from just about anywhere you can think of (Iraq, Japan, Thailand, Brittany) amid the classical recitals.

**Other locations:** 31 rue des Abbesses, 18th.

## La Vieille Grille

*1 rue du Puits-de-l'Ermite, 5th (01.47.07.22.11/ vieille.grille.free.fr). M° Place Monge.* **Open** *Concerts* 8.30pm Mon-Sat; 3pm, 5pm Sun. **Admission** varies. Closed Aug. **No credit cards. Map** p406 K8.

Cosy, artist-run locale, great for theatrical performances of tango, French songs and klezmer, plus operettas, theatre, and children's shows.

## Jazz & blues

## Le Baiser Salé

*58 rue des Lombards, 1st (01.42.33.37.71/ www.lebaisersale.com). M° Châtelet.* **Open** *Chanson concerts* 7pm daily. *Jazz gigs* 10pm daily. **Admission** *in advance* €12-€17. **Credit** AmEx, DC, MC, V. **Map** p406 J6.

The 'salty kiss' divides its time between passing *chansonniers*, world artists and jazzmen of every stripe, from trad to fusion.

## Le Bilboquet

*13 rue St-Benoît, 6th (01.45.48.81.84). M° St-Germain-des-Prés.* **Open** 9am daily. **Admission** (incl 1 drink) €18. **Credit** AmEx, DC, MC, V. **Map** p408 H6.

Latterly revamped in a bid to sharpen up its image, Le Bilboquet is doing a fine job of keeping jazz alive in St-Germain.

## Caveau de la Huchette

*5 rue de la Huchette, 5th (01.43.26.65.05/www. caveaudelahuchette.fr). M° St-Michel.* **Open** 10.15pm daily. **Tickets** €11-€13; €9 students. **Credit** MC, V. **Map** 408 J7.

This medieval cellar has been a Left Bank mainstay for 60 years now. The jazz shows are followed by early-hours performances in a swing, rock, soul or disco vein, and attract a regular student following.

## Caveau des Oubliettes

*52 rue Galande, 5th (01.46.34.23.09). M° Maubert Mutualité or St-Michel/RER St-Michel Notre-Dame.* **Open** 10pm daily. **Admission** free. **Credit** MC, V. **Map** p408 J7.

A foot-tapping frenzy thrives in this medieval dungeon, complete with instruments of torture and underground passages. There are jam sessions in the week if you fancy contributing a note or two to the merry-making.

## Au Duc des Lombards

*42 rue des Lombards, 1st (01.42.33.22.88/www. ducdeslombards.com). M° Châtelet.* **Open** 10pm Mon-Sat. **Admission** €19-€25. **Credit** MC, V. **Map** p406 J6.

Recently refurbished, this small venue is another that has smartened up its act since reopening, although it has always attracted high class players such as Erik Truffaz and Richard Galliano.

## Lionel Hampton Jazz Club

*Hotel Méridien Etoile, 81 bd Gouvion-St-Cyr, 17th (01.40.68.30.42/www.jazzclub-paris.com). M° Porte Maillot.* **Open** 10.30pm Mon-Sat; 10pm Sun. **Admission** (incl 1 drink) €26. **Credit** MC, V. **Map** p400 B2.

This hotel has a strong US bias, with plenty of R&B and gospel, but native acts get a look-in as well. Not particularly progressive, but classy nonetheless.

## New Morning

*7-9 rue des Petites-Ecuries, 10th (01.45.23.51.41/ www.newmorning.com). M° Château d'Eau.* **Open** *Box office* 4-7.30pm Mon-Fri. *Concerts* 9pm daily. **Admission** €15-€21. **Credit** MC, V. **Map** p402 K3.

One of the best for the latest cutting-edge jazz exponents, but with a broad policy embracing *chanson*, blues, world and sophisticated pop.

## Parc Floral de Paris

*Route du Champ de Manoeuvre, Bois de Vincennes, 12th (01.49.57.24.84/www.parcfloraldeparis.com). M° Château de Vincennes.* **Open** *Concerts* (May-July) 4.30pm Sat, Sun. **Admission** €1.50-€3. **No credit cards.**

The most reasonably priced bet for jazz in the summer as the cream of the international jazz world congregate for delightful afternoons in the park. *See also p276.*

## Le Petit Journal Montparnasse

*13 rue du Commandant-René-Mouchotte, 14th (01.43.21.56.70/www.petitjournal-montparnasse.com) M° Gaîté or Montparnasse-*

Cité de la Musique. *See p321.*

Bienvenüe. **Open** *Concerts* 10pm Mon-Sat.
**Admission** (incl 1 drink) €20. **Credit** MC,
V. **Map** p405 F9.
Two-level jazz brasserie in the shadow of the Tour
Montparnasse with Latin sounds, R&B and soul-
gospel. Dinner (€55-€85) starts at 8pm.

### Le Sabot
*6 rue du Sabot, 6th (01.42.22.21.56). M° St-
Germain-des-Prés or St-Sulpice.* **Open** noon-3pm,
6pm-2am Mon-Sat. *Concerts* 9pm. **Admission** free
(drink compulsory). **Credit** MC, V. **Map** p405 G7.
Another tasty jazz-while-you-eat spot, where *gigotin
d'agneau* and jam sessions are on the menu and the
multi-talented owner plays along with guests.

### Les 7 Lézards
*10 rue des Rosiers, 4th (01.48.87.08.97/www.
7lezards.com). M° St-Paul.* **Open** *Concerts* 7pm
& 9pm Mon-Sat. **Admission** free-€18. **No credit
cards. Map** p409 L6.
From fusion to bop, *chanson* to improv, this charming *boîte* in the heart of the Marais provides a nice
alternative to the city's jazz mainstays. Past star
turns include Archie Shepp and Henri Texier. Vocal
or instrumental jams on Sundays (free admission).

### Le Slow Club
*130 rue de Rivoli, 1st (01.42.33.84.30). M° Châtelet.*
**Open** *Concerts* 10pm Fri, Sat. **Admission** €9-€13.
**Credit** MC, V. **Map** p406 J6.
This medieval cellar may be tiny but compensates
with boogie-woogie big bands and dance-friendly
R&B. One of the most famous jazz joints in Europe.

### Le Sunset/Le Sunside
*60 rue des Lombards, 1st (Sunside 01.40.26.21.25/
Sunset 01.40.26.46.60/www.sunset-sunside.com).
M° Châtelet.* **Open** *Concerts* 9pm, 10pm daily.
**Admission** €8-€25. **Credit** MC, V. **Map** p406 J6.
Split-personality venue, with Sunset dealing in electric groups and Sunside catering for acoustic performances. The reputation of both pulls in big names
from both sides of the Atlantic, making this an
essential port of call for any jazz pilgrimage to Paris.

### Théâtre du Châtelet
*1 pl du Châtelet (information 01.40.28.28.00/
booking 01.40.28.28.40/www.chatelet-theatre.com).
M° Châtelet.* **Admission** €16-€69. **Credit** AmEx,
DC, MC, V. **Map** p406 J6.
This venerable theatre and classic music hall has
another life as a jazz and *chanson* venue.

# Nightlife

With Paris DJs and producers rocking the world, see where they head on their days off.

Despite the recent surge in popularity of French electronic music (*see p321* **In the name of Justice**), which has launched a plethora of artists and labels into international stardom over the last year, club life in Paris remains something of an enigma compared to other European cities.

If the new sounds of Paris suggest the city should be jumping with sweat-drenched basements, first appearances are somewhat disappointing. More often than not, however, the parties are going on behind closed doors. Look in the right places, on the right night, and you'll find a deck-diving, dance music mosh pit.

'Over the last year or two the interesting things moved out of the big venues into the smaller 150 capacity venues, with a more specific music programme,' explains DJ Mehdi of Paris dance label Ed Banger. 'It's not rare, for example, to catch [Berlin star DJs] M.A.N.D.Y or Tiefschwarz on a Tuesday night at **Paris Paris**' – not to mention other bijou joints such as **Le Baron** and **La Boule Noire**.

With success has come a discernible reversal of this trend, however, as promoters who were putting on small-but-cool nights a year ago are starting to be snapped up by the bigger venues. The days of finding the whole Ed Banger crew hanging out in a small venue like the tiny but hip Paris Paris are surely numbered.

The advantage of the move into larger spaces is that it makes the scene easier for a visitor to break into: formerly only those with intimate local knowledge would have been able to locate the venue, let alone get past the door. The disadvantage is that bigger nights tend to be one-off events, with the cool labels, DJs and crews – such as Tigersushi, Versatile, Kill The DJ, Bob Sinclar, David Guetta and Dirty Sound system – running their own. But whatever the truth of the matter, clubs like **Rex** and **Point Éphémère** have helped to put Paris back on the global clubbing map after the doldrums of the early noughties.

With Automatik, Rex's leading techno night, celebrating its tenth anniversary, Rex hosting

**La Fourmi**. *See p326.*

a ten-day techno festival in May to mark its 20th birthday, and the reinstated Techno Parade taking place in mid September, 2008 looks set to be a year of almost constant partying. Nights such as the long-running Toxic, the home of veteran DJs Uncle O and Agent Solo, continue to thrive; **Mains d'Oeuvres** is worth keeping an eye on for its infamous occasional parties and regular gigs; and **Le Triptyque** is both somewhere to be seen and to get down in. **Les Bains Douches** is also back on form, drawing a mixed, fashionable crowd.

For big room clubbing the **Mix** is top dog, while the legendary **Queen** continues to pack in a mostly gay crowd. And if you don't know when to stop, there are various after-party options (*see p332* **The city that never sleeps**).

Bastille, the Marais, Oberkampf, the grands boulevards, Pigalle and Canal St-Martin are all littered with bars and small, hip venues. Good starting points for any night out, and useful places to pick up flyers from, are bars such as **La Fourmi**, **Andy Whaloo** and **L'Ile Enchantée**. A number of small venues offer hip hop and Latin nights, although these genres are less well represented in the main clubs, despite an enduring obsession with hip hop. But if dancing to salsa or world beats is your thing, there are options such as the long-serving **La Java** and **La Cabaret Sauvage**.

So, if the streets of Paris sometimes seem a little on the quiet side, don't be fooled. The city is well and truly alive.

## TIPS AND INFORMATION

Useful websites featuring club listings include www.flyersweb.com, www.novaplanct.com, www.radiofg.com and www.lemonsound.com. Radio stations FG (98.2FM) and Nova (101.5FM) also provide listings.

The last métro leaves at around 12.45am and the first one only gets rolling at 5.45am; between those times you'll have to take night buses or taxis. Central Paris is small – it's often possible to walk to your next destination.

## CLUBBING COMMANDMENTS

When clubbing in Paris, local rules apply:
1. Go out late. Parisians like hanging out at home, drinking wine and going for a good meal. This means clubbing generally happens late, so arrive at 1am or 2am.
2. Check flyers in clothes shops and DJ bars for free or reduced entry.
3. Talk loudly in English. Clubs gain kudos for being international and like tourists because they tend to spend more.
4. Order a bottle of spirits at the door at upmarket clubs. It can get you ushered straight past the doorman and is often cheaper than buying a round of drinks by the glass.
5. Avoid turning up with lots of pissed mates. Drunks and large gangs are almost guaranteed not to get in – unless you're all female.

## Club bars

### Andy Whaloo
*69 rue des Gravilliers, 3rd (01.42.71.20.38). M° Arts et Métiers.* **Open** 5pm-2am Tue-Sun. **Admission** free. **Drinks** €2-€10. **Credit** AmEx, MC, V. **Map** p409 K5.
Owned by the people behind Momo and Sketch in London, Andy Whaloo serves sumptuous snack food and is tastefully decorated with Moroccan artifacts. The seating is made from upturned paint cans and the DJs play everything from hip hop to techno. It can be quiet early on (*see p227*), but the atmosphere heats up as the night gets longer.

### Café Chéri(e)
*44 bd de la Villette, 19th (01.42.02.02.05). M° Belleville.* **Open** 11am-2am daily. **Admission** free. **Drinks** €2.80-€6.50. **Credit** MC, V. **Map** p403 M3.
A popular DJ bar, especially in summer, when fashionistas flock to the terrace. Expect anything from DJ Jet Boy's electro punk to house and '80s classics. It's also a chic daytime hangout (*see p232*).

### La Fabrique
*53 rue du Fbg-St-Antoine, 11th (01.43.07.67.07/ www.fabrique.fr). M° Bastille.* **Open** 6pm-5am

Tue-Sat. **Admission** free Tue-Fri; €10 Sat.
**Drinks** €2.50-€11. **Credit** MC, V. **Map** p407 M7.
Local house DJs spin at this bar-club-restaurant on
the busy Fbg St-Antoine stretch. It's surrounded by
several other venues, so you can nip into Sanz Sans
nearby or take your pick of the other bars.

## La Fourmi
*74 rue des Martyrs, 18th (01.42.64.70.35). M° Pigalle.*
**Open** 8.30am-2am Mon-Thur, Sun; 8am-4am Fri, Sat.
**Admission** free. **Drinks** €1.60-€8. **Credit** MC, V.
**Map** p402 H2.
Popular with everyone from in-the-know tourists to
fashionable Parisians, Fourmi was a precursor to the
industrial-design, informal, music-led bars that have
sprung up around Paris – and it's still very much a
style leader. Great throughout the day for coffees
or a beer (*see p226*), it has a small seating area
outside and an always-busy bar with DJ decks. You
can stay into the early hours at weekends, but it's
also a handy pre-club rendezvous and flyer pick-up
point. *Photos p324.*

## L'Ile Enchantée
*65 bd de la Villette, 10th (01.42.01.67.99/http://
lileenchantee.free.fr). M° Colonel Fabien.* **Open** 8am-
2am Mon-Fri; 5pm-2am Sat, Sun. **Admission** free.
**Drinks** €2.20-€6.50. **Credit** MC, V. **Map** p403 M3.
Downstairs this feels like a trendy gastropub;
thanks to an up-to-date music policy, it makes for a
good pre-club drinking venue. Upstairs there's a
bijou disco, which is where you'll find the Paris pre-
club party people taking in the tunes.

## Lizard Lounge
*18 rue du Bourg-Tibourg, 4th (01.42.72.81.34).
M° Hôtel de Ville or St-Paul.* **Open** 4pm-2am daily.
**Admission** free. **Drinks** €6-€8.50. **Credit** AmEx,
MC, V. **Map** p409 K6.
Spread over three levels, Lizard Lounge is a trendy
Marais hangout (*see p229*). There's a boozer upstairs
serving beer in pint glasses and a more full-on DJ
bar in the booth-filled basement – often full, thanks
to its modest proportions. Local jocks play a variety
of contemporary styles.

## La Mezzanine de l'Alcazar
*62 rue Mazarine, 6th (01.53.10.19.99/www.
alcazar.fr). M° Odéon.* **Open** 7pm-2am daily.
**Admission** free. **Drinks** €6-€12. **Credit** AmEx,
DC, MC, V. **Map** p406 H7.
The stylish Conran-owned Mezzanine is the upstairs
posher sister of the Wagg, which is intended to be a
clubbier venue. Naturally both have become well-
heeled hangouts, but the Mezzanine remains the
venue of choice for the suited and booted.

## Project 101
*44 rue de La Rochefoucauld, 9th (01.49.95.95.85/
www.project-101.com). M° Pigalle.* **Open** 10pm-2am
Fri. **Admission** free-€5. **Drinks** €2-€4. **No credit
cards. Map** p401 H2.
While others in Paris have moved on to big times,
this tiny basement venue has kept the bijou vibe.

Connected to an Anglo-French owned shop, it offers
occasional Friday nights featuring experimental
electronic live acts and DJs. Check the website for
details before venturing down.

## Le Troisième Lieu
*62 rue Quincampoix, 4th (01.48.04.85.64/www.
letroisiemelieu.com). M° Rambuteau.* **Open** 6pm-
5am Thur-Sat. **Admission** free. **Drinks** €2.50-€5.
**Credit** MC, V. **Map** p402 K5.
Opened by Les Ginettes Armées, organisers of
renowned Sunday lesbian and mixed events,
Troisième Lieu tends towards electro and house.
The ground floor hosts DJs mixing eclectic sounds
for chatting and relaxing to, while the basement is
more dancefloor-oriented.

## Le Zèbre de Belleville
*63 bd de Belleville, 20th (01.43.55.55.55/
www.lezebre.com). M° Belleville.* **Open** varies.
**Admission** €6-€10. **Drinks** €5-€10. **No credit
cards. Map** p403 N4.
A stylish cabaret/theatre bar used by Dan Ghenacia
and the Freak 'n' Chic posse for after-parties on
Sundays, it's usually a more traditional venue, so
check flyers for event information.

# Cool clubs

## Bateau Concorde Atlantique
*Porte de Solférino, 25 quai Anatole-France, 7th
(01.47.05.71.03/www.concorde-atlantique.com).
M° Assemblée Nationale/RER Musée d'Orsay.*
**Open** *Mid June-mid Sept* 11pm-5am Mon-Fri;
5pm-5am Sat; 6pm-5am Sun. **Admission** free-€10.
**Drinks** €5-€8. **Credit** MC, V. **Map** p401 F5.
With its terrace and voluminous dancefloor, this
two-level boat is a clubbing paradise in the summer.
The legendary Respect crew held a popular, fondly
remembered Wednesday night here and are still,
alongside other cool crews like Ed Banger, involved
in putting on parties at the venue.

## Batofar
*Opposite 11 quai François-Mauriac, 13th (recorded
information 01.53.60.17.30/www.batofar.org).
M° Quai de la Gare.* **Open** 11pm-6am Mon-Sat;
6am-noon 1st Sun of mth. **Admission** €5-€12.
**Drinks** €3.50-€8. **Credit** MC, V. **Map** p407 N10.
In recent years the Batofar has gone through a rapid
succession of management teams, with varying levels of success. The current management has helped
revive the venue's tradition of peddling cutting-edge
music, including electro, dub step, techno and dancehall nights featuring international acts. In summer
clubbers chill on the quayside while DJs play on
deck. Inside are loads of nooks to hide in, and a
robust sound system. It's also a destination for early
morning clubbers determined to dodge their beds.

## Chez Carmen
*53 rue Vivienne, 2nd (01.42.36.45.41). M° Grands
Boulevards.* **Open** 6pm-noon Tue-Sun. **Admission**
free. **Drinks** €5. **Credit** V. **Map** p402 H4.

**Arts & Entertainment**

State-of-the-art sounds at top techno dog **Rex**. *See p330.*

"The *Pink Paradise* The Parisian Dream"
–The Times –

# Pink Paradise

—— PARIS ★ CANNES ★ ST TROPEZ ——

The premiere table dancing club in France presents a dazzling
show with 40 international dancers performing for you
**Monday to Saturday 10 pm - late**

Art Directors : Joanna & Muratt Atik

49-51 rue de ponthieu 75008 Paris – TEL : 01 58 36 19 20 – FAX : 01 58 36 19 21
w w w . p i n k p a r a d i s e . f r  /  m y s p a c e . c o m / s t r i p _ p i n k p a r a d i s e

The tiny but infamous gay-mixed dancefloor is where Paris insomniacs spend their early morning hours hiding from the daylight.

### Le Divan du Monde
*75 rue des Martyrs, 18th (01.42.52.02.46/ www.divandumonde.com). Mº Abbesses or Pigalle.* **Open** 8pm-2am Tue-Thur; 8pm-5am Fri, Sat. **Admission** €6-€30. **Drinks** €3.50-€8. **Credit** AmEx, MC, V. **Map** p402 J2.
Used for one-off parties and regular events, the upstairs specialises in VJ events, while downstairs holds dub, reggae, funk and world music club nights. It's also where the Spoutnik crew holds its rock and electro parties.

### Elysée Montmartre
*72 bd de Rochechouart, 18th (01.44.92.45.38/www. elyseemontmartre.com). Mº Anvers.* **Open** midnight-6am Fri, Sat. **Admission** €10-€15. **Drinks** €4-€10. **Credit** *Bar* MC, V. **Map** p402 J2.
Both a gig venue (*see p318*) and a club, Elysée hosts big nights by outside promoters, such as Open House, Panik and Nightfever, for young clubbers.

### La Flèche d'Or
*102bis rue de Bagnolet, 20th (01.44.64.01.02/ www.flechedor.fr). Mº Alexandre Dumas.* **Open** 8pm-2am Mon-Thur; 8pm-6am Fri, Sat. **Admission** free. **Drinks** €4.50-€11. **Credit** MC, V. **Map** p403 Q6.
This converted railway station reopened under new management and has won over the Paris muso crowd with its adventurous programming, covering everything from electro to punk and *nouvelle chanson. See also p318.*

### Folies Pigalle
*11 pl Pigalle, 9th (01.48.78.55.25/www.folies-pigalle.com). Mº Pigalle.* **Open** midnight-dawn Mon-Thur; midnight-noon Fri, Sat; 6pm-midnight Sun. **Admission** €20 (incl 1 drink); €7 Sun eve. **Drinks** €10. **Credit** AmEx, MC, V. **Map** p402 H2.
The Folies Pigalle's programme includes everything from dancehall and hip hop to techno and electro, fashion shows, go go dancers and striptease shows, plus a gay tea dance on Sunday evenings.

### Le Gibus
*18 rue du Fbg-du-Temple, 11th (01.47.00.78.88/ www.gibus.fr). Mº République or Temple.* **Open** midnight-6am Tue-Sat; 6pm-2am Sun. **Concerts** 8-11.30pm Fri. **Admission** €5-€20. **Drinks** €3-€8. **Credit** *Bar* MC, V. **Map** p402 L4.
A famous 1980s punk venue, Le Gibus has gone through plenty of style changes during its lifetime. Today it takes in R&B, reggae, '80s pop and hip hop on different evenings, plus the occasional 'striptease mixte'.

### Le Glaz'art
*7-15 av de la Porte de-la-Villette, 19th (01.40.36. 55.65/www.glazart.com). Mº Porte de la Villette.* **Open** 8.30pm-2am Thur (occasional Wed); 11pm-5am Fri, Sat. **Admission** €6. **Drinks** €3-€8. **Credit** MC, V. **Map** p403 inset.

This converted Eurolines station is way out north-east, but its strong DJ nights and live acts pull punters in from central Paris. Dub Step, breakbeat, electro and drum 'n' bass nights have made the venue a magnet for breaks fans, and it has a nocturnal garden to chill in. A good destination venue.

### Mains d'Oeuvres
*1 rue Charles-Garnier, 18th (01.40.11.25.25/ www.mainsdoeuvres.org). Mº Garibaldi.* **Open** days and times vary according to event. **Admission** €5-€12. **Drinks** €2-€5. **Credit** *Bar* MC, V.
A rehearsal space and live venue (*see p318*) for new bands. Occasionally the whole building is turned into a club venue with different rooms devoted to different music styles. Look for flyers or keep an eye on the website.

### Nouveau Casino
*109 rue Oberkampf, 11th (01.43.57.57.40/www. nouveaucasino.net). Mº Parmentier.* **Open** midnight-5am Wed-Sat. **Admission** €5-€10. **Drinks** €5-€10. **Credit** *Bar* MC, V. **Map** p403 M5.
Handily surrounded by the numerous bars of rue Oberkampf and tucked behind the legendary Café Charbon (*see p232*), Nouveau Casino is a concert venue (*see p318*) that also hosts some of the city's liveliest club nights from. Local collectives, international names and record labels, such as Versatile, regularly host nights here, making it well worth checking the website for one-offs and after-parties.

Funky mix: **Wagg**. *See p331.*

## Paris Paris
*5 av de l'Opéra, 1st (01.42.60.64.45/www.*
*leparisparis.com). Mᵒ Pyramides.* **Open** 11pm-
5am Tue-Sat. **Admission** free. **Drinks** €10.
**Credit** AmEx, MC, V. **Map** p401 H5.
Still the hottest spot in Paris, and the subject of endless column inches, Paris Paris has the city's club
glitterati regularly passing through its doors, either
to DJ or to enjoy the party – or both. Getting in isn't
easy, but once inside you'll find a bustling basement
where the focus is on having fun, with an on-the-
button music policy.

## Point Ephémère
*200 quai de Valmy, 10th (01.40.34.02.48/www.*
*pointephemere.org). Mᵒ Jaurès or Louis Blanc.*
**Open** 10am-2am daily. **Admission** varies. **Drinks**
€3-€7. **Credit** AmEx, DC, MC, V. **Map** 402 L2.
Generally thought of as a bit of Berlin relocated to
Paris, Point Ephémère is one of the coolest arrivals
on the scene in the last few years. An uncompromising programming policy delivers some of the best
international electronic music to be had in town.
There's also a restaurant and bar with decks and a
gallery, and terrace space by the canal in summer.

## Red Light
*34 rue du Départ, 15th (01.42.79.94.53). Mᵒ Edgar*
*Quinet or Montparnasse Bienvenüe.* **Open** midnight-
11am Fri, Sat. **Admission** (incl 1 drink) €20.
**Drinks** from €10. **Credit** MC, V. **Map** p405 F9.
The former Enfer ('Hell') remains a trance, techno
and house Mecca with local and global DJs spinning
to a young, up-for-it, often gay, well-groomed crowd.
Expect a mixture of local and international DJs.

## Rex
*5 bd Poissonnière, 2nd (01.42.36.10.96/www.*
*rexclub.com). Mᵒ Bonne Nouvelle.* **Open** 11.30pm-
6am Wed-Sat. **Admission** free-€10. **Drinks** €5-€15.
**Credit** Bar MC, V. **Map** p402 J4.
The Rex used its annual August holiday in 2006 to
install a brand new sound system. Revealed to much
fanfare, with over 40 different sound configurations
at the DJ's fingertips, it has proved to be a magnet
for top turntable stars – which isn't surprising. Once
associated with iconic techno pioneer Laurent
Garnier, the Rex has remained at the top of the Paris
techno scene and occupies an unassailable position
as the city's serious club music venue. *Photos p327.*

## La Scène Bastille
*2bis rue des Taillandiers, 11th (01.48.06.50.70/*
*www.la-scene.com). Mᵒ Bastille.* **Open** 7.30pm-
midnight Mon-Thur; 7.30pm-6am Fri-Sun. Closed
Aug. **Admission** €12. **Drinks** €4-€9. **Credit** Bar
MC, V. **Map** p407 M7.
This tastefully decorated club-bar-venue-restaurant
complex holds regular rock concerts (*see p320*), as
well as club events from Thursday to Saturday. The
agenda here changes constantly, so do check what's
on. Popular gay nights too.

## Le Triptyque
*142 rue Montmartre, 2nd (01.40.28.05.55/*
*www.letriptyque.com). Mᵒ Bourse or Grands*
*Boulevards.* **Open** 11.30pm-3am Wed; 11pm-6am
Thur-Sat. **Admission** free-€12. **Drinks** €4-€10.
**Credit** AmEx, MC, V. **Map** p402 J4.
Set amid the hub of club activity around Grands
Boulevards, hip rock venue Le Triptyque has been

**Favela Chic.** *See p332.*

among the top five clubs in Paris since it opened, largely thanks to its varied, spot-on music programming. *See also p320.*

## Wagg

*62 rue Mazarine, 6th (01.55.42.22.00/www.wagg.fr). M° Odéon.* **Open** 11.30pm-6am Fri, Sat; 3pm-midnight Sun. **Admission** €15 Fri, Sat; €10 Sun. **Drinks** €7-€10. **Credit** AmEx, DC, MC, V. **Map** p406 H7.
Refurbished as part of the Conran makeover of La Mezzanine upstairs, Wagg went through a period of attracting big name DJs, but has settled down to be home to a well-to-do Left Bank crowd. Expect funk, house, disco and salsa at weekends. *Photo p329.*

## Glitzy clubs

### Les Bains Douches

*7 rue du Bourg-l'Abbé, 3rd (01.48.87.01.80/ www.lesbainsdouches.net). M° Etienne Marcel.* **Open** midnight-6am Wed-Sun. **Admission** €10-€20. **Drinks** €8-€10. **Credit** AmEx, DC, MC, V. **Map** p402 J5.
Once a global leader, Les Bains lost its way in the 1990s, relying on its reputation to pull in tourists. This all changed recently, and now local star DJs like Busy P and international names such as Erol Alkan grace its decks. It's also home to 6am, one of the city's hottest after-parties, which ends in time for lunch. The clientele is increasingly, but not yet exclusively, gay.

### Le Baron

*6 av Marceau, 8th (01.47.20.04.01/www.cluble baron.com). M° Alma Marceau.* **Open** times vary. **Admission** free. **Drinks** from €10. **Credit** MC, V. **Map** p400 D5.
Owned by André and Lionel, the brains behind Paris Paris, this small but supremely exclusive hangout for the international jet set used to be an upmarket brothel and has the decor to prove it. It only holds 150, most of whom are regulars you'll need to befriend in order to get past the door. But if you manage to get in you'll be rubbing shoulders with celebrities and shiny people.

### Le Cab

*2 pl du Palais-Royal, 1st (01.58.62.56.25/www. cabaret.fr). M° Palais Royal Musée du Louvre.* **Open** 11.30pm-6am Wed-Sat. **Admission** free Tue-Thur; €20 Fri, Sat. **Drinks** €13. **Credit** AmEx, MC, V. **Map** p402 H5.
The Cabaret, now 'Le Cab', is owned by the management behind Club Mix and Queen, and has had an interior facelift by Franco-Japanese designer Ora Ito. R&B and commercial house dominate the playlist.

### L'Etoile

*12 rue de Presbourg, 16th (01.45.00.78.70/www. letoileparis.com). M° Charles de Gaulle Etoile.* **Open** 11pm-5am Mon-Sat. **Admission** €20 (free for women Tue). **Drinks** €16-€20. **Credit** AmEx, DC, MC, V. **Map** p400 C3.

A-list celebrity hangout where guests such as Johnny Halliday, Pamela Anderson and Robbie Williams have been known to show their faces. If you're not A-list, it's seriously hard to get in.

## VIP Room

*76-78 av des Champs-Elysées, 8th (01.58.36.46.00/ www.viproom.fr). M° Franklin D. Roosevelt.* **Open** midnight-5am Tue-Sun. **Admission** free. **Drinks** €20. **Credit** AmEx, DC, MC, V. **Map** p400 D4.
The name says it all for this stylish spot – a hit with the crowd that populates places such as Paris Paris. It has sister venues in Cannes and St Tropez.

## Mainstream clubs

### Club Med World

*39 Cour St-Emilion, 12th (08.10.81.04.10). M° Cour St-Emilion.* **Open** 11pm-2am Tue-Thur; 11.30pm-6am Fri, Sat. **Admission** €15 Tue-Thur; €20 Fri, Sat. Free for women. **Drinks** €9. **Credit** AmEx, MC, V. **Map** p407 N10.
Part of a massive conference, restaurant and club complex in the Bercy Village, Club Med World hosts popular disco and '80s nights at weekends.

### Club Mix

*24 rue de l'Arrivée, 15th (01.56.80.37.37/www. mixclub.fr). M° Montparnasse Bienvenüe.* **Open** 11pm-6am Wed-Sat; 5pm-1am Sun. **Admission** €12-€20. **Drinks** €8. **Credit** MC, V. **Map** p405 F8.
The Mix, formerly Amnesia, has one of the city's biggest dancefloors and DJ booths. Regular international visitors include Erick Morillo's Subliminal and Ministry of Sound parties, while in-house events include David Guetta's 'Fuck Me I'm Famous', 'Hipnotic' and 'One Night With Paulette', plus just about everyone else who's big in France – or anywhere else in the world for that matter.

### La Loco

*90 bd de Clichy, 18th (01.53.41.88.89/www. laloco.com). M° Blanche.* **Open** 11pm-6am daily. **Admission** €10-€20. **Drinks** €6-€8. **Credit** MC, V. **Map** p401 G2.
La Loco has a substantial and youthful following taking advantage of its three dancefloors, which offer different musical genres: house, dance and chart music on weekend nights, and metal and goth concerts during the week.

### Queen

*102 av des Champs-Elysées, 8th (01.53.89.08.90/ www.queen.fr). M° George V.* **Open** midnight-7am Mon-Thur, Sun; midnight-8am Fri, Sat. **Admission** €15 Mon-Thur; €20 Fri, Sat. **Drinks** €10. **Credit** *Bar* AmEx, MC, V. **Map** p400 D4.
Once the citys most fêted gay club (*see p308*) and the only venue that could hold a torch to the Rex, with a roster of top local DJs holding court, Queen's star faded a little in the early noughties, but is now starting to shine more brightly again. Last year it introduced more themed nights and still packs 'em in seven nights a week.

*Arts & Entertainment*

## La Scala

*186bis rue de Rivoli, 1st (01.42.60.45.64/www.
lascalaparis.com). M° Palais Royal Musée du Louvre.*
**Open** 11pm-6am Tue-Sun. **Admission** €12 Tue-
Thur, Sun; €15 Fri, Sat. Free for women Wed-Thur,
Sun. **Drinks** €9. **Credit** MC, V. **Map** p401 H5.

A huge central club with three floors and a commercial music policy that embraces house, techno, R&B,
hip hop, Caribbean music and salsa.

## World, jazz & rock 'n' roll

### Le Cabaret Sauvage

*59 bd Macdonald, 19th (01.42.09.03.09/www.
cabaretsauvage.com). M° Porte de la Villette.*
**Open** 11pm-dawn, days vary. **Admission** €10-€20.
**Drinks** €4-€8. **Credit** AmEx, MC, V. **Map** p403 inset.

A stylish, big top-shaped venue that's taken over by
outside promoters for occasional club nights. In the
old days this often contained a world music element,
but more electronic and drum 'n' bass nights have
begun to be held here and, since the demise of Pulp,
techno label Kill the DJ has started using the venue.
DJ Chloe launched her last album here. Check the
website for one-off nights.

### La Chapelle des Lombards

*19 rue de Lappe, 11th (01.43.57.24.24/http://
chapelle.lombards.free.fr). M° Bastille.* **Open**
11.30pm-6am Tue-Sun. **Admission** free Mon-Wed,
Sun; €15 Thur; €19 Fri, Sat. Free for women Tue-
Thur & before midnight Fri. **Drinks** €6-€12.
**Credit** MC, V. **Map** p407 M7.

With Afrojazz and Latino bands and DJs providing
the music, Latinos and Africans lead the dancefloor
in this popular world music venue.

## Les Etoiles

*61 rue du Château-d'Eau, 10th (01.47.70.60.56).
M° Château d'Eau.* **Open** 9pm-3am Thur-Sat.
**Admission** €10. **Drinks** €4-€6. **Credit** MC, V.
**Map** p402 K3.

Les Etoiles is rumoured to be the oldest music venue
in the city and was home to the burgeoning Paris
salsa scene in the mid 1980s. DJs and bands
still electrify the dancefloor here every weekend,
although these days it's more of a French than a
Latin hangout, and open to beginners – salsa
lessons are available.

### Favela Chic

*18 rue du Fbg-du-Temple, 11th (01.40.21.38.14/
www.favelachic.com). M° République.* **Open** 8pm-2am
Tue-Thur; 8pm-4am Fri, Sat. **Admission** free Tue-
Thur; €10 (incl 1 drink) Fri, Sat. **Drinks**
€6-€19. **Credit** MC, V. **Map** p402 L4.

Situated near the fashionable Canal St-Martin and
Oberkampf, the Brazilian-themed Favela Chic
attracts an international, dressy crowd for some
serious samba and other full-on Latin dancing, DJs,
live acts, plus Brazilian food and drinks. The opening of a sister bar in London has seen the Favela Chic
brand expand into other forms of music, such as
disco punk and electro. *Photo p330.*

### La Java

*105 rue du Fbg-du-Temple, 10th (01.42.02.20.52).
M° Belleville or Goncourt.* **Open** 9pm-3am Wed, Thur;
11pm-6am Fri, Sat; 2pm-2am Sun. **Admission** €5-
€10. **Drinks** €3-€6. **Credit** MC, V. **Map** p403 M4.

Tucked inside the crumbling, disused Belleville market, La Java plays rock, salsa and world music, with
live bands every weekend.

# The city that never sleeps

Compared to London and New York, where
Sunday daytime clubs are an entrenched part
of nightlife activity, Paris after-clubbing is
a relatively small-scale affair. Nevertheless,
after-clubs have played an important role in
the history of the city's club scene. Small
bars and clubs keep the vibe going on a 24-
hour basis, while the established river-based
club scene has become a destination point
for early morning dancing. As with much of
the city's nightlife, after-partying is a matter of
knowing where to look – and that often
requires finding someone with local knowledge
to help out. And remember: in a city that
begins its clubbing activity several hours later
into the night than the UK, even the normal
clubs can feel like an after-party and a night
can feel like it's only just warming up at 5am.

The much-fêted Respect parties, which take
place on the Concorde Atlantique throughout

the summer, begin in the early evening and
don't stop until the sun is high above the
Seine. They're not after-parties as such, but
they will set you up for some sunlit dancing.
For proper after-parties, try smaller venues
such as **Studio 287** (33 av de la Porte
d'Aubervilliers, 18th, 01.49.70.67.27)
or **Le Zèbre de Belleville** (*see p326*).

Closer to the centre, the small, packed
dancefloor of **Chez Carmen** (*see p326*) does
much the same job for a fashionable, sleepy-
shy mixed crowd at the weekend. Also worth
checking out are **Batofar** (*see p326*), which is
historically home of after-parties although
it hosts them less frequently these days,
**Red Light** (*see p330*) and **Nouveau Casino**
(*p329*). Other names to look out for on flyers
include the Families organisation, who like to
keep the crowd rocking 24 hours a day, and
DJ Terry and the Freak 'n' Chic crew.

Arts & Entertainment

# Sport & Fitness

Paris is a city on the move – from Friday night blading to Seine-side bathing.

**Paris St-Germain.** *See p335.*

The modern Olympic Games, as well as football's FIFA, World Cup and European trophies were all planned and developed in the boardrooms of the French capital, and the range of activities available in Paris does justice to the city's proud sporting history.

Much is owed to the dynamic influence of the sports press, particularly the daily newspaper *L'Equipe* and bi-weekly *France Football*. Their fin-de-siècle forebear, *L'Auto*, introduced the world's biggest annual cycling event into the calendar: the **Tour de France** (www.letour.fr). Despite recent doping scandals, the three-week Tour is still a national festival and millions flock to the avenue des Champs-Elysées every July to welcome the riders home. For details of other major sporting events, *see p274-278* **Festivals & Events**.

The Mairie manages many of the facilities across the capital, ensuring very reasonable entry prices. For details, consult its free annual *Parisports: Guide du Sport à Paris* or view the online version at www.sport.paris.fr. If you're looking to buy sportswear and equipment, head for the excellent **Décathlon** (www.decathlon.fr) or **Go Sport** (www.go-sport.com) chain stores.

## Spectator sports

The national stadium is the **Stade de France** (*see p287*), with stations on the RER B (La Plaine Stade de France) and RER D (Stade de France St-Denis) lines one stop from the Gare du Nord. It hosted the memorable football World Cup in 1998 and the rugby World Cup final between England South Africa in 2007.

Indoor events, including judo, basketball, handball and tennis, take place at the **Palais Omnisports de Paris-Bercy** (8 boulevard de Bercy, 12th, 08.92.39.04.90, www.popb.fr, Mº Bercy). The **Stade Roland Garros** (Porte des Mousquetaires, 2 av Gordon-Bennett, 16th, 01.47.43.48.00, www.fft.fr/rolandgarros, Mº Porte d'Auteuil) stages the French tennis open; the **Parc des Princes**, home of Paris St-Germain football club, also hosts rugby and other sporting events.

Tickets for many sports are sold online at www.ticketnet.fr and at branches of **Fnac** and **Virgin Megastore** (for both, *see p272*). For football and rugby internationals held at the Stade de France, contact the respective national associations (www.fff.fr; www.ffr.fr).

**Arts & Entertainment**

# Capital cruising

Parisians take their pastimes very seriously: twice a week rollerbladers take over the city, and cars come to a halt as policemen on skates hold up the traffic.

The city's love affair with skating dates back to the three-week transport strike in 1995, which left train and métro networks paralysed. The rollerblade, previously the preserve of teens with a penchant for speed, became popular as an alternative mode of transport. Sales boomed and skating office-workers became a common sight.

The continued popularity of rollerblading in Paris may have something to do with how manageable the city is on four wheels and a blade. It's possible, for example, to skate from the Bastille in the east to the Eiffel Tower in the west in 40 minutes. Add to this the aesthetic appeal – most of the city's monuments are handily concentrated on the banks of the Seine or tightly packed into the central quarters – and you can begin to understand why skating has become so popular with Parisians of all ages.

Aside from mammoth group skates, the rest of the week sees myriad smaller get-togethers, including moonlit skates, 'wild skates' and processions for the disabled. The two biggest group-skates, **Pari-Roller** (www.pari-roller.com) and **Rollers et Coquillages** (www.rollers-coquillages.org) started out as small meets among friends. Today they are formal associations with thousands of members.

Pari-Roller is for the adrenaline-driven skater. A festive but competitive atmosphere prevails and the 'skate for your life' speed means it is only for the very competent or the foolhardy. Rollerbladers meet at 9.30 pm on Place Raoul Dautry, at the foot of the Tour Montparnasse for the 30km (18-mile) skate around Paris. It lasts until 1am, leaving you enough time to catch the métro home.

If you prefer to take in the sights at a more leisurely speed, you should consider Rollers et Coquillages. The 20km (12.5-mile) skate leaves boulevard Bourdon, by place de la Bastille, every Sunday at 2.30pm. The youngest participants are pushed along in aerodynamic prams and kids as young as seven regularly take part. There's a friendly and supportive atmosphere and staff are happy to help less confident skaters around tricky parts of the circuit. Although both are formal associations, purchasing membership is far from obligatory. And if you'd like to know which sights you will be taking in, both organisations put their planned routes online.

Those who prefer their skating to be done without a police escort have plenty of smaller group skates to chose from. **Rando Plein Lune** meets at the onset of the full moon. The moonlit route is improvised so skaters need to have excellent reflexes and be confident about rolling on any surface the group leader chooses (or else traffic dictates). **321 Bastille Sauvage** meets at 9pm every Wednesday on the steps of the Opéra Bastille and is thought to be the speediest skate.

For those with a physical disability, **Mobil en Ville** (www.mobile-en-ville.asso.fr), an association for people in wheelchairs, frequently joins in the Roller et Coquillage circuit, while the **Montreuillois Rollerskating Club** (RSM http://rs.montreuil.free.fr/handi/hr_index.htm) give rollerblading lessons to the blind and partially sighted.

If you prefer to go at your own pace, the banks of the Seine – from the pont Charles-de-Gaulle to the Quai Tuilleries and from Quai Anatole France to Quai Branly – are closed to traffic on Sunday and bank holidays between 9am and 5pm.

## Basketball

### Paris Basket Racing

*Stade Coubertin, 82 av Georges-Lafont, 16th (01.46.10.93.60/www.parisbasket.net).* M° *Porte de St-Cloud.* **Tickets** from €8. **Credit** MC, V.

PBR are best known as the club where Bruges-born Tony Parker of San Antonio Spurs fame began his career – and this cachet still occasionally brings stars of the NBA to play here.

## Football

### Paris St-Germain

**Stadium** *Parc des Princes, 24 rue du Commandant-Guilbaud, 16th (01.47.43.71.71/tickets & information 32.75/www.psg.fr).* M° *Porte de St-Cloud.* **Tickets** €18-€80. **Credit** MC, V. **Shops** *27 av des Champs-Elysées, 8th (01.56.69.22.22).* M° *Franklin D. Roosevelt.* **Open** 10am-10pm Mon-Thur; 10am-midnight Fri, Sat; noon-8pm Sun. **Credit** AmEx, MC, V. *Parc des Princes.* **Open** 10am-7pm Mon-Sat & 2hrs after game on match days. **Credit** AmEx, MC, V.

Starved of top-class soccer in the capital, a group of donors set up PSG by amalgamating local clubs in 1970. PSG bought top stars to win silverware in the 1980s and '90s, but their star has since faded and the club is now light years away from the Champions League standard set by new superpower Olympique Lyonnais. For tickets, book online and pick them up from any branch of Fnac (*see p272*). *Photo p333.*

## Horse racing

The full racing schedule, the *Calendrier des Courses*, is published by *France Galop* (www.france-galop.com). For information on trotting, consult www.cheval-francais.com. Tickets are €1.50-€8 (free for under-18s). *See also p339* **A day at the races.**

### Hippodrome d'Auteuil

*Route des Lacs, 16th (01.40.71.47.47).* M° *Porte d'Auteuil.*
Steeplechasing in the Bois de Boulogne. The biggest event is the Gras Savoye Grand Steeplechase de Paris on the last Sunday in May.

### Hippodrome de Chantilly

*16 av du Général-Leclerc, 90209 Chantilly (03.44.62.41.00). Train from Gare du Nord.*
Flat racing 40km (25 miles) from Paris. The fashion parade turns out in force for the Prix de Diane Hermès in June; the full length of the course is used for the Prix du Jockey Club the weekend before.

### Hippodrome d'Enghien

*Pl André-Foulon, 95230 Soissy-sous-Montmorency (01.39.89.00.12). Train from Gare du Nord.*
Steeplechasing and floodlit trotting at this course 18km (11 miles) north of Paris.

### Hippodrome de Longchamp

*Route des Tribunes, 16th (01.44.30.75.00).* M° *Porte d'Auteuil then free bus.*
Flat racing in the Bois de Boulogne. This course hosts the racing season's most fashionable social event, the Prix de l'Arc de Triomphe Lucien Barrière. Women in wild hats get in for free.

### Hippodrome de Maisons-Laffitte

*1 av de la Pelouse, 78602 Maisons-Laffitte (01.39.12.81.70). RER Maisons-Laffitte then bus.*
Flat racing.

### Hippodrome de Paris-Vincennes

*2 route de la Ferme, 12th (01.49.77.17.17).* M° *Château de Vincennes/RER Joinville-le-Pont then free bus.*
Trotting in the Bois de Vincennes. Floodlights on winter evenings add to the atmosphere.

### Hippodrome de St-Cloud

*1 rue du Camp Canadien, 92210 St-Cloud (01.47.71.69.26). RER Rueil-Malmaison.*
Flat racing.

## Rugby

### Stade Français Paris

*Stade Jean-Bouin, 26 av du Général-Sarrail, 16th (01.40.71.71.00/www.stade.fr).* M° *Porte d'Auteuil.* **Tickets** €5-€42. **Credit** AmEx, MC, V.
One of the top teams in France. Home matches tend to take place on Saturday evenings.

# Activities & team sports

Some venues require proof of health insurance, ID and passport-sized photos for membership. Note that joining a club usually requires a medical certificate from a doctor.

## All-round sports clubs

The **Standard Athletic Club** (route Forestière du Pavé de Meudon, 92360 Meudon-la-Forêt, 01.46.26.16.09, www.standac.com) is a private sports club aimed at English speakers. Full membership costs €700 per year. There are tennis and squash courts, a heated outdoor pool and workout facilities.

Local multi-sports clubs include **Racing Club de France** (01.45.67.55.86, www.racingclubdefrance.org), **ASPTT de Paris** (01.45.69.01.01, www.aspttparis.com), **Paris Université Club** (01.44.16.62.62, www.puc.asso.fr) and **Stade Français** (01.40.71.33.33, www.stadefrancais.com).

## American football

There are about 15 teams in the suburbs, plus 'no-tackle' flag football teams for men

and women, and cheerleader squads. Contact the **Fédération Française de Football Américain** (01.43.11.14.70, www.fffa.org).

## Athletics & running

Paris has plenty of municipal indoor and outdoor tracks, open to individual runners for a modest monthly subscription; for details see the *Guide du Sport* (*see p333*). Joggers use the banks of the Seine and the parks (Jardin du Luxembourg, Tuileries and Parc de la Villette), as well as the expansive Bois de Boulogne and Bois de Vincennes (which are also gay cruising spots). The Paris Marathon takes place in April (*see p274-278* **Festivals & Events**), while other classic road races include the Paris half-marathon in March and the tough Paris-Versailles in September (www.parisversailles. com). The **Hash House Harriers** organise weekly runs, with four clubs in the Paris region. Log on to parishhh.free.fr or the **Sans Clue HHH** at schhh.free.fr for details.

## Baseball, softball & cricket

Most Paris teams practise in the Bois de Vincennes. The **Fédération Française de Baseball, Softball et Cricket** (01.44. 68.89.30, www.ffbsc.org) has details. An English expat runs the **Château de Thoiry Cricket Club** (78770 Thoiry, 01.34.87.55.70), 40km (25 miles) from Paris. **Paris University Club** (01.44.16.62.62, www.pucbaseball.com) has baseball teams for all ages.

## Basketball

Almost every municipal sports centre has a court and club. Contact the **Fédération Française de Basketball** (01.53.94.25.00, www.basketfrance.com) for details.

## Boules, pool & bowling

For boules or *pétanque*, try square des Arènes de Lutèce (5th) or the *bouludrome* at the Jardin du Luxembourg (6th). Contact the **Fédération Française de Pétanque** (www.petanque.fr) for more information.

Some pool venues require ID or a passport. Paris has 25 ten-pin bowling centres; those listed below rent shoes and stay open late.

### Academy Billard Beaugrenelle
*28 rue Linois, 15th (01.45.79.67.23/www.aka-billard.com)*. **M° Charles Michels. Open** noon-2am Mon-Fri; noon-4am Sat, Sun. **Admission** €10.50-€13.50/hr. **Credit** MC, V. **Map** p404 B8.
The city's largest pool hall has 22 US, five French and four UK tables, plus a DJ.

### Bowling-Mouffetard
*13 rue Gracieuse, 5th (01.43.31.09.35/ perso.orange. fr/bowlingmouffetard)*. **M° Place Monge. Open** 3pm-2am Mon-Fri; 10am-2am Sat, Sun. **Admission** €2-€5.90 per set. *Shoe hire* €1.80. **Credit** AmEx, MC, V. **Map** p406 K9.
Centrally located venue with eight bowling lanes.

### Cercle Clichy Montmartre
*84 rue de Clichy, 9th (01.48.78.32.85/www.academie-billard.com)*. **M° Place de Clichy. Open** 11am-6am daily. **Admission** *Pool* from €10/hr. *Billiards* from €10/hr. **Credit** (€25 minimum) MC, V. **Map** p401 G2.
Historic venue decorated with frescoes, offering a huge bar and pool tables aplenty. No under-18s.

## Climbing

To use any municipal climbing wall, you will need to obtain a personal ID card. Take a photo, your passport, proof of valid insurance and the fee (€4 per month) to the centre you want to use. For the real thing, try the superb boulder formations at the Forêt de Fontainebleau (*see p349*); **Grimporama** (www.grimporama. com) has full details, including maps, on its website. The **Club Alpin Français de Fontainebleau** (01.64.22.67.18, caf77.free.fr) organises group climbs and weekend outings.

### Centre Sportif Poissonnier
*2 rue Jean-Cocteau, 18th (01.42.51.24.68)*. **M° Porte de Clignancourt. Open** 7am-10pm Mon-Sat; 8am-6pm Sun. **Admission** free. **No credit cards.**
The largest of the six municipal walls in Paris.

### MurMur
*55 rue Cartier-Bresson, 93500 Pantin (01.48. 46.11.00/www.murmur.fr)*. **M° Aubervilliers – Pantin Quatre Chemins. Open** noon-11pm Mon-Fri; 9.30am-6.30pm Sat, Sun. **Admission** €12-€14; €6-€7 under-12s. *Joining fee* €23; €12 under-12s. **Credit** AmEx, MC, V.
One of Europe's best climbing walls, with 1,550sq m (16,000sq ft) of wall, 10,000 holds and ice climbing. MurMur also has walls at Issy-les-Moulineaux and Epinay. Hire kit and tuition are available at all sites.

## Cycling

City cycling is growing in popularity thanks to Mayor Delanoë's expansion of bike lanes and the Vélib intiative (*see p164* **Easy rider**). Ideal spots on Sundays and holidays, when roads are traffic-free, are the banks of the Seine, Canal St-Martin and the Bois de Vincennes.

The **Fédération Française de Cyclisme** (01.49.35.69.00, www.ffc.fr) has details of the many local cycle clubs. The **Stade Vélodrome Jacques-Anquetil** (Bois de Vincennes, 12th, 01.43.68.01.27) is regularly open to amateur cyclists, while the circuits by the Hippodromes at **Vincennes** and **Longchamp** (*see p335*)

attract large groups of road cyclists. **Mieux se Déplacer à Bicyclette** (01.43.20.26.02, www.mdb-idf.org) organises free rides for members (€30 per year).

### Gepetto & Vélos
*59 rue du Cardinal-Lemoine, 5th (01.43.54.19.95/ www.gepetto-et-velos.com). Mº Cardinal Lemoine.* **Open** 9am-7.30pm Tue-Sat; 10am-7pm Sun. **Credit** MC, V. **Map** p406 K8.
Rents, sells and repairs all types of bicycles.

### Vélo Bastille
*22 rue Alphonse Baudin, 11th (01.48.87.60.01/ www.parisvelosympa.com). Mº Richard Lenoir.* **Open** 9.30am-6pm Mon, Wed-Fri; 9am-7pm Sat, Sun. **No credit cards**. **Map** p406 L7.
Repairs, rentals and guided cycling tours of the city.

## Diving

Courses for the French diving licence are offered at the **Club de Plongée du 5ème** (01.43.36.07.67), which makes use of the Piscine Jean-Taris (*see p340*) and runs trips to the Med. **Bleu Passion** (94 bd Poniatowski, 12th, 01.43.45.26.29) www.bleu-passion.fr) runs a diving school and sells equipment.

## Fencing

For a list of clubs, consult www.escrime-ffe.fr. The fencing section at the **Racing Club de France** (5 rue Eblé, 7th, 01.45.67.55.86, www.racingclubdefrance.org) is suitable for leisure or competition, with 12 fencing masters and 18 pistes. All levels and ages are welcome.

## Fitness clubs

**Club Med** (www.clubmedgym.fr) dominates the health club scene, with 22 branches in Paris and the western suburbs, including five Waou Clubs with spa facilities. Single visits cost €25 and annual memberships start at €675.

The non-profit **La Gym Suédoise** (01.45.00.18.22, www.gymsuedoise.com) holds one-hour gym sessions in ten locations across Paris. Membership is €75-€110 per term, or €10 per session. Unlike most gyms, there are free trials at specified locations.

There are free weekly 'Sport Nature' sessions of outdoor stretching, aerobics and running, set up by the Mairie at 13 locations around town. Check the annual *Guide du Sport* (*see p333*) or visit www.sport.paris.fr.

### Club Quartier Latin
*19 rue de Pontoise, 5th (01.55.42.77.88/www. clubquartierlatin.com). Mº Maubert Mutualité.* **Open** 9am-midnight Mon-Fri; 9am-7pm Sat, Sun. **Admission** *Pool* from €3.70. *Gym* from €19; from €15 students. **Credit** MC, V. **Map** p406 K7.
Home to the Pontoise pool (*see p340*), this venerable centre off boulevard St-Germain houses no-frills fitness facilities, and has a room for step, aerobics, stretching and yoga classes. There's a sauna too.

Down by the riverside: **Piscine Josephine-Baker**. *See p340.*

## Espace Vit'Halles

*48 rue Rambuteau, 3rd (01.42.77.21.71/*
*www.vithalles.com). M° Rambuteau.* **Open**
8am-10.30pm Mon-Fri; 9am-10pm Sat; 10am-
7pm Sun. **Admission** €25/day. **Credit** AmEx,
MC, V. **Map** p406 K5.

This sunken-level health club has Technogym fitness machines, a sauna and some of the best classes
in the city, particularly for step and spinning; the
classes cost extra.

## Football

For information on the local amateur leagues,
contact the **Ligue Ile de France de Football**
(01.42.44.12.12). To join a weekend kickabout,
try the Bois de Boulogne near Bagatelle, the
Bois de Vincennes or the Champ de Mars.

## Golf

The suburbs are full of top-rated courses
suitable for all levels and budgets. Contact
the **Fédération Française de Golf**
(01.41.49.77.00, www.ffgolf.org) for more info.

### Golf du Bois de Boulogne

*Hippodrome d'Auteuil, 16th (01.44.30.70.00/*
*www.golfduboisdeboulogne.fr). M° Porte d'Auteuil.*
**Open** 8am-8pm daily. **Admission** €4-€5. **Credit**
AmEx, MC, V.

The municipal green has one main course, putting
greens and crazy golf. It's closed on horse-racing
days, so check before you set off.

### Golf National

*2 av du Golf, 78280 Guyancourt (01.30.43.36.00/*
*www.golf-national.com). RER St-Quentin-en-Yvelines*
*then taxi.* **Open** 8am-7pm Mon-Fri; 8am-8pm Sat,
Sun. **Admission** (annual membership €44) €37-€97.
**Credit** MC, V.

The home of the French Open, this has two 18-hole
courses and one nine-hole course.

## Horse riding

To enjoy the horse-riding trails in the Bois de
Boulogne or the Bois de Vincennes, you need
to join a riding club such as **La Société
d'Equitation de Paris** (Centre Hippique
du Bois de Boulogne, 16th, 01.45.01.20.06,
www.equitation-paris.com), the **Centre
Hippique du Touring** (Bois de Boulogne,
16th, 01.45.01.20.88) or the **Cercle Hippique
du Bois de Vincennes** (8 rue de Fontenay,
94130 Nogent-sur-Marne, 01.48.73.01.28).
Beginners can learn at the **Club Bayard
Equitation** in the Bois de Vincennes (Centre
Bayard, UCPA Vincennes, 12th, 01.43.65.46.87,
www.clubbayard.com). Membership runs for
one year (€83), or you can take a special five-
day course in July or August for €275. Out

near Versailles, the **Haras de Jardy**
(boulevard de Jardy, 92430 Marnes-la-
Coquette, 01.47.01.35.30, www.haras-de-
jardy.com) is open every day and offers
lessons by the hour for all ages, with no
membership fee. Leisurely rides in the forests
of Fontainebleau are run by **La Bleausière**
(06.82.01.21.18, la.bleausiere.free.fr).

## Ice skating

The most popular open-air skating rink is the
free one in front of the **Hôtel de Ville**, which
is open from December to February. Smaller
wintertime rinks are also erected at the Tour
Montparnasse and Bilbliothèque. *See also*
*pp274-278* **Festivals & Events**.

### Patinoire de Boulogne

*1 rue Victor-Griffuelhes, 92100 Boulogne-*
*Billancourt (01.46.08.09.09/www.*
*patinoireboulogne.com). M° Marcel Sembat.*
**Open** 4-6pm Mon; 3-6pm Wed; 3.45-5pm Fri;
10.30am-1pm, 3-6pm, 9pm-midnight Sat;
10am-1pm, 3-6pm Sun. **Admission** €5.20;
€4.30 reductions. **No credit cards.**
Year-round indoor rink with free skate rental.

### Patinoire Pailleron

*32 rue Edouard Pailleron, 19th (01.40.40.27.70).*
*M° Bolivar.* **Open** noon-1.30pm, 4-10pm Mon, Tue,
Thur; noon-10pm Wed; noon-1.30pm, 4pm-midnight
Fri; noon-midnight Sat; 10am-6pm Sun. **Admission**
€4; €3 reductions. **No credit cards. Map** p403 N2.

Reopened in 2006, this rink is part of a renovated art
deco sports complex. Skaters can sign up for hockey
and dance lessons on the ice.

### Patinoire Sonja Henie

*Palais Omnisports de Paris-Bercy (01.40.40.27.70/*
*www.bercy.fr). M° Bercy.* **Open** Sept-mid June 3-6pm
Wed; 9.30pm-12.30am Fri; 3-6pm, 9.30pm-12.30am
Sat; 10am-noon, 3-6pm Sun. **Admission** €3-€6. **No
credit cards. Map** p407 N9.

Protection, helmets and skates for hire (€3).

## In-line skating

*See p334* **Capital cruising**.

## Rowing & watersports

Paris residents can row, canoe and kayak for
free on Saturdays at the **Base Nautique
de la Villette** (41bis quai de la Loire, 19th,
01.42.40.29.90). Reserve a week in advance and
bring along proof of residence, two photos and
a swimming certificate (obtainable at any pool).
You can go waterskiing and wakeboarding
at the **Club Nautique du 19ème** (Bassin
de Vitesse de St-Cloud, 92100 Boulogne-
Billancourt, 01.42.03.25.24). Serious rowers
can join the annual **Traversée de Paris,**

**Arts & Entertainment**

part of the Randon'Aviron EDF outings open to the public. Contact the **Ligue Ile-de-France d'Aviron** (94736 Nogent-sur-Marne, 01.48. 75.79.10). For a leisurely paddle, hire a boat at **Lac Daumesnil** or **Lac des Minimes** in the Bois de Vincennes, or at **Lac Supérieur** in the Bois de Boulogne.

## Rugby

For a good standard of play, try the **Athletic Club de Boulogne** (Stade du Saut du Loup, av de la Butte-Mortemart, 16th, 01.46.51.11.91), which fields two teams. The **British Rugby Club of Paris** (58-60 av de la Grande-Armée, 17th, 01.40.55.15.15, www.brfcparis.com) fields two teams in the corporate league.

## Skateboarding

In 2008, the inauguration of the **Espace Glisse de Paris** (Stade des Fillettes, 54 bd Ney, 18th) will provide skateboarders with a space to hone their skills. Among the most popular public places to skate are the riverfront courtyard at the **Palais de Tokyo** (*see p120*), known as 'Le Dôme', and the ledges and steps at **Trocadéro** (16th). **La Défense** (*see p183*) tends to be full of security guards, but is still worth exploring for smooth marble, ledges and rails; the **Palais Omnisports de Paris-Bercy** (*see p333*) has vast ledges and some almighty gaps.

A more relaxed scene is found at the **place des Innocents** (by the Forum des Halles, 1st), with low ledges and smooth ground, and at the **Opéra Bastille** (11th), with small steps. Check www.paris-skate-culture.org or ask at skateshop **Street Machine**, also in Les Halles (12 rue des Halles, 1st, www.streetmachine.fr).

### Cosanostra Skatepark
*18 rue du Tir, 77500 Chelles (01.64.72.14.04/ www.cosanostraskatepark.net). RER Chelles-Gournay.* **Open** *July, Aug* 2-8pm Mon-Wed, Sat; 2-11pm Thur, Fri; 2-7pm Sun. *Sept-June* 4-11pm Tue, Thur, Fri; 2-8pm Sat; 2-7pm Sun. **Admission** €6. *Season ticket* €205; €190 under-13s. **No credit cards.**
A huge indoor street course and micro-ramp, which hosts international competitions.

## Squash

No membership is necessary to play squash at the **Club Quartier Latin** (*see p337*), which charges €17-€25 per match (racket rental from €2.50). The **Standard Athletic Club** (*see p335*) also rents squash courts to members or on payment of a €185 seasonal fee.

### Squash Montmartre
*14 rue Achille-Martinet, 18th (01.42.55.38.30/www. squash-montmartre.com). M° Lamarck Caulaincourt.* **Open** 10am-11pm Mon-Fri; 10am-7pm Sat, Sun. **Admission** from €11. **Credit** V.
Period memberships available, plus equipment hire.

# A day at the races

There are seven racetracks in and around Paris, catering for flat racing, steeplechasing and, a French favourite this, trotting.

The latter takes place at the **Hippodrome de Vincennes** (*see p335*) on the eastern edge of the city. The two-wheeled chariots make for an exciting and colourful spectacle. Racing under floodlights in the winter adds to the atmosphere. Purists, though, may prefer steeplechasing at **Auteuil** (*see p335*) in the Bois de Boulogne. Meetings take place every weekend during the season. Access to the *pelouse* is free, though the facilities are a little basic. It's worth paying for a seat in the *tribune* (grandstand). The season's highlight is the **Gras Savoye Grand Steeplechase de Paris** on the last Sunday in May.

As for flat racing, the most important date in the calendar is the **Prix de l'Arc de Triomphe Lucien Barrière** at Longchamp (*see p335*). The 'Arc' is as much a social

and fashion event as a sporting one (women get in free provided their headgear is sufficiently flamboyant). The same is true of the **Prix de Diane Hermès**, held each June at **Chantilly** (*see p335*). This event attracts a well-heeled crowd as interested in the contents of their picnic hampers as they are in their betting slips.

There are no bookmakers on French racecourses: all betting is done under the auspices of the state-owned PMU. For odds (*la cote*) and tips, visit www.pmu.fr, www. paris-turf.com or buy the day's edition of *L'Equipe*. A *pari simple* is a bet on one horse, for one race, to win (*gagnant*) or to be placed (*placé*). A *jumelé* is two horses in the correct order, a *jumelé placé* two horses placed in the first three past the post. A *trio* is the same for three horses. The *quinté* of five horses in the right order is offered once during every meeting.

# Swimming

Pools are plentiful and cheap. Most require a swimming cap and ban bermudas, and many are open late. Swimming to music is integral to Nuit Blanche in October (see p276 **Up all night**). Times given below may change during school and national holidays.

## Aquaboulevard

*4 rue Louis-Armand, 15th (01.40.60.10.00/ www.aquaboulevard.com). M° Balard.* **Open** 9am-11pm Mon-Thur; 9am-midnight Fri; 8am-midnight Sat; 8am-11pm Sun. **Admission** *6hrs* €25; €10 reductions. **Credit** AmEx, MC, V. **Map** p404 A10.
With year-round summer temperatures, this tropical water park under a giant atrium is great fun for kids. An extra charge gets you a steam bath and three saunas of varying intensity.

## Piscine Butte-aux-Cailles

*5 pl Paul-Verlaine, 13th (01.45.89.60.05). M° Place d'Italie.* **Open** 7-8.30am, 11.30am-1.30pm, 4.30-7pm Tue; 7am-7pm Wed; 7-8.30am, 11.30am-6.30pm Thur, Fri; 7-8.30am, 10am-6.30pm Sat; 8am-6pm Sun. **Admission** €2.60; €1.50 reductions. **Credit** AmEx, MC, V.
This listed complex, built in the 1920s, has one main indoor pool and two outdoor pools (open in the summer). The water is a warm 28°C, thanks to the natural sulphurous spring.

## Piscine Georges-Vallerey

*148 av Gambetta, 20th (01.40.31.15.20). M° Porte des Lilas.* **Open** 10am-6pm Mon, Wed, Fri; 10am-2pm, 3pm-10pm Tue, Thur; 9am-5pm Sat, Sun. **Admission** €2.60; €1.50 concessions. **Credit** (€15 minimum) MC, V.
Built for the 1924 Olympics, this complex features a retractable Plexiglas roof, a 50m pool and one for kids. It reopened in 2005 after renovation.

## Piscine Jean-Taris

*16 rue Thouin, 5th (01.55.42.81.90). M° Cardinal Lemoine.* **Open** 7-8am, 11.30am-1pm Tue, Thur; 7-8am, 11.30am-5.15pm Wed; 7-8am, 11.30am-1pm, 5-7.45pm Fri; 7am-5.15pm Sat; 8am-5.15pm Sun. **Admission** €2.60; €1.50 concessions. **Credit** V. **Map** p406 J8.
This 25m pool has huge bay windows overlooking a sloping garden, with the Panthéon visible just above the trees. Mixed showers and locker area.

## Piscine Josephine-Baker

*Quai François-Mauriac, 13th (01.56.61.96.50). M° Quai de la Gare.* **Open** 7-8.30am, 1-3pm, 5-9pm Mon; noon-5pm, 7pm-midnight Tue; 7-8.30am, 1-9pm Wed; noon-3pm, 5-9pm Thur; 7-8.30am, 1-5pm, 7pm-midnight Fri; 10am-8pm Sat, Sun. **Admission** €2.60; €1.50 reductions. **Credit** MC, V. **Map** p407 M10.
Moored on the Seine by the Bibliothèque Nationale, the Piscine Josephine-Baker boasts a 25m main pool, a paddling pool and café. *Photo 337.*

## Piscine Pontoise Quartier Latin

*18 rue de Pontoise, 5th (01.55.42.77.88/www. clubquartierlatin.com). M° Maubert Mutualité.* **Open** 7-8.30am, 12.15-1.30pm, 4.30-11.45pm Mon, Tue; 7-8.30am, 12.15-11.45pm Wed; 7-8.30am, 12. 15-1.30pm, 4.30-7.15pm, 9-11.45pm Thur; 7-8.45am, noon-1.30pm, 4.30-11.45pm Fri; 10am-7pm Sat; 8am-7pm Sun. **Admission** €3.70; €2.20 reductions; €9.50 for all 9-11.45pm. **No credit cards. Map** p406 K7.
A beautiful art deco pool with two mezzanine levels. It has private locker rooms, plus night swimming to underwater music. Small fee for lockers.

## Piscine Suzanne-Berlioux

*Forum des Halles, 10 pl de la Rotonde, 1st (01.42. 36.98.44). M° Les Halles.* **Open** 11.30am-10pm Mon, Tue; 10am-10pm Wed; 11am-10pm Thur, Fri; 9am-7pm Sat, Sun. **Admission** €3.80; €3 under-16s. **Credit** (€8 minimum) MC, V. **Map** p402 J5.
Although usually busy, this 50m pool with its own tropical greenhouse is good for lane swimming – but there are no lockers (check in your belongings with the attendants).

# Tennis & table tennis

The Paris Tennis system (01.71.71.70.70, www.tennis.paris.fr) allows you to register a password and reserve a court online, €6.50 per hour, €12.50 for indoor courts. Among the 40 municipal courts, the six at the **Jardin du Luxembourg** (01.43.25.79.18) are convenient, but there's a better selection at the **Centre Sportif La Faluère** (route de la Pyramide, 12th, 01.43.74.40.93) in the Bois de Vincennes.
To find public table-tennis tables in parks around town, consult the *Guide du Sport* (see p333). Find club details at www.paristt.com.

## Centre Sportif Suzanne-Lenglen

*2 rue Louis-Armand, 15th (01.44.26.26.50). M° Balard.* **Open** 7am-10pm Mon-Fri; 7am-7pm Sat, Sun. **Admission** from €3. **No credit cards. Map** p404 A10.
Fourteen courts, two of which are covered.

## Club Forest Hill

*4 rue Louis-Armand, 15th (01.40.60.10.00/www. aquaboulevard.com). M° Balard/RER Bd Victor.* **Open** 9am-11pm daily. **Admission** prices vary. **No credit cards. Map** p404 A10.
Tennis, table tennis and other racquet sports at most of the dozen branches in and around Paris.

# Triathlon

The multi-discipline effort of triathlon (swim, bike, run) is one of Europe's fastest growing sports, and the Paris area hosts some of the sport's biggest clubs, including Beauvais, Poissy and Sartrouville. For details of local clubs, contact the Ligue Ile de France de Triathlon (www.idftriathlon.com).

# Theatre

From Peter Brook to *banlieue* fringe, it's a full house in the city of light.

Theatre in Paris is growing ever more global. Brit-born Peter Brook has been spellbinding Paris theatregoers with his programming and directing at the **Théâtre des Bouffes du Nord** since the 1970s, and now the stalwart of French Classical repertoire, the **Théâtre de l'Odéon,** has added the words 'de l'Europe' to its name and is filling its revamped auditorium with performances in a multitude of European languages. Meanwhile, **MC93 Bobigny,** in the suburbs, hosts international companies performing in their own tongues; and John Malkovich is proving a dab hand at directing French actors in adaptations of English-language plays (Terry Johnson's *Hysteria* in 2005 at the **Théâtre Marigny** and Zach Helm's *Good Canary* in 2007 at the **Comédia**).

On the French front, you'll still find highbrow, state-run institutions headed up by the **Comédie Française,** plus a long list of independent theatres that tend to have more populist appeal but provide opportunities for on-the-up thespians to make a bob and a name. There are exceptions, of course: the audience magnet in 2007 was Charlotte Rampling in Strindberg's *La Danse de Mort* (The Dance of Death) at the **Théâtre de la Madeleine.**

As you would expect from the city where Ionesco's absurdist *La Cantatrice Chauve* was premiered (in 1950), and is still running with over 16,000 performances under its belt (at the **Théâtre de la Huchette**), experimental theatre is strong. The **Théâtre National de Chaillot, Théâtre du Rond Point** and **Théâtre de la Ville** all show relentlessly new and exciting spectacles combining off-the-wall theatre with dance or music. In the Bois de Vincennes, a special theatre bus takes you to the **Cartoucherie,** a factory remade as a theatre commune that's home to five exciting and innovative companies. And in the Parc de la Villette, the **Théâtre de la Villette** (211 av Jean-Jaurès, 19th, 01.40.03.72.23, www.theatre-paris-villette.com) presents contemporary, multi-disciplinary productions.

## BEYOND THE PERIPHERIQUE

Culture doesn't just end at the city ring-road (*see pp44-46*): a combination of government funding designed to bring theatre to the masses and extortionate rental rates for independent productions inside Paris has led to the creation of several excellent out-of-town venues. In the north-east, **MC93 Bobigny** (1 bd Lénine, 93000 Bobigny, 01.41.60.72.72, www.mc93.com) is a slick institution dedicated to promoting global cross-cultural exchange with visiting companies from across France and abroad. Its 2008 Standard Idéal festival offers a sweeping panorama of theatrical genres with everything

**Odéon, Théâtre de L'Europe.** *See p344.*

from an adaptation of Michel Houellebecq's controversial novel *Platform*, to a German take on Molière's pessimistic analysis of bourgeois society, *Der Tartuffe*, by the Thalia Theater Hamburg troupe. The **Théâtre Gérard-Philipe** (59 bd Jules-Guesde, 93207 St-Denis, 01.48.13.70.00, www.theatregerardphilipe.com), housed in a century-old building and directed by Alain Ollivier, offers quality fare for the 2008 season, ranging from Corneille to the Et Moi Alors? festival for youngsters. Just beyond La Défense's lofty towers, the **Théatre Nanterre Amandiers** (7 av Pablo Picasso, 92022 Nanterre, 01.46.14.70.00, www.nanterre-amandiers.com, shuttle bus from RER Nanterre-Préfécture 1hr before show) provides an eclectic mix of probing modern theatre (often of a sticky political nature), as well as the great classics and occasional opera.

### PLAYING IN ENGLISH

Catching a play in English in Paris isn't as difficult as you might think. Productions in English, German, Spanish and Italian come to the Théâtre de l'Odéon, Théâtre des Bouffes du Nord, **Théâtre de la Cité Internationale**, MC93 Bobigny and the versatile stage at the Centre Pompidou (pl Georges-Pompidou, 4th, 01.44.78.12.33, www.cnac-gp.com).

Several devoted companies also keep the scene pulsating with a range of English-language shows and English translations of French works: 2008 promises yet more Anglo-American repertoire from the **Glasshouse** (glasshouse.monsite.orange.fr) company, whose previous pieces include a successful revival of Jean Genet's *The Maids* and *Little Women*. Local improv troupe the **Improfessionals** (www.improfessionals.com) have been treading the boards of central Paris for the last six years offering off-the-cuff stuff; the **Mondays at 7** troupe (www.mondaysat7.com) at the Sudden Théâtre (14bis rue Ste-Isaure, 18th, 01.42.62.35.00, www.suddentheatre.fr) puts on plays by British and Irish playwrights most Monday evenings; and in 2008 the **Théâtre en Anglais** group (4 bis rue de Strasbourg, 92600 Asnières, 01.55.02.37.87, theatre.anglais.free.fr) is putting on a well-crafted interpretation of Pinter's *The Dumb Waiter* at the Théâtre Silvia Monfort (106 rue Brancion, 15th, 01.56.08.33.88, www.theatresilvia monfort.com). Shakespeare in English is performed every June in the Bois de Boulogne's Théâtre de Verdure du Jardin Shakespeare (08.20.00.75.75) by the **Tower Theatre Company** (www.towertheatre.org.uk).

If you fancy grabbing a lesson or two while you're in Paris, check out the **Method Acting Center** (115 rue du Fbg-du-Temple, 10th,

01.42.49.78.13, www.methodacting.fr) which offers a wide range of classes for budding actors and seasoned professionals.

### TICKETS AND INFORMATION

For listings, look in the 'Théâtre' section of the weekly *L'Officiel des Spectacles* and *Pariscope*. Further information can be found at www.paris voice.com. Tickets can be bought at the theatres, from **Fnac** or **Virgin Megastore** (for both, *see p272*) or online at www.theatreonline.com. Check out www.theatresprives.com for half-price tickets to performances during the first week of a new show. Two agencies that sell same-day half-price tickets are the **Kiosque de la Madeleine** (15 pl de la Madeleine, 8th, closed Mon) and the **Kiosque Montparnasse** (parvis de la Gare Montparnasse, 15th, closed Mon), although these tend to be for the big commercial shows only. Queues can be long, and there's no way to contact the kiosks by phone or internet. For students, special subscriptions are available at many theatres.

## Right Bank

### Cartoucherie de Vincennes

*Route du Champ de Manoeuvre, Bois de Vincennes, 12th. M° Château de Vincennes, then shuttle bus.*
**Théâtre de l'Aquarium** *(01.43.74.99.61/ www.theatredelaquarium.com).*
**Théâtre du Chaudron** *(01.43.28.97.04/ www.theatreduchaudron.fr).*
**Théâtre de l'Epée de Bois** *(01.48.08.39.74/ www.epeedebois.com).*
**Théâtre du Soleil** *(01.42.74.87.63/ www.theatre-du-soleil.fr).*
**Théâtre de la Tempête** *(01.43.28.36.36/ www.la-tempete.fr).*
Past the Château de Vincennes in the middle of the woods, five independent theatres, each with its own troupe, offer first-class, politically committed fare. This drama-lover's heaven is housed in ex-army munitions warehouses, where you will be met with home-made soup, a forest backdrop and, on a clear night, a starry sky.

### Comédia

*4 bd de Strasbourg, 10th (01.42.38.22.22/www. theatrecomedia.com). M° Strasbourg St-Denis.*
**Box office** 11am-7pm Mon-Sat. **Admission** varies. **Credit** MC, V. **Map** p402 K4.
This former 19th-century music hall hosted the likes of Mistinguett and Maurice Chevalier before being demolished and rebuilt as a cinema in 1933. Revamped back into a theatre in the 1970s, it has hosted musicals and operettas as well as traditional French boulevard comedies. Nowadays the Comédia rents its space to anyone with a wallet and a name. In 2007, that meant a French version of the musical *Fiddler on the Roof* and John Malkovich's take on Zach Helm's *Good Canary*.

# All the world's a stage

Say farewell to red velvet curtains, sneaky tipples during entr'actes, high ceilings, padded seats and gilded cherubs. If you want a real taste of the city's fringe theatre, you'll need a nose for adventure, a penchant for the unconventional and an eye so keen it can actually find the venues, which are more often than not hidden down side streets, and not necessarily in central Paris. You see, Paris has one major problem: there are more troupes than there are places to play in – an unfortunate imbalance that is being addressed by a handful of enterprising thespians willing to turn anything and anywhere into a stage. Venues ranging from factories and multidisciplinary arts squats to old washhouses, psychiatric hospitals and train stations have become the new cradle for some of the city's most original and experimental drama.

The bastion of alternative theatre in the north of Paris is the **Lavoir Moderne Parisien** (35 rue Léon, 18th, 01.42.52.09.14, www.rueleon.net, Mº Château Rouge or Marcadet Poissonniers). Housed in an old washhouse (lavoir) in the Goutte d'Or district, performances cover themes of immigration, identity and potential in modern society.

Further east in the 20th, the near invisible **Confluences** (190 bd de Charonne, 20th, 01.40.24.16.34, www.confluences.net, Mº Alexandre Dumas) – go through a discreet gate and walk to the end of the courtyard – is a veritable cultural laboratory that brings together artists from several disciplines. The pickings here are both unconventional and accessible, giving pride of place to original texts by little-known authors. Just down the road, **Goumen Bis** (2bis Cité Aubry, 20th, Mº Alexandre Dumas) lives life on the edge as an artists' squat constantly threatened with closure. The fare is hard-hitting and political.

**Point Ephemère** (200 quai de Valmy, 10th, 01.40.34.02.48, www.pointephemere.org, Mº Jaurès) is a cool urban arts centre led by its gargantuan older brother **Mains d'Oeuvres**,

set inside an old warehouse in the suburb of St-Ouen (1 rue Charles Garnier, 93400 St Ouen, 01.40.11.25.25, www.mains doeuvres.org, Mº Garibaldi or Porte de Clignancourt). Both stage performances (often surrealist) by some of the most interesting troupes in town, combining theatre, dance, music and the visual arts.

The banlieue is livelier than ever. In Bagnolet, **L'Echangeur** (59 av du General de Gaulle 93170 Bagnolet, 01.43.62.71.20, www.lechangeur.org, Mº Gallieni) and **Le Colombier de Bagnolet** (20 rue Marie-Anne Colombier, 93170 Bagnolet, 01.43.60.72.81, Mº Porte des Lilas) showcase works by up-and-coming authors whose theatrical tendencies cover the wide spectrum between slapstick comedy and dark tragedy.

Housed within the walls of a former metal factory, **Les Laboratoires d'Aubervilliers** (41 rue Lecuyer, 93300 Aubervilliers, 01.53.56.15.90, www.leslaboratoires.org, Mº Pantin-Quatre Chemins) churn out some wonderful, high-concept productions that frequently mix acting with the disciplines of other resident artists (video, sound, dance, etc). For a creepier experience, try **Les Anciennes Cuisines de Ville-Evrard** (202 av Jean-Jaurès, 93330 Neuilly-sur-Marne, 01.43.09.35.58, RER A Neuilly Plaisance then Bus 113 towards Chelles) dilapidated kitchens set in an annexe building of the town's psychiatric hospital, where the Vertical Détour troupe performs contemporary creations that frequently explore the topics of insanity and happiness.

**Gare au Théâtre** (13 rue Pierre Sémard, 94400 Vitry-sur-Seine, 01.55.53.22.22, www.gareautheatre.com, RER C Vitry-sur-Seine), as its name suggests, is an arts centre and theatre in Vitry-sur-Seine's former train station. Once again, performances tend to be of an experimental nature, promoting the arts in general. For more information about fringe theatre in Paris, go to www.actesif.com.

## Comédie Française

*www.comedie-francaise.fr.*
**Salle Richelieu** *2 rue Richelieu, 1st (08.25.10.16.80/01.44.58.15.15). Mº Palais Royal Musée du Louvre.* **Box office** 11am-6.30pm daily. **Admission** €11-€37. *1hr before show* €5 for cheapest seats only; €11 under-27s. **Credit** AmEx, MC, V. **Map** p401 H5.

**Studio-Théâtre** *Galerie du Carrousel du Louvre, 99 rue de Rivoli, 1st (01.44.58.98.54/01.44.58.98.58). Mº Palais Royal Musée du Louvre.* **Box office** 2-5pm on performance day. **Admission** €11-€37. **Credit** MC, V. **Map** p401 H5.
**Théâtre du Vieux Colombier** *21 rue du Vieux Colombier, 6th (01.44.39.87.00/01.44.39.87.01). Mº St-Sulpice.* **Box office** 1-6pm Mon, Sun; 11am-6pm

Arts & Entertainment

Tue-Sat. **Admission** €28. *45 mins before show* €13 under-27s. **Credit** MC, V. **Map** p405 G7.

The gilded mother of French theatres, the Comédie Française turns out season after season of classics, as well as lofty new productions. The red velvet and gold-flecked Salle Richelieu is located right by the Palais-Royal; under the same umbrella are the Studio-Théâtre, a black box inside the Carrousel du Louvre, and the Théâtre du Vieux Colombier. The line-up for 2008 includes Molière's *Le Misanthrope* and Edmond Rostand's *Cyrano de Bergerac.*

## Théâtre de la Bastille

*76 rue de la Roquette, 11th (01.43.57.42.14/ www.theatre-bastille.com). M° Bastille or Voltaire.* **Box office** 10am-6pm Mon-Fri; 2-6pm Sat. **Admission** €13-€20. **Credit** MC, V. **Map** p407 N6.

The Bastille is a little smaller, a little edgier and a little funkier than many Paris theatres, showing plenty of effervescent and exotic productions.

## Théâtre des Bouffes du Nord

*37bis bd de la Chapelle, 10th (01.46.07.34.50/ www.bouffesdunord.com). M° La Chapelle.* **Box office** 11am-6pm Mon-Sat. **Admission** €10-€24. **Credit** MC, V. **Map** p402 K2.

This recently renovated landmark theatre has been Peter Brook's playground for more than 30 years. In 2008, expect epic delights such as Samuel Beckett's *Fragments,* directed by Brook himself.

## Théâtre de la Madeleine

*19 rue de Surène, 8th (01.42.65.07.09/www. theatremadeleine.com). M° Madeleine.* **Box office** 11am-7pm daily. **Admission** €14-€32. **Credit** MC, V. **Map** p401 F4.

Molière and other classic playwrights get a good thrashing here but so do contemporary authors, with everything from Existentialist tragedy to intelligent comedy on show.

## Théâtre Marigny

*Av de Marigny, 8th (01.53.96.70.30/www.theatre marigny.fr). M° Champs Elysées Clemenceau or Franklin D. Roosevelt.* **Box office** 11am-6.30pm Mon-Sat; 11am-3pm Sun. **Admission** €37-€72. **Credit** MC, V. **Map** p401 E4.

Théâtre Marigny is one of the most expensive nights out for theatregoers in Paris. But then not many other theatres can boast a location off the Champs-Elysées, a deluxe interior conceived by Charles Garnier of Opéra fame, high-profile casts and an illustrious pedigree stretching back 150 years.

## Théâtre National de Chaillot

*1 pl du Trocadéro, 16th (01.53.65.30.00/ www.theatre-chaillot.fr). M° Trocadéro.* **Box office** 11am-7pm Mon-Sat. **Admission** €12-€33. **Credit** MC, V. **Map** p400 B4.

Get here early, grab a cocktail and gaze in awe at the Eiffel Tower through the lobby window. Chaillot's three auditoriums range from intimate and experimental to a 2,800-seater amphitheatre. Highlights for 2008 include Shakespeare's *A Midsummer Night's Dream* in German, and Flamenco dance and music.

## Théâtre du Rond Point

*2bis av Franklin D Roosevelt, 8th (01.44.95.98.21/ www.theatredurondpoint.fr). M° Champs-Elysées Clemenceau or Franklin D. Roosevelt.* **Box office** noon-7pm Tue-Sat, noon-4pm Sun. **Admission** €10-€33. **Credit** MC, V. **Map** p401 E4.

More than just a theatre, this historical venue doubles up as a bookshop, tearoom and restaurant. So once you've fed your mind on contemporary, avant-garde and sometimes politically slanted theatre, make a night of it and opt for dinner as well.

## Théâtre de la Ville
## & Théâtre des Abbesses

*01.42.74.22.77/www.theatredelaville-paris.com.* **Box office** 11am-7pm Mon; 11am-8pm Tue-Sat. **Admission** €8-€30. **Credit** MC, V. **Théâtre de la Ville** *2 pl du Châtelet, 4th. M° Châtelet.* **Map** p406 J6. **Théâtre des Abbesses** *31 rue des Abbesses, 18th. M° Abbesses.* **Map** p402 H1.

Between its two sites, the 'City Theatre' turns out the most consistently innovative and stimulating programming in Paris. Instead of running a standard rep company, the house imports music, dance and theatre productions.

# Left Bank

## Odéon, Théâtre de L'Europe

*Pl de l'Odéon, 6th (01.44.85.40.00/bookings 01.44.85.40.40/www.theatre-odeon.fr). M° Odéon.* **Box office** 11am-6.30pm Mon-Sat. **Admission** €7.50-€30. **Credit** MC, V. **Map** p408 H7.

The renovated Odéon has a thrilling programme planned. In early 2008 Daniel Auteuil stars here in *L'Ecole des Femmes* by Molière, followed by Chekhov's *Ivanov* in Hungarian, subtitled in French. Its sister theatre, Les Ateliers Berthier (1 rue André Suarès, 17th, M°/RER Porte de Clichy), is showcasing a colourful interpretation of *Pinocchio. Photo p341.*

## Théâtre de la Cité Internationale

*17 bd Jourdan, 14th (01.43.13.50.50/www.theatre delacite.com). RER Cité Universitaire.* **Box office** 2-7pm Mon-Sat. **Admission** €5-€21. **Credit** MC, V.

A polished, professional theatre on the campus of the Cité Universitaire, the Théâtre de la Cité displays an international flair worthy of its setting. In addition to the main theatre and dance salon, the prestigious Ecole du Théâtre National de Strasbourg occupies the stage for a short stint each summer.

## Théâtre de la Huchette

*23 rue de la Huchette, 5th (01.43.26.38.99/www. theatrehuchette.com). M° Cluny La Sorbonne or St-Michel.* **Box office** 5-9pm Mon-Sat. **Admission** €19.50; €14.50 reductions. **Credit** MC, V. **Map** p408 J7.

Eugene Ionesco's absurdist classic *La Cantatrice Chauve* ('The Bald Soprano') has been playing at this tiny theatre since 1957, running on a double bill with Ionesco's *La Leçon.* Each runs just short of an hour. A reasonable level of French should get you through.

# Trips Out of Town

## Features

## Map

**Fondation Claude Monet**. *See p351.*

# Trips Out of Town

Head out beyond the boulevards to a land of palaces, painters and popping corks.

In this chapter we've listed the local tourist information centres, which can provide further details about specific areas and their attractions. For the main entries – cathedrals, châteaux and other sightseeing attractions – we have included details of opening times, admission and transport, but be aware that these can change without notice: always phone in advance to check.

For a list of mainline railway stations in Paris and their destinations, *see p363.*

## Day Trips

### Auvers-sur-Oise

This charming rural retreat was where Vincent van Gogh spent his last weeks. Many of his best-known works were completed here and are now displayed on illustrated panels around the village.

Van Gogh's tiny attic room at the **Auberge Ravoux** is open to the public. Previous Auvers residents had included fellow artists Camille Pissarro, Paul Cézanne and Charles-François Daubigny. Today you can explore **Daubigny's museum** (Manoir des Colombières, 01.30. 36.80.20) and his studio (61 rue Daubigny, 01.34.48.03.03), which is still decorated with his murals.

A further attraction here, linked with the artistic community of the day, is the **Absinthe Museum** (44 rue Callé, 01.30.36.83.26), a rather modest collection of art and artefacts related to the notorious drink. Banned in France since 1915, the green concoction is not available at the replica café-bar upstairs.

The local artistic legacy has not been overlooked by Auvers' main historical attraction, either. The 17th-century **Château d'Auvers** (rue de Léry, 01.34.48.48.45, www.chateau-auvers.fr) features a walk-through tour (for which visitors must wear a special helmet) themed around the Impressionists and their surroundings.

#### Auberge Ravoux

*1 place de la Mairie, 95430 Auvers-sur-Oise (01.30.36.60.60).* **Open** 10am-6pm Wed-Sun. **Admission** €5. **Credit** *Shop & restaurant* AmEx, MC, V.

## Where to eat & stay

You can always do as Van Gogh might have done, and dine at the **Auberge Ravoux** (*see above*) – today it serves traditional dishes with set menus. Otherwise, try **La Guinguette** (Château d'Auvers, rue de Léry, 01.34.48.43.29), which does cheap lunches. The **Hostellerie du Nord** (6 rue Général-de-Gaulle, 01.30.36.70.74, www.hostelleriedunord.fr, closed dinner Sun) has chef Joël Boilleaut running the kitchen; upstairs are eight comfy doubles (€98-€188).

## Getting there

### By car
35km (22 miles) north from Paris by A15, exit 7, then N184, exit Méry-sur-Oise for Auvers.

### By train
From Gare du Nord, changing at St-Ouen L'Aumone (whole journey takes about 1hr).

## Tourist information

### Office de Tourisme
*Manoir des Colombières, rue de la Sansonne, 95430 Auvers-sur-Oise (01.30.36.10.06/www.auvers-sur-oise.com).* **Open** 9.30am-12.30pm, 2-6pm (Nov-Mar until 5pm) Tue-Sun.

### Chantilly & Senlis

From the 14th century until 1897, the town of **Chantilly** was the domain of the Princes of Condé, the cousins of the French kings. As well as its impressive **château**, Chantilly has a rich equestrian history, with its hunting forests and prestigious horse-racing centres.

Much of the cream-coloured château, a fine example of the French Renaissance, was destroyed during the Revolution, leaving the main wing to be reconstructed in the 19th century by Henri d'Orléans, Duc d'Aumale. When the duke died in 1897, he bequeathed the Domaine de Chantilly – including the Grand Stables, the Hippodrome and the 61sq km (23 square mile) forest – to the Institut de France on the condition that the château be opened to the public as the Musée Condé, and that none of the artworks would be moved or

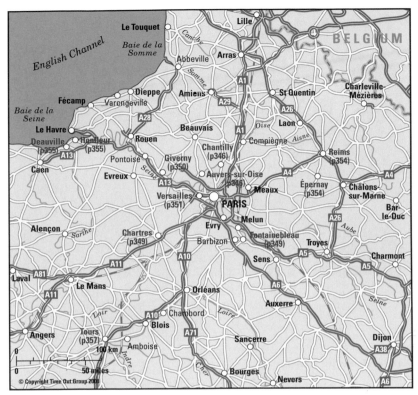

loaned to other museums. His remarkable collection is complemented by the surrounding **park**, beautifully landscaped by André Le Nôtre (of Versailles fame).

The Grandes Ecuries ('great stables') at the château were commissioned in 1719 by Prince Louis-Henri de Bourbon (who believed he would be reincarnated as a horse). Later, they became one of Napoleon's equestrian training grounds, having suffered only light damage during the Revolution. In 1982 the great horseman Yves Bienaimé restored the stables and turned them into the **Musée Vivant du Cheval**. The Bienaimé family has also restored the **Potager des Princes**, the princes' old vegetable garden.

The **Forêt de Chantilly** is full of hiking and cycling trails. A pleasant walk of around seven kilometres (4.5 miles) circles the four small lakes, the Etangs de Commelles, and passes the Château de la Reine Blanche, a mill converted in the 1820s into a pseudo-medieval hunting lodge. For trail details, ask at the Office National des Forêts (1 av de Sylvie, 03.44.57.03.88, www.onf.fr).

**Senlis**, nine kilometres (5.5 miles) east of Chantilly, is known as the birthplace of the French monarchy.

### Château de Chantilly
*Musée Condé, Chantilly (03.44.27.31.80/www. chateaudechantilly.com).* **Open** *Apr-Oct* 10am-6pm Mon, Wed-Sun. *Nov-Mar* 10.30am-5pm Wed-Sun.**Admission** *Château & park* €9; free under-18s. **Credit** MC, V.
The major attraction here is the collection of paintings and drawings at the Musée Condé. It includes three paintings by Raphael, and the *Très Riches Heures du Duc de Berry*, a medieval book of hours.

### Château park
**Open** *mid Mar-Oct* 10am-8pm Mon, Wed-Sun; 10am-12.45pm, 2-8pm Tue. *Nov-mid Mar* 10.30am-6pm Mon, Wed-Sun. **Admission** *Park only* €4; €3.50 12-17s; €2.50 4-11s; free under-4s. *Combined ticket* (boat tour, carriage ride, mini-train rides) from €9. **Credit** MC, V.
The main section of the château's sprawling park, designed by royal landscape architect Le Nôtre, features traditional French formal parterres and an extensive canal system, which allows visitors to see

Home to 14 French kings: **Château de Fontainebleau.** *See p350.*

the park from electric-powered boats. Get off the beaten path to explore the English Garden, the Island of Love, the kangaroo zoo and the original hamlet that inspired Marie-Antoinette to build her own version at Versailles.

### Musée Vivant du Cheval

*Les Grandes Ecuries, Chantilly (03.44.57.40.40/ www.museevivantducheval.fr).* **Open** *Apr-Oct* 10.30am-6.30pm Mon, Wed-Fri; 10.30am-7pm Sat, Sun. *Nov-Mar* 2pm-6pm Mon, Wed-Fri; 10.30am-6.30pm Sat, Sun. **Admission** €9; €7 under-18s. **Credit** MC, V.

This museum is an interactive affair where kids can pet the ponies and everyone gets to learn how the horses are trained to perform in the ring. There are demonstrations every day at 11.30am, 3.30pm and, in summer, also at 5.30pm.

### Potager des Princes

*Parc de la Faisanderie, 17 rue de la Faisanderie, Chantilly (03.44.57.39.66/www.potagerdesprinces. com).* **Open** *Apr-Nov* 2-5pm Mon, Wed-Fri; 2-5.30pm Sat, Sun. **Admission** €7.50; €4.50-€6.50 under-12s. **Credit** MC, V.

The restored princes' kitchen garden is today a 19th-century English garden with vegetable plots, trained fruit trees, a small farmyard and an open-air theatre next to the lake.

## Where to eat & stay

Try the home-style cooking at **Le Goutillon** (61 rue du Connétable, 03.44.58.01.00). **La Capitainerie** (03.44.57.15.89) offers good

French food in the old château kitchens. To sample Chantilly whipped cream, stop by for tea at **Aux Goûters Champêtres** (03.44.57.46.21, closed mid Nov-mid Mar) in the *hameau* at the château.

One of the few hotels in the town centre is the **Hotel du Parc Best Western** (36 av du Maréchal-Joffre, 03.44.58.20.00, www.hotel-parc-chantilly.com, doubles €110-€120, equipped with the essentials for a good night's rest.

## Getting there

### By car

40km (25 miles) from Paris by N16 (direct) or A1 (Chantilly exit).

### By train

SNCF Chantilly-Gouvieux from Gare du Nord (30mins), then 5min walk to town, 20min to château. Some trains stop at Creil, then loop back to Chantilly.

## Tourist information

### Office de Tourisme (Chantilly)

*60 av Maréchal-Joffre, 60500 Chantilly (03.44.67. 37.37/www.chantilly-tourisme.com).* **Open** 9.30am-12.30pm, 1.30-5.30pm Mon-Sat.

### Office de Tourisme (Senlis)

*Pl du parvis Notre-Dame, 60302 Senlis (03.44.53. 06.40/www.ville-senlis.fr).* **Open** 10am-12.30pm, 2-6.15pm Mon-Sat; 10.30am-1pm, 2-6.15pm Sun. Closes 5pm Nov-Feb.

**Trips Out of Town**

# Chartres

Seen from afar, the mismatched spires and dazzling silhouette of **Chartres cathedral** burst out of the Beauce cornfields and dominate the skyline of this modest town some 90 kilometres (56 miles) south-west of Paris.

Chartres was a pilgrimage site long before the cathedral was built, ever since the Sacra Camisia (said to be the Virgin Mary's birthing garment) was donated in 876 by the king. The sublime stained glass of the cathedral, and its doorways bristling with sculpture, embody a complete medieval world view, in which earthly society and civic life reflect the divine order.

The town of Chartres is an attractive tangle of narrow, medieval streets on the banks of the river Eure. Two sights merit a special mention: the **Musée des Beaux-Arts** (29 cloître Notre-Dame, 02.37.90.45.80), which houses a collection of 18th-century French paintings by Watteau and others; and the **memorial to Jean Moulin**, the legendary figure of the Resistance, a wartime prefect of Chartres until he was dismissed by the Vichy government after his refusal to co-operate with the Nazis. He became de Gaulle's man on the ground, and died under torture in Lyon in 1943. Moulin's memorial is a ten-minute walk west of the cathedral, at the corner of rue Collin d'Arleville and boulevard de la Résistance.

### Cathédrale Notre-Dame

*Pl de la Cathédrale (02.37.21.72.02).* **Open** *Cathedral* 8.30am-7.30pm daily. *Tower* 9.30am-noon, 2-4.30pm Mon-Sat; 2-4.30pm Sun. **Admission** *Cathedral* free. *Tower* €6.20; €4.20 students; free under-10s. **No credit cards.**

The west front, or 'Royal Portal', of this High Gothic cathedral modelled in part on St-Denis (*see p179*) has three sculpted doorways. Inside, there's another era of sculpture, represented in the 16th-century scenes of the life of Christ that surround the choir. Note the circular labyrinth of black and white stones in the floor. The cathedral is famed, above all, for its stained-glass windows depicting biblical scenes, saints and medieval trades in brilliant 'Chartres blue', punctuated by rich reds. Climb the tower for a fantastic view.

English-language tours by lecturer Malcolm Miller – one of the world's most knowledgeable and entertaining experts on the cathedral – take place twice daily for most of the year (noon & 2.45pm Mon-Sat, €10, €5 students; enquire in the gift shop. In his absence, audio-guides can be hired. Miller is also available for private tours (02.37.28.15.58, millerchartres@aol.com).

### Where to eat & stay

Tourists flock to the **Café Serpent** (2 cloître Notre-Dame, 02.37.21.68.81), in the shadow of the cathedral – if it's full, there are plenty of easy options nearby. For restaurant cuisine with a riverside view, try **L'Estocade** (1 rue de la Porte Guillaume, 02.37.34.27.17, closed all day Mon & Sun eve). For fireside treats, **La Vieille Maison** (5 rue au Lait, 02.37.34.10.67, closed Mon & Sun) has a cosy 14th-century dining room. For a local speciality, order some Chartres pâté at **Le Saint-Hilaire** (11 rue Pont St-Hilaire, 02.37.30.97.57).

Two chain hotels on the ring road, not far from the town centre, are the **Grand Monarque** (22 pl des Epars, 02.37.18.15.15, www.bw-grand-monarque.com, doubles from €115) and the more basic **Ibis Centre** (pl Drouaise, 02.37.36.06.36, www.ibishotel.com, doubles €73).

## Getting there

### By car

90km (56 miles) from Paris by A10, then A11.

### By train

Direct from Gare Montparnasse (1hr).

## Tourist information

### Office de Tourisme

*Pl de la Cathédrale, 28000 Chartres (02.37.18.26.26/ www.chartres-tourisme.com).* **Open** *Apr-Sept* 9am-7pm Mon-Sat; 9.30am-5.30pm Sun. *Oct-Mar* 10am-6pm Mon-Sat; 10am-1pm, 2.30-4.30pm Sun.

# Fontainebleau

Home to 14 French kings since François I, Fontainebleau was once a sort of aristocratic club where gentlemen of the day came to hunt and learn the art of chivalry. The town grew up around the **château** in the 19th century, and is a pleasant place to visit, circled by hunting forest and rock formations.

The château is bite-sized compared to the sprawling grandeur of Versailles. The style adopted by the Italian artists brought in by François I is still visible, as are the additions by later rulers. The extensive château gardens, park and grand canal, all free for visitors to enter, are also worth exploring.

The 170sq km (66 square mile) **Forêt de Fontainebleau** is part of the Gâtinas regional nature park, which has bizarre geological formations and diverse wildlife. It's the wildest slice of nature to be found near Paris, and is popular with outdoor types. There are a number of well-marked trails, such as the GR1 from Bois-le-Roi train station, but more serious yompers would be better off with an official map such as the TOP25 IGN series 2417-OT, which covers the entire forest, highlighting climbing sites, campsites and picnic areas.

Trail maps are on sale at the **Fontainebleau tourist office**, which rents out bicycles (€20 per day) and has information on the nearby villages of Barbizon and Moret-sur-Loing. Bikes can also be hired from La Petite Reine (32 rue Sablons, 01.60.74.57.57, www.la-petite-reine.fr), as can baby seats – passport or €300 deposit required. La **Bleausière** riding school (06.82.01.21.18, http://la.bleausiere.free.fr) in Barbizon offers year-round short and long guided tours for all ages and levels.

### Château de Fontainebleau

*Pl du Général-de-Gaulle (01.60.71.50.70/www.musee-chateau-fontainebleau.fr).* **Open** *Château* June-Sept 9.30am-6pm Mon, Wed-Sun. Oct-May 9.30am-5pm Mon, Wed-Sun. *Park & gardens* Mar, Apr, Oct 9am-6pm daily. May-Sept 9am-7pm daily. Nov-Feb 9am-5pm daily. **Admission** *Château* €8; €6 18-25s; free under-18s. PMP. *Park & gardens* free. **Credit** AmEx, MC, V.

This former hunting lodge is a real mix of styles. In 1528 François I brought in Italian artists and craftsmen to help architect Gilles le Breton transform a neglected lodge into the finest Italian Mannerist palace in France. This style, noted for its grotesqueries, contorted figures and crazy fireplaces, is still visible in the Ballroom and Long Gallery. Henri IV added a tennis court, Louis XIII built a double-horseshoe entrance staircase, and Louis XIV and XV added classical trimmings. Napoleon and Louis-Philippe also spent a fortune on redecoration. The château gardens include Le Nôtre's Grand Parterre and a carp pond in the Jardin Anglais. There is also an informal château park just outside, with lawns and a canal. *Photo p348.*

### Where to eat & stay

Rue Grande is lined with restaurants such as the inventive, stylish **Au Délice Impérial** (no.1, 01.64.22.20.70) and **Au Bureau** (no.12, 01.60.39.00.01), which has Tex-Mex specialities in a pub setting, with DJs and bands in the evening. At no.92, picnickers can find an array of local cheeses at the sumptuous **Fromagerie Barthélémy** (01.64.22.21.64).

For a blow-out meal, head for **Le Caveau des Ducs** (24 rue Ferrare, 01.64.22.05.05), with traditional French cuisine in a 17th-century interior of heavy oak tables and tapestries.

Some of the dozen rooms at the charming, central **Hôtel de Londres** (1 pl du Général-de-Gaulle, 01.64.22.20.21, www.hoteldelondres.com, doubles €90-€150) have balconies overlooking the château. The elegant **Hôtel Napoleon** (9 rue Grande, 01.60.39.50.50, www.hotelnapoleon-fontainebleau.com, doubles €130-€250) overlooks an interior garden, and provides appropriately grand meals at its restaurant, **La Table des Maréchaux**.

### Getting there

#### By car

60km (37 miles) from Paris by A6, then N7 (about 75mins). Beware of the likelihood of traffic jams when heading back to Paris on Sundays.

#### By train

Gare de Lyon to Fontainebleau-Avon (35mins), then bus AB (marked 'Château'). Ask for a 'Forfait Château de Fontainebleau' (€20.80; €16 10-17s; €7.70 4-9s) at the Gare de Lyon; it includes train fare, château entrance and audio guide.

### Tourist information

#### Office de Tourisme

*4 rue Royale, 77300 Fontainebleau (01.60.74.99.99/ www.fontainebleau-tourisme.com).* **Open** May-Oct 10am-6pm Mon-Sat; 10.30am-1pm, 2pm-5.30pm Sun. Nov-Apr 10am-1pm Mon-Sat.

## Giverny

In 1883 Claude Monet moved his mistress and their eight children into a quaint pink-brick house in bucolic Giverny, and concentrated as much time on cultivating a beautiful garden here as painting the water lilies in it.

The leader of the Impressionist movement thrived on outdoor scenes, whether along the Seine near Argenteuil or by the Thames in London. Having once seen the tiny village of Giverny from the window of a train, he was smitten. By 1890 he had bought his dream home and soon had a pond dug, bridges built and a tableau of greenery created. As Monet's eyesight began to fail, he produced endless impressions of his man-made paradise, each trying to capture how the leaves and water refracted light. He died here in 1926.

Of the hundreds of tourists who visit here every day, not all are art lovers – there are no original Monets here, though you will see the 32 Japanese woodblock prints collected by the artist. Most visitors are simply here for the lilies, and a good photo opportunity. (Giverny is overrun with visitors snapping each other.) The garden is a masterpiece, its famous water-lily pond, weeping willows and Japanese bridge remarkably intact; and the charming house, the **Fondation Claude Monet**, is dotted with touching mementos. But once you're back in the village, be prepared for heated arguments over finding a table and long queues of impatient tourists almost everywhere you turn. Get here early, or book ahead for dinner at the famous **Hôtel Baudy** museum-restaurant (81 rue Claude Monet, 02.32.21.10.03, closed Nov-Mar), where Monet's American disciples (such

First impressions: **Fondation Claude Monet**.

as Willard Metcalf and Dawson-Watson) set up their easels for several decadent years, expanding the old hotel into an *art-atelier extraordinaire*, complete with ballroom, rose garden and tennis courts – Cézanne stayed for a month. Today, booking accommodation for Giverny (*see below*) is essential – but you will be first to the Monet museum in the morning. Up the road, the **Musée d'Art Américain de Giverny** (99 rue Claude-Monet, 02.32.51.94.65, www.maag.org) houses works by the American Impressionist colony.

### Fondation Claude Monet

*84 rue Claude-Monet, 27620 Giverny (02.32. 51.28.21/www.fondation-monet.com).* **Open** *Apr-Oct* 9.30am-6pm Tue-Sun. **Admission** *House & garden* €5.50; €4 students; €3 7-13s; free under-7s. **Credit** AmEx, MC, V.

## Where to stay

For suggestions of hotels and B&Bs in the area, visit www.giverny.org. Pretty **Le Clos Fleuri** (5 rue de la Dîme, 02.32.21.36.51, doubles €75, closed Nov-Mar) is in Giverny, close to the Musée d'Art Américain and Monet's garden.

## Getting there

### By car

80km (50 miles) west of Paris by A13 to Bonnières, then D201.

### By train

Gare St-Lazare to Vernon (45mins), then 5km (3-mile) taxi ride or bus from the station.

## Tourist information

### Comité Départemental du Tourisme de l'Eure

*3 rue du Commandant-Letellier, BP 367, 27003 (02.32.62.04.27/www.cdt-eure.fr).* **Open** 9am-12.30pm, 1.30-6pm Mon-Thur; 9am-1pm, 1.30-6pm Fri.

## Versailles

Centuries of makeovers have made Versailles the most sumptuously clad **château** in the world – a brilliant, unmissable cocktail of extravagance. Architect Louis Le Vau first embellished the original building – a hunting lodge built during Louis XIII's reign – after Louis XIV saw Vaux-le-Vicomte, the impressive residence of his finance minister, Nicolas Fouquet. The Sun King had the unlucky minister jailed, and stole not only his architect but also his painter, Charles Le Brun, and his landscaper, André Le Nôtre, who turned the boggy marshland into terraces, parterres, fountains and lush groves.

After Le Vau's death in 1670, Jules Hardouin-Mansart took over as principal architect, transforming Versailles into the château we know today. He dedicated the last 30 years of his life to adding the two main wings, the Cour des Ministres and the Chapelle Royale. In 1682

**Trips Out of Town**

Louis moved in, accompanied by his court; thereafter, he rarely set foot in Paris. In the 1770s, Louis XV commissioned Jacques-Ange Gabriel to add the sumptuous Opéra Royal, used for concerts by the Centre de Musique Baroque (01.39.20.78.10). The expense of building and running Versailles cost France dear. With the fall of the monarchy in 1792, most of the furniture was lost – but the château was saved from demolition after 1830 by Louis-Philippe.

Versailles has hosted the official signings of many historic treaties – European recognition of the United States, the unification of Germany in 1871, the division of Europe after 1918 – and it is still used by the French government for major summits. In the gardens, the Grand Trianon accommodates heads of state.

The **gardens** are works of art in themselves, their ponds and statues once again embellished by a fully working fountain system. On summer weekends, the spectacular jets of water are set to music, a prelude to the occasional fireworks displays of the Fêtes de Nuit.

Beyond the gardens are the Grand Canal and the wooded parkland and sheep-filled pastures of the estate's park. Outside the château gates are the **Potager du Roi** (the Sun King's vegetable garden), and stables which now house the **Académie du Spectacle Equestre.**

Versailles is currently undergoing a major overhaul, so expect a little chaos for the next few years. As well as sprucing up Marie-Antoinette's residence (*see below*), the French state and several sponsors have funded a restoration of the **Hall of Mirrors** – a 73-metre (240-foot) gallery overlooking the garden, hung with chandeliers. Commissioned in 1678 by Louis XIV and decorated by Le Brun, it is lined with 357 mirrors.

In the town of Versailles, grab a *Historical Places* brochure free from the tourist office (*see p354*) and explore. The Quartier St-Louis opposite the Potager was developed by Louis XV around the Cathédrale St-Louis. Just off rue d'Anjou are the Carrés St-Louis, four market squares surrounded by 18th-century boutiques . North-east of the château is the Quartier Notre-Dame, part of the 'new town' designed by the Sun King himself. Eglise Notre-Dame is where members of the royal family were baptised and married. Around the corner is the Marché Notre-Dame, a market square dating back to 1671 and surrounded by restaurants and cafés. The covered market is closed on Mondays.

Bicycles can be rented from outside RER Versailles-Chantiers (pl Raymond Poincaré, 01.39.20.16.60) for €2 an hour or €12 a day.

### Académie du Spectacle Equestre
*Grandes Ecuries, Château de Versailles (01.39.02.07.14/www.acadequestre.fr).* **Les Matinales des Ecuyers** (*to watch riding practice & visit*) **Viewings** 10.30am, 11.15am Sun. Times vary for groups & during school holidays; call for details. **Admission** €8; €4 5-18s, students. **Credit** MC, V.
**Reprise Musicale** (*performance & visit*) **Performances** 8.30pm Sat; 3pm Sun. **Admission** *Daytime* €16; €8 under-18s, students. *Evening* €20; €10 under-18s, students. **Credit** MC, V.
Across from the château entrance are the Sun King's magnificent stables, restored in 2003. They house the Académie du Spectacle Equestre, which is responsible for the elaborate shows of tightly choreographed theatrics on horseback run by famous horse trainer Bartabas. Visitors can catch a show either at weekends or at special evening performances, or attend training sessions on Sunday mornings to see how the white horses and their young riders learn their tricks.

### Château de Versailles
*78000 Versailles (01.30.83.78.00/advance tickets 08.92.68.46.94/www.chateauversailles.fr).* **Open** *Apr-Oct* 9am-6.30pm Tue-Sun. *Nov-Mar* 9am-5.30pm Tue-Sun. **Admission** €13.50; €10 after 4pm (summer) or 3pm (winter); free under-18s. PMP, Passeport Versailles. **Credit** AmEx, DC, MC, V.
Versailles is a masterpiece – and it's almost always packed with visitors. Allow yourself a whole day to appreciate the sumptuous State Apartments and the Hall of Mirrors, the highlights of any visit – and

Château de Versailles.

mainly accessible with just a day ticket. The Grand Appartement, where Louis XIV held court, consists of six gilded salons (Venus, Mercury, Apollo and so on), all opulent examples of baroque craftsmanship. No less luxurious, the Queen's Apartment includes her bedroom, where royal births took place in full view of the court. Hardouin-Mansart's showpiece, the Hall of Mirrors, where a united Germany was proclaimed in 1871 and the Treaty of Versailles signed in 1919, is flooded with natural light from its 17 vast windows. Designed to catch the last of the day's rays, it was here that the Sun King would hold extravagant receptions. Other private apartments can be seen only as part of a guided tour.

### Domaine de Versailles

**Gardens Open** *Apr-Oct* 7am-dusk daily. *Nov-Mar* 8am-dusk daily. **Admission** *Winter* free (statues covered over). *Summer* €3; €1.50 10-17s; free under-10s. Passeport Versailles.
**Grandes Eaux Musicales** *(01.30.83.78.88).* **Open** *Apr-Sept* Sat, Sun. **Admission** €7; €5.50 10-17s; free under-10s. Passeport Versailles. **Credit** AmEx, DC, MC, V.
**Park Open** dawn-dusk daily. **Admission** free.
Sprawling across 8sq km (3sq miles), the carefully planned gardens consist of formal parterres, ponds, elaborate statues – many commissioned by Colbert in 1674 – and a spectacular series of fountains, served by an ingenious hydraulic system only recently restored to working order. On weekend afternoons in the spring and autumn, the fountains are set in action to music for the Grandes Eaux Musicales – and also serve as a backdrop, seven times a year, for the extravagant Fêtes de Nuit, capturing the regal splendour of the Sun King's celebrations with fireworks, music and theatre.

### Grand Trianon/Petit Trianon/ Domaine de Marie-Antionette

*01.30.83.77.43/weekend reservations 01.30.83.76.50.* **Open** *Apr-Oct* noon-6.30pm daily. *Nov-Mar* noon-5.30pm daily. **Admission** *Summer* €9; €5 after 4pm; free under-18s. *Winter* €5; free under-18s. PMP, Passeport Versailles. **Credit** AmEx, DC, MC, V.
In 1687 Hardouin-Mansart built the pink marble Grand Trianon in the north of the park, away from the protocol of the court. Here Louis XIV and his children's governess and secret second wife, Madame de Maintenon, could admire the intimate gardens from the colonnaded portico. It retains the Empire decor of Napoleon, who stayed here with his second Empress, Marie-Louise.

The Petit Trianon, built for Louis XV's mistress Madame de Pompadour, is a wonderful example of neo-classicism. It later became part of the Domaine de Marie-Antoinette, an exclusive hideaway located beyond the canal in the wooded parkland. Given to Marie-Antoinette as a wedding gift by her husband Louis XVI in 1774, the domain also includes the chapel adjoining the Petit Trianon, plus a theatre, a neo-classical 'Temple d'Amour', and Marie-Antoinette's fairy-tale farm and dairy, known as the Hameau de la Reine. Here, the queen escaped from the discontent of her subjects and the revolutionary fervour of Paris by pretending to be a humble milkmaid. The Domaine opened to the public in summer 2006, but only its gardens will remain fully accessible until April 2008, when renovation work on the buildings is due for completion; call for updates. A stroll can be enlivened by hiring hand-held digital PDA or iPod guides.

### Potager du Roi

*10 rue Maréchal Joffre (011.39.24.62.62/ www.potager-du-roi.fr).* **Open** *Apr-Oct* 10am-6pm Tue-Sun. *Nov-Mar* 10am-6pm Mon-Fri (by guided tour only). **Admission** *Mon-Fri* €4.50; €3 concessions; free under-6s. *Sat, Sun* €6.50; €3 students; free under-6s. **Credit** AmEx, DC, MC, V.
The Potager du Roi, the king's vegetable garden, features 16 small squares surrounded by 5,000 fruit trees espaliered into fabulous shapes.

## Where to eat & stay

Set in a building dating back to the construction of the château, **Le Chapeau Gris** (7 rue Hoche, 01.39.50.10.81, www.auchapeaugris.com, closed dinner Tue, all day Wed, set menus €21-€28) is the oldest restaurant in Versailles, and offers French country cuisine served under wooden beams. **Boeuf à la Mode** (4 rue au Pain, Marché Notre-Dame, 01.39.50.31.99) is an authentic 1930s brasserie serving steak and

# The Fun King

The easiest, although not the cheapest, way to see Versailles is to get a Passeport Versailles. It allows quick access via Porte C to the main section of the château, the audio-guided tour of the Chambre du Roi, the Grand and Petit Trianon, the gardens and their displays. Buy the Passeport in advance from Fnac stores (*see p272*), tourist offices or any RER station (price of journey added to the ticket); or go directly to Porte C2 or D before 2pm. Those who hold a Carte Musées et Monuments (*see p80*) can enter via Porte B2. Those just wanting a day ticket must queue with the masses at Porte A. Any number of guided tours are available from Porte D; it's essential to book early that morning, and then meet by Porte F.

### Passeport Versailles

**Admission** *Apr-Oct* €20 Mon-Fri; free under-18s; €25 Sat, Sun; free under-18s. *Nov-Mar* €16 daily; free under-18s.

**Trips Out of Town**

seafood specialities at mid-range prices. For a proper splurge, consider sampling the Michelin-starred haute cuisine of **Les Trois Marches** (Hôtel Trianon Palace, 1 bd de la Reine, 01.30.84.52.00, closed Mon & Sun, lunch €58, dinner €160). Another long-established eaterie is the traditional **Brasserie du Théâtre** (15 rue des Réservoirs, 01.39.50.03.21, set menu lunch €20), which stays open until 11.30pm for the after-show crowd from the Montansier theatre next door. You'll also find plenty of late-night bars around the Marché Notre-Dame.

The town centre has several reasonably priced hotels. One of the more historic is the **Hôtel du Cheval Rouge** (18 rue André-Chénier, 01.39.50.03.03, www.chevalrouge.fr.st, doubles €73-€89), built in Louis XIV's former livery overlooking the Marché Notre-Dame. Across from the château, the **Hôtel de France** (5 rue Colbert, 01.30.83.92.23, www.hotelfrance-versailles.com, doubles from €141) is set in an 18th-century townhouse and has period decor.

## Getting there

### By car

20km (12.5 miles) from Paris by A13 or D10.

### By train

For the station nearest the château, take the RER C5 (VICK or VERO trains) to Versailles-Rive Gauche; or take a Transilien SNCF train from Gare St-Lazare to Versailles-Rive Droit (10mins on foot to the château).

## Tourist information

### Office de Tourisme

*2bis av de Paris, 78000 Versailles (01.39.24.88.88/ www.versailles-tourisme.com).* **Open** 11am-5pm Mon, Sun; 9am-6pm Tue-Sat.

# Further Afield

## Champagne country

Named after the region in which it's produced, champagne – nearly all 300 million bottles a year of it – comes from the towns of **Reims** (nasally pronounced 'Rrance') and **Epernay**, some 25 kilometres (16 miles) apart. At less than two hours by train from Paris, both are ideal destinations for a day trip or a weekend break. Most champagne cellars give detailed explanations of how the drink is produced – from the grape varieties used to the strict name and quality controls – and tours finish with a sample. Don't forget your woollies, as the cellars are chilly and damp.

Epernay developed in the 19th century as expanding champagne houses moved out from Reims to acquire more space. Today, the aptly named avenue de Champagne is home to most major brands – but the best tours are at **Moët & Chandon** and **Mercier**.

In Reims, most of the major champagne houses are open by appointment only: Krug (03.26.84.44.20); Lanson (03.26.78.50.50); Louis Roederer (by appointment *and* recommendation only, 03.26.40.42.11) and Veuve Clicquot (03.26.89.53.90, www.veuve-clicquot.com). **Champagne Pommery** is set in an intriguing Elizabethan building.

Home of the coronation church of most French monarchs dating back to Clovis in 496, Reims was an important city even in Roman times. Begun in 1211, the present **Cathédrale Notre-Dame** (03.26.47.55.34, www.cathedrale-reims.com) has rich Gothic decoration that includes thousands of well-preserved figures on the portals. Look out, too, for the splendid stained-glass windows in the axial chapel, designed by Chagall. The statues damaged during heavy shelling in World War I can be seen next door in the former archbishop's palace, the Palais de Tau (2 pl du Cardinal-Luçon, 03.26.47.81.79).

**L'Ancien Collège des Jésuites** (1 pl Museux, 03.26.85.51.50, closed all Tue and Sat & Sun mornings) is a classic example of 17th-century baroque architecture, housing a library decorated with religious carvings and paintings by Jean Hélart.

## Champagne Pommery

*5 pl du Général Gouraud, 51100 Reims (03.26.61. 62.55/www.pommery.com).* **Open** *mid Apr-mid Nov* 9.30am-7pm daily. *Mid Nov-mid Apr* (by appointment only) 10am-6pm daily. **Admission** (incl 1 glass) €7.50; (incl 2 glasses) €10. **Credit** MC, V.

Built in 1868, this unusual château was modelled on Elizabethan architecture . The visit takes place some 30m (98ft) underground, in 18km (11 miles) of tunnels linking 120 Gallo-Roman chalk mines.

## Mercier

*68 av de Champagne, 51200 Epernay (03.26.51.22.22/www.champagne-mercier.fr).* **Open** *mid Mar-mid Nov* 9.30-11.30am, 2-4.30pm daily. *Mid Nov-mid Mar* 9.30-11.30am, 2-4.30pm Mon, Thur-Sun. **Admission** (incl 1 glass) €6.50; €3 12-15s; free under-12s. **Credit** MC, V.

Some 7,000 tonnes of chalk were extracted to create the 18km (11 miles) of cellars at Mercier, opened in 1858. Note the 20-tonne champagne barrel at the entrance: it took 24 bulls and 18 horses to drag it all the way from Epernay to Paris for the 1889 Exposition Universelle. The interesting 45-minute underground tour takes place on a little train and covers a stretch of tunnel that was used for mini-car races in the 1950s.

## Moët & Chandon

*20 av de Champagne, 51200 Epernay (03.26.51.*
*20.00/www.moet.com).* **Open** *mid Mar-mid Nov*
9.30-11.30am, 2-4.30pm daily. *Mid Nov-mid Mar*
9.30-11.30am, 2-4.30pm Mon-Fri. **Admission**
(incl 1 glass) €7.50; €4.50 12-16s; free under-12s.
**Credit** AmEx, DC, MC, V.

Moët & Chandon started life in 1743 as champagne
supplier to Madame de Pompadour, Napoleon and
Alexander I of Russia. Since then it has kept pole position, with the largest domaine and more than 250
global outlets. In the hour-long tour, visitors are led
through a section (under the grand house) of the 28km
(17 miles) of chalk tunnels.

## Where to eat & stay

In Reims, countless cafés and brasseries line
lively **place Drouet d'Erlon**, as do many
hotels. If you fancy staying at a working
champagne domaine, contact **Ariston Fils
Champagne** (4-8 Grande-Rue, 51170 Brouillet,
03.26.97.43.46, www.champagne-aristonfils.com,
doubles €45-€48), which offers three rooms and
pampers its guests. To sleep like a king, book
one of the luxuriously extravagant rooms at the
**Château les Crayères** (64 bd Henry Vasnier,
03.26.82.80.80, www.chateaulescrayeres.com,
doubles €275-€475), a grand country-house
hotel set in lush grounds.

In Epernay, **La Cave à Champagne**
(16 rue Gambetta, 03.26.55.50.70) does good
traditional French food, as does **Théâtre** (8
pl Pierre-Mendès-France, 03.26.58.88.19, closed
dinner Tue & Sun, all Wed & 15 Feb-2 Mar,
15 July-2 Aug & 22-28 Dec). Known for its
champagnes, **Les Cépages** (16 rue Fauvette,
03.26.55.16.93, closed Wed & Sun and July &
Christmas) serves homely food.

Set in a 19th-century red-brick mansion,
**Le Clos Raymi** (3 rue Joseph-de-Venoge,
03.26.51.00.58, www.closraymi-hotel.com,
doubles €100-€140) is a cosy mix of traditional
and modern. Part of the international Best
Western chain, the **Hôtel de Champagne**
(30 rue Eugène-Mercier, 03.26.53.10.60,
www.bw-hotel-champagne.com, doubles
€90-€120) is comfy enough, and the **Hôtel
Kyriad** (3bis rue de Lorraine, 03.26.54.17.39,
doubles from €57) has basic, clean rooms.

## Getting there

### By car

150km (93 miles) from Paris by the A4. For Epernay,
exit at Château Thierry and take the N3.

### By train

From Gare de l'Est, trains take about 45mins for
Reims and Epernay.

## Tourist information

### Office de Tourisme (Epernay)

*7 av de Champagne, 51200 Epernay (03.26.*
*53.33.00/www.ot-epernay.fr).* **Open** *Mid Apr-*
*mid Oct* 9.30am-12.30pm, 1.30-7pm Mon-Sat;
11am-4pm Sun. *Mid Oct mid Apr* 9.30am-noon,
1.30-5.30pm Mon-Sat.

### Office de Tourisme (Reims)

*2 rue Guillaume-de-Machault, 51100 Reims*
*(03.26.77.45.00/www.reims-tourisme.com).* **Open**
*Easter-mid Oct* 9.30am-12.30pm, 1.30pm-7pm Mon-
Sat; 11am-4pm Sun. *Mid Oct-Easter* 9am-6pm Mon;
11am-4pm Sun.

# Deauville & the Norman Riviera

Deauville boomed in the 1860s, when Napoleon
III emulated his half-brother, the Duc de Morny,
who built a racecourse on an empty patch of
the Côte Fleurie, just across a narrow stretch
of water from Trouville-sur-Mer. By the early
1900s there was a casino, a spa and grandiose
hotels, welcoming Paris high society and the
British aristocracy. This early growth period
has left its mark on the town's personality: the
bright parasols and bathing huts of the famous
beach-side promenade, designed to protect
ladies' flowing dresses, are a reminder of those

The Cannes of the North: **Deauville**.

days. Today spa centres and the gourmet food market (pl du Marché, Tue, Fri and Sat mornings) attend to seekers of *bien-vivre*.

Compared, not unfavourably, to Cannes, Deauville caters to old-style leisure and wealth: there are two marinas, three golf courses, including the only floodlit course in Europe (02.31.14.42.00), and a yachting school (02.31. 88.38.19). The spending opportunities are endless: plush designer boutiques, top-dollar restaurants and Paris-style cafés line the streets. Then there's the **casino**, just behind the seafront. This massive belle époque edifice stands like a bastion of decadence, and can't be missed (ID is required and, for some rooms, so is formal attire).

In summer, when the population swells from 4,500 to around 75,000, watersports and sand-surfing keep the restless occupied. An energetic social calendar also brings in the crowds; with polo and racing events all year round, and two big film festivals – the Asia Film Festival (www.deauvilleasia.com) in March, and the American Film Festival in September (www.festival-deauville.com).

The nearby 17th-century port town of **Trouville-sur-Mer** shares Deauville's railway station. Family-owned shops, narrow backstreets and a daily fish market lend Trouville an authenticity that its flashier sister lacks. Check out the beach, casino and Napoleon's summer residence, Villa Montebello (64 rue du Maréchal-Leclerc, 02.31.88.16.26), which regularly hosts art exhibitions.

A short drive or bus journey further east is **Honfleur**, a small, very pretty fishing town at the mouth of the Seine. Honfleur has none of Deauville's glitz, but plenty of charm. The old port and the narrow and winding streets leading off it are perfect for exploring on foot; there are two sandy beaches nearby; and the town has a long list of associations with major artistic figures. Baudelaire spent time at his mother's house here, and the Impressionists were frequent visitors – the 'Honfleur School' included Monet and Courbet. The Musée Eugène Boudin (pl Erik-Satie, 02.31.89.54.00, closed Jan-10 Feb) contains paintings by Monet, Boudin, Jongkind and others, as well as sculptures and folk artefacts from the local area. Also worth a look is the 15th-century Eglise Ste-Cathérine (rue des Capucins, 02.31.89.11.83), with its roof built using boat-construction methods and detached belfry.

## Casino Barrière de Deauville

*Rue Edmond-Blanc, 14800 Deauville (02.31. 14.31.14).* **Open** 11am-2am Mon-Thur; 11am-3am Fri; 10am-4am Sat; 10am-3am Sun. **Admission** (over-18s only, formal dress) €14. **Credit** AmEx, MC, V.

## Where to eat & stay

In Deauville, tuck into oysters at **Le Ciro's** (2 rue Edmond-Blanc, 02.31.14.31.31) on the seafront or tackle a roast lobster and rich Normandy treats at **Le Spinnaker** (52 rue Mirabeau, 02.31.88.24.40). The best of Deauville's hotel selection are the palatial **Royal Barrière** (bd Cornuché, 02.31.98.66. 33, doubles €270-€390) and the half-timbered **Normandy Barrière** (38 rue Jean Mermoz, 02.31.98.66.22, doubles from €288), linked by a tunnel to the casino.

Those looking to stay on a budget should head in from the seafront – or find somewhere in Trouville-sur-Mer. A cheapish option is the **Flaubert** (rue Gustave-Flaubert, 02.31.88. 37.23, www.flaubert.fr, doubles €90-€125).

In Honfleur you'll find **La Ferme Saint-Siméon** (rue Adolphe-Marais, 02.31.81.78.00, www.fermesaintsimeon.fr, doubles €220-€450, closed all Mon & lunch Tue), a luxury inn set in landscaped gardens, with a spa and decent restaurant. In the centre, **Les Maisons de Léa** (02.31.14.49.49, www.lesmaisonsdelea.com, doubles €105-€195) occupies four characterful houses on place Ste-Catherine, by the church, and a cottage for four to six people (€295). Centuries-old stonework adds atmosphere to the harbour views from the hotel and restaurant **L'Absinthe** (1 rue de la Ville, 02.31.89.23.23, www.absinthe.fr, doubles €105-€135, closed mid Nov-mid Dec), where the focus is on fish and seafood; the same outfit runs the nearby **La Grenouille Brasserie** (No.16, 02.31. 89.04.24, closed mid Nov-mid Dec).

## Getting there

### By car
195km (121 miles) west from Paris by A13.

### By train
From Gare St-Lazare to Deauville-Trouville (2hrs).

## Tourist information

### Office de Tourisme (Deauville)
*Pl de la Mairie, 14800 Deauville (02.32.14.40.00/ www.deauville.org).* **Open** *July-mid Sept* 9am-7pm Mon-Sat;10am-1pm, 2-5pm Sun. *Mid Sept-June* 9am-12.30pm, 2-6.30pm Mon-Sat; 10am-1pm, 2-5pm Sun.

### Office de Tourisme (Honfleur)
*Quai Lepaulmier, 14600 Honfleur (02.31.89.23.30/ www.ot-honfleur.fr).* **Open** *Easter-June, Sept* 10am-12.30pm, 2-6.30pm Mon-Sat; 10am-5pm Sun. *July, Aug* 10am-7pm Mon-Sat; 10am-5pm Sun. *Oct-Easter* 10am-12.30pm, 2-6pm Mon-Sat; 10am-5pm Sun (during school hols only).

### Office de Tourisme (Trouville-sur-Mer)

*32 quai Fernand-Moureaux, 14360 Trouville-sur-Mer (02.31.14.60.70/www.trouvillesurmer.org).*
**Open** *Apr-June, Sept, Oct* 9.30am-noon, 2-6.30pm Mon-Sat; 10am-1pm Sun. *July, Aug* 9.30am-7pm Mon-Sat; 10am-1pm Sun. *Nov-Mar* 9.30am-noon, 1.30-6pm Mon-Sat; 10am-1pm Sun.

## Tours

Novelist Honoré de Balzac (1799-1850) once described his beloved birthplace as being 'more fresh, flowery and perfumed than any other town in the world'. An easy statement to make when you're living in the comparatively whiffy centre of early-19th century Paris (albeit in a posh mansion). However, Tours has a lot going for it even today – in fact it is a positively pleasant city, bursting with history, medieval quarters, a lively student population, colourful flower markets (Wednesday and Saturday on boulevard Béranger) and enticing bars and restaurants. Only an hour from Paris by TGV, it is the official gateway to the Loire Valley, and a choice place in which to refuel before overdosing on sumptuous Renaissance castles.

Sandwiched between the Loire (north) and the Cher (south) rivers, it began life as a fertile floodplain, prized by the Turones – a Celtic tribe that gave modern Tours its name. In 57 BC Julius Caesar conquered the city, modestly changing its name to Caesarodunum (Caesar's hill). Traces of the third-century Gallo-Roman city wall and amphitheatre can still be seen in the Musée des Beaux-Arts gardens (the left-hand tower of the Archbishop's palace and the curved wall to the east).

When Christianity hit town, St Martin, the founder of France's first monastery (in Ligugé in Poitou), became bishop of Tours and a local superstar. After his death in 397, his relics, laid to rest in the Roman **Basilique St-Martin**, were believed to have healing powers, drawing in thousands of pilgrims en route to Santiago de Campostela in Spain, and prompting the construction of Tours' medieval quarters.

Throughout the 15th and 16th centuries the city vied with Paris as the seat of power: Charles VII, Louis XI (who instated Tours' silk industry), Charles VIII and François I all cherished Tours; Henry IV preferred Paris. Bombarded by the Prussians in 1870 and flattened in World War II, Tours suffered widespread damage, especially to the historic centre, which by the 1960s was a no-go zone of crumbling masonry.

Nowadays, after 40 years of regeneration, the medieval quarters contain some of Tours' most charming streets. Pedestrianised **place Plumereau**, with its exquisitely pretty half-timbered façades housing cafés, galleries and boutiques, is the hub of town. Wander down lanes like rue Briçonnet to find concealed courtyards, more half-timbered houses and the occasional crooked tower. Place St-Pierre-le-Puellier is a concealed square containing sunken Gallo-Roman remains. Nearby on place de Châteauneuf a lone Romanesque tower stands proud as the only intact segment of the

On the waterfront: the harbour at **Honfleur**.

original Basilique-St-Martin (sacked by the Huguenots in 1562). The neo-Byzantine **Basilique St-Martin** (02.47.05.63.87) houses St-Martin's shrine further up the road, opposite the ruined vestiges.

The east of Tours is dominated by the splendid **Cathédrale St-Gatien** (02.47.70.21.00). Work began on it in the 13th century and ended in the 16th century, demonstrating the French Gothic style in its entirety. The early phase is found in the chevet, while the transept and the nave show progression through to the final Flamboyant period. The stained-glass windows inside are often compared to La Sainte-Chapelle in Paris. Next door, the Archbishop's palace and **Musée des Beaux Arts** (18 pl François-Sicard, 02.47.05.68.73, open 9am-12.45 pm, 2-6pm Mon, Wed-Sun) has a surprisingly rich collection of paintings by Degas, Rembrandt and Delacroix, plus several sculptures by Rodin and Bourdelle. Check out the enormous 200-year-old cedar of Lebanon in the garden, the branches of which are so heavy they have to be held up.

North of here, Tours' **Château Royal** looks over the Loire River with dishevelled majesty. You can best take in its assorted architecture by following the river: the **Tour de Guise** (look out for machicolations and a pepper-pot roof) was a 13th-century fortress, and the 15th-century **Logis des Gouverneurs** on the quay has gable dormers and a chunk of Gallo-Roman wall at its base. Further west the **Eglise St-Julien** has managed to insinuate a wine museum, the **Musée des vins de Touraine** (16 rue Nationale, 02.47.61.07.93, open 9am-noon, 2-6pm Mon, Wed-Sun), into its Gothic, monastic cells; and next door, the **Musée du Compagnonnage** (8 rue Nationale, 02.47.21.62.20, open 9am-noon, 2-6pm Mon, Wed-Sun, daily June-Sept) is a dinky museum, showcasing the handiwork of master craftsmen of the guilds. Cross over rue Nationale (the main thoroughfare and shopping district) and you'll get to the fabulous **Hôtel Goüin**, a splendid Renaissance beauty that once belonged to a rich silk merchant and which now contains the **Musée Archéologique de la Touraine** (25 rue de Commerce, 02.47.66.22.32, open 10am-1pm, 2-6pm Tue-Sun) devoted to the history of the Touraine region. Sadly, the only place still keeping the local silk industry alive is the **Manufacture Le Manach** (35 quai Paul Bert, 02.47.54.45.78, www.lemanach.fr), arranged around a pretty, cobbled courtyard, on the right bank of the Loire. The weaving methods here have remained unchanged since the early 19th century and it is one of the only manufacturers in France capable of reproducing authentic fabrics using patterns from the 17th century. Enquire at the tourist office if you fancy a visit.

## Where to eat & stay

For dreamy regional dishes such as *crépine de dinde* (a giant turkey meatball cooked in red wine) and *poire tappé* (poached pear), head to **Le Petit Patrimoine** (58 rue Colbert, 02.47.66.05.81, menus €16-€25). The dining room is long, thin and sparsely clad, but the dishes that come out of the kitchen, plus the hefty wine list, make up for any shortcomings in the decor department. If *moules-frites* is more your thing, the **Taverne de l'Homme Tranquille** has a large selection (22 rue du grand Marché, nr pl Plumereau, 02.47.61.46.04).

For a few sneaky glasses of Touraine wine before you head back, **Au Chien Jaune** (74 rue Bernard Palissy, 02.47.05.10.17), a former brothel turned good, is in a handy spot by the tourist office and railway station. Aside from the wine, it specialises in regional dishes like *tête de veau*.

If you're on a budget, a good, cheap option in a central location is **Hôtel Mondial** (3 pl de la Résistance, 02.47.05.62.68, www.hotelmondialtours.com, doubles €44-€70). Rooms are fairly tastefully decorated and breakfast is copious. For a touch more luxury, follow in the footsteps of Winston Churchill and try Tours' only four-star hotel, **L'Hôtel de l'Univers** (5 bd Heurteloup, 02.47.05.37.15, www.hotel-univers.fr, doubles €197-€398); or for somewhere a little more modest, with decent rooms and a pretty garden, the **Best Western Central Hôtel** (21 rue Berthelot, 02.47.05.46.44, www.bestwesterncentralhotel tours.com, doubles €76-€140), is altogether more charming than many of the other chain hotels in Tours.

## Getting there

### By car
235km (146 miles) west from Paris by A10.

### By train
From Gare Montparnasse to Tours centre (1hr).

## Tourist information

### Office de Tourisme
78-82 rue Bernard Palissy, 37042 Tours (02.47.70.37.37/www.ligeris.com). **Open** *Mid Apr-mid Oct* 8.30am-7pm Mon-Sat; 10am-12.30pm, 2.30-5pm Sun & bank hols. *Mid Oct-mid Apr* 9am-12.30pm, 1.30-6pm Mon-Sat; 10am-1pm Sun & bank hols.
If you're keen to see the châteaux but don't fancy driving all the way, the tourist office runs excellent day trips from Paris to Azat-le-Rideau, Villandry, Chenonceau and Amboise.

# Directory

## Features

# Directory

## Getting Around

### By air

#### Roissy-Charles-de-Gaulle airport

Most international flights use Roissy-Charles-de-Gaulle airport (www.paris-cdg.com), 30km (19 miles) north-east of Paris. Its two main terminals are some way apart, so check which one you need for your return flight; for information in English, call 01.48.62.22.80 or see www.aeroportsdeparis. fr. The **RER B** (SNCF helpline, 08.91.36.20.20) is the quickest way to central Paris (about 40mins to Gare du Nord; 45mins to RER Châtelet-Les Halles; €8.20 single). A new station gives direct access from Terminal 2; from Terminal 1 you take the free shuttle bus. RER trains run every 15mins, 5.24am-11.56pm daily.

   **Air France buses** (08.92.35.08.20, www.cars-airfrance.com; €13 single, €20 return) leave every 15mins, 5.45am-11pm daily, from both terminals, and stop at porte Maillot and place Charles-de-Gaulle (35-50min trip). Air France buses also run to Gare Montparnasse and Gare de Lyon (€14 single, €22 return) every 30mins (45-60min trip), 7am-9pm daily; there's a shuttle bus between Roissy and Orly (€16) every 30mins, 6am-10.30pm Mon-Fri, 7am-10.30pm Sat, Sun. The **RATP Roissybus** (08.92.68.77.14, www.ratp.fr; €8.60) runs every 15mins, 5.45am-11pm daily, between the airport and the corner of rue Scribe/rue Auber (at least 45mins); buy tickets on the bus. **Paris Airports**

**Service** is a door-to-door minibus service between airports and hotels, 24/7. The more passengers on board, the less each one pays. Roissy prices go from €25 for one person to €12.40 each for eight people, 6am-8pm (minimum €34, 5-6am, 8-10pm); book on 01.55.98.10.80, www.paris airportservice.com. **Airport Connection** (01.43.65.55.55, www.airport-connection.com; booking 7am-7.30pm) runs a similar service, 4am-10.30pm. Prices for Roissy are €27 per person, €45 for two, then €15 per extra person. A **taxi** to central Paris can take 30-60mins depending on traffic. Expect to pay €30-€50, plus €1 per item of luggage.

#### Orly airport

Domestic and international flights use Orly airport (English-speaking information service on 01.49.75.15.15, 6am-midnight daily, www.paris-orly.com), 18km (11 miles) south of the city. It has two terminals: Orly-Sud (mainly international) and Orly-Ouest (mainly domestic).

   **Air France buses** (08.92.35.08.20, www.cars-airfrance.com; €9 single, €14 return) leave both terminals every 15mins, 6am-11pm daily, and stop at Invalides and Montparnasse (30-45mins). The **RATP Orlybus** (08.92.68.77.14, www.ratp.fr; €5.80) runs between the airport and Denfert-Rochereau every 15mins, 5.35am-11.05pm daily (30min trip); buy tickets on the bus. The high-speed **Orlyval** (www.orlyval.fr) shuttle train runs every 7mins (6am-11pm daily) to RER B station Antony (Orlyval and RER together cost

€17.05); getting to central Paris takes about 35mins. You could also catch the **Orlyrail** (€5.65) to Pont de Rungis, where you can take the RER C into central Paris. Trains run every 15mins, 6am-11pm daily; 50min trip. Orly prices for the **Paris Airports Service** and **Airport Connection** door-to-door facility (*see left*) are €24 for one person and €9-€14 each for extra passengers depending on numbers. A **taxi** into town takes 20-40mins and costs €16-€26, plus €1 per piece of luggage.

#### Paris Beauvais airport

Beauvais (08.92.68.20.66, www.aeroportbeauvais.com), 70km (44 miles) from Paris, is served by budget airlines such as **Ryanair** (03.44.11. 41.41, www.ryanair.com). Buses (€13) leave for porte Maillot 20mins after each arrival; buses the other way leave 3hrs 15mins before each departure. Get tickets from the arrival lounge or the shop at 1 bd Pershing, 17th (01.58.05.08.45).

#### Airline contacts

**Aer Lingus** 01.70.20.00.72/ www.aerlingus.com.
**Air France** 08.20.32.08.20/ www.airfrance.fr.
**American Airlines** 08.10.87.28.72/ www.americanairlines.fr.
**bmibaby** 08.90.71.00.81/ www.bmibaby.com.
**British Airways** 08.25.82.54.00/ www.britishairways.fr.
**British Midland** 01.41.91.87.04/ www.flybmi.com.
**Continental** 01.71.23.03.35/ www.continental.com.
**Easyjet** 08.26.10.26.11/ www.easyjet.com.
**KLM & NorthWest** 08.90.71.07.10/ www.klm.com.
**United** 08.10.72.72.72/ www.united.fr.

# By car

Options for crossing the Channel with a car include: **Eurotunnel** (08.10.63.03.04, www.eurotunnel.com); **Brittany Ferries** (08.25.82, 88.28. www.brittanyferries. com); **P&O Ferries** (08.25. 12.01.56, www.poferries. com); and **SeaFrance** (08.25. 04.04.45, www.seafrance.com).

### Shared journeys

**Allô-Stop** *1 rue Condorcet, 9th (01.53.20.42.42/08.25.80.36.66/ www.allostop.net). M° Poissonnière.* **Open** 10am-1pm, 2-6pm Mon-Fri; 10am-1pm, 2-4pm Sat. **Credit** MC, V. Call several days ahead to be put in touch with drivers. There's a fee (€4 under 200km, 124 miles; up to €10 over 500km, 310 miles), plus €0.50 per km to the driver.

# By coach

International coach services arrive at the Gare Routière Internationale Paris-Gallieni at Porte de Bagnolet, 20th. For reservations (in English), call **Eurolines** on 08.92.89.90.91 (€0.34/min) or 01.44.63.00.66 (UK 01582 404 511), or visit www.eurolines.fr.

# By rail

Eurostar services to Paris now depart from the new terminal at St Pancras International instead of Waterloo. Thanks to a new high speed track, the journey from London to Paris now takes 2hrs 15mins direct, slightly longer for trains stopping at Ashford and Lille. Eurostar services from the new terminal at Ebbsfleet International, near junction 2 of the M25, take 2hrs 5mins direct. Check in at least 30 mins before departure time. Eurostar trains from London St Pancras (01233 617 575, www.eurostar.com) arrive at Gare du Nord (08.92.35. 35.39, www.sncf.fr), with easy access to public transport and taxi ranks. **Cycles** can be taken as hand luggage if they are dismantled and carried in a bike bag. You can also check them in at the Eurodispatch depot at Waterloo (Esprit Parcel Service, 08705 850 850) or Sernam depot at Gare du Nord (01.55.31.54.54). Check-in must be done 24hrs ahead; a Eurostar ticket must be shown. The service costs £20/€45.39.

# Maps

Free maps of the métro, bus and RER systems are available at airports and métro stations. Other brochures from métro stations are *Paris Visite – Le Guide*, with details of transport tickets and a small map, and *Plan de Paris*, a fold-out one showing *Noctambus* night bus lines. A Paris street map (*Plan de Paris*) can be bought from newsagents. The blue *Paris Pratique* is clear and compact.

# Public transport

Almost all of the Paris public transport system is run by the **RATP** (Régie Autonome des Transports Parisiens; 08.92.68.77.14, in English 08.92.68.41.14, www.ratp.fr): the bus, métro (underground) and suburban tram routes, as well as lines A and B of the RER (Réseau Express Régional) suburban express railway, which connects with the métro within the city centre. National rail operator **SNCF** (08.92.35.35.39, www.sncf.com) runs RER lines C, D and E, and serves the Paris suburbs (*Banlieue*), and French regions and abroad (*Grandes Lignes*).

# Fares & tickets

Paris and suburbs are divided into eight travel zones; zones 1 and 2 cover the city centre. RATP tickets and passes are valid on the métro, bus and RER. Tickets and *carnets* can be bought at métro stations, tourist offices and *tabacs* (tobacconists); single tickets can be bought on buses. Hold on to your ticket in case of spot checks; you'll also need it to exit from RER stations.

● A single ticket costs €1.50, but it's more economical to buy a *carnet* of ten for €11.10.

● A one-day *Mobilis* pass costs from €5.60 for zones 1 and 2 to €18.70 for zones 1-8 (not including airports).

● A one-day *Paris Visite* pass for zones 1-3 is €8.50; a five-day pass is €27.20, with discounts on some attractions.

● One-week or one-month *Carte Orange* passes (passport photo needed) offer unlimited travel in the relevant zones; if bought in zones 1 or 2, each is delivered as a Navigo swipe card. A *forfait mensuel* (monthly *Carte Orange* valid from the first day of the month) for zones 1 and 2 costs €53.50; a weekly *forfait hebdomadaire* (weekly *Carte Orange* valid Mon-Sun inclusive) for zones 1 and 2 costs €16.30 and is better value than *Paris Visite* passes.

# Métro & RER

The Paris **métro** is the fastest and cheapest way of getting around. Trains run daily 5.30am-12.40am. Individual lines are numbered, with each direction named after the last stop. Follow the orange *Correspondance* to change lines. Some interchanges, such as Châtelet, Montparnasse Bienvenüe and République, involve long walks. The exit (*Sortie*) is indicated in blue. The driverless line 14 runs from Gare St-Lazare to Olympiades. Pickpockets and bag-snatchers are rife – pay special attention as the doors are closing.

The five **RER** lines (A, B, C, D and E) run 5.30am-1am daily through Paris and into the suburbs. Within Paris, the RER is useful for faster journeys – Châtelet Les Halles to Gare du Nord is one stop on

# Taking to the water

In its quest to improve public transport on all fronts, the *mairie* has now turned to the water. Mayor Bertrand Delanoë recently unveiled plans to create a boat network composed of regular pick-up and drop-off points along the Seine. A test phase begins in 2008, with the creation of a six-station route between the Gare d'Austerlitz and the eastern *banlieue* of Maisons-Alfort.

While tourists often take to the Seine for guided tours of the city, Parisians have rarely considered the river a viable means for transport. Since 1995, Batobus has been running a boat service within Paris, but the vast majority of its 800,000 annual voyagers are tourists. The company has tried to entice locals by offering an annual pass for just €55 (€35 for children), but there are currently just 500 holders. It must be said that neither the hours (10am-4.30pm in the winter) nor the route (just nine stops between the Eiffel

Tower and the Gare d'Austerlitz) are particularly compatible with commuting. A nocturnal service has, however, proved highly popular during the annual Nuit Blanche festival, while temporary boat services have also met with considerable success during the Paris-Plage festival.

The new project has longer-term ambitions. The idea is for boats to become part of the established Paris travel network. During the test phase, boats are scheduled to run every 20 minutes in rush hour, and will be accessible using existing (métro and bus) transport cards. If the initial trial proves a success, the service will eventually be extended as far as Suresnes in the west and Vitry in the east, helping unite Paris with its various Seine-side communities. Given that the boat's top speed is 15km/h (10mph), however, it is unlikely to win over long-distance commuters.

---

the RER, and six on the métro. Métro tickets are valid for RER journeys within zones 1 and 2.

## Buses

Buses run 6.30am-8.30pm, with some routes continuing until 12.30am, Mon-Sat; limited services operate on selected lines Sun and public holidays. You can use a métro ticket, a ticket bought from the driver (€1.50) or a travel pass. Tickets should be punched in the machine next to the driver; passes should be shown to the driver. When you want to get off, press the red request button.

### Night buses

After the métro and normal buses stop running, the only public transport – apart from taxis – are the 18 **Noctambus** lines, between place du Châtelet and the suburbs (hourly 1.30am-5.35am Mon-Thur; half-hourly 1am-5.35am Fri, Sat); look out for the owl logo on bus stops. Routes A to H, P, T and V serve the Right

Bank and northern suburbs; I to M, R and S serve the Left Bank and southern suburbs. A ticket costs €2.70 with one change; travel passes are valid.

## River transport

### Batobus
*(08.25.05.01.01/www.batobus.com).*
River buses stop every 15-25mins at: Eiffel Tower, Musée d'Orsay, St-Germain-des-Prés (quai Malaquais), Notre-Dame, Jardin des Plantes, Hôtel de Ville, Louvre, Champs-Elysées (Pont Alexandre III). They run Nov-Mar 10.30am-4.30pm; Mar-May & Sept-Nov 10.30am-7pm; June-Aug 10am-9.30pm. A one-day pass is €12 (€6, €8 reductions); two-day pass €14 (€7, €9 reductions); five-day pass €17 (€8, €11 reductions); season-ticket €55 (€35 reductions). Tickets can be bought at Batobus stops, RATP ticket offices and the **Office de Tourisme** (*see p381*).

## Trams

Two modern tram lines operate in the suburbs, running from La Défense to Issy-Val de Seine and from Bobigny Pablo Picasso to St-Denis; a third runs between the Garigliano Bridge in the

west of the city to Porte d'Ivry in the south-east. They connect with the métro and RER; fares are the same as for buses.

## Rail travel

Suburban destinations are served by the RER. Other locations farther from the city are served by the SNCF railway; the TGV high-speed train has slashed journey times and is being extended to all the main regions. There are few long-distance bus services.

Tickets can be bought at any SNCF station (not just the one from which you'll travel), SNCF shops and travel agents. If you reserve online or by phone, you can pay and pick up your tickets from the station or have them sent to your home. SNCF automatic machines (*billeterie automatique*) only work with French credit/debit cards. Regular trains have full-rate White (peak) and cheaper Blue (off-peak) periods. You can save on TGV fares by buying special cards. The *Carte 12/25* gives under-26s a 25-50

per cent reduction; even without it, under-26s are entitled to 25 per cent off. Buy tickets in advance to secure the cheaper fare. Before you board any train, stamp your ticket in the orange *composteur* machines located on the platforms, or you might have to pay a hefty fine.

### SNCF reservations & tickets

*National reservations & information 08.92.35.35.39 (€0.34 per min)/ www.sncf.com.* **Open** 7am-10pm daily. You can also dial 3635 and say 'billet' at the prompt.

### SNCF information

*Ile-de-France (08.91.36.20.20; no reservations).* **Open** 7am-10pm daily.

## Mainline stations

**Gare d'Austerlitz**: Central and south-west France and Spain.
**Gare de l'Est**: Alsace, Champagne and southern Germany.
**Gare de Lyon**: Burgundy, the Alps, Provence and Italy.
**Gare Montparnasse**: West France, Brittany, Bordeaux, the south-west.
**Gare du Nord**: Eurostar, Channel ports, north-east France, Belgium and Holland.
**Gare St-Lazare**: Normandy.

## Taxis

Paris taxi drivers are not known for their flawless knowledge of the Paris street map; if you have a preferred route, say so. Taxis can also be hard to find, especially at rush hour or early in the morning. Your best bet is to find a taxi rank (*station de taxis*, marked with a blue sign) on major roads, crossroads and at stations. A white light on a taxi's roof indicates the car is free; an orange light means the cab is busy. Taxi charges are based on zone and time of day: **A** (10am-5pm Mon-Sat central Paris, €0.62 per km); **B** (5pm-10am Mon-Fri, 5pm-midnight Sat, 7am-midnight Sun central Paris; 7am-7pm Mon-Sat inner suburbs and airports, €1.06 per km); **C** (midnight-7am Sun central Paris; 7pm-7am Mon-

Sat, all day Sun inner suburbs and airports; all times outer suburbs, €1.24 per km). Most journeys in central Paris cost €6-€12; there's a minimum charge of €5.10, plus €0.90 for each piece of luggage over 5kg or bulky objects, and a €0.70 surcharge from mainline stations. Most drivers will not take more than three people, although they should take a couple and two children.

Don't feel obliged to tip, although rounding up to the nearest euro is polite. Taxis are not allowed to refuse rides if they deem them too short and can only refuse to take you in a certain direction during their last half-hour of service (both rules are often ignored). If you want a receipt, ask for *un reçu* or *la note*. Complaints should be made to the **Bureau de la réglementation publique**, 36 rue des Morillons, 75732 Paris Cedex 15.

## Phone cabs

These firms take phone bookings 24/7; you also pay for the time it takes your taxi to reach you. If you wish to pay by credit card (minimum €15), mention this when you order.

**Airportaxis** *to and from Paris airports, 01.41.50.42.50/ www.taxiparisien.fr.*
**Alpha** *01.45.85.85.85/ www.alphataxis.fr.*
**G7** *01.47.39.47.39/www.taxis-g7.fr.*
**Taxis Bleus** *01.49.36.29.48/ 08.91.70.10.10/www.taxis-bleus.com.*

## Driving

If you bring your car to France, you must bring its registration and insurance documents. An insurance green card, available from insurance companies and the AA and RAC in the UK, is not compulsory but is useful. As you come into Paris, you will meet the Périphérique, the giant ring road that carries traffic into, out of and around the city. Intersections, leading on to other main roads, are

called *portes* (gates). Driving on the Périphérique is not as hair-raising as it might look, though it's often congested, especially at rush hour and peak holiday times. If you've come to Paris by car, it may be a good idea to park at the edge of the city and use public transport. Some hotels have parking spaces that can be paid for by the hour, day or by various types of season tickets.

In peak holiday periods, the organisation Bison Futé hands out brochures at motorway *péages* (toll gates), suggesting less crowded routes. French roads are categorised as *Autoroutes* (motorways, with an 'A' in front of the number), *Routes Nationales* (national 'N' roads), *Routes Départementales* (local, 'D' roads) and rural *Routes Communales* ('C' roads). *Autoroutes* are toll roads, though some sections, including most of the area immediately around Paris, are free. *Autoroutes* have a speed limit of 130km/h (80mph); this is not adhered to with any degree of zeal by French motorists. The limit on most *Routes Nationales* is 90km/h (56mph); within urban areas the limit is 50km/h (30mph), and 30km/h (20mph) in selected residential zones.

**Infotrafic** *08.99.70.71.01 (€0.34 per minute)/www.infotrafic.fr.*
**Traffic information service for the Ile-de-France** *08.26.02.20.22/ www.securiteroutiere.gouv.fr.*

## Breakdown services

The AA and RAC do not have reciprocal arrangements with an equivalent organisation in France, so it's advisable to take out additional breakdown insurance cover, for example with a company like **Europ Assistance** (0870 737 5720/ www.europ-assistance.co.uk). If you don't have insurance, you can still use its service (01.41.85.85.85), but it will charge you the full cost. Other

24-hour breakdown services in Paris include: **Action Auto Assistance** (01.45.58.49.58) and **Dan Dépann Auto** (01.40.06.06.53).

## Driving tips

● At junctions where no signposts indicate right of way, the car coming from the right has priority. Many roundabouts now give priority to those on the roundabout. If this is not indicated (by road markings or a sign with the message *Vous n'avez pas la priorité*), priority is for those coming from the right.
● Drivers and all passengers must wear seat belts.
● Children under ten are not allowed to travel in the front of a car, except in baby seats facing backwards.
● You should not stop on an open road; you must pull off to the side.
● When drivers are flashing their lights at you, this often means they will not slow down and are warning you to move out of their path or keep out of the way. But some friendly drivers also flash their lights to warn other drivers when there might be traffic police lurking in the vicinity.
● Try to carry plenty of change, as it's quicker – and less stressful – to make for the exact-money line on *péages*. If you are caught short, some cashiers give change and most *péages* accept credit cards.

## Parking

There are still a few free on-street parking areas in Paris, but they're often full. If you park illegally, you risk getting your car clamped or towed away (*see below*). It's forbidden to park in zones marked for deliveries (*livraisons*) or taxis. Parking meters have now been replaced by *horodateurs*, pay-and-display machines, which take a special card (*carte de*

stationnement at €10 or €30, available from *tabacs*). Parking is often free at weekends, after 7pm and in August. There are plenty of underground car parks in the city centre. Most cost around €2.50 per hour, €22 for 24 hours; some have lower rates after 6pm, and many offer various season tickets – a week from €80 or a month at €150.

**Parking information for Paris**
*www.parkingsdeparis.com.*

## Clamps & car pounds

If your car is clamped, contact the nearest police station. There are eight car pounds (*préfourrières*) in Paris. You'll have to pay a €136 removal fee, plus €10 storage charge per day and a parking fine of €35 for parking in a no-parking zone. Bring your driving licence and insurance papers. Before you can pay, you need to find your vehicle – no small task. Once clamped, your car will be sent to the *préfourrière* nearest to where it was snatched, then moved on to a different pound after 72hrs. To find out where, call 01.53. 73.53.73 or 08.91.01.22.22, or try www.prefecture-police-paris.interieur.gouv.fr

## Car hire

To hire a car you must be 25 or over and have held a licence for at least a year. Some agencies accept drivers aged 21-24, but a supplement of €20-€25 per day is usual. Take your licence and passport with you. There are often good weekend offers (Fri evening to Mon morning). Week-long deals are better at the bigger companies: with Avis or Budget, for example, it's around €300 a week for a small car with insurance and 1,750km (1,090 miles) included. Costlier hire companies allow the return of a car in other French cities and abroad. Bargain companies may have

an extremely high charge for damage: read the small print before signing.

### Hire companies
**Ada** *01.48.06.58.13/ 08.25.16.91.69/www.ada.fr.*
**Avis** *01.44.18.10.54/ 08.20.05.05.05/www.avis.fr.*
**Budget** *01.41.22.19.30/ 08.25.00.35.64/www.budget.fr.*
**EasyRentacar** *www.easycar.com.*
**Europcar** *01.53.64.16.24/ 08.25.82.55.13/www.europcar.fr.*
**Hertz** *01.41.91.95.25/www.hertz.fr.*
**Rent-a-Car** *08.91.70.02.00/ www.rentacar.fr.*

### Chauffeur-driven cars
**Chauffeur Services Paris** *(09.53.09.66.88/www.csparis.com).* **Open** 24hrs daily. **Prices** from €120 airport transfer; €180 for 4 hours. **Credit** AmEx, DC, MC, V.

## Cycling

In 2007 the mayor launched a free bike scheme – Vélib (www.velib.paris.fr). There are now over 20,000 bicycles available 24 hours a day, at nearly 1500 'stations' across the city (*see p164* **Easy rider**). Just swipe your travel card to release the bikes from their stands. The *mairie* actively promotes cycling in the city and the Vélib scheme is complemented by the 353 km (220 miles) of bike lanes snaking their way around Paris. There are even plans for a bicycle 'Périphérique' circling the city.

The Itinéraires Paris-Piétons-Vélos-Rollers – scenic strips of the city that are closed to cars on Sundays and holidays – continue to multiply; the city website (www.paris.fr) can provide an up-to-date list of routes and a downloadable map of cycle lanes. A free *Paris à Vélo* map can be picked up at any mairie or from bike shops. Cycle lanes (*pistes cyclables*) run mostly N-S and E-W. N-S routes include rue de Rennes, av d'Italie, bd Sébastopol and av Marceau.

E-W routes take in the rue de Rivoli, bd St-Germain, bd St-Jacques and av Daumesnil. You could be fined (€22) if you don't use them, which is a bit rich considering the lanes are often blocked by delivery vans and the €135 fine for obstructing a cycle lane is barely enforced. Cyclists are also entitled to use certain bus lanes (especially the new ones, which are set off by a strip of kerb stones); look out for traffic signs with a bike symbol. The Bois de Boulogne and Bois de Vincennes offer paths away from traffic, although they are still criss-crossed by roads bearing menacing motor vehicles.

Don't let the Parisians' blasé attitude to helmets and lights convince you it's not worth using them. Be confident, make your intentions clear and keep moving – and look out for scooter-mounted bag-snatchers. If the thought of pedalling around alone in a city known for the verve of its drivers fazes you, consider joining a guided bike tour.

## Cycles & scooters for hire

Note that bike insurance may not cover theft.

### Freescoot

*63 quai de la Tournelle, 5th (01.44.07.06.72/www.freescoot.com). M° Maubert Mutualité or St-Michel.* **Open** 9am-7pm daily; closed Sun Oct-mid Apr. **Credit** AmEx, MC, V. Scooters €30/day, €40/weekend, €145/week. Deposit of €1,300/€1,600 required, plus passport. **Other locations**: 144 bd Voltaire, 11th (01.44.93.04.03).

### Maison Roue Libre

*1 passage Mondétour, 1st (01.44.76.86.43/08.10.44.15.34). M° Châtelet.* Plus (Mar-Oct) four RATP cyclobuses at Stalingrad, pl du Châtelet, porte d'Auteuil and parc Floral in the Bois de Vincennes (01.48.15.28.88/www.rouelibre.fr). **Open** 9am-7pm daily. **Credit** MC, V (for weekend hire only). Bike hire €4/hour, €10-€15/day, €28/weekend. Helmets free. Passport and deposit of €200 required. **Other locations**: 37 bd Bourdon, 4th (01.42.71.54.54).

### Paris-Vélo

*2 rue du Fer-à-Moulin, 5th (01.43.37.59.22/www.paris-velo-rent-a-bike.fr). M° Censier Daubenton or St Marcel.* **Open** 10am-7pm daily. **Credit** MC, V.

Good selection of mountain bikes (VTT) and 21-speed models for hire. Five hours cost €12, a weekend €30, a month €116. Passport and €300 deposit required.

### Vélib

Free bikes can be hired and deposited at Vélib stations throughout the city (*see* p164 **Easy rider**). including at the following locations: *2 rue Jean Meroz, 8th, M° Franklin D Roosevelt; 12 pl de la Chapelle, 18th, M° La Chapelle; 7 pl de l'Hotel de Ville, 4th, M° Hôtel de Ville; 2 rue de l'Oratoire, 1st, M° Louvre Rivoli; 85 av Bosquet, 7th, M° École Militaire.*

## Walking

Walking is the best way to explore Paris; just remember to remain vigilant at all times. Crossing Paris streets can be a perilous business, as the 3,000 or so pedestrians who end up in hospital – or worse – each year can tell you. Brits should be aware that traffic will be coming from the 'wrong' direction and that zebra crossings mean very little. By law, drivers are only obliged to stop at a red traffic light – and even then, many will take a calculated risk.

# Staying mobile

Even if the Paris transport system has a decent reputation for reliability, buses and métros can still stray from the advertised timetables. No one likes waiting around and wasting time – which is why the RATP has launched a new real-time travel information service. **Ma RATP dans la poche** lets travellers use their mobile phones to instantly find out when the next bus, tram or RER is due at any given station. Users can either consult the WAP site (wap.ratp. fr) or send a text message to 61064 that consists of the word 'Bus', 'Tram' or 'RER', followed by the line number and the name of the desired station/stop. The WAP site also includes RATP news, information about tickets and online games.

To make life even simpler, certain RER stations are experimenting with a barcode system. Travellers with a camera phone

simply scan these barcodes, which are displayed on platforms, to immediately access the latest travel information.

Another mobile phone information service currently in its test phase is the Paris Bluetooth MobiGuide. Certain Vélib stations in the 1st, 2nd and 4th arrondissements have been equipped with Bluetooth technology, allowing Parisians and visitors to download the MobiGuide on to their mobile phone for free. The MobiGuide is a guide to the local area that takes the form of a search engine and map, enabling users to locate the nearest taxi ranks, WiFi hotspots and Vélib stations; access news about municipal activities and events; and search for emergency numbers (cinema and museum programmes, etc) and local services. The idea is to collect feedback on this trial version before launching a city-wide service.

**Directory**

# Resources A-Z

## Addresses

Paris arrondissements are indicated by the last two digits of the postal code: 75002 denotes the second, 75015 the 15th. The 16th arrondissement is divided into two sectors, 75016 and 75116. Some business addresses have a more detailed postcode, followed by a Cedex number, which indicates the arrondissement; *bis* or *ter* is the equivalent of 'b' or 'c' after a building number.

## Age restrictions

For heterosexuals and homosexuals, the age of consent is 15. You must be 18 to drive, and to consume alcohol in a public place. There is no age limit for buying cigarettes.

## Attitude & etiquette

Parisians take manners seriously and are generally more courteous than their reputation may lead you to believe. If someone brushes you accidentally, they will more often than not say *'pardon'*; you can do likewise, or say *'c'est pas grave'* (don't worry). In shops it is normal to greet the assistant with a *'bonjour madame'* or *'bonjour monsieur'* when you enter, and say *'au revoir'* when you leave. The business of *'tu'* and *'vous'* can be tricky for English speakers. Strangers, people significantly older than you and professional contacts should be addressed with the respectful *'vous'*; friends, relatives, children and pets as *'tu'*. Among themselves, young people often launch straight in with *'tu'*.

## Business

The best first stop in Paris for initiating business is the **CCIP** (*see below*). Banks can refer you to lawyers, accountants and tax consultants.

## Conventions & conferences

Paris is the world's leading centre for trade fairs.

**CNIT** *2 pl de la Défense, BP 321, 92053 Paris La Défense (01.72.72.17.00/www.parisexpo.fr). Mᵒ/RER Grande Arche de La Défense.* Mainly computer fairs.
**Palais des Congrès** *2 pl de la Porte-Maillot, 17th (01.40.68.00.05/ www.palais-congres-paris.fr). Mᵒ Porte-Maillot.*
**Parc des Expositions de Paris-Nord Villepinte** *SEPENV 60004, 95970 Roissy-Charles-de-Gaulle (01.48.63.31.31/www. expoparisnord.com). RER Parc des Expositions.* Trade fair centre near Roissy airport.
**Paris-Expo** *Porte de Versailles, 15th (01.72.72.16.17/www. parisexpo.fr). Mᵒ Porte de Versailles.* The city's biggest expo centre, from fashion to pharmaceuticals.

## Courier services

**ATV** *(08.11.65.56.05/www. atoutevitesse.com).* **Open** 24hrs daily. **Credit** MC, V.
Bike or van messengers 24/7. Higher rates apply after 8pm weekdays and at weekends.
**Chronopost** *(Customer service: 08.25.80.18.01/www.chronopost. com).* **Open** 8am-8pm Mon-Fri; 9am-3pm Sat. **Credit** MC, V.
This overnight delivery offshoot of the state-run post office is the most widely used service for parcels.
**UPS** *34 bd Malesherbes, 8th (08.21.23.38.77/www.ups.com). Mᵒ St-Augustin.* **Open** 8am-7pm Mon-Fri; 8am-1pm Sat. **Credit** AmEx, MC, V.
International courier services.

## Secretarial services

**ADECCO International** *50 rue Etienne-Marcel, 2nd (01.55.34.78.20/www.adecco.fr). Mᵒ Etienne Marcel.* **Open** 8.30am-12.30pm, 2-6.30pm Mon-Fri.
International employment agency specialising in bilingual secretaries and office staff – on a permanent or temporary basis.

## Translators & interpreters

Documents such as birth certificates, loan applications and so on must be translated by certified legal translators, listed at the **CCIP** (*see below*) or embassies. For business translations there are dozens of reliable independents.
**Association des Anciens Elèves de l'Esit** *(01.44.05.41.46).* **Open** by phone only, 8am-8pm Mon-Fri; 8am-6pm Sat.
A translation and interpreting co-operative whose 1,000 members are graduates of the Ecole Supérieure d'Interprètes et de Traducteurs.
**International Corporate Communication** *3 rue des Batignolles, 17th (01.43.87.29.29). Mᵒ Place de Clichy.* **Open** 9am-1pm, 2-6pm Mon-Fri.
Translators of financial and corporate documents, plus simultaneous translation.

## Useful organisations

**American Chamber of Commerce** *156 bd Haussmann, 8th (01.56.43.45.67). Mᵒ Miromesnil.* Closed to the public, calls only.
**British Embassy Commercial Library** *35 rue du Fbg-St-Honoré, 8th (01.44.51.34.56/www.amb-grandebretagne.fr). Mᵒ Concorde.* **Open** by appointment.
Stocks trade directories, and assists British companies that wish to develop or set up in France.
**CCIP (Chambre de Commerce et d'Industrie de Paris)** *27 av de Friedland, 8th (08.20.01.21.12/ www.ccip.fr). Mᵒ Charles de Gaulle Etoile.* **Open** 9am-5pm Mon-Fri.
This huge organisation provides a variety of services for people doing business in France and is very useful for small businesses. Pick up the free booklet *Discovering the Chamber of Commerce* from its head office (*above*). There's also a legal advice line (08.92.70.51.00, 9am-4.30pm Mon-Thur; 9am-1pm Fri).
**Other locations**: Bourse du Commerce, 2 rue de Viarmes, 1st (has a free library and bookshop);

2 rue Adolphe-Jullien, 1st (support for businesses wishing to export goods and services to France).
**INSEE (Institut National de la Statistique et des Etudes Economiques)** *Salle de consultation, 195 rue de Bercy, Tour Gamma A, 12th (08.25.88.94.52/ www.insee.fr)* *M° Bercy*. **Open** 9.30am-12.30pm, 2-5pm Mon-Thur; 9.30-12.30pm, 2-4pm Fri.
Source of seemingly every statistic to do with French economy and society.
**US Commercial Service** *Postal address: US Embassy, 2 av Gabriel, 8th. Visit: US Commercial Service, NEO Building, 14 bd Haussmann, 9th (01.43.12.23.83/www.buyusa. gov/france or www.amb-usa.fr).* *M° Richelieu Drouot*. **Open** by appointment 9am-6pm Mon-Fri. Helps American companies looking to trade in France. Advice by fax and email.

## Consumer

In the event of a serious misdemeanour, try one of the following:
**Direction Départmentale de la Concurrence, de la Consommation et de la Répression des Fraudes** *8 rue Froissart, 3rd (01.40.27.16.00).* *M° St-Sébastien Froissart*. **Open** 9am-noon, 2-5pm Mon-Fri.
Come here to file a consumer complaint concerning Paris-based businesses.
**Institut National de la Consommation** *80 rue Lecourbe, 15th (08.92.70.75.92/www.conso. net). M° Sèvres Lecourbe*. **Open** *by phone* 9am-12.30pm Mon-Fri; recorded information at other times. Queries on consumer, regulatory, housing and administrative matters.

## Customs

There are no customs on goods for personal use between EU countries, provided tax has been paid in the country of origin. Quantities accepted as being for personal use are:
● 800 cigarettes or 400 small cigars or 200 cigars or one kilo loose tobacco.
● Ten litres of spirits (over 22% alcohol), 90 litres of wine (under 22% alcohol) or 110 litres of beer.
For goods brought in from outside the EU:
● 200 cigarettes or 100 small cigars or 50 cigars or 250g loose tobacco.
● One litre of spirits (more than 22% alcohol) or two litres of wine and beer.
● 60cc perfume.

## Tax refunds

Non-EU residents can claim a refund or *détaxe* (around 12 per cent) on VAT if they spend over €175 in any one day in one shop and if they live outside the EU for more than six months in the year. At the shop concerned ask for a *bordereau de vente à l'exportation*, and when you leave France have it stamped by customs. Then send the

stamped form back to the shop. *Détaxe* does not cover food, drink, antiques, services or works of art.

## Disabled travellers

It's always wise to check up on a site's accessibility and provision for disabled access before you visit. General information (in French) is available on the Secrétaire d'Etat aux Personnes Handicapées website: www.handicap.gouv.fr, telephone 08.20.03.33.33.
**Association des Paralysés de France** *13 pl de Rungis, 13th (01.53.80.92.98/www.apf.asso.fr).* *M° Place d'Italie*. **Open** 9am-12.30pm, 2-6pm Mon-Fri.
Publishes *Guide 98 Musées, Cinémas* (€3.81) listing accessible museums and cinemas, and a guide to restaurants and sights.
**Fédération APAJH (Association pour Adultes et Jeunes Handicapés)** *185 Bureaux de la Colline, 92213 St-Cloud Cedex (01.55.39.56.00/www.apajh.org).* *M° Marcel Sembat*.
Advice for disabled people living in France.
**Plateforme d'Accueil et d'Information des Personnes Handicapées de la Mairie de Paris** *(08.00.03.37.48/ 01.43.47.77.99).*
Advice available in French to disabled persons living in or visiting Paris. The Office de Tourisme website (www.parisinfo.com) also provides useful information for disabled visitors.

## Getting around

The métro and buses are not wheelchair-accessible, with the exception of métro line 14 (Méteor), and bus lines 20, PC (Petite Ceinture) and some 91s. Forward seats on buses are intended for people with poor mobility. RER lines A and B and some SNCF trains are wheelchair-accessible in parts. All Paris taxis are obliged by law to take passengers in wheelchairs.
**Aihrop** *3 av Paul-Doumer, 92508 Rueil-Malmaison Cedex (01.41.29.01.29/www.aihrop.com).* **Open** 9.30am-12.30pm, 1.30-5.30pm Mon-Fri. Closed Aug.

---

# Travel advice

For current information on travel to a specific country – including the latest news on health issues, safety and security, local laws and customs – contact your home country's government department of foreign affairs. Most have websites with useful advice for would-be travellers.

### Australia
www.smartraveller.gov.au

### Canada
www.voyage.gc.ca

### New Zealand
www.safetravel.govt.nz

### Republic of Ireland
foreignaffairs.gov.ie

### UK
www.fco.gov.uk/travel

### USA
http://travel.state.gov

**Directory**

Transport for the disabled, anywhere in Paris and Ile-de-France; book 48 hours in advance.

## Drugs

French police have the power to stop and search anyone. It's wise to keep prescription drugs in their original containers and, if possible, to carry copies of the original prescriptions. If you're caught in possession of illegal drugs, you can expect a prison sentence and/or a fine. *See also right* **Health**.

## Electricity & gas

Electricity in France runs on 220V. Visitors with British 240V appliances can change the plug or use an adaptor (*adaptateur*). For US 110V appliances, you'll need to use a transformer (*transformateur*), available at BHV or branches of Fnac and Darty. Gas and electricity are supplied by the state-owned Electricité de France-Gaz de France. Contact EDF-GDF (08.10.34.34.75/ www.edf.fr/www.gazdefrance. com) about supply, bills, power failures and gas leaks.

## Embassies & consulates

For a full list of embassies and consulates, see the Pages Jaunes (www.pagesjaunes.fr) under 'Ambassades et Consulats'. Consular services (passports, etc) are for citizens of that country only.

**Australian Embassy** *4 rue Jean-Rey, 15th (01.40.59.33.00/ www.france.embassy.gov.au). M° Bir-Hakeim.* **Open** *Consular services* 9.15am-noon, 2-4.30pm Mon-Fri; *Visas* 10am-noon Mon-Fri.
**British Embassy** *35 rue du Fbg-St-Honoré, 8th (01.44.51.31.00/ www.amb-grandebretagne.fr). M° Concorde. Consular services 18bis rue d'Anjou, 8th. M° Concorde.* **Open** 9.30am-12.30pm, 2.30-4.30pm Mon-Fri. *Visas 16 rue d'Anjou, 8th (01.44.51.31.01).* **Open** 9.30am-noon by phone; 2.30-4.30pm.

British citizens wanting consular services (new passports, etc) should ignore the long queue stretching along rue d'Anjou for the visa department, and instead walk straight in at no.18bis.
**Canadian Embassy** *35 av Montaigne, 8th (01.44.43.29.00/ www.amb-canada.fr). M° Franklin D. Roosevelt.* **Open** 9am-noon, 2-5pm Mon-Fri. *Consular services 01.44.43.29.02.* **Open** 9am-noon Mon-Fri. *Visas 37 av Montaigne, 8th (01.44.43.29.16).* **Open** 8.30-11am Mon-Fri.
**Irish Embassy** *12 av Foch, 16th. Consulate 4 rue Rude, 16th (01.44.17.67.00). M° Charles de Gaulle Etoile.* **Open** *Consular/visas* 9.30am-noon Mon-Fri; by phone 9.30am-1pm, 2.30-5.30pm Mon-Fri.
**New Zealand Embassy** *7ter rue Léonard-de-Vinci, 16th (01.45.01.43.43/www.nzembassy. com/france). M° Victor Hugo.* **Open** 9am-1pm, 2-5.30pm Mon-Fri (closes 4pm Fri). *July, Aug* 9am-1pm, 2-4.30pm Mon-Thur; 9am-2pm Fri. *Visas* 9am-12.30pm Mon-Fri. Visas for travel to New Zealand can be applied for on the website www.immigration.govt.nz.
**South African Embassy** *59 quai d'Orsay, 7th (01.53.59.23.23/ www.afriquesud.net). M° Invalides.* **Open** 8.30am-5.15pm Mon-Fri. *Consulate & visas* 8.30am-noon Mon-Fri.
**US Embassy** *2 av Gabriel, 8th (01.43.12.22.22/www.amb-usa.fr). M° Concorde. Consulate & visas 4 av Gabriel, 8th (01.43.12.22.222). M° Concorde.* **Open** *Consular services* 9am-12.30pm, 1-3pm Mon-Fri. *Visas* (08.92.23.84.72) or check website for non-immigration visas.

## Emergencies

Most of the following services operate 24 hours a day. In a medical emergency, such as a road accident, phone the Sapeurs-Pompiers, who have trained paramedics. *See also* **Health: Accident & Emergency; Doctors; Helplines.**
**Ambulance (SAMU)** 15
**Police** 17
**Fire (Sapeurs-Pompiers)** 18
**Emergency (from a mobile phone)** 112
**GDF (gas leaks)** 08.10.43.32.75/ www.gazdefrance.fr
**EDF (electricity)** 08.10.33.39 + number of arrondissement (01-20)
**Centre anti-poison** 01.40.05.48.48

## Gay & lesbian

For information on HIV and AIDS, *see below* **Health**. *See also pp301-306* **Gay & Lesbian**.

## Health

Nationals of non-EU countries should take out insurance before leaving home. EU nationals staying in France are entitled to use the French Social Security system, which refunds up to 70 per cent of medical expenses. UK residents travelling in Europe require a European National Health Insurance Card (EHIC). This allows them to benefit from free or reduced-cost medical care when travelling in a country belonging to the European Economic Area (EEA) or Switzerland. The EHIC replaces the E111 form and is free of charge. For further information, refer to www.dh.gov.uk/travellers or your local post office.

If you're staying for longer than three months, or working in France but you are still making National Insurance contributions in Britain, you will need form E128 filled in by your employer and stamped by the NI contributions office in order to get a French medical number. Consultations and prescriptions have to be paid for in full on the spot, and are reimbursed on receipt of a completed *fiche*. If you undergo treatment, the doctor will give you a prescription and a *feuille de soins* (bill of treatment). Stick the small stickers from the medication boxes on to the *feuille de soins*. Send this, together with the prescription and details of your EHIC card, to the local **Caisse Primaire d'Assurance Maladie** for a refund. For those resident in France, more and more doctors now accept the **Carte Vitale**, which lets them produce a virtual *feuille de soins* and you

to pay only the non-reimbursable part of the bill. Information on health insurance can be found at www.ameli.fr. You can track refunds with Allosecu (08.20.90.09.00). See also the Ministry of Health's website at www.sante.gouv.fr.

## Accident & emergency

Hospitals specialise in one type of emergency or illness – refer to the Assistance Publique's website (www.aphp.fr). In a medical emergency, call the Sapeurs-Pompiers or SAMU (*see* **Emergencies**). The following (in order of district) have 24hr accident and emergency services:

### Adults
**Hôpital Hôtel Dieu** *1 pl du Parvis Notre-Dame, 4th (01.42.34.82.34).*
**Hôpital St-Louis** *1 av Claude-Vellefaux, 10th (01.53.72.22.98).*
**Hôpital St-Antoine** *184 rue du Fbg-St-Antoine, 12th (01.49.28.20.00).*
**Hôpital de la Pitié-Salpêtrière** *47-83 bd de l'Hôpital, 13th (01.42.16.00.00).*
**Hôpital Cochin** *27 rue du Fbg-St-Jacques, 14th (01.58.41.41.41).*
**Hôpital Européen Georges Pompidou** *20 rue Leblanc, 15th (01.56.09.20.00).*
**Hôpital Bichat-Claude Bernard** *46 rue Henri-Huchard, 18th (01.40.25.80.80).*
**Hôpital Tenon** *4 rue de la Chine, 20th (01.56.01.70.00).*

### Children
**Hôpital Armand Trousseau** *26 av du Dr Arnold-Netter, 12th (01.44.73.74.75).*
**Hôpital St-Vincent de Paul** *74-82 av Denfert-Rocherau, 14th (01.40.48.81.11).*
**Hôpital Necker** *149 rue de Sèvres, 15th (01.44.49.40.00).*
**Hôpital Robert Debré** *48 bd Sérurier, 19th (01.40.03.20.00).*

### Private Hospitals
**American Hospital in Paris** *63 bd Victor-Hugo, 92200 Neuilly (01.46.41.25.25/www.american-hospital.org). Mº Porte Maillot, then bus 82.* **Open** 24hrs daily. English-speaking hospital. French Social Security refunds only a small percentage of treatment costs.

**Hertford British Hospital (Hôpital Franco-Britannique)** *3 rue Barbès, 92300 Levallois-Perret (01.46.39.22.22/www.british-hospital.org). Mº Anatole-France.* **Open** 24hrs daily. Most of the staff here speak English.

## Complementary medicine

**Centre de Médecine Naturelle** *2 rue d'Isly, 8th (01.43.87.60.33). Mº St-Lazare.* **Open** by appointment 9am-8pm Mon-Fri; 9am-1pm Sat. Health services include acupuncture, aromatherapy and homeopathy.

## Contraception & abortion

To get the pill (*la pilule*) or coil (*stérilet*), you need a prescription, available on appointment from the two places listed below, from a *médecin généraliste* (GP) or from a gynaecologist. The morning-after pill (*la pilule du lendemain*) can be had from pharmacies without prescription but is not reimbursed. Condoms (*préservatifs*) and spermicides are sold in pharmacies and supermarkets, and there are condom machines in most métro stations, club lavatories and on some street corners.

If you're considering an abortion (IVG – *interruption volontaire de grossesse*) but want to discuss options in detail, you may get better information and counselling from the *orthogénie* (family planning) department of a hospital than from the two organisations below (see www.aphp.fr for IVG services). While abortion rights are strongly grounded in France, there are some doctors who remain opposed. Ultrasound examinations to ascertain the exact stage of pregnancy are obligatory.

**Centre de Planification et d'Education Familiales** *27 rue Curnonsky, 17th (01.48.88.07.28). Mº Porte de Champerret.* **Open** 9am-5pm Mon-Fri.

Free consultations on family planning and abortion. Abortion counselling on demand; otherwise phone for an appointment.
**MFPF (Mouvement Français pour le Planning Familial)** *10 rue Vivienne, 2nd (08.00.80.38.03/01.42.60.93.20/www.planning-familial.org). Mº Bourse.* **Open** 9.30am-5.30pm Mon, Tue, Thur, Fri; 9.30am-7.30am Wed.
Phone for an appointment for prescriptions and contraception advice. For abortion advice, turn up at the centre at one of the designated time slots. The approach here, however, is brusque.
**Other locations:** 94 bd Masséna, 13th (01.45.84.28.25).

## Dentists

Dentists are found in the *Pages Jaunes* under *Dentistes*. For emergencies, contact:
**Hôpital de la Pitié-Salpêtrière** *(see left);* also offers 24hr emergency dental care.
**SOS Dentaire** *87 bd Port-Royal, 13th (01.43.36.36.00). Mº Les Gobelins/RER Port-Royal.* **Open** *by phone* 9am-midnight.
Phone service for emergency dental care.

## Doctors

You'll find a list of GPs in the *Pages Jaunes* under *Médecins: Médecine générale.* For a social security refund, choose a doctor or dentist who is *conventionné* (state registered). Consultations cost €20 or more, of which a proportion can be reimbursed. Seeing a specialist costs more still.

**Centre Médical Europe** *44 rue d'Amsterdam, 9th (01.42.81.93.33). Mº St-Lazare.* **Open** 8am-7pm Mon-Fri; 8am-6pm Sat.
Practitioners in all fields; modest consultation fees.

### House calls
**SOS Médecins** *(01.47.07.77.77 or 08.20.33.24.24).* House calls cost €35 before 7pm; from €50 after and on holidays; prices are higher if you don't have French social security.
**Urgences Médicales de Paris** *(01.53.94.94.94).* Doctors make house calls for €35 during the day (€60 if you don't have French social security); €50/€80 until midnight; €63.50/€90 after midnight. Some of them speak English.

**Directory**

## Opticians

Branches of **Alain Afflelou** (www.alainafflelou.com) and **Lissac** (www.lissac.com) stock hundreds of frames and can make prescription glasses within the hour. For an eye test, you'll need to go to an *ophtalmologiste* – ask the optician for a list. Contact lenses can be bought over the counter if you have your prescription details.

**Hôpital des Quinze-Vingts**
*28 rue de Charenton, 12th (01.40.02.15.20).*
Specialist eye hospital offers on-the-spot consultations for eye problems.
**SOS Optique** *(01.48.07.22.00/ www.sosoptique.com).*
24hr repair service for glasses.

## Pharmacies

French *pharmacies* sport a green neon cross. A rota of *pharmacies de garde* operate at night and on Sundays. If closed, a pharmacy will have a sign indicating the nearest one open. Staff can provide basic medical services such as bandaging wounds (for a small fee) and will indicate the nearest doctor on duty. *Parapharmacies* sell almost everything pharmacies do but cannot dispense prescription medication. Toiletries and sanitary products are often cheaper in supermarkets.

### Night pharmacies

**Grande Pharmacie de la Nation**
*13 pl de la Nation, 11th (01.43.73.24.03). M° Nation.*
Open 8am-11pm daily.
**Matignon** *2 rue Jean-Mermoz, 8th (01.43.59.86.55). M° Franklin D. Roosevelt.* Open 8.30am-2am daily.
**Pharmacie des Champs-Elysées** *84 av des Champs-Elysées, 8th (01.45.62.02.41). M° George V.* Open 24hrs daily.
**Pharmacie Européene de la Place de Clichy** *6 pl de Clichy, 9th (01.48.74.65.18). M° Place de Clichy.* Open 24hrs daily.
**Pharmacie des Halles** *10 bd de Sébastopol, 4th (01.42.72.03.23). M° Châtelet.* Open 9am-midnight Mon-Sat; 9am-10pm Sun.
**Pharmacie d'Italie** *61 av d'Italie, 13th (01.44.24.19.72). M° Tolbiac.* Open 8am-2am daily.

**Pharma Presto** *(01.61.04.04.03/ www.pharma-presto.com).* Open 24hrs daily. Delivery (€40 8am-6pm; €55 6pm-8am & weekends) of medication. Will also chauffeur your ailing pet to the vet.

## STDs, HIV & AIDS

**Cabinet Médical (Mairie de Paris)** *2 rue Figuier, 4th (01.49.96.62.70). M° Pont-Marie.*
Open 9am-5.30pm Mon, Tue, Thur; noon-5.30pm Wed; 1.30-5.30pm Fri; 9.30-10.30am Sat.
Free, anonymous tests (*dépistages*) for HIV, hepatitis B and C and syphilis (wait one week for results). Good counselling service too.
**Le Kiosque Infos Sida-Toxicomanie** *36 rue Geoffroy-l'Asnier, 4th (0148.04.95.20). M° St-Paul.* Open 10am-7pm Mon-Fri; 2-7pm Sat.
Youth association that offers information on AIDS and sexuality, drug addiction and abuse. Face-to-face counselling service.
**SIDA Info Service** *(08.00.84.08.00/www.sida-info-service.org).* Open 24hrs daily. Confidential AIDS information in French. English-speaking counsellors available 2-7pm Mon, Wed, Fri.

## Helplines

### Alcoholics Anonymous in English

*(01.46.34.59.65/www.aaparis.org).*
24hr recorded message gives details of AA meetings at the American Cathedral or American Church (for both, *see p376*).

### Allô Service Public

*(39.39/www.service-public.fr).* Open 8am-7pm Mon-Fri; 9am-2pm Sat.
A source of information and contacts for all aspects of tax, work and administration matters. They even claim to be able to help if you have problems with neighbours. The catch: you can only dial from inside France, and operators speak only French.

### The Counseling Center

*(01.47.23.61.13).*
English-language counselling service, based at the American Cathedral.

### Drogues Alcool Tabac Info Service

*(08.00.23.13.13/www.drogues.gouv.fr).*
Phone service, in French, for help with drug, alcohol and tobacco problems.

### Narcotics Anonymous

*(01.43.72.12.72/www.nafrance.org).*
The helpline is open daily 6-8pm. Meetings in English are held three times a week.

### SOS Dépression

*(01.40.47.95.95/http://sos.depression.free.fr).* Open 24hrs daily.
People listen and/or give advice. Can send round a counsellor or psychiatrist in case of a crisis.

### SOS Help

*(01.46.21.46.46/www.soshelpline.org).* Open 3-11pm daily.
English-language helpline.

## ID

French law requires that some form of identification be carried at all times. Be prepared to produce your passport or **EHIC** card (*see p368*).

## Insurance

*See p368* **Health**.

## Internet

### ISPs

**America Online** *(08.26.02.60.00/ www.aol.fr).*
**Club-Internet** *(08.05.50.05.55/ www.club-internet.fr).*
**Free** *(08.92.13.51.51/www.free.fr).*
**Neuf** *(08.00.97.59.75/ www.neuf.fr).*
**Orange** *(32.20/www.orange.fr).*

### Internet access

Many hotels offer internet access, some from your own room – and an increasing number of public spaces are setting themselves up as Wi-Fi hotspots.
**Milk** *31 bd de Sébastopol, 1st (08.20.00.10.00/www.milkinternethall.com). M° Châtelet or Rambuteau/RER Châtelet Les Halles.* Open 24hrs daily.
**Other locations**: throughout the city.

## Language

*See p383* **Vocabulary**; for food terms, *see p210* **Menu lexicon**.

## Left luggage

### Gare du Nord

There are self-locking luggage lockers (6.15am-11.15pm daily) on Level -1 under the main station concourse: small (€3.50), medium (€7) and large (€9.50) for 48 hours.

### Roissy-Charles-de-Gaulle airport

**Bagages du Monde**
*(01.34.38.58.90/www.bagagesdu monde.com)*. **Terminal 1** *Niveau Départ, Porte 20 (01.34.38.58.82)*. **Open** 8am-8pm daily. **Terminal 2A** *Niveau Départ, Porte 3-4 (01.34.38.58.80)*. **Open** 8am-8pm daily. **Terminal 2F** *Niveau Arrivée, Porte 4-5 (0134.38.58.81)*. **Open** 7am-7pm daily.
Company with counters in CDG terminals and an office in Paris (102 rue de Chemin-Vert, 11th, 01.43.57.30.90, open 2-6pm Mon; 9am-noon, 2-6pm Tue-Thur; 10am-1pm Sat) that can ship excess baggage anywhere in the world, or store luggage.

## Legal help

*Mairies* can answer some legal enquiries; ask for times of their free *consultations juridiques*.

**Direction Départmentale de la Concurrence, de la Consommation et de la Répression des Fraudes** *8 rue Froissart, 3rd (01.40.27.16.00)*. *Mº St-Sébastien Froissart*. **Open** 9am-noon, 2-5pm Mon-Fri.
Part of the Ministry of Finance; deals with consumer complaints.

**Palais de Justice Galerie de Harlay** *Escalier S, 4 bd du Palais, 4th (01.44.32.51.51)*. *Mº Cité*. **Open** 9am-noon Mon-Fri.
Free legal consultation. Arrive early and obtain a ticket for the queue.

**SOS Avocats** *(08.25.39.33.00)*. **Open** 7-11.30pm Mon-Fri. Closed July, Aug.
Free legal advice by phone.

## Libraries

Every arrondissement has a free public library. To get hold of a library card, you need ID and evidence of a fixed address in Paris.

**American Library** *10 rue du Général-Camou, 7th (01.53.59.12.60/ www.americanlibraryinparis.org)*. *Mº Ecole-Militaire/RER Pont de l'Alma*. **Open** 10am-7pm Tue-Sat (shorter hours in Aug). **Admission** day pass €12; annual €100; discount for students.
A useful resource: this is the largest English-language lending library on the Continent. It receives 400 periodicals, as well as popular magazines and newspapers (mainly American).

**Bibliothèque Historique de la Ville de Paris** *Hôtel Lamoignon, 24 rue Pavée, 4th (01.44.59.29.40)*. *Mº St-Paul*. **Open** 1-6pm Mon-Fri; 9.30am-6pm Sat. Closed 1st 2wks Aug. **Admission** free (bring passport photo and ID).
Books and documents on Paris history in a Marais mansion.

**Bibliothèque Marguerite Durand** *79 rue Nationale, 13th (01.53.82.76.77)*. *Mº Tolbiac*. **Open** 2-6pm Tue-Sat. Closed 3wks Sept. **Admission** free.
40,000 books and 120 periodicals on women's history. The feminism collection includes letters of Colette and Louise Michel.

**Bibliothèque Nationale de France François Mitterrand** *quai François-Mauriac, 13th (01.53.79.59.59/www.bnf.fr)*. *Mº Bibliothèque*. **Open** 10am-8pm Tue-Sat; noon-7pm Sun. Closed 2wks Sept & bank holidays. **Admission** day pass €3.50; annual €35.
Books, papers and periodicals, plus titles in English. An audio-visual room lets you browse photo, film and sound archives.

**Bibliothèque Publique d'Information (BPI)** *Centre Pompidou, 4th (01.44.78.12.33/ www.bpi.fr)*. *Mº Hôtel de Ville/RER Châtelet Les Halles*. **Open** noon-10pm Mon, Wed-Fri; 11am-10pm Sat, Sun. Closed 1 May. **Admission** free.
Now on three levels, the Centre Pompidou's vast library has a huge global press section, reference books and language-learning facilities.

**BIFI (Bibliothèque du Film)** *51 rue de Bercy, 12th (01.71.19.32.32/ www.bifi.fr)*. *Mº Bercy*. **Open** 10am-7pm Mon-Fri. Closed 2wks Aug. **Admission** €3.50 day pass; €34 annual; €15 students annual.
Housed in the same building as the **Cinémathèque Française** (*see p296*), this world-class researchers' and film buffs' library offers books, magazines, film stills and posters, as well as films on video and DVD.

**Documentation Française** *29-31 quai Voltaire, 7th (01.40.15.71.10/ www.ladocumentationfrancaise.fr)*. *Mº Rue du Bac*. **Open** 9am-6pm Mon-Fri. Closed Aug & 1st wk Sept.
The official government archive and central reference library has information on French politics and economy since 1945.

## Locksmiths

Numerous round-the-clock repair services handle locks, plumbing and, sometimes, car repairs. Most charge a minimum €18-€20 call-out (*déplacement*) and €30 per hour, plus parts. Charges are higher on Sunday and at night.

**Allô Assistance Dépannage** *(01.42.49.05.81/www.allocentral depannage.com)*.
**SOS Dépannage** *(08.20.22.23.33/www.okservice.fr)*.
Double the price of most services, but claims to be twice as reliable.

## Lost property

### Bureau des Objets Trouvés

*36 rue des Morillons, 15th (08.21.00.25.25/www.prefecture-police-paris.interieur.gouv.fr)*. *Mº Convention*. **Open** 8.30am-5pm Mon-Thur; 8.30am-4.30pm Fri.
Visit in person to fill in a form specifying details of the loss. This may have been the first lost property office in the world, but it is far from the most efficient. Huge delays in processing claims mean that if your trip to Paris is short, you may need to nominate a proxy to collect found objects after you leave, although small items can be posted. If your passport was among the items lost, you'll need to go to your consulate to get a single-entry temporary passport in order to leave the country.

### SNCF lost property

Some mainline SNCF stations have their own lost property offices.

## Media

*See also p385* **Websites**.

## Magazines

### Arts & listings

Two modest local publications compete for consumers of basic Wednesday-to-Tuesday listings: the handbag-sized **L'Officiel des Spectacles** (€0.35) and **Pariscope** (€0.40). Look out also for **Lylo**, a free bi-monthly booklet distributed around bars and clubs, for information on gigs and DJ nights. Affiliated to Radio

**Directory**

Nova, monthly **Nova** gives multi-ethnic information on where to drink, dance and hang out. **Technikart** tries – not entirely successfully – to mix clubbing with the arts. Highbrow TV guide **Télérama** has superb arts coverage and comes with **Sortir**, a Paris listings insert. **Les Inrockuptibles** (fondly known as *Les Inrocks*) deals with contemporary music scenes at home and abroad; it has strong coverage of film and books too.

There are specialist arts magazines for every interest. The choice of film-related titles, in particular, is wide, and includes long-established intellectual heavyweights **Les Cahiers du Cinéma**, **Positif** and **Trafic**, fluffy **Studio** and celebrity-heavy **Première**.

## Business

**Capital**, its sister magazine **Management** and weightier **L'Expansion** are the notable monthlies. **Défis** has tips for the entrepreneur; **Initiatives** is for the self-employed.

## English

The springtime **Time Out Paris Free Guide** is widely distributed in visitor venues such as hotels, and the **Time Out Paris Visitors' Guide** is on sale in newsagents across the city. **FUSAC** (France-USA Contacts) is a small-ads magazine that lists flat rentals, job ads and appliances for sale.

## Gossip

The French love gossip. **Public** gives weekly celebrity updates; **Oh Là!** (sister of Spain's *Hola!* and UK's *Hello!*) showcases celebs. **Voici** is the juiciest scandal sheet; **Gala** tells the same stories without the sleaze. **Paris Match** is a French institution founded in 1948, packed with society gossip, celeb interviews and regular photo scoops. **Point de Vue** specialises in royalty (no showbiz fluff). Monthly

**Entrevue** aims to titillate and tends toward features on nonconformist sex.

## News

Weekly news magazines are an important sector in France, offering news and cultural sections as well as in-depth reports; they range from respected organs **L'Express**, **Le Point** and **Le Nouvel Observateur** to the sardonic, chaotically arranged **Marianne**. Weekly **Courrier International** publishes an interesting selection of articles, translated into French, from newspapers all over the world.

## Women, men & fashion

**Elle** was a pioneer among women's mags and has editions across the globe. In France it's a weekly, and spot-on for interviews and fashion. Monthly **Marie-Claire** takes a more feminist, campaigning line. Both have design spin-offs (**Elle Décoration**, **Marie-Claire Maison**), and *Elle* has also spawned foodie **Elle à Table**. DS has lots to read and coverage of social issues. **Vogue**, bought for its fashion coverage and big-name guests, is rivalled during fashion week by **L'Officiel de la Mode**. Meanwhile the underground prefers to buy more radical publications such as **Purple** (six-monthly art, literature and fashion tome), **Crash** and the new wave of fashion/lifestyle mags: **WAD** (stands for We Are Different), **Citizen K**, **Jalouse** and **Numéro**. Men's mags include the naughty-bizarre **Echo des Savanes** and French versions of lad bibles **FHM**, **Maximal** and **Men's Health**.

## Newspapers

French national dailies, with relatively high prices and low print runs, are in dire straits. Only 20 per cent of France read

a national paper; regional dailies dominate outside Paris. Serious, centre-left **Le Monde** is must-read material for business types, politicians and intellectuals; despite its lofty reputation, subject matter is eclectic. The conservative upper and middle classes go for daily broadsheet **Le Figaro**, which has a devotion to politics, shopping, food and sport. Taken over in 2004 by the head of the Dassault defence and media group, it steers clear of controversial industrial issues. Its sales are aided by pages of property and job ads and Wednesday's **Figaroscope** Paris listings. The Saturday edition has three magazines. Founded in the aftershocks of 1968 by a group that included Sartre and de Beauvoir, **Libération**, once affectionately known as *Libé*, is shedding readers and yet to find a modern identity. In early 2005, its staff accepted a plan for financier Edouard de Rothschild to take a 39 per cent stake in the paper – only to go on a three-day strike when he later proposed 52 job cuts across the board. It is still the preferred read of the *gauche caviar* (champagne socialists) and worth buying for wide news and arts coverage. For business and financial news, the French dailies **La Tribune**, **Les Echos** and the weekly **Investir** are the tried and trusted sources. The easy-read tabloid **Le Parisien** is strong on consumer affairs, social issues, local news, events and vox pops. Downmarket **France Soir** has gone tabloid. **La Croix** is a Catholic, right-wing daily. The Communist Party **L'Humanité** (shortened to *L'Huma*) struggles on. Sunday broadsheet **Le Journal du Dimanche** comes with **Fémina** mag and a Paris section. **L'Equipe** is the doyen of European sports dailies – Saturday's edition comes with

a magazine. Its sister bi-weekly **France Football** is the bible of world soccer. Each was instrumental in setting up the game's top competitions during the golden age of French sports journalism after the war. **Paris-Turf** is for horse fans.

### English-language papers

Paris-based **International Herald Tribune** is on sale throughout the city; British dailies, Sundays and **USA Today** are widely available on the day of issue at larger kiosks in the centre, though often without their supplements. The most popular (and many esoteric) English and US newspapers and magazines can be found in central bookshops (*see pp241-242*).

### Satirical papers

Wednesday institution **Le Canard Enchaîné** is the Gallic *Private Eye* – in fact it was the inspiration for the *Eye*. It's a broadly left-wing satirical weekly broadsheet that's full of in-jokes and breaks political scandals.

## Radio

For a complete list of all Paris radio frequencies, go to www.bric-a-brac.org/radio. Many of the following can be heard online at their respective websites. A mandatory state-defined minimum of 40 per cent French music has led to overplay of Gallic pop oldies and to the creation of dubious hybrids by local groups that mix words in French with a refrain in English. Trashy phone-in shows also proliferate. Wavelengths are given in MHz.

**87.8 France Inter** Highbrow, state-run; jazz, international news and discussion slots aplenty. Good cultural coverage.
**90.4 Nostalgie** As you'd expect.
**90.9 Chante France** 100 per cent French *chanson*.
**91.3 Chérie FM** Lots of oldies.

**91.7 France Musiques** State classical music channel: highbrow concerts and top jazz.
**92.1 Le Mouv'** New public station aimed at luring the young with pop and rock music.
**93.1 Aligre** From local Paris news to literary chat.
**93.5/93.9 France Culture** Talky state culture station.
**94.8 RCJ/Radio J/Judaïque FM/Radio Shalom** Shared wavelength for Jewish stations.
**95.2 Ici et Maintenant/ Neo** New stations hoping to stir local public debate about current events.
**96.0 Skyrock** Pop station with loudmouth presenters. Lots of rap.
**96.4 BFM** Business and economics.
**96.9 Voltage FM** Dance music.
**97.4 Rire et Chansons** A non-stop diet of jokes and pop oldies.
**97.8 Ado** Music for teenagers.
**98.2 Radio FG** Beloved of clubbers for its on-the-pulse tips, this station ditched its all-gay remit back in 1999.
**99.0 Radio Latina** Great Latin and salsa music.
**100.3 NRJ** 'Energy' – geddit? National leader with the under-30s.
**101.1 Radio Classique** Top-notch, state-run classical music station.
**101.5 Radio Nova** Hip hop, trip hop, world, jazz.
**101.9 Fun Radio** Now embracing techno alongside Anglo pop hits.
**102.3 Ouï FM** Ouï will rock you.
**103.9 RFM** Easy listening.
**104.3 RTL** The most popular French station nationwide mixes music and talk programmes.
**104.7 Europe 1** News, press reviews, sports, business, entertainment. Much the best weekday breakfast news broadcast, with politicians interviewed live.
**105.1 FIP** Traffic and weather information, what's on in Paris and a mix of jazz, classical, world and pop. 'Fipettes', female continuity announcers employed for their come-to-bed voices, are a much-loved feature.
**105.5 France Info** 24hr news, weather, economic updates and sports bulletins. Reports get repeated every 15 minutes: useful if you're learning French.
**106.7 Beur FM** North African music and discussion.

### English

You can receive the **BBC World Service** (648 KHz AM), with its English-language international news, current events, pop and drama; also on 198KHz LW, from midnight to 5.30am daily. At other times

198KHz LW carries **BBC Radio 4**, with British news, talk and *The Archers*. **RFI** (738 KHz AM; www.rfi.fr) has an English-language programme of news and music 7-8am, 2.30-3.30pm and 4.30-5pm daily. There's also the French capital's first all-English radio station, **Paris Live** (www.paris-live.net).

## Television

In 2005, the choice of free TV channels available in France more than doubled. Under the explosive acronym TNT (Télévision Numérique Terrestre, or terrestrial digital television), seven new channels – available via the traditional rooftop aerial with a decoder that costs about €100, or automatically to cable and satellite customers – began broadcasting. For more information, go to www.tdf.fr or pick up a copy of weekly mag *Télérama*. The channels listed below are the six 'core' stations available on an unenhanced TV set:

**TF1** *(www.tf1.fr)*. The country's biggest channel, first to be privatised (in 1987). Reality shows, dubbed soaps and football are staples.
**France 2** *(www.france2.fr)*. This state-owned station mixes game shows, chat, documentaries and the usual cop series and films.
**France 3** *(www.france3.fr)*. This, the more heavyweight of the two state channels, offers wildlife and sports coverage, debates, *Cinéma de Minuit* – classic films in V.O. (*version originale*, or original language) – and the endearing cookery show *Bon Appétit Bien Sûr*, fronted by superchef Joël Robuchon.
**Canal+** *(www.canalplus.fr)*. Subscription channel shows recent films, exclusive sport and late-night porn. A week's worth of the satirical puppets show *Les Guignols* is broadcast unscrambled on Sundays at 1.40pm.
**Arte/France 5** *(www.arte-tv.com)*. The intellectual Franco-German hybrid Arte shares its wavelength with educational channel France 5 (3am-7pm).
**M6** *(www.m6.fr)*. Dubbed US sci-fi series and made-for TV movies, plus investigative reportage, popular science and kids' shows.

## Cable TV & satellite

France offers a decent range of cable and satellite channels but content in English is still limited. CNN and BBC World offer round-the-clock news coverage. BBC Prime keeps you up to date on *EastEnders* (omnibus Sun 2pm), while Teva supplies comedy such as *Sex and the City*.
**Numericable** *(08.92.02.00.10/ www.numericable.fr)*.
The first cable provider to offer an interactive video service via internet.

## Money

The amount of currency visitors may carry is not limited. However, sums worth over €7,600 must be declared to customs when entering or leaving the country.

## The euro

Non-French debit and credit cards can be used to withdraw and pay in euros, and currency withdrawn in France can be used subsequently all over the euro zone. Daylight robbery occurs, however, if you try to deposit a euro cheque from any country other than France in a French bank: they are currently charging around €15 for this service, and the European parliament has backed down on its original decision that cross-border payments should be in line with domestic ones across the euro zone. Good news for Brits, though: if you transfer money from the UK to France in euros, you will pay the same charges as if Britain were within the euro zone (but watch the exchange rate carefully). For useful euro information online, *see p385*.

## ATMs

Withdrawals in euros can be made from bank and post office automatic cash machines. The specific cards accepted are marked on each machine, and most can give instructions in English. Credit card companies charge a fee for cash advances, but rates are often better than banks.

## Banks

French banks usually open 9am-5pm Mon-Fri (some close at lunch); some banks also open on Sat. All are closed on public holidays, and from noon on the previous day. Note that not all banks have foreign exchange counters. The commission rates vary between banks; the state-owned Banque de France usually offers good rates. Most banks accept travellers' cheques, but may be reluctant to accept personal cheques even with the Eurocheque guarantee card, which is not widely used in France.

### Bank accounts

To open an account (*ouvrir un compte*), French banks require proof of identity, address and your income (if any). You'll probably be required to show your passport, an electricity, gas or phone bill in your name and a payslip/letter from your employer. Students need a student card and may need a letter from their parents. Of the major national banks (BNP, Crédit Lyonnais, Société Générale, Banque Populaire, Crédit Agricole), Société Générale tends to be the most foreigner-friendly. Most banks don't hand out a Carte Bleue/Visa card until several weeks after you've opened an account. A chequebook (*chéquier*) is usually issued in about a week. Payments made with a Carte Bleue are debited directly from your current account, but you can arrange for purchases to be debited at the end of every month. French banks are tough on overdrafts, so try to anticipate any cash crisis in advance and work out a deal for an authorised

overdraft (*découvert autorisé*) or you risk being blacklisted as '*interdit bancaire*' – forbidden from having a current account – for anything up to ten years. Depositing foreign currency cheques can be slow, so try to use wire transfer or a bank draft in euros to receive funds from abroad.

## Bureaux de change

If you happen to be arriving in Paris early in the morning or late at night, you will be able to change money at the **American Express** bureaux de change in terminals 1 (01.48.16.13.26), 2A, 2B, 2C and 2D (01.48.16.48.40) and 2E (01.48.16.63.81) at Roissy, and at Orly Sud (01.49.75.77.37); all open 6.30am-11pm daily. **Travelex** (*see right*) has bureaux de change at the following train stations:
**Gare Montparnasse** *01.42.79.03.88.* **Open** 8am-6.30pm daily.
**Gare du Nord** *01.42.80.11.50.* **Open** 6.30am-10pm daily.

## Credit cards

Major international credit cards are widely used in France; Visa (more commonly known in France as *Carte Bleue*) is the most readily accepted. French-issued credit cards have a security microchip (*puce*) in each card. The card is slotted into a reader, and the holder keys in a PIN to authorise the transaction. Non-French cards work, but generate a credit slip to sign. In case of credit card loss or theft, call one of the following 24hr services which have English-speaking staff:
**American Express** *01.47.77.70.00.*
**Diners Club** *01.49.06.17.50.*
**MasterCard/Visa** *08.36.69.08.80.*

## Foreign affairs

**American Express** *11 rue Scribe, 9th (01.47.77.70.00/www.americanexpress.com). M° Opéra.* **Open** 9am-6.30pm Mon-Sat.

Travel agency, bureau de change, *poste restante* (you can leave messages for other card holders), card replacement, travellers' cheque refund service, international money transfers and a cash machine for AmEx cardholders.

**Barclays** *6 rond-point des Champs-Elysées, 8th (01.44.95.13.80/ 08.10.06.06.06/www.barclays.fr).* *M° Franklin D. Roosevelt.* **Open** 9.15am-4.30pm Mon-Fri.
Barclays' international Expat Service handles direct debits, international transfer of funds, etc.

**Citibank** *15 rue Paul Cézanne, 8th (01.70.75.50.00/www.citibank.fr).* *M° St-Philippe-du-Roule.* **Open** 10am-5.30pm Mon-Fri.
Clients get good rates for international money transfers, preferential exchange rates and no commission on travellers' cheques.

**Travelex** *52 av des Champs-Elysées, 8th (01.42.89.80.33/www.travelex. fr). M° Franklin D. Roosevelt.* **Open** 9am-10.30pm daily. Hours of other branches (over 20 in Paris) vary.
Issues travellers' cheques and insurance; deals with bank transfers.

**Western Union Money Transfer** *(www.westernunion.com).* Many post offices in town *(see right)* provide Western Union services. Transfers from abroad should arrive within 15 minutes; charges paid by the sender.

## Tax

French VAT *(taxe sur la valeur ajoutée* or TVA) is arranged in three bands: 2.1 per cent for items of medication and newspapers; 5.5 per cent for food, books, CDs and DVDs; and 19.6 per cent for all other types of goods and services.

## Natural hazards

Paris has no natural hazards as such, though in recent years the town hall has produced evacuation plans to cover flooding. The deadly heatwave of 2003 led to *anti-canicule* measures for 2004, though these were ridiculed in the press. *See also p365* **Walking**.

## Opening hours

Standard opening hours for shops are 9/10am-7/8pm Mon-Sat. Some shops close on Monday. Shops and businesses often close at lunch, usually

12.30-2pm; many shops close in August. While Paris doesn't have the 24hr consumer culture beloved of some capitals, some branches of Monoprix stay open until 10pm. Also most areas have a local grocer that stays open into the night and will often open on Sundays and public holidays too.

**24hr florist** Elyfleur *82 av de Wagram, 17th (01.47.66.87.19). M° Wagram.* **Credit** MC, V.
**24hr garage** Shell *6 bd Raspail, 7th (01.45.48.43.12). M° Rue du Bac.* This round-the-clock garage has an extensive if pricey array of supermarket standards from the Casino chain. No alcohol sold 10pm-6am.
**24hr newsagents** include: *33 av des Champs-Elysées, 8th, M° Franklin D. Roosevelt.* 2 *bd Montmartre, 9th, M° Grands Boulevards.*
**Late-night *tabacs*** Le Brazza *86 bd du Montparnasse, 14th (01.43.35.42.65). M° Montparnasse-Bienvenüe.* **Open** 6am-2am daily.
La Favorite *3 bd St-Michel, 5th (01.43.54.08.02). M° St-Michel.* **Open** 7am-2am daily.

## Photo labs

Photo developing can often be more expensive than in the UK or USA (although developing slide films can often be cheaper). **Fnac Service** (www.fnacphoto.com), **Photo Station** (www.photostation.fr) and **Photo Service** (www. photoservice.com) have many branches around the city.

## Police

The French equivalent of 999 or 911 is **17** (**112** from a mobile), but don't expect a speedy response. That said, the Préfecture de Police has no fewer than 94 outposts in the city. If you're assaulted or robbed, report the incident as soon as possible. You'll need to make a statement *(procès verbal)* at the *point d'accueil* closest to the site of the crime. To find the nearest, call the Préfecture Centrale (08.91.01.22.22) day or night, or go to www.prefecture-

police.paris.interieur.gouv.fr. Stolen goods are unlikely to be recovered, but you'll need a police statement for insurance purposes.

## Postal services

Post offices *(bureaux de poste)* are open 8am-7pm Mon-Fri; 8am-noon Sat, apart from the 24-hour one listed below. Details of all branches are included in the phone book: under 'Administration des PTT' in the *Pages Jaunes*; under 'Poste' in the *Pages Blanches*. Most post offices contain automatic machines (in French and English) that weigh your letter, print out a stamp and give change, thus saving you from wasting time in an enormous queue. You can also usually buy stamps and sometimes envelopes at a tobacconist *(tabac)*. For more information refer to www.laposte.fr.

**Main Post Office** *52 rue du Louvre, 75001 Paris, 1st (01.40.28.76.00). M° Les Halles or Louvre Rivoli.* **Open** 24hrs daily for poste restante, telephones, stamps, faxes, photocopying and a modest amount of banking operations.
This is the best place to arrange to have your mail sent to if you haven't got a fixed address in Paris. Mail should be addressed to you in block capitals, followed by Poste Restante, then the post office's address. There will be a charge of €0.50 for each letter received.

## Recycling & rubbish

The city has a recently established system of colour-coded domestic recycling bins. A yellow-lidded bin can take paper, cardboard cartons, tins and small electrical items; a white-lidded bin takes glass. All other rubbish goes in the green-lidded bins, except for used batteries (all shops that sell batteries should accept them), medication (take it back to a pharmacy), toxic products (call 08.20.00.75.75 to have

them picked up) or car batteries (take them to an official tip or return to garages exhibiting the 'Relais Verts Auto' sign). Green, hive-shaped bottle banks can be found on many street corners. More information is available at www.environnement.paris.fr.

## Religion

Churches and religious centres are listed in the *Pages Jaunes* under 'Eglises' and 'Cultes'. Paris has several English-speaking churches. The *International Herald Tribune*'s Saturday edition lists Sunday church services in English.

**American Cathedral** *23 av George V, 8th (01.53.23.84.00/ www.americancathedral.org). Mº George V.*

**American Church in Paris** *65 quai d'Orsay, 7th (01.40.62.05.00/ www.acparis.org). Mº Invalides.*

**Emmanuel International Church of Paris** *56 rue des Bons Raisins, Rueil-Malmaison (01.47.51.29.63/http://perso.orange. fr/ebcparis/). RER Reuil-Malmaison, then bus 244.*

**Kehilat Gesher** *10 rue de Pologne, 78100 St-Germain-en-Laye (01.39.21.97.19/www.kehilatgesher. org). RER St-Germain-en-Laye.* The Liberal English-speaking Jewish community have rotating services in Paris and the western suburbs.

**La Mosquée de Paris** *2 pl du Puits de l'Ermite, 5th (01.45.35.97.33/www.mosquee-de-paris.org). Mº Place Monge.*

**St George's Anglican Church** *7 rue Auguste-Vacquerie, 16th (01.47.20.22.51/www.stgeorgesparis. com). Mº Charles de Gaulle Etoile.*

**St Joseph's Roman Catholic Church** *50 av Hoche, 8th (01.42.27.28.56/www.stjoeparis.org). Mº Charles de Gaulle Etoile.*

**St Michael's Church of England** *5 rue d'Aguesseau, 8th (01.47.42.70.88/www.saintmichaels paris.org). Mº Madeleine.*

## Renting a flat

Flats are generally cheapest in northern, eastern and south-eastern Paris. You can expect to pay approximately €20 per square metre per month (so, for example, €700 per month for a modest 35sq m apartment).

Studios and one bedroom flats fetch the highest prices proportionally; the provision of lifts and cellars will also boost the rent.

### Flat hunting

Given the scarcity of housing in Paris, it's a landlord's world; you'll need to search actively, or even frenetically, in order to find an apartment. The internet is a decent place to start: www.explorimmo.fr lists rental ads from *Le Figaro* and specialist real estate magazines; you can place a classified ad or check lettings on www.avendrealouer.fr. Thursday morning's *De Particulier à Particulier* (www.pap.fr) is a must for those who want to rent directly from the owner, but be warned – most flats go within hours. Fortnightly *Se Loger* (www.seloger.com) is also worth getting, though most of its ads are placed by agencies. Landlords keen to let to foreigners advertise in the *International Herald Tribune* and English-language *FUSAC* (www.fusac.fr); rents tend to be higher than in the French press. There are also assorted free ad brochures that can be picked up from agencies. Private landlords often set a visiting time; prepare to meet hordes of other flat-seekers and have your documents and cheque book to hand.

There's also the option of flat-sharing – one that's been growing in popularity in recent years. To look for housemates, pick up a copy of *FUSAC* or browse the 3,000-odd weekly announcements found at www.colocation.fr, which also organises monthly soirée Le Jeudi de la Colocation, a chance to meet potential flatmates in the flesh.

### Rental laws

The minimum lease (*bail de location*) on an unfurnished flat is three years (though the

tenant can give notice and leave before this period is up); furnished flats are generally let on one-year leases. During this period the landlord can only raise the rent by the official construction inflation index. At the end of the lease, the rent can be adjusted, but tenants can object before a rent board. Tenants can be evicted for non-payment, or if the landlord wishes to sell the property or use it as his own residence. It is illegal to throw people out in winter. Landlords will probably insist you present a dossier with pay slips (*fiches de paie/bulletins de salaire*) showing income equivalent to three to four times the monthly rent, and for foreigners in particular, provide a financial guarantor (someone who will sign a document promising to pay the rent if you abscond). When taking out a lease, payments usually include the first month's rent, a deposit (*caution*) of the equivalent of two months' rent, and an agency fee, if applicable.

It's customary to have an inspection of the premises (*état des lieux*) at the start and end of the rental, the cost of which (around €150) is shared by landlord and tenant. Landlords may try to rent their flats *non-déclaré* – without a written lease – and get rent in cash. This can make it hard for tenants to establish their rights – which is one reason why landlords do it.

**Centre d'information et de défense des locataires** *9 rue Severo, 14th (01.45.41.47.76). Mº Pernety.* **Open** *by appointment* 10am-12.30pm, 2.30-3.30pm Mon-Thur. Helps sort out problems with landlords, rent hikes, etc.

## Safety & security

Beware of pickpockets, especially around crowded tourist hotspots. *See also p361* **Métro & RER** *and p375* **Police**.

## Shipping services

### Hedley's Humpers

*6 bd de la Libération, 93284 St-Denis (01.48.13.01.02/www.hedleys humpers.com). M° Carrefour Pleyel.* **Open** 9am-1pm, 2-6pm Mon-Fri. Closed 2wks Aug. Specialist in transport of furniture and antiques. **In** UK: 3 St Leonards Road, London NW10 6SX (020 8965 8733). **In** USA: 21-41 45th Road, Long Island City, New York NY 11101 (1-718-433-4005).

## Smoking

Although smoking seems to be an essential part of French life (and death), the French state and public health groups have recently waged war against the cigarette on several fronts. Smoking is now banned in most public spaces, such as theatres, cinemas and public transport (including TGV trains), and there are increasingly strident anti-smoking campaigns. Health warnings on cigarette packets are now unignorable, and prices have soared. Restaurants are obliged to have a non-smoking area (*espace non-fumeurs*) – though it will often be the worst corner in the house, and there's no guarantee other people seated in the section won't light up anyway. A fairly modest number of restaurateurs, encouraged by the Mairie, have opted for the *100% sans tabac* label, making their establishments entirely non-smoking.

For information about stopping smoking, contact the Tabac Info Service (08.25.30.93.10/www.tabac-info.net). If you're a dedicated smoker, you'll soon learn that most *tabacs* close at 8pm (for a few that don't, *see p375* **Opening hours**). Some bars sell cigarettes behind the counter, generally only to customers who have a drink.

## Study

### Language

Most large multinational language schools, such as **Berlitz** (08.25.04.34.30/ www.berlitz.com), have at least one branch in Paris. **Konversando** (01.47.70.21.64/ www.konversando.fr) specialises in international exchanges and talk.

**Alliance Française** *101 bd Raspail, 6th (01.42.84.90.00/ www.alliancefr.org). M° St-Placide.*

# Wireless and the digital future

In 2007, 400 free WiFi access points were installed in public places around Paris. Residents and visitors equipped with a WiFi-compatible laptop can now check their email or surf the web free of charge in 250 Paris parks and gardens, 150 municipal libraries and local town halls, and at a scattering of big-name tourist locations, such as the square in front of the Hôtel de Ville.

While Paris has long benefited from a network of privately owned hotspots (wireless access points) in airports, train stations, cafés and eateries, this new initiative represents the first large-scale deployment by the Mairie de Paris. Furthermore, it has made sure it does not upset the private sector: the 400 connection points function only during park and library opening hours, and signals can't be used by inhabitants of neighbouring buildings.

The venture forms part of Mayor Delanoë's city-wide programme (dubbed PARVI or Paris Ville Numérique) to plot out the city's digital future. As long ago as 2003, the Mairie began experimenting with public hotspots in the third arrondissement, and it has already made provisions for the next few years. Public benches will become laptop-friendly by incorporating small tables and solar-powered power points, while another initiative aims to create 'digital knowledge gardens': any green spaces located near a library will offer laptop users access to a whole range of educational tools and resources, including online dictionaries, encyclopaedias, library catalogues and digital documents.

As part of PARVI, the Mairie has also established a number of Espaces Publics Numériques (EPN), public centres that offer locals a chance to hone their IT skills. The training courses on offer cover everything from internet use to programming and creating websites.

Another major objective of PARVI is to provide Parisians with faster internet connections. Today, some 60 per cent of Paris households have a high-speed connection (ADSL or cable), making the French capital one of the most connected cities in the world. With PARVI, Delanoë aims to equip 80 per cent of Paris buildings with an 'ultra high-speed' fibre connection by 2010. Fibre-optic cables can deliver up to 100Mbps download speeds, which is roughly five times faster than ADSL. To achieve this goal, Delanoë is offering fibre-optic companies access to the Paris sewers – as well as major tax reductions.

**Directory**

Non-profit French-language school. Beginner and specialist courses start every month. Film club and lectures.

**Ecole Eiffel** *3 rue Crocé-Spinelli, 14th (01.43.20.37.41/www.ecole-eiffel.fr). M° Pernety.*
Intensive classes, business French and phonetics.

**Institut Catholique de Paris** *12 rue Cassette, 6th (01.44.39.52.68/ www.icp.fr/ilcf). M° St-Sulpice.*
Courses in French culture and language. You must hold a *baccalauréat*-level qualification and be 18 or over (but don't have to be Catholic).

**Institut Parisien** *29 rue de Lisbonne, 8th (01.40.56.09.53). M° Monceau.*
Dynamic private school offering courses in language, French civilisation and business French.

**La Sorbonne – Cours de Langue et Civilisation** *47 rue des Ecoles, 5th (01.40.46.22.11/www.ccfs-sorbonne.fr). M° Cluny-La Sorbonne/ RER Luxembourg.*
Classes for foreigners ride on the name of this eminent institution. Teaching is grammar-based. Courses are open to anyone over 18 and fill up quickly.

**University of London Institute in Paris** *9-11 rue Constantine, 7th (01.44.11.73.73/www.ulip.lon.ac.uk). M° Invalides.*
Linked to the University of London, this 4,000-student institute offers English courses for Parisians, and French courses at university level. Also offers a degree course and MAs.

## Specialised

Many of the prestigious Ecoles Nationales Supérieures (including film schools La FEMIS and ENS Louis Lumière) offer summer courses in addition to their full-time degree courses – ask for *formation continue.*

**Adult education courses**
*Information: www.paris.fr or from your local mairie.*
A huge range of inexpensive adult education classes is run by the city of Paris, including French as a foreign language, computer skills and applied arts.

**American University of Paris** *31 av Bosquet, 7th (01.40.62.06.00/ www.aup.edu). M° Ecole-Militaire/ RER Pont de l'Alma.*
International college awarding four-year American liberal arts degrees (BA/BSc).

**Cordon Bleu** *8 rue Léon-Delhomme, 15th (01.53.68.22.50/ www.cordonbleu.edu). M° Vaugirard.*

Courses range from three-hour sessions on classical and regional cuisine to a nine-month diploma for those starting a culinary career.

**Ecole du Louvre** *Palais du Louvre, porte Jaugard, place du Carrousel, 1st (01.55.35.18.00/www. ecoledulouvre.fr). M° Palais Royal Musée du Louvre.*
Art history and archaeology courses. Foreign students not wanting to take a degree can attend lectures.

**INSEAD** *bd de Constance, 77305 Fontainebleau (01.60.72.40.00/ www.insead.edu).*
Highly regarded international business school offering a ten-month MBA course in English as well as PhDs in a range of business subjects.

**Parsons School of Design** *14 rue Letellier, 15th (01.45.77.39.66/www.parsons-paris.com). M° La Motte-Picquet-Grenelle.*
Subsidiary of the New York art college offering BFA programmes in fine art, photography, fashion, marketing and interior design.

**Ritz-Escoffier Ecole de Gastronomie Française** *38 rue Cambon, 1st (01.43.16.30.50/ www.ritzparis.com). M° Madeleine.*
Everything from afternoon demonstrations in the Ritz kitchens to diplomas. Courses are in French with English translation.

---

# Student life

## Long-term visas & housing benefit

UK and other students from the EU may stay in France for as long as their passport is valid. To also work legally during their course in Paris, they can find out more information about their rights at www.droitsdesjeunes.gouv.fr.

Foreign students from outside the EU wishing to study in Paris for longer than three months must apply for a long-term visa through the French embassy in their particular country.

Some students may be eligible to receive housing benefit, the ALS (*allocation de logement à caractère social*), which is dealt with by four CAFs (*caisses d'allocations familiales*). The '*Aide au logement étudiant*' feature of the French-only website (www.caf.fr) allows you see

how much you are entitled to receive; enter your postcode on the site to find which office you should contact. The section www.paris.caf.fr deals with enquiries related to Paris.

### Accommodation

The simplest budget accommodation for medium-to-long stays can be found at the **Cité Universitaire** or *foyers* (student hostels). There are 37 halls of residence set in landscaped gardens, with sports facilities and a theatre (*see p344*). Another option is a *chambre contre travail* – free board in exchange for childcare, housework or English lessons; for this, look out for ads at language schools and the American Church. For cheap hotels and youth hostels, *see pp48-78* **Where to Stay.** As students often cannot provide proof of income, a *porte-garant* (guarantor) who will guarantee payment of rent and bills is required.

**Cité Universitaire** *17 bd Jourdan, 14th (01.44.16.64.00/www.ciup.fr). RER Cité Universitaire.* **Open** *Offices* 8am-6pm Mon-Fri.
Foreign students enrolled on a university course, or interns who are also studying, can apply for a place at this campus of halls of residence (but be warned: only about ten per cent of the students who apply are successful). Rooms can be booked for a week, a month or for an entire academic year. Rents are approximately €300-€400 per month for a single, €200-€300 per person for a double. UK citizens must apply to the Collège Franco-Britannique, and Americans to the Fondation des Etats-Unis.

**CROUS (Centre Régional des Oeuvres Universitaires et Scolaires)** *39 av Georges-Bernanos, 5th (01.40.51.36.00/ 08.92.25.75.75/www.crous-paris.fr). Service du Logement: (01.40.51.55.55). RER Port-Royal.* **Open** 9am-5pm Mon-Fri.
Manages all University of Paris student residences, posts ads for rooms and has a list of hostels. Requests for rooms must be made by 1 April for the next academic year. CROUS also runs cheap canteens (listed on website) and is the clearing house for all *bourses* (grants) and to foreign students. Call the Service des Bourses on 01.40.51.55.55.

**UCRIF (Union des Centres de Rencontres Internationales de France)** *27 rue de Turbigo, 2nd (01.40.26.57.64/www.ucrif.asso.fr). M° Etienne Marcel.* **Open** 9am-6pm Mon-Fri.
Operates cheap, short-stay hostels from five help centres: 5th (01.43.29.34.80); 12th (01.44.75.60.06); 13th (01.43.36.00.63); 14th (01.43.13.17.00); 20th (01.40.31.45.45).

## Student & youth discounts

To claim a *tarif étudiant* (around €1.50 off cinema seats, up to 50 per cent off museums and standby theatre tickets), you must have a French student card or International Student Identity Card (ISIC), available from **CROUS** (*see p378*), student travel agents and the **Cité Universitaire** (*see p378*). ISIC cards are valid in France only if you are under 26. Under-26s can get up to 50 per cent off rail travel on some trains with the SNCF's Carte 12/25 and the same reduction on the RATP network with the Imagine R card.

## Working

Foreign students can legally work up to 20 hours per week. Non-EU members studying in Paris must apply for an *autorisation provisoire de travail* from the DDTEFT. The job service at CROUS (01.40.51.37.52-57) finds part-time jobs for students.
**DDTEFT (Direction Départementale du Travail, d'Emploi et du Formation Professionelle)** *109 rue Montmartre, 2nd (08.21.34.73.47/ 01.44.84.41.00/www.travail.gouv.fr). M° Bourse.*

## Useful organisations

**CIDJ (Centre d'Information et de Documentation Jeunesse)** *101 quai Branly, 15th (08.25.09.06.30/01.44.49.12.00/ www.cidj.com). M° Bir-Hakeim/RER Champ de Mars.* **Open** 10am-6pm Mon-Wed, Fri; 1-6pm Thur; 9.30am-1pm Sat.
The library gives students advice on courses and careers; the youth bureau of ANPE (Agence Nationale pour l'Emploi/www.anpe.fr) can assist with job applications.

**Maison des Initiatives Etudiantes (MIE)** *50 rue des Tournelles, 3rd (01.49.96.65.30/ www.paris.fr).* **Open** 10am-10pm Mon-Fri; 2-9pm Sat.
Provides student associations with logistical assistance and Paris-based resources like meeting rooms, grants and computers. Radio Campus Paris, a radio station for students, has been broadcasting since September 2004.
**Socrates-Erasmus Programme**
*Britain: UK Socrates-Erasmus Council, British Council, 10 Spring Gardens, London, SW1A 2BN (020 7389 4910/www.erasmus.ac.uk). France: Agence Socrates-Leonardo Da Vinci, 25 quai des Chartrons, 33080 Bordeaux Cedex (05.56.00.94.00/www.socrates-leonardo.fr).*
The international Socrates-Erasmus scheme lets EU students with reasonable written and spoken French spend a year of their degree in the French university system. Applications must be made via the Erasmus co-ordinator at your home university. Non-EU students should find out from their university whether it has an agreement with the French university system.
American students can find out more from the following:
**MICEFA** (*26 rue du Fbg-St-Jacques, 14th, 01.40.51.76.96/ www.micefa.org*).
**Relais d'accueil** (Foreign students helpdesk) *Cité Universitaire, 17 bd Jourdan, 14th. RER Cité Universitaire. CROUS de Paris, 39 av Georges-Bernanos, 5th (014.051.36.00). RER Port-Royal.* **Open** *Sept-Nov* 8.30am-4pm Mon-Fri (Cité); 9am-4.30pm Mon-Fri (CROUS). Advice on housing, getting a bank account, visa requirements, social security and university registration is available (by appointment) to foreign students at the two addresses above.

# Telephones

## Mobile phones

A subscription (*abonnement*) will normally get you a free phone if you sign up for at least one year. Two hours' calling time a month costs about €35 per month. International calls are normally charged extra – a lot extra. The three companies that rule the cell phone market in France are:
**Bouyges Télécom** *(08.25.82.56.14/ www.bouyguestelecom.fr).*

**France Télécom/Orange** *(08.25.00.57.00/www.orange.fr).*
**SFR** *(01.71.24.00.00/www.sfr.fr).*

## Dialling & codes

All French phone numbers have ten digits. Paris and Ile-de-France numbers begin with 01; the rest of France is divided into four zones (02-05). Mobile phone numbers start with 06. 08 indicates a special rate (*see p380*); numbers beginning with 08 can only be reached from inside France. If you are calling France from abroad, leave off the 0 at the start of the ten-digit number. The country code is 33. To call abroad from France dial 00, then the country code, then the number. Since 1998 other phone companies have been allowed to enter the market, but France Télécom still has the monopoly on basic service. It has a useful website with information on rates and contracts: www. agence.francetelecom.com.
**France Télécom English-Speaking Customer Service** *(08.00.36.47.75/from abroad +33 1.55.78.60.56).* **Open** 9am-5.30pm Mon-Fri.
Freephone information line in English on phone services, bills, payment, internet.

## Public phones

Most public phones in Paris, almost all of which are maintained by France Télécom, use *télécartes* (phonecards). Sold at post offices, *tabacs*, airports and train and métro stations, they cost €7.50 for 50 units and €15 for 120 units. For cheap international calls, you can also buy a *télécarte à puce* (card with a microchip) or a *télécarte pré-payée*, which features a numerical code you dial before making a call; these can be used on domestic phones too. Travelex's International Telephone Card can be used in more than 80 countries (available from

Travelex agencies, *see p375*). Cafés have coin phones, while post offices usually have card phones. In a phone box, the display screen will read 'Décrochez'. Pick up the phone. When 'Introduisez votre carte' appears, put your card into the slot; the screen should read 'Patientez SVP'. 'Numérotez' is your signal to dial. 'Crédit épuisé' means you have no more units left. Hang up ('Raccrochez') – and don't forget your card. Some public phones take credit cards. If you're using a credit card, insert the card, enter your PIN number and 'Patientez SVP' will appear.

## Operator services

**Operator assistance, French directory enquiries**
(*renseignements*) *12*. To make a reverse-charge call within France, ask to make a call *en PCV*.
**Airparif** (*01.44.59.47.64/www. airparif.asso.fr*).
Information about pollution levels and air quality in Paris and Ile-de-France: invaluable for asthmatics.
**International directory enquiries** *32.12*, then country code. €3 per call.
**International news** (France Inter recorded message, in French), *08.92.68.10.33* (€0.34 per min).
**Telegram** *all languages, international 08.00.33.44.11; within France 36.55*.
**Telephone engineer** *10.13*.
**Time** *36.99*.
**Traffic news** *08.26.02.20.22*.
**Weather** *08.99.70.12.34* (€1.39 then €0.34 per min) for enquiries on weather in France and abroad, in French or English; you can also dial 08.92.68.02.75 (€0.34 per min) for a recorded weather announcement for Paris and region.

## Telephone directories

Telephone books can be found in all post offices and most cafés. The *Pages Blanches* (White Pages) list people and businesses alphabetically; the *Pages Jaunes* (Yellow Pages) list businesses and services by category order. Online versions can be found at www.pagesjaunes.fr.

## Telephone charges

All local calls in Paris and Ile-de-France (to numbers beginning with 01) cost €0.11 for three minutes, standard rate and €0.04/min thereafter. This only applies to calls to other landlines. Calls beyond a 100km radius (*province*) are charged at €0.11 for the first 39 seconds, then €0.24 per minute.

International destinations are divided into 16 zones. Reduced-rate periods for calls within France and Europe are 7pm-8am during the week and all day Saturday and Sunday. Reduced-rate periods for the US and Canada are 7pm to 1pm Monday to Friday and all day Saturday and Sunday.

## Cheap providers

Getting wise to the market demand, smaller telephone providers are becoming increasingly popular, as rates from giant France Télécom are not exactly bargain-basement. The following can offer alternative rates for calls – although you will still need to rent your telephone line from France Télécom:
**AT&T Direct** (local access) *08.00.99.00.11*.
**Free** *www.free.fr*. With the Freebox (Free's modem for ADSL connection), €29.99 per month gets you ten hours of free calls to landlines (additional calls: €0.01 per minute), €0.19 per minute to mobiles and €0.03 per minute for most international calls.
**IC Télécom** *08.05.13.26.26/ www.ictelecom.fr*.
**Neuf Télécom** *08.92.79.00.19/ www.neuf.fr*.
**Onetel** *08.92.13.50.50/ www.onetel.fr*.
**Télé 2** *www.tele2.fr*.

## Special-rate numbers

**0800 Numéro Vert** Freephone.
**0810 Numéro Azur** €0.11 under three minutes, then €0.04/min.
**0820 Numéro Indigo I** €0.118/min.
**0825 Numéro Indigo II** €0.15/min.
**0836.64/0890.64/0890.70** €0.112/min.

**0890.71** €0.15/min.
**0891.67/0891.70** €0.225/min.
**0836/0892** €0.337/min. This is for the likes of ticket agencies, cinema and transport information.
**10.14** France Télécom information; free (except from mobile phones).

## Minitel

France Télécom's Minitel, launched in the 1980s, is an enduring dinosaur: a videotext service available to any telephone subscriber. The internet has made it virtually redundant. If you come across one of these beige plastic boxes, type in 3611 for Minitel directory in English, wait for the beep, press 'Connexion', type MGS, then hit 'Envoi'. Then type 'Minitel en anglais' for the English service.

## Ticket agencies

The easiest way to reserve and buy tickets for concerts, plays and matches is from a **Fnac** store. You can also reserve on www.fnac.com or by phone (08.92.68.36.22; 9am-8pm Mon-Sat) and pick them up at one of their *points de vente* (see site for full list) – or pay with your credit card and have them sent to your home. **Virgin** has teamed up with **Ticketnet** to create an online ticket office (www.virginmega.fr). Tickets can also be purchased by phone (08.25.12.91.39) and sent to your home for a €5.50 fee.
**Fnac Forum** *Forum des Halles, Porte Lescot, 1st 08.25.02.00.20/ www.fnac.com*). *M° Les Halles/ RER Châtelet Les Halles*. **Open** 10am-7.30pm Mon-Sat. **Credit** AmEx, MC, V.
**Virgin Megastore** *52-60 av des Champs-Elysées, 8th (01.49.53.50.00). M° Franklin D. Roosevelt*. **Open** 10am-midnight Mon-Sat; noon-midnight Sun. **Credit** AmEx, MC, V.

## Time & seasons

France is one hour ahead of Greenwich Mean Time (GMT). France uses the 24hr system (for example 18h means 6pm).

## Tipping

A service charge of ten to 15 per cent is legally included in your bill at all restaurants, cafés and bars. However, it is polite to either round up the final amount for drinks, or to leave a cash tip of €1-€2 or more for a meal, depending on the restaurant and, of course, the quality of the service.

## Toilets

The city's automatic street toilets are not as terrifying as they look. You put your coin in the slot, and open sesame. Each loo is completely washed down and disinfected after use, so don't try to avoid paying by sneaking in as someone is leaving: you'll get covered in bleach. Once inside, you have 15 minutes. If a space age-style lavatory experience doesn't appeal, you can always nip into the toilets of a café; although theoretically reserved for customers' use, a polite request should win sympathy with the waiter – and you may find you have to put a €0.20 coin into a slot in the door-handle mechanism, customer or not. Fast-food chain toilets often have a code on their toilet doors that is made known to paying customers only.

## Tourist information

### Espace du Tourisme d'Ile de France

*Carrousel du Louvre, 99 rue de Rivoli, 1st (08.26.16.66.66/ www.paris-ile-de-france.com). M° Palais Royal Musée du Louvre or Pyramides.* **Open** 8.30am-7pm Mon-Fri.
This is the information showcase for Paris and the Ile-de-France.

### Maison de la France

*20 av de l'Opéra, 1st (01.42.96.70.00/www.franceguide. com). M° Opéra or Pyramides.* **Open** 10am-6pm Mon-Fri; 10am-5pm Sat.
The state organisation for tourism in France: information galore.

### Office de Tourisme et des Congrès de Paris

*Carrousel du Louvre, 99 rue de Rivoli, 1st (08.92.68.30.00 recorded information in English & French/www.parisinfo.com). M° Palais Royal Musée du Louvre or Pyramides.* **Open** 9am-7pm daily. Information on Paris and the suburbs, shop, bureau de change, hotel reservations, phonecards, museum cards, travel passes and tickets. Multilingual staff. **Other locations**: *Gare de Lyon* 20 bd Diderot, 12th. M° Gare de Lyon. **Open** 8am-6pm Mon-Sat. *Gare du Nord* 18 rue de Dunkerque, 10th. M° Gare du Nord. **Open** 8am-6pm daily. *Montmartre* 21 pl du Tertre, 18th. M° Abbesses. **Open** 10am-7pm daily. *Opéra* 11 rue Scribe, 9th. M° Opéra. **Open** 9am-6.30pm Mon-Sat. *Pyramides* 25 rue des Pyramides, 1st, M° Pyramides. **Open** 9am-7pm daily. *Tour Eiffel* Champ de Mars, 7th. M° Bir-Hakeim. **Open** late Mar-Oct 11am-6.40pm daily.

## Visas

EU nationals don't need a visa to enter France, nor do US, Canadian, Australian, New Zealand or South African citizens for stays of up to three months. Nationals of other countries should enquire at the nearest French embassy or consulate before leaving home. If they are travelling to France from one of the countries in the Schengen agreement (most of the EU, but not Britain or Ireland), the visa from that country should be sufficient.

EU citizens may stay in France for as long as their passport is valid. For non-EU citizens who wish to stay for longer than three months, they must apply to the French embassy or consulate in their own country for a long-term visa. For more information, contact these two offices:

**CIRA (Centre Interministeriel de Renseignements Administratifs)** *(0821.08.09.10 0.12€/min/www.service-public.fr).* **Open** 8am-7pm Mon-Fri; 8am-noon Sat.
Advice on most French administrative procedures.

**Préfecture de Police de Paris Service Etrangers** *7-9 bd du Palais, 4th (01.53.71.51.68/ www.prefecture-police-paris. interieur. gouv.fr). M° Cité.* **Open** 9am-4pm Mon-Fri.
Information on residency and work permits for foreigners.

# Average monthly climate

| Month | High temp (C°/F°) | Low temp (C°/F°) | Rainfall |
|---|---|---|---|
| Jan | 7/45 | 2/36 | 53cm |
| Feb | 10/50 | 2/36 | 43cm |
| Mar | 13/55 | 4/39 | 49cm |
| Apr | 17/63 | 6/43 | 53cm |
| May | 20/68 | 9/48 | 65cm |
| June | 23/73 | 12/54 | 54cm |
| July | 25/77 | 15/59 | 62cm |
| Aug | 26/79 | 16/61 | 42cm |
| Sept | 23/73 | 12/54 | 54cm |
| Oct | 20/68 | 8/46 | 60cm |
| Nov | 14/57 | 4/39 | 51cm |
| Dec | 7/45 | 3/37 | 59cm |

**Directory**

## Weights & measures

France uses only the metric system; remember that all speed limits are in kilometres per hour. One kilometre is equivalent to 0.62 miles (1 mile = 1.6km). Petrol, like other liquids, is measured in litres (one UK gallon = 4.54 litres; 1 US gallon = 3.79 litres).

## What to take

Binoculars for studying high-altitude details of monuments, a pocket knife with corkscrew (for improvised picnics) and – vital – comfortable shoes. If you're staying in cheap hotels, a universal sink plug is handy.

## When to go

In July and August, when there are deals on hotels and a good range of free events; the city seems more relaxed than usual. Avoid October, with its fashion weeks and trade shows.

## Women in Paris

Though Paris is not especially threatening for women, the precautions you would take in any major city apply: be careful at night in areas like Pigalle, the rue St-Denis, Stalingrad, La Chapelle, Château Rouge, Gare de l'Est, Gare du Nord, the Bois de Boulogne and Bois de Vincennes. If you receive unwanted attention, a politely scathing *N'insistez pas!* (Don't push it!) makes your feelings clear. If things get too heavy, go into the nearest shop or café.

**CIDFF (Centre d'Information et des Droits des Femmes et de la Famille)** *7 rue du Jura, 13th (01.42.17.12.00). M° Gobelins.* **Open** visits by appointment only.
The CIDFF offers health, legal and professional advice for women.
**Violence Conjugale: Femmes Info Service** *(01.40.33.80.60).* **Open** 7.30am-11.30pm Mon-Sat.
Hotline for battered women, directing them towards medical aid or shelters.
**Viols Femmes Informations** *(08.00.05.95.95).* **Open** 10am-7pm Mon-Fri. Freephone service.
Help and advice available, in French, to rape victims.

## Working in Paris

Most EU nationals can work legally in France, including UK and Irish citizens, but should apply for a French social security number. Some job ads can be found at branches of the French national employment bureau, the **Agence Nationale pour l'Emploi** (ANPE), or on its website (www.anpe.fr). Branches are also the place to sign up as a *demandeur d'emploi*, to be placed on file as ready for work and possibly to qualify for French unemployment benefits. Britons can only claim French unemployment benefit if they were already signed on before leaving the UK. Non-EU nationals need a work permit and cannot use the ANPE network without having valid work papers.

**Club des Quatre Vents** *1 rue Gozlin, 6th (01.43.29.60.20). M° St-Germain-des-Prés.* **Open** 9am-6pm Mon-Fri.
Provides three-month work permits for US citizens at university or recent graduates.
**Espace Emploi International (OMI et ANPE)** *48 bd de la Bastille, 12th (01.53.02.25.50/www.emploi-international.org). M° Bastille.* **Open** 9am-5pm Mon, Wed-Fri; 9am-noon Tue.
Provides work permits of up to 18 months for Americans aged 18-35.
**The Language Network** *(01.44.64.82.23).*
Helps native English speakers who wish to find work teaching.

## Job ads

Help wanted ads sometimes appear in the *International Herald Tribune*, in *FUSAC* and on noticeboards at language schools and the **American Church** (*see p376*). Bilingual secretarial/PA work is available for those with good written French. If you're looking for professional work, have your CV translated, including French equivalents for any qualifications. Most job applications require a photo and a handwritten letter.

# Size charts

## Women's clothes

| British | French | US |
| --- | --- | --- |
| 4 | 32 | 2 |
| 6 | 34 | 4 |
| 8 | 36 | 6 |
| 10 | 38 | 8 |
| 12 | 40 | 10 |
| 14 | 42 | 12 |
| 16 | 44 | 14 |
| 18 | 46 | 16 |
| 20 | 48 | 18 |

## Women's shoes

| British | French | US |
| --- | --- | --- |
| 3 | 36 | 5 |
| 4 | 37 | 6 |
| 5 | 38 | 7 |
| 6 | 39 | 8 |
| 7 | 40 | 9 |
| 8 | 41 | 10 |
| 9 | 42 | 11 |

## Men's clothes

| British | French | US |
| --- | --- | --- |
| 34 | 44 | 34 |
| 36 | 46 | 36 |
| 38 | 48 | 38 |
| 40 | 50 | 40 |
| 42 | 52 | 42 |
| 44 | 54 | 44 |
| 46 | 56 | 46 |
| 48 | 58 | 48 |

## Men's shoes

| British | French | US |
| --- | --- | --- |
| 6 | 39 | 7 |
| 7.5 | 40 | 7.5 |
| 8 | 41 | 8 |
| 8 | 42 | 8.5 |
| 9 | 43 | 9.5 |
| 10 | 44 | 10.5 |
| 11 | 45 | 11 |
| 12 | 46 | 11.5 |

**Directory**

# Vocabulary

In French the second person singular (you) has two forms. Phrases here are given in the more polite *vous* form. The *tu* form is used with family, friends, children and pets; you should be careful not to use it with people you do not know sufficiently well. Courtesies such as *monsieur, madame* and *mademoiselle* are used more than their English equivalents.

## General

**good morning/afternoon, hello** bonjour; **good evening** bonsoir; **goodbye** au revoir; **OK** d'accord; **yes** oui; **no** non; **how are you?** comment allez vous?/vous allez bien?; **how's it going?** comment ça va?/ça va? (familiar); **sir/Mr** monsieur (Mr); **madam/Mrs** madame (Mme); **miss** mademoiselle (Mlle); **please** s'il vous plaît; **thank you** merci; **sorry** pardon; **excuse me** excusez-moi; **do you speak English?** parlez-vous anglais?; **I don't speak French** je ne parle pas français; **I don't understand** je ne comprends pas; **speak more slowly, please** parlez plus lentement, s'il vous plaît; **I am going to pay** je vais payer; **it is** c'est; **it isn't** ce n'est pas; **good** bon/bonne; **bad** mauvais/mauvaise; **small** petit/petite; **big** grand/grande; **beautiful** beau/belle; **well** bien; **badly** mal; **a bit** un peu; **a lot** beaucoup; **very** très; **with** avec; **without** sans; **and** et; **or** ou; **because** parce que; **who?** qui?; **when?** quand?; **what?** quoi?; **which?** quel?; **where?** où?; **why?** pourquoi?; **how?** comment?; **at what time/when?** à quelle heure?; **forbidden** interdit/défendu; **out of order** hors service (HS)/en panne; **daily** tous les jours (tlj).

## On the phone

**hello** allô; **who's calling?** c'est de la part de qui?/qui est à l'appareil?; **this is... speaking** c'est... à l'appareil; **I'd like to speak to...** j'aurais voulu parler avec...; **hold the line** ne quittez pas; **please call back later** rappellez plus tard s'il vous plaît; **you must have the wrong number** vous avez dû composer un mauvais numéro.

## Getting around

**where is the (nearest) métro?** où est le métro (le plus proche)?; **when is the next train for...?** c'est quand le prochain train pour...?; **ticket** un billet; **station** la gare; **platform** le quai; **entrance** entrée; **exit** sortie; **left** gauche; **right** droite; **straight on** tout droit; **far** loin; **near** pas loin/près d'ici; **street map** un plan; **road map** une carte; **bank** la banque; **is there a bank near here?** est-ce qu'il y a une banque près d'ici?

## Sightseeing

**museum** un musée; **church** une église; **exhibition** une exposition; **ticket** (*for museum*) un billet; (*for theatre, concert*) une place; **open** ouvert; **closed** fermé; **free** gratuit; **reduced price** un tarif réduit.

## Accommodation

**do you have a room (for this evening/for two people)?** avez-vous une chambre (pour ce soir/pour deux personnes)?; **full** complet; **room** une chambre; **bed** un lit; **double bed** un grand lit; **(a room with) twin beds** (une chambre à) deux lits; **with bath(room)/shower** avec (salle de) bain/douche; **breakfast** le petit déjeuner; **included** compris.

## At the café or restaurant

**I'd like to book a table (for three/at 8pm)** je voudrais réserver une table (pour trois personnes/à vingt heures); **lunch** le déjeuner; **dinner** le dîner; **coffee** (espresso) un café; **tea** un thé; **wine** le vin; **beer** une bière; **mineral water** eau minérale; **tap water** eau du robinet/une carafe d'eau; **the bill, please** l'addition, s'il vous plaît.

## Shopping

**cheap** pas cher; **expensive** cher; **how much?/how many?** combien?; **have you got change?** avez-vous de la monnaie? **I would like...** je voudrais...; **may I try this on?** est-ce que je pourrais essayer cet article?; **do you have a smaller/larger size?** auriez-vous la taille en-dessous/au dessus?; **I'm a size 38** je fais du 38; **I'll take it** je le prends.

## The come-on

**do you have a light?** avez-vous du feu?; **what's your name?** comment vous vous appellez?; **would you like a drink?** voulez vous boire un verre?; **your place or mine?** chez toi ou chez moi?

## The brush-off

**leave me alone** laissez-moi tranquille; **get lost, you cretin** casse-toi, imbécile.

## Staying alive

**be cool** restez calme; **I don't want any trouble** je ne veux pas d'ennuis; **I only do safe sex** je ne pratique que le safe sex.

## Numbers

**0** zéro; **1** un, une; **2** deux; **3** trois; **4** quatre; **5** cinq; **6** six; **7** sept; **8** huit; **9** neuf; **10** dix; **11** onze; **12** douze; **13** treize; **14** quatorze; **15** quinze; **16** seize; **17** dix-sept; **18** dix-huit; **19** dix-neuf; **20** vingt; **21** vingt-et-un; **22** vingt-deux; **30** trente; **40** quarante; **50** cinquante; **60** soixante; **70** soixante-dix; **80** quatre-vingts; **90** quatre-vingt-dix; **100** cent; **1000** mille; **10,000** dix mille; **1,000,000** un million.

## Days, months & seasons

**Monday** lundi; **Tuesday** mardi; **Wednesday** mercredi; **Thursday** jeudi; **Friday** vendredi; **Saturday** samedi; **Sunday** dimanche; **January** janvier; **February** février; **March** mars; **April** avril; **May** mai; **June** juin; **July** juillet; **August** août; **September** septembre; **October** octobre; **November** novembre; **December** décembre; **spring** le printemps; **summer** l'été; **autumn** l'automne; **winter** l'hiver.

**Directory**

# Further Reference

## Books

### Non-fiction

**Petrus Abaelardus & Heloise** *Letters* The full details of Paris' first great romantic drama.

**Robert Baldick** *The Siege of Paris* The bloodshed, the hunger, the rats for supper: a gripping account of the Paris Commune of 1871.

**Antony Beevor & Artemis Cooper** *Paris after the Liberation* Rationing, freedom and Existentialism.

**NT Binh** *Paris au cinéma* Gorgeous coffee-table round-up of Paris sights on film.

**Henri Cartier-Bresson** *A propos de Paris* Classic black and white shots by a giant among snappers.

**Danielle Chadych, Dominique Leborgne** *Atlas de Paris* Lavishly appointed survey of Paris bricks and blocks and their movements through the centuries.

**Rupert Christiansen** *Tales of the New Babylon* Blood and sleaze in Napoléon III's Paris.

**Vincent Cronin** *Napoleon* A fine bio of the emperor.

**Christian Dupavillon** *Paris Côté Seine* Nicely illustrated history of riverside Paris.

**Julien Green** *Paris* Personal account of Green's city.

**Alastair Horne** *The Fall of Paris* Detailed chronicle of the Siege and Commune 1870-71.

**Andrew Hussey** *Paris: A Secret History* Entertaining, street-level description of Paris through the ages.

**J-K Huysmans** *Croquis Parisiens* The world that Toulouse-Lautrec painted.

**Douglas Johnson & Madeleine Johnson** *Age of Illusion: Art & Politics in France 1918-1940* French culture in a Paris at the forefront of modernity.

**Marc Lemonier, Jacques Lebar** *Fascinating Paris* The city in colour photographs.

**Ian Littlewood** *Paris: Architecture, History, Art* Paris' history and its treasures.

**Colin MacCabe** *Godard* A bio and accessible introduction to intellectual life in late 20th-century France.

**Patrick Marnham** *Crime & the Académie Française* Scandals in Mitterrand-era Paris.

**François Maspero** *RoissyExpress: Journey Through the Paris Suburbs* Take the train: Maspero examines day-to-day life in mid-1990s Paris with photographer in tow.

**Nancy Mitford** *The Sun King; Madame de Pompadour* Great gossipy accounts of the courts of the *ancien régime*.

**Noel Riley Fitch** *Literary Cafés of Paris* Who drank what, where and when.

**Virginia Rounding** *Les Grandes Horizontales* Racy, entertaining lives of four 19th-century courtesans.

**Renzo Salvadori** *Architect's Guide to Paris* Plans, maps and a guide to Paris's growth.

**Simon Schama** *Citizens* Epic, wonderfully readable account of the Revolution.

**William Shirer** *The Collapse of the Third Republic* Forensic account of the reasons for France's humiliating 1940 defeat.

### Fiction & poetry

**Louis Aragon** *Le Paysan de Paris* A great Surrealist view of the city.

**Honoré de Balzac** *Illusions perdues*; *La Peau de chagrin*; *Le Père Goriot*; *Splendeurs et misères des courtisanes* Many of the best-known novels in the 'Comédie Humaine' cycle are set in Paris.

**Charles Baudelaire** *Le Spleen de Paris* Prose poems with Paris settings.

**Simone de Beauvoir** *Les Mandarins* Paris intellectuals and idealists just after the Liberation.

**Louis-Ferdinand Céline** *Mort à crédit* Vivid, splenetic account of an impoverished Paris childhood.

**Victor Hugo** *Notre Dame de Paris* Romantic vision of medieval Paris. Quasimodo! Esmeralda! The bells!

**Guy de Maupassant** *Bel-Ami* Ruthless ambition in 19th-century Paris.

**Patrick Modiano** *Honeymoon* Evocative story of two lives that cross in Paris.

**Gérard de Nerval** *Les Nuits d'octobre* Late-night Les Halles and environs, mid 19th-century.

**Georges Perec** *La Vie, mode d'emploi* Cheek-by-jowl life in a Haussmannian apartment building.

**Raymond Queneau** *Zazie dans le Métro* Paris in the 1950s: bright and very *nouvelle vague*.

**Nicolas Restif de la Bretonne** *Les Nuits de Paris* The sexual underworld of Louis XV's Paris, by one of France's most famous defrocked priests.

**Jean-Paul Sartre** *Les Carnets de la drôle de guerre* Existential angst as the German army takes over Paris.

**Georges Simenon** The Maigret books. Many of Simenon's novels featuring his laconic detective provide vivid pictures of Paris and its underworld. See also *L'Homme qui regardait passer les trains*.

**Emile Zola** *L'Assommoir; Nana; Le Ventre de Paris* Accounts of the underside of the Second Empire from the master Realist.

## The ex-pat angle

**Adam Gopnik** *From Paris to the Moon* A New Yorker raises a family in this alien city.

**Ernest Hemingway** *A Moveable Feast* Big Ern chronicles 1920s Paris.

**Henry Miller** *Tropic of Cancer* Love, lust, lice and low life: bawdy, yes. Funny, too.

**Anaïs Nin** *Henry & June* More lust in Montparnasse with Henry Miller and his wife.

**George Orwell** *Down and Out in Paris and London* Work in a Paris restaurant (it's hardly changed), hunger in a Paris hovel, suffering in a Paris hospital.

**Edmund White** *The Flaneur: a Stroll through the Paradoxes of Paris* US ex-pat maps out some of the hidden nooks of the city's history.

## Film

**Olivier Assayas** *Irma Vep* Jean-Pierre Léaud and Maggie Cheung endeavour to remake Feuillade's vampire classic in 1990s Paris. And fail.

**Luc Besson** *Subway* Christophe Lambert goes underground. Hokum, but easy on the eye.

**Marcel Carné** *Hôtel du Nord* Arletty's finest hour.

**Jean-Luc Godard** *A Bout de Souffle* Belmondo, Seberg, Godard, the Champs-Elysées, the attitude, the famous ending. Essential.

**Jean-Luc Godard** *Une Femme est une femme* Belmondo and Karina, and Godard's first feature in colour – the Grands Boulevards, the attitude, the music.

**Edouard Molinaro** *Un Témoin dans la ville* Lino

Ventura on the run in 1950s nocturnal Paris. Superb *noir*.

**Bertrand Tavernier** *L.627* The drugs war in the 1990s, as seen from the cops' side. Gritty and polemic-making.

**François Truffaut** *Les 400 Coups* The first of the Antoine Doinel cycle.

**Agnès Varda** *Cléo de 5 à 7* The *nouvelle vague* heroine spends an anxious afternoon drifting around Paris.

**Claude Zidi** *Les Ripoux (Le Cop)* Cops Philippe Noiret and Thierry Lhermitte scam the whole of the Goutte d'Or.

## Music

**Air** *Moon Safari* Relaxing, ambient beeps and sonics from that rara avis, a credible French pop group.

**Serge Gainsbourg** *Le Poinçonneur des Lilas* Classic early Gainsbourg: jazzy, elegant, mordant.

**Thelonius Monk** *The Paris Concert* A blend of the experimental and the romantically gentle.

**Pink Martini** *Sympathique* 'Je ne veux pas travailler' and other dinner-party starters by some French-singing Americans.

## Websites

**paris.webcity.fr** Cultural calendar, plus small ads and information on shops, hotels, restaurants, traffic conditions and more.

**www.culture.fr** Current and forthcoming cultural events of all kinds, in Paris and other big French cities.

**www.edible-paris.com** Customised gastronomic itineraries in Paris – you send your requirements before you arrive – by the editor of Time Out's *Eating & Drinking in Paris* guide.

**www.fnac.com** Browse and buy the multidisciplinary

Fnac's books, CDs, DVDs and electronics – and reserve tickets for all sorts of events.

**www.fusac.org** Online version of the free fortnightly small ads mag: jobs, removals, personals, classes and more.

**www.gogoparis.com** Online version of free monthly Anglo listings mag.

**www.mappy.fr** Maps of Paris and France.

**www.meteo.fr** Weather forecasts and stats from the state meteorology office.

**www.pagesjaunes.fr** The Paris yellow pages, with maps and multi-angle photos of every address in the city. Also has a link to the Pages Blanches phone directory.

**www.paris-anglo.com** An abundance of nuts-and-bolts information, in English, on living in Paris.

**www.paris-art.com** Contemporary art exhibitions and galleries.

**www.parisdigest.com** Paris listings, shopping tips and general information in English.

**www.parissi.com** Films, concerts and a strong calendar of clubbing events.

**www.paris-touristoffice.com** Official site of the Office de Tourisme et des Congrès de Paris.

**www.pidf.com** Official site of the Paris regional tourist board: a gold mine of info on museums, events, transport, shopping et al.

**www.quidonc.fr** The phone book in reverse: type in a number, it tells you the owner. Can only be used in France.

**www.ratp.com** Everything you'll need to know about using the buses, métro, RER and trams.

**www.timeout.com/paris** A pick of the best current events and good hotels, eateries and shops.

**Directory**

Index

Note page numbers in **bold** indicate section(s) giving key information on a topic; *italics* indicate photographs.

**a**

Abbesses 220
Abélard, Pierre 89, 149
Académie Cinq Sens 196
Académie Française 19, 32, **156**
Académie de la Grande-Chaumière 162
Académie du Spectacle Equestre, Versailles 352
accident & emergency 369
**Accommodation 47-77**
  apart-hotels & flat rental 77
  bed & breakfast 77
  he best 51
  boutique hotels 55
  by price
    *budget* 49, 54, 57, 65, 66, 67, 69, 71, 74, 75, 77
    *deluxe* 51, 54, 57, 63, 65, 71, 75
    *expensive* 48, 62, 63, 65, 67, 73, 74, 75
    *moderate* 49, 53, 57, 62, 63, 66, 67, 69, 73, 74, 75
  gay & lesbian 310
  hotel bars 228
  youth accommodation 77
Adam Mickiewicz library-museum 92
addresses 366
African culture 128
Africolor 278
Age d'Or, L' 125
age restrictions 366
air, arriving & leaving Paris by 360
Albert, Edouard 42
Alexander Nevsky Cathedral 120
Alexander III, Pope 89
Algerian War, the **29**, 33, 128
*Amants du Pont Neuf, Les* 87
American football 335
Anziutti, Jacques 43
apart-hotels & flat rental 77
Apollinaire, Guillaume 37
aquaria 287-288
Aragon, Louis 27, 107
**Arc de Triomphe** 32, 41, 83, 102, **117**, 177
Arc du Carrousel 41, **102**
architecture **39-43**
  walk 121, **122-123**
Archives Nationaux 132
Arènes de Lutèce 13, 83, 147, **153**
Armée du Salut hostel 43
Armistice Day 278
**arriving & leaving Paris** 360-361
  by air 360
  by car 361
  by coach 361
  by rail 361
art fairs 299
art nouveau 41
**arts & entertainment** 273-340
  for children 288
shops 270
Arts Florissants, Les 311, **312**
Assemblée Nationale 20, 109, 169, **170**

Assumption Day procession 89, **274**
Atelier Brancusi 130
Atelier des Chefs, L' 196
Atelier des Sens 196
athletics 336
ATMs 374
Attila the Hun **13**, 32
attitude 366
Auberge Ravoux, Auvers-sur-Oise 346
Auditorium du Louvre 295, **312**
Auteuil 121-124
Auvers-sur-Oise 346
Avenue Montaigne 239
Azéma, Léon 123

**b**

babies, Paris for 285
bag shops 259
bakeries 260
Baldwin, James 159
Baltard 112
Balzac, Honoré de 121, 162, 357
banks 374
banlieue see suburbs
banlieue riots 44
Banlieues Bleues festival 46, **274**
bars *see* cafés & bars
Bartholdi 166
baseball 336
**Basilique St-Denis** 39, 178, **179**, 179
basketball 335, 336
Bastille, the 17, 20, 137
**Bastille area** 81, **137-139**
  accommodation 67
  cafés & bars 229-231
  restaurants 205-206
  shopping 267
Bastille Day *see* Quatorze Juillet, Le
Bastille Day ball 137, **277**
Bateaux Parisiens 90
Bateaux-Mouches 90
bathroom shops 270
Batignolles 120-121
batobus 362
Batobus Tour Eiffel 90
Batofar 86, **326**
Baudelaire, Charles 92, 156, 159
**Beaubourg** 130-132
  accommodation 65-67
  cafés & bars 227-229
  galleries 300-303
  restaurants 202-205
Beauvert, Thierry 311
bed & breakfast 77
*Belle Hélène, La* 111
Belleville 81, *144*, **145-146**
Bercy 81, **139-140**
Bercy Village 241
Berger, Patrick 43
Besson, Luc 46
BHV (Bazar de L'Hôtel de Ville) 130, **240**
Bibliothèque Forney 17, **136**
Bibliothèque Historique de la Ville de Paris 132
Bibliothèque Nationale de France – François Mitterrand 31, 176, **177**
Bibliothèque Nationale de France – Richelieu 19, **108**
Bibliothèque Ste-Geneviève 41

bicycle/cycling 36, 283, 336, 364-365
  hire 164, 365
  tours 80, **85**
Bizet 111, 311
Black Death, the 17
Blaise, Jean 276
blues music 322-323
Blum, Léon **25**, 33
boat tours 90
Bobin'O 279
Bofill, Ricardo 163
Boileau, Louis-Hippolyte 123
**Bois de Boulogne** 83, **124**, 283
**Bois de Vincennes 139**, 180, 283
Bon Marché, Le 33, 169, **240**
Bonaparte, Louis-Napoleon **23**, 33
Bonaparte, Napoléon *see* Napoléon
Bonsergent, Jacques 26
books *see* literature
Borges, Jorge Luis 159
Bouchard, Henri 123
Bouchardon, Edmé 168
boules 336
Boulez, Pierre 311
Boulogne & the west 181-183
Boulogne-Billancourt 181
Bourbon dynasty 18
Bourbon, Françoise-Marie de 146
Bourse 12, 22, 106, **109**
Bourse de Commerce *108*, 115
boutique & concept fashion shops 250
boutique hotels 55
bowling 336
Brasillach, Robert 27
breastfeeding 285
Breton, André 25, 37, 150
bridges, The 86
British Embassy 117
Brook, Peter 341
Brosse, Salomon de 40
Brown, Dan 93
Budé, Guillaume 149
Buñuel, Luis 125
bureaux de change 374
Burroughs, William 156, 158
bus, getting around Paris by 262
Bush, George 31
business 366
Butte-aux-Cailles, La 176

**c**

**cabaret, circus & comedy** 279-282
Caesar, Julius 12
café-théâtre 279, **281**
**cafés & bars** 220-238
  the best 222
  club bars 325-326
  gay & lesbian 306-307
  hotel bars 228
  rock in bars 322
Caillebotte 111
Canal St-Martin 83, 85, 141, **143-144**, 220
Canal de l'Ourcq 41, 83, **143**
Canauxrama 90
Canopée, La 41
*Cantatrice Chauve, La* 147
Capet, Count Hugues **15**, 32
Capetian dynasty 15

Carax, Leos 87
Carlu, Jacques 123
*Carmen* 33, 111, 311
Carpeaux 111
car 36
  arriving & leaving Paris by 361
  getting around Paris by 363-364
Cars Rouges, Les 84
Cartoucherie theatre complex 139, 341, **342**
Castel Béranger 41, 122, **124**
Catacombes, Les 83, **166**
Cathédrale Notre-Dame, Chartres 349
**Cathédrale Notre-Dame de Paris** 15, 32, 87, **89**, *89*, 285
CD shops 270
*Centaur* 157
Centre Culturel Irlandais **81**, 150
Centre Gai et Lesbien 305
Centre National de la Danse 46, 179, **290**
**Centre Pompidou** 33, 43, 83, 130, **131**, *131*, 295
Centre Pompidou – Galerie des Enfants 286
César 157
Champagne country 354-355
Champagne Pommery 354
**Champs-Elysées** 102, **116-120**
  accommodation 57-63
  cafés & bars 225-226
  galleries 303
  restaurants 194-197
  shopping 266
  *chanson* 317, **320**
Chantilly 346-348
Chapelle Expiatoire 109
Chapelle du Martyr 125
Chapelle de la Médaille Miraculeuse 169, **170**
Chapelle Notre-Dame de l'Assomption 103
Chapelle St-Louis-de-la-Salpêtrière 175
Charlemagne **13**, 32
Charles II 'the Bald', King 13
Charles III 'the Fat', King 15
Charles IV, King 96
Charles V 32, 87, 92, 96, 181
Charles VII, King 17
Charles IX, King 16
Charles X, King 22, 32
Charonne 145-146
Charter of Liberties (1814) 22, 32
Chartres 349
Château de Chantilly 347
Château de Fontainebleau 348, 350
Château de Malmaison 181
Château de Monte-Cristo 181
Château park 347
Château de Versailles 352, 352
Château de Vincennes 139, 180, 183
**Châtelet** 114, **130**
  shopping 266
Châtelet – Théâtre Musical de Paris 311, 353
*Chaufferie avec cheminée* 46
cheese chops 262
Chemin de la Croix, Le 274
Childebert I 89
**children 283-289**

**386** Time Out Paris

Fondation Mona Bismarck 117
Fondation Pierre Bergé Yves Saint Laurent 83, **118**
Fontaine des Innocents 112
Fontaine des Quatre Saisons 168
Fontaine Stravinsky 130
Fontaine du Trahoir, The 112
Fontainebleau 17, 40, **349-350**
food & drink shops 260
football 335, 338
Forum des Halles 112, *114*, **115**
Forum des Images 196
Fouquet 32
Fournier, Alain 158
Fourth Republic **26**, 33
48 hours in Paris 84-85
François I, King **17**, 32, 40, 96, 149, 181
Franco-Prussian War (1870) 24
French Tennis Open 275
Fréteval (1194), Battle of 15
fringe theatre 281
frites 201
'Fronde' rebellion (1648-53) 19, 32
Front Populaire **25**, 33

## g

Galberg, Antoine de 139
Galerie du Carrousel du Louvre, La 241
Galerie-Musée Baccarat 83, **118**
Galeries Lafayette 109, 240, **241**, 285
Galeries Nationales du Grand Palais 83, 118
**galleries 299-304**
alternative spaces 304
commercial galleries 300-304
*see also* Museums & Galleries
Gambetta, Léon 24
Garcia, Jacques 159
gardens see parks, gardens & theme parks
**Gare du Nord** 41, 83, **141-143**
Gare d'Orsay 25
Gare St-Lazare 111
Garnier, Tony 181
gas 368
Gaudin, Henri & Bruno 178
Gauguin 129
Gauls, the 12
Gaulle, Charles de **26**, 29, 31, 33
Gaunier, Charles 24
Gautier, Théophile 92
Gautrand, Manuelle 43
**gay & lesbian 305-310**
accommodation 310
cafés & bars 306-307
clubs 307-308
festivals & events 276
resources 368
restaurants 307
sex clubs & saunas 308-309
shops & services 309-310
Gay Pride March 276, 305
Gehry, Frank 43
Geneviève 13
Géode 288, **294**
gift shops 264
Gill, André 126
Girondins, the 22
Giverny 350-351
Glasshouse 342
*Go Tell It on the Mountain* 159
Gobelins, Les 175-176
Golden Triangle 239
Goldenberg, Jo 134
golf 338
Gothic architecture 39
Gouin, Félix 29
Goujon, Jean 112
Goulue, La 127
Goutte d'Or, La 126
Goutte d'Or en Fête, La 127, **276**
Gozlin, Bishop of Paris 15
Grand Boulevards, The 106, **111**
shopping 266
Grand Concerts Sacrés 311
*Grand Meaulnes, Le* 158
Grand Palais 25, 33, 116, **118**, 169
Grand Pont 15
Grand Rex, Le 112, **330**, 294
Grand Trianon/Petit Trianon/Domaine de Marie-Antoinette, Versailles 353
**Grande Arche de La Défense, La** 31, 102, 183
Grande Galerie de l'Evolution at Museum National d'Histoire Naturelle 83, 153, **154**, 285, **287**
*Grande Jatte, La* 181
Grands Boulevards 32, 81
Gréco, Juliette 155
Grévin 111, **286**
Guillotin, Dr Joseph-Ignace 156
guillotine, the 22
Guimard, Hector 41, 122, 125, 133
Guise, Duc de **16**, 18

## h

Haïm, Emmanuelle 311
**Halles, Les** 16, 32, 81, 112-115
accommodation 54-57
cafés & bars 222-225
restaurants 191-194
shopping 266
Hardouin-Mansart 106
hat shops 257
Haussmann, Baron Georges-Eugène **23**, 33, 39, 41, 87, 125
hazards, natural 375
health 368
health & beauty shops 265
Héloïse 89
helplines 370
Hemingway, Ernest 26, 150, 159
Henri I, King 15, 112
Henri II, King 18, 96, 135, 181
Henri III, King **18**, 32, 87, 96
Henry IV, King 16, 18, 32, 39, 40, 87, 96, 112, 132, 143
Henry V of England, King 32, 91, 139
Henry VI of England, King 17
**history 12-34**
Hitler, Adolf 25, 26
HIV & AIDS 370
Honfleur 356, 357
Hôpital St-Louis 143
horse racing 335, 339
horse riding 338
Hôtel d'Alsace 156
Hôtel d'Angny 111
Hôtel Borghèse 117
Hôtel Carnavalet 40, 132, **135**
Hôtel de Cluny 40
Hôtel-Dieu 89
Hôtel Donon 132
Hôtel Drouot auction house 111, **112**
Hôtel des Grands Hommes 150
Hôtel Guénégaud 132
Hôtel Henri IV 87
Hôtel des Invalides 19, 32
Hôtel de Lamoignon 40, 132
Hôtel La Louisiane 159
Hôtel Matignon 169
Hôtel Mezzara 122
Hôtel St-Germain-des-Prés 159
Hôtel Salé 40, **132**
Hôtel de Sens 17, 40, **136**
Hôtel de Soubise 40, 132
Hôtel de Sully 40, 41, 132, **133**
Hôtel de Ville 130-132
hotels *see* accommodation
Houllebecq, Michel 37
house & home shops 269
Hugo, Victor 87, 89, 132, 153, 175
Huguenots, the 18
Hundred Years War **17**, 32

## i

ice skating 288, 338
ID 370
Ile de Chatou 181
**Ile de la Cité** 12, 15, 81, **87-92**
Ile de la Grande Jatte 181
**Ile St-Louis** 40, 81, **92**
IMAX cinema 183
immigrants 37, 44
Impressionists, the 24, 33
Improfessionals 342
in-line skating 334
Innocent III, Pope 149
Institut de France 156, *157*
Institut du Monde Arabe 83, 84, 153, **154**, 321
Institut Océanographique 150
internet 370
**Invalides, Les** 168, 169, **170**, 285
Ionesco 147
IRCAM 311
IRCAM music institute 130, 314
**Islands 87-92**
accommodation 48-51
restaurants 187-191

## j

Jacobins, the 21, **22**, 32
Jakob and MacFarlance 43
James II 150, 181
Jardin d'Acclimatation 284, **288**
Jardin Atlantique 161, **165**
Jardin des Enfants aux Halles **112**, 284
**Jardin du Luxembourg** 83, 85, 150, 158, **160**, 284, 285
**Jardin des Plantes** 83, *151*, 153, **154**, 287
Jardin des Plantes district, the 153-154
Jardin des Serres d'Auteuil, Le 124
Jardin Tino-Rossi 86, 153, **154**
**Jardin des Tuileries** 102, **105**, 284
Jardins des Halles 112
Jardins de l'Observatoire 162
Järvi, Paavo 311
Jaurès, Jean 108
Jazz à Villette 277
jazz music 316-321, 322-323
Jean II, King 17
Jeanne d'Arc *see* Joan of Arc
Jeu de Paume 20, 102, **105**
jewellery shops 257
Jewish community 112, 132, **134**
Joan of Arc 17, 91 103
Joël, Nicolas 311
Jospin, Lionel 33
*Journal of My Journey to Paris* 159
Journées du Patrimoine 132, 168, **277**
Joyce, James 150, 159
Julian, Emperor **13**, 32
'June Days' 23
Justice 321

## k

'Katangais', the 28
kitchen shops 270
Kouchner, Bernard 34

## l

La Fayette, General 139
Labienus 12
Labrouste, Henri 41
Lacroix, Christian 48
Lagerfeld, Karl 155
Langlois, Henri 295
Lapin Agile, Au 126, **281**
**Latin Quarter, The 147-154**
accommodation 69-71
cafés & bars 235-236
restaurants 209-213
Latina, Le 133, **297**
Laughing Matters 279, **282**
Laval, Pierre 26
League of Nations 25
Ledoux, Nicolas 40
left luggage 371
legal help 371
lesbian Paris 310
*see also* gay & lesbian
libraries 371
Lido, Le 279
lingerie shops 258
*Lion de Belfort* 166
literature
bookshops 241
film bookshops 298
further reference 384
walk 158-159
locksmiths 371
Loo, Adolphe 43
Loos, Adolf 126
lost property 371
Louis IV, King 39
Louis VI, King 126
Louis IX, King 16, 32, 96
Louis XII, King 93
Louis XIII, King 18, 87, 92, 96, 351
Louis XIV, King **19**, 32, 40, 93, 96, 101, 111, 137, 146, 169, 181, 351
Louis XV, King 20, 40, 103, 149, 173
Louis XVI, King **20**, 32, 109
Louis XVIII, King 20, 32
Louis-Philippe d'Orléans **23**, 32, 33
Louis Vuitton Art Foundation 43
Louvin, Gérard 279
Louvre Pyramid 93
**Louvre, the** 13, 32, 40, 80, **93-96**, 101, 156, 285
**Louvre district, the**
accommodation 51-54
cafés & bars 220-222
restaurants 187
Lumière brothers 33
Lutetia **13**, 32
Luxembourg, the 157
Lycée Henri IV 150

## m

MAC/VAL contemporary art museum 45, 178, **180**
**Madeleine** (church), la 22, **109**
Madeleine district 81, **109-111**
magazine shops 241

# Advertisers' Index

Please refer to the relevant pages for contact details

| | |
|---|---|
| Place of interest and/or entertainment . . . . . . | |
| Hospital or college . . . . . . . . . . . . . . . . . . . . . . . | |
| Railway station . . . . . . . . . . . . . . . . . . . . . . . . . | |
| Park . . . . . . . . . . . . . . . . . . . . . . . . . . . . . . . . . . | |
| River . . . . . . . . . . . . . . . . . . . . . . . . . . . . . . . . | |
| Autoroute . . . . . . . . . . . . . . . . . . . . . . . . . . . . . | ═══ |
| Main road . . . . . . . . . . . . . . . . . . . . . . . . . . . . . | |
| Main road tunnel . . . . . . . . . . . . . . . . . . . . . . . . | |
| Pedestrian road . . . . . . . . . . . . . . . . . . . . . . . . . | |
| Arrondissement boundary . . . . . . . . . . . . . . . . . | — |
| Airport . . . . . . . . . . . . . . . . . . . . . . . . . . . . . . . | ✈ |
| Church . . . . . . . . . . . . . . . . . . . . . . . . . . . . . . . | ✚ |
| Métro station . . . . . . . . . . . . . . . . . . . . . . . . . . | Ⓜ |
| RER station . . . . . . . . . . . . . . . . . . . . . . . . . . . . | ⓇⒺⓇ |
| Area name . . . . . . . . . . . . . . . . . . . . LES HALLES | |
| Hotel . . . . . . . . . . . . . . . . . . . . . . . . . . . . . . . . . | ➊ |
| Restaurant . . . . . . . . . . . . . . . . . . . . . . . . . . . . | ➊ |
| Cafés & Bars . . . . . . . . . . . . . . . . . . . . . . . . . . . | ➊ |

# Maps

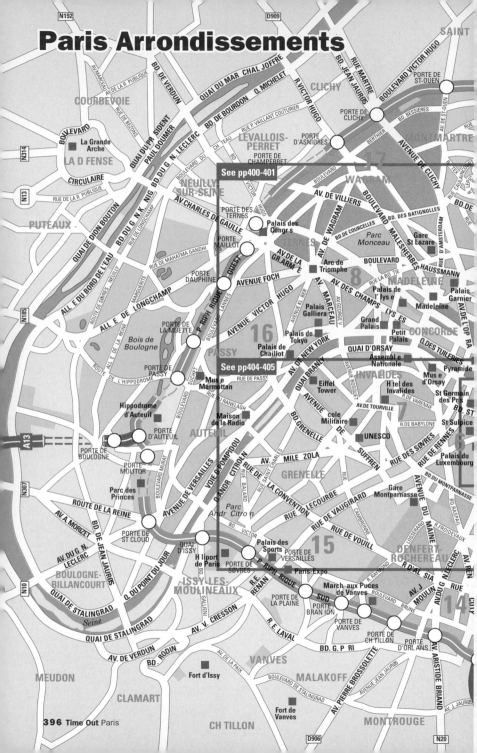

# Paris Arrondissements

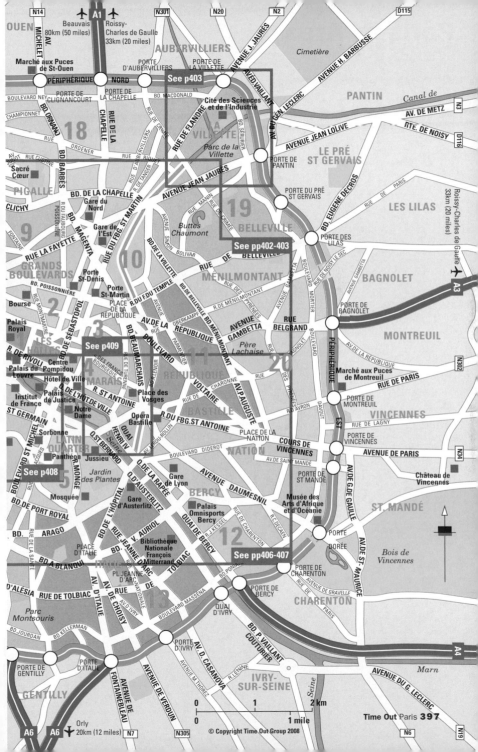

© Copyright Time Out Group 2008

# Paris by Area

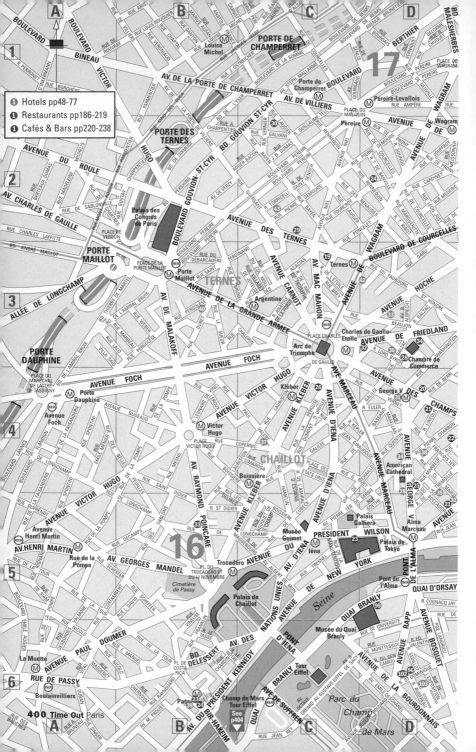

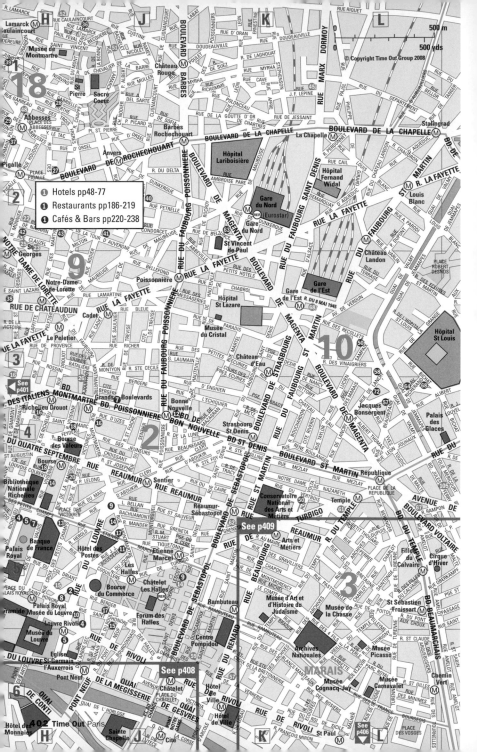

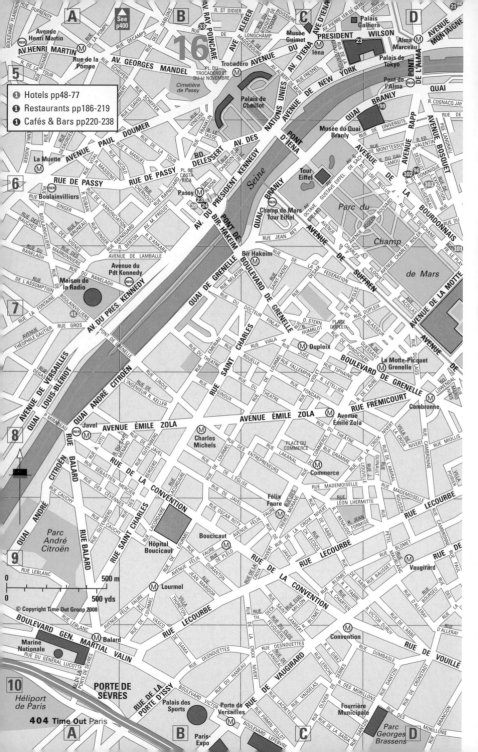

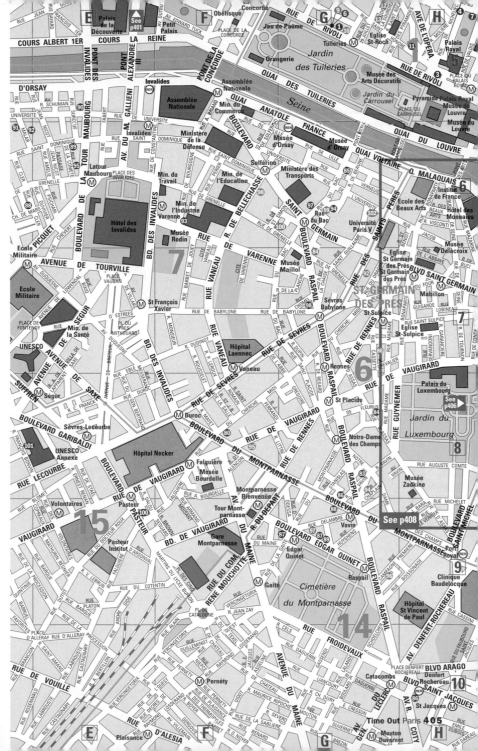

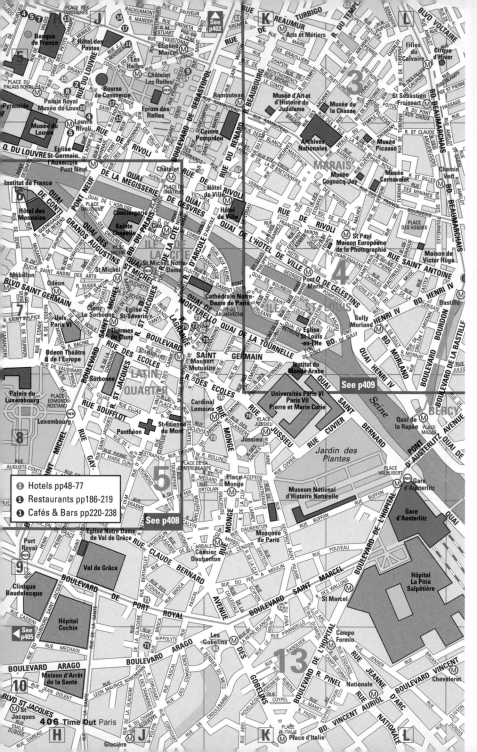

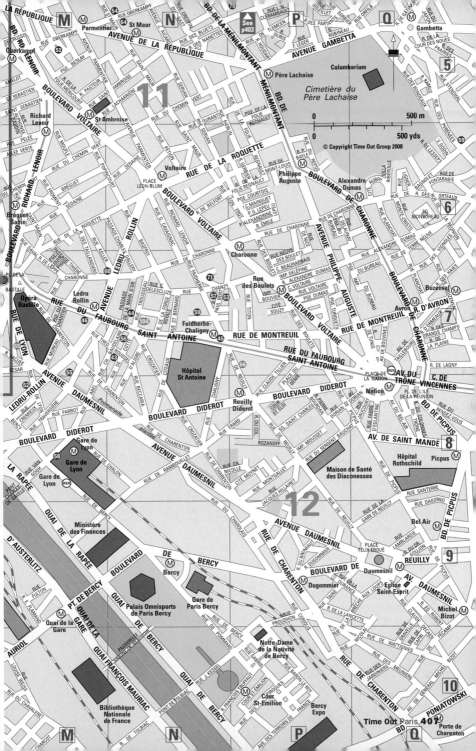

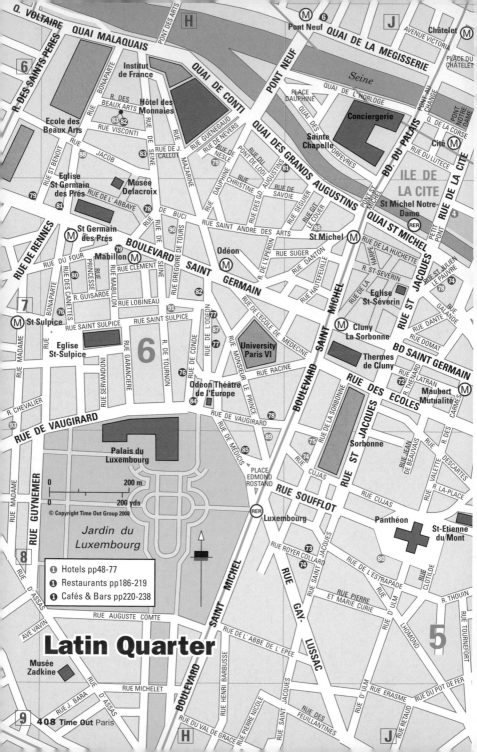

# Latin Quarter

❶ Hotels pp48-77
❶ Restaurants pp186-219
❶ Cafés & Bars pp220-238

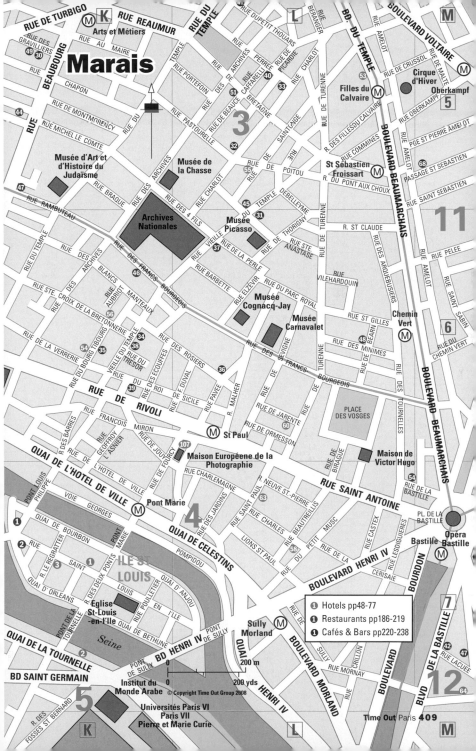

RUE DE TURBIGO
RUE REAUMUR
K
M Arts et Métiers
RUE DU TEMPLE
L
BD. DU TEMPLE
BOULEVARD VOLTAIRE
M

RUE DES GRAVILLIERS
49 30
BEAUBOURG
RUE AU MAIRE
RUE DUPETIT THOUARS
BERANGER
RUE AMELOT
RUE DE MALTE
RUE DE CRUSSOL

**Marais**

CHAPON
RUE PORTEFOIN
TEMPLE
RUE DES ARCHIVES
PERRÉE
RUE DE PICARDIE
RUE CHARLOT
Filles du Calvaire
M
Cirque d'Hiver
Oberkampf

44
RUE DE MONTMORENCY
RUE DU
RUE CAFFARELLI
40
33
RUE DE BRETAGNE
RUE DE TURENNE
RUE DES FILLES DU CALVAIRE
RUE OBERKAMPF
5

RUE MICHEL LE COMTE
51
RUE DE BEAUCE
SAINT-GAGE
RUE COMMINES
PGE ST PIERRE AMELOT
68

47
RUE RAMBUTEAU
Musée d'Art et d'Histoire du Judaïsme
Musée de la Chasse
3
32
55
RUE DE POITOU
St Sébastien Froissart
M
R. DU PONT AUX CHOUX
RUE SAINT SEBASTIEN
PASSAGE ST SEBASTIEN
RUE SAINT SEBASTIEN

RUE BRAQUE
RUE CHARLOT
DU TEMPLE
45
RUE DEBELLEYME
11
RUE DES 4 FILS
Musée Picasso
31
RUE DE THORIGNY
R. ST CLAUDE

RUE DU TEMPLE
RUE DES ARCHIVES
RUE DES FRANCS
**Archives Nationales**
46
37
RUE VIEILLE
RUE DE LA PERLE
RUE STE ANASTASE
RUE VILEHARDOUIN
RUE DES ARQUEBUSIERS
RUE PELEE

RUE STE CROIX DE LA BRETONNERIE
BLANCS MANTEAUX
RUE AUBRIOT
56
RUE BARBETTE
RUE ELZÉVIR
RUE DU PARC ROYAL
Musée Cognacq-Jay
Chemin Vert
M
6
RUE SAINT SABIN

RUE DE LA VERRERIE
54
35
RUE DU BOURG TIBOURG
VIEILLE DU TEMPLE
38
34
RUE DU TRESOR
RUE DES ROSIERS
Musée Carnavalet
RUE ST GILLES
49
RUE DE BÉARN
RUE DES MINIMES
RUE DU CHEMIN VERT

RUE DE RIVOLI
39
RUE DU ROI
RUE D'ECOUFFES
RUE DE SICILE
RUE PAVÉE
R. MALHER
36
RUE DE SÉVIGNÉ
RUE DES FRANCS
BOURGEOIS
RUE DE TURENNE
PLACE DES VOSGES
BOULEVARD BEAUMARCHAIS

FRANCOIS MIRON
RUE DES BARRES
RUE GEOFFROY L'ASNIER
RUE DE-JOUY
St Paul
M
RUE DE JARENTE
60
RUE DE ORMESSON
Maison de Victor Hugo
RUE DE LA BASTILLE
54

QUAI DE L'HOTEL DE VILLE
L'HOTEL DE VILLE
107
Maison Européene de la Photographie
RUE CHARLEMAGNE
RUE SAINT ANTOINE
Opéra Bastille

PONT LOUIS PHILIPPE
VOIE GEORGES
Pont Marie
M
RUE DES JARDINS
RUE SAINT PAUL
RUE NEUVE ST-PIERRE
63
RUE BEAUTREILLIS
**4**
PL. DE LA BASTILLE
M
Bastille

1
QUAI DE BOURBON
RUE
SAINT
QUAI DE CELESTINS
RUE CHARLES
LIONS ST PAUL
58
RUE DU PETIT MUSC
RUE CASTEX
RUE DE LESDIGUIERES
7

2
R. LE REGRATTIER
**ILE ST LOUIS**
POMPIDOU
BOULEVARD HENRI IV
CERISAIE
BOURDON
42
RUE LACUEE

3
QUAI D'ORLEANS
RUE DES DEUX PONTS
QUAI D'ANJOU
RUE POULLETIER
EN L'ILE
PONT MARIE
❶ Hotels pp48-77
❶ Restaurants pp186-219
❶ Cafés & Bars pp220-238
64

PONT DE LA TOURNELLE
Église St-Louis-en-l'Île
QUAI DE BETHUNE
BD HENRI IV
Sully Morland
M
RUE DE LA
RUE CRILLON
RUE MORNAY
BOULEVARD MORLAND
BLVD DE LA BASTILLE
**12**

QUAI DE LA TOURNELLE
Seine
PONT DE SULLY
QUAI
HENRI IV

BD SAINT GERMAIN
**5**
K
Institut du Monde Arabe
© Copyright Time Out Group 2008
0        200 m
0        200 yds
Universités Paris VI Paris VII Pierre et Marie Curie
L
M

# Street Index